WOMEN AND MEN
IN ORGANIZATIONS

Sex and Gender
Issues at Work

SERIES IN APPLIED PSYCHOLOGY
Edwin A. Fleishman, George Mason University
Series Editor

WOMEN AND MEN
IN ORGANIZATIONS
Sex and Gender
Issues at Work

Jeanette N. Cleveland
Colorado State University

Margaret Stockdale
Southern Illinois University, Carbondale

Kevin R. Murphy
Colorado State University

LEA LAWRENCE ERLBAUM ASSOCIATES, PUBLISHERS
2000 Mahwah, New Jersey   London

Lawrence Erlbaum Associates, Inc., Publishers
10 Industrial Avenue
Mahwah, NJ 07430

cover design by Kathryn Houghtaling Lacey

Library of Congress Cataloging-in-Publication Data

Cleveland, Jeanette.
    Women and men in organizations : sex and gender issues at work / Jeanette N. Cleveland, Margaret Stockdale, Kevin R. Murphy.
        p.   cm. — (Applied psychology series)
    Includes bibliographical references and index.
    ISBN 0-8058-1267-9 (cloth : alk. paper). — ISBN 0-8058-1268-7 (pbk. : alk. paper)
        1. Sex role in the work environment—United States.
    I. Stockdale, Margaret S.   II. Murphy, Kevin R., 1952–
    III. Title.   IV. Series.
    HD6060.65.U5C58   1999
    331.11′43--dc21   99-37807
                                                                                CIP

Books published by Lawrence Erlbaum Associates are printed on acid-free paper, and their bindings are chosen for strength and durability.

Printed in the United States of America
10   9   8   7   6   5   4   3   2   1

This book is dedicated to our parents and our children.

One gave us roots and wings; the other gives us hopes and dreams.

> Robert and Kathleen
> Tom and Pat
> Frederick and Joan
>
> Kathleen and Michael
> Sarah, Susan, and Geoffrey

Contents

**PART II: PROCESSES UNDERLYING
             MALE–FEMALE ATTITUDES AND
             BEHAVIOR IN THE WORKPLACE**

               and Women at Work   41

       Gender Stereotypes   42
       Gender Stereotypes and Stereotypes of Race, Age,
           Appearance, and Disability   50
       Effects of Gender Stereotypes in the Workplace   56
       Summary   63

Chapter 4   Physical Attractiveness, Interpersonal
               Relationships, and Romance at Work   67

       Gender and Physical Attractiveness   69
       Physical Attractiveness and Interpersonal Relations   71
       Interpersonal Attraction in the Workplace   76
       Workplace Romance   82
       Summary   90

Chapter 5   Language and Communication Among
               Organizational Members   93

       Female and Male Ways of Speaking: Data
           Versus Stereotypes   95
       Understanding Gender Differences in Language   99
       Women and Men Speaking in Groups   102
       Gender and Nonverbal Language   106
       A Social–Psychological Approach to Understanding
           Language and Linguistic Groups   112
       Additional Issues Concerning Language in the Workplace   118
       Summary   121

Chapter 6   Power and Relationships at Work   125

       Definitions and Sources of Power and Influence   126
       The Effects of Power and Influence   137
       Gender and Power in the Workplace   143
       Summary   149

**PART III: WOMEN AND MEN IN THE
               WORKPLACE: IMPORTANT
               INDIVIDUAL AND
               ORGANIZATIONAL OUTCOMES**

Series Foreword

Edwin A. Fleishman

Series Editor

There is a compelling need for innovative approaches to the solution of many pressing problems involving human relationships in today's society. Such approaches are more likely to be successful when they are based on sound research and applications. This *Series in Applied Psychology* offers publications which emphasize state-of-the-art research and its application to important issues of human behavior in a variety of societal settings. The objective is to bridge both academic and applied interests. This book accomplishes this objective with respect to the increasing diversity occurring in the workplace.

Women now make up over 45% of the U.S. workforce and this proportion is likely to increase. Working women are a diverse group (e.g., White women, minorities, women with children, immigrants, older workers) with widely varying needs, values, experiences, and expectations. Yet often when employees or workers are discussed, implicitly (or often explicitly) it is male workers that are described. Furthermore, when working women are discussed they are often discussed separately and in comparison to men.

This book is intended to discuss women and men within the context of applied work psychology and management. It is the authors' hope that the book can be used for courses in industrial and organizational psychology, applied work psychology, human resources management, and organizational behavior. It is difficult to imagine that students of industrial and organizational psychology has an accurate or complete grasp of leadership unless they know the literature based on research on both men and women as leaders. Any discussion of careers would be misleading, and perhaps inaccurate, if it excluded material on women's careers. To the extent that these discussions ignore the research literature on women in the workplace, traditional texts used in the courses just mentioned reflect information on only a subset of the workforce.

The authors discuss four basic processes that substantially influence men's and women's experiences at work—stereotyping, the role of attractiveness in evaluating others, the ways men and women communicate, and the acquisition and exercise of power and influence in organizations. They show how these processes can be linked to gender discrimination, sexual harassment in organizations, men's and women's career development, leadership and leader–follower interactions, and stress. They discuss how programs to "manage" gender diversity might benefit from paying explicit attention to these issues.

This book draws from a number of disciplines, including psychology, sociology, women's studies, economics, and linguistics to help the reader understand relationships between gender and work. Each discipline carries its own assumptions and favors its own particular approaches to research and scholarship. It is clear that the issues facing men and women at work extend beyond the boundaries of specific academic fields of study. The approach taken in this important book helps to capture the complexity of the relationships between women, men, and work organizations.

Preface

The gender and racial composition of the U.S. workforce is rapidly changing. As more women enter the workforce and as they enter jobs that have traditionally been dominated by men, issues related to sex and gender in work settings become increasingly important and complex. Research addressing sex and gender in the workplace is conducted in several distinct disciplines, ranging from psychology and sociology to management and economics. Books on gender at work often reflect either a more traditional management perspective or a more recent feminist perspective; rarely are these two orientations on women and work acknowledged within the same text. However, given the incredible challenges facing organizations today in terms of full and effective utilization of quality employees, the traditional literature and feminist research literature must be brought together.

The goal of this book is to communicate a variety of social–psychological research on gender issues that affect work behaviors to upper level undergraduate and graduate students in applied psychology and business. The book is designed to supplement upper level undergraduate courses in industrial and organizational (I/O) psychology, organizational behavior, management in organizations, personnel administration, career and vocational counseling, women's studies (particularly those addressing work issues), and selected topics. Furthermore, it can serve as a centerpiece in a topics course devoted to gender in the workplace that might be offered within the curriculum of I/O, vocational psychology, or management, where it can be supplemented by primary research articles or selected book chapters.

ACKNOWLEDGMENTS

This book could not have been completed without the help of a number of colleagues and institutions. First, we are extremely grateful to Frank (Skip) Saal and Barbara Gutek, both of whom collaborated in the earlier stages of this project. Their suggestions, insights, and contributions were extremely valuable and helped to shape the book. Second, we are grateful for the support we received from Colorado State University (specifically, Scott Hamilton as chair of the Department of Psychology) and Southern Illinois University in all of the phases of producing this book. Some of the early work on this book was done while on visiting appointments to the University of California, Berkeley (Cleveland and Murphy), and the University of Arizona (Stockdale); we greatly appreciate the use of their facilities and the opportunities to interact with colleagues in several related disciplines. We (Cleveland and Murphy) completed this book while on sabbatical at the University of Limerick, Ireland; we thank the university, the College of Business, and the Department of Personnel and Employment Relations, particularly Joe Wallace, for their help and support.

Finally, we appreciate the help and encouragement of Ray O'Connell and Anne Duffy, who have been patient and supportive throughout the process of writing and publishing this book.

I

INTRODUCTION

1

Introduction to Women and Men in Organizations

The family picture is on HIS desk.
Ah, a solid, responsible family man.
>   The family picture is on HER desk.
>   *Umm, her family will come before her career.*

HE is talking with his co-workers.
He must be discussing the latest deal.
>   SHE is talking with her co-workers.
>   *She must be gossiping.*

HE's not in the office.
He's meeting customers.
>   SHE's not in the office.
>   *She must be out shopping.*

HE's having lunch with the boss.
He's on this way up.
>   SHE's having lunch with the boss.
>   *They must be having an affair.*

HE got an unfair deal.
Did he get angry?
>   SHE got an unfair deal.
>   *Did she cry?*

HE's getting married.
He'll get more settled.
>   SHE's getting married.
>   *She'll get pregnant and leave.*

HE's having a baby.
He'll need a raise.
>   SHE's having a baby.
>   *She'll cost the company money in maternity benefits.*

HE's leaving for a better job.
He knows how to recognize a good opportunity.
>   SHE's leaving for a better job.
>   *Women are not dependable.*

—(Gardenswartz & Rowe, 1994)

Women make up more than 45% of the U.S. workforce (W.B. Johnson & Packer, 1987; U.S. Department of Commerce, 1997), and this proportion is likely to grow. Working women are a diverse group (e.g., White women, minorities, women with children, immigrants, older workers) with widely varying needs, values, experiences, and expectations. However, working women share a common bond in that, until recently, the world of work was primarily oriented toward men. Historically, women have been segregated into jobs that provided very limited access to the top levels of organizations, and this segregation persists in many sectors of the economy. More recently, however, there has been an influx of women into nontraditional, higher status occupations, and it appears that traditional patterns of occupational segregation may be slowly changing.

Changes in the workforce pose both opportunities and challenges to organizations, and **human resource management** (HRM) experts have devoted increasing levels of attention to the issues and problems that individuals and groups bring to and encounter in the workplace. Researchers in applied work psychology, organizational behavior, and other related fields (social psychology, sociology, and economics) are also showing greater interest in the roles of gender and sex at work. Furthermore, there is a rich tradition of research and scholarship in the area of women's studies dealing with similarities and differences in men's and women's workplace experiences. Each perspective brings its own set of assumptions, insight, and conclusions to bear, and there is a good deal to be learned by bridging the many disciplines concerned with women and men in the workplace.

One goal of this book is to cover a range of issues that both women and men encounter in the workplace but that are not commonly explored in any depth in management or work psychology textbooks. We hope to expand the conceptualization of "human" in HRM to include both women and men. We believe that gender and sex issues have important implications for work-related and HRM issues. Unfortunately, discussions of work often refer (explicitly or implicitly) to workers as men. Therefore, any discussion of another group of workers (in this case women) is at risk of being dismissed as a specialty book (about women). However, this book is not simply about women at work.

This is a book about people interacting with each other in the context of work organizations. Our discussion includes literature that reveals similarities and differences between men and women at work and, wherever possible, among men and women of color and of varying socioeconomic status. We hope to identify what we know about employed men and women as well as what we do not know concerning gender and important work and organizational problems.

Throughout the book, we identify important human resource issues and topics that have not traditionally been treated as mainstream topics in industrial and organizational (I/O) psychology or HRM. Among the topics that have historically been perceived (and sometimes dismissed) as women's issues, yet are now increasingly of concern to both male and female HRM and I/O professionals, are sexual harassment, child-care and childbearing issues, career progress, and stress and health. We believe the entrance of increasing numbers of women into the workforce renders these issues important to men, women, and organizations.

This text is intended primarily for upper level undergraduate and entry-level graduate students and researchers in management, psychology, women's studies, sociology, and related fields. Although the book draws heavily from data-based research findings, we hope that it appeals to teachers and students who are interested in a more general understanding of the processes and issues encountered by employed women and men.

Chapter 1 defines what we mean by the sets of activities that we call *work* and provides a brief historical perspective on the participation of men and women in the workplace. As the definition of work has evolved over the years, so have the type and the extent of male and female involvement in the workforce.

WHAT DO WE MEAN BY WORK?

A look at *Webster's Dictionary* reveals 20 definitions of the noun and 30 definitions of the verb *work* (Neff, 1985). Overall, the definitions tend to have "purposeful activity" in common. However, determining the set of activities we include in a definition of work is complex. As is seen in the review of the history of gender and work, men and women have always worked (Nieva & Gutek, 1981b). Before the Industrial Revolution, both men and women worked, not for wages, but for family survival and maintenance. In this context, women and men were considered partners. However, with the occurrence of the Industrial Revolution, labor was divided into a male work sphere that was paid, public, and external to the family and a female family sphere that was unpaid and private (i.e., work in the home). Therefore, prior to the Industrial Revolution, the definition of work we often use today (i.e., what people do to earn a living) would have been inadequate because it does not include a number of activities that historically were considered work. This definition probably reflects what many people in our society currently view as work, "the means of subsistence" (Schwimmer, 1980). However, the meaning of work, or specifically the definition of work, is historically relative (Brief & Nord, 1990).

Activities that one does for pay have also been called occupational work (G. Miller, 1980). The characteristics of occupational work are "(1) its existence as a role discreet and separate from other roles occupied by the individual, and (2) the primary use of such direct financial rewards as salaries or wages to obtain a minimal level of involvement in the role by the worker" (G. Miller, 1980, p. 382). This definition of occupational work is consistent with what most people today mean by the term *work* (Brief & Nord, 1990). However, there are at least two problems with this definition of work. First, the term *financial* does not describe all possible compensation arrangements. For example, informal work can include bartering and social exchange of services (Brief & Nord, 1990). The second problem is that work–nonwork role separation is rarely complete; many types of occupational work involve interrelated roles. Furthermore, in the 1990s, both women and men became increasingly aware that they were members of two "work groups," one external to the home and one within the home.

In this book, we recognize that the term *work* covers both paid and unpaid activities in both public and private areas of our lives. However, much of the material reviewed in the management, psychology, and sociology literatures is based on work that is defined as paid work. Therefore, when using the term **work or employment**, we refer to activities or tasks that one engages in for pay.

Whenever possible, we distinguish among research findings and theories that are based largely on blue-collar, pink-collar, and white-collar, professional/managerial jobs. We recognize that what may be true for one occupational group may not hold for another. Furthermore, race, gender, and, to some extent, age are confounded with occupational type as well as socioeconomic status. Therefore, we attempt to highlight the characteristics of the occupations and the subjects used in the research we review.

HISTORY OF MALE AND FEMALE WORKFORCE PARTICIPATION

The meaning of work has evolved considerably over the centuries (Brief & Nord, 1990), and our current conception of work as a set of structured, paid activities is relatively new. Simply put, women as well as men have always worked (F.D. Blau & Ferber, 1985; Harris-Kessler, 1985; R. Marshall & R. Paulin, 1987). However, the types of activities and for whom one works have changed dramatically. In preindustrial society, the family was the unit or focus of work. The woman and the tasks she performed were an integral part of that unit (R. Marshall & Paulin, 1987). Men largely obtained goods external to the family. However, at this point, both women and men engaged in family-work activities that were either paid work (e.g., women selling produce that their husbands had harvested) or exchange of goods for other desired goods. The preindustrial society was oriented toward largely agricultural labor and home manufacture. Home or domestic life was nearly indistinguishable from economic life. This economic period was called the "family economy."

Through industrialization, the labor market expanded and paid work became work external to the family. Here is where we observe a split between what is called private (i.e., family), nonpaid work performed primarily by women and public (i.e., external), paid work largely performed by men. Women's work inside the home became viewed as supplemental to the presumably more important and prestigious external and paid employment of men. Furthermore, once men left the private sphere of family work for public employment and women remained within the family sphere, perceptions and expectations developed that reinforced this segregation of private and public, women and men, and secondary and primary facets of work. Women were considered as, at best, temporary participants in a male-dominated public realm of work.

During early stages of industrialization, when women worked for pay outside the home the situation typically involved single women working in low-paying jobs that were gender segregated. When a woman married, she was strongly expected to relinquish the few rights (especially economic independence) she had as a single woman. Few married women were employed outside the home, although occasionally a woman might work for money if her father or husband was unable to provide adequately. Additionally, during early industrial times, the meaning of work for men and women was very different especially if one focused on the social aspects of work. For a woman, there was limited power over her own destiny; the husband's occupation and social standing defined the woman socially. The woman's work was supposed to be for the benefit of the family, not for herself. For the man, work defined him socially and economically. Women were frequently prevented from entering the workforce because men feared that their entry would decrease their own wages. The social attitudes during this period conveyed to women that the only way to achieve womanliness was to bear and nurture children.

Three factors contributed to the entrance of women into the workforce by 1940: demographic changes, the war, and the increase in labor force participation of married women (R. Marshall & Paulin, 1987). The demographic trend involved population growth and a redistribution of women in various age categories, increasing the number of working women between 20 and 64 years of age. In 1870, married women made up 15% of the female labor force, whereas by 1940, the proportion was 35.5% (R. Marshall & Paulin, 1987). Why were more married women entering the workforce in 1940? The reasons included mandatory schooling for young children, decreasing fertility rates, and inadequacy of the male income to sustain the family (i.e., the need to have a second income).

Interestingly, we see precisely these factors cited in the popular press today as explanations for continued participation of women in the workforce.

With the onset of World War II, women increased their presence in such fields as teaching, nursing, and clothing manufacture. Additionally, women entered lumber mills, auto and aircraft factories, electrical and munitions industries, and telephone operation. However, women's experiences in these traditionally masculine jobs during the war were transitory. Once the war was over, women returned to more female-dominated work (R. Marshall & Paulin, 1987). During this postwar period, **occupational sex segregation** was once again prevalent. In 1900, approximately 90.2% of working women worked in only 25 of 252 occupations. Forty years later, not much had changed, for 86.7% of working women were employed in these occupations (Hooks, 1947). Women were a majority (90%) in only 11 of 451 occupations in 1940.

Although held back by racial discrimination, Black women and men also entered new occupations and industries during this period. However, as late as 1910, 95% of all Black women continued to work in agriculture and domestic and personal service. Black women entered the lower levels of the work hierarchy (e.g., textile, clothing, and food industries; tobacco factories; and wood product manufacture) as White women left traditional jobs for better occupations during the war (R. Marshall & Paulin, 1987). In the same way that White women lost many of their gains to men after the war, Black women lost these gains as White women moved back into these prewar occupations.

As a result of great changes in technology during World War II, women again made significant progress in labor force participation, occupational integration, and earnings. From 1940 to 1944, women increased in the workforce by almost 50%, up 6 million to 20.6 million (24.7%–35%). In 1944, the number of married women in the workforce exceeded the number of single women for the first time (44% vs. 43%). The greatest increase of women occurred in war-related manufacturing (R. Marshall & Paulin, 1987).

Black women also made significant gains during World War II. Again, they initially moved into jobs at the lower end of the work hierarchy (jobs left by White women) and then filtered into war industries. During this time there was a parallel decrease in the percentage of Black women in farming, domestics, personal service, and so forth. This was a time of much change and numerous societal and legal contradictions. For example, whereas the men in our nation were called on to be patriotic and to fight for freedom and equality, women were shut out of many occupations and industries in many states. A woman was not allowed to make property transactions without her husband's consent, to enter into contracts, or even obtain legal guardianship of children. Further, Black people were barred from certain restaurants and hotels. Economically, women (White or Black) were not paid the same wages in jobs held by White males.

During the postwar period of the 1960s to 1970s, women became permanent participants in the workforce. Furthermore, during the 1970s, married women participated in the workforce at rates similar to those of single and divorced women (Reskin & Padavic, 1994). Through a combination of economic, social, and technical changes, women moved from the margin to the mainstream in terms of participation. Rather than being incidental workers, women were a significant core of the workforce. By 1985, men provided the sole income in less than 15% of U.S. households. Historically, Black and minority women have had higher participation rates in the workforce than White women. White women typically are pulled into the workforce due to labor market demands (Iglehart, 1979). Furthermore, traditional sex-role norms, especially regarding work and gender (discussed in chapter 3), cannot be generalized from one racial group to another, as many do not hold for Black women (King, 1975). When writers in the popular press described the dramatic increase of women in the workforce during the 1980s, they often were referring to the statistics on White women. There was, as Table 1.1 shows, a dramatic increase in the participation of White women in paid work between 1963 and 1998. Although both Black women (48–64%) and White women (37–59%) showed significant inroads into the workforce between 1963 and 1998, Black women historically show greater labor force participation than White women. By 1998, 79% of men and 60% of women participated in the labor force. Furthermore, more than 75% of women 35 to 44 years old participated in the labor force (Reskin & Padavic, 1994). Figure 1.1

TABLE 1.1
Proportion of Men and Women in Paid Work

Year	Men	Women	Men		Women	
			White	Black & Other	White	Black & Other
1963	81.4	38.3	81.5	80.2	37.7	48.1
1970	79.7	43.3	80.0	76.5	42.6	49.5
1980	77.4	51.5	78.2	70.6	51.2	53.2
1990	76.4	57.5	77.1	71.0	57.4	58.3
1998	79.0	60.0	77.5	73.1	59.3	64.3

Note: 1963–1976 data from *U.S. Working Women: A Databook*, U.S. Department of Labor, Bureau of Labor Statistics, 1977, Washington, DC: U.S. Government Printing Office. 1977–1982 data from *Statistical Abstracts*, U.S. Department of Commerce, Bureau of the Census, 1991, 1997, Washington, DC: U.S Department of Commerce. 1990 data from *Bulletin 2307*, U.S. Bureau of Labor Statistics, 1995, Washington, DC: U.S. Government Printing Office. 1998 data from *The Employment Situation*, [on-line], 1998, July 2, available: stats.bls.gov.newrels.htms.

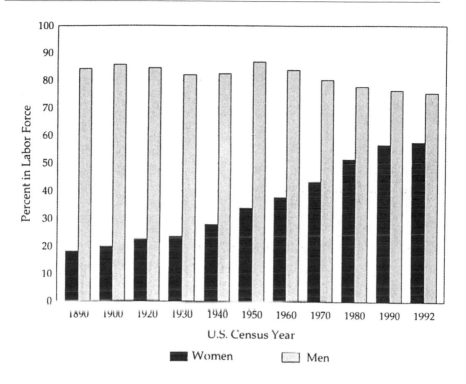

FIG. 1.1. Trends in U.S. labor force participation rates by sex, 1890 to 1992. Data from U.S. Bureau of the Census, 1975, pp. 131–132; U.S. Bureau of the Census, 1992d, Table 609; U.S. Women's Bureau, 1993, p. 1. *Source:* Reskin, B. and Padavic, I (1994). *Women and men at work.* pp. 24, copyright © 1999 by Pine Forge Press. Reprinted by permission of Pine Forge Press.

shows male and female participation rates in the U.S. workforce from 1890 to 1992. Participation rates in 1990 of men and women from around the world are shown in Fig. 1.2.

MODEL FOR UNDERSTANDING MEN AND WOMEN IN A DIVERSE WORKFORCE

A framework outlined in Table 1.2 is proposed for examining sex and gender issues at work. The framework organizes the material presented in this text in the way that we see the linkages among the chapters. Although this framework is straightforward, it conveys the notion that behavior at work is complexly determined by both personal and situational factors, some of which are more mutable or modifiable than others. The

12

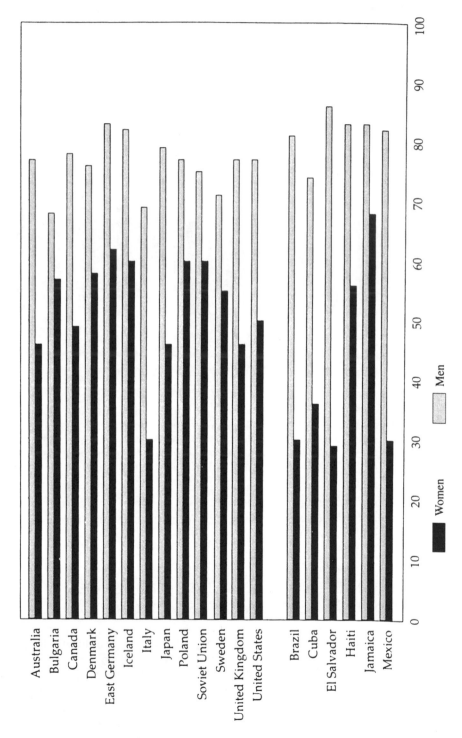

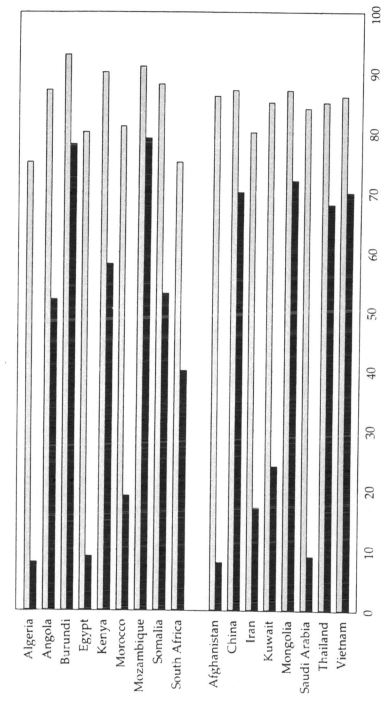

FIG. 1.2. Percentage of economically active women and men ages 15 and over for selected countries, 1990. From United Nations, 1991, Table 8, pp. 104–107. *Source:* Reskin, B. and Padavic, I (1994). *Women and men at work.* pp. 28–28. copyright © 1999 by Pine Forge Press. Reprinted by permission of Pine Forge Press.

13

TABLE 1.2
Framework Depicting Linkages Among Chapters Presented in This Book

Context	*Causes or Independent* *Processes* *variables*	*Outcomes, Effects* Individual and Organizational Outcomes
	Stereotypes (chapter 3)	Discrimination/occupational segregation (chapters 7 & 8)
Culture	Physical attractiveness (chapter 4)	Sexual harassment (chapter 9)
Society	Language and communication (chapter 5)	Career management (chapter 10)
Organization	Power and work relationships (chapter 6)	Leadership (chapter 11)
		Stress and health (chapter 12)

book describes topics in terms of both **person-centered** and **situation-centered** explanations, but the emphasis varies from one chapter to the next. Attributes of the individual are used as the primary causes of outcomes when person-centered explanations are employed. These individual factors can include one's physical attractiveness, the way one speaks, and how feminine or masculine one appears to be. On the other hand, when characteristics of the situation are employed as primary explanatory agents, then a more situation-centered approach is taken.

As Table 1.2 suggests, the society and culture in which we live and the organizations in which we work reflect the context or situation, and this context influences several basic processes that in turn influence behaviors and outcomes in the workplace. Examples of basic processes include stereotypes (especially male and female sex-role stereotypes), the effects of attractiveness on men and women in organizations, male–female similarities and differences in the use of language and in communication styles, and male–female similarities and differences in access to and use of power in organizations. These basic process variables influence a number of organizational outcomes, including discrimination and occupational segregation in the workplace, sexual harassment, male–female differences in career development, the exercise and the effects of leadership in organizational settings, and stress.

Structure of the Book

The principal goal of this book is to integrate research literatures on gender issues that affect workplace behaviors and communicate these findings to upper level undergraduate and graduate students in applied psychology and business. Current social psychological and management theories and empirical research on the processes and basic issues related to sex and gender in organizations are presented. The first two chapters lay the groundwork for discussing the range of topics in this book. Following these introductory chapters, the book is organized into two parts. In Part I, the basic social psychological and societal elements that set the stage for male–female interactions in the workplace are presented. Research on social stereotypes of women and men is reviewed in chapter 3. This chapter considers the influence of such stereotypes on one's sense of self and on others' expectations and behaviors. Chapter 4 covers the empirical literature on attractiveness, a key physical characteristic that affects both men's and women's behaviors and interactions. This also considers the links between attractiveness and interpersonal relationships and one facet of sexuality—romance in the workplace. In chapter 5, similarities and differences in women's and men's use of language and communication in the workplace are presented. Because oral communication is a basic channel for conveying information, differences between men and women in styles or content of communication may lead to misperceptions, misunderstanding, and perpetuation of counterproductive stereotypes and attitudes in the workplace. The final chapter in Part I (chapter 6) examines research on power in the workplace, including various bases of power and perceptions and reactions by others to the exercise of power by women and men.

Part II focuses on work-related domains where the processes described in Part I are likely to affect work behavior. In chapter 7, psychological explanations underlying discrimination at work are discussed. Research on occupational segregation and gender discrimination is reviewed, and different explanations for discrimination are compared. Chapter 8 presents legal issues and laws protecting the status of women and men in the workplace. Chapter 9 presents psychological research and theory dealing with sexual harassment in the workplace. Our examination of sexual harassment pays particular attention to the conditions under which it is more likely to occur and its effects on women and men.

One of the most critical issues to emerge from changing patterns of women's employment is the need for both men and women to balance work and family. The career development cycle is described in chapter 10 as well as some unique factors that influence and shape women's careers. In addition, such issues as mentoring, pregnancy and child care, and dual-career issues are discussed as they impact career experiences of women and men. In chapter 11, the discussion turns to leadership. There has been much popular literature on the need for new leadership styles that will be effective for an increasingly diverse workforce. Research on male and female leadership behaviors is reviewed in chapter 11, with special emphasis on studies examining gender comparisons in leader styles, decision making, and glass-ceiling effects. Chapter 12 examines stress and health-related factors that affect male and female workers, including stress research conducted using biological and psychological perspectives.

The final chapter of the book (chapter 13) examines what organizations and individuals can do to turn diversity from a problem into an opportunity, enhancing the responsiveness of the workplace to individual differences, and ways in which organizations can enhance the productivity and satisfaction of all their members.

SUMMARY

Although women and men have always engaged in purposeful activity, the set of activities that many people consider work or employment is not always clear. Historically, men and women worked side by side together in the fields. Today, however, a distinction is made between paid, public work external to the family and unpaid, private work in the home. Each of these spheres of work has come to be sex-typed, with paid work being viewed by many as the domain of males and unpaid work in the home the domain of females. These perceptions are changing but are still deep-seated in many respects.

Historically, men and women have had very different experiences of work. Men have either secured goods or worked external to the family unit, whereas women often have worked more integrally as part of that unit. Beginning with industrialization and continuing to the workplace today, men's and women's experiences of work have varied significantly, largely due to the continuing sex segregation of occupations. However, with the onset of two world wars, both Black and White women steadily increased their numbers in the external, paid workforce. During the 1990s, the majority of both men and women, Black and White, were employed outside of the family unit.

With the influx of women into the workforce during the last 20 years, there has been increased attention to comparisons between men and women on a number of work-related attributes and behaviors. This book is designed to integrate research from a number of fields to provide multiple perspectives on the issues facing men and women in today's workplace. The format of this book is guided by a multilevel model of factors that shape and influence the relationships and behaviors among men and women at work. Key factors that provide the foundation for male–female, male–male, and female–female interactions at work are discussed in chapters 3 through 6 (gender stereotyping, physical attractiveness and interpersonal relations, language and communication, and power relations). These factors are critical in understanding how men and women behave and compare to each other in terms of more traditional and work-related concerns such as sexual harassment, workplace discrimination, leadership, careers and dual-career issues, and work stress and health, topics that are addressed in chapters 7 through 13.

GLOSSARY

Employment: Activities or tasks that one engages in for pay.

Human resource management: Section within an organization whose function is to attract and select qualified job applicants, develop performance management and compensation systems that align employee behaviors with organizational goals, and assist in the development and retention of a diverse workforce to meet current and future organizational requirements.

Occupational sex segregation: The concentration of women in occupations that are predominantly female and the concentration of men in occupations that are largely male.

Person-centered explanations: Explanations that use attributes of the individual as the primary causes of important outcomes or differences.

Situation-centered explanations: Explanations that use characteristics of the situation as primary explanatory agents of similarities or differences in important behaviors and outcomes.

Work: Purposeful activity, usually for pay, gain, or maintenance.

2

Understanding Men's and Women's Experiences in the Workplace: Methods and Theoretical Perspectives

Before we examine research and theory on the ways men and women deal with, progress in, and interact in the workplace, it is useful to step back and examine the ways we talk about, think about, and write about sex, gender, and sexuality. Some authors would have us believe men and women are so fundamentally different that they might as well inhabit different planets (e.g., *Men Are From Mars, Women Are From Venus* by Gray, 1992), whereas others suggest that there are no real differences and that what we see as essential differences in the behaviors of men and women are in fact nothing more than social conventions. Theory and research on sex, gender, and sexuality are greatly complicated by the number of perspectives on how we should view whether men and women are similar or different and how we should integrate research on similarities and differences at one level (e.g., adult men and women show similar levels of verbal ability) with similarities and differences at another (e.g., regardless of occupation, women are more likely than men to take greater responsibility for child care).

MEN'S AND WOMEN'S EXPERIENCES OF WORK

In recent years, the influx of women into the workforce in general, and into **nontraditional occupations** in particular, has led to increased attention in the popular media. One result of the recent profusion of books, magazine articles, and newspaper stories dealing with these topics is an increasing level of confusion about whether there are, in fact, sex or gender differences between women and men; or if there are such differences, in what ways (i.e., personality, skills, leadership, intelligence, etc.) men and women differ, how much they differ, and whether the differences really mean anything. Although it would be convenient to place much of this confusion on the doorstep of the media, the responsibility can be equally shared both by the scientific community and by the media in attempting to interpret research findings, and communicate them to the public.

There are at least three sources of confusion in understanding and interpreting research findings comparing men and women:

1. The approaches, theories, or explanations for observed or unobserved differences between women and men.
2. The terms used to describe such comparisons (i.e., sex or gender differences).
3. Research biases associated with comparing men and women at work and in other settings.

These three sources of confusion are not completely independent from either the researcher investigating gender comparisons or the student learning about them. For example, an individual may believe, as part of his or her value system, that men and women do differ substantially from each other because, "Gee, just look at them. They look different, so their biological makeup must be different." Given this belief about the source of differences between men and women, an individual may use words or languages that connotes or implies that all differences between men and women are biological and perhaps immutable.

Both one's beliefs about explanations for observed gender differences and the words one uses to reinforce those beliefs influence and, perhaps to some extent, determine the information that both the researcher and the student gather about the actual behavior of men and women. For example, if a researcher believed that all differences between women and men were the result of an unfair educational system and a discriminatory work environment, then programs could be designed and implemented at the early school-age level as well as within organizations to combat such behavior. On the other hand, if a researcher believed that male and female behavior was biologically determined, there would be little incentive to design or implement such programs. Each of these three sources of confusion in understanding gender comparisons is discussed next. In addition, the notion of sexuality in organizations is addressed as a much-ignored issue in the organizational research literature.

Approaches to Understanding Sex and Gender Comparisons

Numerous theories and models exist to explain how sex- and gender-related behaviors emerge or are acquired (Deaux & Major, 1987). These approaches can be grouped into three major categories: biological, socialization, and structural–cultural models. These perspectives are not mutually exclusive. As Table 2.1 indicates, each perspective makes certain assumptions about the bases and changeability of different behaviors among men and women.

Biological Models. The focus of the **biological models** of sex- and gender-related behavior is to identify genetic, hormonal, and physical factors that determine the behavior of men and women (e.g., E.O. Wilson, 1975). Few people doubt that biological differences between men and women influence behavior at least to some degree. However, there is disagreement both among experts in this field and among the public as to the degree to which our behavior, especially social behavior, is determined by our sex. Two assumptions of the biological approaches are

TABLE 2.1

Key Features of the Perspectives for Understanding Sex
and Gender Comparisons

Perspective Key Features	
Biological	Implicitly assumes existing differences between women and men.
	Differences are due to genetic, hormonal, and physical factors.
	Differences are immutable.
	Differences are necessary for survival.
	Research goal is to reinforce detecting differences between men and women.
	Drawback is that differences may be exaggerated.
Socialization	Acknowledges observed differences between men and women.
	Assumes that men and women behave differently as a result of learning.
	Differences observed are not immutable and are subject to change.
	Differences emerge as part of social and cognitive development process.
	Research focus is on describing ways children and adults learn gender identity and social rules that contribute to observed differences.
	Drawback is that small, systematic biological variations among men and women might be ignored.
Structural/cultural	Assumes few inherent differences between men and women.
	Differences observed are the result of social structures and systems that reinforce such differences to reinforce current power hierarchy.
	Differences are changeable.
	Differences exist to keep the powerful in control and the powerless without power.
	Research focus is on identifying similarity or sameness between men and women in similar or identical contexts.
	Drawback is potential to ignore small yet real individual variation among men and women.

that differences exist between men and women, and that maleness and femaleness are given characteristics of the individual that provide the foundation for differences in social behavior (Hess & Ferree, 1987).

Using the biological approach, researchers tend to expect, look for, and confirm differences between men and women and to use these differences to explain male superiority and dominance by implying that such differences are "large, socially significant and consistently favor men" (Hess & Ferree, 1987, p. 14). For example, early research on the topic of intelligence focused on identifying differences between men and women in intellectual function. The popular argument was that brain size was a direct indicator of intelligence; therefore, women, who on average have smaller brains, must be less intelligent than men (Hyde, 1990). Although actual evidence of this was mixed, researchers "refining" this logic then hypothesized that various functions of the brain were located in different regions. It was further believed at this time that the frontal lobes of the brain were the location of the highest mental abilities; not surprisingly, researchers claimed that men had larger frontal lobes than women. When empirical data once again failed to support this claim, researchers reconsidered and asserted that the parietal lobes were the site of intelligence. Once again, because women possessed smaller parietal lobes than men, they were therefore deemed less intelligent (Shields, 1975; Unger & Crawford, 1992). In 1910, a review of the psychological research on gender differences in intelligence found no support for the argument that brain size was an indicator of intelligence. Furthermore, research in this area was found to be flawed and to reflect "flagrant personal bias . . . and unfounded assertions" (Woolley, 1910, p. 340). After correcting for body size, there simply is no significant difference between the brain sizes of women and men (Gould, 1981; Unger & Crawford, 1992).

There are at least two variations of the biological approach to explaining differences among men and women. **Functionalism** (Lips, 1988; Shields, 1975) involves understanding how animal behaviors and mental processes are functional for survival. It is assumed that men and women have different and complementary functions to ensure survival and that they have each evolved in ways that address these different functions (Lips, 1988). For example, according to functionalism, women are naturally more nurturant than men and men are naturally more aggressive than women, to facilitate human survival through childrearing and providing food and shelter. Although functionalism is seductively (no pun intended) simple, there is little evidence supporting its assumptions.

A second biological perspective that has emerged recently is known as **sociobiology**. According to this approach, men and women have evolved different methods of sexual selection and reproduction to ensure the survival of their own genes (Lips, 1988). That is, it is believed that men have an innate tendency to try to reproduce their own genes with as many women as possible. Women, on the other hand, tend to be more selective and attempt to choose only the best males for reproduction; because women commit more time and energy to reproduction (i.e., bearing and nurturing the child). Sociobiologists state that our social behaviors and characteristics are genetically based, which makes social patterns of behavior predetermined or "wired in." Whereas Darwin was concerned with survival of the fittest with respect to physical characteristics, sociobiologists are concerned with the genetic bases of social behavior. Therefore, the theory implies that social behaviors such as war, rape, and racism are largely inevitable and that fundamental changes in the social behaviors of men and women are unlikely (Lips, 1988). Scientific opponents of this position emphasize three themes:

1. Complete lack of evidence that specific social behaviors are linked to given genes or subgroups of genes.

2. Use of circular logic—if a behavior continues across generations, it is genetic and because it is genetic, the behavior will persist.
3. Selective inclusion or omission of data based on animal research to support claims for the genetic bases of human behavior (Lips, 1988).

One contribution of the biological determinists is their recognition that men and women are not biologically alike and that there may be links between our bodies, our minds, and our behaviors. However, biological determinists erroneously infer that biological differences between men and women predict specific actions or behaviors. Experience, learning, and cultural structures in our society can affect and may dominate the influence of biological factors on our behavior. For example, people interpret and label bodily changes consistent with cultural and social norms and the cues provided in the immediate social context (Averill, 1982; Mandler, 1984; Tavris & Wade, 1984). Furthermore, when people believe that a trait is sex linked, the biological approach suggests that all members of one sex and none of the other sex possess it. This certainly is not true. Finally, because we tend to become immersed in our own viewpoint (Tavris & Wade, 1984), biological researchers may exaggerate sex differences or assume sex differences in areas where they have not been documented. There may also be a tendency to infer inappropriately from research on brain cells to complex social and behavioral differences.

Socialization Models. The socialization models suggest that **gender identity** and differences between women and men are acquired by how we pass through various developmental stages. Sex differences in gender identity and roles result from a learning process that involves modeling, imitation, and reinforcement. For example, knowledge of gender stereotypes increases between preschool and college (Del Boca & Ashmore, 1980), and same-sex modeling also increases during the same period (Bussey & Bandura, 1984) with boys watching other boys and men to learn acceptable behavior and girls observing other girls and women. The learning process may be more complex than simply modeling and imitation, however. There is evidence that children are active participants in learning and actively strive to understand social rules and to be viewed as socially competent. However, gender-role expectations cannot be learned until the child has reached a specific stage of intellectual development. Once the child has learned to categorize him- or herself as male or female, the gender category will be used to recognize, organize, and attach value to other behaviors. The child actively searches for cues regarding competent and correct behavior rather than being a passive recipient in the learning process (Lips, 1988).

The socialization models have received empirical support (Bussey & Bandura, 1984; Bussey & Perry, 1982; Coker, 1984; Del Boca & Ashmore, 1980; Leahy & Shirk, 1984; Reis & Wright, 1982) although some research findings are mixed (Bussey & Bandura, 1984; C.L. Martin & Halverson, 1983; O'Keefe & Hyde, 1983). Two examples of this approach, social learning and cognitive development theories, focus more on how gender similarities and differences occur rather than on why such differences occur (Lips, 1988). For a more detailed discussion of these approaches, refer to Lips (1988). One contribution of the socialization models is the view that behaviors among women and men can and do change. Furthermore, this approach suggests that learning at various developmental stages may be one method for implementing or affecting behavior change among men and women.

Social Structural–Cultural Models of Gender.   Biologists, phys-iologists, and psychophysiologists have been the source of biological theories of sex and gender, whereas social learning and socialization theories have been popular among psychologists. The social structural approach, which is gaining acceptance in psychology, has long been popular among sociologists and anthropologists (Lips, 1988). This ap-proach focuses on the social structure, systems, and arrangements that define and support gender differences and on the reasons why our society supports little boys and girls learning these messages (Lips, 1988). The features of social structure that have been examined often are power and status differences between men and women (Gitter, Black, & Mostofsky, 1972; Henley, 1972; Kanter, 1975, 1977a; Weitz, 1976) and the division of labor reflecting men's work and women's work (W.T. Bielby & Baron, 1984; Nieva & Gutek, 1981b; Walby, 1986).

According to this perspective, numerous institutions (e.g., educational, political, military, and religious, among others) have traditional ways of performing their functions. These traditions have become institutionalized as the correct or right ways to operate (Lipmen-Blumen, 1984). Societal members, including those who acquired and maintain power through these traditions and those who are rendered powerless through such traditions, come to accept them as natural (Cleveland & Kerst, 1993; Lips, 1991). The natural appearance of societal systems is a source of institutionalized or societal power that helps to keep the powerful in power and the power-less docile. Structural or institutional power appears so natural that it is difficult for either the powerful or the powerless to question it. There is evidence that it is particularly difficult for women to see their powerless-ness at work because they frequently join more powerful men in other sex–gender systems including marriage and childbearing (Lipmen-Blu-men, 1984). That is, especially White women may have difficulty seeing their powerlessness because they are not separate or segregated from the more powerful group. Because these women derive some advantage from more powerful males, it is difficult to identify their own weakness.

On the other hand, when the less powerful live apart from the powerful (e.g., racial segregation), there is increased awareness of power imbalances (Lipmen-Blumen, 1984). Power is the "infrastructure" of the sex–gender system. Gender roles provide the basis for all other power relations including power relations between generations, socioeconomic classes, and religious, racial, and ethnic groups (Lipmen-Blumen, 1984). Therefore, reinforcement and support for gender roles are very important for maintaining the status quo and impeding real change.

A second way the cultural–structural approach has been applied to comparisons between men and women is to investigate the sex structure and segregation of men and women in work activities—paid and unpaid, internal and external to the home. This line of research is not completely independent of the research on power. For example, Kanter (1977a) and others (Eagly, 1983; Ragins & Sundstrom, 1989) found that the structure of jobs in organizations affects one's ability to exercise power and influence. Women are more likely to occupy jobs that lack power and, therefore, find little opportunity to exercise it. There is evidence that women are also excluded from informal power and opportunity structures within organizations (Kanter, 1977a). The ways in which women are treated in organizations perpetuate this structural segregation. For example, although there is little evidence of gender bias in performance appraisal based on past performance, there is consistent bias in selection, promotion, and perceived causes of performance that favors men (Cleveland & Kerst, 1993; Nieva & Gutek, 1981a). Furthermore, women find it difficult to gain power by either personal strategies (e.g., being assertive or having control over rewards) or by structural ones (e.g., being in a position to secure valued organizational information). Personal power cannot overcome structural barriers (H.L. Smith & Grenier, 1982). For example, although a woman personally can be assertive and have control over the allocations of rewards, she will remain less powerful if she occupies a position or occupation that is not vital to organizational survival or is housed within a department that is not central to the organization's mission (Kanter, 1977a; Ragins & Sundstrom, 1989; V.E. Schein, 1977).

Sex segregation in most occupations has been resistant to change (Colwill, 1982). Given the percentage of women who would be required to change jobs in order to balance the proportion of men and women in occupations within the workplace (F.D. Blau, 1978), there was little change between 1900 and 1970. Although women have been entering professional schools in increasing numbers since 1970, estimates suggest that it would take 100 years at the current rate of change before women's representation in managerial jobs equals their representation in the job market (Colwill, 1982). The highest percentages of employed women are secretaries, nurses, teachers, and social workers; they are also married. Furthermore, increases in female employment may reinforce and exacerbate sex segregation of jobs because most women continue to enter service positions that entail nurturing and caretaking or positions that require physical beauty (Colwill, 1982; Prather, 1971). Job segregation by sex provides the basis and justification for lower wages for women (Hartmann, 1979). Furthermore, it is a primary means by which our society maintains men's power over women. Occupational segregation will be discussed in relation to workplace discrimination in chapter 7.

Implications of Sex Segregation of Work.   Sex segregation of work has implications, beyond women's and men's employment, for socialization, educational aspirations, discrimination, and organization structure (Colwill, 1982). Socialization does not end once one leaves childhood and enters the workforce. Women are socially reinforced for abilities necessary for caretaking jobs, abilities that are seen as natural for women. Men at work are also reinforced for such stereotypical abilities or traits as assertiveness, leadership, and strength. Beyond these social rewards, organizations economically reward and reinforce displays of sex or gender roles and behaviors that perpetuate the segregation of work. Sex segregation of occupations contributes to different educational and training aspirations among young girls and boys. Girls learn early to avoid high-prestige jobs, whereas boys prefer such occupations. These preferences may prompt boys and girls to seek different training and education consistent with their sex roles (Barnett, 1975; Colwill, 1982). Sex segregation of occupations provides the foundation for sex-based discrimination in at least two ways: access to jobs (e.g., refusing to hire individuals for specific positions on the basis of sex, or discriminatory recruiting), and preferential treatment on the job with respect to pay or promotion (Levitin, Quinn, & Staines, 1971). Finally, organizational structures reflect the structure of the U.S. society and shape women's and men's behaviors (Colwill, 1982). That is, the structure of organizations (including occupational structures) and society provides differential opportunities and resources to men and women, which differentially influence their aspirations, ambitions, and commitment to work, which in turn perpetuates gender differences and reinforces societal expectations of male and female behavior at work. Occupational sex segregation is discussed in terms of links to discrimination in the workplace in chapter 6.

Proponents of the structural approach maintain that too much attention has been given to identifying differences between men and women and explaining those observed differences as genetically based, immutable to cultural influences. Structural proponents point to research evidence that social training can overcome traditional sex-typing and to psychological and physiological data showing a significant overlap between men and women on sex-linked traits that may be more important than the average differences between them (Maccoby & Jacklin, 1974). For example, some researchers have found that 40% of women may show greater assertiveness than males, whereas a similar percentage of men exhibit more interdependence (or dependence on others) than females (McCleland, 1975). However, these research findings tend to be ignored in both the scientific and popular press (Lipmen-Blumen, 1984).

Connotations of "Sex Differences" and "Gender Differences"

The debates in the media over the use of terms such as *gender* versus *sex*, *comparisons* versus *differences*, may seem like splitting hairs. However, a number of important issues are involved in the choice of terms and in the specific language used to describe the issues faced by both women and men in what was once the exclusive domain of the male, that is, the world of paid work. Specifically, the term **sex** is defined by biological differences in genetic composition and reproductive anatomy and function (Unger & Crawford, 1992). The term **gender** reflects a society's or culture's interpretations of or constructions based on the characteristics associated with biological sex. Biological sex serves as a physical cue to begin the process of socializing a human being into male or female beginning at birth based on the appearance of the infant's genitals.

Although *gender* and *sex* are often used interchangeably (as well as *gender differences* and *sex differences*), experts on research on men and women (e.g., Unger, 1979) recommended that sex be distinguished from gender in research for two reasons. First, by using them interchangeably, one can easily slip into believing that differences in traits between men and women are biologically determined and immutable when such traits or behavioral differences may be attributable to society or culture. Second, by keeping them distinct, we are better able to remember that human behavior is determined in complex ways. Biological approaches tend to describe observed differences as "sex differences," implying genetic, immutable differences, whereas socialization and social structural/cultural models refer to such observations as "gender differences," implying they are not immutable but are socially determined.

The term *gender* is complex and can be reflected at three levels: individual, interpersonal, and societal (Unger & Crawford, 1992). At the individual level, gender refers to the notions of masculinity and femininity. We have come to associate certain characteristics and behaviors with men and women and assume they are appropriate to each sex. Furthermore, gender is assumed to be **dichotomous**; an individual is either masculine or feminine, but not both. Gender at the individual level reflects a form of stereotyping. For example, it is difficult for most people to believe that a person could have two opposite traits (e.g., be competitive and nurturing). On the other hand, the concept of **androgyny** suggests that men and women can possess seemingly opposite traits (e.g., both masculine and feminine characteristics; Bem, 1979). At the interpersonal level, gender informs us how to behave properly in interactions with others. Often when men and women behave identically, their behaviors are interpreted very differently. The same behavior by a woman and a man may elicit very different reactions by others, reactions that may differentially inhibit or enhance subsequent behaviors by the man or woman. That is, others' reactions may reinforce and thereby increase the occurrence of certain behaviors or may discourage and thereby eliminate the behavior. At the societal and structural level, gender can serve as a system of power relations in that it reflects a system of social classification or status. As such, gender influences one's access to power and resources (Unger & Crawford, 1992). For example, various work tasks have come to be known as "men's work" or "women's work." The value, prestige, and economic rewards associated with these gendered tasks vary dramatically with men's work more often linked with greater power and financial rewards.

Not only is it important to articulate clearly the underlying distinctions between sex and gender, it is critical to note (and keep in mind throughout this book) the dramatic **individual differences** that characterize men's and women's behaviors. Simply put, men are diverse and differ on a wide variety of physical, mental, and emotional characteristics; women are equally diverse. We often neglect or forget this diversity within groups of people. For example, in our society, we often have spokespersons for the "women's view" or for the "Black community view," a practice that minimizes the reality of diversity within these groups. Yet there rarely is only one spokesperson representing the diverse views found in the majority group.

Considerations in the Conduct of Research on Sex and Gender

In this section, we discuss the assumptions of scientific paradigms used in psychological and sociological research and how our orientations to research and the world can influence each phase of the scientific process. These phases include problem identification, formulation of research questions, research design, analysis of results, and interpretation of findings.

Many students and researchers are unaware of how their own beliefs and values affect their perceptions, the problems they select to investigate, and the research methods they employ (Unger, 1983).

Theoretical Paradigms.   **Logical positivism** (Wittig, 1985), or the positivist empiricist model, is important to psychology and management because it guides most of the research in their fields. Logical positivism assumes that scientific facts exist, that the scientist's job is to uncover those true facts, and that the process of fact finding is value neutral (Unger, 1983; Wittig, 1985). This approach focuses on analyzing observable behaviors so that experimenters' own beliefs are not imposed on the process. That is, what we study and how we study it are assumed to be independent. However, this assumption of objectivity may be inaccurate and may lead to faulty conclusions. For example, animal and human behaviors are often studied in laboratories even though this practice removes subjects from their natural surroundings and reduces or ignores the historical contexts of their behaviors. Psychologists and researchers who deny that perceptions of the world depend on the observer's viewpoint may also be unable (or unwilling) to assess their impact on their own research (Unger, 1983). Furthermore, psychological training leads us to look within the person for explanations of social problems rather than equally considering situational factors. For example, only 16% of the studies dealing with Black Americans that appeared in six issues of the 1970 *Psychological Abstracts* looked at situational variables as possible causal factors of behaviors, and no study examined both situational variables and personal factors simultaneously (N. Caplan & Nelson, 1973; Unger, 1983). According to some, the tendency to explain behavior from a person-oriented perspective is stronger among psychologists than among the general public (R.L. Kahn, 1972).

Although not as often embraced, (Wittig, 1985), there are other theoretical perspectives on research in psychology. **Subjective relativism** assumes that fact-finding, analysis, and conclusions are subjective in scientific research. Thus, it is asserted that researchers are quite capable of validating their own prejudices through data collection. Consistent with this theoretical perspective, psychology and related disciplines are affected by the researcher's values because explanatory methods and the objects of research (e.g., human beings in a social context) are value sensitive.

A third theoretical approach to psychological research has emerged in recent years. The major assumption underlying **constructionism** is that human beings invent reality. The role assigned to theory here is more circumscribed in that we attempt to explain psychological and social phenomena but not necessarily to predict them. More complex causal relationships are explored and encouraged, while less emphasis is placed on trying to identify universal principles and deterministic laws (Wittig, 1985).

Each of these theoretical paradigms acknowledges in varying degrees inherent biases that accompany each approach. However, the logical positivist paradigm continues to be the more widely used approach to the scientific study of men and women at work. Yet with its assumption of scientific objectivity, researchers who enthusiastically embrace logical positivism may lull themselves into believing that their research is without bias. Sexist biases have been identified, however, in each stage of scientific experimentation and are discussed next.

Biases in the Stages of Research.   Early feminist psychologists focused on the omission of both historical context and the situation from psychological experimentation, especially in the study of sex and gender comparisons. Historically, women were not included as subjects in research (e.g., research on heart disease), the effects of the experimenter's sex on behavior were ignored (e.g., men often do not admit feelings of weakness or incompetence to other males but may be more inclined with females), there was a tendency to generalize research results to humankind when findings were solely based on male samples (e.g., characteristics of successful leadership), and there were sex biases in how constructs were operationalized depending on which sex was studied (e.g., aggressive behavior defined as physical behavior for men and verbal behavior women).

Furthermore, sexist biases can affect psychological research more specifically at each of the four stages of the research process (Denmark, Russo, Frieze, & Sechzer, 1988; Hyde, 1985; McHugh, Koeske, & Frieze, 1986; Riger, 1992). In order to more fully appreciate and interpret the research literature reviewed in this book, we believe it is critical to convey the potential for such biases to our readers. We understand that, in doing so, we risk being perceived as biased ourselves (i.e., anti-scientific method, anti-male as norm, etc.). However, we hope that readers will not "kill the messenger." Although we readily admit our own biases, we do not believe we are supporting one perspective over another. Our only goal is to illuminate some of the alternative perspectives and biases that affect research on sex and gender comparisons.

Biased views on sex and gender enter each stage of the research process, including question formulation, research methods, data analysis, and conclusions (Denmark et al., 1988). At the question formulation stage, four potentially biasing factors have been identified. First, gender stereotypes may be associated with specific research topics. These stereotypes can bias the manner in which a question is formulated or asked and the outcomes of research. Until recently, for example, leadership was defined using traits that are consistent with the male stereotype (Loden, 1985), including strong, forceful, competent, and logical. Today, leadership characteristics also include supportiveness, openness to alternative perspectives, facilitating others, and team orientation, which reflect behaviors associated more with women (Loden, 1985). Second, new theories depend heavily on existing theory and research, which is based largely on male samples. For example, current conceptualizations of job satisfaction often ignore work–family flexibility or job-discrimination factors at work, both of which are often facets of women's levels of satisfaction. Third, women's experiences in research areas are often not taken into account or are marginalized. When women's experiences are acknowledged, topics more closely associated with white males are viewed as more important and more basic to study. Women's and minority-group issues are viewed as specialized or as exceptions rather than as reflecting the norm. Topics relevant to women are considered less valued, more applied, less basic, taboo, or trivial and receive less attention because there are fewer female researchers (McHugh et al., 1986). Fourth, even current reviews of previous research findings perpetuate biases in question or problem formulation. These reviews are frequently insensitive to subject selection and other methodological biases of earlier research on sex and gender. Additionally, within scientific experimentation, there is a preference for objectivity where the experimenter can be viewed as "neutral, disinterested and nondisclosing" (McHugh et al., 1986). One drawback of this assumption of complete objectivity is that topics with social significance may be ignored, and those choosing to engage in such research may be accused of being "involved, passionate, or enthusiastic" about their research. Another consideration is whether it is realistic to have disinterested or dispassionate people conducting scientific research on biological, social, and organizational problems. Do we really expect scientists to dedicate years of their work lives to studying phenomena about which they have no enthusiasm or passion?

A number of concerns have been raised about the research methods used to study sex or gender issues (Denmark et al., 1988). These include the populations studied, including selection of subjects based on stereotypical assumptions that do not allow for generalization to other groups; selection of subjects that is limited to one sex on the basis of convenience; and elimination of females as subjects when an unexpected sex or gender difference emerges. In addition, gender and gender identity are often confounded with other variables including sex, race, and age; and often the sex, race, and other demographic characteristics of experimenters are not specified, leaving the possibility of unexplored potential combinations of demographic variables, sex composition of groups, and so forth. Finally, the selection of research or stimulus tasks and materials is often biased in that materials reflect stereotypical masculine tasks.

Within a given research method, variables can also be inappropriately conceptualized and operationalized or measured (Denmark et al., 1988; McHugh et al., 1986). The measurement of variables can be influenced and guided by stereotypes. For example, women are stereotypically perceived as more dependent than men, yet this may reflect how independence is defined. Men are not labeled as dependent even though they rely on others to cook, clean, and write thank-you notes for them. Furthermore, nontraditional behavior exhibited by men and women is often perceived and evaluated negatively. For example, women who speak up at meetings or engage in debates are called aggressive or rude rather than independent (McHugh et al., 1986).

In terms of data analysis, there is more of an emphasis on reporting differences among people or between groups than on examining similarities. Few journals (if any) make a practice of publishing nonsignificant results (Hyde, 1985). This data analytic bias selectively screens out research highlighting similarities among men and women and thereby perpetuates a potentially biased research literature. Thus, gender differences are reported when found, but explicit references in research to an absence of gender differences are rare. When gender differences are found, some are magnified inaccurately. There is a need to differentiate in our analyses between statistical significance and substantive or practical significance of male–female differences (Denmark et al., 1988). Finally, journals in the discipline of psychology do not encourage replication of findings, including those pertaining to sex or gender differences. Oddly enough, when researchers have attempted to replicate reported sex and gender differences, especially in the area of intelligence, the initially reported differences are often not found (Tavris, 1992).

Our interpretation of results and the conclusions we draw on the basis of our analyses can reflect bias. Medical research results (Tavris, 1992) are commonly based on one sex (males) and are generalized to both groups. Differences in specific task performance are interpreted as reflecting general gender differences in global ability. Person-centered conclusions (e.g., it is because she is female) are drawn more frequently than situation-centered conclusions (e.g., it is because the jobs have little reward power) or conclusions based on an integration of the two explanations. Using person-centered explanations of gender differences, psychologists and practitioners could conclude that difference means "deficient" and recommend remedial action for the group (often women) that was different. Evaluative labeling of research results often uses males as the standard or norm (e.g., male levels of aggressiveness are the norm and are viewed as acceptable; Hare-Mustin & Marecek, 1988). Finally, there are few references to subject-based limitations of studies in research titles or abstracts, thereby implying that results have broader implications than are warranted by the data (Denmark et al., 1988; Gannon, Luchetta, Rhodes, Pardee, & Segrist, 1992; Riger, 1992).

Even with the explicit assumption of scientific objectivity, logical positivist paradigms for experimentation involve biases associated with every phase of research. It is important to question the validity or accuracy of research outcomes and also ask why a research question is framed as it is, who is asking the questions, and how the results are interpreted.

Evolution of Research on Gender Comparisons.

One way to identify sources of bias in research on gender and sex is to use the stages of scientific inquiry as we have just done and identify potential biases that enter at each stage. Another way is to examine some basic assumptions that researchers have made throughout the last 30 or more years, and continue to make, in their approach to gender comparisons (Tavris, 1992). During the 1960s, research on women and work treated women as a problem (Crawford & Marecek, 1989; Tavris, 1992). That is, women were compared with men, and when differences occurred, attempts were made to explain why women were deficient or why their behaviors deviated from men's and how to "correct" them. Men's (masculine) behavior was regarded as the norm: as normal and correct and better. On the other hand, feminist researchers at the time were attempting to show that there were, in fact, trivial differences between men and women. During the 1970s and 1980s, with the rise of women's studies programs and feminist researchers examining gender similarities and differences, women's behavior came to be viewed as the solution. Specifically, differences between men's and women's behaviors were acknowledged, and women's ways were deemed better. Today's research on gender seems to have adopted the perspective that one never really knows the essence or essential qualities of men and women because they are constantly changing (Tavris, 1991; Tiefer, 1987). Today the question of male–female differences has shifted to, "Why are we so interested in differences and what are the functions that beliefs in differences serve?" (Tavris, 1992, p. 92).

All three of these approaches continue to exist today and are reflected in contemporary gender research. They exist in the context of what has been called the "paradox of gender" (Crosby, 1989)—the persistent belief that males and females differ in important qualities despite many studies that have failed to find or replicate those differences (Tavris, 1991, 1992). Tavris stated that this paradox of gender is the result of (a) using male behavior as the norm; (b) the types of skills, behaviors, and qualities that researchers have selected as important to study; and (c) the scientific practice of attempting to attribute gender differences to biology, personality, or person-centered explanations rather than life experiences, resources, and power. The latter group of factors, of course, is subject to both cultural and historical changes (Tavris, 1992). The overriding problem with all these perspectives is not the study of differences. We recognize that people differ. The problem is that one group's behavior is viewed as the standard or norm according to which all other behaviors are compared, and if the other behaviors differ, they are judged as deficient.

UNDERSTANDING SEXUALITY IN ORGANIZATIONS

"Enter most organizations and you enter a world of sexuality" (Hearn & Parkin, 1987, p. 3). This book concerns issues surrounding gender and employment. Traditionally, most texts in management or industrial and organizational psychology ignore the issue of sexuality at work. In fact, two British management researchers stated that organizational scholars avoid the issue of gender in a "way that is bizarre" (Hearn & Parkin, 1987, p. 4). Sexuality is one of the most obvious aspects of gender relations. Therefore, we would be remiss if we excluded a brief discussion of the notion of sexuality within work organizations. Some have suggested that ignoring sexuality at work in the industrial sociology, industrial and organizational psychology, sociology, organizational theory, management theory, and industrial relations literatures reflects blatant sexism (Hearn & Parkin, 1987). In any case, there is a great void on this topic as it pertains to organizations.

Gender and sexuality are conceptually distinct but very closely related (Hearn, Sheppard, Tancred-Sheriff, & Burrell, 1989). The precise nature of each is highly debatable, and there are many interpretations as to what each is, including what is meant by *sexuality*, especially at work. Sexuality at work refers to "the various ways in which a male (worker) sees himself as a sexual male and responds to the sexuality of a female coworker—and the ways a female (worker) experiences her own sexuality in responding to male workers" (Bradford, Sargent, & Sprague, 1980, p. 18). Furthermore, sexuality at work includes such issues as sexual attraction, office affairs, self-awareness, and other-awareness of sexual attitudes and behaviors (Lobel, 1993).

One reason for the dearth of research on sexuality in organizations is that many perspectives on organizational research suggest or imply the need to remove sexuality from the workplace (Hearn & Parkin, 1987; Lobel, 1993). For example, the bureaucratic ideal suggests that coworkers relate to each other not as individuals but as position incumbents (Smelser,

1980). Work roles and personal relationships should be distinguished within the work context. Although personal relationships may dominate outside of work, the "suppression of sexuality is one of the first tasks the bureaucracy sets itself" (Burrell, 1984, p. 98). One way of suppressing sexuality in organizations is to exclude women from participating in various work activities (e.g., job segregation; Burrell, 1984; Hacker & Hacker, 1987). Consistent with the bureaucratic ideal, sexuality is viewed as an irrational behavior that is best kept in the private and personal domains (Lobel, 1993).

Both contemporary Western society (Mead, 1980) and contemporary organizational experts (Gabarro, 1986; Gutek, Morasch, & Cohen, 1983; Kram, 1985; Lobel, 1993) argue for the prohibition of sexuality at work. For example, to reduce sexual tension between mentor and protégé, there should be an emphasis on a "father–daughter" relationship, which can benefit from incest taboos (Kram, 1985). This is consistent with the recommendation that taboos be developed or evoked to limit sexual behavior at work (Mead, 1980). Again, sexuality is viewed as personal and therefore has little place in the public work organization.

Many feminists also view prohibition of sexuality at work as desirable. However, they assert that sexuality has not been suppressed at work but rather is asserted in terms of male power and control over women in forms of widespread sex segregation of jobs and sexualization of jobs. On the other hand, there is increasing evidence that personal relationships, including sexual ones, may support rather than conflict with organizational goals (Lobel, 1993). Data suggest that interpersonal caring and trust can benefit both the organization (in terms of bottom line productivity, and corporate health) and the individual (Kaplan, 1991; Lobel, 1993). Interpersonal concerns and caring among workers could become part of one's work role (M. Bell, 1984; Mumby & Putnam, 1992). For example, a more feminine approach to leadership, which typically involves more openness and self-disclosure, may be an effective way to lead increasingly diverse groups of employees (Loden, 1985). In chapters 4 and 9, the impact of male–female interpersonal relationships, workplace romance, and sexual harassment on worker behavior is discussed.

A second line of argument supports the importance of considering sexuality at work. Sexuality cannot be confined to nonwork private relations because social and work roles are permeable (D.T. Hall & Richter, 1988). In fact, flexibility between work and nonwork roles may increase as more women enter the workforce. People at work have generally favorable attitudes toward nonharassing sexual behaviors (Gutek, Cohen, & Konrad, 1990; Mainiero, 1989; Rapp, 1992). In a survey conducted by the Society for Human Resources Management (cited in Rapp, 1992), 70% of 1,550 human resources managers reported that their companies accept dating among coworkers, 60% said dating was not a problem, and 92% had no policies prohibiting dating between coworkers.

Sexuality can be directed toward another person as an expression of caring. This is especially true when the target is capable of consent or dissent. Obviously, the degree of choice may be severely limited in various cultural contexts (Lobel, 1993) and organizational settings. Rather than unilateral prohibition of sexuality at work, new social norms in the workplace can be developed and then the organization can determine which ones have positive or negative consequences. Because women are at greater risk to experience negative consequences of sexuality at work, the use of a "reasonable women" standard may be advisable (Conte, 1997). That is, men and women may not agree about which behaviors are negative or noxious and which are not. Women tend to find more behaviors offensive and disruptive, so women should play important roles in formulating new social norms at work regarding sexuality in organizations.

SUMMARY

With the influx of women into the workforce during the last 20 years, there has been increased attention to comparisons between men and women on a number of work-related attributes and behaviors. With this increased attention, there has also been some confusion about whether women and men differ to a significant degree, how much they differ, and whether these differences truly are meaningful regarding behavior at work. Three sources of confusion in understanding or interpreting research comparing women and men are presented in this chapter.

First, there are at least three approaches to explaining how sex- and gender-related behaviors emerge or are acquired: biological, socialization, and structural/cultural models. These approaches vary in terms of a number of assumptions about the similarities and differences among men and women. One perspective makes the assumption that not only do women and men differ in important ways but that these differences are genetic, immutable, and necessary for survival (biological approach). On the other hand, the structural/cultural perspective assumes there are few inherent differences between women and men, those differences that are observed are due to the social structure of society, and such differences are mutable. These explanations have significantly different implications for the types of research questions asked and for the evaluation of workplace behavior.

A second source of confusion is that the use and connotations of such terms as *sex differences* and *gender differences* have contributed to misinterpreting results of research on gender in the workplace. The term *sex* often connotes that observed differences between men and women are biological or genetic in nature and thus less amenable to change. *Gender*, on the other hand, reflects individual, interpersonal, and societal notions of masculinity and femininity. A third source of confusion involves the biases associated with the very research methodologies we use to investigate behavior among and between women and men.

The chapter concludes with a brief discussion of sexuality in organizations. Sexuality is an important consideration in the discussion of women and men at work; nevertheless, most management and applied psychology texts do not include a discussion of sexuality as it affects the work environment.

GLOSSARY

Androgyny: Concept that people can combine traits traditionally assigned to one or the other sex.

Constructionism: A theoretical perspective on research in psychology which assumes that human beings invent or construct reality, and that the role of theory reflects scientists' attempts to explain psychological phenomena but not necessarily to predict them.

Dichotomous: Extreme opposites of a given attribute, skill, or trait (e.g., strong vs. weak, passive vs. aggressive).

Functionalism: A school of psychology concerned with how an organism's or person's behavior and consciousness are functional for its survival.

Gender: What culture makes out of the "raw material" of biological sex. All known societies recognize biological differentiation and use it as the basis for social distinction. Gender is based on sex.

Gender identity: Degree to which one sees oneself as female or male or masculine or feminine.

Individual differences: Differences among individuals on a wide range of behaviors, skills, abilities, and personalities.

Logical positivism: A scientific model that assumes scientific facts exist and it is the psychologist's job to discover those facts. Further, the model assumes that the scientific process for uncovering those facts is value neutral.

Nontraditional occupation: An occupation that a person holds where the predominant incumbent is the opposite sex.

Proximal context variables: Factors close in time and space that directly influence an individual's behavior.

Sex: Biological differences in genetic composition and reproductive anatomy and function.

Sociobiology: Perspective that the behavior of humans is due to the interests of the survival of their own particular genes; social behavior has a large genetic basis and is largely unchangeable.

Subjective relativism: Another scientific perspective on psychological research which assumes, quite unlike logical positivism, that fact-finding, analysis, and conclusions are subjective in scientific research.

II

PROCESSES UNDERLYING
MALE–FEMALE ATTITUDES
AND BEHAVIOR
IN THE WORKPLACE

3

How Stereotypes Affect Our Perception of Men and Women at Work

MEN ARE TAUGHT TO APOLOGIZE
FOR THEIR WEAKNESSES, WOMEN
FOR THEIR STRENGTHS.
—Lois Wyse, b. 1926, American advertising executive
(*Women's Wit and Wisdom*, 1991, p.   )

The terms *male, female, Black, Anglo, Asian,* and *Native American* carry powerful images of the characteristics or attributes of specific groups. Such labels or stereotypes not only carry messages about how various groups are perceived but also convey expectations about how various group members should behave and what characteristics or attributes are valued by the dominant group. Stereotypes, especially gender stereotypes, influence our expectations and evaluations of what is appropriate for ourselves as well as for others. Stereotypes can limit the types of careers that people select and can facilitate or inhibit the perceptions of an individual's effectiveness.

Individuals hold numerous beliefs about what constitutes masculinity and femininity, and these beliefs shape our perceptions of who is likely to perform certain behaviors and what behaviors are appropriate at work. We start this chapter by describing gender stereotypes and then relate these to stereotypes based on race, age, appearance, and disability. There is evidence that stereotypes influence both people's behavior and others' perceptions of that behavior, and we describe some of these findings. Furthermore, stereotypes not only refer to perceptions of individuals but also are associated with perceptions of occupations, specifically, men and women in nontraditional roles or jobs including leadership roles. Finally, we conclude the chapter by discussing the influence of stereotypes on personnel decisions affecting men and women.

GENDER STEREOTYPES

Stereotyping involves generalizing beliefs about groups as a whole to members of those groups. For example, if you believe that older people are more likely to resist change than younger people, you may infer that an older person you have just met is likely to be rigid and to have a hard time adapting to changes. Through stereotyping, we can categorize people into groups on numerous demographic bases, including gender, race, age, religion, social class, and so forth, and our perceptions of specific individuals will be influenced by what we know or think we know about the group as a whole. **Gender stereotypes** are socially shared beliefs about the characteristics or attributes of men and women in general that influence our perceptions of individual men and women.

Stereotypes tend to exaggerate both the perceived differences of members of different groups (e.g., men and women) and the perceived similarities of a particular man or woman to the general categories of *male* and *female* (Lips, 1988). That is, men and women who are objectively similar in many ways (e.g., similar appearance, behavior, interests, values, etc.) often will be seen as quite different because they are members of two quite different categories. The oppositional nature of masculine and feminine stereotypes implies that men and women should be separate from each other in a variety of contexts including work (e.g., occupational segregation) and family (e.g., cooking vs. mowing lawn) activities, and these stereotypes can have a powerful influence on both men's and women's workplace experiences.

Since the early 1950s, a large number of studies have been conducted on gender stereotypes. Most gender stereotype studies in psychology were conducted by individuals interested in personality (Ashmore & Del Boca, 1986), for example, Sherriffs and McKee (1957) in *Journal of Personality;* Rosenkrantz, Vogel, Bee, Broverman, and Broverman (1968) in *Journal of Consulting and Clinical Psychology;* and Spence, Helmreich, and Stapp (1974) in *Journal of Applied Psychology Catalog of Selected Documents in Psychology* (a multidisciplinary journal, not a social psychology journal). The personality orientation has had two implications (Ashmore & Del Boca, 1986) for research on gender stereotypes. First, it influences the questions that are asked involving gender stereotypes and focuses largely on questions pertinent to the clinical setting (e.g., Is emotional dysfunction influenced by gender stereotypes, or are therapists' recommendations for therapy guided by gender stereotypes?) Second, it influences how gender stereotypes are studied. For example, the personality approach relies heavily on the use of traits and adjectives to measure gender stereotypes. This person-based focus may exacerbate perceived differences between men and women and ignore important social and situational factors.

Gender stereotype research has had three major goals: to assess the content of sex stereotypes, determine the degree to which characteristics associated with men and women are evaluated favorably, and to determine the pervasiveness of such stereotypes (Ashmore & Del Boca, 1986). Each of these goals warrants further discussion.

Stereotypes of Women and Men

Sex stereotypes work at two levels: **sex-role stereotypes** and **sex-trait stereotypes** (D. Williams & Best, 1990). Sex-role stereotypes are beliefs about the appropriateness of various **roles** and activities for men and

Sidelight 3.1   Masculinity: The Male
Sex Role

The meaning of masculinity in the United States is described as a function of three factors: the nature of the relationship between men and women, the nature of the relationship between men and other men, and the nature of the relationship between men and themselves (Franklin, 1984). Two fundamental themes in the male role include **achievement** and the **suppression of affect** (Pleck, 1976). In the traditional male role, the major forms of achievement that validate masculinity are physical (Pleck, 1976). At times, achievement may translate into physical power over others, especially women. The traditional male expects women to acknowledge and defer to his authority. Masculinity is characterized, traditionally, as aggressiveness, dominance, and competitiveness (Franklin, 1984). In the modern male role, male achievement may take other forms including behaviors that require more interpersonal and intellectual skills rather than exclusively physical strength (Pleck, 1976).

There has been a significant amount of research on the relationship between gender stereotypes and ethnic stereotypes, and this research suggests that these two sets of roles can sometimes conflict or can interact in ways that pose significant problems for individuals. For example, Franklin (1984) suggested that Black males' masculine experience can be life threatening and psychologically damaging. Black males have higher rates of heart disease, strokes, and accidents than White males. Dominance is expressed within Black male–female relationships because Black men often have fewer opportunities to express dominance outside the Black culture (Franklin, 1984). Black men must internalize dominance and competitiveness and control themselves both physically and mentally. In describing themselves, Black males tend to endorse both feminine and masculine traits more than White males (Pettigrew, 1964).

Black males tend to be inhibited in efforts to fulfill the provider–protector aspect of masculinity due to societal structural barriers such as racial discrimination. Yet, society (including the Black culture) considers the internalization of the work ethic as a necessary trait of masculinity. That is, in order to "be a man," a young Black or White man must provide for his family and develop the training and skills needed for work. However, Black males receive the contradictory message that White society will not allow them the opportunities to fulfill that work role. These contradictory messages may inhibit development of a work ethic and security of masculinity among Black males. Black males may be expected to demonstrate dominance, aggressiveness, and violence within the Black cultures while simultaneously being expected to show submissiveness outside the culture (Franklin, 1984).

Numerous aspects of traditional masculinity are generally hazardous to both Black and White men's health (Pleck, 1981). Aggressiveness and competitiveness encourage men to place themselves in dangerous situations. Emotional inexpressiveness or suppression among males may lead to psychosomatic and other health problems. Men take greater risks than women. Although risk taking may be viewed as an asset in some circumstances (e.g., managerial decision-making leadership), it can have negative consequences as well. Men's jobs expose them to more physical danger and psychological stress. Furthermore, the traditional male role socializes men to have personality characteristics associated with high mortality (e.g., **Type A behaviors,** especially an anger component; Pleck 1981). The responsibilities associated with being a sole family breadwinner contribute to male psychological stress. The male role encourages specific behaviors that are known to endanger health including smoking and alcohol consumption. Finally, the male role discourages men from taking adequate medical care of themselves (Pleck, 1981).

women (e.g., the two sexes participate in these activities with differential frequency). Sex-trait stereotypes are beliefs that psychological and behavioral characteristics describe the majority of men to a greater or lesser degree than the majority of women. We focus on sex-trait stereotypes or the content of general gender stereotypes in this section. Subsequent sections in the chapter address stereotypes or beliefs about the appropriateness of various behaviors by men and women.

A large number of traits have been associated with women and men. In the late 1950s, after researchers gave participants over 200 adjectives to evaluate, men were described as frank, straightforward in social relations, intellectually rational, and competent, bold, and effective in dealing with the environment. Stereotypes of women included such descriptors as emotional, warm, concerned about issues besides the material, and concerned about social amenities (J.P. McKee & Sheriffs, 1957). These clusters of traits are often referred to as **adaptive–instrumental** (male traits) and **integrative–expressive** (female traits; Parsons & Bales, 1955). A second major group of sex-stereotype studies were conducted in the 1960s and 1970s (Broverman, Vogel, Broverman, Clarkson, & Rosenkrantz, 1972), with results similar to those found in the late 1950s. Consistent with previous research, instrumental items were associated with men and expressive traits were associated with women (Bem, 1974, 1975). More recently, the assessment of gender stereotypes shows remarkable consistency and resistance to change. In the late 1980s, women were described as affectionate, attractive, flirtatious or sexy, and dreamy, whereas men were described as rational, realistic, tough, aggressive, and dominant (Williams & Best, 1990).

Favorability of Masculine and Feminine Stereotypes.   Numerous researchers have attempted to assess the relative favorability of stereotypes for each sex, and most have found that the masculine stereotype is more positively valued than the feminine stereotype (Broverman et al., 1972; McKee & Sherriffs, 1957). However, not all evidence supports this conclusion. Although a higher proportion of stereotypically male attributes than female have been found to be socially desirable, the favorability of the two sex stereotypes is not necessarily significantly different (Rosenkrantz et al., 1968). Furthermore, assessments of stereotype favorability may depend on the method used to define gender stereotypes.

For example, gender stereotypes can be either **"focused"** or **"expanded"** (J.E. Williams & Bennett, 1975). Attributes that are assigned to one gender by a great majority of the population (i.e., 75%) represent focused stereotypes of females and males. Attributes assigned to either gender by a smaller majority (i.e., 60%) reflect an expanded stereotype. Although the male focused stereotype includes a greater proportion of positive traits than the female focused stereotype, the female expanded stereotype compares favorably to the male expanded stereotype (Williams & Bennett, 1975).

Even when stereotypes of one gender contain more positive attributes than stereotypes of another, overall assessments of male and female stereotypes may be more complex than a simple count of attributes would suggest. In the Williams and Bennett (1975) study, both expanded and focused stereotypes were analyzed by a trained clinician. This clinical assessment indicated that although both stereotypes reflected "immaturity" and **"pathology,"** the stereotypical male was rated as more disturbed than the stereotypical female (Williams & Bennett, 1975). In sum, the evidence regarding the favorability of male and female stereotypes is mixed, and conclusions vary. Furthermore, the bases for a given study's conclusions are equivocal. The masculine stereotype is rated more favorably than the feminine stereotype when the total number of favorable attributes for each sex is compared. One reason for this is that the male stereotype often comprises a large number of attributes and, therefore, is more likely to contain a larger number of favorable attributes. When comparison procedures are used that correct for the number of items within stereotypes, male and female stereotypes tend not to show great differences in favorability (Ashmore & Del Boca, 1986).

However, the difference between male and female stereotypes in the number of items that they contain has an important implication. Men are given a wider range of socially desirable and acceptable behaviors or characteristics that they can exhibit. Women are more limited by a feminine stereotype to demonstrate socially desirable behavior. This is depicted in a quote by Marlo Thomas: "A man has to be Joe McCarthy to be called ruthless. All a woman has to do is put you on hold" (*Women's Wit and Wisdom*, 1991, p. 11). Given the greater behavioral latitude for men and the more restricted set of positive behaviors for women, the male stereotype in practice may be more positive than the female stereotype (Ashmore & Del Boca, 1986).

Pervasiveness of Gender Stereotypes.   Assessments of gender stereotypes in the United States have shown remarkably consistent results. Again, women are often described as affectionate, attractive, charming, dreamy, emotional, flirtatious, and sentimental. Men are often described as aggressive, assertive, dominant, handsome, masculine, strong, tough, rational, and realistic. This research has been extended to 25 countries to assess sex-trait stereotypes cross-culturally (Best & Williams, 1990). In all 25 countries surveyed, women were described as sentimental, submissive, and superstitious, and in 22 countries they were described as sexy. For men in all 25 countries, masculine stereotypes included adventurous, independent, masculine, and strong. This consistent pattern of findings across studies and across countries suggests that gender stereotypes are quite pervasive.

Another way of tapping the pervasiveness of gender stereotypes is to understand the notion of the "person = male" bias. The **prototype** in our culture is male (Silveira, 1980). That is, in the absence of any contrary information, there is a greater likelihood that when one pictures an individual, that person will be male (Henley, 1989). So, if you do not know an individual's gender (e.g., you receive a memo from Pat Jones), you are more likely to refer to this person as "he" than as "she." This does not always occur, but there is empirical support for this pro-male bias in a number of settings (M.C. Hamilton, 1991; O'Sullivan, Cole, & Moseley, 1982).

Are Gender Stereotypes Valid?

Stereotypes can be very useful, in the sense that they help us understand the world. They are particularly useful when they are based on facts and when the generalizations they lead to are quite likely to be correct. For example, if we see someone in an airport reading a philosophy text, this might lead to a stereotype such as "student" or "scholar," which might also lead us to believe that this person is reasonably intelligent, is able to follow complex arguments, and is interested in academic pursuits. If our categorization of this person is correct, the other guesses we make based on that characterization (e.g., intelligent, studious) might also be correct. On the other hand, stereotypes that are based on incorrect information, biases (e.g., derogatory stereotypes of racial, ethnic, or religious groups), or outmoded ideas may do more harm than good in that they may lead us to make incorrect inferences about people. Therefore, the question of whether stereotypes are valid (e.g., is it true that women are more emotional than men?) is important.

An even more important question, and one that is often difficult to answer on the basis of empirical research, is exactly how accurate or inaccurate are the inferences based on gender stereotypes? For example, suppose that women are more affectionate than men. Unless you know how large the differences between groups are, compared to the differences within genders (some men are certainly more affectionate than others), it might be very difficult to determine whether this stereotype will help you assess others or will mislead you. Consider the situation illustrated in Fig. 3.1. In this hypothetical example, there is a small difference between the average level of affectionate behavior shown by men and women, but there is extensive variability within groups. This means that many men will be more affectionate than many women, and reliance on the stereotype that women are more affectionate will lead to many errors in perceptions of specific individuals.

On the whole, research evidence on the validity of gender stereotypes suggests that they are often poor representations of individual men or

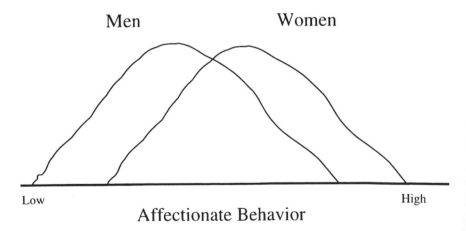

FIG. 3.1.   Illustration of overlap among groups that differ in their average level of affectionate behavior.

women. For example, male–female differences in most cognitive abilities and in most basic personality traits (except for traits such as masculinity vs. femininity, which are directly linked to sex and gender) are generally small, in comparison with the variability within genders. In areas where there are relatively large male–female differences (e.g., likelihood of working in child-care settings), it is likely that stereotypes and socially constructed definitions of what men and women should do are themselves significant causes of these differences. Although male-female differences in many areas are relatively small, reliance on stereotypes can lead people to exaggerate these differences and to perceive men's and women's behavior quite differently, even if the behavior itself is quite similar across gender lines.

Androgyny. Gender stereotypes sort people into one of two mutually exclusive categories: male versus female. However, few men possess all of the characteristics that are stereotypically male and none of those that are stereotypically female. That is, there are relatively few men who are extremely aggressive, assertive, dominant, handsome, masculine, strong, tough, rational, and realistic but not at all affectionate, attractive, charming, dreamy, emotional, flirtatious, and sentimental. There are probably even fewer women who are extremely affectionate, attractive, charming, dreamy, emotional, flirtatious, and sentimental but not at all aggressive, assertive, dominant, handsome, masculine, strong, tough, rational, and realistic. The masculine and feminine stereotypes describe extremes of a continuum, and it is likely that many men and women possess a mix of stereotypically masculine and stereotypically feminine traits. To be sure, there are some people who are highly masculine or highly feminine. There are also some individuals who demonstrate few of any of the traits listed previously.

People who possess high levels of both masculine and feminine traits are referred to as androgynous. **Androgyny** is sometimes thought of as the best of both worlds, in the sense that androgynous individuals may be able to draw on a wider array of strengths and talents in dealing with the world around them. There is some research support for the notion that androgyny is related to success and to social adjustment (Bem, 1979), and the idea that androgyny is beneficial has certainly been picked up by the popular media (e.g., think of all of the stories of men who succeed by getting in touch with their "feminine side"). It is less clear how people become androgynous or whether androgyny can or should be taught or developed in the same way we try to develop other social skills. However, people who are tightly locked in narrow or extreme definitions of their appropriate gender roles may find it easier to succeed in environments where their particular roles are emphasized and harder to succeed in contexts where there is less emphasis on stereotypically defined masculinity or femininity.

GENDER STEREOTYPES AND STEREOTYPES OF RACE, AGE, APPEARANCE, AND DISABILITY

It is difficult to think of a "typical" man or woman without also imagining that the individual has a specific race and age and, perhaps, a certain degree of physical attractiveness (Landrine, 1985; Lips, 1988). In North America, such an image is likely to be someone who is White, relatively young, of average attractiveness, and nondisabled. However, holding gender stereotypes based on the "typical" man or woman may contribute to perceptions that people who are not typical are somehow "different and less," thereby perpetuating stereotypes based on race, age, appearance, or disability as well. Furthermore, there is a possibility that gender stereotypes combine with other stereotypes so that work perceptions and outcomes are complexly determined.

Gender Stereotypes and Race

Women of color may experience sexism differently than White women, and men and women of color may experience racism differently from each other (A. Smith & Stewart, 1983). We are only beginning to understand the joint dynamics of racism and sexism by investigating the experiences of various gender-role groups (Lips, 1988).

Commonly reported gender stereotypes include the belief that Black women may be viewed as less feminine than their White counterparts (O'Leary, 1977) when one uses the feminine stereotype generated based on all-White female samples. Black women are stereotyped as strong, self-reliant, and having a strong achievement orientation (Epstein, 1973; Fleming, 1983a) in addition to being more dominant, assertive, and self-reliant than Black males (called the "Black matriarchy" theory). Although this appears to be a positive stereotype, it characterizes Black women's strength only within the context of the family. Furthermore, this stereotype of Black women has been used by many commentators in U.S. society to hold women responsible for many of the problems associated with Black men and young adults. Although the existence of such a stereotype has been documented, it is based on both misleading and flawed evidence (Fleming, 1983b; Lips, 1988).

Both White men and women rate White women more negatively than Black women are rated by Black men and women (O'Leary & Harrison, 1975). Furthermore, Black subjects identify fewer traits that distinguish men and women than Whites, suggesting that Blacks may be less likely to devalue women on a stereotypical basis. There is some evidence that the feminine stereotype in the United States largely reflects views of White, middle-class females. Although Black and White middle- and working-class women are rated similarly on the female stereotype, stereotypical descriptions differ significantly by race and social class. Black and White women are described similarly on traits including ambitious, competent, intelligent, self-confident, and hostile, but White women are described more similarly to the traditional feminine stereotype (e.g., higher on characteristics such as dependent, emotional, and passive). Therefore, although race and class affect gender stereotypes to some degree, gender stereotypes emerge beyond these variables (Lips, 1988).

Older Women

Stereotypes of femininity are strongest when they are applied to younger women. Both women and men describe themselves in less stereotypical terms as they age. Furthermore, older men perceive older women as more active, hardy, involved, and stable than themselves (Feldman, Biringen, & Nash, 1981). Age stereotypes may replace the salience of gender stereotypes as people grow older (Lips, 1988). How does this occur? One of the widely accepted stereotypes of the aged is that they are no longer interested in (or perhaps capable of) sex (Kay & Neeley, 1982). Sexuality is one of the major bases for masculinity and femininity (i.e., to be sexually attractive). If sexuality becomes dissociated with men and women, then perhaps so do stereotypes of masculinity and femininity (Lips, 1988). Although there is evidence that sexuality is not unimportant to older individuals, the belief that it is may lessen the salience of gender stereotypes.

There is, however, evidence of a double standard regarding the interchange between age and gender stereotypes, placing women at a disadvantage (Abu-Laban, 1981). Because in North America so much of a woman's worth is based on her attractiveness, she may find herself devalued as she ages. This does not appear to hold for aging men, whose worth is based on other factors including power and prestige via financial achievement, occupational success, and so forth (Lips, 1988) that are likely to increase with one's age. Women who hold more traditional feminine stereotypes may handle aging less well and may view themselves more critically as they age (Lowenthal, Thurnber, & Chiriboga, 1975; Maas & Kuypers, 1974).

Gender Stereotypes and Appearance

Physical appearance is a critical component of gender stereotyping (Mc-Arthur, 1982). Perceptions of both one's own appearance and the appearance of others can have strong implications for how masculine or feminine an individual is believed to be (Lips, 1988). A tall, large-boned woman may be viewed as more masculine than a short, petitely built woman, whereas a short male may perceive himself as less masculine than a tall male.

Although appearance is important to men and women, attractiveness and the preoccupation with one's appearance are viewed as important aspects of the female or feminine stereotype (Rodin, Silberstein, & Striegel-Moore, 1984). Such bodily parts as breast size, hips, and the shape of a woman's legs are all signals used in our society to denote a woman's femininity and sexuality (Brownmiller, 1984; Lips, 1988). Furthermore, especially for women, weight is a critical aspect of physical appearance. Fat is viewed as unfeminine, unattractive, and nonsexual, whereas a thinner body is viewed as attractive (Gillen & Sherman, 1980). College women most frequently cited being overweight as the item that would make them feel less feminine (Lips, 1986).

Not only is physical attractiveness a central component of gender stereotype, but it is also a central part of self-concept for women more than men (M.J. Lerner & Karabenick, 1974; R.M. Lerner, Orlos, & Knapp, 1976). Weight and body shape are central determinants of women's perceptions of their physical attractiveness (Rodin, Silberstein, & Striegel-Moore, 1984). College-age women report more dissatisfaction and concern with their bodies than men (Fallon & Rozin, 1985). Furthermore, obesity among women is associated with more negative evaluations for women than for men (Spigelman & Schultz, 1981). The importance of weight in shaping stereotypes of femininity is supported further by a study of women who value nontraditional roles for women. The influence of slenderness is powerful. Even women who rejected many of the traditional views of femininity were found to prefer a smaller, thinner female body shape and associated a larger, rounder shape with the "wife and mother" stereotype (Beck, Ward-Hull, & McLear, 1976).

Traditional sex-role stereotypes may interact with individuals' age and gender to affect their self-ratings of attractiveness (Friedman & Zebrowitz, 1992; Sorell & Nowak, 1981). For example, men at midlife are often at the peak of their success, and signs of aging may be viewed as evidence of years of socially valued experiences (Sorell & Nowak, 1981). For women, midlife signals that the traditional role of motherhood is coming to an end. Signs of aging may therefore symbolize diminishing social usefulness. Middle-aged women consider themselves less attractive than younger or older women and young, middle-aged, or older men (Nowak, 1976; Nowak, Karuza, & Namikas, 1976). Middle-aged men see themselves as less attractive than younger people but as more attractive than older men or women.

Gender differences have been found in regard to eating, weight, physical appearance, and appearance self-esteem across the life span (Pliner, Chaiken, & Flett, 1990). Women at all ages have significantly lower appearance self-esteem than males, which may suggest that the standards for female attractiveness are higher than for male attractiveness (Pliner et al., 1990). Women are also more concerned about eating and body weight, which the authors suggested comes from the larger cultural context that emphasizes greater importance of physical attractiveness for females than for males. Traditionally (and stereotypically), a woman's occupation is to provide a man with affection, sexual responsiveness, and care of the home and children. Men are expected to be economic providers. Physical appearance is assumed to be more relevant to the woman's role than to the man's (Pliner et al., 1990)

Sexuality and Gender Stereotypes. In a multinational study, participants from 22 of 25 countries included the adjectives *affectionate, sexy, flirtatious,* and *attractive* as part of the stereotype of women (J.E. Williams & Best, 1990). These findings suggest that women are viewed in more sexual terms than men. However, men not only are more sexually active but also perceive male–female interactions as more sexual than do women.

Studies on **sexual harassment** consistently show that men perceive a woman's behavior as more sexual than do women perceivers (Saal, Johnson, & Weber, 1989). Men are more likely than women to view "friendly" behavior in mixed-sex settings as indicating sexual interest (A. Abbey & Melby, 1986; N. Abbey, 1982; E.G.C. Collins & Blodgett, 1981; Saal, 1996). Men also believe that such sexual behaviors are more typical of and acceptable by individuals in the workplace. Men may more quickly label women's behavior as sexual than do women (Saal 1996). To test this conclusion within the context of sexual harassment, C.B. Johnson, Stockdale, and Saal (1991) presented subjects with 12 versions of a scenario depicting a professor interacting with a student of the opposite sex, in which sex of the powerholder, level of harassment, and response to harassment were manipulated. Regardless of the harassment condition and the response of the victim, male subjects rated the actors using more sexual terms than did female subjects. Men more than women believed that the female actor, whether she portrayed the student or the professor, was trying to behave in a more promiscuous, seductive, and sexy manner.

Men also believed that the male student was trying to behave in a more sexy manner. In the most harassing condition, women viewed the male professor in more sexual terms than did men.

These results suggest that men have more difficulty than women in differentiating between the sexual intentions of a more severe male harasser and those of a less severe one (in the more harassing conditions, males were clearly behaving more sexually). Even when the female target refused to submit to what clearly seemed to be harassing behavior, males persisted in rating the female target as trying to act in a more sexual manner than did female subjects (C.B. Johnson et al., 1991). In general, men's sexuality-based ratings of female targets were higher than the women's ratings. Men's sexuality-based perceptions of male targets did not differ from women's perceptions. These results suggest that men may misperceive women's behaviors but not other men's to the same degree (C.B. Johnson et al., 1991). On the other hand, the results also indicate that women may not be quite as sensitive to the harassing behavior of other women as they are to the harassing behavior of men.

Power and Gender Stereotypes

Major components of the traditional masculine stereotype include such adjectives as *strong, dominant, aggressive,* and *powerful.* Powerful figures in North America are perceived to be almost exclusively male. In fact, the idea of a powerful woman is disconcerting and uncomfortable for many, both male and female. Men's reactions to female power appear to contain "sincere horror as well as a conscious attempt to control and diminish that power by defining it as illegitimate and unnatural and by making it sound ridiculous or offensive" (Garlick, Dixon, & Allen, 1992, pp. 210–211). Stereotypical images of women in power include such negative phrases as "dowager empress," "powerful poisonous witches, and murdering mothers," "iron butterfly" (referring to Imelda Marcos), "domineering dowager," "scheming concubines," or "terrible woman" (Garlick et al., 1992). The implicit assumption that women close to power exert undue and inappropriate influence arises from the view that the political woman is a paradox. A powerful woman is viewed by many as somehow unnatural, and it is often assumed that a woman's means to power are somehow dubious (Garlick et al., 1992). Sidelight 3.2 on First Lady Hillary Clinton is an example of the disconnection between the notion of a women of power and the feminine stereotype.

Stereotypes of Working Women. Men are somewhat more likely to be regularly employed than women, but most women are employed for significant portions of their adult years. Nearly 75% of women with

Sidelight 3.2   The First Lady

The wife of the U.S. President occupies the special role of "First Lady." Most First Ladies have concentrated on traditionally feminine activities, such as hosting dinners and functions or decorating the White House, and even their public activities have often been restricted to areas that are viewed as feminine (e.g., "Lady Bird" Johnson was widely known for work on highway beautification; many other First Ladies have concentrated on issues involving children). However, a few First Ladies have achieved power and influence outside of traditionally feminine spheres, and public reactions to their activities reveal a great deal about stereotypical views of women.

Two first ladies have achieved notable influence outside of traditionally feminine spheres: Eleanor Roosevelt and Hillary Clinton. (Near the end of Woodrow Wilson's presidency, he had a series of strokes and his wife had a significant role in running the White House, but this was largely done behind closed doors.) Eleanor Roosevelt and Hillary Clinton are admired by a number of commentators, but both have also been the target of vicious criticism. Both of these women have been referred to as the most admired and the most hated First Ladies in U.S. history

Evolving views of Hillary Clinton illustrate how behavior that conflicts with or conforms with sex-role stereotypes can influence public perceptions. Her involvement in the health care debate during the President's first term alarmed many conservatives and many who viewed such behavior as inappropriate for women, and criticism of the First Lady was especially severe. Later, during the impeachment controversy, she was widely praised for "standing by her man" and providing public support, even when her husband's behavior involved well-publicized infidelities. Perceptions of Hillary Clinton were more negative when she was behaving in ways that are not consistent with the feminine stereotype (e.g., taking a lead in health care reform) than when her behavior was consistent with that stereotype (e.g., providing unconditional support to her husband).

---

school-aged children are expected to be in the labor force in the next decade (Silverstein, 1991; U.S. Bureau of Labor Statistics, 1987a), and the figure is even higher for women without young children. Given women's extensive involvement in the workforce, it is surprising that stereotypes of working women are still relatively negative and are still based on the assumption that the workplace is not the normal environment for women. Common stereotypes of working women include a non-job-involved, uncommitted, young, single woman who is looking for a husband; a sad, unhealthy middle-aged or older woman who has given up on men and will be a spinster; and a stressed-out career women uninterested in male–female relationships or having children. Stereotypes of working mothers often stress the conflicts between work and family, focusing either on the ways family will detract from work (e.g., working mothers are often assumed to be less involved in their work, less reliable, etc.) or on the ways that work will detract from family (e.g., working mothers are sometimes assumed to have less interest in or dedication to their children).

Contrary to the negative stereotypes many people hold about working women, there is evidence that work is beneficial to women much in the same way it is beneficial to men. Women who work outside the home report better physical and emotional health than do women who are full-time homemakers (Barnett & Baruch, 1987; we discuss gender, stress, and health in greater detail in chapter 12). The presence of children has positive effects on working mothers including less restricted views of sex roles (Hoffman, 1986). Furthermore, when negative findings are reported, other factors such as attitudes toward childrearing, sex-role definitions, and social class are more important in explaining those findings than whether a mother is working outside the home (Hoffman, 1989).

EFFECTS OF GENDER STEREOTYPES IN THE WORKPLACE

The stereotype literature suggests that our general beliefs about groups of people can affect our assessments of individual group members (Biernat, 1991). Stereotypes can contribute to shared misperceptions of coworkers, job candidates, performance, and credentials (Deaux & Major, 1987; D.L. Hamilton, 1979; Nieva & Gutek, 1980). Stereotypes not only affect the decisions we make about men and women but also affect self-perceptions, decisions, and choices made by those men and women. Furthermore, gender stereotypes can create a self-fulfilling prophecy, in the sense that both men and women may feel pressure to behave in ways that correspond to gender stereotypes. Thus, stereotypes can affect both how men and women behave in the workplace and how their behavior is perceived.

In chapter 7, we examine in some detail the processes that lead to gender discrimination in the workplace and note the important role of stereotypes in discrimination. Here, we provide a brief overview of how gender stereotypes can influence judgments and decisions that are made about men and women, and then we discuss several ways that stereotypes can affect the behavior of men and women in the workplace in ways that can limit women's effectiveness and success.

Influence of Stereotypes on Evaluations of and Decisions About Men and Women

Although conscious beliefs about men and women may be changing (McBroom, 1987), stereotypes still operate as implicit knowledge (Basow, 1986). We draw on them, and they influence our perceptions and evaluations of men and women, Anglo, Black, Hispanic, or Asian. There is evidence that stereotypes influence a number of work-related outcomes.

Hiring and Promotion Decisions. Research has repeatedly demonstrated that men are more likely to be hired for professional and managerial positions than similarly qualified women (R.D. Arvey, 1979; Cohen & Bunker, 1975; Powell & Posner, 1983; Rosen & Jerdee, 1974). For example, in studies of hiring decisions in academic settings, chairpersons of university departments evaluated female job candidates as more appropriate for assistant professor, a rank without job security, whereas male candidates with identical credentials were ranked as meriting associate professor, a higher rank with more job security and higher salary (Fidell, 1975; Haslett, Geis, & Carter, 1992). In general, women are perceived as less competent and subsequently are less likely to be promoted or are promoted at a slower rate than men with the same qualifications (Nieva & Gutek, 1981b). In fact, even when women receive higher performance ratings than men, men receive more promotions (Gupta, Jenkins, & Beehr, 1983). There is continued evidence that in business, government, and professional occupations, the proportion of women present decreases as the rank or status of the occupation increases (F.D. Blau & Ferber, 1985). The exclusion of women from higher status jobs is called "the glass ceiling" (Morrison, White, Van Velsor, and the Center for Creative Leadership, 1987), and there is evidence that this glass ceiling is at least in part the result of biases in the perception of men and women with objectively similar credentials (Haslett et al., 1992).

Interviews and Performance Evaluation. Research in the 1970s suggested that demographic characteristics of applicants (e.g., sex and race) significantly influenced interview outcomes. In more recent studies, demographic factors have shown much smaller effects (if any) on selection interview outcomes. Kacmar and Hochwarter (1992) suggested that this change reflects changes in both the contexts in which interviews occur and in the methods used to conduct interviews. Women and minorities may encounter less discrimination in the selection interview due to an increase in racial and gender diversity in the workplace, increases in interviewer training, and the use of structured interviews.

Although **access discrimination** (e.g., discrimination in hiring) seems to be declining in organizations, gender stereotypes still affect evaluations of men's and women's performance. For example, in studies where subjects were asked to evaluate critical reading exercises (P. Goldberg, 1968; Paludi & Strayer, 1985) or paintings (Pheterson, Kiesler, & Goldberg, 1971), products were evaluated more favorably when attributed to a male than to a female. Critical reading essays written by men were judged to be more important, authoritative, and convincing than those written by women.

There is evidence that the same job behavior by men and women is sometimes evaluated differently, in part because raters have different expectations about how men and women should perform and assume that men and women are likely to succeed for different reasons (Bartol & Butterfield, 1976; Deaux & Taynor, 1973; Dobbins, Stuart, Pence, & Sgro, 1985; Vaughn & Wittig, 1981). When a man succeeds, evaluators attribute it to the man's ability. When he fails, evaluators are likely to attribute it to less stable external causes, such as lack of effort, a difficult task, or even bad luck (Deaux, 1976; Deaux & Emswiller, 1974; Frieze, Fisher, Hanusa, McHugh, & Valle, 1978). The reverse appears to occur with women. A woman's success is attributed by others to external factors (e.g., she was just lucky), whereas her failures are attributed to lack of ability. Stereotypes lead us to expect that women fail (due to lack of ability) and that men succeed (because they are competent). When the unexpected occurs, evaluators discount the event as something odd and unlikely to occur again. As a result, even with identical performance credentials, evaluators will have more positive expectations regarding the future of men than women (Cash, Gillen, & Burns, 1977). Even when similar **attributions** are made about the causes for men's and women's success, men are consistently ranked higher than women (Pazy, 1986).

Access to Resources and Support.   Access to organizational resources and support (e.g., financial support to attend a professional development conference, permission to fire a subordinate, access to opportunities, resources, power, and autonomy) is critical to career mobility and success (Haslett et al., 1992). There is evidence that formal requests for such support are more likely to be approved by superiors when these requests come from male subordinates than from females (Rosen, Templeton, & Kirchline, 1981). There is also evidence of systematic differences in the types of informal support received by men and women. Research on male–female interactions in tasks performed by mixed-sex groups illustrates subtle but pervasive differences in nonverbal behavior that encourage participation by men and discourage participation by women.

Men distance themselves from a female partner by turning their heads or bodies away from her (Lott, 1987), but they do not do the same with male partners. In a study on problem solving using mix-sexed groups, when a man had the correct answer (which secretly had been provided by the researchers), the group accepted and applauded the individual. However, when a woman offered the same correct answer, it was ignored and rejected (Altemeyer & Jones, 1974). In discussions generally, women are interrupted, overlooked, ignored, or not "heard" more than men (Bunker & Seashore, 1975).

Ignoring or not supporting equally the contributions of women and men in a mixed group involves both female and male members. Both female and male members showed fewer facial expressions of approval and more expressions of disapproval for women's contributions than for the same contributions from men (Butler & Geis, 1990). By contributing to the group, the woman was violating stereotypical expectations of women. Even subtle reinforcers (or chastizers) can be misinterpreted as indicating whether a contribution is good or poor (V. Brown & Geis, 1984) and can influence subsequent behavior and performance of women and men.

Can Negative Perceptions of Women in the Workforce Be Eliminated? Although stereotypes appear to have substantial effects, there is evidence that the effects of these stereotypes can be sharply reduced. In particular, people are willing to view an individual as an exception to the stereotype about that person's social group when **individuating information** contradicts the stereotype (Locksley, Borgida, Brekke, & Hepburn, 1980). Individuating information that is directly relevant to job qualifications can reduce sex discrimination (Glick, Zion, & Nelson, 1988; Heilman, 1984). For example, women described as successful female managers (performing effectively) are not perceived in traditionally stereotypical ways (Heilman, Block, Martell, & Simon, 1989). That is, when a woman is depicted as a manager, the correspondence between descriptions of managers and women increases; the similarity increases further when the woman is depicted as a successful manager (Heilman et al., 1989). Furthermore, these women are described using masculine attributes typically associated with the managerial role.

Although the individuating information can affect decisions, it does not eliminate sex discrimination. For example, Glick et al. (1988) found that male and female applicants with identical resumes were perceived to be equally masculine and feminine with respect to their personality traits yet were still matched to jobs according to their gender. This suggests that stereotypes about occupations are unlikely to change unless the actual proportions of men and women in sex-typed jobs are altered so that each group is more equally represented (Glick et al., 1988).

Self-Limiting Effects of Stereotyping on Women's Performance

Gender stereotypes not only influence others' perceptions of women but also influence women's behavior, often in ways that limit their effectiveness in the workplace. For example, women consistently speak less than men and offer fewer contributions for the task in mixed-sex group tasks (Kimble, Yoshikowa, & Zehr, 1981). This gender difference cannot be due to intelligence or verbal skills (evidence indicates that women are as intelligent as men and have equal or better verbal skills; Maccoby & Jacklin, 1974). The difference may be due, in part, to task-related knowledge. Often, task group discussions utilize tasks or problems that tap more masculine areas of knowledge or expertise. When more stereotypical feminine topics are discussed, women participate more than men (Wentworth & Anderson, 1984). A second potential explanation for differences is that social expectations based on gender stereotypes suggest that men should be dominant and that women should be more passive and deferential to men (Haslett et al., 1992). These expectations can inhibit women's contributions in two ways. First, they discourage women, so that women limit their contributions and allow men to dominate. Second, these expectations encourage men and possibly other women within the group to ignore the woman's contribution and to treat such participation as unimportant or unwelcome (Haslett et al., 1992). Even when a dominant woman is paired with a nondominant man, the man usually becomes the leader. One interpretation of this behavior is that the woman is using her dominance to ensure that social expectations (formed by gender stereotypes) are met (Megargee, 1969).

Women report similar levels of self-esteem as men when responding to general questions about self-worth, but they have lower confidence in succeeding on specific tasks and in male-dominated jobs (J.S. Bridges, 1988; Erkert, 1983; Maccoby & Jacklin, 1974). The differences between men and women may be due to the effects of the stereotype that men are more competent than women (Vollmer, 1976). As mentioned earlier, women's explanations for the causes of their successes and failures may reflect such stereotypes. That is, women attribute their own successes to luck or an easy task and their failures to a lack of ability, which could explain why a woman has lower self-efficacy in her ability to succeed on a new problem or task (Haslett et al., 1992).

Stereotypes about the abilities, interests, and behaviors appropriate to women may lead women to behave in ways that limit their effectiveness in the workforce. As noted, they may participate less in mixed-sex tasks and may show less confidence and lower self-evaluation, even when their performance is objectively similar to that of their male colleagues. The hypothesis that gender stereotypes may lead to self-limiting behaviors has been examined closely in the areas of gender and achievement and in research on the relationship between gender and expectations regarding rewards.

Gender Stereotypes and Achievements. Although females achieve at relatively high levels in childhood, their ultimate levels of achievement, especially academic and occupational achievement, are considerably lower than those of males (Stein & Bailey, 1973). Too often, women are viewed as "deficit" males, that is, they are described in terms of falling short in comparison to males. On the other hand, it may be that achievement has been operationalized in a restrictive fashion (Offerman & Beil, 1992). The measures used to assess achievement consistently include student grades, college major, selection of nontraditional courses/careers, or performance on individual short term laboratory tasks. The intrinsic value of tasks for the individual is ignored. Furthermore, tasks that require long-term cooperation and teamwork as critical features for success have not been examined. Yet research using a limited range of measures finds that the ratio of female to male underachievers increases with age until college, when the proportion of female underachievers exceeds the proportion of male underachievers (Raph, Goldberg, & Passow, 1966).

Historically, achievement motivation has been defined as a relatively stable disposition to strive for success in any situation where standards of excellence are applicable (McCleland et al., 1953). The construct has received reasonably sound support in studies using males but less support among females (Stein & Bailey, 1973). Achievement, including societal leadership roles, may require a range of skills broader than the traditionally studied achievement outcome variables. As a result of their socialization or their experiences, women and men may define achievement in different ways and may seek to achieve in ways consistent with their own conceptions of success. Such conceptions may not be the same as traditional definitions, which adopt a largely masculine view of what achievement is or should be (Offerman & Beil, 1992; Stein & Bailey, 1973). Achievement styles are characteristic ways in which individuals approach achievement situations. The satisfactions people derive from these situations relate to sex-role socialization and sex-linked occupational choice. Women are more likely to take intrinsic pleasure in task accomplishments even if others do not recognize the accomplishment, whereas men are more likely to emphasize social comparison and power mastery (Kipnis, 1974;

Sutherland & Veroff, 1985). Female achievement behaviors may be stimulated by **affiliation motivation** or a **need for social approval** rather
than achievement motivation (Stein & Bailey, 1973). Social skills and
interpersonal relations are often important areas of achievement for females (V.C. Crandall, 1963). The goal is to attain a standard of excellence,
but the areas in which attainment are most important differ for females
and males. Females may not be more sensitive to social approval; rather,
they may receive social approval for a more social pattern of achievement
behavior than do males (Veroff, 1969).

Achievement motivation is often in conflict with many of the stereotypical personality characteristics associated with femininity, including nonas-
sertiveness, avoidance of competition, and dependency. There are limited
avenues a woman can pursue that are highly rewarded and relatively free
from conflict with feminine stereotypes. However, some women appear
to define achievement-related behavior as more feminine than others.
When they define achievement as feminine, women are more likely to
exhibit achievement-oriented behaviors (Stein, 1971).

Competence, Performance, and Pay Expectations.

Males typi-
cally have higher performance expectations than do females (Levy &
Baumgardner, 1991). A series of studies using various age groups showed
that females had lower expectations of success than males even when
their performance was superior (V.C. Crandall, 1969). One reason for the
lower female performance expectations may be the generalized sex-role
stereotype in our society that females are less competent than males.
Women and girls themselves may in part accept the stereotype that females
are less competent. Expectancy measures an individual's belief of what he
or she will be able to do. An individual's expectations predict achievement
behavior and performance for adolescent and college females about as
well as for males (V.C. Crandall, 1969). Gender-related expectations
for performance and competence influence self-expectations about the
likelihood for success.

In addition, such expectations influence others' perceptions about the
performance competence and success of males and females. There is
extensive evidence supporting the notion that, regardless of task, men are
generally perceived by both genders as more competent and that the
performance of men is generally superior to that of women (Wood, 1987).
In studies of men and women who were equally competent, men were
judged or perceived to be more competent (Deaux & Taynor, 1973;
Vaughn & Wittig, 1981), and men's responses to problems were perceived
as more logical than the identical responses by women (Taynor & Deaux,
1975). Generally, this research shows that gender stereotypes may influence perceptions of the quality of opinions, project proposals, academic

courses, leadership, and handling administrative responsibilities (Haslett et al., 1992).

Gender stereotypes influence not only self-expectations regarding performance and likelihood of success but also expectations about the levels of pay an individual expects (Jackson, Gardner, & Sullivan, 1992). Women earn on average from approximately 50% to 75% of what men earn depending, in part, on the occupation (National Committee on Pay Equity, 1986). Gender differences in self-pay expectations may contribute to the gender wage gap, in part, by causing women to be more content with less pay (Crosby, 1982). Across a wide variety of jobs and tasks, women have lower performance expectations, evaluate their performance less favorably, and attribute their success more to external causes such as more effort, easy task, or luck than do men (e.g., Deaux & Farris, 1977; R.D. Hansen & O'Leary, 1985; Nieva & Gutek, 1981b).

Women believe that less pay is "fair pay" for a variety of occupations that vary in both prestige and gender composition, and regardless of the gender of the target employee (L.A. Jackson & Grabski, 1988). Women report lower pay expectations than men in careers for such majors as agriculture, business, education, engineering, human ecology, and nursing (no difference for social science). The gender gap is greatest in the male-dominated field of engineering, where women are expected to earn approximately $35,000 less at career peak than men. In female-dominated occupations such as nursing and education, women are expected to earn about $20,000 less at career peak than men. Furthermore, these female subjects have higher grade point averages and standardized test scores of verbal ability than men. On the other hand, men perceive themselves as having greater business sophistication and expect to perform better on the job than do the women regardless of the occupational field (L.A. Jackson, Gardner, & Sullivan, 1992). Women expect to take more time out from the workforce for childbearing than do men. Furthermore, women place greater importance on interpersonal and comfort factors on the job than do men. Men's higher self-pay expectations may be attributable, in part, to greater self-perceived business sophistication, whereas women's lower self-pay expectations may be due, in part, to the importance placed on job accommodations and family life (L.A. Jackson, Gardiner, & Sullivan, 1992).

SUMMARY

Gender stereotypes are widely shared beliefs about the characteristics and attributes associated with men and women. These beliefs influence numerous perceptions about what behavior to expect, the appropriateness of such behavior, and the sanctions for engaging in behaviors contrary to the stereotype. Traits associated with women have been characterized as integrative–expressive, reflecting an emotional, nurturing component, whereas traits associated with men are characterized as more adaptive–instrumental, reflecting a competence theme. The stereotype of masculinity involves both achievement and the suppression of affect. Although there is evidence that stereotypes of women and men do not differ in terms of perceived favorability, women may be more limited in the quantity and range of behaviors they can engage in and continue to be viewed as acceptable. There is multinational evidence that gender stereotypes are internationally pervasive. Furthermore, gender stereotypes at times conflict with actual behaviors of men and women. For example, the female stereotype features characteristics such as attractive, affectionate, and sexy, but there is clear evidence that males focus on sexuality in a wide range of interactions with females, including those in which the female has done little to suggest sexual interest.

Gender stereotypes historically resulted from research using White or Anglo male and female college-age subjects. However, gender stereotypes may differ in content or lessen in strength when we focus on groups other than White, college-age men and women. There is evidence that race and age combine with gender stereotypes with varying intensity. For example, young White women are most strongly stereotyped as feminine, yet as men and women age, gender stereotypes become less salient. Also, one's physical appearance is important in activating gender stereotypes and subsequent decisions or judgments about a person. Other research provides additional support that gender stereotypes are complex and multifaceted. Within the gender stereotype, there are generalized beliefs about gender and sexuality, power, and the working or career woman.

Given our social expectations of men and women based on gender stereotypes, it is not surprising to observe some differences between men and women in numerous domains at work and home. For example, men and women differ in their expectations for success on specific tasks, and these expectations are related to achievement motivation on the task. This finding has been interpreted as meaning that women have lower expectations for success than men, and that is why they do not attempt new tasks or perform as well as men on subsequent tasks. However, an equally plausible explanation is that women face more barriers than men on the job, especially sex discrimination, and are less likely to be successful due in part to biased evaluations. Furthermore, women may take this into account when forming their expectations about occupations that do not require lengthy training programs or extensive time commitment. That is, success expectations for a woman may include an implicit assessment of the sexism within her current environment as well as an assessment of her ability to perform a given task. There is evidence (from studies conducted in the 1970s and again in the 1990s) suggesting a small but consistent impact of gender stereotypes on work-related decisions and on men's and women's self-perceptions of their behavior, performance, and worth (including expectations for pay).

However, the observed differences must be interpreted with much caution. One conclusion drawn from these differences is that women are deficient in some ways compared to men. It is easy to attribute the cause of such differences to internal, skill, personality, or biological explanations. The reliance on internal or person-based explanations inhibit and often precludes the search for equally compelling external, situation-based explanations for gender differences (Tavris, 1991). Most behaviors that reflect gender differences are learned behaviors, and by labeling them as masculine and feminine, scientists may reinforce the association of that behavior with gender (Lott, 1981). It may be more constructive to think about sex and gender in terms of what women and men bring to a situation as individuals, not in terms of a series of traits (Sagrestano, 1991).

GLOSSARY

Access discrimination: The behavioral manifestation of stereotypes and prejudicial attitudes; refers to negative (sometimes positive) actions taken toward a particular group to limit members' access into an organization because of their membership in that group.

Achievement: Attainment of outstanding results in pursuits of socially recognized significance.

Affiliation motivation: The need to seek and sustain numerous personal friendships.

Adaptive–instrumental: Male-associated traits that comprise the male stereotype, including frank and straightforward in social relations, intellectually rational and competent, and bold and effective in dealing with the environment.

Attribution: Process by which people seek information to know and understand the causes behind others' behaviors.

Expanded gender stereotypes: Attributes assigned to either gender by 60% of subjects.

Focused gender stereotypes: Attributes assigned to either gender by 75% of subjects.

Gender stereotypes (or sex stereotypes): Socially shared beliefs about the characteristics, traits, skills, or attributes of women and men.

Individuating information: Information describing one person's unique skills and abilities that is not based on that person's membership in various demographic groups (e.g., gender or race).

Integrative–expressive: Female-associated traits that comprise the female stereotype including social amentities, emotional warmth, and a concern for nonmaterial matters.

Need for social approval: An individual's need to receive positive interpersonal feedback for his or her behavior.

Pathology: All conditions, processes, or results of a particular disease.

Perceptual bias: Psychological process whereby individuals are more likely perceive what they expect to see.

Prototype: The original, model, or pattern from which all other things of the same kind are made.

Roles: Tasks or activities that different individuals are expected to accomplish.

Sex-role stereotypes: Socially shared beliefs about the appropriateness of various roles and activities for men and women.

Sex-trait stereotypes: The psychological and behavioral characteristics that are believed to describe the majority of men and not the majority of women and vice versa.

Sexual harassment: Unwelcome sexual advances, requests for sexual favors, and other verbal or physical conduct of a sexual nature when (a) submission to such conduct is made either explicitly or implicitly a term or condition of an individual's employment, (b) submission to or rejection of such conduct by an individual is used as the basis for employment decisions affecting the individual, or (c) such conduct substantially interferes with an individual's work performance or creates an intimidating, hostile, or offensive working environment.

Suppression of affect: Conscious or unconscious attempts to suppress or not demonstrate or convey one's emotions to others.

Type A behavior: Behavior pattern characterized by competitiveness, impatience, and a tendency toward frustration and hostility. Individuals who are Type A appear driven, habitually trying to do better than others, and they are verbally and nonverbally hostile if they are prevented from reaching a goal.

4

Physical Attractiveness, Interpersonal Relationships, and Romance at Work

"I live by a man's code, designed to fit a man's world, yet at the same time I never forget that a woman's first job is to choose the right shade of lipstick."
—Carole Lombard, American actress (1908–1942)

"When a man gets up to speak, people listen, then look. When a woman gets up, people look, then if they like what they see, they listen."
—Pauline Frederick, American news correspondent (1908–1990)

(*Women's Wit and Wisdom*, 1991, pp. 96 and 15).

"Work is fundamentally one of the sexiest things that people can do together and it is high time we started taking advantage of all that energy in some constructive way."
—Eyler (1994), cited in Fisher (1994)

Physical attractiveness is one of the most visible and obvious traits we possess. It conveys information, both accurate and inaccurate, and plays a tremendous role in our interactions with others in our personal and work lives (Patzer, 1985). There is evidence that our physical attractiveness plays a significant role in what people expect from us, how people respond to us, and what decisions are made about us by ourselves and others. "What is beautiful is good" depicts the attractiveness stereotype.

In this chapter we review research on the influence of physical attractiveness on work-related outcomes for both women and men and explore reasons why it may play a more significant role for women than men in developing relationships both in and outside of work. Physical attractiveness is an important factor in interpersonal attraction between people. However, an individual's physical attractiveness is also associated with many outcomes including perceptions of one's social power, extent to which one is liked, extent to which one is assumed to have other positive traits and characteristics, and work decisions. Variations in the role of attractiveness and the development of friendships among women and men may set the stage for variations and interpersonal challenges in the workplace. Gender differences in friendship characteristics have implications for same-sex male and female friendships, cross-sex friendships, and romantic relationships at work.

This chapter ends with a discussion of romance in the workplace. Depending on your perspective, workplace romance can be disruptive or it can be the best thing about going to work. However, romance in the workplace often has different implications for males and females, and the effects of romance may depend on factors such as one's level in the organization, organizational climates, and the nature of the work.

GENDER AND PHYSICAL
ATTRACTIVENESS

A person who is physically attractive is likely to be more positively perceived, more favorably responded to, and more successful in his or her personal and professional life than a less attractive individual (Patzer, 1985). Furthermore, there is evidence that physical attractiveness is even more important and influential for women than for men.

Surprisingly, given the pervasive impact of attractiveness on both men and women, there is significant disagreement about exactly what defines attractiveness. First, attractiveness is a socially defined construct, and different societies may prize different attributes. Second, attractiveness is complexly determined, and evaluations of attractiveness are likely to be influenced by a number of physical features. Much of the social–psychological research in this area has focused on facial appearance, which some researchers believe to be the most important determinant of a person's physical attractiveness (Bridges, 1981). There is no complete definition of attractiveness; however, some aspects of the attractiveness stereotype can be articulated.

The Attractiveness Stereotype

Although there is some disagreement about precisely what defines attractiveness, there is remarkable consistency in describing the characteristics that attractive people are assumed to possess. The core of the attractiveness stereotype is the notion that "what is beautiful is good" (Dion, Berscheid, & Walster, 1972). More concretely, individuals perceived as physically attractive are thought to have more socially desirable traits, live better lives, and have more successful marriages and jobs than those perceived as less attractive (Berscheid & Walster, 1972).

In many instances, the effects of physical attractiveness are similar for females and males (although we present important exceptions to this statement in a later section in this chapter). For example, attractive women are perceived as more feminine and attractive men as more masculine than their less attractive counterparts (Gillen, 1981). For both men and women, as physical attractiveness increases, so do perceptions of social desirability. Attractive individuals are viewed as more intelligent, sensitive, kind, interesting, sociable, and likely to attend college than less attractive people (Clifford & Walster, 1973; Smits & Cherhoniak, 1976; Walster, Aaronson, Abrahams, & Rottman, 1966). Furthermore, the less physically attractive a person is the less the person is liked (Korabik, 1981) and the less the person is preferred as a working, dating, or marriage partner (Blood, 1956; Brislin & Lewis, 1968; Huston, 1973; Stroebe,

Sidelight 4.1   Public and General Scientific View of the Role of Attractiveness

Although there is little agreement on the definition of physical attractiveness, there is evidence that physical attractiveness plays a key role in communication and interaction with people. However, most people resist the notion that they are influenced by a person's physical appearance. Even the general scientific community has not examined this issue as much as one might think (Patzer, 1985). A pioneering researcher on attractiveness perhaps best captured the sentiment of the scientific community and the public about the denial of the role of attractiveness in our lives:

> In a democracy, we like to feel that with hard work and a good deal of motivation, a person can accomplish almost anything. But, alas, (most of us believe), hard work cannot make an ugly woman beautiful. Because of this suspicion, perhaps most social psychologists implicitly would prefer to believe that beauty is indeed, only skin deep—and avoid the investigation of its social impact for fear that they might learn otherwise. (Aronson, 1969, p. 160)

The implicit belief that attractiveness shouldn't have such a decisive impact on evaluation of individuals has contributed to the relatively incomplete literature on the nature and determinants of physical attractiveness. Some aspects of physical attractiveness are well understood (e.g., in U.S. culture, thin is almost always preferred to fat), but basic questions such as why some facial structures are viewed as more attractive than others are still not fully answered.

Insko, Thompson, & Layton, 1971). Attractive and unattractive individuals also receive differential attention, with attractive persons receiving more positive looks and smiles (Kleck & Rubenstein, 1975). In general, social interactions for physically attractive persons are often positive while those for the less attractive are often negative (Patzer, 1985).

Pervasiveness.   Physical attractiveness stereotypes are not restricted to specific age groups. This stereotype appears to hold across ages and situations, ranging from infancy to late adulthood and elderly stages (Dushenko, Perry, Schilling, & Smolarski, 1978). However, most research in this area has focused on young adults. Using young parents as subjects, researchers have found that the physical attractiveness of children influences the parents' expectations in a number of ways. Parents expect attractive children to be more popular, to be more successful socially, and to have more positive attitudes (Adams & LaVoie, 1974). Middle-aged persons are perceived as more honest, as more sociable, and as having higher self-esteem and vocational status as a function of attractiveness (Adams & Huston, 1975). Similar results have been found with couples aged 64 to 86 years (J.L. Peterson & Miller, 1980). One reason for the pervasiveness and power of the attractiveness stereotype is that along with race and sex, it is so readily observable (Patzer, 1985). It is simply one of the few traits that people first notice.

Subtleness.   People vehemently deny the influence of physical attractiveness on their perceptions, judgments, and behaviors even in the face of evidence to the contrary. For example, when college students were asked to list characteristics desirable in a date, they placed physical attractiveness near the bottom (Hudson & Henze, 1969). Yet experimental studies show that choice of and attraction to a date are largely a function of the date's physical attractiveness. In fact, attractiveness has been shown to be the only predictor of liking a date (Walster et al., 1966). Therefore, the effects of physical attractiveness may be subtle. Even if attractiveness per se is not an important social cue, the fact that attractiveness is linked (at least sterotypically linked) to so many other socially valued attributes ensures that attractive people will often be preferred to their less attractive counterparts.

Socialization.   Discrimination based on physical attractiveness may be as pervasive as other forms of discrimination including sex, race, and religion (Patzer, 1985). One reason for this assertion is that most children are taught that what is ugly is bad and what is beautiful is good or innocent. For example, in children's stories, the bad witch is always ugly or grotesquely formed; royalty including the prince or princess is invariably described as handsome or beautiful. Children as young as 3 years old are more likely to select a photograph of a peer who is higher in attractiveness than one who is lower (Dion, 1977).

PHYSICAL ATTRACTIVENESS
AND INTERPERSONAL RELATIONS

There are four general research findings concerning physical attractiveness and interpersonal (and intrapersonal) relations (Patzer, 1985). First, greater physical attractiveness is associated with greater social acceptance.

Second, physically attractive people are liked more than less attractive people, all other things being equal. Third, more physically attractive people are assumed to possess more positive and favorable characteristics. Fourth, highly attractive individuals elicit different reactions from others and receive different responses from others than individuals who are less attractive. The research in each of these areas is reviewed.

Attractiveness and Social Acceptance

Physical attractiveness influences **expectations** that we have about each other. Physically attractive people are rated as more curious versus indifferent, complex versus simple, perceptive versus insensitive, happy versus sad, active versus passive, amiable versus aloof, humorous versus serious, pleasure-seeking versus self-controlled, outspoken versus reserved, and flexible versus rigid (A.G. Miller, 1970). Also, more attractive individuals are associated with greater excitement, emotional stability, and active social orientation (Bassili, 1981).

From the educational literature there is strong evidence that teachers' expectations of students vary by the students' physical attractiveness. The more attractive the student is, the greater the perceived intelligence, parental interest, peer relations, and self-concept (Clifford, 1975). This could contribute to a **self-fulfilling prophecy.** Perceptions of social deviance are also influenced by physical attractiveness. A misdeed by an attractive child is viewed as less serious and more short-lived than the same misdeed by a less attractive child (Dion, 1972, 1974). Furthermore, people are more lenient when punishing an attractive child.

Among adults operating within the legal system, the more physically attractive individual is less likely to be judged by others as having committed negative or harmful behaviors. Physically attractive people are viewed as more caring, responsible, and independent and are also less likely to be assigned guilt or punishment. For both legal crimes and social offenses, the more physically attractive are treated more leniently (Jacobson & Berger, 1974) and are given less harsh punishment (Cavoir & Howard, 1973; Efran, 1974; Friend & Vinson, 1974). Finally, people low in physical attractiveness receive less sympathy and less help even when they have no control over their predicament (Shaw, 1972). Interestingly, however, fewer people approach individuals high in physical attractiveness to request aid or assistance (Stokes & Bickman, 1974). It appears that highly attractive individuals may also be somewhat intimidating—"What is beautiful is unapproachable" (Stokes & Bickman, 1974, p. 292).

Attractiveness, Liking, and Loving

Physical attractiveness plays a role in three stages of romantic attraction including the time prior to and including the first meeting, the period of dating, and a period of committed relationship like marriage (Patzer, 1985). The role of physical attractiveness appears to decline as the stages of the attraction or friendship unfold, yet research shows a persistent effect. In the stage prior to meeting, the desire to be friends or to date is higher for individuals with higher physical attractiveness (Black, 1974; Pellegrini, Hicks, & Meyers-Winton, 1979). Physical attractiveness appears to influence expectations and preferences, which, in turn, influence the desire to meet only certain individuals (within the context of romantic relationships). During the dating stage, physical attractiveness plays the most influential role (Berscheid, Dion, Walster, & Walster, 1971; Byrne, Ervin, & Lamberth, 1970; Mathes, 1975; Walster et al., 1966), whereas during later stages, physical attractiveness appears to be the second most important factor in the developing relationship. Time spent together is the first most important factor (R.M. Kramer, 1978).

Physical attractiveness is also an important factor in **nonromantic attraction.** Attractiveness effects are found for both same-sex and opposite-sex friendships. Physical attraction is one of the best predictors of attraction (Kornbik, 1981; Thornton & Linnstaedter, 1975, 1980). The positive link between nonintimate liking and physical attractiveness has been demonstrated in numerous settings (Byrne et al., 1970). Physical attractiveness continues to influence interactions (although it may not be the most important factor) even after the initial phases of attraction and after people have had time to interact and learn about each other (Byrne & Clore, 1970; Kleck, Richardson, & Ronald, 1974).

Although the influence of attractiveness on liking is pervasive, some individuals are more influenced by attractiveness than others. People who most like physically attractive others tend to be more thrill seeking (Horai, 1976) and tend to place importance on sexuality and physical appearance (Touhey, 1979). There is evidence that men are more influenced by attractiveness than women and that women are more influenced by character description and attributions of the target person than men (McKelvie & Matthews, 1976). Yet women are more concerned about their own attractiveness than are men (Wagman, 1967). Furthermore, men consider the physical attractiveness of their partner as more important than women view it for their partner (Coombs & Kenkel, 1966). One interpretation of these findings is that women may be aware of the importance that men place on women's attractiveness and respond by valuing it for themselves.

However, in the United States, men may be growing as concerned as women about their physical appearance. For example, men's magazines that promote a "standard of male beauty as unforgiving and unrealistic as the female version . . ." are becoming increasingly popular (Cottle, 1998, p. 30). Furthermore, the saturated women's fashion and glamour industries appear to have targeted men. Although research evidence suggests that women place greater importance on their physical appearance than do men, this may be a thing of the past. Physical appearance is increasingly being marketed as "a guy thing," and the way appearance has been packaged as a guy thing is to link it to the rationale of a wise career move. "Whatever a man's cosmetic shortcomings, it's apt to be a career liability," says Alan Farnham (cited in Fortune, September 1996). "The business world is prejudiced against the ugly."

Finally, the rationale used to justify the importance of physical attractiveness for men and women is divided along sex stereotype lines in business related magazines. For example, in an effort to distinguish between male and female vanity, *Forbes* magazine reported (Dec. 1, 1996), "Plastic surgery is more of a cosmetic thing for women. They have a thing about aging. For men, it's an investment that pays a pretty good dividend." This implies that one's concern about appearance is seen as a frivolous issue for women, but is a legitimate one for men.

Attractiveness and Self-Perception

The level of one's attractiveness affects responses from others, and these responses may be internalized and may influence the way an individual develops (Patzer, 1985). For example, there is evidence that the more physically attractive exhibit greater individuality, adjust better socially, and are less socially anxious. There may be a self-fulfilling prophecy effect concerning attractiveness. Attractiveness is more important in love relationships than many personality characteristics (Maroldo, 1982). Generally, people who rate themselves low in physical attractiveness also report more difficult interpersonal relations (Mitchell & Orr, 1976). People with greater attractiveness receive greater acceptance by others and are more popular (Dion & Berscheid, 1974; Kleck et al., 1974).

Attractiveness and Work Decisions

The positive expectations associated with physical attractiveness generalize beyond interpersonal relationships such as dating and marriage into the work setting. Perceptions of attractiveness have a moderate effect on perceptions of the person's intellectual competence (Eagly, Ashmore, Makhijani, & Longo, 1991; Feingold, 1990). The link between attractiveness and perceptions of intelligence appears to be similar for both men and women. However, attractiveness appears to have a stronger effect for women than for men on perceptions of job performance (at least when men are the evaluators; R. Anderson & Nida, 1978; Kaplan, 1978; K.E. Lewis & Bierly, 1990). Applicants and employees with higher physical attractiveness are expected to do better work. Once completed, their work is evaluated more positively than identical work by less attractive individuals. In one study, highly attractive authors were evaluated as having better ideas, demonstrating better style, being more creative, and generally producing higher quality work (Landy & Sigall, 1974).

In the interviewing setting, if an interviewer believes that physical attractiveness is an important job attribute, then being attractive is an advantage (Beehr & Gilmore, 1982). There is extensive research evidence that attractiveness positively influences entry-level employment decisions (Cash et al., 1977; Dipboye, Arvey, & Terpstra, 1977; Dipboye, Fromkin, & Wiback, 1975; Heilman & Saruwatari, 1979; L. Jackson, 1983; Riggio & Throckmorton, 1988; Snyder, Berscheid, & Matwychuk, 1988). Other research has shown few significant effects (Boor, Wartman, & Reuben, 1983; Caballero & Pride, 1984).

Although there is some evidence to the contrary (see L. Jackson, 1983), physical attractiveness appears to interact with the sex-type of the job to influence work evaluations (Cash et al., 1977). Physical attractiveness is a positive feature for women when applying to lower level positions (e.g., clerical) but not for higher level positions (e.g., management), whereas physical attractiveness is advantageous for men in a wider range of positions. These advantages and disadvantages are similar for such work decisions as evaluations of applicant qualifications, hiring recommendations, starting salary, and rankings of hiring preferences (Dipboye et al., 1977; Marvelle & Green, 1980).

Attractiveness may be especially advantageous when the position is stereotypically appropriate for gender (e.g., male for car sales position, female for office receptionist; Cash et al., 1977). In nontraditional occupations, attractiveness may not be such an asset. For example, physical attractiveness is associated with more favorable outcomes (e.g., performance evaluations, salary) for men in professional jobs (J. Ross & Ferris, 1981), but for professional women, attractiveness can be a liability. Biases against women working in professional jobs appear to be enhanced by physical attractiveness; male associates may patronize or be sexually attracted to them; female associates may respond to them with jealousy and contempt (Ancker-Johnson, 1975; Kaslow & Schwartz, 1978; "Woman as Bosses," 1983). Physically attractive women may have a double "handicap"—their gender and their attractiveness. They may have to double their efforts to demonstrate their commitment and competence in the work setting, especially in traditionally masculine and high-status occupations.

In a survey of successful women in business, media, and academia, physical attractiveness in general was perceived as a positive quality for initial interactions and initial access to job opportunities and was the reason given by organizations for selecting the women for high-visibility positions (Kaslow & Schwartz, 1978). Yet, once on the job, women reported problems with other women who were less attractive as well as with males who resented the women's achievements or were sexually attracted to them. Some women complained that they were looked upon as a date rather than as a serious colleague, or that the men "looked at me rather than my product" (p. 413). Attractive women felt excluded from high-level decision making due to male paternalistic and protective attitudes. These women believed that their friendliness was often misinterpreted and that some men desired a sexual relationship rather than a professional one.

At work, physical attractiveness is usually an advantage for women and men, but for women, there are limits to these positive consequences. Attractiveness is most beneficial for women working in traditional feminine areas or just entering an organization. However, when women enter more traditionally masculine work, physical attractiveness can be a liability (Spencer & Taylor, 1988). One interpretation of these findings is that because women who are physically attractive are also perceived as more feminine (Heilman & Stopeck, 1985), the negative female stereotype of being less intelligent or competent may be activated or salient. Especially in masculine occupations where competence is of great perceived importance, attractive women may face discrimination.

INTERPERSONAL ATTRACTION
IN THE WORKPLACE

Physical appearance is one factor that influences a person's interpersonal attraction. Just what is **interpersonal attraction?** Attraction tends to refer to a person's initial responses to a stranger rather than to long-term relationships (Bryne, 1971). Occasionally, however, it refers to "liking." Generally, interpersonal attraction covers any instance of personal relationships with positive overtones (Berscheid & Walster, 1969; Huston, 1974). **Workplace romance,** on the other hand, is defined as any relationship between two members of the same organization that entails mutual sexual attraction (Dillard & Witteman, 1985; L.A. Mainiero, 1986; Powell, 1993). Although interpersonal attraction often refers to "liking," workplace romance often involves loving feelings. However, interpersonal attraction does not necessarily have sexual connotations, nor does it necessarily lead to romance. Rather, interpersonal attraction is a basis for a wide array of positive interpersonal interactions at work, including workplace friendships.

Antecedents of Interpersonal Attraction

The factors that predict whether we will like someone can be distinguished from those factors that predict loving (Rubin, 1973; Sternberg, 1988).

Although liking and loving can be distinguished from each other, when individuals like each other, this can lead to more intense romantic feelings (Hendrick & Hendrick, 1983; Pierce, Byrne, & Aguinis, 1996). The factors that are linked to interpersonal attraction including liking are described as follows.

Proximity or Propinquity. Proximity provides the opportunity for friendships to develop. It is the degree to which people are geographically close to one another, and it plays a large role in determining who we like (Byrne & Neuman, 1992). In organizations, individuals who work near each other are more likely to interact with each other and have more opportunity to become attracted to each other (Quinn & Judge, 1978). People are more likely to initiate relationships at work both when there is physical proximity (the actual physical distance between two individuals) and when there is functional proximity (how easy it is for two individuals to interact). When coworkers are required to spend many hours together on the job, propinquity is especially influential (Mainiero, 1986).

Repeated Exposure or Familiarity. Repeated exposure to a person or a stimulus increases the positivity of its evaluation (R. Crandall, 1972; Zajonc, 1968). This phenomenon has been called the **mere exposure effect.** Employees who work together and have repeated contact can become attracted to each other. Contrary to the expression "familiarity breeds contempt," research evidence indicates that the more people are exposed to something, the more likely they are to like it (Bornstein, 1989). One reason for the familiarity or mere exposure effect in the workplace is that it builds mutual trust and respect between employees, which may enhance interpersonal attraction (E.G.C. Collins, 1983).

Social contact and repeated exposure outside of the workplace can also enhance the likelihood of interpersonal attraction and a romantic relationship. Such activities as traveling with an opposite-sex partner or attending corporate cocktail parties and conventions can relax social barriers (Mainiero, 1989; Spruell, 1985). Although social psychologists are still not certain what is the underlying cause of the mere exposure effect, it appears clear that repeated exposure can enhance interpersonal attraction.

Attitude Similarity. With few exceptions, people like other people who are similar to themselves (Feldman 1998). Similarity can contribute to interpersonal attraction regardless of whether we are referring to similarity in attitudes, values, or personality traits. The clearest example of the similarity-attraction relationship involves attitude and value similarity. Despite a few inconsistencies in the literature (Rosenbaum, 1986a, 1986b; Sunnafrank, 1992), there is substantial evidence that the greater proportion of similar attitudes shared between two people, the greater the likelihood that the two individuals will like each other (Byrne, 1992; Byrne, Clore, & Smeaton, 1986).

Personnel selection in an organization has been described as a process by which employees are attracted to and selected based on their fit within the culture of the organization (B. Schneider, 1987). Therefore, the selection process results in employees who express similar attitudes and values (Pierce et al., 1996). The organization can be thought of as a large group of potential romantic partners based on their similarity of attitudes (Mainiero, 1989). When we make new acquaintances, we assess how similar or dissimilar they are to us (Byrne et al., 1986). If they are too dissimilar, we avoid them. If they pass our initial assessment, we take attitude similarity into account, liking best those who are most similar (Feldman, 1998).

Reciprocity of Liking.   When we learn that another person likes us, whether it is demonstrated through nonverbal behavior or deeds or spoken directly, we tend to like that person in return (Feldman, 1998). Reciprocity of liking means that you like those who like you. Furthermore, when you like someone, you tend to believe that person likes you in return (Condon & Crano, 1988). However, there is one exception to the reciprocity of liking rule. When people suspect that others are saying positive things to ingratiate themselves, interpersonal attraction is not likely to result. **Ingratiation** is a deliberate attempt to make a favorable impression often by flattering another person (Jones & Pittman, 1982).

Physical Attractiveness and Interpersonal Attraction.   One commonality among the antecedents of interpersonal attraction is that each increases the likelihood that another person will be noticed. Besides one's sex, a person's level of physical attractiveness is one of the first characteristics others notice about the individual. As we noted earlier, individuals who are attractive are more likely to be noticed by others, to have a larger circle of friends, and to have higher ratings of likability. Men tend to place more emphasis on physical attractiveness than do women; the physical attractiveness of the female partner is a more important determinant of interpersonal attraction than the physical attractiveness of the male. However, females tend to place more emphasis on specific physical characteristics (e.g., stature or height) than do males (Feingold, 1990; Pierce, 1994).

Gender and Friendships

The essential difference between male and female same-sex friendships can be described in the following way: female friendships are "face-to-face," whereas male friendships are "side-by-side" (Winstead, 1986; P.H. Wright, 1982). This characterization of male and female same- and mixed-sex friendships is played out in the types of nonsexual relationships men and women form both in and outside work. Implications for friendships formed and maintained at work involving men and women are discussed subsequently.

Same-Sex Friendships and Mixed-Sex Friendships. Verbal communication is a central activity and feature of women's same-sex friendships. Friendships among women are more intimate and self-disclosing than male friendships. Women are more likely to study together and talk about friends, family, and personal problems, whereas men are more likely to watch movies or play sports together. Women converse more frequently and in greater depth about issues involving themselves and their close relationships, whereas men talk more about activity-oriented topics (F.L. Johnson & Aries, 1983). Men, on the other hand, prefer to do things together (i.e., activities other than talking). They will share activities, like sports, in which their attention is focused on a third party but not on one another.

Consistent with this, factors most central to female friendships include mutual helping and support, whereas males emphasize similar interests and shared experiences (Weiss & Lowenthal, 1975). Similarity in values is an important antecedent to friendships for women, but men are more concerned about similarity in interests (Hill & Stull, 1981). In general, women appear to have more in-depth friendships whereas men have friendships that reflect less intimacy and more activities.

Male and female differences in friendships begin as early as age 3 or 4. At this time, girls and boys begin to show a preference for same-sex friends (Rubin, 1980). Gender differences emerge regarding the number of friends or playmates, with girls preferring one to two other friends and boys playing in groups. This pattern is well-established by kindergarten and among elementary school-age children (Eder & Hallinan, 1978). Furthermore, the most socially successful boys have the most extensive peer relationships (i.e., greater numbers of relationships), whereas the most successful girls have the most intensive peer relationships, playing with one girl. Boys' play also tends to be more structured and complex, often involving competition (Lever, 1978). Girls are likely to take turns playing games where there is little role hierarchy and little competition. Boys also prefer outcomes that are equitable but not necessarily equal, whereas girls prefer an equal distribution of rewards. Equitable rewards are more associated with groups or teams based on individual contribution.

Generally, girls know more factual information about their best friends (McAdams & Losoff, 1984) and show higher ratings of attachment, giving and sharing, and trust and loyalty (Sharabany, Gershoni, & Hoffman, 1981). There is some indication that power motives more stereotypically associated with males may inhibit one-to-one relationships (McAdams, 1982).

Friendships at Work.   At work, individuals have a variety of choices in the types of relationships that they can establish with coworkers. These range from working on tasks with no communication to forming intimate relationships (G.A. Fine, 1986). However, most relationships at work fall in between these extremes and include friendly relations. Many times these friendly relations begin at work and develop into close friendships (Kurth, 1970), and the organizational culture may sometimes require friendly relations. Friendly relations can facilitate cooperation. Also, the content of work can facilitate friendship development especially if the work is socially situated, where there are times of intense activity when one must help others and other times when people can leisurely chat. Furthermore, professional occupations involve more job autonomy, allowing greater choice in opportunities to interact with others.

Although friendships can develop among persons at different levels of an organizational hierarchy, it is easier to develop friendships among individuals at equal status levels (G.A. Fine, 1986). Friendships are give-and-take relationships, and individuals with relatively similar resources find it easier to establish relationships of exchange (Schutte & Light, 1978). People with highly disparate resources must overcome barriers caused by unequal exchange relations. High-status people may base their friendships more on status characteristics of others, whereas those in lower status positions may select friends based more on proximity (they may be less occupationally mobile; Schutte & Light, 1978). Some experts suggest that executives are characterized by their strategic use of friends. Executives recognize that whom they befriend influences how they are perceived by others (Goffman, 1959). When an individual is promoted, especially with a change in status, that person's social networks often change. Old acquaintances tend to be dropped, and patterns of friendships change. Occupational mobility provokes a dilemma with interpersonal relations; when individuals are promoted, they are out of tune with former friends and not yet accepted by new ones (P. Blau, 1956).

Three peer friendship types have been identified that differ in level of closeness: the **information peer** (lowest level), the **collegial peer,** and the **special peer** (highest level; Kram & Isabella, 1985). The information peer level reflects low levels of self-disclosure and trust, little emotional support, and little personal feedback. It appears to be the most frequent type of organizational relationship and serves as a source of information about the organization and work or task concerns. The collegial peer level reflects moderate levels of trust and self-disclosure (Fritz, 1997). The collegial peer exhibits information sharing and emotional support, feedback, and confirmation. For example, topics of wider content are discussed, including work and family. The functions of the collegial peer include career strategizing, job-related feedback, friendship, some information sharing, especially about career options and strategy, and emotional support. Finally, the special peer is the most intimate form of peer relationship found in organizations. It is characterized by high levels of self-disclosure and self-expression and offers intimacy as well as stability and continuity. Additionally, this type of friendship takes longer to develop and is relatively rare (Kram & Isabella, 1985).

Possible Benefits and Drawbacks of Friendships at Work. Friendships are highly valued relationships. As our discussion suggests, there are many kinds of interpersonal attractions and friendships that may or may not lead to a romantic relationship at work. There are both benefits and limitations to friendships within an organizational context. First, in terms of benefits, friendships among employees can provide social support, which is an important buffer from stress and stress-related illness. Furthermore, friendship such as the ones discussed previously (Kram & Isabella, 1985) can develop into valuable mentoring relationships (the reverse can occur as well, with formal mentoring relationships developing into friendships). There is also some evidence that such relationships can bolster work attitudes and performances, especially those of the participants. Finally, formal or informal relationships can be positive for the organization by creating a more open and positive organizational culture with managers and employees who are helpful and supportive (Fisher, 1994; Lobel, Quinn, St. Clair, & Warfield, 1994).

On the other hand, there are some dangers associated with friendships, both nonsexual and sexual, for the participants, coworkers, and the organization. These negative consequences can include gossip and jealousy among coworkers. Especially with manager–employee friendships, there are perceptions that formal performance evaluations will be biased. Coworkers may resent the friendship even when it is platonic and may perceive sexual intimacy even when there is none (Lobel et al., 1994). Finally, the organization may suffer lawsuits, especially if there are manager–subordinate relationships. Coworkers may perceive that sexual favors are being exchanged for career advancements and may resent the special privileges that apparently come from a close relationship (Lobel et al., 1994). Therefore, organizations must exercise balanced judgment when developing policies about the range of appropriate behaviors at work.

WORKPLACE ROMANCE

"The office has become the dating service of the '90s," says Lisa Mainiero, author of the 1989 book *Office Romance: Love, Power and Sex in the Workplace* (Alderman, 1995).

With increasing numbers of women in the workforce, there is increased frequency of intimate contact between male and female employees (Dillard, 1987). Indeed, over 80% of employees in the United States report some social or sexual experiences on the job including fun, mutually desired relationships with their coworkers (Gutek 1985), whereas nearly 75% of individuals indicate that they either observed or participated in a romantic relationship at work (Dillard & Witteman, 1985). Given the greater numbers of women and men interacting closely and over an extended period of time, under sometimes stimulating and often stressful work circumstances, it is not surprising that interpersonal attraction between women and men occurs in the workplace. Furthermore, sexual interest in a coworker may not always be unwelcome (Powell, 1993). However, romance in the workplace is sometimes frowned upon. Margaret Mead argued that taboos against sexual involvements at work are necessary in order for men and women to work together effectively (Mead, 1980). It often happens that both individuals in such relationships suffer in terms of career prospects, or that the more "valuable person" survives while the other partner suffers (E.G.C. Collins, 1983). Others have argued that people do not need protection from sexual or romantic relationships at works but rather need mutual respect for the freedom of others, including the freedom to participate in an organizational romance (Powell, 1993). These views suggest that there are possibly both positive and negative effects of romantic relationships on the participants, their coworkers, and the organization. Our discussion of workplace romance examines the impact of such behavior on participants, coworkers, and organizations.

Engaging in Sexual Behavior at Work

We have discussed the factors that lead to interpersonal attraction in the workplace and, by extension, to romantic attraction. However, both interpersonal attraction and romantic attraction are attitudes that two people have toward each other, not actual behavior. Employees who are attracted to each other must decide whether they will initiate a close, romantic relationship in the workplace (Pierce et al., 1996). Three factors have been suggested that lead two employees who are attracted to each other to engage in a workplace romance: attitudes toward workplace romance, organizational culture, and job autonomy.

Attitudes Toward Workplace Romance.   The beliefs that managers and subordinates have regarding workplace romances can impact the occurrence of such behavior (Spelman, Crary, Kram, & Clawson, 1986). Top management attitudes can influence subordinates' attitudes about romantic relationships (Horn & Horn, 1982), and these attitudes can affect how individuals manage their feelings about attraction (Crary, 1987). There is evidence that individuals who believe flirting at work is acceptable also have positive attitudes toward workplace romances (Haavio-Mannila, Kauppinen-Toropainen, & Kandolin, 1988). However, more research is needed to examine the influence of attitudes toward romance in the workplace.

Organizational Culture.   **Organizational culture** has been defined as the "personality" of an organization (Hatch, 1993; E.H. Schein, 1990, 1991) and as an invisible force that guides employee behavior (Westhoff, 1985). The organization's culture conveys to employees the attitudes, values, beliefs, norms, and standards that develop regarding those who work in the organization (Mainicro, 1989; Spelman et al , 1986; Westhoff, 1985). Organizational culture is believed to influence workplace romance because it conveys to employees what is and is not appropriate behavior. There is some evidence that slow-paced, conventional, traditional, conservative cultures typically discourage workplace romances. On the other hand, fast-paced, action-oriented, dynamic, liberal cultures that include a climate of intense pressure and activity that stimulates sexual excitement (Pietropinto, 1986; Quinn & Judge, 1978) tend to accept such behavior. For example, Microsoft CEO Bill Gates courted and married marketing executive Melinda French. When there is a tense work environment with 18-hour days and you practically live at work, relationships are bound to occur. In many respects, the Gates–French relationship may be typical of the 90s (Fisher, 1994).

Job Autonomy.   Job autonomy in the context of workplace romance has been defined as the ability to make "decisions about one's own work" and the "freedom to move in the work environment and to make contacts with coworkers" (Haavio-Mannila et al., 1988, p. 126). In autonomous jobs, employees may find it easier to initiate romantic behavior with other coworkers. The autonomous job may allow employees to have more frequent one-to-one interactions with opposite-sex members of the work group. For example, researchers found that 40% of women in autonomous jobs had been involved in a workplace romance, whereas only 25% of women with less autonomous jobs had been involved in the same type of romantic affair (Haavio-Mannila et al., 1988). Although high job autonomy is positively associated with involvement in a romantic relationship, especially for men, more research is needed to understand this relationship.

Beliefs and Experiences of Workplace Romance

In a survey of undergraduate and evening MBA students, sexual intimacy and work were perceived to have an uneasy coexistence (Powell, 1986). Participants believed that sexual relations interfere with communications but also that sexual intimacy makes for a more harmonious work environment. Although a relationship that leads to marriage was regarded in this survey more positively, there was a general belief that such relationships lead to few benefits (Powell, 1986). Respondents believed strongly that management should try to discourage sexual propositions toward coworkers and should actually reprimand supervisors who proposition their subordinates. Although there was tolerance for some attempts to satisfy needs for intimacy, flirting with one's supervisor met with more disapproval than having as a coworker as a sexual partner. Overall, respondents agreed that some forms of sexual intimacy are acceptable in the workplace as long as they are not extreme and have no negative effects on productivity. However, there were considerable differences in beliefs among men and women. Women held more negative perceptions of workplace romance. Women perceived less benefit or value in sexual intimacy in the workplace, desired more managerial action to discourage sexually oriented behavior, regarded sexually oriented behavior by others as less acceptable, and were less inclined than men to get involved in organizational romance (Powell, 1986). These more negative reactions by women are not surprising, because women are also more likely to evaluate sexual behavior at work as harassment. (Perceptions and reactions to sexual harassment are discussed more in chap. 8.) Furthermore, given their relatively lower status and power at work, women are more likely to suffer negative consequences once sexual liaisons become public knowledge.

Types of Organizational Romance and Experiences of Romance

The beliefs that women and men hold about romantic relationships at work may depend in part on the precise nature of the romance. Three types of organizational romances have been identified (Quinn & Lees, 1984): **true love, the fling,** and the **utilitarian relationship.** True love involves two people who have a sincere, long-term interest in each other and usually leads to marriage. This type of workplace relationship yields the fewest objections from coworkers, especially when it occurs between peers. The fling involves two participants who become very excited and involved, but the relationship ends quickly (Powell, 1993). Although a fling results in less approval from coworkers than true love, it receives more approval than the utilitarian relationship. This third type of organizational romance involves some trade-off between sexual adventure and ego satisfaction for one employee and job or career advancement for the other. This tradeoff, which is not based on job-related skills or performance, violates coworkers' sense of equity in the workplace and results in the most negative reactions.

How are these types of romances played out in organizations? Most organizational romances are between higher status men and lower status women. In a survey of white-collar workers, 62% of romances involved a man in a higher position, 30% involved men and women at the same level, and only 8% involved a woman in a higher position (perhaps because there are more men in management positions, especially at upper levels). A large majority of these romances involve men and women at different organizational levels, involving power differentials and issues of dependency. The more powerful employee in the relationship is the one who is giving more than he or she is getting and is less dependent on the relationship. Three kinds of dependency may characterize romantic relationships at work (Powell, 1993): **task dependency, career dependency,** and **romantic dependency.** Task dependency exists when a worker depends on another to perform his or her function effectively, whereas career dependency involves individuals who desire advancement in organizations that depend on the consent of another. In nonromantic relationships, these two dependencies operate in usual manager–subordinate relations. Employees work hard to accomplish work activities (and thereby satisfy their managers' task dependency) for the reward of career advancement (for which the employee depends on the manager). When an organizational romance occurs, the relationship between the manager and subordinate is complicated by a romantic dependency. Romance dependency can threaten the balance between task and career dependency, which can trigger negative reactions from peers. Furthermore, when there is an imbalance of power in a romantic relationship, there is potential for exploitation of whoever is more dependent on the relationship. The higher level employee can use the relationship to force the lower level employee to increase performance or engage in tasks not normally part of the job. On the other hand, lower level employees can pressure the higher level participant for favorable assignments. Regardless, when these types of relationships occur at work, they threaten the careers and self-image of employees and the morale and productivity of coworkers (Powell, 1993).

Utilitarian romances are the most disruptive for coworkers. Coworker morale and organizational effectiveness can be adversely affected when rewards are intentionally granted on the basis of personal relationships and not job-related skills. Although flings can be disruptive, they tend to pass quickly and tend not to be motivated by job or power enhancement. Romances based on true love are the least threatening, especially between peers, and they may contribute positively to the couple's productivity (Powell, 1993).

Impact of Workplace Romance on Participants, Coworkers, and the Organization

There have been reports of both positive and negative effects of workplace romance on the participants, their coworkers, and the organization. However, more information needs to be gathered to fully understand the impact of such relationships within the workplace.

Participant Responses. Workplace romance appears to influence job productivity, worker attitudes, and worker motivation. Several studies show that an employee who is involved in a romantic relationship can be more productive on the job (Bureau of National Affairs, 1988; Eyler & Baridon, 1992) at least in the short term. Specifically, members of mixed-sex work teams often increase productivity in comparison to same-sex teams, and this may be due, in part, to stimulating effects of attraction (Clawson & Kram, 1984; Crary, 1987). Consistent with this, 15% of women and 9 to 17% of men in workplace romances were more productive (C.I. Anderson & Hunsaker, 1985).

However, not all participants in workplace romances are more productive. When couples are initiating or developing their relationship, performance may decline (Westhoff, 1985). In later stages of the relationship, especially once it has been stabilized, participants may show a renewed interest in work and increased productivity (Rubin, 1973). Therefore, the stage of a workplace romance may influence whether participants increase their productivity. Another factor that might influence the degree to which a person in a romantic relationship is more productive is the motive for engaging in a romance (C.I. Anderson & Hunsaker, 1985; Dillard, 1987; Dillard & Broetzmann, 1989). Those participating with a love motive that involves a sincere desire for companionship tend to increase in productivity. Those participating with an ego motive (e.g., desire for excitement and adventure) or with a job-related motive (e.g., desire for advancement, security, power, financial rewards, or lighter or more challenging work-loads) show little or no change in performance.

Although the previously mentioned literature documents the benefits of romantic relationships, it is more common to observe a decline in participant productivity due to missed meetings, late arrivals, early departures, and costly errors (Pierce et al., 1996). Again, these findings are largely based on surveys of employees (not just participants) regarding the effects of workplace romances. In one survey, 79% of the respondents indicated that romances decrease performance due to excessive employee chatting, long lunches, and lengthy discussion behind closed doors (C.I. Anderson & Hunsaker, 1985). These general results have been replicated in numerous studies (Colwill & Lips, 1988; Mishra & Harell, 1989; Pietropinto, 1986; Rapp, 1992), yet they are largely based on perceptions.

The effects of workplace romance on productivity may depend upon the type of romantic relationship, that is, supervisor–subordinate (hierarchical) or peer (lateral). For example, couples involved in a lateral romance, between peers, are more productive than those involved in a hierarchical romance (Devine & Markiewicz, 1990). It has been suggested that hierarchical relationships impede the performance of both peers and participants because coworkers may perceive inequity due to unjust managerial decisions and procedures, may feel resentful, and thereby may decrease their performance (Mainiero, 1989; Powell & Mainiero, 1990).

One question in the workplace romance literature is whether such interactions influence worker attitudes such as motivation, job satisfaction, and job involvement. Self-report data indicate that romances can make workers feel better about themselves and willing to work longer hours together (Eyler & Baridon, 1992a; Mainiero, 1989). Thirty-three percent of workers reported an increased motivation to work (Mainiero, 1989), whereas 40% of men and 57% of women showed a significant increase in work-related enthusiasm (Dillard & Broetzmann, 1989). Although involvement in a workplace romance appears to increase worker motivation, it may depend upon other factors such as the stage of the relationship. More research needs to be conducted on how the stage of a romantic relationship affects worker motivation (Pierce et al., 1996).

Job satisfaction is an important work outcome and reflects "an affective . . . reaction to a job that results from the incumbent's comparison of actual outcomes with those that are desired" (Cranny, Smith, & Stone, 1992, p. 1). A number of theories (e.g., Thibaut & Kelley's social exchange theory) suggest that an employee who perceives the outcomes of a workplace romance as exceeding his or her expectations will be more satisfied with his or her partner and, possibly, more satisfied with certain aspects of his or her job (Pierce et al., 1993). That is, an individual happily in a relationship with a coworker may be particularly satisfied with that component of work. On the other hand, if the relationship is viewed as unsatisfactory or inequitable, employee dissatisfaction may result, possibly leading to a failed relationship, job dissatisfaction, and voluntary organizational exit (Pierce et al., 1993). Although, theoretically, workplace romances influence job satisfaction, more research is needed to provide empirical links.

Additional research is needed that examines job involvement in the context of workplace romance (Pierce et al., 1993). Job involvement is defined as the importance of work to an individual or the extent to which the individual psychologically identifies with work (Lodahl & Kejner, 1965) or the personal value that a person invests in his or her work (Alliger & Williams, 1993). There is some evidence that individuals who enter a workplace romance with ego or job-related motives show no change in job involvement, whereas those with love motives increase their job involvement (Dillard, 1987).

Coworker Reactions.   In general, participating in a workplace romance is risky. In relationships where one person is more senior or at a higher organizational level, other workers may lose respect for the higher level employee, believing his or her judgment is flawed (Powell, 1993). The lower level employee may question whether his or her progress within the organization is due to competence or the romantic relationship. The mood of a work group can be heightened or lowered because of workplace romance. Although there is some anecdotal evidence (e.g., Colwill & Lips, 1988) that a workplace romance can energize employee morale, most of the evidence indicates that morale is adversely affected (Staff, 1988). In a survey of 756 respondents, 8% indicated that workplace romances angered others, and 47% reported that such behavior created an awkward or uncomfortable work environment (Staff, 1988). One key factor here is the type of workplace romance. Supervisor–subordinate romances tend to be more disruptive than peer romances (Colwill & Lips, 1988; Mainiero, 1989; Powell & Mainiero, 1990). In one survey, 78% of female executives resented supervisor–subordinate relationships, whereas only 21% resented romantic peer relationships (Mainiero, 1989). One reason for the perception of greater disruption with supervisor–subordinate romances is that members of the work group may fear that the subordinate involved will receive task and career rewards in exchange for providing sexual favors, which in turn results in perceptions of unfairness and lowers group morale (Powell, 1993).

Gossip is another coworker reaction to organizational romances. The tone of the employee gossip depends once again on the perceived motive of the office romance. Dillard (1987) found that females entering a relationship with a job-related motive (e.g., desire for advancement, security, power, financial rewards, etc.) stimulated negative gossip, whereas male employees who initiated a relationship with a sincere love motive prompted more positive gossip. Therefore, coworker reactions in terms of office gossip depend in part on the gender and the perceived motives of the participants.

Implications for the Organization. Workplace romance can influence organizational effectiveness in a number of ways, including the breakdown of the legitimacy of organizational promotions and structure, excessive transfers, and more terminations (Pierce et al., 1993). Especially when a romantic relationship involves a supervisor and a subordinate, it is likely to result in perceptions of favoritism and inequity concerning promotions among coworkers. When coworkers perceive such favoritism they can become both alienated from the work group (Chesanow, 1992) and envious (Schultz, 1982), which can result in an imbalance of power within the organization (Mainiero, 1989; Quinn & Lees, 1984). Furthermore, when the power structure within an organization breaks down, channels for advancement become closed off and promotion and raise decisions become distorted and unpredictable (Jamison, 1983; Mainiero, 1989; Pierce et al., 1996; Rapp, 1992). When one investigates the basis for promotions and who is promoted, it is important to examine the values, informal guidelines, and norms surrounding such decisions. Therefore, the relationship between workplace romance and promotion decisions may depend, in part, on the culture of the organization.

Should employees participating in a workplace romance be transferred or relocated? Managers appear to perceive job relocation as a reasonable intervention to workplace romance (Westhoff, 1985), especially when employees engage in such behavior against formal organizational policy. Furthermore, employees might expect such transfers as a consequence. Some experts (Colby, 1991; E.G.C. Collins, 1983; Spruell, 1985) suggest that management should offer relocation as one option for couples to consider. However, female participants are more frequently relocated than males (Josefowitz, 1982; Rapp, 1992), and fewer of these women occupy top-level management or higher status positions (Spruell, 1985). Therefore, organizational relocation decisions in situations of workplace romance may be discriminatory based on the employees' gender or organizational positions (Pierce et al., 1993).

The decision to terminate or dismiss an employee because of his or her involvement in a workplace romance may also be viewed as a detrimental managerial action, one representing a punitive form of organizational intervention. Yet employees are often dismissed for participating in a workplace romance (Powell, 1986; Powell & Mainiero, 1990; Rapp, 1992). Furthermore, a female participant is more likely to be terminated than a male participant (Anderson & Fisher, 1991; Horn & Horn, 1982; Westhoff, 1985), the participant who is lower in status or less "valuable" to the organization is more often terminated (E.G.C. Collins, 1983; Westhoff, 1985), and extramarital affairs are more likely to result in employee termination as compared to other types of affairs (Mainiero, 1989; Westhoff, 1985). However, there is a need to identify managerial prejudices and inequitable decisions based on gender, so that if terminations are made within the context of workplace romance, an employee is terminated based on poor performance rather than gender or organizational status (Pierce et al., 1993).

SUMMARY

Our personal physical attractiveness plays a tremendous role in our interactions with others in our personal and work lives. There is evidence that attractiveness influences what people expect from us, how people respond to us, and what decisions we make are made about us. Yet many organizational texts do not address this topic. We believe that physical attractiveness is a pivotal factor in the development of relationships, friendships, and romances in the workplace. Furthermore, these relationships greatly shape men's and women's experiences of work.

The physical attractiveness stereotype is generally, "What is beautiful is good." This view appears to hold for younger and older persons and for men and women. Yet the stereotype is subtle, and often we deny its influence on our behavior. Attractiveness appears to influence the expectations we have about each other including intelligence, interpersonal skills, honesty, and guilt or innocence of a crime. Furthermore, attractiveness appears to influence a number of work-related decisions including hiring decisions, work evaluations, interview ratings, and salaries.

Physical attractiveness is a key factor in interpersonal attraction and liking as well as in the development of romantic relationships at work. Although such factors as propinquity, familiarity, attitude similarity, and reciprocity of liking are important, an attractive individual is more likely to engage in interpersonal relationships than a less attractive individual. Furthermore, interpersonal attraction is one antecedent of sexually intimate relationships including romantic relationships at work.

Workplace romances appear to be increasing among American workers. The rise seems to be associated with greater acceptance of office dating, especially among coworkers (less so between a manager and subordinate), and organizational cultures that convey more liberal attitudes about the appropriateness of such behavior. There are numerous outcomes or consequences of workplace romances, and such outcomes may depend, in part, on the type of romance occurring: true love, the fling, or a utilitarian relationship. More negative coworker and organizational reactions occur with utilitarian relationships, followed by flings and true love. Although workplace romances can promote perceptions of inequity among coworkers and increased legal liability for the organization, these reactions are usually is associated with manager–subordinate romances and perceptions of sexual harassment.

GLOSSARY

Career dependency: An individual's advancement in an organization depends on the consent of another.

Defendant: The person accused of wrongdoing in a legal matter.

Expectation: Anticipation of a particular reaction or set of characteristics that can actually shape perceptions of and feelings about an event or stimulus.

Fling: A type of organizational romance where two participants become very excited and involved, but the relationship ends quickly.

Ingratiation: Efforts by individuals to enhance their attractiveness to a target so that this person will be more susceptible to their requests.

Interpersonal attraction: A person's initial responses to a stranger.

Mere exposure effect: The effect that repeated exposure to any stimulus increases the positivity of its evaluation.

Nonromantic attraction: Same- and opposite-sex platonic friendships.

Organizational culture: Shared beliefs, expectations, and values held by members of a given organization and to which all newcomers must adjust.

Romantic dependency: When an individual depends on another to fulfill need within an organizational romance. Romantic dependency especially can disrupt a supervisor–subordinate relationship.

Self-fulfilling prophecy: Phenomenon that when others hold and communicate negative expectations about a person, this may undermine the person's confidence and self-esteem and lead the person to act in ways that confirm expectations.

Task dependency: When a worker depends on another to perform his or her function effectively.

True love: A type of organizational romance where two people have a sincere, long-term interest in each other; usually leads to marriage.

Utilitarian relationship: A type of organizational romance where there is some trade-off between sexual adventure and ego satisfaction for one employee and job or career advancement for the other.

Workplace romance: Any relationship between two members of the same organization that entails mutual sexual attraction.

5

Language and Communication Among Organizational Members

"Sticks and stones may break my bones but words will never hurt me."

Managers, psychologists, women, and men all know that this is not true. Words can hurt. Importantly, words can shape our self-perceptions, our perceptions of others, and our behavior at work.

Few applied psychology texts include a chapter on language and similarities and differences in language styles across groups. There are two reasons why we have included one. First, language provides the basis for communication and miscommunication in work organizations. Numerous studies have shown that a person's speech characteristics or style influences the way the person is perceived and evaluated by others. In this chapter, we suggest that the "trivia" of everyday interactions (e.g., smiling, downcast eyes, interruptions, deep-pitched voice, touching, swearing) play a key role in shaping the larger context of work (Haslett et al., 1992; Henley & Thorne, 1977). Second, the speech styles that men and women use or are expected to use reinforce sex or gender stereotypes, and if expectations are violated or not met, this can result in negative consequences for both sexes. How men and women speak influences the degree to which others view them as powerful or powerless or effective as a leader.

In chapter 1 and 2, we noted that issues related to gender and work can be addressed and defined at several levels of analysis, from individual differences to broad societal trends. In this chapter, we note the relevance of language at each of several levels, focusing particularly on interpersonal interactions involving same- or mixed-sex groups. However, we also address societal issues relating to the use and function of language as a function of gender. This chapter focuses on the perceptions of the ways men and women speak including characteristics of both verbal speech and nonverbal behavior. Because men and women interact with each other in groups at work, we discuss language behavior in same-sex and mixed-sex groups. A key theme that pervades the **sociolinguistic** literature as we apply it to language in organizations involves speech styles associated with power. One reason power and dominance are so relevant is that organizations are power hierarchies, and language helps move certain individuals through the hierarchy as well as reinforcing that hierarchy. We review some of the research in this area as well as research on perceptions of individuals who are viewed as using appropriate or inappropriate language styles. One social psychological theory, the speech styles approach (Giles & Powesland, 1975; Kramarae, 1981) is presented, which provides a framework for understanding how various linguistic groups develop. It can be applied to understand both men and women in communication as well as other linguistic groups including U.S. Blacks, French Canadians, Irish, and so forth.

FEMALE AND MALES WAYS
OF SPEAKING: DATA
VERSUS STEREOTYPES

A review of the literature on **sociolinguistics** shows that few of the expected sex differences in language are substantiated by empirical evidence (Thorne, Kramarae, & Henley, 1983). For example, gender stereotypes associated with language suggest that women talk more than men, but there is little evidence of this. Yet inaccurate stereotypes regarding differences in the use of language can affect our perceptions of communication as early as the infant stage. For example, a baby's cries are described differently depending on whether subjects are told the child is a boy or a girl. Subjects who believe the baby is a boy are likely to perceive crying as a reflection of anger, but subjects who believe the baby is a girl perceive crying as an expression of fear.

Despite the limited evidence of sex differences in communication, researchers continue to look for such differences (Thorne et al., 1983). Although evidence indicates more similarity of speech among women and among men than the stereotypes suggest, there appear to be differences in the degree to which men and women use language. More recent approaches have examined language within the contexts of actual use, including one-to-one communication in same- or mixed-sex groups in the home, at work, or in the classroom, and have focused on language use in terms of strategies. For example, when men and women speak, they intend to achieve certain objectives including creating rapport or asserting and resisting control (Thorne et al., 1983). Men and women appear to differ in the frequency with which they use certain language forms and styles. We discuss some of these comparisons next.

Comparisons of Male and Female
Communication Styles

According to both the popular literature (e.g., *Men Are From Mars, Women Are From Venus,* Gray, 1992) and selected language research, there is enough evidence to suggest that two separate language styles exist: one for men and one for women (Haslett et al., 1992; Kramer, 1974a, 1974b). However, this statement is based on evidence that suggests greater perceived differences than actual differences in language characteristics.

Nevertheless, a few generalizations can be made about male–female differences in language use.

Gender Differences in Speech. Characteristics associated with male speech include more use of joking (Coser, 1960), hostile verbs (Gilley & Summers, 1970), more interruption in cross-sex conversation, a greater amount of talking (Swacker, 1975), and lower pitch levels than females (even when accounting for physiological factors; Sachs, Lieberman, & Erickson, 1973; Scott, 1980). Traits associated more frequently with the speech of women include use of correct forms of speech (i.e., politeness; Labov, 1972); dynamic intonations including wider range of pitch variations in loudness and frequent changes of rate; polite and cheerful intonations; higher pitch levels than expected on the basis of female physiological factors (Sachs et al., 1973); use of expressive **intensifiers** such as "so," "such," "adorable," and "lovely" (Crosby & Nyquist, 1977; Lakoff, 1973; McGrath, & Gale, 1977); and use of questions to express opinions (Crosby & Nyquist, 1977; Lakoff, 1973). The anecdote presented in Sidelight 4.1 reflects one example of a stereotypical female pattern of speech, which is perceived as more tentative. The second example presented in Sidelight 4.1 shows that women and men might disagree on the labeling of various colors. Further, this example suggests, as we discuss later in this chapter, that the acceptance of some language may depend on the situation or task. In this case, publicity may be a more nontraditional field.

Perceived Differences Among Men and Women. Although there are few actual differences in speech use between men and women, there is ample evidence of perceived differences. Samples of high school and college-age students describe female speech as friendly, gentle, enthusiastic, smooth, gibberish, and devoted to trivial topics (C. Kramer, 1977). On the other hand, male speech is depicted as forceful, loud, dominating, and direct, including short replies (Bradac, Hemphill, & Tardy, 1981). Female speech is sometimes viewed as "kind and correct, but unimportant and ineffective" (C. Kramer, 1977, p. 159) and by some experts as inferior (Lakoff, 1973).

Although many discussions of male and female ways of speaking concentrate on the difficulties that can result from following a female style in a male-dominated context (e.g., the workplace), many qualities of female speech are desirable. Some characteristics stereotypically associated with female speech make it better for **affective communication** than characteristics associated with male speech (Scott, 1980). These characteristics include a concern for the listener and good grammar. Undesirable characteristics of male speech include perceptions of boastfulness

---

Sidelight 5.1 Speech Styles Are Not Always Easy to Predict

As Personnel Director of an electronics company, I distributed training seminar pamphlets to the middle management staff. One woman sent me back a memo requesting a spot in the assertiveness-training course. "All the topics sound interesting," she wrote, "but I think I'd benefit most from the assertiveness seminar—if that's all right with you."

—Contributed by Pat O'Reilly
(*Reader's Digest,* January 1997, p. 118)

In preparation for an upcoming drama festival, my friend David and I were creating publicity posters for the event. After studying a wide selection of papers and inks, we decided on a color but could not agree on its name. I argued that it was goldenrod, while David claimed it was orange–yellow, adding that it was just like a woman to give a basic color a fancy name. Calling a truce, we took the sample to our printer.

"So," he commented, examining our choice, "you've decided on the marigold?"

—Contributed by Rebecca Petruck
(*Reader's Digest,* May 1997, p. 68)

(Passage written by a male author).

A new car
Reality: 331-horsepower five-speed V-8, four valves per cylinder, dual overhead cam, twin turbocharger. She-speak: It's red.

A new apartment
She-speak: only four closets, but lots of light, and a huge bathtub. The floor's kinda shot, but at least it has the original moldings. Two people can fit in the kitchen at the same time. Seems good, but let's look at the next twenty on the list. Reality: I can hang my bike on the left wall, and it's close to a good bar. Where do we sign?"

(Sheidlower, 1997, p. 29)

---

and aggressiveness. Many of these results are from U.S.-based research. A number of characteristics associated with male speech may inhibit effective cross-cultural communication. When an ideal speaker is considered, more male characteristics deviate from the ideal than female characteristics (Kramer, 1977). Scott (1980) suggested that many female speech traits are effective for addressing affiliative interactions where warmth, cooperation, and self-expression are important. Where expressive or socioemotional competency is needed, female speech may be evaluated as more effective.

In a **meta-analysis** of male and female communication styles, Pruett (1989) found that men were perceived as more dominant and contentious than women, whereas women were perceived as more attentive. Men perceived themselves as more dramatic than women, whereas women perceived their style as more open. Although others did not see them as more so, men perceived themselves as more relaxed. Women's styles were seen by observers as more animated and friendly. In organizational settings, male managers (compared to females) are perceived to be more dominant, quick to challenge others, more likely to ignore comments of others if others are in control of the conversation, and more often directing the course of the conversation (Baird & Bradley, 1979). Female managers, on the other hand, are rated higher on showing concern and being attentive to others.

Not surprisingly, actual gender differences in speech are linked to stereotypically perceived differences in speech between men and women (Newcombe & Arnkoff, 1979). For example, the use of tag questions (e.g., "We are going to leave now for work, OK?"), qualifies, hedges, hesitations, and compound requests, all of which are part of the stereotype of female language, is perceived as less powerful. The use of qualifiers is associated with ratings of greater speaker warmth. Women ask more questions than men and do more of the "maintenance work" in keeping conversations going (Fishman 1983). Women also use more positive responses like "uhmmm," use silence as a response to interruptions, and use more pronouns like *you* and *we* that acknowledge the other person. Men tend to ignore previous remarks made by others, but women refer to previous remarks. Women tend to evaluate verbal aggression as negative, disruptive, and personally directed. Men use it as a strategy for conversation. Men give advice as experts, whereas women share their experiences and offer reassurance (Haslett et al., 1992). Furthermore, the same communication behavior is sometimes used differently by men and women. Women use tag questions to maintain an interaction, while men use them as requests for information. Although researchers found that sex of speaker had small effects on evaluations, changes in how one speaks might allow both women and men to change the way they are perceived (Newcombe & Arnkoff, 1979).

Summary and Note of Caution. Although there is evidence that women and men use different language or communication styles with varying frequency, we would like to highlight some cautions noted in this literature. First, there is a reasonably consistent finding that perceived differences in communication of language between women and men are greater than actual differences. For example, **pitch level** depends on the length, tension, and weight of one's vocal cords. Although women's vocal cords tend to be shorter, lighter, and stretched more tightly, resulting in higher pitch (C. Kramer, 1974b), differences in vocal cord structure do not account for the range of differences between men and women. That is, a woman's speaking voice range includes higher pitches or voice than expected given vocal cord structure, whereas a man's range includes a lower voice than expected from the size of his vocal cords. Therefore, the difference may reflect social influences or learning by men and women to sound a gender-specific way. Second, numerous researchers point out the tendency to exaggerate differences between men and women. Although there are large variations within male and female groups and across situations or contexts (refer to Fig. 3.1 in chap. 3), there are contextual variations in the occurrence or use of such forms of speech as tag questions and pauses that may be misattributed to gender.

The need to be sensitive to the context of speech cannot be overemphasized (A. Haas, 1979; Kramarae, 1982; Kramarae, Thorne, & Henley, 1978). In studies using a **correlational approach,** voice quality including pitch has been found to differ depending upon one's sex, age, status, and occupation (Crystal, 1971, cited in Thorne & Henley, 1975). These are variables that are often neglected in research on gender and language (Thorne & Henley, 1975). Furthermore, the social situation and components of the communication process including characteristics of the participants, forms of the message, and so forth may be relevant to the understanding of sex differences in language (Hymes, 1974).

UNDERSTANDING GENDER
DIFFERENCES IN LANGUAGE

To fully understand sex differences in language, leading experts Thorne and Henley (1975) recommend that researchers shift their focus from language differences among women and men to larger societal gender differences. For example, they note that a number of societal themes account for the apparent sex differences in language, including social elaboration of gender, structure of male dominance and the division of labor by sex (Thorne & Henley, 1975).

First, one of the most obvious differences between male and female speech involves its pitch, and most people assume that this reflects physiological differences between men and women. This is not necessarily the case. **Pitch** apparently has a learned component (Thorne & Henley, 1975). **Acoustical differences** are greater than differences accounted for by anatomical differences between men and women (Sachs, Lieberman, & Erickson, 1973). That is, differences in voice we hear among men and women are greater than what we would expect given modest vocal cord differences between the genders. The popular stereotypes of men and women perpetuate, reinforce, and exacerbate larger differences in male and female pitch than would be expected if there was no societal belief that women should talk with a higher pitch (Kramer, 1974b, 1974c).

Second, several forms of male dominance are built into the economic, family, political, and legal structures of society, including linguistic dominance. Dominance is revealed through the words used to describe men and women. Men are described using more positive words, words that connote power, strength, prestige, and leadership. Women are described with negative words that connote weakness, inferiority, immaturity, and a sense of the trivial. Sexism in our language plays a central role in influencing our thoughts and behavior by ignoring, defining, and depreciating women (Henley & Thorne, 1977). Language ignores women by the use of the generic *he* to refer to all humankind. Advocates of the use of the generic *he* state that this male term includes all women (e.g., spokesman, working man, etc.). However, women are largely ignored in most school textbooks (Graham, 1973). Even when *he* is used generically, it is often interpreted by others as depicting men (Henley & Thorne, 1977; Schneider & Hacker, 1973). Interestingly, prior to the 18th century, *they* was widely used to refer to someone whose sex was unspecified (Bodine, 1975). Yet today, some grammar experts (**grammarians**) insist that the use of *they* is clumsy and inaccurate. We are taught that the use of *he* is accurate even when referring to women as *he* (Henley & Thorne, 1977). Yet, the pronoun *she* is used when we discuss traditionally feminine occupations like school teacher, nurse, or homemaker.

Language defines women by helping to maintain women's place and secondary status (Henley & Thorne, 1977). Women are labeled or defined in relation to or as a possession of men. For example, at marriage, a woman often changes her name to her husband's, and children take his name as his possessions. Women are referred to in relational terms (in relation to men) as Miss or Mrs., yet men, married or single, are referred to in occupational terms or simply as Mr. Language also defines women into groupings: women and children, his and hers, or he and she, rather than women and men, hers and his, or she and he. *Lady surgeon, woman astronaut*—all denote exceptions, not the rule, even in occupations that are feminine. Men in traditionally female fields make up their own terms (e.g., *chef* vs. *cook*) that often connote greater status and prestige.

Sexism is transmitted through our language by **deprecating connotations.** *Virtue* is a term that comes from an old root meaning man or virtuous, being manly (Henley & Thorne, 1977). Can there be virtuous women? Maleness implies leadership, power, and strength, whereas words associated with femaleness connote "unpredictability or treachery," like hurricanes and other natural disasters. A woman's sex is treated as one of her most salient characteristics. Words associated with men imply importance, whereas those associated with women refer to the unimportant or trivial (e.g., *ess* or *ette: poetess, usherette, majorette*).

Third, and finally, the societal division of work or labor by sex reflects a broader societal perspective of sex difference in language (Thorne & Henley, 1975). In every society, tasks, activities, and rights are allocated by sex. Although women have higher status in some societies than others, there are no societies where women are publicly recognized as equal to or more powerful than men (Rosaldo, 1974). Women's tasks are defined by their relationship to men. Men are portrayed in books more frequently and as engaging in a wider variety of tasks than women. Women, when mentioned at all, are referred to as mother or wife (again mother depicting a relationship to others rather than simply an individual description).

The link between gender differences in language and sex segregation of labor is exemplified in differences in conversational topics for men and women. For example, in the 1960s, extensive sex segregation among U.S. blue-collar couples was found to affect patterns of conversation (Komarovsky, 1962). Among these couples, males and females "split up" for conversation. Men and women had little to say to each other even in social situations. Women talked about interpersonal issues, whereas men discussed cars, sports, work, and so forth. Men ridiculed female talk as "dirty diaper stuff" (Thorne & Henley, 1975). Furthermore, men and women knew terms associated with their sex-stereotypical realm of activities (Conklin, 1974) such that women were more likely to know about terms associated with child care, cooking, and house decorating and men to know terms about sports and cars. These findings suggest that historically, a woman's style of communication was more confined in time and territory (Thorne & Henley, 1975). A woman's setting was most likely the home, whereas a man's territory included a variety of settings (e.g., home, work, outdoors) including foreign places. As more women enter the workforce, will the topics of male–female conversation converge? Unfortunately, there is evidence that women in the workforce continue to be concentrated in a small total number of occupations whereas men occupy a wide range of occupations (we examine the topic of occupational segregation more in chap. 7).

In sum, although there is some evidence that female characteristics of speech are viewed as positive, other factors may influence speaking outcomes including personal effectiveness and influence (R.M. Kramer et al., 1978). For example, men are perceived to have greater personal and position power (see chap. 6 for a discussion of power and gender). Social desirability of communication may not be as important to the final outcome of a communication exchange as relative power. Some language experts (Lakoff, 1973) suggest that women adopt male speech, especially as more women enter the workforce and male-dominated occupations. Others argue that the female style has strength including the expression of emotion and self-disclosure, and that new patterns or styles should be created (Thorne & Henley, 1975). However, women in the workplace may find themselves in a double-bind. Men may be more effective in situations where power differentials are important, in part because power and dominance are natural parts of their style of speaking. If women continue to use more feminine styles, they may be viewed as less effective, powerful, and influential. Yet when women use the style linked with men, they may be viewed as unfeminine and may risk being disliked (Goodman, 1979; Scott, 1980).

WOMEN AND MEN SPEAKING IN GROUPS

Numerous myths are associated with language or communication styles of men and women (Henley & Thorne, 1977). As mentioned at the beginning of this chapter, the popular view is that women speak more frequently and longer than men. Actually, men speak more often, speak at greater length, and interrupt others more than do women. These findings occur in numerous contexts: alone, and in single-sex or mixed-sex pairs and groups. In a study of male–female dyads, men spoke more than 59% of the time (Hilpert, Kramer, & Clark, 1975). The same results were found in a laboratory study (Swacker, 1975) where females averaged 3 minutes of speaking whereas men averaged approximately 13 minutes. An important finding in regard to work meetings and committees, men outtalked women, and in general, women had a difficult time "getting the floor" (i.e., having an opportunity to speak) in groups and were interrupted more (Bernard, 1972). This may be due to perceptions that women have less powerful voices, so they have difficulty securing attention. Women also are more likely to lose attention by successful interruptions from men. In studies of conversations of same-sex and mixed-sex pairs in natural situations, 98% of the interruptions and 100% of the overlaps in conversation were made by men (Zimmerman & West, 1975). Communication within mixed-sex groups in terms of turn-taking showed that males tended to control the conversation (Zimmerman & West, 1975). Conversation and language are one component of social interaction between women and men. Interruptions, lapses in the flow of communication, and inattentiveness are all used by men to control conversation, reflecting greater power and dominance (Sacks, Schegloff, & Jefferson, 1974).

Stereotypes, Context, and Language

Stereotypical beliefs about the appropriate language styles for men and women influence the behavior and perceptions of behavior of women and men working in groups. Communication patterns among women and men vary depending on the sex composition of the group and the nature of the group task (i.e., social vs. task oriented). Consistent with sex-role stereotypes, women are perceived to be (and, according to stereotypes, are supposed to be) expressive, nurturant, and supportive in their social interactions whereas men are concerned with leadership, power, and influence (Aries, 1977). In hierarchically structured interactions, men tend to dominate (Edelsky, 1981). In more collaborative mixed-sex interactions, women participate more equally with men. In general, in same sex groups, women share interactions equally, tend to develop and pursue a single topic cooperatively, discuss topics of intimacy and interpersonal relations, support others' remarks, and give more attention to socioemotional issues than men in all-male groups. Men in all-male groups establish a relatively stable dominance hierarchy and discuss a range of general, nonintimate topics on which a few men dominate. Men express competition and leadership, and their talk focuses on competition and status. Power, then, appears to play a central role in all-male groups. In both male and female same-sex groups, however, amount of task talk increases over time whereas the amount of socioemotional talk decreases (Aries, 1977; Carli, 1982).

In mixed-sex groups, men and women tend to accommodate each other's style (Haslett et al., 1992). Men become less dominating and women less supportive than their behaviors in same-sex groups. Yet, when sex differences occur, they are consistent with sex-role expectations. Men tend to talk more, initiate more topics, make more contributions, and receive more comments from others than women. Women increase their communication with men in mixed-sex groups but not with other women. Men's talk becomes more personal and less competitive in mixed-sex groups, but men continue to express more dominance and competition than women. Women continue to express more concern for others and more affection than men.

However, many of these stereotypical perceptions in communication are not supported. There is evidence that most people, including both women and men, are capable of a wider range of behaviors, and they select from this repertoire (Megargee, 1969). For example, it has been found that high-dominant women exert leadership over low-dominant women but not over low-dominant men. Women conform more to group pressure in mixed-sex groups than in all-female groups (Tuddenham, McBride, & Zahn, 1958). Further, women are more socioemotional (i.e., nurturing, supportive) and men more task-oriented in both family interactions and mixed-task groups (Strodtbeck & Mann, 1956). However, a similar task/socioemotional role differentiation occurs in all-male task groups as well (Bales & Slater, 1955). That is, men are capable of task and emotional behavior, suggesting once again that people develop a repertoire of language behavior and draw from it depending on the requirements of the situation.

In general, men initiate and receive more interaction in groups than women (Aries, 1977). Aries (1977) found that in all-male groups, a more stable dominance hierarchy among members emerged. The same men within the group were most active or least active across time. This was not the case in the all-female groups. In the all-female groups, there was greater flexibility over time in the rank order of members. The most active speakers sometimes felt they took up too much of the group's time, and they would draw out the more silent members.

Furthermore, men addressed significantly more of their remarks to the group as a whole in the all-male group than when interacting with women (Aries, 1977). This behavior in the all-male group may reflect less intimacy in the all-male group or a need to establish oneself. For women, the (female) style of addressing individuals remained similar in the all-female and mixed-sex groups. Interestingly, there was little interaction among women in mixed-sex groups. However, there was an upward flow of communication from inactive to more active speakers (e.g., women directing their comments toward men), so there was a low likelihood of female-to-female interactions (Aries, 1977). Yet in sessions where women initiated a more equal amount of interaction, there was more cross-sex than same-sex interaction (Aries, 1977). The increased participation by women was associated with increased male communication with women, not greater interaction among women. One conclusion from these findings is that women may compete with each other in interactions with men (Aries, 1977). An alternative explanation is that as a less powerful minority, women avoid threatening the more powerful male members by showing solidarity with the males rather than with other females.

In general, more awkward silences occur in mixed-sex groups than in all-female or all-male groups (Aries, 1977). Men often reveal little of themselves personally, compete with each other, size each other up, and engage in teasing to express superiority and aggression. Women, on the other hand, are more self-disclosing, discuss home and family issues, and, in mixed-sex groups, tend to favor men more in terms of the types of topics covered. Furthermore, women have slightly fewer topics for conversation than men in task-related conversations (S.K. Murphy, 1989).

Context, Gender, and Perceptions
of the Speaker

As indicated earlier in this chapter, there is disagreement over the extent to which female and male patterns of speech truly differ. Some experts argue that female speech is less powerful (Lakoff, 1975), whereas others suggest there are few consistent differences (Phelps, 1980, cited in Bartol & Martin, 1986). However, there is evidence that our reactions to speakers depend, in part, on their gender, their style of speaking, and the characteristics of the situation. For example, different speech strategies appear to affect the influence of female and male speech on others (Bradley, 1981). Both females and males are viewed as more influential and are viewed more positively when their opinions are accompanied by supportive arguments. The use of tag questions such as "Don't you think so?" or disclaimers ("I'm no expert but . . . ") has negative effects when used by women but not when used by men. Women using these qualifiers have lower influence and are perceived as having lower intelligence and little knowledge.

However, many studies contradict each other. For example, in some studies, women used more tag questions than men, making them sound more uncertain and less powerful (Lakoff, 1975), or used tag questions when trying to obtain responses from an uncommunicative conversational partner (Fishman, 1983). Other studies show no difference between men and women in the use of tag questions in the classroom (Baumann, 1976). The point is that the same language technique appears to be used differently depending on the gender composition of the group and the situation, suggesting that language is used to achieve certain goals. Consistent with this, in mixed-sex groups, situational characteristics such as task groups versus unstructured groups influenced the perceptions of female assertiveness (Kimble et al., 1981). However, situational characteristics do not have as much influence on perceptions of women in all-female groups.

Although men appear to use more masculine language and women a more feminine pattern, a more accurate description may be that there is a range of speech that varies from very masculine to very feminine (Case, 1988), and that the frequency of use of a specific pattern depends on the context of the interaction (Case, 1988; Giles, Robinson, & Smith, 1980; Kimble et al., 1981). Furthermore, the same word or gesture may be interpreted one way if used by a woman and another way if used by a man. For example, a greater rate of talking by men appears to influence others but by women does not influence others (Kenkel, 1963). It seems the expression "the more one talks, the greater the influence" holds for men but not for women. In addition, some female managers use a "stronger" masculine style of speaking (Case, 1988). However, the women who adopt the masculine style (consistent with the masculine managerial context) are not treated as equal to men. Self-confident, assertive, masculine speech when used by women is perceived as aggressive and overbearing (Fulmer, 1977; P.B. Johnson & Goodchild, 1976). Men sometimes resent assertive, unemotional women and perceive them to be acting like men. Yet, men also judge women who are passive and emotional as being unsuitable for management (Kanter, 1977a).

On the other hand, women's speech allows them to invite the expression of different value positions by others through supportive listening, sensitivity to others' needs, and mutual sharing of emotions and personal knowledge (Case, 1988). Certainly these characteristics of women's speech can serve a useful organizational function (Case, 1988). Women's speech can be useful in organizations that are evolving, especially in multicultural organizations. Women's speech seems to be appropriate when a response to change is needed, when a situation is ambiguous, when problems require a long-range perspective, when a variety of values need to be understood, and when goals are needed (Case, 1988). Men in groups use a more impersonal, authority-oriented, dominating, and controlling style. Although masculine norms pervade American management (e.g., individualism, achievement striving), they may not reflect the most optimum style in managing organizational members from a diverse workforce or in multicultural contexts. Such masculine norms do not appear to work as well in such cultures as Israel, Thailand, Taiwan, and Scandinavian countries as in the United States (Case, 1988; Hofstede, 1984).

GENDER AND NONVERBAL LANGUAGE

According to Nancy Henley (1973–1974), a leading expert on the social psychology of language and communication among women and men, the micropolitical cues or "trivia" of everyday life are important in studying women's and men's places and behaviors at work. The trivia Henley refers to include using "sir," surnames, or first names, touching others, dropping one's eyes, smiling, interrupting, and so forth. There is evidence that nonverbal messages can often overpower verbal messages (Argyle, Salter, Nicholson, Williams, & Burgess, 1970).

The literature on nonverbal behavior focuses on friendship, liking, and relationships (Morris, 1971; Scheflen, 1972). However, N.M. Henley and colleagues have discussed nonverbal behaviors extensively as reflections of power and powerlessness. In this section, we will begin with gender comparisons in nonverbal behavior and sensitivity, followed by a discussion of how nonverbal displays reflect dominance and submission.

Gender Comparisons of Nonverbal Language

Research evidence suggests a number of male–female differences in nonverbal behavior including **demeanor,** use of space, looking or staring, smiling, and touching.

Demeanor. In general, societal norms allow men to exhibit a wider range of behaviors that are considered appropriate or acceptable. Men can be "cool" and informal. Women are more restricted in what behavior is acceptable and are expected to be more proper. For example, men can swear, tell jokes, change the topic of conversation, and sit in undignified positions. Women show greater body tension including sitting upright ("don't slouch"!) with feet together and hands clasped together. Furthermore, it is generally viewed as negative and improper for a woman to swear or sit in an undignified position. Men use more open, relaxed positions as reflected by trunk relaxation, greater backward lean, and open-leg positioning (Dierks-Stewart, 1980). Women display more closed bodily positions such as hands in the lap, legs crossed at the knees or ankles, elbows closer to the body, and more trunk rigidity (P. Peterson, 1975). Higher status individuals are allowed more latitude in demeanor whereas lower status individuals are expected to show greater circumspection (N.M. Henley, 1973–1974).

Space. Women are approached more closely than are men by both other women and men (Willis, 1966). (Other research indicates that women may prefer closer positions and may possess smaller personal space than men) (Evans & Howard, 1973). In general, women tend to be more restrained and restricted in the space they use, whereas men take up more space. Have you ever noticed whose elbow you bump into when seated next to someone on a bus or airplane? Chances are it is a male passenger, because men control territorial space. For example, Silveira (1972) found that women moved out of men's way in 12 of 19 mixed-sex encounters when passing on the sidewalk. When women approached other women or men approached men, both moved out of each other's way about 50% of the time.

Eye Contact and Visibility. Eye contact is the most extensively researched nonverbal behavior (N.M. Henley, 1973–1974). People maintain greater eye contact with those from whom they want approval (Rubin,

1970). However, there is also the finding that listeners look more at speakers, and as noted earlier in this chapter, men are more often speakers. In general, women look more at other people than men (Exline, 1963; Rubin, 1970). Women avert their gaze from others, especially men; stares are a dominant and aggressive gesture among humans, as among other animals. Yet, women also have a greater percentage of mutual looking, which is interpreted as reflecting more inclusive and affectionate interpersonal relations (Exline, Gray, & Schuette, 1965). Dominance through eye contact is communicated by staring (Ellsworth, Carlsmith, & Henson, 1972; O'Connor, 1970), whereas submission may be reflected through averted glances or gaze (Hutt & Ounsted, 1966).

Related to eye contact and self-disclosure is visibility, which refers to the availability of visual cues or information about oneself to others. When subjects could not see the other person, females appeared to have more difficulty communicating. In one study, women decreased their speech by 40% when invisible, whereas men increased their speech by 40% in addition to talking more than women generally (Argyle, Lalljee, & Cook, 1968).

Touching and Smiling.   Touching and smiling are also gestures of dominance and submission. Touching is a gesture of dominance, and cuddling is the complementary gesture of submission (N. Henley, 1972). Women are touched more than men. If women touch men, it is viewed as sexual; the same interpretation is made when men touch other men. Touching has not only sexual connotations but also status connotations. It is one of the most direct invasions of one's personal space. Touching is a more physical threat than space violation, pointing, or staring. In fact, it is expected that women accept touching by others as normal behavior. Yet when women initiate touch, it is often interpreted by men as conveying sexual intent.

However, sexual attraction is not sufficient to explain men's more frequent touching of women (N.M. Henley, 1973–1974). There is little evidence that men have greater sex drives than women. Gender differences in touch may be due to women's inhibition to display sexual interest in this way. Status differences may be the best explanation of differences in touch. Touch may be a nonverbal equivalent of calling someone by her or his first name (N.M. Henley, 1973–1974). Smiling, on the other hand, is viewed as a gesture of submission. Women appear to smile more than men whether they are happy or not. However, there is little empirical evidence on the actual frequency of male and female smiling (N.M. Henley, 1973–1974). Our culture supports two classes of nonverbal behavior; one communicates dominance and status and the other involves the expression of emotional warmth (Frieze & Ramsey, 1976). Both of these groups of nonverbal behavior are consistent with sex-role stereotypes (Dierks-Stewart, 1980).

After an extensive review of the literature, J.A. Hall (1978; Barton & Martin, 1986) concluded that women are more facile at recognizing the meaning of nonverbal cues of emotion than men. Women's greater sensitivity to nonverbal cues may be an advantage to women entering nontraditional roles and work, because it may allow them to be aware of resistance from others. On the other hand, this increased awareness of resistance may also undermine their self-confidence. For example, there is evidence that women may respond more than men to the biases of interviewers in ways that confirm the interviewers' biases (Bartol & Martin, 1986; Christensen & Rosenthal, 1982).

Perceptions of Power and Powerlessness

Power is also created and communicated both verbally and nonverbally (Haslett et al., 1992). In general, powerless speech is characterized by hedges, tag questions, intensifiers, politeness, and hesitations. Powerful forms of speech are direct, including short replies (Bradac et al., 1981). As cited earlier in this chapter, men interrupt more, challenge others' statements more, tend to ignore comments if other speakers control the topic, and make more direct declarations than do women. In this section, we briefly discuss how power levels are communicated and examine power issues in language that occurs in groups.

A number of studies have described women's style of speaking as powerless and men's as more powerful (Bradac et al., 1981; Lakoff, 1973). Two people of unequal status use different patterns of eye contact (Dovidio & Ellyson, 1982). The lower status individual gazes attentively at the high-status person while the high-status individual is speaking. When the lower status person speaks, his or her gaze is averted from the other's face. Higher status individuals do not gaze so attentively at a lower status person while he or she is speaking, but they do look their partner in the eye when they themselves are speaking. In a related study of nonverbal dominance using pairs of men and women working on a neutral task, men used dominant, high-status visual patterns of communication (Dovidio, Ellyson, Keating, Heltman & Brown, 1988). However, the same women talking with the same male partners used dominant high-status visual patterns when they had situational role power (i.e., expertise or assigned status). Further, the men used a low-status pattern when the situation role placed them in a low-power position. Results indicated that situational role power can override internal personality factors in shaping some forms of nonverbal dominance display (Dovidio et al., 1988).

Men use inexpressiveness to maintain positions of power (Sattell, 1983). Male inexpressiveness is a culturally produced personality trait that is learned by boys as a major characteristic of their adult masculinity (Balswick & Peek, 1971; see Sidelight 3.1 in chap. 3). Inexpressiveness manifests itself in two ways: in adult male behavior that does not show affection, tenderness, or emotion, and in men's tendency to not support the affective expectations of others. Inexpressiveness as a characteristic of adult masculinity implies that boys and men devalue expressive behavior in others as nonmasculine (Sattell, 1983). Men are socialized into inexpressiveness through taunts and put-downs. However, boys are also socialized to learn that inexpressiveness is associated with power and prestige. Keeping "cool" is a strategy for maintaining power. Power can be exercised through inexpressiveness and can be used against women, for example, by not indicating to others why the male is silent. It can be used to withhold vital information within a given context. Paradoxically, men also are perceived as more vocally assertive and influential than women, which may, in part, be due to women's use of tag questions more in mixed-sex groups than in same-sex groups (McMillan et al., 1977). The active assertive role associated with power is demonstrated more by males than by females.

On the flip side of power, men yield less to others, especially in mixed-sex groups, because men yield less to women than to other men. Women also yield more in mixed-sex groups because women too yield less to other women than to men (Haslett et al., 1992). Consistent with sex-role expectations, men focus on task contributions (asking and giving opinions) whereas women tend to be more friendly and agree more (providing socioemotional support). However, this sex-role-consistent behavior does depend on the gender characteristics of the task. When the topic is related more to the interests and knowledge of one sex, the favored sex engages in more task behavior (Aries, 1977; Bernard, 1972; Carli, 1982; Piliavin & Martin, 1978). This suggests that men and women may communicate and perform differently on different types of tasks. Women perform better at tasks that require discussion, negotiation, or creative, integrative solutions, whereas men perform better at tasks requiring a large amount of information (W. Wood, Polek, & Aiken, 1985).

Because men have higher status than women in the larger society, men also have greater status and power in work groups within organizations (Berger & Zelditch, 1985). Status, authority, and power are all part of the masculine stereotype. To level the power among men and women in organizations, it may be necessary for a well-accepted authority (e.g., upper level management or a person with a legitimate authority) to intervene in a mixed-sex group so that initial and external societal status differences between men and women do not control the structure and power distribution within the work group (Lockheed & Hall, 1976). For example, when the experimenter in a study (Piliavin & Martin, 1978) asked men to speak more, gender-role stereotypical behaviors increased, with women speaking even less. When the experimenter asked women to speak more, stereotypical behavior decreased for both men and women. These results highlight the importance of an authority figure's support for women's contributions.

(Consistent with stereotypical expectations of men and women, a meta-analysis of sex differences in leader communication showed that men demonstrated greater emergent leader behaviors: behaviors that facilitated communication including giving suggestions and explanations, autocratic leader behavior like domination, influence strategies reflecting persuasive message, and negative affect including displaying tension. Women showed more democratic leader behavior than men, including attending to the socioemotional needs of the group and positive affects like friendliness.) When the behavior among men and women in groups is examined, it is important to keep in mind the status of men and women in the larger society as well as the organizational culture and the status of group members within the organization itself (Haslett et al., 1992). For example, women in leadership positions behave in more task oriented ways than those in nonauthority positions. Furthermore, for women, there may be a conflict between task-oriented group behavior (associated with power and leadership) and gender-role expectations for women, a conflict that is not present for men. If a woman behaves in a task-oriented way, she may be viewed as masculine or unfeminine. If she exhibits gender-role-consistent behavior, she may be viewed as unsuitable for higher levels of management and leadership positions, thus creating a double-bind. According to N.M. Henley (1973–1974), nonverbal behavior that often suggests greater power for men may be perceived by others as sexual intent or availability when exhibited by women. Because powerful women are perceived as violations of sex-status norms, women's nonverbal behavior including touch, stares, physical closeness, or less formal demeanor may be interpreted as sexual availability.

Another area where power plays a role in communication involves the use of humor. People in higher status positions and with greater power initiated the use of humor more than individuals in lower status positions (Coser, 1960). In one study, humor was used by medical personnel to relax the social structure of work without upsetting it. In terms of the hierarchy of joking, senior staff members joked more than junior staff; men used humor more than women, but women laughed harder. It appears that women with a good sense of humor are the ones who laugh at jokes, whereas men with a sense of humor tell good jokes and provide witty remarks. "Man provides, woman receives" (Coser, 1960, p. 85). Using humor as a communication tool is discussed in more detail at the end of this chapter.

A SOCIAL–PSYCHOLOGICAL APPROACH TO UNDERSTANDING LANGUAGE AND LINGUISTIC GROUPS

Numerous studies have shown that a person's speech pattern and style affect the way the person is perceived and evaluated by others (Seligman, Tucker & Lambert, 1972; Triandis, Loh, & Levin, 1966). Furthermore, there is evidence that we change our ways of speaking depending on the context and our audience. One perspective or framework for investigating speech behaviors of women and men, including the changes in those behaviors, is called the *speech styles approach* (Giles & Powesland, 1975; Kramarae, 1981). This framework uses a social-psychological approach to understand the relationships between linguistic groups and gender (and ethnic groups). It is a useful framework to examine the communication behaviors of men and women as members of dominant and subordinate groups.

The speech styles approach is based on the premise that certain speech styles are associated with specific social groups (e.g., women, Blacks, etc.) and serve as cues or indicators of the individual's group membership. According to Kramarae (1981), this model becomes more dynamic when three areas are emphasized:

1. The ways that distinctive speech can be used by group members to create solidarity and to exclude members of outgroups from inter-actions.
2. The ways that dominant group members use the distinctive features of speech (actual or perceived) of subordinate groups as a focus for ridicule.
3. The ways that speakers manipulate their speaking styles to empha-size or deemphasize particular social identities.

This approach to language is based on Tajfel's (1974) theory of inter-group behavior and social change. It assumes that psychological group distinctiveness is the result of the convergence of three processes: **social categorization, social identity,** and **social comparison** (J. Williams & Giles, 1978).

Individuals are assumed to be actively attempting to define themselves in relation to the world. Social categorization is one of the cognitive tools that people use to define and categorize themselves as well as define and categorize others. Social identity is a part of one's self-concept and in-volves the knowledge of one's membership in various social categories (e.g., male or female, African-American or Asian) and the value that a given society attaches to those social categories. Social identity acquires meaning through social comparisons or in relation to other groups (J. Williams & Giles, 1978). That is, members of a social group perceive their interactions with other social groups in ways that allow them to view their own group as positive and distinct from others. Positive social identity of the group results from this positive social comparison and distinction from other groups.

The relationships between language and intergroup relations depend, in part, on psychological, social, and situational variables including group status, group size, institutional support for the group, and its language. For example, members of a subordinate group may assert their language in a society or social context. The movement in some states to recognize languages other than English as the accepted spoken language is one example of this. The dominant group may respond to the subgroup in ways that block the development of their own language distinctiveness. As a result, members of these subgroups may develop more negative social identities (Tajfel, 1978) by accepting negative characteristics associated with lower status or may attempt to change their situation (Tajfel, 1974). For example, if members of a group recognize their lower status and consider it to be fair and legitimate, they may seek to develop a positive self-identity or image through individual means. There are two ways of achieving positive distinctiveness at the individual level: by comparing one's own position with ingroup members rather than with those in the superior group, or by attempting to leave the group and move into a superior one (i.e., social mobility).

If group members are aware of their lower status and view this as unfair, they may attempt to obtain a positive social identity by taking collective group actions. Specifically, a lower status group can use three strategies to develop a positive group identity through group action and social change (Tajfel, 1974). First, the group can attempt to assimilate both culturally and psychologically into the majority groups or try to achieve equally with these groups on important characteristics. Often this is the strategy initially used by lower status groups. Second, lower status group members may redefine characteristics that previously were negatively valued (e.g., skin color, gender, dialect) in positive terms, for example, emphasizing that women are more inclusive than men rather than less competitive, or using such expressions as "Black is beautiful!" Third, the group may identify new or alternative dimensions, not used previously in intergroup comparisons, from which the group may perceive a positive distinctiveness from others. This theory is dynamic because it assumes that collective social change action by a lower status group will meet with strong reactions by the dominant group (which is trying to maintain distinctiveness as well). Giles et al. (1978) stated that a distinct language style is a key feature of a group. This distinctiveness will be heightened when members of one group are in competition with, are compared to, and live in close proximity with the other group.

Men and Women as Linguistic Groups

Evidence that women and men compose two linguistic groups can be used as a basis for Tajfel's (1974) intergroup analyses (Giles et al., 1978; Kramarae, 1981). The relationship between men and women has been compared to relationships between Blacks and Whites and children and adults, groups with subordinate–dominant relationships. Furthermore, there are pervasive beliefs that males and females speak differently. Women are members of a subordinate or inferior group in our society. Like Blacks, women earn less outside the home, are not represented proportionately in organizations, and are more dependent on the actions of others. Intelligence and speech patterns of Blacks, women, and children are perceived more negatively than those of White males. Therefore, women are a minority based on power differences rather than absolute numbers. Women's and Blacks' speech has been described by White males as emotional, intuitive, and involving the use of words not spoken or not spoken often by the dominant group (Zimmerman & West, 1975). Both groups have been described as using more touch and nonverbal communication. Women, like children, are interrupted more.

Combining Tajfel's (1974) theory of intergroup relations and Giles' (1977) theory of speech accommodation provides a framework for understanding the role of language in group and interpersonal relationships (Kramarae, 1981). The theory of speech accommodation (Giles, Taylor, & Bourhis, 1973) suggests that one member of a dyad tends to adopt the speech patterns of the person to whom she or he is talking. The logic of speech accommodation rests on the **similarity-attraction theory** in social psychology (Byrne, 1971), where a person can enhance an evaluation of self by reducing dissimilarities. The similarity-attraction notion suggests that if a speaker desires a positive interaction, the speaker accommodates his or her own speech style to that of the individual with whom she or he is interacting. Social approval is one goal of accommodation (Giles & Powesland, 1975).

People continuously adjust their speech styles depending on to whom they are speaking. We can adopt speech to reduce or accentuate differences—to convey social similarity, differences, approval, or disapproval (Giles et al., 1973). When a person wants approval, there will be more convergence or match to the other person's speech or speech expectations. Convergence and divergence in speech involve both what is said and how it is said. In interactions where both parties want approval, one person may shift upward toward high-prestige speech and the other downward toward low-prestige speech. Women do more speech accommodating than men, especially in male–female interactions. Women do not accommodate in female–female interactions, nor do men in male–female interactions (Henley & Thorne, 1977; Kramarae, 1981). However, men and women may seek approval by using complementary speech styles rather than matching ones when highlighting gender differences in order to win approval. For example, in dating situations, it may be important for the man to convey his masculinity and the woman to show her femininity.

Language, Intergroup Theory, and Social Change

Members of minority or lower power groups can assert themselves on two levels: individual and group (Giles et al., 1973; Tajfel, 1974). The objective of this assertion is to enhance self-identity. For centuries, women have acted on an individual level by comparing themselves with each other, primarily with other domestic housewives. Historically, women could advance themselves individually through marriage more than men could through occupational achievement (Chase, 1975). A married woman's status depended on her husband's, so women worked to improve their husbands' status. These efforts were and are often successful and are considered deterrents to unified group social action. Unlike other minority groups, women do not live separately from the majority group. Separation and inferior living conditions are conducive to the development of a collective group consciousness. Women often live with the dominant group and derive many benefits from such close associations (Williams & Giles, 1978).

Another strategy that women can use at the individual level to enhance self-identity is called the "Queen Bee" syndrome (Staines, Tavris, & Epstein-Jayarantne, 1974). In this situation, the woman is concerned with personal success in a male-dominated activity. Men become her referent group. She does not identify with other women and views herself as an exception to her gender. She may accept the dominant group's negative view of her group, but she considers herself different from other women and attempts to convey to men that she is different from other members of her group and that she recognizes the inferiority of most members of her group. This is similar to the process of **assimilation.** Although individual assimilation into the dominant group may be a necessary initial change strategy for women, it is full of pitfalls and tends to preserve the status quo (J. Williams & Giles, 1978). By assimilating, the woman is evaluated using outgroup or masculine values. Females tend to accept the criteria used by the dominant group as superior to their own standards. When applying this approach to language, women who assimilate tend to accept the male way of speaking as superior and adopt that speaking style. Assimilation appears to move women away from self-definitions to definitions of self based on male standards. Consistent with assimilation is the recommendation (often by dominant groups) that women adopt a more male speech, implying that such speech is better (Lakoff, 1973).

If members of a group become aware that the group's status is illegitimate, and that they are capable of change, there is a tendency to redefine the group by collective action (J. Williams & Giles, 1978). This awareness can lead to a redefinition of the group's social identities through social movements. The women who made the most significant efforts to alter social roles during the last century were from the upper classes. Their awareness of social inequity was stimulated by two conflicting perceptions. On the one hand, upper class women received the respect due to their class-position and education. On the other hand, their status as women exposed them to a different type of social response—disregard. These conflicting experiences led these women to question the status quo. Such questioning resulted from blocked goals that upper class women possessed and believed to be legitimate (Galtung, 1974). They compared themselves to men and became aware of legal, political, and work injustices. In order for collective action changes to occur, the minority members need to view inferior comparisons with the majority as unsupported (Tajfel, 1974). However, redefining or creating new dimensions on which the minority group compares favorably with the majority group is difficult.

A controversy in Oakland involved elements of intergroup theory and social change. In December 1996, the Oakland School Board recognized the language spoken by many African-American students called **Ebonics** and agreed to use it as a starting point to teach standard English in schools. In a school district that was 92% minority, African-Americans were performing poorly in school, and by recognizing Ebonics, Oakland officials hoped to improve the way Black students were taught to read and write standard English. The move by the Oakland School Board may be one example of a minority group becoming aware of social inequity and creating a new dimension (i.e., legitimizing Ebonics) on which the minority group compares favorably. The attempt to recognize Ebonics as a separate language has its roots in the Black pride movement of the 1960s (Lubman, 1996). As one linguist states, "One way to say you're proud to be an African-American is by the way you talk" (Guy Bailey, University of

Texas, Arlington, cited in Lubman, 1996, p. A06). Another linguist states that the public's reaction to this controversy suggests a failure to realize that the linguistic changes reflect deeper cultural problems. Most of the differences in White and Black English are occurring among young people who criticize their elders for "speaking too white" (Toner, 1998). Furthermore, these language differences may reflect decreasing interaction among ethnic groups. We continue our discussion of the majority group's reactions to the Oakland School Board decision in the next section.

Responses of the Dominant Majority Group to Minority Collective Action

Reactions to assertions by women (feminists) and ethnic minorities for acceptance of a new group identity can vary substantially. First, the majority group can appear to accept changes that minorities advocate but then redefine the situation so that these changes become trivial (e.g., use of *chairman* vs. *chairperson* where the latter is used to denote women only; Kramarae, 1981). Second, majority group members can use humor or ridicule to diminish changes in language asserted by women. Although violence is generally used as a tool in resistance to racial desegregation, ridicule, which is violence's "psychic counterpart" (p. 229), is used to combat sexual equality (Murray, 1971). Humor and laughter are responses men use to avoid seriously examining the issue of language change (Hole & Levine, 1971; Kramarae, 1981; Williams & Giles, 1978). Laughter can be used by the dominant group when their social identity is threatened. For example, the media and newspaper columnists poked fun of feminists' concerns about the use of the generic *man* and *he* by moving the issue to the extreme and marginalizing it (e.g., *foreman* vs. *foreperson*). In addition, the reaction to the December 1996 Oakland School Board decision on Ebonics was equally swift. Initially, reactions were negative from both Blacks and Whites, including the Rev. Jesse Jackson and poet Maya Angelou. Jackson later met with school board officials and indicated he agreed with some of their goals. However, comments such as "We're the laughingstock of the nation" and "Your policy that attempts to legitimatize poor grammar and identify it with Black America will set us back 100 years" were made once the decision was announced ("Oakland school board amends ebonics' policy," (1997, January 16), CNN Interactive. CNN.com).

Finally, women or minorities who threaten the status quo (in terms of behavior but also in the use of language) often are accused of being sexually, emotionally, or physically defective or deviant. For example, such women are accused of not being "real" women; rather they are lesbian, insane, crazy, or not intelligent. The majority group may respond to collective action by saying that changes in language proposed by feminists are not "natural." The greatest changes in language are likely to occur when men accept the positive group distinctiveness that women claim for themselves, and when the integration of male and female roles does not involve or is perceived not to involve a loss of positive social identity for the majority group (J. Williams & Giles, 1978).

ADDITIONAL ISSUES CONCERNING
LANGUAGE IN THE WORKPLACE

The language and communication literatures provide a rich basis for application to the workplace; therefore, two additional topics warrant attention. First, as women increasingly enter more male-dominated occupations, it is important to understand how they will be perceived if they adopt more male language styles, as recommended by some linguists (Lakoff, 1975). In the next section we briefly describe some of the reactions to "sex-inappropriate" language. Second, humor is an effective communication tool but is also a potential source of misunderstanding and conflict between men and women in the workplace.

"Sex-Inappropriate" Language

Is a woman perceived as strong and confident when she employs a more male style of speaking? Or is she viewed as unfeminine? Is a man using a more female style viewed as more open and nurturing or as weak and inferior? More research is needed to fully address these questions. Yet women who use male styles of speaking are often categorized as unfeminine (Thorne & Henley, 1975). Men who speak like women are perceived as effeminate and are regarded with disdain. When speech forms of men and women merge, women usually adopt male language (Conklin, 1974). Although there are barriers for both women and men, women can more freely use both forms. In some settings, women can obtain social rewards for using male styles including being taken more seriously (Lakoff, 1973). However, although women may benefit from speaking to a male supervisor using a strong, masculine style (including promoting their strengths), self-promoting to another woman may be met with a negative reaction (Elias, 1995).

Men who reject the traditional American masculine image are more likely to use speech associated with females, including homosexuals, hippies, and academic men (Lakoff, 1973). Men who use female styles are more stigmatized than are women (Thorne & Henley, 1975). That is, we tend to view men who use a female style of speaking much more negatively than a woman using a more masculine style. Men appear to be more stigmatized for using feminine styles of speech because such use reflects downward mobility for men. For women, using the male style reflects upward mobility. Furthermore, central to the male identity is the need for men to demonstrate their masculinity and to assert themselves firmly as not feminine (Thorne & Henley, 1975). Maintaining and using male styles of speaking, a masculine symbol, may be one way of doing this. Women, on the other hand, may not have the need to prove their femininity, or prove that they are not masculine.

Research findings on perceptions of men and women using sex-inappropriate language are mixed. In mixed-sex groups where females were encouraged to talk more, females exhibited more leadership and greater participation (Schwartz, 1970). On the other hand, males in the group disliked the talkative female more than a similarly behaving male. Males continued to dislike these women even after the women stopped behaving in a sex-inappropriate manner (Schwartz, 1970). Furthermore, there is evidence that women have been fired from their jobs because their language was perceived as too strong or inappropriate for their gender (Kramarae, 1981).

Other research indicates that the use of sex-appropriate and -inappropriate language differentially affects males and females (Berryman, 1980). In Berryman's (1980) study, male speakers using sex-appropriate language (i.e., male speech) were rated as more extroverted, less credible, and less active. Males using sex-inappropriate language (i.e., female speech) were viewed as less extroverted and more credible and active. Females using sex-appropriate language (i.e., female speech) were viewed as more credible and less extroverted and confident. Females using sex-inappropriate speech (i.e., male speech) were rated as less credible and more extroverted and confident. In general, regardless of gender, men and women using female features of language were rated as more credible communicators; users of male language were rated as more extroverted.

Clearly, more research is needed on the effects of gender and language appropriateness on perceptions of competence and liking. It may be that the use of one style is associated with more positive rewards and perceptions, yet we may be less comfortable when a given individual uses a language style that we expect from the opposite gender. Regardless, it is clear that men and women do not use simply one style of speaking. Consistent with theories presented in this chapter, women and men use variations of masculine and feminine styles. Competence and ease of movement from masculine to feminine or integrating both styles may enable individuals to meet challenges within the workplace (Berryman-Fink & Wheeless, 1987).

Gender and Humor

Most of us believe we have a reasonable sense of humor. In fact, most of us believe we possess an above-average sense of humor (Mackie, 1987). Humor reflects a shared set of experiences and communicates attitudes and evaluation (Lindesmith, Strauss, & Denzin, 1977). Due to its ambiguous nature, humor allows people to express beliefs and feelings without being held accountable for them (Sanford & Eder, 1984). One can communicate a message and then "take it all back" by saying "it was only a joke" (Kane, Suls, & Tedeschi, 1977, p. 13).

Humor is an extension of language generally. In the United States, it reflects an antifemale bias reinforcing women's inferior status (Cantor, 1976; McGhee, 1979; Zimbardo & Meadow, 1974). Humor strengthens ingroup ties and solidarity. Differences between groups serve as a basis for laughter, and ingroup humor is often kept from outgroup members. For example, women rarely tell jokes about men in men's presence. In mixed-sex groups, women use self-deprecating humor (Walker, 1981). On the other hand, men do tell jokes to women that denigrate women, and women laugh at these jokes (Cantor, 1976). Why would women laugh at such denigrating jokes? Laughter is a form of ingratiation (Mackie, 1987). This is an impression management technique that people use to increase their own likability, especially to be liked by someone more powerful (Kane et al., 1977). Therefore, in order to be liked by males, women may laugh even at their own expense.

A humorous interaction can often be divided along traditional sex-role lines. Men initiate it, while women receive or respond. A man who has a good sense of humor is one who tells funny jokes; a woman with a good sense of humor, however, is one who laughs at them (Eakins & Eakins, 1978). Women's attempts at being funny often meet with male disapproval, especially when female humor is interpreted as undermining male authority. Jokes that denigrate or are said at the expense of others increase among individuals with higher status (McGhee, 1979). Women tend to use self-deprecating humor, which is tied to lower status (Eakins & Eakins, 1978). Feminists tend not to laugh at jokes that denigrate women and, consequently, are perceived as having no sense of humor at all (Walker, 1981).

Why is humor in the workplace a serious topic for applied psychologists and HRM professionals? First, there is some evidence that male and female supervisors who use humor receive higher overall effectiveness ratings than those who do not (Fisher, 1996). In addition, humor is the delineation of ingroup and outgroup status. It can identify individuals who are "one of the gang" and clearly convey to others that they are not "one of us." For example, one of the more prevalent forms of sexual harassment of women at work includes sexual jokes and teasing. Forty to sixty percent of all complaints reflect this type of harassment (Alberts, 1992). Joking and teasing can reflect a hostile work environment although often not the (legally) more serious form of harassment called quid pro quo. Teasing can be viewed as harassment because it includes playfulness/ joking and derogation/aggression (Alberts, 1992). It is an aggressive behavior that is embedded within a situation with cues signaling that play is occurring. The interpretation of teasing is very important yet is often ambiguous. When a man teases a woman, his intentions are highly uncertain. The man may believe he is being playful. The woman may feel harassed or she may believe it is joking, only to find out just the opposite (Alberts, 1992). See the examples of interchanges between men and women in Sidelight 4.2. Which do you find more humorous? More impolite or rude? The perpetrator of teasing can also deny culpability. This form of harassment can be effective in terms of inflicting harm upon its target and can be difficult to eradicate because the harasser can always claim that he was "only joking." Sexual harassment is discussed more fully in chapter 9.

SUMMARY

Although there appear to be some actual differences in the way women and men speak, perceived differences are far greater than actual differences. Women tend to have higher and men lower pitch levels than expected on the basis of female and male physiology. Women tend to speak more politely whereas men speak more forcefully. Descriptions and characterizations of male and female speaking styles closely follow stereotypical notions of men and women in our society. For example, words associated with men reflect dominance and are positive in content. Such words connote power, strength, prestige and leadership. Female words reflect weakness, inferiority, and a sense of the trivial.

The link between gender differences in language and sex segregation of the workforce is exemplified by the content of male and female conversations. Especially among blue-collar workers, men and women split up for conversation and rarely have much to say to each other. The topics of conversation for women include interpersonal matters, whereas men discuss work, sports, and cars.

Sidelight 5.2   Males and Females Seem to Use Humor Differently

The Regional Vice President at my company, a middle-aged man with a receding hairline, never missed an opportunity to get in a dig at the engineers in my department. One day at our staff meeting, he zeroed in on a young single guy who often tried out different hairstyles and grooming products. "You keep spending money on your hair," the vice president said with a smirk, "and you'll have to take out a loan."

"Thankfully," the young man responded coolly, "with the money you are saving on your hair, you'll be able to give me one."

—Contributed by Sharon A. Peterson
(*Reader's Digest,* March 1998, p. 36)

Between her sophomore and junior years at college, my daughter Laurie waited tables at a rather seedy steakhouse. One evening she waited on a well-dressed young couple. In a rather condescending tone, the man asked her, "Have you ever thought of going college?"

"Actually, I *do* go to college," Laurie replied.

"Well, I went to Harvard," he said, surveying the restaurant, "and I'd *never* work in a place like this."

"I go to Vassar," Laurie retorted, "and I'd never *eat* in a place like this."

—Contributed by Nancy Kuusela
(*Readers Digest,* December 1997, p. 75)

In group interactions, stereotypical patterns of verbal and nonverbal interactions among men and women emerge. Men tend to initiate conversation within the group, interrupt women more, talk more, and establish a hierarchy of dominance. Women, especially in all-female groups, tend to take turns speaking, ensuring that everyone has the opportunity to speak. Even with nonverbal behavior, women reflect a more formal, restrictive set of nonverbal behaviors. Women show more body tension and closed body positions, whereas men reflect a more relaxed manner. As a result, women take up less space physically, avert their gaze from others especially men, and touch others less than men. Men use inexpressiveness to maintain positions of power, and women ask more questions and exert more effort at keeping conversations going.

The speech styles approach to understanding language and gender suggests that certain speech styles are associated with specific social groups including men and women, Blacks and Whites, and so forth. Based on Tajfel's theory of intergroup behavior, language is one way a group develops its own distinctiveness and identity. In attempts to develop a positive social identity, a group of lower status may take collective group action to change its negative circumstances. Examples of these include the women's movement in the 1960s and the 1996 Oakland School Board decision regarding Ebonics. Collective social action by a lower status group will likely meet with strong reactions by the dominant group.

Other important language issues include using sex-inappropriate language and humor in the workplace. Men using a more feminine style appear to be more negatively stigmatized than women using a more masculine style. Specifically, women using a masculine style are perceived more positively in some circumstances by men but not by other women. Women may need to move from more feminine to masculine styles depending upon their listeners. Finally, humor in the workplace is becoming an increasingly serious topic. Although there may not be significant gender differences in sense of humor, the behaviors in which men and women engage in order to be perceived as having a sense of humor appear to be quite different. Men with a sense of humor tell jokes; women with a sense of humor laugh at them. However, humor, especially teasing and joking, can have serious repercussions in the workplace if misperceived. More on misperceptions of humor and sexual harassment is presented in chapter 9.

GLOSSARY

Acoustical differences: Differences in heard sound.

Affective communication: Sending and receiving information regarding feelings and emotions.

Demeanor: One's outward behavior.

Deprecating connotations: Words, phrases, or expressions that convey disapproval.

Dyad: A pair or a unit of two.

Grammarian: A specialist in grammar or the study of rules for speaking and writing in a language.

Hedge: To hide behind words or refuse to commit oneself.

Intensifier: Word that implies an increase in degree or strength of force or vividness.

Meta-analysis: A procedure in which the outcomes of different studies are quantified so that they may be compared and summarized.

Pitch level: Level or quality of a tone or sound determined by the frequency of vibration of the sound waves reaching the ear.

Social categorization: Process of classifying people according to particular social characteristics.

Social comparison: Social process of comparing one's opinions and abilities with other people's and making evaluations based on this comparison.

Social identity: Use of group membership (including gender, racial, and religious groups) as a source of personal identity or definition and self-esteem.

Sociolinguistics: Science of social languages.

6

Power and Relationships at Work

A little girl and a little boy are in a sandbox. The little boy wants to compete with the girl, and so he tells her about how his family owns a color TV set. The girl says her parents own a color TV set. He says they own a boat. She replies that her parents also own a boat. He pulls down his trousers asnd declares, "I have this!" She pulls down her pants, looks, and runs home crying. The next day they are back in the sandbox. Having enjoyed himself the previous day, the little boy says that his parents have two cars. She replies that her parents have two cars. He says that they have a big house. She counters that her family too has a big house. Figuring it worked before, the little boy pulls down his pants. The little girl looks him in the eye and says, "My mommy says that when I'm big I can have as many of those as I want!"

—(Barreca, 1991, pp. 92–93)

Power is the capacity to influence others. Supervisors praise or punish workers, senior employees selectively share their expertise, and organizational leaders filter information to the rank and file in order to influence their behaviors, beliefs, and attitudes. Power is a ubiquitous feature of relationships both within and outside organizational settings. The prudent and effective use of power to forward legitimate organizational goals is the hallmark of a healthy organization. However, power can be used for inappropriate purposes, individuals or groups can exercise power only to gain more power, and powerful actions can have unintended negative consequences for individuals, groups, and organizations.

This chapter describes power and its related concepts (e.g., influence, dependency, control, and authority) as they affect organizational functioning and interpersonal relationships within organizations. Various definitions and theories of power are discussed as well as the effects of power and influence strategies on gender and various power-related topics. We conclude by focusing on the implications of power imbalances between women and men and on women's strategies to gain power in organizations.

DEFINITIONS AND SOURCES OF POWER AND INFLUENCE

In work organizations, it is easy to mistake formal authority for power, in the sense that people higher on the organizational chart are often assumed to have more power, and people at equivalent levels are assumed to have the same power. In fact, formal authority is only one aspect, and sometimes a small one, of power. That is, people at the same organizational level may have vastly different levels of power, because of their different access to resources, because of their personal characteristics (including gender), and because of the types of subordinates they work with (if subordinates won't follow you, you are not a very powerful leader). In this chapter, we distinguish between structural and personal sources of power and also between sources of power that are explicit and "visible" and those that are more subtle and less clearly visible to external observers.

Conceptualizations of Power

From a personal perspective, power is the potential to get something that you want from someone else who may unwilling to relinquish it. Thus, power is the potential to influence, but as Emerson (1962) noted, power is not a static characteristic of an individual. It is a property of a social relationship; that is, one individual has power over another individual (but not necessarily over a different individual). According to Emerson, when a person has desirable resources, such as the ability to control rewards like job promotions, she or he has power over those who desire those resources (e.g., an ambitious subordinate) The ambitious subordinate, therefore, depends on the supervisor for a job promotion. The first definition of power that we offer, then, describes **power-dependence relations:** "The power of actor A over actor B is the amount of resistance on the part of B which can be potentially overcome by A" (Emerson, 1962, p. 32). The more dependent the second person is on the first, the great the potential the first person has to overcome the second's resistance to his or her requests. For example, if the ambitious subordinate depends entirely on his supervisor's recommendation for the promotion, he is likely to do whatever his supervisor asks him to do regardless of how unpleasant the task. If the supervisor is only one of several people who have input on job promotions, the ambitious subordinate is not so strongly compelled to acquiesce to the supervisor's every demand.

Related to dependency is scarcity or nonsubstitutability. To the extent that one person depends on scarce resources controlled by another, the person controlling the valued resource has power over the person who needs the resource (Kipnis, 1990). Thus, if the job market is tight and only one or two promotions will be granted in a given year, the ambitious subordinate becomes particularly dependent on his supervisor, and the supervisor has considerable power over the subordinate. However, if there are several opportunities for advancement in an organization, or if higher paying, higher prestige jobs are readily available elsewhere, the ambitious subordinate is not so dependent on the supervisor for the particular job promotion she or he controls.

Three general models of power have been developed in various disciplines, such as philosophy, psychology, and sociology (Hiley, 1987). The *behavioral model* views power as "the intentional and overt behavior of individuals or groups where there is explicit conflict or resistance, and where the resolution is explained in terms of the power one individual has over another in achieving consensus" (Hiley, 1987, p. 345). Emerson's power-dependence model is an example of a theory within the behavioral model. In the *ideological model,* power "operates through the way a belief system or set of values figures in structuring or fostering the conditions for certain explicit outcomes" (Hiley, 1987, p. 345). For example, an organization's **corporate culture** may indicate that certain beliefs and patterns of behavior are valued over others. Organizational members think and act accordingly due to the "power" of the corporate culture. An organization that places a high value on loyalty and is known by all members to reward loyal employees (or punish disloyal employees) may be able to influence employees to conform to company norms no matter what the cost. Gender stereotypes might represent an ideological basis for power, in the sense that they convey the idea that men should have power or influence over women, particularly when interacting in what has historically been the man's domain—the workplace. In the *disciplinary model* (Hiley, 1987), power is focused on the way the rules, policies, structure, and workplace design of an organization produce efficient and conforming behavior. Hiley described how routinization and the separation of people in work cubicles or evenly spaced assembly line positions destroy a sense of collective identity and produce uncritical conformity and allegiance to organizational goals. It is ironic that the hallmarks of discipline hailed by bureaucratic and scientific management principles that were designed to diminish the role of power became, in fact, a form of power.

We focus on the behavioral conceptualization of power in this chapter primarily because it has received the most theoretical and research attention in the organizational literature. It also provides a useful framework for understanding similarities and differences between women and men in their acquisition, use, perceptions, and consequences of power. The reader is advised, however, to keep the ideological and disciplinary models of power in mind throughout our discussion. These perspectives will become more important when we discuss feminist perspectives on power.

Acquiring Power

One way of articulating the different sorts of power is to describe how people get power. As we note subsequently, power may be the result of the position one occupies, the information, talents, or resources one brings to that position, relationships with subordinates, and so forth.

Bases of Power.   Individuals or groups can acquire power through a variety of means. French and Raven (1959) developed a general and widely recognized taxonomy of power bases that include six types of power: legitimate, reward, coercive, expert, referent, and informational. **Legitimate power** is based on an individual's formal authority in an organization. Both the power holder and the target recognize and accept the rights the former has in making requests of the latter because such requests are sanctioned by the organization. A supervisor has legitimate power over subordinates because the organization vests authority in the supervisory position. Reward and coercive power are derived from an individual's or group's ability to offer rewards or dole out punishments to others in return for their compliance. Because supervisors control rewards such as pay, promotions, and job assignments, and because they can also legitimately punish workers by docking their pay or demoting or firing them, supervisors have considerable power on the basis of reward and punishment. This base of power, however, is not solely the province of supervisors, who, for example, may be affected by rewards and punishments controlled by subordinates (e.g., their social approval or threats to strike). Thus, individuals or groups with no legitimate power may acquire power through the control of such resources. **Expert power** derives from an individual's or group's skills, abilities, and specialized knowledge that are needed by others. Again, because supervisors typically know more than subordinates about the technical and/or political environment of their department, they possess greater power on the basis of this expertise. A coworker or subordinate who has greater expertise on a matter of importance to others, however, gains power over his or her peers or bosses. A charming, attractive, popular individual who draws others possesses **referent power.** Transformational leaders, that is, those who inspire trust, commitment, and value changes in others, are considered to have referent power (e.g., Burns, 1978). Finally, **informational power** stems from the ability to provide or control important information. Individuals who hold central positions in communication networks possess informational power because they can control the flow and type of information passed from one individual or group to another.

Although each type of power has been widely discussed in the organizational literature, researchers have raised questions about the validity of this taxonomy (Kipnis & Schmidt, 1983; Kipnis, Schmidt, & Wilkinson, 1980; Koslowsky & Schwarzwald, 1993). Among their concerns are that the bases are not clearly defined or that empirical analyses do not support the original conceptualizations. Koslowsky and Schwarzwald (1993), for example, found that there may be fewer than six conceptually distinct types of power bases. Coercion, reward, and expertise power bases were consistent with their original descriptions, but legitimacy, informational, and reference bases seemed to group together. It might be that informational and referent tactics are often used to legitimate a request or a demand. Similarly, when we attempt to influence others, we often rely on various combinations of power bases that vary across situations and targets (Hinkin & Schriesheim, 1989). Yukl (1981) suggested that power sources can be more succinctly categorized as three types:

1. *Position power,* wherein power derives from the formal role an individual occupies such as the ability to control rewards and punishments and to have one's power legitimated by the role (e.g., supervisor).
2. *Interpersonal power,* wherein one individual's attractiveness, charisma, and informal influence over another are sources of power in that relationship.
3. *Individual power,* which comes from individual disposition and skills that are independent of the job and interpersonal context (e.g., expertise).

Strategic Contingencies.   As described earlier in this chapter, one important source of power is the ability to control resources that others depend on. Power and dependency in a relationship are inversely related. An individual or group gains power by acquiring resources that are needed or wanted by others and that cannot be obtained elsewhere. Salancik and Pfeffer (1977) developed the **strategic contingencies theory** to explain why organizational groups gain and lose power. Groups or individuals who can control or provide information and solutions to areas of uncertainty in an organization become powerful because they provide an important resource (control over uncertainty) that other groups need. The more important the issue over which there is uncertainty, the greater the power of the group who can control this uncertainty. The case of "Sputnik" provides a good example of power by strategic contingencies. Research and development divisions of organizations gained considerable power during the 1950s and 60s because they could provide ways to be technologically competitive. Because the United States was embarrassed that the Soviet Union had launched the first spaceship, Sputnik, the goal of becoming technologically superior was highly salient to governments, businesses, and the general public. Therefore, research and development groups could wield considerable influence. In more recent history, the American automobile industry suffered from the perception that American cars were lower in quality than foreign competitors. Although perceptions are managed through a variety of means (including actually making better cars), one important method is marketing: positioning a product or service to influence consumers' perceptions that it is worth buying. Thus, according to strategic contingencies theory, individuals or groups with savvy marketing expertise should have gained considerable power in influencing automobile corporations' decisions during this precarious time in this industry. Conversely, groups lose power when the functions they control are no longer of strategic importance to the organization.

Conceptualizations of Influence and Influence Tactics

If power is the potential to influence, influence is the exercise of that potential. Influence tactics are the "actual means used by power holders to change the behavior of other people" (Kipnis, 1990, p. 16). A person may offer rewards in exchange for favors, appeal to reason and logic, compliment the other person, or coerce and threaten in order to change another's behavior. The success of any of these strategies depends on the influencer's power over the target. A substantial body of research examines influence tactics, the conditions under which they are used, and their effectiveness.

Influence Tactics.   Individuals with power over others can influence others in a variety of ways. To better understand influence tactics, people are asked to describe what they do to influence others (e.g., Kipnis, 1984; Kipnis & Consentino, 1969; Kipnis, et al., 1980). These studies have been conducted in the context of supervisor–subordinate relationships (Kipnis & Schmidt, 1983; Kipnis et al., 1980), friendships and dating relationships (Falbo & Peplau, 1980; Kipnis, 1984), and meetings (Littlepage, Nixon, & Gibson, 1992), among other settings. Although there are many ways to influence other people, most strategies boil down to a few basic methods. We can forcibly influence others (assertiveness) or use friendship and kindness (ingratiation). Furthermore, it's reasonable that some, if not many, people are swayed by logic and evidence (rationality). These and other basic influence tactics are summarized in Table 6.1.

Researchers have examined the frequency with which these influence tactics are used and the conditions under which they are used. People change their influence strategies depending upon the outcomes they are trying to obtain (Kipnis et al., 1980). Ingratiation and negative sanctions (e.g., punishments and other coercive tactics) are used to achieve personal goals. Logic and rational discussion (rationality) are most likely to be used when the goal is to initiate change, and sanctions and assertive tactics

TABLE 6.1
Common Influence Tactics

Tactic	Definition	Examples
Assertiveness[a]	Directly eliciting a response from others by demanding, ordering, or setting deadlines.	Pointing out rules to a subordinate that need to be followed; setting a deadline for a project to be completed; showing anger verbally.
Ingratiation[a]	Weak, unobtrusive influence tactics aimed at getting others to comply with your requests out of friendship and liking.	Sympathizing with a subordinate about the burdens a request you have made has caused; making someone feel good before requesting a favor from that person.
Reason–based[a]	Use of rationality influence tactics.	Presenting a logical, well-reasoned argument to convince others to pursue a strategy or option; presenting data and evidence to support an argument or position.
Exchange of benefits[a]	Exchange of positive reinforcement between parties for mutual gain.	Providing a manager access to a senior-level executive in exchange for that manager's support for your proposal. Reminding your supervisor of the weekend you spent on her project in order to take off early from work this week.
Upward appeal[a]	Appealing to a higher authority to obtain additional pressure for conformity on a target.	Obtaining support from a senior-level executive before you pitch an idea to your supervisor; filing a report about your supervisor with a high-level official in the organization.
Coalition[a]	Use of steady pressure for compliance by obtaining the support of coworkers, subordinates, or others with similar goals.	Gaining the support of your coworkers to back up your idea, proposal, or complaint; forming a group of female managers who support initiatives to enhance women's career development in the organization.
Blocking[a]	Attempts to stop the target person from carrying out some action.	Threatening to notify the Equal Opportunity Employment Commission if the organization doesn't take steps to end discrimination against women; engaging in a work slowdown until management concedes to union demands.
Sanction[a]	Use of administrative enforcement to induce compliance.	Threatening a subordinate with a low performance evaluation if work quality does not improve; withholding a raise from a subordinate who refuses to use new procedures.
Inspirational appeal[b]	Emotional request or proposal that arouses enthusiasm by appealing to one's values and ideals or by increasing one's confidence.	Describing a proposal with enthusiasm and conviction that it is worthwhile and important; giving a motivational speech in support of a proposal or new strategy.
Indirect[c]	Disguising attempts to influence others.	Dropping a subtle hint that you would like your manager to nominate you for a leadership role or a special project.

[a]Kipnis et al. (1980); Hinkin & Schriesheim (1990). [b] Yukl & Falbe (1990). [c]Offermann & Schrier (1985).

are most commonly used to improve a target's performance. People in cultures that stress status and power tend to rely on more emotional influence tactics, such as assertiveness and ingratiation, than do people in cultures less marked by status and power differentials (Kipnis & Schmidt, 1983). In the latter, nonemotional forms of influence, such as rationality, are more commonly used than emotional forms. People who are attempting to influence their subordinates (i.e., downward influence) or peers and coworkers (i.e., lateral influence) tend to rely on assertiveness, ingratiation, upward appeals, and exchange tactics more than those attempting to influence supervisors (i.e., upward influence; Kipnis et al., 1980; Yukl & Falbe, 1990). Coalition tactics, such as gaining support from influential colleagues, tend to be used equally often in all three directions of influence, and rational persuasion tends to be used more in upward influence attempts than in downward and lateral influence attempts (Kipnis et al., 1980), Although there are exceptions to this latter finding (Yukl & Falbe, 1990). In addition to describing these general types of influence tactics, researchers have also found that different types of people tend to rely on different types of influence tactics (Kipnis & Schmidt, 1983, 1988). These styles are summarized in Sidelight 6.1.

People who possess broad bases of power, such as supervisors, are more likely to than others to use influence tactics. When power differentials are particularly strong or salient in comparison to more egalitarian settings, power holders tend to rely on strong influence tactics, such as assertiveness and pressure tactics. Individuals in relatively powerless positions, such as subordinates, are likely to use influence tactics based on their available power base (i.e., rationality and ingratiation).

Gender Similarities and Differences in Use of Influence Tactics. Stereotypically, strong influence tactics, such as assertion, coercion, bargaining, and making legitimate requests, are associated with men, and weaker influence tactics, such as personal rewards and sexual intimations, are associated with women (Gruber & White, 1986; P. Johnson, 1976). When asked to indicate how they might respond to a hypothetical scenario, men report more willingness than women to use more forms of influence, such as giving misleading information, convincing and persuading, using assertion, bargaining, and coercion (Ansari, 1989; Gruber & White, 1986; Offermann & Schrier, 1985). Comparatively, women report greater likelihood of pleading, begging and praying (Gruber & White, 1986) or using personal/dependent tactics (similar to ingratiating) and negotiation tactics (Offermann & Schrier, 1985). Kipnis et al. (1980), however, found no gender differences in self-reports of influence tactics.

Sidelight 6.1   Types of Influence Strategies

Can you classify people by the type of influence strategies they use? Individuals in similar positions may differ in their preference for using various influence tactics. Kipnis and Schmidt (1983, 1988) used a statistical technique called **cluster analysis** to group people according to the way they attempt to influence others. They then surveyed managers in different organizations to determine what types of influencers were most effective and liked most by their peers and supervisors, and other characteristics of these different types of people. What kind of influencer are you?

Type	Influence Tactics Used	Characteristics
Shotguns	Influence primarily with assertiveness, bargaining, upward appeals, and moderate levels of other influence tactics.	Young, relatively new managers who desire to gain influence and power in their organizations. Shotguns tend to not be liked by their peers and report high levels of stress.
Tacticians	Influence primarily with reason and with other influence tactics to a moderate degree.	Found in critical, strategically important positions where they control large budgets and make important decisions. Male tacticians are preferred by their supervisors over other types of men, and they tend to have high power.
Ingratiators	Influence primarily with ingratiation tactics (friendliness). Use other influence tactics to a moderate degree.	Tend to be in lower organizational positions and have moderate skills. Their salaries are also moderate in comparison to other types of influencers. Supervisors tend to favor ingratiator females over ingratiator males.
Bystanders	Use few, if any, influence tactics.	Tend to be in units that conduct routine work and have little organizational power. Bystanders report having few wants or needs to satisfy in comparison to others.

The actual behaviors of women and men reveal fewer clear-cut differences in the amount or type of influence used. To discover how men and women influence those who have greater powers, Mainiero (1986b) conducted a series of **critical incidents interviews** with men and women. She found that women were more likely to use acquiescence strategies (doing nothing) than men, and men were more likely to use persuasion tactics than women. However, there were no gender differences in the use of coalition formation, finding other alternatives, or ingratiation. In **laboratory studies,** male and female research participants were instructed to influence another participant in order to gain some kind of reward for themselves (Molm, 1985, 1986; J.W. White, 1988). In one set of studies, no gender differences in the amount of influence exercised were demonstrated (Molm 1985, 1986). J.W. White (1988), however, found that men tended to use reward-based influence strategies more than other forms, whereas women tended to use request-based strategies. The extent to which these influence strategies were used, however, depended on other conditions. Men, but not women, tended to use more coercion when they were verbally insulted by the target. Also, when access to valued resources was limited, both men and women increased their use of coercion. Similarly, regardless of gender, individuals who possess greater power are more likely to report using strong influence tactics than those with less power (Offermann & Schrier, 1985). Thus, although women and men tend to use stereotypical forms of influence, the influencer's role or status position or other outside conditions tend to have a stronger effect than gender on the type of influence strategy used.

Three theories have been advanced to explain similarities and differences in women's and men's use of influence tactics. *Sex-role socialization theory* (e.g., Weitzman, 1979) posits that differences in women's and men's socialization experiences lead to different styles of influence strategies. Women are taught to use weak and passive forms of influence, whereas men are taught to use strong and assertive forms of influence. This theory predicts that men and women will differ on both the type and amount of influence exercised. *Structural theory* (e.g., Eagly, 1983; Kanter, 1977a) focuses on the role of contextual factors in determining power use. According to this theory, men and women use different influence tactics because men and women have different status levels in organizations and have access to different kinds and amounts of resources. Men use stronger forms of influence than women because they hold positions of greater authority in organizations, have greater control over budgets, personnel, and strategic decisions, and are accorded higher status. If these **structural features** were equally distributed among women and men, there would be no gender differences in influence. Structural theory predicts, for example, that individuals occupying higher organizational positions will exert greater influence than individuals at lower positions, regardless of gender.

A more complicated perspective is offered by *expectation states theory* (also known as *status characteristics theory;* e.g., Berger, Fisek, Norman, & Zelditch, 1977). When information is grouped into categories, one or more of those categories are often accorded greater status (value) than contrasting categories. Two types of status information are available. **Diffuse status** is information about an object (person) that is constant and transportable across situations. Gender, race, and attractiveness are examples of diffuse status characteristics. **Specific status** is information about an object that is context dependent, such as organizational position (supervisor vs. subordinate). When two or more people are compared in a given situation, the status characteristic on which they vary (diffuse or specific) becomes the salient feature on which differential perceptions of them are based. For example, if a male and a female manager are compared, all else being equal, they will be evaluated on gender-based characteristics—a diffuse status characteristic. Similarly, if a female subordinate is compared to a female supervisor, they will be judged on the basis of formal position—a specific status characteristic.[1] When both diffuse information and specific information are available, they combine to affect others' perceptions of the targets (as well as the targets' own behavior). For example, superiors are expected to use stronger forms of influence than subordinates, but male superiors (by virtue of sex-role socialization) may be more coercive than female superiors because men are socialized to use more coercive forms of influence than women. Expectation states theory suggests that we can better predict the type and amount of influence someone will use when we know both the gender of the influence agent and the critical contextual variables than when we know only one of these variables.

Each of these three theories has received some support from **empirical research** on influence strategies. As noted earlier, both gender and formal position directly predict the use of influence strategies (Gruber & White, 1986; Offermann & Schrier, 1985), supporting sex-role socialization and structural theories. Moreover, gender interacts with structural and contextual features to affect choice of influence strategies (Johnson, 1993; Molm, 1985, 1986; J.W. White, 1988), supporting expectation states theory. These studies are limited, however, by their reliance on **self-report** and/ or **laboratory-based methodology.** We understand very little about the ways men and women influence others in ongoing, complex, organizational environments. However, to describe men as strong and direct and women as weak and passive in influencing others is overly simplistic.

---

[1] Expectation states theory accounts not only for differences in others' perceptions of target individuals but also for differences in the targets' behaviors. When others hold different expectations for targets on the basis of status information, targets will normally conform to their expectations through **self-fulfilling prophecies** (Darley & Fazio, 1980).

THE EFFECTS OF POWER
AND INFLUENCE

The exercise of power and influence not only gets others to do what the power users want them to do, resolves conflicts, or gains more resources for the powerful; how power is exercised also affects the behaviors of the power users, the way they perceive others, and the way they are perceived by others. This section reviews research on the effects of power use on these other consequences. We end by examining the question, "Does power corrupt?"

Effects on Targets' Commitment to their Organizations

Employees' level of involvement and commitment to their organization is directly related to the way power is exercised in the organization (Etzioni, 1975). Organizational power holders, such as managers and chief executives, who use coercive influence tactics can expect that their employees will do the least they can get away with to avoid punishment. This is called **alienative involvement.** An organization's reliance on exchange or **quid pro quo** bases of power engenders **calculative involvement,** wherein employees are motivated to maximize personal gain. Such employees are likely to give little, if any, service to the organization outside what is normally expected for the job. Finally, organizations that rely on referent or **"normative" power** produce **moral involvement,** where individuals are committed to the values and beliefs of the organization and are likely perform in their jobs and provide service to the organization beyond what is expected of them. Etzioni's conceptualization of organizational influence strategies and employee involvement is broad and perhaps overly general. Kelman (1961) offered a similar analysis to predict an individual's level of commitment to an influence agent as a function of the agent's style of influence, but little empirical testing has been conducted.

Effects on Nonverbal Behaviors

In addition to predicting how employees respond to their organization, power has a number of interesting effects on subtle, nonverbal behavior. In chapter 5, we discussed male–female similarities and differences in nonverbal behaviors. A number of researchers have examined the differences in nonverbal behaviors of powerful and nonpowerful people, and these overlap somewhat with male–female differences. Interestingly, these nonverbal behaviors mirror dominance behaviors of nonhuman primates

(Ellyson & Dovidio, 1985). Powerful persons, for example, are much more likely to touch less powerful persons than vice versa (Henley, 1972). In a naturalistic observation study, Henley found that higher status individuals compared to others were more likely to touch other people but not to be touched themselves. Thus, men, older individuals, and people of higher socioeconomic status were more likely to touch others than to be touched by others. Henley noted that nonreciprocal touch serves as a **dominance cue;** it informs others about who has more power. Summerhayes and Suchner (1978) examined the implications of touch in male–female relationships and found that generally men are perceived to be more dominant than women, higher status individuals to be more dominant than lower status individuals, and touchers to be more dominant than those being touched. Their study showed that both women and men who are being touched are perceived as less dominant than when they are not being touched. Comparatively, a person who is touching is perceived as only slightly more dominant than a person who is not touching. Thus, touching made the touched person appear less dominant, as opposed to raising the perceptions of the toucher. A male who was touched by a woman, for example, appeared to be less dominant than a man who was not touched.

Eye contact is another nonverbal dominance cue. When they are speaking, high-status individuals maintain contact with lower status individuals but tend to look away when they are being spoken to (Henley, 1972). (The ratio of the amount of time a person spends looking at his or her target while speaking compared to looking while listening is termed a **visual dominance ratio;** Exline, Ellyson, & Long, 1975.) Conversely, low-status individuals tend not to maintain eye contact regardless of whether they are speaking or being spoken to. Dovidio, Ellyson, Keating, Heltman, and Brown (1988) examined associations between gender and visual dominance in a social influence situation. In line with expectation states theory, the authors predicted that when dyads differed on amount of expertise or reward power, the more powerful person would display a higher visual dominance ratio than the other. When there was no power difference, gender, acting as a diffuse status characteristic, would predict visual dominance with men displaying greater dominance than women. In this behavioral study (i.e., actual eye contact was measured, as opposed to self-report), both women and men with either reward or expert power maintained visual dominance over their less powerful partners. However, as predicted, when these bases of power were equivalent among members of the dyad, men generally maintained greater visual dominance than women (Dovidio et al., 1988). Thus, with no other information to the contrary, men behave as if they have more power than women (and similarly, women aquiesce to these perceptions).

Thus, the amount and type of influence exercised affect both how power holders behave and how their targets respond. **Strong tactics** such as assertiveness and coercion force targets to behaviorally comply with power holders' demands. Conversely, **weak tactics,** such as reason, rationality, and friendliness, evoke internal commitment from targets. Additionally, power holders display nonverbal behaviors and speech styles that convey their status to others. Henley (1977) argued that gender differences in behaviors such as touch, eye contact, and speech styles can be accounted for by gender differences in power, and empirical research has generally supported this claim. When women and men possess power, they tend to act similarly (direct and assertive) in their interpersonal interactions. When they both lack power, they both act passively and deferently. When no power information is provided, diffuse status differences between men and women are activated, giving men greater power over women. Men and women, then, respond in kind. Often as important as the actual amount and use of power, if not more so, is the perception of power. How others perceive power holders, how power holders perceive their targets, and the effects of these perceptions are the focus of the next section.

Effects on Perceptions of the Power Holder

Generally, the more power holders use strong influence tactics, the more they are viewed as aggressive and domineering and the more they are disliked by subordinates (Kipnis, 1990). Rahim and Afza (1993) examined associations between accountants' perceptions of their supervisors' bases of power (i.e., French & Raven's [1959] bases of social power) and job attitudes. Perceptions that bosses used personal bases of power (i.e., referent and expert) were positively related to accountants' organizational commitment, job satisfaction, and attitudinal compliance with supervisory wishes. Referent and legitimate bases of supervisory power were positively associated with behavioral compliance. That is, accountants were more likely to do what their bosses requested if their bosses relied on their influence and charm or made reasonable supervisory requests than when supervisors did not use these forms of influence. Supervisors' uses of reward and coercive power were not associated with respondents' job attitudes (Rahim & Afza, 1993).

Use of various influence strategies affects subordinates' perceptions of their bosses' power. Hinkin and Schriesheim (1990) demonstrated that bosses using rational influence tactics were perceived by subordinates to possess legitimate, expert, and referent power. Conversely, bosses who used upward appeals and sanction-based influence tactics were perceived to possess less legitimate, expert, and referent power compared to bosses using other strategies to influence their subordinates. Use of assertiveness was associated with perceptions of coercive bases of power. Use of ingratiation, exchange, and coalition tactics was not associated with perceptions of power bases. This latter finding lends credence to Kipnis et al.'s (1980) assertion that powerful people are less likely to use such tactics than those who are less powerful.

An interesting question is whether women who use strong influence tactics are equally disliked or whether they are more disliked than men who use such tactics. Well-known female leaders such as Hillary Rodham Clinton and Margaret Thatcher have been heavily criticized for their use of direct, assertive influence strategies. Thatcher, for example, who is not known for her feminist tendencies, has had her share of thinly disguised hostile comments on her style and tactics of influence. When she received the following backhanded compliment from a Labour Party official (the opposing political group), "May I congratulate you on being the only man on your team," she replied, "That's one more than you've got on yours!" (Barreca, 1991, p. 84).

Researchers have studied this question under controlled, laboratory conditions. LaFrance (1992) examined people's perceptions of men and women who interrupted a conversation partner. Interruption, like visual dominance (e.g., staring) and touching, is a dominance-cue reminder. Interrupters were viewed as more confrontative, disrespectful, and assertive than noninterrupters. These perceptions were strongest when a woman interrupted a man. Consistent with expectation states theory, the observation of a woman interrupting a man violated sex-role stereotypes that women should act passively, which generated particularly negative opinions about the woman. Using the same logic, Kipnis and Schmidt (1988) expected to find that female shotguns would be less favorably evaluated than male shotguns (see Sidelight 6.1). Both male and female shotguns, however, were equally disliked by their supervisors. Geddes (1992) had male and female speakers use either powerful style (i.e., direct, masculine style), powerless style (indirect, feminine style), or a mix of powerful and powerless styles. Raters found that both male and female speakers who used a mixed style were more effective and satisfactory than those using either the powerful or powerless style. The most severe ratings were given to a female speaker who used a powerless style, contradicting LaFrance's (1992) finding that violating sex-role expectations negatively impacts perceptions. Falbo, Hazen, and Linimon (1982), however, found that both male and female speakers who used power bases associated with the opposite sex were regarded as less competent and qualified than speakers who used sex-appropriate power bases. The sex-role inappropriate cases involved women using expertise to talk about gun control and men using helplessness to address day care. Raters, however, felt that

---

Sidelight 6.2   Gray Power: Assertive Women and Nurturant Men Are Acceptable in Their Senior Years

Although men are expected to influence others with strong and assertive tactics whereas women are expected to use weak and friendly strategies, there is evidence that perceptions of male and female influence tactics change as a function of age. That is, as women get older they are perceived as having greater strength, self-confidence, and interpersonal power, whereas men's power is perceived to decrease with age (e.g., A. Friedman, 1987; Gutmann, 1987). Gutmann theorized that during parenting age, women are biologically inclined to use softer, nurturant forms of influence, giving them the appearance of powerlessness, whereas men at this age are inclined to express aggressive resource-acquisition characteristics (i.e., powerfulness). As women get older and grow out of the parenting role, they can begin to express their dominance and strength because they do not interfere with nurturant mothering demands. Aging men, on the other hand, do not need to express the dominance and asssertiveness required of their bread-winning role during the parenting years; thus, they can begin to express their emerging nurturant side.

The perception that women gain and men lose power with age appears to be a function of our stereotypes and beliefs about aging and gender as opposed to biological functions. Friedman, Tzukerman, Wienberg, and Todd (1992) found that ideology toward parenting predicted perceptions of powerfulness and powerlessness more than did biological age. Research participants who came from an egalitarian, communal child-care culture (an Israeli kibbutz) did not perceive female parents to be less powerful than male parents. Participants from Israeli cities, where more traditional attitudes and gender roles were present, associated parenthood with perceptions of women's powerlessness (and men's powerfulness).

---

speakers were most qualified if they relied on expertise than any other form of power. It is particularly troubling, then, that women were devalued for using expertise on a male sex-type topic. What do people think of women experts in nontraditional fields such as engineering, construction, and management? Finally, there is evidence that perceptions of men and women and their uses of various power strategies change as a function of age. Sidelight 6.2 provides a review of this research.

To summarize, people who depend on strong aggressive forms of influence are disliked by others and are perceived to have only coercion as their basis of power. Conversely, those who use reason and personal qualities and who exercise authority within legitimate bounds are more satisfactory to others. This appears to hold true for both women and men, although there is inconclusive evidence that women who act either too powerfully (e.g., by interrupting others) or too passively (e.g., by using a powerless speech style) are negatively evaluated in comparison to men who use these styles. As illustrated in Sidelight 6.2, the relationship between aging and respective perceptions of power gain and power less for women and men is interesting and, again, appears to reflect our cultural beliefs about gender and power.

The Metamorphic Effect of Power: Power Holders' Perceptions of Others

Why do power holders often regard those whose favors they are seeking with disdain? One need only look at historical events, such as slavery or the Holocaust, as well as everyday life to know that powerful people often view their subjects as contemptible, worthless, incapable beings. Yet, it is from these subjects that power holders expect to gain deference, compliance, and devotion. Kipnis (1990) posed this question in his exploration of the corrupting effects of power. Not only can the use of power to influence others lead to the pursuit of greater power as an end to itself, or can the possession of power alter one's view of self as being above norms, laws, and morals that apply to everyone else; the abuse of certain forms of power also leads to fundamental changes in how the power holder perceives her or his targets of influence. Kipnis termed this perceptual change the **metamorphic** effect of power. Zimbardo's infamous prison experiment (1972) demonstrated that normal individuals (male research participants randomly assigned to prison guard roles) who attained legitimate coercive bases of power quickly viewed and treated research participants who had been assigned to prisoner roles like animals. Kipnis (1990) explained that metamorphic effects of power occur because it is easier to influence others if psychological distance is maintained. If targets are viewed as worthless and lazy, distasteful requests feel justifiable. Also, the act of influence, especially with strong influence tactics, leads to the perception that targets are not in control of themselves. By definition, strong influence tactics are those that do not give targets choice in how to respond. Therefore, when targets do what the power holders request, a type of **fundamental attribution error** is made. That is, the power holder disregards the situational influences on the target's behavior (i.e., that the target was given no choice) and views the target as being so incapable of making decisions that she or he must be constantly controlled by the power holder.

Given these corrupting effects of power use, a more plausible question might be, "Why don't all power holders become corrupt?" A psychological answer to this question is complex. At the most basic level, influence tactics that preserve the feelings and perceptions of the target's own control are required, that is, weak influence tactics such as reason and ingratiation. It would be difficult for power holders to despise and maliciously treat others who they viewed as competent, autonomous, and self-reliant. Yet, can centuries of prejudice, ethnic hatred, and gender stereotypes be unraveled with a simple change from strong to weaker forms of influence? It is at this point that the simple behavioral view of power becomes inadequate to fully explain the consequences of power. Feminist scholars argue that power differentials are at the root of women's inequality with men and their subsequent mistreatment. Yet, if there are few gender differences in power bases and influence tactics, is such an explanation sufficient? The following section explores gender dynamics and feminist views on power in more detail. We briefly review issues regarding women and power and feminist conceptualizations of these issues. Finally, we discuss implications of power differentials on the status of women in the workplace with regard to top leadership, pay inequity, and sexual harassment.

GENDER AND POWER
IN THE WORKPLACE

Men and women in organizations typically have different levels of authority; men are more likely to hold managerial positions than women, and male–female differences become more dramatic the higher one goes in the organization (chap. 7 reviews research on gender discrimination and occupational segregation). In addition to differences in structural power, males and females may have different levels of personal power and may acquire power in different ways. It is useful to examine in some detail the relationship between gender and power in the workplace.

Bases of Power for Women

Under many circumstances, men and women use different styles of influence. As explained earlier, however, this may be due, in part, to the structural differences in our society that have segregated men and women into roles that differ in terms of access to resources and status (i.e., power). For example, corporate executives, by virtue of their position in organizations, are capable of wielding much more influence in organizations than others. Because most executives are men, it is easy to assume that such influence is a function of being a man as much as (or more than) a function of the positions they hold. The amount of power an individual possesses in a given situation, however, is a much stronger predictor of the type of influence that is exercised than her or his gender. Thus, to gain a fuller understanding of the obstacles women face in achieving equality with men in our society, we must analyze the bases of power on which women rely. The following section reviews the commonly known social bases of power (i.e., expert, reward, etc.) as they apply to women and offers alternative explanations of women and power.

On almost all bases of power commonly reported in the literature, women come up short compared to men. First and foremost, women have less access to valued resources than men. Men dominate political, economic, and intellectual spheres, as noted by the predominance of men in authoritative occupations in our society. Thus, women have less power than men (Frieze, Parsons, Johnson, Ruble, & Zellman, 1978; A. Kahn, 1984). They are less able to control rewards, to be in legitimate positions of power, to be considered "expert" unless they receive formal, external recognition of their expertise (see A. Kahn, 1984), and to dole out punishments. Also, because women are less likely to be in influential positions, they are less likely to be viewed as role models and to possess referent power. A. Kahn (1984) reported that it was more likely for women to list a man as a role model than for men to list a woman. Finally, because men are more central than women in important, influential communications networks in organizations (Ibarra, 1992), they possess greater informational power than women. Given these real disparities, one would expect greater differences between men and women in the use and type of influence strategies than are reported in the literature.

Access to and the use of power are more consistent with male sex-role stereotypes, which emphasize dominance and achievement, than with female sex-role stereotypes, which emphasize helping and cooperation. Furthermore, characteristics of women that are sometimes critical for gaining influence (e.g., physical attractiveness) are not seen as valid bases for achieving or exerting power. Both our stereotypes of male and female sex roles and a survey of the organizational realities experienced by men and women suggest that women are less likely than men to have power, and the power and influence they do have is more likely to be resented and undermined.

Yet, women do use power, and they influence others. Consistent with the structural model, however, women use influence strategies commonly found among those who are less powerful. Friendliness, helplessness and dependency, and other indirect strategies are commonly associated with women (Falbo & Peplau, 1980; P. Johnson, 1976) and those who are in subordinate positions (Kipnis et al., 1980). Many studies have demonstrated, however, that when women possess the same bases of power as men, they are likely to use the same forms of influence to the same degree as men (e.g., Rosenthal & Hautaluoma, 1988; Sagrestano, 1992). Still others argue that women possess "power in powerlessness" (see Griscom, 1992). That is, from seeing the world from the bottom up (in terms of power), women possess keener awareness of the abuses of power and its metamorphic effects. Thus, they may be more likely to use softer (weaker) influence tactics that preserve the dignity and integrity of others. For example, women are more likely than men to share power with others through the use of consultative and participative decision-making modes (i.e., empowerment; Denmark, 1993; Jago & Vroom, 1982). Furthermore, subordinates are much more satisfied with democratic bosses who lead participatively as opposed to autocratic, directive leaders. Thus women, with their reliance on weaker, empowerment-type strategies, may be more successful than men, with their use of strong, directive influence strategies. For example, a sample of female executives nominated women more often than men as "best bosses." These best bosses were those who relied on reference, reward, informational, and expert (i.e., weaker) bases of power (Oyster, 1992).

But, do women actually endorse or prefer to use weaker forms of power that involve sharing power with others (i.e., empowerment-type forms of power), or are they locked into this style because of their lower status in our society? In an effort to understand how women conceptualize power, C.L. Miller and Cummins (1992) asked a sample of women to describe what made them feel powerful and powerless, and how they believed power was defined in our society. Responses to both open-ended items (participants could freely respond to the question) and closed-ended items (participants rated their level of agreement with a number of statements) tapping these questions revealed the following themes: *control over* (resources and other people), *personal authority* (owning yourself, ability to make own choices), *evaluation* (viewing power as positive or negative), resources (having money and material possessions), *self-enhancement* (attractiveness and positive self-image), and *work/men* (rewarded at work, being with men).[2] Women felt that society defines power in terms of "control over" but that personal authority is most important in their own lives and should be emphasized more in society. Self-enhancement and men/work issues made them feel most powerful, and loss of personal authority made them feel powerless. Contrary to predictions, empowerment did not emerge as a salient theme in women's definitions and experiences of power. These findings need to be viewed with caution because

---

[2]Other, less salient factors were reproductive issues (being pregnant, dealing with children) and relationships (being in a relationship, in a group of women).

the sample of women surveyed was not representative. Yet the findings pose interesting questions for future research: Do women's conceptualizations of power vary as a function of their standing on various structural and personal indices, such as degree of formal authority, age, and sex-role attitudes?

To summarize, in terms of traditional measures of power, women, compared to men, have less access to resources needed to exert influence. As a consequence, women tend to use influence tactics associated with the powerless, such as ingratiation and reason. However, when women have access to important resources, giving them the same power bases as men, they tend to use the same influence strategies as men. But because of the structural inequalities in our society, women are on the whole more likely to view and use power from a position of powerlessness. Some have argued that women's powerlessness gives them an advantage in their greater willingness and adeptness, compared to men, in using softer, power-sharing, relationship-preserving forms of influence. It appears, however, that women themselves do not view this as a form of power. Much remains to be learned about men, women, and power.

Although women have made major advances toward gender equality, men simply have more power than women. This final section briefly reviews the implications of this power difference on workplace issues, such as leadership and advancement, pay equity, and sexual harassment. Each topic is examined in more detail in other chapters of this book. The purpose here is to explicate the role of power in shaping these phenomena.

Power Implications for Women in the Workplace

Male–female differences in both structural power and personal power may have profound implications for understanding men's and women's experiences in the workplace, especially in such areas as leadership, pay, and sexual harassment.

Power and Top-Level Leadership. Women are relatively well represented in lower and midlevel management positions in American and European organizations but are woefully underrepresented in top-level executive positions (F.D. Blau & Ferber, 1987). A number of theories have been forwarded to account for this phenomenon, but power remains an important consideration. Ragins and Sundstrom (1989) argued that individual, interpersonal, organizational, and societal factors impinge on processes affecting women's and men's ability to advance to the top, most powerful positions in organizations. Each factor has a different impact on women and men at each rung on the organizational ladder (i.e., entry to the job market, entry into an organization, and promotion to powerful positions). For example, young adults respond to sex-role expectations when they make career choices. Men are more likely than women to choose careers that have more central routes to top management positions (social level of analysis). Upon entering a particular organization, women may be more likely than men to be placed in peripheral, less critical positions from which they have little hope of acquiring necessary resources for power (organizational level of analysis). Men's relative ease in comparison to women in gaining access to important informal networks and to mentors both helps create the perception that they are more powerful than women and actually provides men greater access to important resources (i.e., other powerful people; interpersonal level of analysis). Finally, small but reliable differences in women's and men's job experiences, motives, interpersonal styles, and responses to power affect selection and promotion decisions (individual level of analysis). The cumulative effect of gender-based socialization, stereotyping, discrimination, and behavior is to provide considerable barriers to gender-equity in the boardroom.

Once obtained, men's strong use of power may provide yet another barrier for women. Because of the metamorphic effects of power, women, who are more likely to be in powerless positions compared to men, may be perceived as weak, ineffective, and unable to influence others. Indeed, decades of stereotyping research, as discussed in chapter 3, shows that given no specific information to the contrary, women are perceived to be weak, dependent, passive, and unmanagerial (e.g., Broverman et al., 1972; Heilman et al., 1989; E.H. Schein, 1973). Thus, women are deemed to be poorly suited for top management positions. Finally, those who demonstrate malelike characteristics of assertiveness, dominance, and directiveness (and thus seem suitable for top management) are likewise viewed as poor executive candidates (Fiske, 1993). Expectation states theory predicts that women who violate gender-linked expectations for power use (i.e., aggressive instead of passive) are harshly judged by others. Studies have shown that those women who have attained top leadership positions have done so by towing the fine line between appearing too feminine and too masculine, or similarly, too weak and too powerful (e.g., Morrison et al., 1987; U.S. Department of Labor, 1991).

Power and Pay Inequity. Reaching positions of structural equality with men has not meant that women enjoy the same degree of financial reward from these positions. Women are significantly underpaid compared to men in the same occupations and with the same level of qualifications (e.g., Dreher & Ash, 1990; Stroh, Brett, & Reilly, 1992). Central to our discussion here is the role of power in explaining the gender wage gap. Recall that power comes from the ability to control valued and scarce resources (Salancik & Pfeffer, 1977). To the extent that men are more likely than women to be in positions of authority and to control monetary and labor resources, men earn higher incomes than women. Spaeth (1985) examined a random sample of working adults in Illinois and found that men who were in positions where they made important decisions about budgets earned greater salaries than men who did not. For women, salary levels were impacted by budgetary control, like men, but also by the number of subordinates they supervised. However, together monetary and personnel control did not yield the same earnings benefit for women as monetary control alone did for men. Thus, to the extent that men are accorded greater control over monetary resources in organizations, their earnings are greater than women's.

Power and pay interact with gender in another interesting analysis. It is possible to predict managers' salaries from knowing which style of upward influence managers use (Dreher, Dougherty, & Whitely, 1989). However, salary predictions differ for men and women depending on the type of influence tactic used. Men benefited (with an average dollar increase per unit increase on the exchange tactic subscale of $5,000) from their use of exchange-type bargaining tactics with their supervisors, such as offering to make a personal sacrifice to a superior if he or she would do what they wanted. Women benefited (by $3,000) from their use of rationality tactics, such as writing a detailed plan to justify their ideas, but were penalized (by a decrease of $4,000) for using exchange tactics. Thus, men who influenced by means of exchange and bargaining earned more whereas women who did the same earned less than their same-sex peers who were less inclined to influence in this manner. Because the data are **cross-sectional,** causality cannot be determined, but it is interesting to note the associations between types of influence tactics and job earnings. Further research exploring these connections is warranted.

Power and Sexual Harassment.   Nearly 50% of working women and female students are subjected to sexualized behavior from men that they did not welcome and did not invite (Fitzgerald & Shullman, 1993). Examples of sexually harassing treatment range from sexual jokes and teasing aimed at debasing female audiences to inappropriate sexual advances to threatening job security to gain sexual access (chap. 9 provides a full discussion of sexual harassment). The role of power and its associated processes in explaining this irascible problem is briefly discussed here.

Recall that individuals who possess significant sources of power (e.g., men) are more likely to use strong, possibly coercive influence tactics. Sexual harassment is an influence tactic. Many victims of harassment report quitting their jobs or transferring to another job site in order to avoid the harasser (Gutek & Koss, 1993). Thus, the harasser has succeeded in influencing the target to leave the field. Furthermore, harassers who offer organizational rewards or threaten job-related punishments are directly using reward and coercion power to gain sexual compliance. Recall also that the use of strong influence tactics can cause a metamorphic change in the power holder's perception of the target. By using sexual harassment, the harasser's view of the target as a weak, ineffectual, sexual object may intensify, promoting an endless cycle of sexual debasement. Not all forms of sexual harassment, however, can be explained by these phenomena, and Cleveland and Kerst (1993) have more thoroughly delineated the role of power in sexual harassment.

Finally, sexual harassment can be viewed as a response to men's power loss. A. Kahn (1984) theorized that as women gain more power in our society as well as in the workplace, men who feel particularly threatened by this loss may respond with one of the few power bases they perceive themselves to hold onto—sexual and physical coercion. Studies of domestic violence show that batterers tend to be men who are economically dependent on women (among other characteristics). Such dependence places men in a position of powerlessness, to which they respond with violence. Although the settings and circumstances of domestic violence and sexual harassment are quite different, the processes are quite similar (see Cleveland & McNamara, 1996). Research is needed to empirically examine whether men experience power loss as women gain power and status and whether power loss is related to sexual harassment.

Leadership, pay equity, and sexual harassment are only a few workplace issues affecting women and men for which power and its related concepts play a role. It is beyond the scope of this chapter to delineate how power affects and is affected by all gender-related issues. The reader is invited, however, to apply the framework for understanding power outlined in this chapter to analyze other issues of interest. We also caution the reader to recognize the boundaries of power as a construct. Although power is a ubiquitous phenomenon, to relate power to everything would yield a meaningless concept.

SUMMARY

In this chapter, we have discussed the concept of power, how it is critical in understanding organizational as well as interpersonal processes, and why an understanding of power is necessary to explain differences in the status of women and men in organizations. Power is most commonly defined as the ability to influence others and is obtained by having access to scarce, important resources desired by others. Power can be exercised in a variety of ways. Strong, assertive influence tactics provide little option for targets' response; they must comply or face serious consequences. In responding this way, targets are perceived as weak and ineffectual, thus perpetuating a cycle of strong influence tactics. In return, however, targets of strong influence tactics show less commitment to satisfaction with, and liking for power holders. In comparison, weaker influence tactics such as rationality, ingratiation, and requests provide targets options for responding and thus preserve their dignity and sense of control. In return, these targets are more loyal to, committed to, and satisfied with their influencers.

For a variety of reasons, men generally have greater access to these resources and thus have more power than women. This difference in power accounts to a large degree for many of the observed differences between women and men (e.g., that men are more likely to be in leadership positions, and that men act more powerfully and are perceived to be more powerful than women). It is also arguable that power differences account for discriminatory practices against women such as sexual harassment and pay inequity. Some feminist scholars have challenged the notion that power means the ability to outcompete others and have argued that women gain strength from their connectedness to others and their ability to empower others. Empirical studies do not universally support this position, so it will be some time before our conceptualizations of power change for women and men.

GLOSSARY

Alienative involvement: A low level of commitment to an organization, leader, or manager; employees comply with the leader's request to a minimal degree to avoid punishment.

Calculative involvement: A moderate level of commitment to an organization, leader, or manager; employees comply with the leader's requests to the extent that they perceive they will benefit from their compliance.

Cluster analysis: Statistical technique that groups objects, such as people, on the basis of the degree to which they are similar to one another on one or more characteristics.

Corporate culture: Shared beliefs, expectations, and core values of people in an organization.

Critical incidents interview: Type of interview in which the interviewer elicits instances of specific behaviors of interest. An example would be asking a manager to describe all the ways she or he tries to get subordinates to perform special requests.

Cross-sectional research: Collecting data on a process at one point in time but across different categories relevant to the process. Causality cannot be determined from cross-sectional research designs. For example, a study in which male and female managers (i.e., different categories of managers) are surveyed about their use of influence strategies (i.e., different categories of influence strategies) and simultaneously about their salaries is cross-sectional. Although a relationship between gender, influence strategies, and salary can be assessed, one cannot determine whether use of different influence strategies causes salaries to be higher or lower for women or men.

Diffuse status: A characteristic about a person that cannot be easily changed, that is true about the person regardless of level of education, job status, and achievements. Most diffuse status characteristics are biological or cultural (e.g., gender, race, nationality).

Dominance cue: Information that informs others about who has more power.

Empirical research: Process of collecting and analyzing data to support or refute a hypothesis. Empirical studies must be able to disconfirm (provide evidence that does not support) a research question.

Expert power: Power derived from an individual's recognized superior skills and abilities in a certain area.

Fundamental attribution error: Tendency to believe that others act in a certain way because of their own desires or internal motives (i.e., dispositions) while discounting the situational pressures for them to act that way.

Informational power: Power based on the extent to which a person controls information that is valuable to someone else.

Laboratory studies/laboratory-based methodologies: Research conducted under controlled conditions typically apart from the environment in which the behavior normally occurs. Researchers conducting laboratory studies are able to manipulate a variable of interest (i.e., independent variable) while keeping all other variables constant for all conditions of the experiment.

Legitimate power: Power granted by virtue of one's position in the organization.

Metamorphic: Change of form. With regard to power, a metamorphic change can be the change in one's perception of subordinates as competent individuals to the perception that they are ignorant and lazy.

Moral involvement: A high level of commitment to an organization, leader, or manager that is based on the belief that the organization's or leader's requests are consistent with and support one's own values and philosophies.

Normative power: Power based on the perception that the organization has the right to govern employees.

Power dependence relations: Theory of power which states that the amount of power an individual (A) has over another individual (B) is based on the degree to which B depends on A for valued resources or outcomes.

Quid pro quo: Latin term meaning one thing in return for another.

Referent power: Power based on the extent to which others like, admire, and want to emulate oneself.

Self-fulfilling prophecies: Tendency to fulfill expectations that others have of you.

Self-report: Research strategy in which research participants report their own thoughts, feelings, or behaviors (usually by way of a survey) on a subject as opposed to the researcher directly observing the behavior or characteristic or having others report about the participants' thoughts, feelings, or behaviors.

Specific status: Characteristics of individuals based on the particular circumstances they are in, such as their job titles or roles.

Strategic contingencies theory: Theory of how people or groups gain or lose power. An entity gains power when it is able to control resources that are valuable to others, scarce, and nonsubstitutable. Similarly, entities lose power when the resources they control are no longer valuable or can be obtained elsewhere or by some other means.

Strong tactics: Influence tactics that give little or no option for how targets may respond (e.g., assertiveness and coercion).

Structural features: Situational characteristics that define a position that people occupy, such as level in an organizational hierarchy (level), degree to which a job holder has control over primary business functions (centrality), or amount of authority an individual has to direct the activities of others (authority).

Visual dominance ratio: Ratio of the amount of time a person spends looking at a target while speaking to him or her to the amount of time the person spends looking at the target when being spoken to by the target. The higher the ratio (i.e., more time looking while speaking than looking while listening), the more dominant the person is perceived to be.

Weak tactics: Influence tactics that allow targets to decide how they want to respond (e.g., ingratiation and rationality).

III

WOMEN AND MEN
IN THE WORKPLACE:
IMPORTANT INDIVIDUAL
AND ORGANIZATIONAL
OUTCOMES

7

Gender Discrimination in the Workplace

The Help Wanted ads in a local newspaper included the following:

DANCERS
Have fun and get paid!

No experience necessary, will train.
Must be at least 18 years of age. Can
earn up to $400/week to start.

Housekeepers

Now hiring FT. Exp. not necessary. Top
wages! M-F, 8-5.

During the same week, the *Sunday Times of India* (New Delhi) carried the following ad:

Female

Office Assistant and Personal Secretary. Willing
for local travel, typing not required.

There is a striking difference in these ads. The ad for dancers was taken out by a club that features female exotic dancers, but the ad doesn't mention gender; neither does the housekeeping ad. Everyone reading these ads is likely to expect almost all of the applicants and all of those hired (especially in response to the ad for dancers) will be women, but the ads are carefully written to be gender-neutral.

In contrast, the ad taken out in the *Sunday Times of India* explicitly calls for a female applicant. It is not clear exactly what the duties of this job might be (personal secretary, willing to travel with employer, but no typing required), but it is clear that only women will be considered. What does this tell us about gender discrimination in the United States versus India?

There are broad cross-cultural differences in both the type and the amount of gender discrimination practiced and accepted in the workplace. In more traditional countries, jobs might be explicitly set aside for men and for women. In most Western countries, there are relatively few formal barriers to women's entry into a wide range of jobs and professions, but that does not necessarily mean that there is no gender discrimination. As shown in this chapter, gender discrimination can have a substantial effect on men's and women's work lives, even if formal barriers to the entry of men or women into particular jobs or occupations are removed.

Men and women are treated differently in the workplace. Sometimes, men receive favorable treatment and women are discriminated against. Sometimes, it is the other way around. Sometimes, differences in treatment and outcomes are related to real and meaningful gender differences, and sometimes they are related to inaccurate perceptions of differences between men and women. When people are treated differently because of race, ethnicity, gender, or other similar characteristics, this is often labeled "discrimination." This chapter examines the causes and possible consequences of gender discrimination in the workplace.

We begin by defining prejudice and discrimination and go on to discuss specific features of the workplace that may lead to or strengthen gender discrimination. A recurring theme of this section is that widely held stereotypes of women are sometimes inconsistent with stereotypes of jobs, and this lack of fit can lead directly to discriminatory actions. The second section of this chapter examines the segregation of the workforce by gender. A number of occupations are strongly sex-segregated (e.g., almost all secretaries and receptionists are women), and even within occupations, men and women often draw different job assignments. We consider economic models that attempt to explain occupational segregation and finally consider alternative explanations for differences in men's and women's work. We end this chapter by asking whether differences in the pay, work assignments, and career paths of men and women are in fact the result of gender discrimination, and if so, how gender discrimination might operate.

PREJUDICE AND DISCRIMINATION

One of the most basic human tendencies is for people to favor those whom they perceive to be similar to themselves and discriminate against those they perceive to be different (Allport, 1954). This has both positive and negative effects. On the positive side, it enhances feelings of solidarity and cohesiveness in groups, families, and nations. The negative side of this basic human tendency is prejudice and **discrimination.**

Prejudice and discrimination are virtually universal phenomena, and people find all sorts of reasons (race, ethnicity, religion, language) to discriminate against others who differ and to discriminate in favor of those they see as similar. Discrimination on the basis of gender is not a unique phenomenon, but some aspects of the workplace are important for understanding how and why gender discrimination operates. Before looking at features of the workplace that might lead to (or work against) gender discrimination, we first define some important terms.

Defining Prejudice and Discrimination

Social psychologists (Baron & Byrne, 1994) distinguish between prejudice and discrimination. *Prejudice* is usually defined as an attitude toward members of a group. Most discussions of prejudice focus on negative attitudes, but clearly prejudice could cut both ways: Women might be favored in some settings (e.g., primary school education) because they are women. Nevertheless, there are good reasons to focus on negative attitudes. Prejudice against members of different groups appears to contribute to widespread segregation in the workplace and in society in general and probably fosters racism, sexism, and many of the other "isms" that are of concern to society.

Discrimination involves action toward individuals on the basis of their group membership; Baron and Byrne (1994) defined discrimination as prejudice in action. Discrimination can take a very overt form (e.g., refusal to hire women into certain jobs), but in many instances, gender discrimination involves the degree to which the workplace is open to versus resistant to the participation of women. Although many discussions of gender discrimination have focused on the ways managers and supervisors treat men and women, gender discrimination could involve managers, coworkers, subordinates, clients, or customers. In general, gender discrimination includes behaviors occurring in the workplace that limit the target person's ability to enter, remain in, succeed in, or progress in a job and that are primarily the result of the target person's gender. In chapters 8 and 9, we discuss the concept of a hostile work environment, especially as it relates to women's experiences of sexual harassment. This chapter outlines some of the factors that can contribute to a hostile work environment.

There are two reasons why gender discrimination is an especially important topic. First, the likely presence of systemic discrimination on the basis of gender suggests that the number of people who might be affected is huge (i.e., discrimination against women would put half the population at a disadvantage). Given the potential impact of gender discrimination, the possibility that gender is an important influence on people's work lives must be considered. Second, there is a good deal of evidence that men and women are treated differently in the workplace. Women receive lower wages than men, are segregated into low-level jobs, and are less likely to be promoted. As we note in sections that follow, it is sometimes difficult to determine exactly why men and women enter different jobs or receive different pay, and what appears to be gender discrimination in the workplace may in fact reflect much broader societal trends. Nevertheless, there are enough data to suggest that gender is very important in predicting a person's occupation, pay, and progress, and that discrimination is at least a partial explanation for this disparity. Additionally, some specific features of the workplace appear to contribute to prejudice and discrimination against both men and women.

Features of the Workplace That Contribute to Gender Discrimination

Gender discrimination occurs in a number of settings. Men and women are perceived differently, are assigned different roles and are assumed to have different characteristics in most settings (e.g., around the house, cooking, cleaning, and caring for children are usually the woman's role, whereas home repairs, mowing the lawn, and maintaining the car are the man's role). To some extent, gender discrimination in the workplace can be thought of as a simple extension of beliefs most of us hold about the roles men and women should have in society (sex-role spillover). However, specific features of the workplace heighten the influence of gender on attitudes and actions, particularly the stereotypes assigned to men, women, and jobs, and the relative rarity of women in many work settings.

Sex-Role Spillover. The term *female worker* describes two roles (woman and worker) that involve different behaviors, different demands, and different assumptions. The traditional role of a woman involves caring for others, self-sacrifice, submissiveness, and social facilitation, whereas the worker role often involves technical accomplishment, competition, development and exercise of skills, and leadership. Barbara Gutek (1985, 1992) noted that beliefs about the appropriate roles for men and women are likely to "spill over" into a work setting. That is, our expectations regarding female workers will be determined in part by our expectations and beliefs regarding women in general. Even in situations where the work has little to do with stereotypically female roles, expectations about the typical roles of men and women will likely have some influence on the way we perceive and treat male and female workers. For example, in a meeting that involves several men and one woman, it is not unusual to find that both the men and the woman assume that it is the woman's job to serve coffee, take notes, and carry out other "feminine" tasks.

You can think of **sex-role spillover** as a specific instance of a much more general issue, which is that everyone carries out a number of roles that may or may not be fully compatible. A female faculty member might have the roles of teacher, advisor, parent, wife, and young woman, and her interactions with others in the workplace are likely to be affected by the way she is seen in relation to each of these roles. What, then, is so special about sex roles? Why should we be more concerned with sex-role spillover than with spillover between the roles of, for example, parent and worker?

One reason for paying attention to sex-role spillover is that sex roles are both powerfully ingrained and highly salient. Unlike many other roles (e.g., teacher, parent), sex roles are just about universally applicable, and gender is usually a highly salient feature of a person. For example, if you were describing a colleague to someone else, you might fail to mention many characteristics, but you would probably not forget to mention whether you were talking about a man or a woman.

Some environments may be especially conducive to sex-role spillover. For example, work environments can become sexualized in the sense that they feature relatively high levels of sexual behavior (e.g., sexual jokes, flirting). These work environments seem to encourage people to emphasize sex roles when thinking about coworkers (Gutek, 1985), which may lead to an undue generalization of general societal expectations about men and women in the specialized setting of the workplace. Environments might also highlight gender differences (e.g., with dress codes) in ways that lead people to think of each other in terms of their sex roles rather than in terms of their roles as workers. In general, the more cues in the environment that point to a worker's gender, the higher the likelihood that men and women will be treated differently.

Stereotypes of People and Jobs.   Table 7.1 lists a number of traits that could be used to describe a person. Many of these seem to "fit" better when applied to men than to women (or vice versa). Decisiveness, confidence, ambition, and recklessness are traits we expect to find in men, whereas warmth, sensitivity, understanding, and dependence are stereotypically feminine traits. The stereotypes of some traits are so strongly sex-typed that traits viewed as positive in men (e.g., assertiveness) may be viewed as negative for women. Similarly, traits that are viewed as positive in women (e.g., sensitivity) may be viewed as negative in men.

These same words might be used to describe jobs or, more precisely, the sort of person we would expect to find in a job (e.g., decisive executive, sensitive nurse). The same adjective can be positive when applied to some jobs (e.g., aggressive sales manager) and negative when applied to others (e.g., aggressive kindergarten teacher). The same adjective can take on different connotations when paired with both a job and a person. For example, "assertive nurse" probably brings to mind a different image when the nurse is male than when the nurse is female.

TABLE 7.1
Traits That Might be Used to Describe Men, Women, or Typical Job Holders

Decisiveness	Warmth
Confidence	Sensitivity
Ambition	Understanding
Recklessness	Dependence

Sidelight 7.1   Are We Closing the Wage Gap?

One of the most persistent concerns in discussions of gender and work is the long-standing wage gap between men and women. The U.S. Department of Labor has tracked the earnings of full-time male and female workers, as illustrated in the following figure:

Median Weekly Earnings - Full-Time Wage and Salary Workers

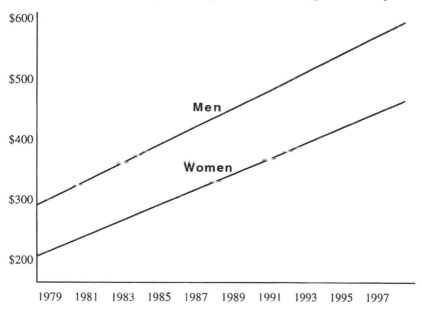

In 1979, the average weekly earnings for men and women were $285 and $177, respectively. That is, at that time, women earned a bit under 62 cents for every dollar earned by men. In the first quarter of 1998, average weekly earnings for men and women were $596 and $455, respectively. That is, women earned a bit over 76 cents for every dollar earned by men. The trend over time is not quite as simple as depicted in the figure; there have been years when the gap was relatively larger or relatively smaller. However, there is still a large gap, and there is no sign that it is likely to close in the near future.

The size and nature of the wage gap depend substantially on another demographic characteristic—race. In 1983, White women earned 66.7% as much as White men, whereas in 1995, the gap had closed to 75.5%. For Black women, the gap hardly closed at all (59.7% in 1983 vs. 62.7% in 1995). For Hispanic women, there is no evidence that the wage gap is closing; in both 1983 and 1995, they earned 54% of that earned by White men.

Sidelight 7.2   What Defines "Valuable" Work?

The person who takes away your garbage is probably more highly paid than the person who teaches your children. The person who fixes your refrigerator probably makes more than the local librarian. It is not universally true, but work that is typically performed by women is usually viewed as less valuable than work typically performed by men. If you ask, "Who decides what work is valuable or important?", the answer is likely to be "the market." It is important to note that "the market" is shorthand for decisions made by millions of individuals in a society. The definition of what type of work is valuable and important and what type is peripheral or trivial is a value judgment that reflects widely shared cultural assumptions about the worth, centrality, and importance of different activities.

Judgments about what is valuable, good, and important in a society usually reflect the preferences, biases, experiences, and values of the groups in society that have the most power and influence. That is, judgments about what literature is worth reading (e.g., what books are regarded as classics), what sorts of art are preferred, or what sorts of houses are better naturally reflect the views of groups who have more power and influence, and the same is true in the world of work. It should come as no surprise that the activities which are most valuable and which are seen as most important in the workplace (e.g., leading others, exercising authority, controlling resources, dealing with things rather than people) are all consistent with the male stereotype, whereas activities that are seen as less valuable (e.g., dealing with children, helping others) are often consistent with the female stereotype. The workplace has historically been the domain of males, and widely accepted definitions of the types of work that are more or less valuable are value judgments that reflect the preferences, experiences, and biases of males.

Judgments about the value of different types of work are essentially subjective, and as societies change and evolve, these judgments may also change. There often is little about the work itself that determines its value (often, people's willingness to work in a job is more important than the work itself in defining market value), and it is likely that judgments about what sorts of work are more or less valuable will change over time. Whether "women's work" will be perceived as more valuable in the future remains to be seen.

Finally, these descriptors take on different meanings when used to describe men or women in the same job. For example, "ambitious executive" might suggest different traits when used to describe men than when used to describe women. (Stereotypes of successful female executives are often negative, focusing on the sacrifices they have made and on the out-of-stereotype behavior needed to succeed in this man's world.) Similarly, "sensitive teacher" is probably more positive when applied to females than to males. For a man, this characteristic may violate typical sex-role stereotypes and is unlikely to be viewed as an asset, whereas for women, sensitivity will probably be seen as a strength.

That jobs can often be described in terms that are strongly sex-typed has fundamental implications for understanding gender discrimination in the workplace. If you believe that men are more likely than women to possess some attribute thought to be necessary for a job, you will probably discriminate against women (and in favor of men) when evaluating applicants or incumbents in that job. For example, a person who thinks that dominance is an important part of police work will probably favor men over women as police officers (dominance is strongly sex-typed). Stereo typing of men, women, and jobs is not inevitable; people are often able to look past stereotypes and evaluate individuals strictly on their individual merits. (For a review of factors that moderate stereotyping, see Fiske & Taylor, 1991; Martell, 1996). However, there is compelling evidence that stereotypes do influence evaluations of men and women at work. The role of gender stereotypes in the evaluation of male and female managers has been studied extensively and offers a case in point.

Research suggests that women and men do not differ in management ability or motivation (Dipboye, 1987), but women are generally seen as less attractive candidates for managerial positions. Even when they have similar backgrounds and credentials, women are perceived to have fewer of the attributes associated with managerial effectiveness (Brenner, Tom-kiewicz, & Schein, 1989; Heilman et al., 1989). Our stereotype of managerial success includes traits like decisiveness, confidence, and ambition, and women are usually assumed to be less decisive, less confident, and less ambitious than men. It is not clear whether this is really true or whether these traits contribute much to success as a manager, but the fact that the stereotype of a man fits the stereotype of a manager, whereas the stereotype of a woman does not, spells trouble for women attempting to enter and succeed in the managerial ranks.

A Lack of Fit. Madeline Heilman (1983) developed a "**lack of fit**" model to identify the conditions under which gender discrimination might be more or less likely to occur. Consistent with the preceding discussion, this model suggests that perceptions of jobs may be a critical issue in determining the extent to which gender influences work outcomes. Heilman noted that some jobs are more strongly sex-stereotyped than others. One basis for such stereotypes may be simple workforce demographics. Jobs that are mainly held by men tend to have male stereotypes, whereas jobs that are mainly held by women tend to have female stereotypes, almost independent of the content of the job. A second basis for such stereotypes is the content of the job. Jobs that include activities that are stereotypically masculine (e.g., working outdoors, working with heavy equipment) are likely to be viewed as more masculine than jobs that include stereotypically feminine activities (e.g., working with children, caring for others). Finally, jobs might have sex stereotypes because of attributes that are thought to be critical for success. As noted previously, successful managers are often described as ambitious, competitive, analytical, and interested in power, all of which are stereotypically masculine traits. Women are thought to have a number of very different skills (e.g., interpersonal skills, interest in consensus) that are clearly work related, but few of which correspond to the stereotype of a manager. In terms of this model, there is a poor fit between the stereotype of the manager and popular stereotypes of women.

Heilman suggested that gender discrimination is most likely to occur when the characteristics of the person do not fit with the stereotype of the job. That is, women are most likely to encounter gender discrimination when the job is seen as masculine. Conversely, men are most likely to encounter gender discrimination when entering jobs or occupations that are stereotypically feminine. Sackett, DuBois, and Noe (1991) provided striking confirmation for some of the predictions of the lack of fit model. They found that when women made up less than 20% of a work group, their performance evaluations were substantially lower than those received by men. In groups that were 50% or more female, women received slightly higher performance ratings.

Although the lack of fit model suggests some symmetry in gender discrimination (i.e., women are at a disadvantage in masculine jobs and men are at a disadvantage in feminine jobs), wage surveys suggest that lack of fit is a more serious issue for women than for men. That is, men in stereotypically feminine jobs (e.g., nurse, librarian) may receive lower ratings, lower salaries, and fewer opportunities for advancement than they would in the absence of any gender discrimination, but the effects of lack of fit are consistently stronger for women than for men. As we note subsequently, one reason for this is that stereotypically feminine jobs tend to be lower in prestige, responsibility, and pay than stereotypically masculine jobs, meaning that there is less to lose or to gain in these jobs as the result of systematic gender discrimination.

Tokenism. The relationships among members of a work group can be quite different, depending on the composition of the work group. The social dynamics of an all-male work group are very different from those of an all-female group, and mixed-gender groups show different patterns of interpersonal relationships than either all-male or all-female groups. In some settings, (e.g., traditionally male occupations), women may be very much in the minority, and their status as **tokens** may lead to higher levels of gender discrimination.

Kanter (1977a) defined *token* as an individual representing a particular group that accounts for less than 15% of an organization's members (other researchers suggest that token status is not determined solely by numerical representation; see Yoder, 1991). One of the most basic research findings on the effects of token status is that characteristics which separate the few from the many tend to be unduly emphasized (Kanter, 1977). If, for example, women make up 10% of a work group, the very rarity of women may lead others to pay more attention to gender and less attention to job-related characteristics than they would in groups with equal numbers of men and women.

Kanter suggested that three processes can lead to gender discrimination when women are tokens. First, token status increases stereotyping. When members of one group are in a distinct minority, others tend to perceive a stronger fit between the characteristics of tokens and the assumed characteristics of the group (Kanter, 1977a). For example, in a work group that contains only a few women, those individuals may be more readily thought of in stereotypically feminine terms (warmth, interpersonal concern, dependence) than when there are many women. As the number of women increases, the probability that they will be thought of as individuals who differ rather than as exemplars of a social group seems to increase. Second, token status increases **visibility.** That is, token status increases awareness and scrutiny of a person's behavior, particularly when that behavior conforms to a stereotype. If a token woman gets emotional at a staff meeting, people notice and remember this. The same behavior in a man will not draw the same scrutiny. Third, token status leads to **polarization, an exaggeration of differences between members of the minority group and members of the majority group.** That is, people tend to notice differences and ignore similarities between tokens and members of the majority.

The accomplishments of tokens are often underestimated by members of the majority group (Sackett et al., 1991; Spangler, Gordon, & Pipkin, 1978). It is easy to see why, when you consider the effects of stereotyping, visibility, and polarization. As noted at the beginning of this chapter, there is a nearly universal tendency to think of people who are different from you in a somewhat negative light. As a result, the stereotypes people hold about groups other than their own are often negative (i.e., few people hold the stereotype that some other group is better than them). Token status increases the probability that a person will be thought of in stereotypical terms, increases public scrutiny of the token's behavior (especially faults), and exaggerates differences between members of the token group and members of the majority group.

Token status also is likely to affect the token's behavior. There is considerable evidence that people who are members of token groups make conscious efforts to downplay their presence and their activities (Deaux, 1979; Ely, 1994; Sarason, 1973). Again, this is easy to understand. A person under constant scrutiny will probably go out of her or his way to escape further notice. The problem with this strategy is that it may hide the person's successes as well as mistakes and miscues.

The basic processes that affect the perceptions of tokens seem to work in similar ways no matter which group is in the minority and which is in the majority. That is, perceptions of a lone male in a female-dominated work group may also be affected by processes of stereotyping, visibility, and polarity. However, the net effect of token status may not be the same for all groups. Widely held stereotypes of some groups are more favorable than others. For example, the stereotypes associated with Asians are somewhat more positive than the stereotypes associated with other ethnic and racial minorities. The more positive the stereotype, the lower the likelihood that token status will lead to negative perceptions.

As noted subsequently, women are often found in occupations that are strongly female-dominated, which means that most working women will not serve as tokens. However, women who enter male-dominated occupations may encounter situations that increase the influence of gender stereotypes (i.e., situations where they are tokens), and the effects of these stereotypes could be substantial. Heilman's lack of fit model suggests that stereotypes are most likely to influence perceptions of individual workers when the characteristics of the person do not fit the characteristics of the job. Male-dominated occupations often have strongly masculine stereotypes (e.g., construction worker, truck driver), and women entering these occupations might encounter a doubly negative set of circumstances. First, the lack of fit between their gender and the stereotypes of the job may increase people's reliance on gender stereotypes when observing and evaluating women. Second, women's status as tokens may exaggerate male–female differences and increase scrutiny of the behavior of the small number of women entering the workforce.

OCCUPATIONAL SEGREGATION
AND GENDER DISCRIMINATION

The term *segregation* is often associated with discrimination on the basis of race or ethnicity, and in many contexts (e.g., analyses of housing patterns in urban areas) race still is the primary basis for segregation. In the workplace, however, gender may be a more potent force in the segregation of the workforce than race, ethnicity, age, or other factors.

It is possible to find men and women doing just about any job in the U.S. economy. Jobs that are completely sex-segregated (e.g., Roman Catholic priest, NFL player, combat infantryman) do exist, but they are clear exceptions. However, although there are relatively few formal barriers to the equal participation of men and women in most occupations, men and women do fundamentally different types of work. It is not completely clear whether this is due to gender discrimination or to other factors (e.g., differences in training and skills). Before we consider why jobs and occupations are segregated by gender, it is useful to consider both the data on sex-segregation in the workplace and models (primarily economic models) that attempt to explain these data in terms of factors other than gender discrimination.

Segregation by Occupation

Historically, women have been concentrated in a relatively small number of occupations, particularly in service sector work, clerical work, and retail sales. Jobs in these categories are so female-dominated that they are sometimes referred to as "pink-collar" work. A number of indices of gender segregation in the workplace exist, but they all tell essentially the same story. A woman entering the workforce is very likely to be found in an occupation where the majority of workers are women; about half of all working women are employed in occupations that are more than 75% female (Dunn, 1997b; Jacobs, 1993).

Jobs that are held primarily by women tend to involve lower levels of technical skill and responsibility than jobs held primarily by men and are generally not as highly valued by organizations (P. England, 1992). In fact, one of the best predictors of the status and pay level of a job is the proportion of women holding that job. The more women found in a particular job, the lower the average pay (Dunn, 1997a). As we note later, one explanation for this trend is that women, for whatever reason, are concentrated in jobs that are of less value to organizations. An alternative, suggested by feminist scholars, is that the work done by women is simply devalued by organizations (Acker, 1989).

Occupational segregation is increasingly obvious the higher in the organization one goes. Surveys show that 95 to 98% of executive-level positions are filled by men (U.S. Department of Labor, 1995). The Federal Glass Ceiling Commission (U.S. Department of Labor, 1991; U.S. Department of Labor, 1995) concluded that equally qualified women are being denied advancement to top levels in organizations on the basis of gender (see also Powell & Butterfield, 1994). Male stereotypes of women and male-dominated culture (i.e., sociocultural factors) often are cited by women as explanations for this glass ceiling (Bucholz, 1996; Dobrzynski, 1996) whereas men sometimes cite lack of motivation (Maupin, 1993) or preparation (Dobrzynski, 1996) (i.e., individual-level factors) as explanations for the small number of female executives.

Devaluing Women's Work.   Many of the jobs that are dominated by women appear to require relatively high levels of interpersonal or nurturant skills (Kilbourne & England, 1997). Female-dominated jobs often involve serving, helping, or supporting others, and these jobs require a number of special skills and abilities. Although interpersonal and nurturant skills are clearly relevant to successful performance in many jobs and roles, there is evidence that these skills are not valued in the same way as technical skills. Kilbourne and England (1997) noted that jobs involving high levels of interpersonal and nurturant skills tend, on average, to involve lower wages than jobs that demand lower levels of these skills. The negative relationship between the level of interpersonal skill required in a job and the average pay level for that job is a concrete indicator of just how little value is assigned to the skills that often characterize "women's work."

Well-run organizations are likely to use careful and systematic processes in making decisions about pay levels assigned to different jobs and career tracks, and it is sometimes difficult to understand how gender discrimination could affect these decisions. Decisions about compensation often start with a systematic **job analysis, which is a study of the tasks, duties, responsibilities, and content of a job.** On the basis of job analysis, jobs might be classified into families and levels, and by combining information about job content with a careful analysis of movement from job to job and the skills required and developed by different jobs in an organization, career tracks might be identified. **The process of making decisions about the compensation levels assigned to different jobs and job families is referred to as job evaluation,** and it often incorporates both information about the content of the job and information about market pay rates into the formulas that are used to determine pay levels. Pay levels for different jobs are often linked to the degree to which **compensable factors** (such as responsibility, autonomy, working in stressful environments, technical skills, etc.) are present in each job.

Job evaluation seems so objective and thorough that many people question whether stereotypes and biases could affect decisions about the worth of different jobs. However, gender discrimination can enter into the process in at least two places. First, the use of market data perpetuates any historical bias that exists in the system. Suppose, for example, that garbage truck drivers have historically received higher pay than elementary school teachers (they have). If you define *worth* in terms of what people are willing to pay for something, you might conclude that garbage truck drivers should be paid more than elementary school teachers (see Sidelight 7.1). The very fact that they are paid more will lead some people to argue that they are in fact worth more. An alternative point of view is that the market has historically discriminated against "women's work" and that the continued reliance on market data simply further entrenches this discrimination.

Second, questions can be raised about the values that drive compensation systems. Typically, jobs that involve more responsibility offer higher pay than jobs involving less responsibility. This reflects a value statement—that responsibility is something that should be rewarded. On the other hand, jobs that involve working with children typically offer lower pay than similar jobs that involve working with adults. This also reflects a value statement—that working with children is not a valued activity (again, see Sidelight 7.1). Whenever you see a statement of values, it is useful to ask whose values are being reflected. Some scholars (e.g., Acker, 1989) suggest that assumptions about what aspects of work are or are not valuable themselves reflect broader societal biases. That is, the decision that level of responsibility is valued and rewarded whereas working with children is not may simply reflect dominant cultural assumptions that, on the whole, tend to assign more value to male-stereotyped activities than to female-stereotyped activities.

Suppose you accept the conclusion that at a broad societal level, the type of work done by women is not valued as much as the type of work done by men. It still might not be clear whether this reflects bias and discrimination or whether it reflects real differences in the work performed and the contribution of that work to organizations and society. If differences in the value assigned to work were based exclusively on the content of men's and women's jobs, it might be impossible to sort out competing explanations for differences in the perceived value of jobs. However, it is not only the activities done by women that tend to be devalued. There is also evidence that the very fact a job is done by women will lead to lower pay, lower status, and lower value. The clearest case for this phenomenon is the job of secretary.

Secretaries are almost always women, and given the skills required, the stress levels encountered, and the work expected from secretaries, it seems reasonable to argue that they are undervalued by organizations and by society. The job of secretary has relatively low pay and relatively low status, but this was not always the case. Prior to World War I, secretaries were almost always male, and the job of secretary had relatively high status. This job often brought young men into close proximity with the power elite, allowed them to work in comfortable surroundings, and provided good pay. As women entered the secretarial ranks, the status and pay of this job declined, even though the essential functions did not change much. This is a case where the feminization of a job seems to have directly reduced the pay, prestige, and status associated with the job.

Is Occupational Segregation Decreasing?   There have been substantial changes in gender segregation in recent years, at least for some high-status jobs. By 1990, approximately 50% of the bachelor's degrees and approximately 35% of the PhD degrees granted in the United States went to women. About 33% of the MD and 40% of the law degrees went to women. A number of professions have seen substantial growth in female representation, and as women take greater advantage of educational opportunities (e.g., college, professional school, and graduate school), the likelihood that they will inhabit the "pink-collar ghetto" has decreased. However, occupational segregation is still a fact of life for women with lower levels of education and training. The gender composition of fields like law and medicine is changing rapidly, but traditionally pink-collar jobs are still dominated by women. Despite the gains made by women with higher levels of education or socioeconomic status, it is still a good bet that receptionists, secretaries, dietitians, and day-care workers will be women.

Patterns of occupational segregation appear to differ as a function of socioeconomic variables, such as education and income. On the whole, women from relatively privileged backgrounds are less likely to find themselves in pink-collar jobs than women with less access to education and business contacts. However, even when women enter the occupations that are not strongly dominated by men or women, they may still encounter a sex-segregated workplace.

Segregation by Job

Sex segregation in the workplace is most obvious when you compare broad occupations (e.g., clerical work vs. engineering). However, often there is also sex segregation in jobs and duties within the same occupation (Bielby & Baron, 1986). For example, female managers often lead less prestigious or less powerful departments, female bank managers tend to work in smaller, more remote branches, and female clerks have less prestige and less discretion than male clerks (Stover, 1997). Bielby and Baron's (1986) survey suggested that men and women performing similar duties in the same organization sometimes have different job titles (male-dominated jobs usually having more prestige) and different career tracks (female-dominated jobs having fewer promotion prospects).

In addition to holding jobs that are often less desirable than men's, women are increasingly likely to hold part-time jobs (Shockley, 1997). Even when job titles and career tracks are formally equivalent, women are more likely to hold jobs that have more tenuous status and prospects. Jobs held by women not only have lower pay than similar jobs held by men but are less likely to provide adequate benefits or job security.

Within professional fields, it is not unusual to find sex segregation by speciality. For example, the authors of this book are industrial/organizational (I/O) psychologists. Twenty-five years ago, I/O psychologists were overwhelmingly male. Today, the proportions of males and females entering the field are roughly equal. Other fields of psychology (e.g., developmental psychology, counseling psychology) are dominated by women, but a few (e.g., mathematical psychology) are still largely male enclaves.

Economic Models of Gender Discrimination

Economists sometimes argue that if gender discrimination exists at all, it reflects true differences in the productivity of male versus female workers. For example, if you assume that labor markets are productive and competitive, it would be very difficult for an individual firm to systematically discriminate against female workers. An organization that did not pay women fairly or that denied them opportunities would lose its best female workers and would be unable to attract high-quality replacements. At least, this is the assumption sometimes made by economists.

Human Capital Theory. Economists argue that education, training, skills, and experience all increase a worker's present and future productivity and that firms recognize and reward these differences in **human capital.** The analogy to financial capital is deliberate, reflecting the idea that people who invest their time and energy in developing job-related skills should expect to see a return on their investment. One possible explanation for differences in the wages earned by men and women is that they differ both in the skills they acquire and in the time and energy they invest in developing new job-related skills (Polacheck, 1981).

Human capital theorists, for example, note that women are more likely than men to interrupt their careers during childbearing years. If unbroken experience on the job does indeed lead one to develop skills that are not developed by people who enter, leave, then reenter the labor market (a common pattern for some women), it might be reasonable to argue that people who do not leave the labor market (often men) should receive better pay than people who leave and reenter (often women). Furthermore, employers might be unwilling to invest in extensive training for workers who are less likely to remain in the labor market, further increasing the skills gap between men and women (Cohn, 1996).

Cohn (1996) noted that one key assumption of human capital models is that women are more likely than men to leave their jobs (thus experiencing more career interruptions and providing less attractive candidates for advanced training). In certain segments of the population, this assumption is probably true. For example, women with young children are probably more likely to experience career interruptions than men in similar age groups. However, across the board, there is little evidence that women are more likely to leave organizations or jobs than men (Cohn, 1996). Thus, the argument that men are likely to be more valuable to organizations because they suffer fewer career interruptions is probably not realistic. Men and women may leave organizations at different times or for different reasons, but there are few data to support the belief that gender is substantially related to turnover.

Even in cases where there are differences in work experience, human capital theory may not sufficiently explain wage differentials. There is little doubt that experience is related to job performance and productivity, but there are sharply diminishing returns for increased levels of experience. Workers with 2 years of experience are rarely twice as valuable to an organization as workers with 1 year of experience, and the value of each additional year of experience tends to diminish sharply (e.g., differences in the skills and productivity of workers with 1 year vs. 2 years of job experience are typically much larger than differences between workers with 20 years vs. 21 years of experience). Thus, when differences in job experience are used to explain differences in wages, careful attention needs to be paid to both the absolute and the relative amounts of experience of men and women.

Can Human Capital Theory Explain Wage Differentials?
There have been attempts to reformulate human capital theory to use

Sidelight 7.3   Closing the Gap
By External Movement?

A basic assumption of many economic models is that competitive labor markets will sort out true differences, if any, in the value of what men and women do. In particular, if women are undervalued when they enter the job market, it is possible that they can recover lost value by moving from one job to another. Often, the most successful strategy for gaining a substantial raise is to move from your current organization to a competitor. Both men and women use this external market strategy, and it is possible that movement through the labor market might diminish the effects of initial differences in male and female salaries.

Brett and Stroh (1997) examined the use of external versus internal labor market strategies by men and women, and their analysis suggests that use of an external labor market strategy does not solve but rather magnifies the problem of male–female pay differences. Data from their study are shown in the following figure.

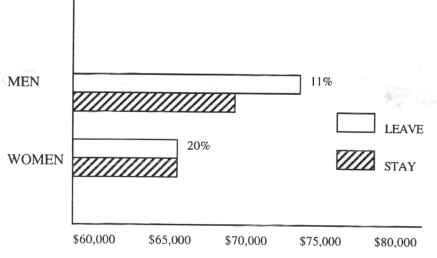

In this study, women were more likely than men to "jump ship" (i.e., leave the organization for a job elsewhere), but the effects of following an external labor market strategy were quite different for men than for women. Men who moved to other organizations gained substantially in salary, whereas women's salaries (which were in any case lower than men's) were not affected by their choice to move or stay.

These data suggest that an external labor market strategy will not address differences in the wages earned by men and women. On the contrary, movement in the labor market seems likely to increase rather than decrease the salary gap.

perceptions and beliefs about turnover rather than actual turnover as explanatory variables. Suppose, for example, managers believe that female employees are more likely to leave the organization. As a result, managers might be less willing to give women valued assignments or expensive training, fearing that their "investment" in these women will be lost. A theory like this might explain why women receive fewer developmental opportunities and, at a broad societal level, might even explain why women are less likely to hold jobs at the top of the organization. However, this sort of extension of human capital theory does not explain why men and women in similar jobs often receive dissimilar salaries.

The most potent criticism of human capital theory is that it simply does not explain the data. The differences in wages earned by men and women cannot be explained by objective differences in their credentials, interrupted work histories, or training shortfalls (Cohn, 1996). Bielby and Baron (1986) studied the distribution of males and females in jobs within a large number of firms and found that human capital variables explained only about 15% of the variance in sex segregation. Even if you control for differences in the occupations and jobs held by men and women (which themselves might be influenced by gender discrimination), significant wage differentials remain (Madden, 1985). The best single explanation for male–female wage differentials is that women tend to enter occupations with low pay, low prestige, and low mobility (Jacobs, 1993). This suggests that strategies such as increasing training, strictly enforcing equal pay laws, and encouraging greater job mobility may do little to reduce differences in the wages received by men and women. To understand how and why men and women receive markedly different salaries, we must first ask how they end up in such different occupations, careers, and jobs.

Accounting for Occupational Segregation

Thirty-five or 40 years ago, it would be much easier to explain occupational segregation. In the 1950s and early 1960s, it was common to reserve some jobs for men and others for women, and occupational segregation could be largely explained in terms of formal barriers to the employment of women in most workplaces. Today, there are few absolute barriers to men's or women's participation in most occupations, and there is less occupational segregation in the current workforce than at any time since the 1940s (during World War II, many women worked in traditional male occupations; "**Rosie the Riveter**" was a very popular image during this era). However, occupational segregation is still a fact of life for many women, and it is important to ask whether this is the result of limited opportunities for women or of choices made by women and by society (or some combination) that lead to persistent male–female differences in occupations and careers.

Four factors are commonly cited to explain differences in the occupations chosen by men and women: differences in socialization; differences in education; differences in interests, values, and preferences; and differences in emphasis on work and family roles.

Gender-Role Socialization.   Women are prepared from childhood for traditional roles such as mother, wife, and helper and are socialized into patterns of behavior that do not foster competition, achievement, or mastery (B.F. Reskin, 1984). Sex-role socialization literature suggests that girls and young women are exposed to numerous messages from family, friends, teachers, and the media that orient them toward female roles and away from traditionally male roles. Thus, women who choose traditionally feminine occupations make choices that are most compatible with messages they have received from society almost from birth.

Another aspect of gender-role socialization is that women are exposed to many role models who have chosen traditional paths (e.g., mothers, grandmothers) and fewer who have chosen nontraditional occupations. There is clear evidence that the availability of female role models increases interest in and persistence in nontraditional occupations (Betz & Fitzgerald, 1987). Many organizations and educational institutions use mentoring programs to increase women's exposure to role models of this sort.

Educational Experiences.   Surveys of the educational backgrounds of men and women show substantial differences in their training in mathematics, science, and computers. In an increasingly complex job market, lower levels of skill and experience in math and science can significantly limit career opportunities, and these educational differences may explain some of the differences in the occupations pursued by men and women. The question, then, is why women are less likely to pursue training in these areas.

In grade school and junior high school, boys and girls seem to have similar levels of interest and success in math, science, and related fields. However, large differences in interest and success in these fields emerge in high school and college (R. Hall & Sandler, 1982; Vetter, 1973). R. Hall and Sandlers' report suggests that the classroom environment in math- and science-related fields becomes increasingly "chilly" for women the further they go (i.e., there is more open hostility to women in college math courses than in high school courses), and women are often quite actively encouraged to consider areas other than science and math. In fact, this is exactly what happens. In college, women are heavily concentrated in the humanities and social sciences and are much less likely to major in engineering, math, science, or other technology-related fields. Patterns of occupational segregation that women will encounter later in life are often mirrored by their segregation into different areas of study in high school and college.

Heilman's lack of fit model might explain the hostility women some-times encounter in advanced math, science, and technology courses. These areas are all stereotypically masculine and are more strongly so at advanced levels than at introductory levels. For example, the stereotype of a com-puter systems analyst is probably more masculine than the stereotype of a worker who uses a computer occasionally. As women move into more advanced levels of training in math and science, the fit between the stereotype of women and the stereotype of the field may decrease, leading to greater salience for gender in evaluating others and more exclusion of individuals on the basis of gender. We might think of college and graduate school as being more open to diversity than some other, more conservative segments of society, but when it comes to advanced training in traditionally male-dominated fields, the college classroom may not be all that receptive to women, either as students or as faculty.

The Role of Interests, Values, and Preferences.   Another reason for differences in the occupations chosen by men and women is that they differ in their **vocational interests**, that is, work-related values and preferences. Vocational interests tend to develop and crystallize during childhood, adolescence, and early adulthood (all periods during which gender–role sexualization is especially intense), and the vocational inter-ests of men and women are substantially different.

Table 7.2 describes Holland's model of vocational interests. This widely cited theory is the foundation for many interest inventories and has been extensively tested. On the whole, women show lower realistic and conven-tional interests than men and higher social interests; evidence of differences in investigative, artistic, and enterprising interests is somewhat mixed, although women show lower investigative and enterprising and higher artistic interests than men in some studies (Betz & Fitzgerald, 1987). Sex differences in vocational interests emerge relatively early in life (typically, systematic differences in men's and women's interests can be detected by the time they finish high school), and they probably reflect the influence of gender-role socialization (Erez, Borochov, & Mannheim, 1989). By

TABLE 7.2
Holland's Taxonomy of Vocational Interests

Interest	Characteristics	Typical jobs
Realistic	Enjoys working outdoors, working with tools and machines, dealing with things rather than people or ideas.	Construction worker, forestry
Investigative	Enjoys solving abstract problems, scientific research; not especially interested in working with others.	Chemist, mathematician
Artistic	Enjoys creative work, self-expression, and unstructured activities; less interested in abstract problem solving.	Designer, commercial artist
Social	Enjoys working with others, arranging interpersonal activities, and solving problems by discussion with others.	Social worker, teacher
Enterprising	Enjoys influencing, dominating, and leading others; interested in persuasion and sales, power and status.	Sales manager, real estate agent
Conventional	Enjoys highly ordered activities, detail-oriented work, and structured situations; less interested in physical activities or social relationships.	Accountant, banker

the time the women make occupational choices, they tend to prefer occupations that are most consistent with social interests and are less attracted to occupations most consistent with realistic or conventional interests. Vocational interests represent one specific type of work orientation that can influence occupational choice. In addition to studies of male–female differences in vocational interests, there are numerous studies of more general differences in work-related values and preferences. In general, men's values and preferences center on competition and dominance, whereas women's center on social relationships. For example, men show greater interest in income, leadership, and advancement, whereas women show greater interest in exercising values and skills, working with others, and helping people (Betz & O'Connell, 1989).

It is clear that differences in interests, values, and preferences are related to differences in occupational choices. What is less clear is whether these differences are the cause or the effect of occupational segregation. For example, it is possible that women choose different occupations because they have different interests from men. However, it is also possible that the interests women develop reflect their perception of what the world is like. Interests are often defined as a "response of liking," and it is easy to imagine that people learn to like things they think they will succeed in and develop less attraction toward things they think will be a source of failure and frustration. If you believe that pursuing a career as a mathematician is likely to lead to failure, rejection, and hostility, you probably will not be very attracted to that career. Girls and young women who frequently hear the message that some careers are more appropriate for women than others may internalize this message and develop stronger interests in careers that fit the female stereotype.

Family-Friendly Work Roles.   Some occupations require you to spend long hours at work, to be available at a moment's notice, or to travel for days or weeks at a time, whereas others impose fewer demands, provide more flexibility, and offer less of a chance that work will interfere substantially with nonwork roles. Although this is not always the case, jobs that require lower levels of involvement and time commitment are usually also lower in pay, prestige, and opportunities for advancement. However, jobs that do not demand high levels of involvement or commitment have one advantage over jobs that provide a great salary in return for an 80-hour week: They allow you to devote time and energy to family life rather than to your career.

It is sometimes argued that women are willing to settle for jobs with lower pay and lower prestige because those jobs do not interfere with family obligations. Another version of this argument is that women have to settle for jobs of this sort if they want to have a family. The demands of a career in upper management or in many of the more high-powered professions may leave little time for family life and provide little of the flexibility that is necessary when normal family crises (e.g., childhood illnesses) occur.

In theory, work–family issues should be of concern to both men and women, but in fact, women are likely to take the primary responsibility for most of the traditional family-centered roles (e.g., caring for children, cooking, cleaning). Even in families that espouse relatively egalitarian ideologies, traditional divisions of family roles are likely to occur (Apostal & Helland, 1993). Men are socialized to seek and accept work roles that substantially interfere with their roles as husbands and fathers, but women are on the whole less likely to make this choice and less comfortable when they do make it. For many women, career choice boils down a decision about the relative importance of career versus marriage and children (Nieva & Gutek, 1981a).

There are three ways that men or women can deal with potential conflicts between work and family roles. First, they can minimize their involvement in one role. For women, this often involves seeking low-pay, low-prestige jobs, but for men this often involves cutting back on family commitments. This is not always the case; there are plenty of women who choose not to have families or to minimize their involvement in the family and there are plenty of men who choose to become "house-husbands." Nevertheless, if the choice is to minimize the centrality of one role, it is a reasonable guess that women will minimize work in favor of family whereas men will minimize family in favor of work.

Rather than trying to meet the demands of work and family simultaneously, a number of men and women attempt to carry out these roles sequentially. That is, a person may enter the workforce for a period, leave the workforce when children are born, and return to the workforce when the children are grown. One possible explanation for women's choice of occupations that are lower in skills, pay, and prestige is that women are more likely than men to leave the workforce to care for young children. If you anticipate that you are likely to enter, leave, and reenter the workforce, it is unlikely that you will be drawn toward occupations that demand high levels of skill (e.g., job-related skills would probably become outdated during the years you are out of the paid workforce) or experience. You would probably find occupations that are intensely competitive unappealing, especially because your possible position on the "mommy track" would put you at a competitive disadvantage as compared with your peers. In short, people who anticipate that they will leave the workforce for long periods but eventually reenter may find low-skill, low-prestige jobs the only realistic possibility. In a job of this sort, there may not be a substantial penalty for leaving the workforce, but in many high-skill, high-paying jobs, individuals who attempt to leave and reenter the job after long periods of absence may find it impossible to succeed.

A number of employers have made efforts to develop a more family-friendly workplace. These efforts include on-site day care, attractive family leave options (as we note in chap. 8, family leave policies that are mandated by law provide only the most minimal help to working families), flexible working hours, and telecommunicating arrangements. These efforts often reflect a combination of good-faith efforts by employers to respond to the conflicts that often emerge between work and family roles and a recognition of the economic costs of failing to provide such benefits. Organizations that do not make at least minimal accommodations for work–family conflicts may find it difficult to attract and retain the most talented employees.

Is Discrimination to Blame for Occupational Segregation?

The only sensible answer to this question is "yes and no." The research evidence suggests that occupational segregation is not, for the most part, the result of individual employers' decisions not to hire women. As discussed in chapter 8, stiff legal penalties can be imposed on employers who discriminate on the basis of gender in hiring, promotion, salary, and assignment to working conditions. If we define discrimination as a conscious and intentional decision on an individual level to treat similarly situated men and women differently when making hiring, job assignment, and promotion decisions, it is probably fair to say that gender discrimination is not the major cause of occupational segregation. Changes in the law and changes in society have removed many of the formal barriers to equal employment opportunities for men and women.

If we define discrimination as differences in the way men and women are treated when as they prepare for, aspire to, seeking training for, or perform in various jobs, it seems clear that gender discrimination defined in these terms is a critically important factor in occupational and job segregation. Differences in men's and women's vocational interests, work values, job preferences, and educational choices are rarely a matter of biology; whatever the causes of male–female differences in occupational choice, it is probably not the Y (or the second X) chromosome that explains occupational segregation. Rather, male–female differences in a number of occupationally relevant skills, values, interests, and experiences seem to be a function of differences in the way society treats men and women. As noted at the beginning of this chapter, discrimination is sometimes defined as "prejudice in action." It seems reasonable to argue that discrimination (i.e., differences in the treatment of males and females) at a societal level is the most critical factor in determining the similarities and differences of the careers and career choices of men and women.

There is a useful distinction between individual and **structural discrimination.** Gender discrimination by a specific individual at a specific point in time is easier to recognize (see chap. 8). Structural discrimination on the basis of gender may be a much trickier issue. First, if men and women make different occupational choices because of the influence of their respective sex-role socialization experiences, it may be impossible to pinpoint the specific behaviors that constitute discrimination or the specific individuals who actively discriminate against women. If gender discrimination is part of the basic structure of society, it will be impossible to identify the responsible parties or the discriminatory acts. This does not mean that gender discrimination is not occurring. Rather, it is likely to mean that gender discrimination is such a part of the social fabric that the culprit is likely to be society and social systems in general rather than some individual.

Individual acts of discrimination in the workplace certainly do occur. However, the most potent form of gender discrimination is probably the form that occurs well before men and women enter the workplace—

sex-role socialization. The idea that different patterns of behavior are appropriate for males and females is such a basic part of how boys and girls are raised that it is natural to believe they will have different attitudes toward, preferences for, interests in, and orientations toward the world of work. These differences are likely to become especially salient as the demands of work conflict with the demands of family, and men and women are socialized to deal with this conflict in different ways.

If one accepts the argument that occupational segregation is largely a result of how we as a society define and communicate sex roles, one might also accept the argument that fundamental change in occupational segregation is unlikely to occur soon. A great deal can be accomplished by insisting that employers apply fair and equal standards when making decisions about individual job applicants and incumbents (see chap. 8), yet it may be less reasonable to hold employers strictly accountable for broader societal differences in how we view men and women or in how men and women view their own roles. There are many reasons to believe that the socialization of men and women is less restrictive (at least with regard to their socialization into work-related roles) today than it was 50 years ago, and it is likely that a long-term trend toward a more gender-integrated workplace will continue. However, the process of societal change is always slow, and it is likely that differences in the way males and female are prepared for and oriented to the world of work will persist for some time.

In addition to the societal factors that influence our beliefs and attitudes about men and women (and our perceptions of our own sex roles and work roles), there is an even deeper structural explanation for gender discrimination in the workplace. Work has traditionally been a male domain, and our definitions of what sort of work is valuable, the relative importance of work and nonwork roles, and the sorts of behaviors that contribute to or detract from organizations all reflect a male-oriented perspective. As we noted in our discussion of differences in the value attached to "men's work" and "women's work," the assumption that supervising 10 subordinates is more valuable and more important than teaching 10 children reflects the values of the dominant culture, in this case the "male" culture. Our assumptions about what work means in our lives; how, when, and where people should work; how organizations should be structured; and how conflicts between work and nonwork roles should be juggled tend to reflect and reinforce a particular perspective on the world that seems more in tune with male sex roles than with female sex roles. On the whole, the world of work seems friendlier and more comfortable to men than to women, and this should come as no surprise. Feminist scholars argue that the world of work was designed by and for men, and that efforts to improve the fit between people and work should not be limited to changing sex roles but should also include a reconsideration of fundamental assumptions we make about work itself (Kessler-Harris, 1985; Lorber, 1986).

SUMMARY

Discrimination occurs when people are treated differently on the basis of their membership in a particular group. A number of features of the workplace lead to or enhance gender discrimination. In particular, the stereotypes people have of men and women often differ in terms of their compatibility with stereotypes of work. If you believe that a job requires a competitive attitude, a desire for power and dominance, and interest in things rather than in people, you are likely to think that men are better suited for that job than women. If you believe that a job requires interpersonal skill, concern for others, and a willingness to subordinate one's own needs to the needs of others, you are likely to think that women are better suited for that job than men.

Structural features of the workplace strengthen the effects of stereotypes on the evaluation of male and female workers. In particular, when women (or men) represent only a small minority of the work group, their very rarity may lead people to think about them in terms of their sex roles rather than in terms of their work roles. The extensive sex segregation of the workplace suggests that many women are either a distinct minority in a male-dominated job or are confined to jobs that are heavily dominated by females (i.e., pink-collar jobs).

The clearest evidence of gender segregation is found when examining the occupations of men and women. The majority of working women are found in a relatively small number of female-dominated occupations (e.g., clerical work, service work) that are characterized by low pay, low prestige, and low skill demands. Even within occupations, there is evidence of segregation. Men and women in the same general occupational group (e.g., college professors) are often found in different types of jobs (e.g., women are more likely to be found in the social sciences and humanities and less likely in mathematics and the hard sciences).

Differences in the pay, benefits, and career progression of men and women reflect a number of factors, but a large part of the variance in these outcomes is explained by the gender segregation of occupations and jobs. A number of factors, including sex-role socialization, differences in education (particularly in math and science), and differences in vocational interests and work-related values and preferences play an important role in the sex segregation of the workplace.

Your conclusions about the role of gender discrimination in determining differences in the pay, benefits, and careers of men and women depend substantially on how you define discrimination. Definitions of discrimination that focus on the actions of organizational decision-makers suggest that gender discrimination is not a major factor in occupational segregation. Definitions of discrimination that focus on broad societal structures (e.g., the way men and women are socialized, the structure of work roles) suggest that gender discrimination is a major factor in determining men's and women's experiences in the workplace.

GLOSSARY

Compensable factors: Features of a job, such as the level of responsibility required, autonomy, stress of the environment, and technical skills required, that are accepted by organizations as bases for awarding higher pay to one job than to another.
Discrimination: Action (usually negative) toward individuals on the basis of their group membership.
Human capital: Job-related credentials, training, and skills that represent investments by current or potential employees in increasing their productivity.
Job analysis: Systematic study of the tasks, duties, responsibilities, and content of a job.
Job evaluation: The process of making decisions about compensation levels by analyzing the job and the relevant labor market.
Lack of fit: A model for studying gender discrimination developed by Madeline Heilman. The model suggests that gender discrimination is most likely to occur when the characteristics of the person do not fit with the stereotype of the job.
Polarization: Psychological process involving exaggeration of differences between members of a minority group and members of the majority group.
Rosie the Riveter: Popular image used during World War II to represent women who stepped into war production jobs as males were drawn into the Armed Forces.
Sex-role spillover: When interactions with female workers are influenced by assumptions and beliefs about their sex roles (i.e., the fact that they are women) rather than about their roles as workers.
Structural discrimination: Persistent patterns of discrimination that are the result of broad societal values, role definitions, and socialization practices.

Tokens: An individual representing a particular group that accounts for less than 15% of an organization's members.

Visibility: Psychological process involving increased awareness and scrutiny of the behavior of a token, particularly when that behavior conforms to a stereotype.

Vocational interests: Responses of liking to particular types of occupations or particular types of work.

8

Gender and the Legal Context in Which Men and Women Work

Hopkins, an associate in a prestigious accounting firm, was being considered for partner. Evaluations of Hopkins included phrases like "outstanding performance," "strong character, independence, and integrity," "highly competent project leader," and "deft touch." Nevertheless, despite having more billable hours than any of the other 87 candidates for the status of partner, and despite generating $25 million in business, Hopkins was soundly disliked by many of the partners. One criticism of Hopkins involved dress and grooming: They just were not up to the standards expected by the partners. Another involved interpersonal skills. Hopkins was criticized as aggressive, harsh, difficult to work with, and impatient with staff. Hopkins was passed over for partner, while coworkers with records that seemed less stellar were promoted.

A subsequent lawsuit suggests that the problem with Hopkins was gender (*Price-Waterhouse v. Hopkins*, 1989). Ann Hopkins was simply not (in the male partners' eyes) very feminine. She was criticized as "macho" and for using foul language (which the partners found unbecoming in a lady), and one partner advised her to "take a course at charm school." Another advised her that she would have a better chance of advancement if she walked, talked, and dressed more femininely. There was no suggestion that being aggressive, using foul language, and dressing in a somewhat masculine style were frowned on at Price-Waterhouse, only that these behaviors were viewed as negative when coming from a woman.

In *Price-Waterhouse v. Hopkins* (1989), the Supreme Court accepted the argument that decisions made about Ann Hopkins reflected sex stereotypes rather than job-related evaluations. What was particularly telling in this case was that many of the same behaviors that were seen as a problem when evaluating Hopkins (e.g., aggressiveness) were seen as beneficial in male candidates. As the court noted, this created an impossible situation for women at Price-Waterhouse (Bennett-Alexander & Pincus, 1998). Women who were not aggressive did not bring in enough business to succeed, but those who were aggressive were seen as unladylike. This double-bind still plagues women in many work settings.

This chapter examines how the legal system deals with, or fails to deal with, gender discrimination in the workplace. As noted in chapter 7, federal antidiscrimination laws are for the most part concerned with specific acts of individual employers and not with broad societal tendencies to treat men and women differently and thus often fail to address structural discrimination. However, these laws do offer potentially powerful protection to the rights of men and women who encounter different treatment or different work-related outcomes because of their gender, and have opened a wider range of options for women in the workplace.

We start by examining the legal framework for dealing with claims of gender discrimination in the workplace. Laws such as the Equal Pay

Act and The Civil Rights Acts of 1964 and 1991 specifically address discrimination against women in hiring, firing, pay, and conditions of employment. We then discuss the enforcement of these laws by federal, state, and local agencies and through litigation. In particular, we discuss the sorts of issues that often arise in lawsuits charging sex discrimination in the workplace.

In addition to antidiscrimination laws, several laws deal specifically with potential conflicts between work and family. In particular, recent laws granting family leave as well as laws forbidding discrimination because of pregnancy are described. The final section of this chapter describes the nature and scope of affirmative action programs and considers the possibility that these programs may harm their intended beneficiaries more than help them.

THE LEGAL FRAMEWORK FOR DEALING WITH GENDER DISCRIMINATION IN THE WORKPLACE

Men and women work in a societal context that promotes and condones discrimination against women (e.g., by establishing and reinforcing gender stereotypes, or by devaluing "women's work") while vigorously condemning and punishing job discrimination based on gender, race, religious origin, or other demographic factors (e.g., through antidiscrimination laws). The legal arena represents a very special facet of the broader cultural context in which men and women work, and it is useful to understand why cultural norms regarding the treatment of men and women in the workplace might not always lead to the same conclusions as legal norms.

Laws banning discrimination in schools and the workplace reflect basic ideals about fairness in dealing with each other in a civil society. In a sense, these laws reflect the "conscience" of society, at least in this particular area. Thus, there is some consensus in society that you should not treat a person differently solely on account of that person's gender or race. Cultural beliefs and stereotypes about men and women, on the other hand, reflect a wide array of information, observations, and preconceptions about what men and women are like, how they should behave, and their appropriate roles. Although the legal system is part of a broader cultural context in which men and women work, it is one in which specialized ideas about what is fair, equitable, or proper are given precedence over other sorts of norms, beliefs, or ideas. So, even though many people believe that women should place higher priority on the home than on the career, should be expected to work in traditionally female-dominated occupations, and should give deference to men in the work-place, people will also often believe that women should not be forced to choose home over work, to avoid male-dominated occupations, or to put up with boorish or inappropriate behavior from supervisors. Thus, even in a societal context where widely held beliefs about men and women can substantially bar women's success in the workplace, women have been able to take advantage of a number of laws that support equality of rights of men and women in this male-dominated context.

Two major laws deal with gender discrimination in the workplace (the Equal Pay Act of 1963 and the Civil Rights Act of 1964), and there are numerous additional sources of legal protection (e.g., the Civil Rights Act of 1991). Important features of these laws, and of similar laws that have been passed in other countries, are reviewed next.

Equal Pay Act

Prior to 1963, organizations would sometimes post separate pay rates for men and women, even for identical jobs. The **Equal Pay Act of 1963** represents one of the first post–World War II attempts to address gender discrimination in the workplace. The act forbids paying men and women different rates for "equal work on jobs the performance of which requires equal skill, effort, and responsibility, and which are performed under similar working conditions." Although this law addresses an important concern (i.e., different pay for men and women), its effects are limited by a number of factors. First, different pay can be given for work that is "equal" if pay inequalities are the result of a seniority system, a merit system, or a system that ties earnings directly to the quantity or quality of production. More generally, pay differentials for male and female workers doing highly similar work are not illegal if it can be shown that they are based on a factor other than sex.

The most important limitation of the Equal Pay Act is not the set of exceptions previously listed (i.e., seniority, merit, etc.) but rather the fact that the act applies only to jobs that are essentially equal. In lawsuits brought under this act, the **plaintiff** has the burden of showing that work is equal, and unless both the work itself and the conditions of work can be shown to be essentially identical, the Equal Pay Act does not apply.[1]

---

[1]In equal employment litigation, the plaintiff generally refers to the individual or group who is alleging harm due to some unlawful employment procedure, and the defendant is usually the employer.

The World War II Labor Board required equal pay for "comparable work" performed by men and women, but under the Equal Pay Act a higher standard is required (Player, 1988).

Player (1988) noted that the Equal Pay Act does not require that pay rates be rational or defensible. For example, if one job requires more skill, more effort, or more responsibility than another, there is no legal requirement that it offer more pay. Employers who pay lower rates in jobs dominated by women (e.g., receptionist) than in jobs dominated by men (e.g., truck driver) are not violating this act.

Although the Equal Pay Act is sharply limited in its coverage, a number of cases are brought each year. For example, in 1994, over 1,600 suits were brought under the Equal Pay Act. This is not necessarily a large number given the size of the U.S. workforce, but given the egregious nature of the practices covered by this act (i.e., paying men and women differently for essentially identical work performed under essentially identical conditions), this number is still surprisingly high.

Comparable Worth. Often, the complaint is not that men and women are paid differently for essentially the same work, but rather that jobs held by women tend to be undervalued by organizations and that pay rates often fail to reflect the skills required in different jobs, the importance and complexity of the activities included in each job, and the conditions under which work is performed. It is often argued that jobs of **comparable worth** should offer comparable pay.

Intentional discrimination in pay on the basis of sex can be illegal under certain circumstances (*County of Washington v. Gunther*, 1981), but there is no federal law requiring organizations to pay on the basis of comparable worth. Labor market surveys often show substantial differences in pay rates for jobs that involve comparable (but not identical) skills, levels of responsibility, and complexity, and these market differences can be used as legal defense of gender differences in pay across jobs. Organizations may adopt compensation systems based on assessments of comparable worth at their discretion but are not required to do so (*State, County and Municipal Employees v. Washington*, 1985). Some of the steps involved in assessing comparable worth are illustrated in Sidelight 8.1.

The key idea in comparable worth analyses is that the worth of a job should be systematically related to the content of that job. Analyses of comparable worth help, for example, in determining whether male–female differences in pay rates can be explained by differences in job requirements and activities. Barker (1997) and Acker (1989) noted that there are many places gender discrimination could enter into the process of assessing comparable worth (see Sidelight 7.1), and it is naive to see comparable

Sidelight 8.1   Assessing Comparable Worth

Pay systems based on assessments of comparable worth are still relatively rare in the private sector but have been implemented in a number of public-sector organizations (Barker, 1997). The point factor method of job evaluation is sometimes used to link the pay level associated with each job in an organization with the content of the job and the conditions under which people are required to work. There are four steps in implementing this method of job evaluation.

First, decisions must be made about which features of a job should be considered when determining pay (i.e., compensable factors). For example, organizations often offer higher pay for jobs that involve higher levels of responsibility, more complex problem solving, or more stringent skill and training requirements or that require individuals to work in stressful environments. (In chap. 7, we noted that decisions about what factors are "compensable" are value judgments that may reflect the preferences and experiences of men more closely than those of women.) Second, levels for each factor are defined, and points are awarded to levels based on subjective or analytic evaluation of worth of each factor and level. For example, a job that requires extensive training might receive 50 points; if high levels of responsibility for decisions and resources are required, 100 points might be awarded. Third, jobs are analyzed to determine exactly what is required in each. Fourth, this job-analytic information is used to make a statement about the worth of each job on the basis of the content of the job and the conditions under which people work.

Once point totals are obtained for each job in an organization, it is possible to determine the relationship between the content and requirements of different jobs and the pay rates for those jobs. The following figure illustrates one form this analysis might take.

This figure illustrates a common pattern of findings in assessments of comparable worth. If compensation decisions were based solely on the content of the job and the requirements of different jobs, most jobs would fall very near the regression line shown in the figure. That is, the higher the job in terms of specific compensable factors, the more it should pay. What is often found is that jobs held by men pay more than they would if compensation decisions were made solely on the basis of an analysis of what the job entails, whereas jobs held primarily by women often pay less than would be predicted based on an analysis of the job and its associated working conditions. These differences are often attributed to market factors, and it is not clear whether an employer can safely ignore the going labor market rates for different jobs when designing compensation

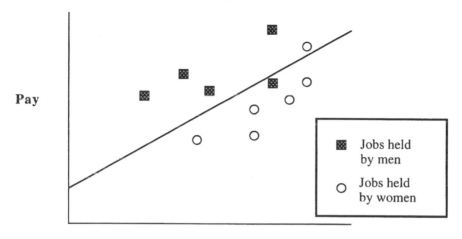

Total Points

packages. Nevertheless, results similar to those shown in this figure are what fire the debate about comparable worth.

worth analyses as statements of the objective worth of different jobs. Nevertheless, analyses of the relationships between job content and pay levels do provide valuable information for understanding why jobs held primarily by men or primarily by women might entail such different rates of pay.

Civil Rights Act of 1964

The **Civil Rights Act of 1964** states that it is illegal for an employer to "fail to hire or discharge an individual, or to discriminate with respect to compensation, terms, conditions, or privileges of employment because of such individual's race, color, gender, religion or national origin." The act covers discrimination in hiring, firing, training, discipline, compensation, benefits, classification, and other terms or conditions of employment for employers who are engaged in interstate commerce and/or who have 15 or more employees. In addition to covering employees in the United States, the Civil Rights Act of 1964 covers U.S. citizens working outside of the United States for U.S. employers. Bennett-Alexander and Pincus (1998) discussed specific employer actions that might be considered evidence of sex discrimination; Table 8.1 includes a number of examples of discriminatory actions covered by the act.

TABLE 8.1

Employer Actions That Might Constitute Sex Discrimination

Specifying a particular gender as preferred in a job advertisement.

Refusing to hire a person of particular gender for a job.

Refusing to hire women who are pregnant, who have children under a certain age, or who are not married.

Asking different questions of men and women in applications or interviews (e.g., asking women but not men about child-care issues).

Restricting hours, assignments, or positions to one gender.

Disciplining one gender for acts that are tolerated when committed by the other gender.

Providing different types or levels of training by gender.

Providing different benefits by gender.

Requiring different conditions of employment by gender (e.g., setting dress codes for female but not for male employees).

The Civil Right Act is divided into several sections of "titles"; **Title VII** covers discrimination in the workplace. The original version of Title VII did not forbid or even mention sex discrimination. This was added as an amendment to the statute in a spirit of satire by the chairman of the House Rules Committee (Player, 1988), quite probably in an attempt to kill the bill (R. Arvey, 1979). In 1963, the idea of forbidding discrimination on the basis of sex was such a radical notion that some people believed adding gender to the bill would doom its chances in the Senate. Ironically, given that gender was included in an attempt to derail the bill, sex discrimination cases have become one of the largest sources of equal employment litigation (Arvey & Faley, 1988). In 1995, the **Equal Employment Opportunity Commission** (EEOC) received over 25,000 sex discrimination claims (EEOC, 1995), representing roughly one third the caseload under Title VII.

As we note in chapter 9, the Civil Rights Act forbids sexual harassment in the workplace, on the theory that such harassment constitutes sex discrimination. That is, if a woman is treated differently in the workplace because of her gender (which would include sexual harassment), this can constitute employment discrimination. Furthermore, the harassment does not have to take the form of direct threats, assaults, or even offers of jobs, promotions, or pay raises in exchange for sexual favors. As has been shown in several landmark cases (e.g., *Jenson v. Eveleth Taconite Co.,* 1993; *Meritor Savings Bank, FSB v. Vinson,* 1986; *Robinson v. Jacksonville Shipyards, Inc.,* 1991), if the level of sexual harassment present in the work environment is sufficiently severe and pervasive to limit women's ability to function effectively or to progress (i.e., if harassment creates a **hostile work environment**), the courts are likely to find that this harassment constitutes gender discrimination. Again, the theory is that the behavior is directly a function of the recipient's gender, and that it reduces her opportunity to perform effectively on the job.

Gender-based differences in assignments or conditions of employment are often found to be discriminatory even when their purpose is seemingly benign. In *UAW v. Johnson Controls* (1991), employees in a particular class of jobs ran the risk of exposure to high levels of lead. Women who might become pregnant were barred from this job and were allowed to occupy the job only if their infertility could be medically proven. Because lead exposure can be very dangerous for a fetus, this policy might be seen as being in the interests of the employee (or at least of her offspring). In *UAW v. Johnson Controls* (1991), however, this policy was ruled to be discriminatory. The court argued that prospective parents, not employers, should make decisions about protecting their reproductive health, and that a policy that affected women but not men (men were not barred from this job, even if they expressed concerns about their reproductive health) was clearly discriminatory.

The Civil Rights Act also addresses what has been referred to as **gender-plus discrimination** (Bennett-Alexander & Pincus, 1998). Policies that place different limitations on some women than on men in general represent instances of gender-plus discrimination. For example, in *Phillips v. Martin-Marietta* (1971), the company had a policy of not accepting job applications from women with preschool-age children. The court found that the application of this policy to women, but not to men, was discriminatory. Companies do have a right to establish performance standards and do have a right to require that employees adhere to those standards, regardless of whether they are parents. For working parents, this implies that some mechanism for child care must be worked out. However, companies cannot use the stereotype that child care is the mother's responsibility to place this limitation on women only. That is, treating a woman with small children differently than you treat a man with small children usually constitutes discrimination.

Civil Rights Act of 1991

A series of Supreme Court decisions during the 1980s seemed to sharply limit the applicability and enforceability of the Civil Rights Act of 1964. The Civil Rights Act of 1991 was designed primarily to overturn these decisions (the text of the act includes specific reference to decisions that seemed to misrepresent the intent of Congress) and to resolve some procedural limitations of the Civil Rights Act of 1964.

Lawsuits brought under the Civil Rights Act of 1964 are heard as bench trials; that is, they are heard before a judge. The Civil Rights Act of 1991 allows jury trials, which many believe will benefit plaintiffs (juries may be sympathetic to plaintiffs who seem to have been treated unfairly, even if the admissible facts do not strongly support the complaint). It also provides for compensatory and punitive damages to employees who can prove intentional discrimination. This act applies only to violations occurring after November 21, 1991, and its impact on the legal system is still to be seen.

Additional Legal Protection

An amendment to the Civil Rights Act of 1964, **Title IX**—Education Amendments of 1972, prohibits discrimination on the basis of sex in administration of educational programs. The most visible effect of Title IX has been in efforts to equalize support for men's and women's athletic programs in high schools and colleges, but the law is by no means limited to this specific application. Complaints of sexual harassment in the classroom have been litigated under Title IX (a recent Supreme Court ruling absolves school districts from liability for sexual harassment of pupils by teachers if the district does not know that the harassment has occurred), and Title IX may provide broad protection against unequal treatment in educational programs of just about any sort.

The State and Local Fiscal Assistance Act and the Omnibus Crime Control and Safe Streets Act prohibit discrimination on the basis of race, national origin, sex, age, or religion by state or local governments in programs funded by these acts. As we note subsequently, this is a specific instance of a broader principle that discrimination is generally forbidden in any program that is funded, even in part, by the federal government.

In addition to specific statutes protecting the rights of women and minorities, employees often have a good deal of legal protection under common law. For example, courts routinely uphold employers' obligation to act in good faith and deal fairly when negotiating and designing employment relationships. Good faith and fair dealing requirements apply most clearly to terminations; employers are not allowed to terminate employees solely to secure an unwarranted economic advantage or to terminate for reasons that are inconsistent with community standards of reasonableness. Although not specifically aimed at sex discrimination, these common law protections can be a useful supplement to the specific statutes considered by the courts.

Individuals can sometimes be protected from discrimination through the obligations imposed under tort law (i.e., contract law). For example, an employer who signs a contract that includes a duty to evaluate employee performance, and then conducts those evaluations negligently or discharges employees without notice or opportunity to challenge and remedy unfavorable evaluations, may face a legal claim for negligent performance of a duty. Employee handbooks and manuals describing personnel policies often include fairly specific descriptions of employers' and employees' rights and duties, and the statements in those manuals can become the basis for legal complaints if those policies are not adequately carried out.

Finally, there are constitutional protections against discrimination. For example, gender distinctions that do not bear a close and substantial relationship to important governmental objectives are usually subject to "heightened scrutiny" by the courts. In general, constitutional protections are relevant to the acts of governmental agencies and not to private employers. However, many private employers are also government contractors and in this role may be subject to additional scrutiny when discrimination is alleged.

International Trends. Many other nations have antidiscrimination laws, although the scope and coverage of these laws are not always as extensive as in the United States (Sowell, 1990). Increasing attention is being devoted to the **United Nations Universal Declaration on Human Rights**, which seeks to guarantee equal rights for men and women, and for racial and ethnic groups. Although the U.N. declaration is not itself legally binding, many nations have adopted antidiscrimination laws based on its provisions (e.g., the recent agreement between the Republic of Ireland, the United Kingdom, and Northern Ireland is likely to lead to antidiscrimination laws patterned after this declaration in both the Republic and Northern Ireland). Groups such as Amnesty International have criticized the U.S. record on gender discrimination, noting that important terms of the U.N. declaration have not been met in this country. The argument made by Amnesty International is that structural discrimination against women is just as harmful as individual discrimination (and its effects are more pervasive), and that U.S. laws which ignore structural discrimination do not do enough to reduce sex discrimination in the workplace.

Sex Discrimination in the Workplace: Areas of Special Concern

The laws previously cited are relatively broad in scope and can be applied to a wide variety of specific actions. Furthermore, there are a number of reasons why employers might (intentionally or unintentionally) treat men and women differently in the workplace. As a result, the range of issues that have been raised in sex discrimination complaints is extremely broad. Nevertheless, some specific issues arise quite frequently in sex discrimination complaints and lawsuits, and it is useful to examine a few of these.

Sidelight 8.2   The Equal Rights Amendment

The **Equal Rights Amendment** (ERA) was proposed as the 27th Amendment to the Constitution. Surprisingly brief and simple, it stated that "equality of rights under the law shall not be denied or abridged by the United States or any State on account of sex." Originally proposed in 1923, the ERA was approved by the House of Representatives in 1971 and the Senate in 1972. It was ratified by 35 states (this total was reached only after the deadline for ratification was extended), but ratification by 38 states is needed to amend the constitution, and the ERA failed. It was reintroduced to Congress in 1982, but it did not gain congressional approval and was never again submitted to the states for ratification.

The defeat of the ERA can be attributed to a number of factors, including belief that it would lead to radical federal mandates (e.g., same-sex toilets) and that it would undermine social institutions that revolve around sex differentiation (e.g., marriage, family). Another factor in its defeat was the belief that the ERA would have few real benefits for women, based on the assumption that women were already adequately protected by the 5th and 14th Amendments of the Constitution (which guarantee equal protection under the law) and the Civil Rights Act (which outlaws sex discrimination in the workplace and in educational programs).

It is difficult to predict what effects passage of the ERA would have had on sex discrimination in the workplace. The argument that direct, individual acts of discrimination are already covered by the Civil Rights Act is probably correct. Adding a layer of constitutional protection to that already provided by the Civil Rights Act might not really change the scope or the effects of federal efforts to prevent sex discrimination. However, the ERA might have provided a useful tool for addressing some of the indirect and structural factors that lead to gender discrimination. A specific statement in the Constitution that men and women should be treated equally could be a significant step in changing societal attitudes and practices that foster gender discrimination.

It is important to recognize some of the potential limitations of the ERA and of constitutional protections in general. The ERA was designed to forbid differences in treatment by "the United States or any State" on account of sex. Acts of discrimination by private individuals, employers, or other nongovernmental entities might not be directly affected by the ERA or any similar change to the constitution. Although the defeat of the ERA was a significant setback to women's rights in many other contexts, it might not have substantially impacted specific efforts to reduce sex discrimination in the workplace.

Sex Differences in Compensation: Civil Rights Act Versus Equal Pay Act. As we noted in chapter 7, women earn substantially lower wages than men, sometimes for what appears to be quite similar work. Differences in men's and women's pay is often an important consideration in evaluating sex discrimination claims.

Sex discrimination in pay is covered by both the Equal Pay Act and the Civil Rights Act. In some cases, gender discrimination in pay that would be authorized under the Equal Pay Act (specifically gender discrimination that results from the application of a factor other than sex in making pay decisions) might also be authorized under the Civil Rights Act. For example, salaries might be based in part on past experience, education, or prior salary. These seemingly neutral criteria can lead to substantial differences in the average salary received by men and women, but such salary differences are not necessarily evidence of gender discrimination, regardless of which law (i.e., Equal Pay Act vs. Civil Rights Act) is applied. In general, if policies that base pay on factors of this sort are uniformly applied, and the employer can articulate a valid business-related reason for including these factors in pay decisions, pay differentials for jobs held by men and women are permissible under both the Civil Rights Act and the Equal Pay Act.

Plaintiffs who believe they are paid lower rates because they are women might find it easier to proceed under the Civil Rights Act than under the Equal Pay Act. As we note subsequently, the Civil Rights Act allows legal action in response to both intentional and unintentional discrimination and provides a relatively simple structure for presenting and prosecuting lawsuits. It also may provide harsher penalties to employers if intentional discrimination can be proven in a court of law.

Subjective Hiring or Promotion Criteria. Hiring and promotion decisions are sometimes based on relatively objective criteria, such as test scores, credentials, and seniority. These criteria are subject to challenge, particularly if it can be shown that their application leads to different employment outcomes as a function of race, sex, national origin, or other similar criteria. In other cases, these decisions are made on the basis of more **subjective criteria,** such as an interviewer's impression that you would be a good fit for a job, a manager's recommendation that you receive a promotion, and so forth. Employment decisions made on the basis of such subjective criteria have been a frequent focus of sex discrimination complaints.

There are two reasons why the use of subjective criteria in making employment decisions has been a special concern in sex discrimination litigation. First, employment tests and other objective criteria often show relatively small sex differences. For example, if selection decisions are made on the basis of well-validated tests of cognitive ability, men and women will usually be selected at about the same rate in most jobs (Jensen, 1980). The same is not always true for subjective measures. Second, many experts believe that subjective methods of assessment provide more leeway for stereotypes and biases to operate (R.D. Arvey, 1979). So, an interviewer who believes that women don't, in general, fit a particular job may be more likely to evaluate female interviewees poorly, even if their behavior is essentially identical to that of male candidates (R.D. Arvey & Faley, 1988; Baron & Byrne, 1994; Heilman et al., 1989).

A number of cases have examined the role of subjective evaluation methods in sex discrimination (e.g., *Rowe v. General Motors,* 1972). On the whole, the courts are more receptive to the use of subjective criteria in hiring and promotion for white-collar than for blue-collar jobs (Sedmak & Vidas, 1994). Subjective evaluation methods that adversely affect women, minorities, or members of other **protected groups** must be validated, and it is sometimes much harder to defend apparently discriminatory employment decisions that depend on such methods. However, subjective evaluation methods that have shown an adverse impact against women have survived legal scrutiny (*Harless v. Duck,* 1977). The particular selection tool examined in that case was a well-developed structured interview, and it is likely that the care with which this interview protocol was developed figured largely in its successful defense. In general, employment decisions that rely on subjective evaluations or assessments should be scrutinized carefully. Sex discrimination may be more likely to occur when subjective rather than objective criteria are used to make employment decisions, and the very subjectivity of those criteria can make them difficult to defend.

Physical Requirements. A number of jobs, particularly in public safety occupations (e.g., police, firefighter) have minimum height, weight, and/or strength requirements, and these requirements often have a disproportionate effect on women. For example, if you require job candidates to be 6 feet tall, to weigh 200 pounds, and to lift very heavy objects from a standing position, you will probably screen out the majority of female applicants. As we note later, requirements of this sort are legal if it can be shown that they are indeed related to effective or safe job performance, and requirements that disqualify almost all women from a job can be legal under a variety of circumstances. Nevertheless, the fact that height, weight, and/or strength requirements can have such a substantial impact on female applicants (and on job applicants from ethnic or racial groups whose members tend to be smaller, lighter, etc.) has led to substantial scrutiny of these requirements.

Height, weight, and strength requirements for specific jobs have all been challenged, with mixed success (*Blake v. City of Los Angeles,* 1977; *Dothard v. Rawlinson,* 1977; *Harless v. Duck,* 1977; *Officers for Justice v. Civil Service Commission,* 1975). The general method for defending these requirements is similar to that established for other tests, assessments, or minimum qualifications. Employers should be cautious in setting minimum requirements for height, weight, or strength, because these requirements will almost certainly have a different impact on men than on women. Employers who want to establish and enforce such requirements should have clear evidence that the specific requirements they have put in place can be justified in terms of the individual's ability to perform the job effectively or the individual's safety.

ENFORCING GENDER DISCRIMINATION LAWS

Two important groups are involved in enforcing antidiscrimination laws. First, a number of federal, state, and local agencies have specific enforcement responsibilities. Second, sex discrimination lawsuits filed by individuals and groups of individuals (**class action** lawsuits) have an important role in defining and enforcing antidiscrimination laws. The roles of enforcement agencies and of litigation in the enforcement of antidiscrimination laws are described next.

Federal Enforcement Agencies and Procedures

Numerous state, local, and federal agencies are responsible for enforcing specific antidiscrimination statutes (e.g., the Department of Labor Wage and Hour Division enforces the Family and Medical Leave Act). However, most claims of sex discrimination in the workplace are handled by one of two federal agencies: the Equal Employment Opportunity Commission and the Office of Federal Contract Compliance Programs.

Equal Employment Opportunity Commission. The Equal Employment Opportunity Commission (EEOC) is the federal agency responsible for enforcing Title VII of the Civil Rights Act. The EEOC is charged with investigating, conciliating, and litigating violations of Title VII and with developing guidelines for enforcement of Title VII (although not having the force of law, these guidelines are granted great deference by the courts). The EEOC can bring suits in its own name or intervene in suits filed by private individuals.

The EEOC investigates the charges it receives to determine whether there is reasonable cause to believe that discrimination has occurred. Between half and two thirds of the claims received by the EEOC are dismissed, suggesting that the agency does differentiate credible claims from those that are either frivolous or unsubstantiated. (However, this figure may say more about the relatively limited resources of the commission than about the merits of the cases it receives.) Currently, the EEOC handles about 80,000 complaints a year and has a backlog of approximately 70,000 cases. The commission employs about 750 investigators, and the typical caseload for each investigator is 100 to 150 cases.

If, after investigation, the EEOC finds "cause," it must first seek to reach a voluntary resolution between the charging party and the respondent. The EEOC may bring suit in federal court only if conciliation is not successful.

In 1994, analyses provided by the Bureau of Labor Statistics showed that there were approximately 1.5 claims per 1,000 employees nationwide. Although the percentage of employees filing claims is relatively low, the total number of claims is large. In 1995, there were over 70,000 complaints filed and approximately 17,500 cases were filed in federal courts.

Office of Federal Contract Compliance Programs. The U.S. Department of Labor **Office of Federal Contract Compliance Programs** (OFCCP) enforces the executive orders that define federal affirmative action policies, along with several work-related statutes (e.g., the Rehabilitation Act). This office is primarily responsible for monitoring discrimination in federal contracts and for helping organizations develop and implement affirmative action plans. It also has the power to investigate discrimination complaints and to impose contract remedy sanctions on offending employers.

Whereas the EEOC is concerned with violations of federal law, the OFCCP is largely concerned with enforcing specific provisions of federal contracts. Unlike EEOC lawsuits, which are typically heard in federal court, OFCCP hearings are generally held before a Department of Labor administrative law judge. Despite their differences in focus, the EEOC and the OFCCP often handle similar cases, and the hearings carried out by the OFCCP often deal with the same sets of issues as encountered in enforcing Title VII.

Litigating Gender Discrimination Claims

Suppose a woman applies for and meets all the posted qualifications for a particular job. She goes to an interview and is asked vague and general questions by an interviewer who seems to exhibit a patronizing attitude toward women. She does not get the job, even though men with similar

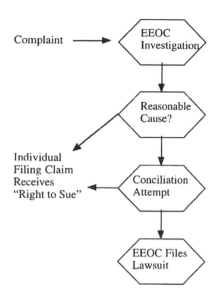

FIG. 8.1   Typical process for filing a discrimination suit.

qualifications are hired. She believes that she has been discriminated against because of her gender and decides to sue the employer. What happens next?

Although there are a number of paths a suit might take, the procedure for filing a discrimination lawsuit is well defined and usually takes the form shown in Figure 8.1. First, the woman must file a timely complaint with the EEOC or an approved state agency. After an investigation, the EEOC determines whether there is a reasonable cause to believe that a violation has occurred (suits are possible even without a finding of probable cause, but in many cases, such a finding will terminate the complaint).

If the EEOC concludes that there is reasonable cause to believe that a violation has occurred, it is required by Title VII to attempt to conciliate between the parties and reach a voluntary agreement to deal with the complaint. If this conciliation fails, the EEOC can bring a suit in federal court.

An individual or group of individuals can bring a suit, but they must first file a complaint with the EEOC. If the EEOC decides not to pursue a complaint itself, it may issue a "right to sue" notice to the party or parties bringing the charge. Regardless of whether the suit is filed by an individual or by the EEOC, the charge can be litigated under theories of "disparate treatment" and/or theories of "disparate impact."

Disparate Treatment Versus Disparate Impact.   The term **disparate treatment** usually refers to intentional discrimination on the part of an employer. An individual who claims to be treated differently than other similarly situated applicants or employees because of sex or race has made a claim of disparate treatment. Except in those rare cases where a "smoking gun" exists (e.g., a memo to interviewers instructing them to treat women differently than they treat men), disparate treatment can be difficult to prove. If you hope to improve intentional discrimination, you may have to establish that the employer's actions cannot be explained on any plausible job-related grounds (*McDonnell Douglas Corp. v. Green*, 1973). A claim of disparate treatment can be difficult to prove, especially because it can be rebutted if the employer can produce a valid business-related reason for the decision in question. Many employment discrimination cases are argued under an alternate approach: the theory of **disparate impact.**

Seemingly neutral procedures (e.g., an employment test that is given to all applicants) can have a substantially different effect on one group than on another. For example, you might give a test of auto and shop procedure knowledge to applicants for the job of machine operator and find that women fail the test more often than men. (The Armed Services Vocational Aptitude battery has a subtest of this sort, and pass rates for males and females are consistently different; Murphy & Davidshofer, 1998.) Employment procedures that have different effects for men and women or Whites and Blacks may be illegal under Title VII.

Claims that an employment procedure has disparate impact usually start with a demonstration that there are meaningful differences in passing rates, **selection rates,** or some other employment-related outcome. J.M. O'Connor (1997) noted that in disparate impact cases, credible statistical evidence that the practice being challenged has an impact, and that its impact is substantial enough to be statistically reliable, is absolutely crucial. Without such evidence, disparate impact cases will almost certainly fail.

Returning to our example, to show that the interview had a disparate impact on women, the plaintiff would have to produce credible evidence that women applicants typically did worse in the interview than men. This by itself would not be enough to show that the interview illegally discriminated against women. Rather, as we describe next, charges that an employment procedure has disparate impact can often be defended by showing that the procedure is related to job performance or some other valid business interest of the employer.

How Disparate Impact Cases Work. Most sex discrimination cases are argued under the theory of disparate impact, and it is useful to describe in detail how these cases work. In general, these cases involve a two-step procedure, where the plaintiff presents evidence that a procedure

TABLE 8.2
Assessing Adverse Impact

	Applicant	Hired	Selection ratio	Adverse impact ratio
Male	120	45	.375	
Female	90	21	.233	.233/.375 = .621

Note. If the selection rate for females is less than 80% as large as the selection rate for males, this is accepted as evidence of adverse impact. Here, the female selection rate is 62.1% as large as the selection rate for males.

has different impact on members of different groups, and the **defendant** presents evidence that the procedure is related to job performance or to the safe and efficient operation of the business.

To succeed in a discrimination claim, the plaintiff must first prove that the procedure in question has **adverse impact,** that is, that it has a substantially different impact on one group of applicants than on another. Table 8.2 illustrates one method that might be used to determine whether the interview described in this example in fact had adverse impact.

To evaluate adverse impact, we compare passing rates attained by males and females. For example, if 120 men were interviewed and 45 were hired, the passing rate (or selection ratio) for men would be 37.5%. If 90 women were interviewed and 21 were selected for the job, the passing rate for women would be 23.3%. Statistical tests are available to determine whether this difference in passing rates (i.e., 37.5% vs. 23.3%) is large enough to be statistically reliable, but the Uniform Guidelines on Employee Selection Criteria suggest a simple rule that is widely followed by the courts. The passing rate for women will be judged to be meaningfully lower than the rate for men if it is less than 80% as large as the men's rate.

In this example, the selection rate for men is .375. This means that any selection rate for women that is lower than .300 (i.e., .80 × .375) will be accepted as evidence that the selection procedure really does have adverse impact on women. In our example, the women's selection rate (.233) is substantially lower than .300, and the adverse impact ratio (i.e., a comparison of the selection rate for women and men) is far below .80 (here, the selection rate for women is 62% as large as the selection rate for men). Evidence of this sort establishes a **prima facie case** that the interview has an adverse effect on female applicants.

The plaintiff must establish this prima facie case to have any hope of succeeding; without credible evidence of adverse impact, the employer will almost always prevail in disparate impact cases. Once the plaintiff has demonstrated adverse impact, the burden of proof shifts to the employer. The employer can successfully defend an employment practice that has adverse impact if he or she can show that the practice has **business necessity** or that gender is a **bona fide occupational qualification** (BFOQ).

There are only a few instances in which gender is a valid job requirement, in the sense that a job can only be performed by males (e.g., sperm donor) or females (e.g., wet nurse). However, it is usually very difficult to establish gender as a BFOQ. Even if customers, coworkers, and managers strongly prefer to do business with males rather than females, sex is generally not itself an essential requirement of most jobs, and employment practices that are challenged on the basis of sex discrimination are rarely defended with the argument that gender is a BFOQ. Rather, they are much more likely to be defended with the argument that business necessity justifies the employment practices in question. An employer can follow two strategies in demonstrating business necessity. First, if the employer can show that the procedure being challenged (e.g., the interview described in our example) is related to the job, either in terms of its content or in terms of a significant relationship between interview outcomes and job performance, the procedure will generally be upheld as legal even though it has an adverse impact on women. As long as an employer can demonstrate that a test or assessment is job related, the fact that it adversely affects women will not be enough to show that it illegally discriminates. On the contrary, as long as employers can demonstrate that they are making decisions based on criteria that are relevant to the job, they are often free to use procedures that appear to discriminate against women and minorities.

Evidence of job-relatedness is not the only method of showing the business necessity of an employment practice. For example, a business that involves substantial contact with the public may impose dress and grooming standards on employees. These standards may have little relevance to the performance of specific job duties, but the employer may argue that they are necessary to the success of the business. Note, however, that imposing substantially different standards on men and women might constitute sex discrimination.

Trends in Litigation: You Don't Have to Win to Win

Both federal agencies (EEOC and OFCCP) and private individuals have filed numerous lawsuits challenging employment practices that appear to discriminate against women (and occasionally men) because of their gender. These suits can take years to investigate, litigate, and appeal, and

Sidelight 8.3 Can You Be Fired For No Reason?

The simple answer is yes. In many cases, if your employer decides he or she doesn't like you, doesn't want you to remain in the organization, doesn't like the color of your car, and so on, your employment can be terminated. If there is no agreement (implied or actual) or contract to the contrary, employment is usually considered to be at will. That is, there is no obligation on either side to remain in the relationship. Under the at-will employment doctrine, either the employer or the employee can terminate the employment relationship at any time and for virtually any reason, as long as the reason for termination is not prohibited by law (e.g., discrimination on the basis of race or gender). The practical effect is that in many situations, anyone can be fired, and the employer is under no obligation to provide a rationale for firing that individual.

Organizations that are wary of firing employees will sometimes create conditions that are so intolerable that the employee has no real option but to quit. This is referred to as *constructive discharge* (Bennett-Alexander & Pincus, 1998), under the theory that the employer's actions rather than a free decision of the employee lead to the discharge. Employers are forbidden to engage in constructive discharge when such acts are based on the sex or race of an employee, but there is no broad prohibition against employers making your life so miserable that you feel forced to quit. Constructive discharges are, in general, handled like ordinary discharges.

Employment at will is not assumed where there is a breach of promise or where the discharge violates some recognized public policy. For example, an individual who is fired because he or she refused to engage in some criminal act on the behalf of an employer (e.g., people who refuse to go along with white-collar crime in the organization) can usually sue for wrongful discharge. However, unless you can show that an actual or implied contract exists, or that the discharge occurred because of sex, gender, or national origin or that it was in violation of some public policy, you often have no legal basis for challenging a termination decision.

many plaintiffs can be discouraged from suing by the mere fact that the process is often so long and difficult. However, the recent trend in large-scale gender discrimination lawsuits has been for organizations to offer very substantial settlements in cases before they go to trial or before a trial is completed. For example, in 1997, Home Depot U.S.A. announced a $65 million settlement in a class action suit alleging that women were discriminated against by being forced into dead-end jobs (e.g., 80% of the cashiers in Home Depot stores were women, whereas 66% of the employees were men) and denied opportunities to move to supervisory and management positions. Public Supermarkets paid $81.5 million to settle a similar gender discrimination suit. Mitsubishi Motors Manufacturing of America recently agreed to pay $34 million to settle a sexual harassment case (the largest settlement to date for a sexual harassment case).

Why are organizations willing to settle for such large sums? There are several possible explanations, but the two most plausible theories include public relations concerns and the sheer expense and difficulty of defending a complex lawsuit. For example, there was extensive publicity concerning the lawsuits filed against Home Depot and Mitsubishi, and their public images suffered considerably. At some point, executives in both organizations might have decided that the damage to their image was far more costly than the settlements they offered. No executive wants to see stories of apparently egregious discrimination at his or her organization become a staple in the nightly news.

A second explanation for organizations' willingness to settle is that litigation of this sort is unbelievably expensive and time-consuming. Between depositions, discovery, meetings with lawyers, and the trial itself, the costs in terms of time spent by managers and executives alone is quite high. If you add legal fees and all the costs of preparing and presenting a defense, it is easy to understand why some organizations are nervous about taking lawsuits to court. Even if they win, the costs can be staggering, and if they lose, there is a real possibility that very large awards will be granted to the plaintiffs.

What all of this means is that women do not necessarily have to win or even to file a lawsuit to gain important concessions from organizations. An important factor in enforcing these laws is organizations' awareness of the substantial costs that even a small lawsuit might involve. A credible threat of legal action (i.e., one that is backed up by believable evidence that discrimination has occurred) is increasingly likely to get the attention of top management, and if the trend in multimillion-dollar settlements continues, this threat is likely to become increasingly effective. This does not mean that women or members of minority groups can get what they want simply by threatening to sue (although this tactic can be surprisingly effective). As Figure 8.1 illustrates, employment discrimination lawsuits are first evaluated by the EEOC or similar agencies, and if these agencies find no probable cause to believe that discrimination has occurred, threats to sue may not be viewed as credible. However, an individual who can assemble concrete evidence that discrimination has occurred will probably find that the recent trend toward large-scale settlements will enhance his or her bargaining power in attempting to resolve discrimination claims without going to court.

FAMILY-RELATED LEGISLATION

Employment policies in the United States are often substantially less family friendly than in other countries. In particular, many European countries provide long and well-subsidized parental leave, strict regulations guaranteeing that a woman's career will not be substantially harmed by taking leave for childbirth, and policies that encourage rearranging work duties and schedules during a child's early years. Prior to 1993, there were few federal laws protecting job security for women who took more than a minimal family leave, and even today, the laws that provide such protection are considerably less family friendly than in most industrialized countries (e.g., federal law guarantees some rights to family leave but does not require that it be paid leave). Nevertheless, there has been some progress in the United States in developing legal protections for men and women whose family roles may not always be completely consistent with (or at the mercy of) their work roles.

Family and Medical Leave Act (1993)

The **Family and Medical Leave Act** (FMLA) provides up to 12 weeks of unpaid family or medical leave for birth or adoption; to care for an ill child, spouse, or parent; or for an employee's own illness. The FMLA applies to employers with 50 employees or more and covers a significantly smaller portion of the workforce than most federal antidiscrimination laws (note that the Civil Rights Act applies when there are 15 employees or more). Bennett-Alexander and Pincus (1998) noted that the FMLA applies to about 5% of U.S. employers and about 40% of U.S. employees. Simply put, most U.S. employees are not protected under the FMLA.

In general, the FMLA protects a person's right to return to his or her old job or to an equivalent job (with equivalent pay) in the organization, but there is an important exception. Highly compensated employees (those in the top 10% of an organization's employees) are not required to be restored if their return would cause "substantial and grievous economic injury to the operations of the employer." The act also requires employers to maintain health care benefits at their normal level during the leave. Employers are allowed to count paid vacation, sick leave, personal leave, or other sorts of leave toward the 12-week total, so that an employer who already offered 2 weeks of vacation, 1 week of paid sick leave, and 1 week of paid personal leave would not be required to provide another 12 weeks of family leave. This employer would be required to provide an additional 8 weeks of unpaid leave, provided that leave was requested for one of the specific purposes described in the act.

There are several reasons why the FMLA was not extended to smaller businesses (i.e., 15–49 employees), but the most important one was a concern among business owners that mandated leave would severely hurt their ability to compete. For example, if you have 10 employees and 2 take 3-month leaves at the same time, you could find it very difficult to get adequate temporary replacements or to function effectively with a 20% reduction in your workforce.

Despite concerns expressed by some business owners, the FMLA has not proved to be burdensome. Department of Labor (DOL) Surveys show that 90% of employers report that compliance costs little or nothing; less than 2% of employers report reducing other benefits to comply with the law. One reason for the low cost is the relatively low utilization rate. DOL surveys suggest that the median length of time away from work while on family and/or medical leave is 10 days, and that only 2 to 3% of employees actually take leave (58% of the leaves provided under FMLA are granted to women). Because the leaves granted under this act are often unpaid, it can be a significant hardship to take the full 12 weeks allowed by law, and even leaves of 2 weeks or more may be beyond the means of many employees. Again, there is legal protection on the books, but in practice it is less than effective in addressing work–family realities that women face.

Pregnancy Discrimination Act

Approximately 50% of the workforce is female, and about 75% of those of childbearing age will have children sometime during their working years, which suggests that allowing organizations to discriminate against pregnant workers could cause substantial problems. Nevertheless, in 1976, the Supreme Court ruled (*General Electric Co. v. Gilbert*) that discrimination on the basis of pregnancy was not sex discrimination under Title VII. Two years after this decision, Congress passed the Pregnancy Discrimination Act, which prohibits termination or refusal to hire because of pregnancy and protects reinstatement rights of women on leave for pregnancy-related reasons.

The Pregnancy Discrimination Act of 1978 requires employers to treat pregnancy like they would treat any other short-term disability. In particular, employers cannot refuse to allow a pregnant employee to work if she wishes to and is physically able to, nor can they refuse to provide accommodations to pregnant employees that they would provide to employees with other short-term disabilities (e.g., if an employee who strains his or her back is placed on temporarily light duties, similar accommodations must be made for pregnant employees). Also, the act forbids employers who make accommodations for pregnant employees to use those accommodations as a pretext for a subsequent negative employment decision. Thus, an employer cannot assign pregnant employees to light duties and then fire them because they have not been as productive as regular-duty employees.

IS AFFIRMATIVE ACTION A HELP OR A HINDRANCE TO WOMEN IN THE WORKPLACE?

A series of executive orders (starting with Executive Order 11246, signed by Lyndon Johnson) and laws passed over the last 25 to 30 years have created what is probably the most vaguely defined and poorly understood strategy for dealing with employment discrimination: **affirmative action**. People appear to have very different ideas about what affirmative action actually involves, and their attitudes toward affirmative action are sometimes decisively shaped by their misperceptions of key aspects of these programs (Kravitz et al., 1997). In the following sections, we define affirmative action and consider the hypothesis that affirmative action may do more to harm than to help its supposed beneficiaries.

What Is Affirmative Action?

Federal law requires companies with government contracts over $50,000 and more than 50 employees to comply with nondiscrimination requirements and establish affirmative action plans. The components of these plans vary, but they usually emphasize action to increase access and opportunities for women and minorities (e.g., utilization analysis, enhanced recruitment, and setting goals and timetables). Employers are required to establish affirmative action goals and targets and to make good-faith efforts to reach self-defined goals, and failure to adopt or comply with an affirmative action plan can be treated as breach of contract with the government. However, there are generally no penalties for failing to reach affirmative action goals.

As the term *affirmative action* implies, these programs are designed to do more than simply remove existing barriers to equal employment. The key idea of affirmative action is outreach, that is, specific efforts to ensure that qualified members of underrepresented groups are considered when hiring and promotion decisions are made. **Preferential treatment** is not required as part of affirmative action and in fact is usually illegal (e.g., the Civil Rights Act of 1964 specifically noted that employers are not required to remedy workforce imbalances by preferential treatment of the less-favored group). Quotas are not required in establishing affirmative action programs and in many settings are specifically forbidden by law.

One of the most significant misunderstandings of affirmative action programs is the belief that they require preferential treatment for women and minority group members. As previously noted, this is not true. Thus, the fact that women may be discriminated against in the workplace is not a sufficient justification for preferential hiring or promotion. Gender-conscious employment policies are legal only if three conditions are met:

1.   There has been a competent finding of illegal treatment of women in a specific setting.
2.   The plan is designed to remediate that specific discriminatory treatment.
3.   The plan does not require the discharge of males or exclude them from consideration for employment (Player, 1988).

Furthermore, even when gender-conscious hiring is permitted, it is generally illegal to hire an unqualified woman over a qualified man. Courts can order hiring and promotion goals and ratios to remedy specific effects of discrimination, but courts cannot mandate layoffs to redress past discrimination. Affirmative action goals under Executive Order 11246 are treated solely as targets, and evidence of good-faith efforts to meet these targets is sufficient to document compliance.

Affirmative action efforts can be implemented at the individual level (e.g., programs to increase outreach to female applicants) or at the organizational level. Various government agencies have established set-aside programs, that is, programs which reserve a certain proportion of government contracts for businesses owned by women and/or minority-group members. As is true for preferential hiring procedures, set-aside programs are often illegal unless they are designed to remediate proven discrimination in a particular sector of the economy. Even here, firm set-aside programs (i.e., ones that limit applications to firms owned by women or members of minority groups) are often not allowed (*Adarand Constructors, Inc. v. Peña,* 1995). Rather than setting firm quotas, current set-aside programs are likely to focus on enhancing the competitiveness of proposals from firms owned by women or members of minority groups (e.g., a price break of up to 10% when calculating low bidder on government contracts).

Although affirmative action is often attacked by politicians, there is strong support for this concept in the business community. This is in part because it represents a visible action to correct past discrimination, and perhaps also because it can limit liability for such discrimination. Organizations that are engaged in a well-developed affirmative action effort seem less likely to be sued for discrimination or to be subject to strict scrutiny by agencies such as the EEOC or OFCCP.

Although affirmative action does not require quotas or preferential treatment, the public perception that these programs might lead to reverse discrimination is not entirely illusory. Organizations are required to make good-faith efforts to meet their own affirmative action goals, and a company that has consistently failed in hiring or promoting women or members of minority groups may conclude that its liability would be lower if its "numbers" were more representative. Although there is rarely pressure from enforcement agencies to grant preferential treatment, it does appear that some organizations whose hiring policies are under scrutiny may do exactly that. However, data on the effects of affirmative action on both its intended beneficiaries (i.e., women, minority group members) and on those not considered beneficiaries (essentially, White males) are hard to come by. For example, despite the widespread public concern over reverse discrimination, fewer than 2% of all discrimination cases involve complaints of sex discrimination filed by males and/or complaints of racial discrimination filed by Whites, and relatively few of these complaints are upheld in court. Similarly, there is clear evidence that employment outcomes for women and members of minority groups have improved, but it is difficult to determine how much (if any) of this improvement is due to affirmative action (*Affirmative Action Review,* 1995; Kravitz et al., 1997).

Backlash and Unintended Consequences

In theory, affirmative action represents little more than an attempt to make sure that fully qualified women and minority group members are given a fair shake in the employment process. Proponents of these programs emphasize activities like outreach (e.g., running employment ads in places where a wide range of potential applicants are likely to read them) and also emphasize the idea that preferential treatment, quotas, and reverse discrimination are not part of affirmative action. However, this is not the image of affirmative action held by the general public.

Surveys of attitudes toward affirmative action consistently show three things:

1. A large percentage of the population believe that affirmative action involves or requires the preferential treatment of women and minority group members.
2. These beliefs are not limited to White males but are held to varying degrees by virtually all demographic groups in the population.
3. The stronger the belief that affirmative action involves preference, quotas, reverse discrimination, and the like, the more negative attitudes toward affirmative action become (Kravitz et al., 1997; Kravitz & Platania, 1993; Turner & Pratkanis, 1994).

One very concrete indication of the public perception that affirmative action involves preferential treatment and reverse discrimination is the debate over a recent ballot initiative passed in California. In 1996, California voters approved Proposition 209, which bans preferential selection, promotion, and contracting on the basis of race, sex, or national origin. This law is almost universally described as "outlawing affirmative action," but in fact the relationship of this law to affirmative action programs is not clear. The law does not address or even mention the components of traditional affirmative action programs (e.g., outreach, recruitment, and antidiscrimination policies), and many of the actions covered by this law are, in theory, already illegal under the Civil Rights Acts of 1964 and 1991.[2] The text of this proposition speaks of the need to remove discrimination on the basis of sex, race, ethnicity, and the like and in many respects overlaps with the Civil Rights Act of 1964.

In general, research shows that the beneficiaries of affirmative action are more likely to have positive attitudes about these programs than those who do not benefit (Kravitz et al., 1997). This, however, does not mean that affirmative action enjoys widespread support, even among those who stand to benefit. For example, surveys generally show that about two out of three women and about three out of four men oppose affirmative action programs if they believe that these plans include preferential treatment of women.

---

[2]A ballot initiative in the City of Houston suggests that public perceptions of affirmative action activities can be decisively influenced by how they are labeled and described. The voters in Houston decisively defeated Proposition A, which would have amended "the Charter of the City of Houston ... to end the use of Affirmative Action for women and minorities in the operation of City of Houston employment and contracting, including ending the current program and any similar programs in the future." This suggests that "affirmative action" might be seen in more positive terms than "preferential treatment." To further complicate matters, on June 26, 1998, Texas District Court Judge Sharolyn Wood threw out the results of this election, on the grounds that the city had purposely worded this initiative in terms of "affirmative action" rather than "preferential selection." The original proponents of this initiative had proposed a law modeled on Proposition 209, and the city changed the wording of the initiative to refer to affirmative action rather than preferential treatment.

Negative perceptions of affirmative action itself may lead to a much more serious problem: negative perceptions of the supposed beneficiaries of affirmative efforts. Madeline Heilman and her colleagues have extensively researched the **"stigma of incompetence"** (Heilman, 1994; Heilman, Lucas, & Kaplow, 1990; Heilman, McCullough, & Gilbert, 1996; Heilman, Rivero, & Brett, 1991; Heilman, Simon, & Repper, 1987). These studies show that the belief that you have gained a position because of preferential selection can lead to the devaluation of your abilities, skills, and accomplishments. That is, if people believe you have been selected, promoted, and positively evaluated because you are a woman, they are also likely to believe that you are less competent, less skilled, and less likely to perform well than a man. (Other scholars, including Truax, Cordova, Wood, Wright, & Crosby, 1998, question whether such devaluation occurs in real-life contexts.) Furthermore, this effect shows up in self-perceptions as well as perceptions of others. That is, individuals who believe that their own success is in part due to preferential treatment are likely to devalue their own abilities, skills, and accomplishments. One of the most potent arguments against affirmative action is that it may do more harm than good. That is, it may lead to more negative perceptions of women even if their selection or success has nothing to do with race or sex. Opponents of affirmative action note that many women and members of minority groups whose success came because of their abilities, skills, and hard work will nevertheless be dismissed as incompetent, based on the assumption that they are the beneficiaries of reverse discrimination. Research on backlash associated with affirmative action suggests that this sometimes occurs for women, but there is little evidence of these effects for other minorities.

Opponents of affirmative action have made considerable headway with the arguments that discrimination on the basis of race or sex is wrong (even when the motives for such discrimination are benign) and that affirmative action can harm its intended beneficiaries. Proponents of affirmative action note that there is some irony in this sudden concern for discrimination and for the stigma of incompetence. A review of our recent history suggests that discrimination on the basis of race and sex did not seem to be a burning concern to political conservatives until they believed that White males might suffer from discrimination. Similarly, concern that preferential selection might harm its intended beneficiaries was never raised until someone other than White males was seen to benefit.

The United States had a long-standing program of preferential selection, reserving most desirable jobs for White males, that lasted for over 350 years. To our knowledge, there is little research about the stigma of incompetence as it applied to White males prior to 1964. You could certainly argue that many of these individuals were successful because they did not have to compete with the majority of the population (i.e., women, members of minority groups) for jobs, capital, and education, and that they would not have been so successful in a free and open competition. While the "stigma of incompetence" observed by Heilman and her colleagues is a real and important problem, we are not convinced that the possibility of such a stigma should be used to end affirmative action efforts to decrease discrimination in the workplace. The beneficiaries of the preferential selection programs in place prior to 1964 seemed to survive without anyone assuming they were incompetent, and it is not completely clear why this stigma should be a problem now if it was not a problem before the passage of the Civil Rights Act.

Finally, to reiterate a point made in chapter 7, equal employment opportunity laws and affirmative action efforts are likely to address only some of the causes of sex discrimination in the workplace. Sex discrimination is likely to reflect a mix of intentional decisions on the part of employers (disparate treatment); unintentional discrimination that results from using tests, assessments, or decision criteria that tend to screen out women (disparate impact); and occupational segregation that results from sex role socialization and differences in male–female interests and values. Litigation and affirmative action interventions are likely to address discrimination by employers but are unlikely to address the broader question of discrimination by society.

SUMMARY

In this chapter we examine the legal framework for dealing with gender discrimination in the workplace. The legal context of work can be an important factor in shaping organizational actions and, in part, larger societal attitudes. Title VII of the Civil Rights Act of 1964 is the single most important law dealing with employment discrimination, but there are a number of other specific laws (e.g., Equal Pay Act) as well as constitutional, common law, and tort law remedies available for dealing with discrimination by employers. Employment discrimination complaints can involve a wide range of issues, but some issues arise with sufficient frequency that a series of laws or relevant cases can be cited (e.g., male–female differences in pay, the use of subjective employment criteria, or height, weight, and strength requirements).

We discuss the roles of federal agencies versus individual and class action lawsuits in enforcing antidiscrimination laws and described the steps involved in filing and litigating discrimination claims. We distinguish between intentional and potentially unintentional discrimination and discuss the steps in a typical suit alleging unintentional discrimination. Finally, we note a recent trend for organizations to offer large settlements rather than risk the outcome of sex discrimination cases in court.

In contrast to other industrialized democracies, the United States does relatively little to accommodate work with having and raising children. However, federal laws protect female workers against discrimination on the basis of pregnancy and provide at least some minimal family leave. We discuss these laws and comment on reasons for the relatively low use of family leave provisions.

Finally, we discuss affirmative action. Despite its long history and its widespread implementation, affirmative action policies are poorly understood by the public. Although preferential selection and reverse discrimination are often forbidden by law, most public discussions of affirmative action are based on the assumption that these programs favor women and members of minority groups over more qualified White males. This assumption, in turn, can lead to a "stigma of incompetence," a tendency to devalue the abilities, skills, and accomplishments of women and members of minority groups, on the assumption that they have received scholarships, jobs, and promotions solely because of their sex or race. There is evidence that affirmative action programs can have negative consequences for their intended beneficiaries, although the extent of this problem is far from clear.

GLOSSARY

Adverse impact: Situation in which an employment criterion leads to substantially different employment outcomes for different groups in the population.

Affirmative action: Program under which government contractors and large employers are required to develop programs to increase employment opportunities for qualified women and members of minority groups. These programs often include tools such as utilization analysis, enhanced recruitment, and employment goals and timetables.

Bona fide occupational qualification: A criterion that appropriately restricts employment opportunities to particular groups, based on the argument that a characteristic such as sex is an essential requirement for performing the duties of a job (e.g., sperm donor, wet nurse).

Business necessity: Test, assessment, or employment requirement that is demonstrably related to job performance or that can be shown to be necessary for the safe or efficient operation of a business.

Civil Rights Act of 1964: Federal law forbidding discrimination on the basis of sex, race, ethnicity, national origin, or religion.

Class action: Legal action taken on behalf of a group or class of similarly situated individuals.

Comparable worth: Setting pay rates on the basis of the requirements, duties, or working conditions of jobs.

Defendant: Individual or group accused of violating civil or contract law.

Disparate impact: Theory under which seemingly neutral employment criteria that have adverse impacts against protected groups are often litigated.

Disparate treatment: Intentional discrimination on the basis of sex, race, or national origin.

Equal Employment Opportunity Commission: Federal agency responsible for enforcing the Civil Rights Act.

Equal Pay Act: Federal law forbidding different pay for men and women doing essentially identical jobs.

Equal Rights Amendment: Proposed constitutional amendment (never ratified) that called for equal rights under the law for men and women.

Family and Medical Leave Act: Federal law guaranteeing 12 weeks of unpaid family leave per year.

Hostile work environment: Work environment in which the level of sexual harassment is sufficiently severe and pervasive to limit women's ability to function effectively.

Gender-plus discrimination: Discriminatory policies that treat some women (e.g., women with small children) differently than they treat men.

Office of Federal Contract Compliance Programs: Federal agency responsible for enforcing nondiscrimination clauses and affirmative action provisions of federal contracts.

Plaintiff: Individual or group bring a legal action.

Prima facie case: Presentation of evidence that an individual or a group has been adversely affected by an employment procedure (e.g., selection test, promotion process).

Preferential treatment: Granting members of protected groups preference over equally qualified or more highly qualified White males when making employment decisions.

Protected groups: Demographic groups protected from employment discrimination by specific federal laws (e.g., women, racial minorities).

Selection rates: Proportion of applicants selected by an organization.

Stigma of incompetence: Assumption that women and members of minority groups owe their success to preferential treatment rather than to their own abilities, skills, or accomplishments.

Subjective criteria: Methods of making decisions that rely on the judgment of interviewers and managers.

Title VII: Section of the Civil Rights Act of 1964 dealing with discrimination in employment.

Title IX: Amendment to the Civil Rights Act of 1964 dealing with discrimination in educational programs.

United Nations Universal Declaration on Human Rights: Statement of principles developed by the United Nations that seeks to guarantee equal rights for men and women and racial and ethnic groups.

9

Sexual Harassment

In September 1990, "sports reporter Lisa Olson was going about business as usual. She was reporting on the New England Patriots football game against the Indianapolis Colts for her paper *The Boston Herald.* But on that day, business was anything but usual. While covering her 'beat,' which as with all sports reporters includes the locker room, five naked men approached her and began making lewd and threatening gestures to her. Olson tried to continue her interview, but finally, shaken and confused, she left the room. The ordeal only lasted a few minutes, but the aftermath will haunt her for quite some time."

—(Burley, 1990, p. 23)

"In lurid detail, [Anita Hill] described [then–U.S. Supreme Court nominee Clarence] Thomas as a boss who pestered her for dates and spoke graphically about pornography, bestiality, rape and his skills as a lover. 'He talked about pornographic materials depicting individuals with large penises or large breasts involved in various sex acts.' "

—("Anatomy of a Debacle," 1991, p. 26)

" 'All the nice girls love a sailor,' as the song goes. Not so the 26 women sailors and officers at the Tailhook convention [in September 1991], who found, on the third floor of the Las Vegas Hilton, a melee of drunken and groping naval aviators.

—("Sexual Harassment," 1992, p. 29)

"Just days after [Senator Robert Packwood, Republican, Oregon] won re-election in a closely fought race . . . Bob Packwood was accused of sexual harassment by a number of women who had worked for him. It seems the senator had a penchant for seizing young women and kissing them, after literally chasing them around the desk. It further seems that this had been going on unabated for years."

—(J. L. Symons, 1993, p. 56)

"As early as 1992 female employees at Mitsubishi . . . reported obscene, crude sketches of genital organs and sex acts, and names of female workers scratched into unpainted car bodies moving along the assembly line. Women were called sluts, whores and bitches and subjected to groping, forced sex play and male flashing. Explicit sexual graffiti such as 'Kill the Slut Mary' were scrawled on rest-area and bathroom walls."

—(Jaroff, 1996, p. 56)

"On May 8, 1991, . . . Paula Corbin [now Paula Jones] . . . , an eye-catching 24-year old with a clerical job at the Arkansas Industrial Development Commission, . . . [was told by one of then-Governor Bill Clinton's state troopers] that 'The governor said you make his knees knock'; The trooper later returned with the number of a suite in the hotel where Mr. Clinton wanted to meet her. In the Jones version of what followed, she naively allowed herself to be accompanied to the room where she found herself alone with Mr. Clinton. After some small talk . . . he put his hand on her leg and tried to kiss her, saying 'I love your curves.' Despite her rejections, she claims, Mr. Clinton exposed himself and asked for oral sex" ("Scandal," 1997, p. 21). A U.S. District court judge, however, ruled that Ms. Jones did not have a legal case of sexual harassment against Mr. Clinton because the alleged conduct was only brief and isolated.

—(Rankin & Cannon, 1998)

Lisa Olson and the New England Patriots, Clarence Thomas and Anita Hill, Tailhook, Packwood, Mitsubishi, President Clinton and Paula Jones. Although people had already begun to recognize **sexual harassment** as a serious workplace issue, these widely publicized events have had the effect of a national slap in the face, forcing us to focus our attention on this problem. Although people's opinions and theories regarding sexual harassment have been wide-ranging, they certainly have not been neutral. The sexual harassment controversy is fueled by the many interpretations afforded by various definitions of sexual harassment. What appears to be blatant harassment to one person is nothing more than innocent flirtation to another. What clearly represents male domination over women to some is simply old-fashioned courtesy for others. In this chapter we organize and present cross-disciplinary research on sexual harassment. We summarize different viewpoints about what constitutes sexual harassment, its prevalence, its cost to the individual and organization, possible explanations for its occurrence, and ways to combat and eliminate such behavior. Consistent with the overall model of studying sex and gender issues in the workplace presented in chapters 1 and 2, we discuss sexual harassment from individual, group, and organizational perspectives. We hope this chapter will contribute to reasoned dialogue and discussion.

EMERGING AWARENESS AND LABELING OF SEXUAL HARASSMENT

Before the phenomenon was named, presumably by the Working Women United Institute in 1976 (MacKinnon, 1979; cf. Farley, 1978), sexual harassment was just part of everyday life for working women. Such treatment was considered "business as usual." Mary Bulzarik (1978) recounted 19th-century female factory workers' daily fears: "There in the office I sat on a chair, the boss stood near me with my pay in his hand, speaking to me in a velvety, soft voice. Alas! Nobody around. I sat trembling with fear" (p. 32).

Lyn Farley's (1978) book, entitled *Sexual Shakedown: The Sexual Harassment of Women on the Job,* poignantly relabeled "business as usual" as "sexual harassment." On the heels of Farley's book, Catherine MacKinnon, a feminist legal scholar, offered a compelling argument that sexual harassment is a form of sexual discrimination, because it is much more likely to affect women than men. Within a year of publication of MacKinnon's book, the Equal Employment Opportunity Commission (EEOC) adopted guidelines consistent with MacKinnon's position: Targets of such behavior should receive legal protection from Title VII (Gutek, 1993). Furthermore, several important legal decisions have upheld the view that sexual harassment is discriminatory and illegal and that substantial penalties can be imposed on the perpetrators and employing organizations. Thus, sexual harassment has a long past but a short history. Within two decades, what was "business as usual" is now widely understood to be morally and legally reprehensible.

Despite this awareness, sexual harassment continues to be a serious threat to gender equality. Numerous surveys have been conducted to determine the prevalence of sexual harassment in the workplace and in educational settings. The following section summarizes current conceptualizations of sexual harassment and survey research addressing its prevalence.

Definition and Measurement

Whenever a social issue emerges as a public concern, much controversy and debate over its definition and boundaries ensue (Gillespie & Leffler, 1987). Sexual harassment has been no exception. In the early years of sexual harassment scholarship, the definitions used by researchers ranged from the occurrence of very specific events (e.g., actual or attempted rape or assault; United States Merit Systems Protection Board [USMSPB], 1981), to broad generalizations such as "unwanted sexual overtures" (see Gutek, 1985). Scholars, practitioners, and laypersons alike have expressed concern about the vagueness and ambiguity of these definitions. Arvey and Cavanaugh (1995) and Lengnick-Hall (1995) argued that ambiguous and inconsistent definitions contribute to poor theoretical development and imprecise measurement instruments. For example, how can research on the causes of sexual harassment progress without a precise, commonly accepted definition? Furthermore, how valid are the research instruments developed to study sexual-harassment-related phenomena, such as incident rates and psychological or organizational outcomes? Human resources officers and other practitioners in organizations charged with developing and enforcing sexual harassment policies are concerned with whether their policies cover enough ground or perhaps go too far in drawing the boundaries of acceptable behavior. Finally, the average person on the street wants to know what acts constitute sexual harassment; when is that line between sensible social–sexual interactions and sexual harassment crossed?

Unfortunately, a clear, unambiguous, unanimously agreed upon definition of sexual harassment does not exist nor is it likely that one will be developed. Because the heart of the matter is whether the recipient of potentially harassing behavior feels that she or he was treated in a sexually inappropriate manner in a work- or school-related context, sexual harassment definitions must allow for subjectivity. Fortunately, however, both legal theory and psychological theory have advanced considerably in the past two decades resulting in clearer (but not absolute) consensus on the definition of sexual harassment. As the following review demonstrates, today we are better able to address the concerns raised by scholars, practitioners, and laypersons.

Legal Definition of Sexual Harassment

The EEOC definition developed in 1980 has been adopted by courts, organizations, and universities and implicitly by most social scientists. According to the EEOC, sexual harassment is defined as follows:

> Unwelcome sexual advances, requests for sexual favors, and other verbal or physical conduct of a sexual nature constitute sexual harassment when (1) submission to such conduct is made either explicitly or implicitly a term or condition of an individual's employment, (2) submission to or rejection of such conduct by an individual is used as the basis for employment decisions affecting such individual, or (3) such conduct has the purpose or effect of substantially interfering with an individual's work performance or creating an intimidating, hostile, or offensive working environment. (EEOC, 1980, p. 33)

Conditions 1 and 2 of this definition are termed **quid pro quo** harassment, and Condition 3 is often termed "hostile work environment" harassment. This definition of sexual harassment is not limited to harassment of women by men but rather applies equally if harassment is carried out by women (e.g., women harassing men) or if it involves same-sex harassment. Regardless of the gender of the harasser or the target of harassment, behavior that fits the EEOC's definition constitutes sexual harassment, and it can substantially interfere with the recipient's ability to function in the workplace.

In this chapter, we focus on the harassment of women by male coworkers, supervisors, and even subordinates. Our reason for focusing on this type of harassment is simple; over 90% of the reported cases of sexual harassment in the workplace involve male harassers and female recipients. To be sure, there are instances in which women sexually harass men, in which women sexually harass other women, or in which men sexually harass other men, but these are all rare in comparison to the harassment of women by men.

Quid Pro Quo.   Conditions satisfying quid pro quo harassment are more clear-cut than those relating to hostile work environment harassment (Paetzold & O'Leary-Kelly, 1996). Examples include requiring an employee to provide sexual favors for a supervisor, such as sexual intercourse, in order to maintain employment, or firing an employee who refuses to provide sexual favors. Subtle forms of quid pro quo sexual harassment, such as hinting that an employee may be treated better on the job if she provides sexual favors to the boss, are also illegal. The requirements for meeting the legal definition of quid pro quo sexual harassment are that employment consequences are conditioned on sexual conduct, and that the offender is an employer or supervisor.

Hostile Work Environment.   This form of sexual harassment has been more difficult to define. For hostile work environment (HWE) sexual harassment to exist, a tangible employment benefit (such as keeping a job or gaining a promotion) does not have to be at stake. Examples of HWE include working in an area where sexual jokes, teasing, pornographic materials, and other "sexual stimuli" are part of the daily work environment. Repeatedly asking a person for a date or making unwanted telephone calls of a sexual nature to a coworker or employee are also forms of HWE sexual harassment, as are sexual touching, staring, grabbing, and kissing. Ramona Paetzold and Anne O'Leary-Kelly (1996) reviewed U.S. Federal Courts of Appeals cases of sexual harassment (which deal with issues of law, as opposed to fact) that were bracketed by the two U.S. Supreme Court cases that dealt with hostile environment cases (*Meritor Savings Bank, FSB v. Vinson,* 1986; *Harris v. Forklift Systems, Inc.,* 1993). These cases are particularly important because they shed light on the legal theory regarding hostile work environment harassment that has evolved in this time frame.

To establish a case of hostile environment sexual harassment, the plaintiff must show four things:

1. She or he was subjected to unwelcome harassment (the plaintiff must not have invited or enticed the conduct).
2. The allegedly harassing conduct occurred because of the plaintiff's sex (i.e., the behavior would not have reasonably been directed toward an opposite member of the plaintiff's sex).
3. The conduct was severe or pervasive (the plaintiff was adversely affected by the alleged harassment and can show that a "**reasonable**

person" (called the reasonable-person standard) would also be adversely affected by the same treatment).

4. The employer is held liable for the action (the employer either had actual knowledge of the harassment or should have been aware of the harassment due to its nature or changes in the plaintiff's behavior) (Paetzold & O'Leary-Kelly, 1996).

Of these elements, the plaintiff's ability to prove that the harassment was severe or pervasive and that the employer had actual knowledge of the mistreatment but failed to act adequately are strongly related to federal court decisions favoring the plaintiff (Terpstra & Baker, 1992).

As relatively straightforward as these elements appear, however, considerable debate has ensued over how some of these elements should be operationally defined. For example, in establishing the "unwelcomeness" element, some triers of fact (e.g., jurors and judges) have concluded that an alleged sexual harassment recipient who does not formally complain about the misconduct at the onset must not have minded the treatment (or, conversely, "welcomed" it). To wit, *U.S.A. Today* polls indicated that only 25% of Americans believed Anita Hill's testimony. The disbelief was centered on the fact that she did not officially report the behavior she complained about in her testimony. Yet, social science research has consistently shown that only a few targets of harassment and other sex-related crimes, including rape, report these incidents to institutional or legal authorities (Fitzgerald et al., 1988; Fitzgerald, Swan, & Fischer, 1995; Koss, 1990). Moreover, considerable (although not fully tested) theory exists to explain why targets are disinclined to actively report sexual harassment. A brief review of these theories is presented in Table 9.1.

The "severity" element also proves problematic. Plaintiffs are usually required to prove that they suffered job- or school-related, economic, physical, and/or psychological consequences as a result of the alleged harassment. Because many targets of harassment experience at least one if not many measurable adverse consequences (Gutek & Koss, 1993; Pryor, 1995), it is often possible to present concrete evidence of this sort. The case of Paula Jones versus Bill Clinton, however, was thrown out by a U.S. District Court judge because the plaintiff (Ms. Jones) conceded that alleged behavior was brief and isolated and did not result in a level of distress that a reasonable person would find unbearable.

There are substantial individual differences in how targets react to harassment. Some people are able to withstand a lot of abuse without physically or psychologically suffering, whereas others are much more vulnerable to these effects. Should a target's reactions to alleged harassment be the proof that harassment occurred (as opposed to the facts of the harassing behavior itself)? Fortunately, the U.S. Supreme Court, aided

TABLE 9.1

Explanations for Targets' Reluctance to Report Sexual Harassment

Fear of negative consequences	Active reporting may lead to direct or indirect retaliation against the victim or a worsening of psychological or work/school-related consequences. (Fitzgerald, Swan et al., 1995; Gutek & Koss, 1993; Stockdale, 1997)
"Just world" hypothesis	By denying that a bad thing has happened (e.g., sexual harassment), the target maintains the belief that the world is just and people get what they deserve. (Koss, 1990)
Escalation of commitment	Target initially interprets harasser's (typically more benign) behavior as friendly or professional and becomes committed to the workplace relationship. The target's acceptance signals the harasser to escalate his behavior. In turn, the target becomes confused about whether the harasser's intentions are professional or sexual and is thus trapped and unable to make a proactive complaint. (Williams & Cyr, 1992)
Gender differences in appraisal of coping effectiveness	Individuals differ in their opinions about what coping strategies will effectively deter the harassing treatment and restore a sense of safety. Although many men believe in active confrontation and assertive strategies, women perceive that ignoring, avoiding, or going along with the behavior will be more effective than active confrontation. (Fitzgerald, Swan et al., 1995)
Gender differences in dispute resolution preferences	Women are less likely than men to use formal dispute resolution systems, such as formal reporting channels for dealing with workplace dispute, due to either differential socialization experiences and/or dissatisfaction with prior experiences with formal dispute channels. (Lach & Gwartney-Gibbs, 1993; Riger, 1991)

by an amicus curiae brief from the American Psychological Association, opined in *Harris* that proof of psychological suffering is not necessary to establish a case of sexual harassment. Although it is not necessary to demonstrate physical or psychological suffering, the requirement that the plaintiff present concrete evidence that she has suffered harm ensures that the plaintiff's assertion of sexual harassment is not trivial or hypersensitive. This reasonable-person standard, however, has also been the center of considerable debate.

In their review of the social–psychological research bearing on this issue, Gutek and O'Connor (1995) stated that many courts have relied on the reasonable-person standard, asking whether a reasonable person would find the work environment hostile or abusive (e.g., *Rabidue v. Osceola Refining Co.,* 1986/1987; *Radtke v. Everett,* 1993). This standard helps determine whether the alleged sexual harassment had the "effect of substantially interfering with an individual's work performance or created an intimidating, hostile, or offensive working environment" (EEOC,

1980). The Ninth Circuit Court of Appeals in *Ellison v. Brady* (1991), however, modified this standard by asserting that sexual harassment can be defined as conduct that a "reasonable woman" would find severe or pervasive. The argument for the **reasonable-woman standard** is based on two assumptions:

- Women (who are typically the targets of sexual harassment) perceive and experience sexual conduct differently (more severely) than do men.
- When asked to evaluate alleged sexually harassing conduct from a reasonable-person perspective, decision makers, such as judges and juries, are more likely to adopt a normative male perspective than a female perspective.

One argument for the latter assumption is that most judges are men and may be less sensitive to viewing sexual harassment from a woman's perspective than from a man's perspective (*Ellison v. Brady,* 1991).

In arguing the merits of the reasonable-woman versus reasonable-person perspective, feminist scholars sit on both sides of the fence, with some desiring to eradicate the reasonableness standard altogether, whether "person," "woman," or "victim" (Paetzold & Shaw, 1994). Proponents of the reasonable-woman standard (or, more generally, the reasonable-victim standard) argue that women and men have consistently perceived and experienced social–sexual behavior differently (with women typically more sensitive than men to the aversive nature of these experiences), and that the reasonable-woman standard will help judges and jurors take the perspective of and be more sympathetic to the typical victims of sexual harassment (i.e., women). Backing their argument is a rather substantial body of research showing that women and men reliably differ in their perceptions of social–sexual behavior (see Frazier, Cochran, & Olson, 1995, for a thorough review). Skeptics of the reasonable-woman standard argue that highlighting the distinction between "reasonable person" and "reasonable woman" only reinforces gender stereotypes and strengthens the view that there are natural, unalterable differences between women and men (Gutek & O'Connor, 1995; Paetzold & Shaw, 1994). Gutek and O'Connor supported their position by carefully analyzing the existing research on gender differences in perceptions of sexual-harassment-related phenomena and noted that gender differences are typically very small, albeit significant. More potent factors include the severity of the act(s) and the power differential between the harasser and the target. Furthermore, gender differences are more likely to be found in studies that rely on short, ambiguous written scenarios than in studies that strive to provide more realistic, complex stimuli (see Sidelight 9.1). Thus, there does not appear to be consensus, even among feminist scholars, about which standard (if any) should be used to judge claims of sexual harassment.

To summarize, the legal definition of sexual harassment has been generally laid out by the EEOC (1980). This definition includes both quid pro quo and hostile work environment forms of sexual harassment. The courts have recognized both forms (e.g., *Meritor Savings Bank, FSB vs. Vinson,* 1986), but of these, hostile work environment forms of sexual harassment have been more difficult to define and are open to wider interpretation. Courts typically invoke several criteria for judging claims of hostile work environment sexual harassment, but the critical components, unwelcomeness and severity, contain subjective elements that remain enigmatic. The courts, as well as organizations and individuals striving to eradicate sexual harassment, need to look to social science research and theory to better understand the complexities underlying these issues (Wiener, 1995). Thus, we look next at the social science research that has addressed these definitional and measurement concerns.

Psychological Definition of Sexual Harassment

Fitzgerald argued that sexual harassment has both a legal and a psychological definition (Fitzgerald, Gelfand, & Drasgow, 1995). The legal definition, outlined previously, is used to determine whether a particular case of sexual harassment is worthy of being tried in a court of law. Many people, however, are subjected to treatment that may be considered sexual harassment but does not meet the legal definition. Nonetheless, their experiences may result in negative consequences such as lowered productivity, absenteeism, depression, and/or physical disturbances that merit concern of researchers and practitioners. Moreover, the existence of these events may be symptomatic of a wider set of processes that may lead to litigation or other serious consequences and thus may be worthy of an organization's attention (Fitzgerald, Gelfand, et al., 1995). In this section, we review the psychological definition of sexual harassment and the instruments that have been developed to measure it.

Although scholars began querying various groups of women (typically) about their experiences very early in the "discovery" of sexual harassment, more systematic attempts were made after publication of the EEOC's definition of sexual harassment. Various survey instruments were developed based implicitly on this definition. A common approach was to

Sidelight 9.1   Using Long Scenarios and Videotapes to More Accurately Assess Perceptions of Sexual Harassment

"Jane is walking slowly down the hall at work. Mr. Davidson, Jane's boss, walks up from behind. As Mr. Davidson passes Jane, he pats her on the fanny and says, 'Hurry up, you'll never get everything done today' " (from Gutek et al., 1983, p. 35). Is this sexual harassment? Many studies have used short, fairly context-void scenarios such as this one to determine how people view sexual harassment. However, if you are a human resources officer, a coworker, or a member of a jury, you would not likely learn about the purported facts of a sexual harassment in such a limited and omniscient manner. It is more likely that you would have much more information about the context in which the alleged harassment occurred and the nature of the relationship between the two (or more) parties, and you would have several versions of the story (e.g., "he said, she said"). How valid, then, is our knowledge about factors affecting perceptions of sexual harassment that comes from the studies which use these short, unnaturalistic scenarios? Barbara Gutek and her colleagues (Gutek, O'Connor, Melancon, & Greer, 1998) recently studied perceptions of sexual harassment using a much more complex and detailed scenario of an alleged sexual harassment incident. The scenario was created both as a written account (1½ pages, typed, single-spaced) and as a 1½-hour videotape of a court trial based on the facts of the case. The scenario was based on a real harassment case tried in a West Coast court. The scenario (both the written and videotape forms) provided extensive details about the organization in which the harassment occurred and provided the target's (plaintiff's) version of the story as well as the defendant's view. Groups of both college students and adults (people waiting to serve jury duty and participants in a supervisory training program on sexual harassment) viewed the written or videotape versions and completed questionnaires about their perceptions of case. The findings suggest that many of the factors thought to be important in influencing perceptions of sexual harassment, such as the research participant's gender, the status of the defendant (supervisor or coworker), and the manner in which the target responds to the harassment (does nothing, goes along with the behavior, or reports the behavior immediately), have only very small effects on perceptions of the case. Therefore, researchers may not have captured or identified all the important factors associated with this problem. This may explain why many people are still confused about what is sexual harassment and why there is still considerable uncertainty in the outcome of sexual harassment cases.

generate a list of possible quid pro quo and hostile-environment situations and ask respondents to indicate whether they had experienced them within a certain time frame and context (e.g., on the job in the last 2 years; Fitzgerald et al., 1988; Gutek, 1985; Working Women's Institute, 1975). Sometimes these items are grouped in categories (e.g., job consequences related to expected sexual activity). Unfortunately, it becomes difficult to determine the prevalence of different forms of sexual harassment when a given behavior can be classified in more than one category. For this reason, some researchers have attempted to evaluate definitions of sexual harassment systematically and devise categorization schemes that are both exhaustive and mutually exclusive. The efforts of Fitzgerald et al. (1988) and Gruber (1992), summarized as follows, are noteworthy.

Based on earlier work by Till (1980), Fitzgerald et al. (1988) developed a comprehensive survey to measure five forms of sexual harassment:

1. Gender harassment: generalized sexist remarks and behavior
2. Seductive behavior: inappropriate and offensive but essentially sanction-free sexual advances
3. Sexual bribery: solicitation of sexual activity or other sex-linked behavior by promise of rewards
4. Sexual coercion: coercion of sexual activity by threat of punishment
5. Sexual assault: gross imposition or assault (Fitzgerald et al., 1988, p. 157)

On the basis of statistical evidence, Fitzgerald, Gelfand, et al. (1995), classified Category 1 as **gender harassment** and Categories 2 and 5 as **unwanted sexual attention,** both of which are aspects of a hostile work environment. Categories 3 and 4 were combined and labeled **sexual coercion** or quid pro quo. Thus, this system provides specific definitions for the forms of sexual harassment covered in the EEOC definition.

The Sexual Experiences Questionnaire (SEQ; Fitzgerald et al., 1988; now revised as the SEQ–W [employee form] or SEQ–E [student form]; Gelfand, Fitzgerald, & Drasgow, 1995) contains behavioral items corresponding to these three forms of harassment. Because individuals' definitions of and thresholds for labeling an event as sexual harassment vary (Fitzgerald et al., 1988; Stockdale & Vaux, 1993), the SEQ does not require respondents to indicate whether they experienced "sexual harassment" per se. Instead they indicate whether they experienced a given event (e.g., "Have you ever been in a situation where a coworker directly offered you some sort of reward for being sexually cooperative?"). Because the SEQ is based on a sound conceptualization of sexual harassment and because it eliminates a serious response bias associated with the emotionally laden term *sexual harassment,* the SEQ is one of the best sexual harassment survey instruments available.

Gruber (1992) created a sexual harassment taxonomy based on a content analysis of 17 published surveys of sexual harassment. Noting that researchers used different terms to mean the same behavior (e.g., expected sexual activity, verbal negotiations, sexual bribery) and that many researchers omitted important forms of sexual harassment (e.g., sexual bribery), Gruber included in the taxonomy 11 forms divided into three broad categories of harassment: verbal requests (goal-oriented statements, including threats, intended to establish sexual or relational intimacy); verbal remarks and comments (personally demeaning statements, questions, or remarks about women); and nonverbal displays (nonverbal ways of sexually harassing women, ranging from pornographic pictures to sexual assault). Although Gruber's taxonomy has not been subjected to empirical testing and validating, the thoroughness of the content-analysis strategy suggests that important contributions will evolve from this work.

Prevalence of Sexual Harassment

A number of scientifically sound studies based on different populations within the United States have been conducted to determine how widespread is sexual harassment in the workplace and in academic settings. In a **stratified random sample** of 23,964 federal workers, the U.S. Merit Systems Protection Board (USMSPB, 1981) estimated that 42% of the female respondents and 15% of the male respondents had experienced some form of sexual harassment within a 2-year period. Surveyors asked respondents if they had experienced one or more of the following events in the last 2 years on the job: unwelcome sexual remarks, deliberate touching, pressure for dates, pressure for sexual cooperation, unwelcome letters and telephone calls, and actual or attempted sexual assault/rape. Although women reported experiencing all of the surveyed forms of sexual harassment more than men, both groups reported higher rates of less serious forms of sexual harassment, such as unwelcome sexual remarks, than more serious forms of sexual harassment, such as assault. A follow-up study conducted in 1987 yielded very similar prevalence rates (USMSPB, 1988) as did a more recent follow-up study in 1994 (USMSPB, 1995). Table 9.2 presents the prevalence rates of seven major forms of sexual harassment from five large-scale studies.

Gutek (1985) conducted a random telephone survey of working adults in Los Angeles county. Her methodology employed a hybrid of the **behavioral-experiences approach** and the **direct-query approach.** She asked respondents to indicate whether they had experienced any of several forms of social–sexual behavior during their working lives, and then she asked

TABLE 9.2

Estimates of the Prevalence (Percentage of Sample) of Several Forms
of Sexual Harassment Across Several Large-Scale Studies

Form of harassment	Federal gov. 1987[a] (N = 8,523)	Federal gov. 1994[b] (N = 8,052)	U.S. military 1988[c] (N = 22,800)	U.S. Navy 1989[d] (N = 6,042)	Midwestern university 1994[e] (N = 1,147)
Rape/sexual assault					
Female	0.8	4.0	5.0	6.0	6.0
Male	0.3	2.0	1.0	0.4	3.0
Request for sexual favors					
Female	9.0	7.0	15.0	14.0	2.0
Male	3.0	2.0	2.0	1.0	2.0
Deliberate touching					
Female	26.0	24.0	38.0	29.0	27.0
Male	8.0	8.0	9.0	3.0	18.0
Letters and calls					
Female	12.0	10.0	14.0	17.0	19.0
Male	4.0	4.0	3.0	1.0	15.0
Pressure for dates					
Female	15.0	13.0	26.0	27.0	14.0
Male	4.0	4.0	3.0	2.0	9.0
Suggestive looks, gestures					
Female	28.0	29.0	44.0	37.0	38.0
Male	9.0	9.0	10.0	2.0	24.0
Sexual remarks					
Female	35.0	37.0	52.0	39.0	41.0
Male	12.0	14.0	13.0	3.0	37.0

[a]USMSPB (1988). [b]USMSPB (1995). [c]Martindale (1991). Note: Three additional forms of sexual harassment were measured on this survey, but not reported in this table: whistles and calls, attempts to get participation, and other attention. [d]Culbertson et al. (1992). Note: Only data from enlisted officers are reported. The category whistles and calls is not reported in this table. [e]Cashin et al. (1993).

them the degree to which they considered each form to be sexual harassment. She reported that 53% of the female respondents indicated experiencing at least one form of sexual harassment during their working lives.

One other set of sexual harassment surveys that merits discussion was conducted by Gruber and his colleagues (Gruber, Smith, & Kauppinen-Toropainen, 1996). Although random sampling procedures were not employed, these surveys compared incidents of sexual harassment under Gruber's (1992) taxonomy in samples of U.S., Canadian, and European (former Soviets) working women. Consistent with patterns of results found in surveys of U.S. federal and private-sector workers, the incident rates of "less severe" forms of sexual harassment such as sexual jokes, teasing, and categorical remarks about women were high in all samples, ranging

Sidelight 9.2   Does Asking "Have You Been Sexually Harassed" Affect Prevalence Rates?

Many people who indicate on surveys that they have experienced at least one form of "unwanted sexual attention or advance" in the workplace or in an academic setting do not claim to have been sexually harassed (Stockdale & Vaux, 1993). There appears to be a threshold that differs across individuals concerning the severity or pervasiveness of unwanted sexual attention one will experience before claiming to have been sexually harassed. Therefore, if a survey measures the prevalence of sexual harassment on the basis of the question, "Have you been sexually harassed?" it is likely to underestimate the amount of potentially sexually harassing behavior that exists in the workplace (or in academia). Researchers at the Navy Personnel Research and Development Center (Newell, Rosenfeld, & Culbertson, 1995) wanted to know how the type of question affected sexual harassment prevalence rates.

Using two different approaches, the researchers examined the prevalence of sexual harassment in a **stratified random sample** of 12,000 active-duty members of the U.S. Navy. In the first approach, the EEOC definition of sexual harassment was provided and respondents were directly asked if they had been sexually harassed on or off duty on a base or ship in the year preceding the survey. This method of eliciting responses is termed the **direct-query** approach. Prevalence was measured by counting the number of people who agreed with the statement, "I have been sexually harassed." In the second version, respondents were not directly asked if they had been sexually harassed. Instead, they were asked if they had experienced any of eight specific types of events in the year preceding the survey (unwanted sexual teasing, sexual looks, or sexual whistles, etc.; deliberate touching; pressure for dates; letters and phone calls; pressure for sexual favors; or attempted rape/assault). This method is termed the **behavioral-experiences** approach. Prevalence is determined by counting the number of people who report sexual harassment experiences.

Culbertson et al. (1993) found that prevalence estimates between the two forms varied considerably. The rates of harassment calculated from the direct-query approach were 44% of females enlisted and 33% of female officers. Eight percent of males enlisted and 2% of male officers indicated being sexually harassed. Comparatively, prevalence estimates calculated from the behavioral-experiences approach were 74% and 60% of females enlisted and female officers, respectively, and 21% and 7% of males enlisted and male officers, respectively. On average, the behavioral-experiences approach yielded prevalence estimates that were 55% higher than the direct-query approach. These data clearly show that estimates of prevalence are affected by the survey methodology employed.

from 24% (former Soviets) to 75% (U.S. workers). Furthermore, rates of severe forms of harassment such as sexual bribery and sexual assault were relatively low (e.g., bribery ranged from 5% for former Soviets to 16% for U.S. workers). Moreover, the rank order of 10 forms of sexual harassment in terms of prevalence was very similar across all three samples, suggesting that patterns of sexual harassment are universal (at least among these international comparisons).

Thus, the experience of sexual harassment is widespread, especially for women. The pervasiveness of sexual harassment is similar across several different cultures, across several different subpopulations within the U.S. culture, and across 2 decades of research on this topic. What is the cost of this widespread workplace stressor?

MULTIFACETED IMPACT OF SEXUAL HARASSMENT

How harmful is one tasteless joke or an occasional "hey, babe?" Furthermore, doesn't a little sexual tension in the office make work more interesting? It is no easy task to determine the costs of sexual harassment, let alone convince others of these costs.

In government-level studies, costs have been assessed in terms of turnover, absenteeism, individual and group productivity loss, and estimates of insurance benefits to cover emotional and physical distress (USM-SPB 1981, 1988, 1995). Although these cost projections involved much speculation, they were based on relatively straightforward assumptions about damages to individuals who identified themselves through survey responses as targets of sexual harassment. Parameters not yet considered include the implications of sexual harassment for workplace morale or climate and its effects on the attitudes and behaviors of individuals who observe others being sexually harassed. Attaching dollar values to these and other outcomes will prove difficult.

In addition to the difficulty of understanding and adequately measuring the range of potential outcomes, sexual harassment (like other forms of sexual violence) is peculiar because the harm induced by a particular type of harassment varies across targets (i.e., targets are differentially sensitive to different forms of sexual harassment). "Unrecognized harm" (Vaux, 1993) represents a related but distinct issue. Less sensitive targets may not understand that their tolerance can perpetuate sexual harassment. Interestingly, individuals who experience noxious treatment vary greatly in their tendencies to label the experience as sexual harassment (Stockdale & Vaux, 1993). The likelihood of labeling one's own experience as sexual harassment appears to be no greater for more severe incidents, such as sexual imposition, than for conceptually milder forms of treatment, such as sexual seduction. Respondents' feelings of distress and emotional disturbance associated with the experience, regardless of what type it was, have been related to acknowledgement that the treatment was sexually harassing (Stockdale, Vaux, & Cashin, 1995). Thus, these studies underscore the importance of listening to the target's opinion about the severity of her or his experiences before forming judgments about what types of harassment are or are not harmful. Keeping these issues in mind, we now review available information on the impacts of sexual harassment on both individuals and organizations.

Individual Costs

Koss (1990) reviewed survey-based as well as anecdotal and clinical data to examine effects of sexual harassment on targets. Among the behavioral outcomes of harassment, Koss reported that a substantial number of acknowledged targets reported adverse employment effects such as poor working conditions, diminished opportunities for advancement, and job changes. Losing one's job or quitting out of frustration were also reported. Furthermore, decreased morale, absenteeism, job dissatisfaction (Culbertson, Rosenfeld, Booth-Kewley, & Magnusson, 1992; Gruber & Bjorn, 1982, 1986), and loss of concentration have also been reported (Gutek & Koss, 1993; Koss, 1990).

Mental and physical health effects are common. Emotions range from "anger, fear, depression, anxiety, irritability, loss of self-esteem, feelings of humiliation and alienation, and a sense of helplessness and vulnerability" (Koss, 1990, p. 78; see also Loy & Stewart, 1984). Deteriorated interpersonal relationships have also been reported (e.g., Bandy, 1989). Physical symptoms include gastrointestinal attacks, stress-induced jaw tightness and teeth grinding, sleep and eating disorders, nausea, and crying spells (e.g., Crull, 1982; Loy & Stewart, 1984). Preliminary but impressive data link sexual harassment to post-traumatic stress disorder (PTSD) and depression. PTSD involves exposure to an extreme stressor, reexperience of the trauma, avoidance of situations that resemble the traumatic event, and heightened arousal. Gutek and Koss (1993) reported a preliminary study by Kilpatrick (1992) in which a nationally representative sample of employed women were surveyed regarding PTSD, depression, and harassment experiences. Women suffering from PTSD and depression were significantly more likely to have reported sexual harassment experiences than were women in general. This was true across the full range of harassment experiences (from mild to severe).

Most of the studies reviewed by Koss (1990) were based on small samples of select (i.e., not randomly selected) women. Often these studies do not rely on theoretically and psychometrically sound indices of physical, attitudinal, and/or emotional states. It is telling that no matter what sample of women are surveyed, a wide range of aversive consequences are always found. Nonetheless, more weight should be given to rigorous research that uses sound sampling techniques and instrumentation. Fortunately, research of this nature has recently been conducted.

The U.S. government's surveys of U.S. federal government employees (USMSPB, 1981, 1988, 1995) and the U.S. military (Martindale, 1991) are among the most comprehensive surveys of sexual harassment to date. Both sets of surveys used sophisticated, comprehensive survey techniques. Sample sizes ranged from 8,000 to almost 24,000, and all received high return rates (e.g., 66%). Although each survey measured various work- and health- (both physical and emotional) related outcomes, the validity of these measures was not reported. Nonetheless, these findings provide very useful information about the range of outcomes experienced by targets of sexual harassment.

Most people who indicated that they had had at least one sexually harassing experience (regardless of whether they labeled it as so) reported no change in their working conditions (United States Merit System Protection Board, 1981, 1986, 1995). The working conditions of roughly 10% of both male and female targets worsened, however, with 7% of female targets and 5% of male targets being denied a promotion or other positive resource action. Feelings regarding work worsened for 36% of female targets and 19% of male targets as did emotional and/or physical conditions for 33% of female targets and 21% of male targets. Percentages of targets experiencing these outcomes were not reported in the USMSPB 1988 and 1995 reports, although the data were collected.

The military study (Martindale, 1991) was modeled very closely after the federal government surveys (e.g., USMSPB, 1981). Pryor (1995) analyzed the responses of over 20,000 individuals to determine the psychological impact of sexual harassment on women in the military and found that sexual harassment affected four areas:

1. Forty-two percent of the female targets experienced productivity problems (quantity and quality of work, attitudes, and feelings of control about work).
2. Sixty percent experienced negative attitudes about the military (e.g., feelings about the military in general and about her unit and supervisors).
3. Fifty-eight percent experienced emotional distress (e.g., loss of self-esteem, more negative opinions about others, diminished emotional and physical condition.)

4. Eight percent experienced family problems (e.g., relations with spouse and other family problems).

Although the U.S. government has conducted the most comprehensive surveys of sexual harassment and its effects, scientifically sound studies have been carried out in the private sector (Schneider, Swan, & Fitzgerald, 1997). Schneider et al. found that 68% of the women surveyed reported at least one sexually harassing incident. Harassed women reported significantly lower job satisfaction, lower intrinsic commitment to the organization, and greater work and job withdrawal compared to nonharassed women. In all comparisons, harassed women were worse off than nonharassed women. Both life satisfaction and general mental health were negatively affected by harassment experiences. Finally, women experiencing any form of sexual harassment were more likely to report symptoms of PTSD than women who had not been harassed.

Organizational Costs

The USMSPB studies (1981, 1988, 1995) also attempted to estimate the financial costs of sexual harassment to the federal government. These costs were measured in terms of absenteeism, medical costs, turnover, and productivity loss. The USMSPB (1981) estimated that sexual harassment cost the federal government from $200 million to $327 million 1981 dollars over each 2-year period covered in the three studies. Researchers analyzing the U.S. military survey (Martindale, 1991) examined specific costs associated with hiring, transfers, training, and so forth, for each job represented in the survey (Faley, Knapp, Kustis, & Dubois, 1994). They calculated the total cost of sexual harassment to be close to $500 million (1993 dollars). Hanisch (1996) noted, however, that neither the USMSPB surveys nor the Faley et al. study provided sufficient information to evaluate the accuracy of their cost estimates. Nonetheless, it is reasonable to conclude that the organizational price tag for sexual harassment is very high.

Because a disproportionate number of women in traditionally male occupations are harassed (Gruber & Bjorn, 1982; Gutek, 1985; Gutek et al., 1990), another indirect organizational cost (as well as a personal cost) is the loss of talented, productive women in these occupations. The cost of losing a substantial number of talented individuals because of sexual harassment could be staggering. This is particularly salient at a time when organizations are concerned about the changing demographics of the workplace, when White women and minorities are projected to represent the majority of new workforce entrants (Bolick & Nestleroth, 1988; Johnston & Packer, 1987).

Sidelight 9.3   Does Harassment Have Different Implications for Women Than for Men?

Men often claim that they would not be offended by, would enjoy, or would even be complimented by sexual attention from their female coworkers. Furthermore, the same behaviors are sometimes interpreted differently when coming from men than when coming from women. Women who are the targets of suggestive looks from male coworkers often report feeling offended and harassed, whereas men who are the targets of suggestive looks from female coworkers might feel aroused or complimented. Is it reasonable for the same behaviors to be interpreted as harassment when directed toward women but as acceptable when directed toward men?

Earlier, we discussed differences between the reasonable-person standard and the reasonable-woman standard, and this distinction may help explain why the same behaviors can have different implications when directed toward men versus women. Sexual harassment represents an inappropriate and unwelcome sexualization of the workplace. In chapter 4, we noted that sexual interactions in the workplace are common and often welcome. One important issue, therefore, is to understand the conditions under which sexual behaviors in the workplace are likely to be welcome.

In chapter 3, we noted that men are more likely than women to interpret friendly behavior from the opposite sex in romantic terms and to welcome sexual attention of this sort. On the whole, men are more likely to welcome unsolicited sexual attention than women. However, male–female differences in acceptance of sexual attention are only part of the story. A much more important issue is likely to be the different implications of harassment for men and for women. Women who are the targets of sexual harassment are put in a situation in which others exercise power and control (i.e., by engaging in unwanted behaviors that are detrimental to the recipient) and which reinforces the stereotype that women should be considered as sexual objects rather than as people in the workplace. Men have not traditionally been in positions of diminished power and control, and they are very unlikely to feel that their primary purpose in the workplace is to provide sexual outlets for their female colleagues (think of all the jokes and cartoons about the boss' attractive, well-endowed secretary). For women, sexual harassment tends to maintain and reinforce their subservient position in the workplace, but men are less likely to feel that their position or status is threatened or demeaned as a result of sexual attention from their coworkers.

The impetus to change the workplace may be facilitated by legal precedent and decisions, but specific guidelines for change should be informed by theory and research driven by theories or models of sexual harassment. The following section examines various explanations of sexual harassment.

BAD APPLES OR BAD BARRELS?
THEORIES AND MODELS
OF SEXUAL HARASSMENT

Are sexual harassers "dirty old men" for whom the workplace is a convenient setting in which to express their various perversions (bad apples)? Is sexual harassment of women a manifestation of power inequalities condoned and perpetuated by a patriarchical society (bad barrels)? What organizational, situational, or individual characteristics influence harassment behavior? This section reviews current theories of sexual harassment.

Biology or Sociology? Macro Theories
of Sexual Harassment

Tangri, Burt, and Johnson (1982) described three broad theories of sexual harassment: the biological model, the organizational model, and the sociocultural model. They also tested some general hypotheses derived from each model using data from the 1981 USMSPB survey of federal workers. These models are similar to the general approaches presented in chapter 1 designed to explain similarities and differences between women and men.

According to Tangri et al. (1982), the **biological model** posits that sexual harassment is a manifestation of biologically based human courtship patterns. This model suggests that sexual harassment victims are likely to be women who are attractive sexual targets for men (i.e., similar in age and race, not married). Furthermore, harassment behaviors should resemble normal courtship behaviors that targets would not find offensive or harmful. These assumptions were not supported in Tangri et al.'s (1982) analyses. Neither the characteristics of harassers, their actions, nor the victims' responses were consistent with the biological model's predictions. Specifically, harassers tended to be older, married men rather than younger, mate-seeking men. They tended to harass more than one person, as opposed to seeking one-on-one relationships; and victims tended to have negative reactions to the men's behaviors, as opposed to being flattered. The biological model has since been dismissed as a viable explanation of sexual harassment (cf. Studd & Gattiker, 1991).

The **organizational model** posits that institutions provide opportunities to use power and dominance to obtain sexual gratification. That is, sexual harassment occurs because existing organizational features such as power hierarchies, skewed gender ratios in work groups (Kanter, 1977b), and gendered organizational norms (e.g., waitresses, receptionists, and women in other female-dominated occupations are viewed as sex objects within their organizations) provide a structure that facilitates sexual harassment. Tangri et al. hypothesized that if this model is viable, victims should tend to occupy low-power positions (e.g., temporary or part-time workers, those in low grade levels, newcomers, and tokens). In U.S. organizations, these "vulnerable" people are more likely to be women than men. Furthermore, because of their powerlessness, victims should feel unable to respond assertively. These predictions were partially supported in Tangri et al.'s (1982) analyses. Women trainees experienced more sexual harassment than women in other job categories. Women were also likely to find the harassing events more offensive than flattering and felt that it would be futile to respond assertively.

The sociocultural model posits that a **patriarchal society** establishes gender norms of male dominance and female subservience. Men, therefore, are socialized to be aggressive, whereas women are socialized to be acquiescent. Sexual harassment is a means for men to express dominance. This model predicts that women, regardless of organizational status, are more likely to be victims than men. Women in positions where their "femaleness" is a salient feature, such as the only woman in an all-male work group, or women who work in a traditionally female occupation, should be even more likely to experience sexual harassment. Again, these predictions were partially supported in Tangri et al.'s (1982) analyses of the USMSPB data. Women were four times more likely to experience sexual harassment than men, and only women who occupied the highest job grades were partially shielded from being sexually harassed.

Personality, Motives, and Situations: Micro Theories of Sexual Harassment

Sandra Tangri and her colleagues (Tangri et al., 1982) explored three very broad theories of sexual harassment, and found that no single approach adequately explained why sexual harassment occurs. In recent years, the focus has shifted from trying to understand sexual harassment from a broad perspective, such as sociocultural or organizational power, to more subtle, personality-based explanations. John Pryor, a prominent social psychologist, found that sexual harassment may be a function of both personality and situational factors. His theory is labeled the *person X situation* model. Specifically, he found that men who have very negative

Sidelight 9.4   If Women Gain as Much
                 Power as Men (or More)
                 in the Workplace, Will They
                 Be as Likely to Sexually
                 Harass as Men Currently Are?

In the popular novel (and movie) *Disclosure,* Michael Crighton dramatizes
the possibility that when women gain power in organizations, they will
be as likely as men to use sexual harassment as a tool of dominance. Is
this likely? Although only time can tell, research conducted in the past
decade casts doubt on this hypothesis. In one study, researchers analyzed
data from the U.S. federal government's national survey of its employees
(USMSPB, 1981) and found that factors related to an individual's power
(or powerlessness) in the organization, such as occupational status and
type of occupation, were not as important in predicting who would be
sexually harassed than more general characteristics such as age and marital
status (Fain & Anderson, 1987). Young, unmarried women were more
likely to be sexually harassed than others regardless of how powerful
they were in the organization. In another study of sexual harassment in
Israel, researchers believed that women who lived and worked in egalitarian sections of Israeli society (i.e., the *Kibbutzim*) would be less likely
to be sexually harassed than women who lived and worked in more
traditional, nonegalitarian areas (Barak, Pitterman, & Yitzhaki, 1995).
Contrary to researchers' expectations, however, Kibbutzim women were
as likely to experience sexual harassment as traditional women. Although
these two studies do not directly address the question of whether women
will be more likely to sexually harass if they gain organizational power,
they do show that organizational power does not seem to be a very
important explanation for sexual harassment.

attitudes toward women and have a high **need for power** are more likely
to sexually harass women than are other men (Pryor, 1987). He created
a survey that measures men's **likelihood to sexually harass** (LSH). Scores
on the LSH measure are correlated with the type of **misogynistic** attitudes
and personality previously described. Pryor theorized that men who score
high on the LSH measure (and thus have a high propensity to sexually
harass) tend to look for situations where they can "disguise" their motives
to get away with sexual harassment. For example, if a situation arises
where touching a woman is appropriate (e.g., in teaching her how to hold
a golf club), these men tend to touch her in more sexual ways than do
other men in the same situation. Or, if these men observe other men

engaging in potentially harassing behavior, they are more likely than others to "model" that behavior (Pryor, LaVite, & Stoller, 1993).

Building on Pryor's work, Bargh and his colleagues (Bargh & Raymond, 1995; Bargh, Raymond, Pryor, & Strack, 1995) developed a theory that links power and sex-related motives. Using Pryor's (1987) LSH measure, Bargh and his colleagues found that men who are more likely to sexually harass automatically (i.e., subconsciously) associate sex and power cues. As Bargh and Raymond (1995) noted, "When [these men] are in a situation in which they have power over a woman, the concept or motive of sex will become active automatically" (p. 87). This may explain why some men do not think that their behavior toward women is sexually harassing even when women tell them that it is.

Sex-role spillover theory (Gutek, 1985; Gutek & Morasch, 1982) is based on the supposition that gender norms are so well established, stable, and salient that they "spill over" into the work role, and therefore people respond to women in their **sex role** (or gender role) instead of their **work role**. In chapter 7, we noted that sex-role spillover could lead to gender discrimination in the workplace. It can also lead to inappropriate sexualiza tion of the workplace. Because the female gender role still includes a sex-object component (as discussed in chapter 3 on stereotypes; Williams & Best, 1982), men can be expected to sometimes treat women in the workplace as sexual objects rather than as coworkers.

Sex-role spillover is more likely to occur when ratios of women to men in occupations and jobs are skewed (Gutek & Morasch, 1982). An individual's gender becomes a more salient attribute when one is in a **token** position that strengthens traditional sex-role expectations (Kanter, 1977a). According to this approach, women in male-dominated occupations and work groups should experience more sexual attention than women in gender-balanced occupations and work groups. Women in traditionally feminine occupations but who work primarily with men (e.g., secretaries, nurses, receptionists) should also experience sex-role spillover. In these cases, the occupations themselves are the targets of spillover because the work role becomes entwined with female sex-role expectations. Gutek and her colleagues suggest that such women also experience more sexual attention than women in gender-balanced occupations and work groups.

The sex-role spillover theory was tested in a survey of women who worked outside the home (Gutek & Morasch, 1982). Gutek and Morasch found that women in nontraditional jobs (i.e., male-dominated occupations or jobs) were more likely to receive both complimentary and insulting sexual comments, gestures, looks, touches, and requests for dating and sex than women in gender-integrated occupations (i.e., where the ratio of women to men in the job or occupation is roughly 50:50). Sexual behavior was personally directed at these women, and they experienced more negative consequences (e.g., were forced to quit their jobs) than the rest of the sample. Comparatively, women in traditionally female occupations (i.e., female-dominated occupations or jobs) experienced both complimentary and insulting sexual attention more than did women in gender-integrated occupations. Women in these occupations were more likely than others to report that physical attractiveness was important both in getting hired and in how they were treated on the job. They believed that women in their occupations were expected to dress in a sexually attractive manner and that sexual comments and jokes were common. Give these findings, one conclusion is that sexuality becomes a part of the informal atmosphere in traditionally female occupations (Gutek & Morasch, 1982).

A relatively straightforward alternative explanation for women's sexual harassment experiences in gender-skewed occupations such as factory jobs or upper level management is the notion that increased contact with men leads to greater likelihood of being sexually harassed. This has been termed the "contact hypothesis" (Gutek et al., 1990). It is commonly observed that men sexualize their environments more than women. Compared to women, men are more likely to tell sexually based jokes, hang pin-ups, comment about sexual exploits, and pursue sexual stimuli (Gutek et al., 1990). Some research evidence supports both the contact hypothesis and the sex-role spillover model (Gutek et al., 1990). Women who had more contact with men were more likely than others to perceive that their work environment was sexualized, which in turn led to reports of sexual behavior, both harassing and nonharassing. Men's reports of sexualized work environments, however, did not change as a function of their level of contact with women.

Whether strong societal gender roles spill over into the workplace may depend on other factors. For example, Ragins and Scandura (1992) found that women in nontraditional occupations where the gender composition of work groups was highly skewed were not more likely to report sexual harassment than women in integrated or traditionally female occupations. However, among the nontraditional women in their sample, those in blue-collar occupations were more likely to report harassment than women in all other classifications. The researchers stated that the mere ratio of men to women in a job setting is not sufficient to explain sex-role spillover. Another factor, **occupational culture,** may be necessary to explain sex-role spillover and sexual-harassment experiences. In occupational cultures where masculine, "physical" attributes are valued, the perception that women are sex objects prevails. This physical culture, which values toughness, sends a message to women that sexual harassment is a part of the job that they must prove they can handle. The effects that physical, "macho" cultures found in blue-collar jobs have on sexual harassment experiences have been documented by others who have studied blue-collar occupations (Gruber & Bjorn, 1982; Yount, 1991; see also the description of harassment at Mitsubishi at the beginning of this chapter).

Theoretical Summary

Three broad explanations for sexual harassment, the biological, organizational, and sociocultural models, have been debated by scholars for over a decade. These models, however, have been supplemented by more specific explanations. Although more theoretical precision and research are needed, it is becoming clear that both personality and situational factors are important in understanding sexual harassment. Some men (certainly not all) have personalities and attitudes that dispose them to view women in negative, hostile ways. When these men are in work environments that tolerate, condone, or facilitate sexual harassment or are in other ways sexualized, these men will likely act on their harassing impulses. Moreover, it appears that these men are not aware that they are acting hostilely toward women because they believe they are acting on benevolent sexual impulses. As discussed next, identifying such men and the sexualized environments they work in and retraining them to think and behave more appropriately are among the strategies an organization can take to deal with sexual harassment.

COMBATING SEXUAL HARASSMENT

Throughout this book we emphasize that equitable treatment of women and men in the workplace is necessary to ensure that all organizational members have equal access to the full benefits of employment and thereby to promote healthy, functional, competitive organizations. Organizations have no choice about whether to deal with sexual harassment. Sexual harassment is illegal under two federal statutes (Title VII of the Civil Rights Act of 1963 [and now under the Civil Rights Act of 1991] and Title IX of the Education Amendments of 1972), and courts have found organizations liable for actions of their employees or representatives (*Burlington Industries, Inc., v. Ellerth,* 1998; & *Faragher v. Boca Raton,* 1998). Organizations that have failed to vigorously combat sexual harassment are likely to be held accountable by the courts (Terpstra & Baker, 1992).

In this chapter, we document the insidious, discriminatory, and costly effects of sexual harassment on individuals and organizations, and we summarize existing explanations for sexual harassment. Certainly, more research is needed to obtain complete information about these experiences. We do have sufficient information based on both research and legal precedent, however, to offer some general advice for combating sexual harassment. The last section briefly outlines these strategies.

Societal and Legislative Strategies

To the extent that sexual harassment is a means of social control, like other forms of sexual violence (Fitzgerald, 1993), women are targeted because they are accorded less power and lower status in our society (Cleveland & Kerst, 1993; Farley, 1978; Grauerholz, 1989). Thus, efforts to combat sexual harassment should include strategies to empower women. Electing and appointing women to high public, governmental, and judicial offices; removing barriers to executive positions in organizations; eliminating gender-biased education; and increasing multicultural awareness and values represent empowerment strategies that may not only reduce sexual harassment but also improve the quality of women's lives in general.

In addition to these broad-based approaches, the actions and attitudes of the legal and legislative systems toward sexual harassment strongly influence women's empowerment. Already we have seen that social-science research has been used (at least in some circuits) to alter the reasonable-person standard to the reasonable-woman standard for determining severity of harassment claims. It is too early to tell whether switching to a reasonable-woman standard will help judges and jurors emphasize more with women's views of harassment. Certainly, triers of fact should be educated about the differences as well as the similarities in how women and men view harassment. In addition, Fitzgerald (1993) called for the following legislative initiatives and legal reform:

1. Remove caps on available damages and consider ways to encourage the award of substantial punitive damages that fit the seriousness of the offense.
2. Reform unemployment compensation statutes to ensure that [people] who quit their jobs due to harassment can receive unemployment compensation.
3. Extend the statute of limitations for filing sexual harassment charges.
4. Ensure that the legal system does not continue to revictimize harassment victims (p. 1074).

Organizational Strategies

Organizations with strong policies against harassment and managers who act swiftly and judiciously to enforce those policies are less vulnerable to claims of sexual harassment than other organizations (Terpstra & Baker, 1992). More importantly, the more an organization fosters a climate that disdains such offensive treatment, the less likely is sexual harassment to occur (Hulin, Fitzgerald, & Drasgow, 1996; Pryor et al., 1993). Several writers have provided strong guidelines to help organizations curtail and deal effectively with harassment.

1.   Have a clear policy against harassment and effective grievance procedures that are made known to all employees (Biaggio, Watts, & Brownell, 1990; Fitzgerald, 1993).
2.   Design a flexible dispute-resolution system that provides various informal and formal mechanisms for resolving conflict (Rowe, 1996).
3.   Train everyone in the organization. Depending on the audience, training should serve a variety of purposes, such as increasing awareness and sensitivity to sexual harassment, promoting understanding of the organization's policy and reporting procedures, and developing strategies for monitoring hostile environments (Stockdale, 1996).
4.   Develop interventions to challenge attitudes that perpetuate sexual harassment. Biaggio et al. (1990) offered numerous suggestions relevant to harassment in academic environments, such as training student leaders whose enlightened attitudes may influence others. Items related to sexist comments and sexual invitations should be included in teaching evaluations. Results of surveys indicating the prevalence of sexual harassment at particular universities should be publicly displayed. Many of these suggestions can be adapted for organizational use. For example, sexual-harassment-related criteria can be incorporated into performance appraisals.

Recently the Supreme Court made it clear that organizations can be held responsible for the harassing activities of their employees (*Burlington Industries, Inc. v. Ellerth*, 1988; *Faragher v. Boca Raton*, 1988). The court further suggested that the best defense an organization can have against being held liable for sexual harassment is a strong policy against sexual harassment. Furthermore, companies should make sure that everyone in the company knows and understands the policy and is trained to recognize and combat sexual harassment. Gutek (1997) suggested the following goals of a sexual harassment policy:

(1) Take a stand on sexual harassment, that is, to show the organization cares; (2) make the stance public knowledge; (3) discourage employees from engaging in harassing behavior; (4) encourage targets of harassment

to come forward and inform management; (5) educate people about sexual harassment; (6) provide guidelines for dealing with allegations of harassment; and (7) be able to defend the organization in the event that it is taken to court in a sexual harassment case. (p. 188–189)

Individual Strategies

Without societal and organizational or structural interventions to reduce sexism and power imbalances, sexual harassment may never be eliminated completely. However, individuals may be able to reduce the serious consequences of sexual harassment. Recently, researchers have focused on various types of response or coping strategies for sexual harassment and their relative effectiveness. Early studies reported that targets of sexual harassment who took assertive action against the offender (e.g., told the person to stop, reported the offense to an authority) found these methods to "make things better" compared to targets who took less assertive actions, such as going along with the behavior or avoiding the harasser (USMSPB, 1981). Later studies found that coping assertiveness tended to be associated with more severe or distressing forms of sexual harassment and with more severe outcomes (Gruber, 1989). These findings suggest that harassed individuals reserve more assertive forms of coping for serious levels of sexual harassment. But do these assertive methods of dealing with sexual harassment help alleviate the serious consequences of sexual harassment? Stockdale (1997) studied the coping responses of 1,782 women and 553 men in government jobs who indicated experiencing at least one form of unwanted sexual treatment on the job. She found that individuals who dealt with their harasser in an assertive manner (e.g., telling him or her to stop or threatening to report the behavior) experienced more negative consequences, such as quitting their jobs or taking leaves of absence, than did people who experienced the same amount of harassment but who did not respond assertively. This was especially true for men, moreover. Thus, better individual strategies for responding to sexual harassment need to be developed and tested.

In the meantime, the recommended individual strategy is to monitor the work environment for conditions that may lead to sexual harassment. Sexualized work environments (e.g., abundance of flattery, sexual overtures, jokes, and teasing) tend to lead to a greater incidence of sexual harassment than nonsexualized settings (Gutek, 1985). Supervisors who are responsible for work environments must understand how to recognize sexual harassment and inform others that it is not acceptable.

Finally, although sexual harassment was only recently labeled and thus only recently scrutinized systematically, it is neither a recent nor an isolated phenomenon. Scholars, practitioners, and activists must incorporate knowledge from core areas of the social sciences (e.g., aggression, altruism, social influence, and group dynamics) to improve our understanding of sexual harassment. Not only will this integration help us to eradicate sexual harassment, but sexual harassment scholarship can help us understand broader issues of human interaction.

SUMMARY

Before it was labeled as such, sexual harassment was considered "business as usual" in the lives of working women. However, during the late 1970s, sexual harassment was formally labeled and recognized as a form of sexual discrimination that could be successfully litigated under Title VII of the 1964 Civil Rights Act. Although 2 decades have passed, debate continues on what specifically constitutes sexual harassment. Sexual harassment has been defined in legal terms, although many behaviors that are perceived as harassing would not fall under the legal definitions. Therefore, more systematic, psychological definitions of sexual harassment have emerged. This research suggests that behaviors considered harassing take a wide range and vary in terms of severity and frequency including gender harassment, unwanted sexual attention, and sexual coercion (listed from less severe to more severe). Furthermore, it appears that the supposedly less severe forms of harassment occur most frequently, that all forms of harassment are much more frequently targeted toward women than men, and that the frequency of such behaviors toward male and female targets may be similar across countries.

Through both military and government surveys, it is clear that sexual harassment exacts a toll on both the organization and the individual. Organizational costs include those associated with turnover, absenteeism, and productivity loss. Such cost estimates do not include the impact of sexual harassment on organizational morale or coworker reactions. On the individual level, targets of harassment report job loss, quitting, decreased morale, and job dissatisfaction. Negative mental, emotional, and physical health effects are common. Given that a disproportionate number of women in male occupations are harassed and that women and minorities are projected to represent the majority of new workforce entrants, harassment incurs a particular toll on both the organization and the individual.

Numerous theories have been offered to explain why sexual harassment exists. Macro theories of sexual harassment largely reflect three approaches similar to those described in chapter 1: the biological model, the organizational model, and the sociocultural model. The biological model suggests that sexual harassment is a manifestation of human courtship patterns.

Whereas this approach has been dismissed as a credible explanation, the other two models have provided partial explanations for sexual harassment. The organization model posits that institutions such as work organizations and their accompanying structure provide opportunities to use power and dominance to obtain sexual gratification. Organizational features such as power hierarchies (of jobs or occupations), skewed gender ratios in work groups, and gendered organizational norms facilitate sexual harassment. The sociocultural model posits that the patriarchal society establishes and reinforces norms of male dominance and female subservience and that sexual harassment is an expression of male dominance. Aspects of both of these models have been empirically supported.

Although these macro models provide some explanation for sexual harassment, more recent micro explanations have emerged to supplement them. It is becoming clear that both personality and situational factors are important in understanding sexual harassment. It appears that some men who link power and sex-related motives are more likely to view sexual behavior at work as appropriate and to be willing to engage in such behavior.

Finally, combating sexual harassment requires action and strategies targeted at multiple levels within our society. Certainly, female employees can use individual strategies to avoid sexual harassment and if this fails can directly address harassing behavior. However, individual coping strategies alone are doomed to failure. Organizations must also develop strong policies against harassment and create organizational climates that prevent such behavior. A number of organizational strategies are suggested in this chapter. Further action is necessary at both the legislative and societal levels as well, including, for example, shifting to the reasonable-woman standard from the reasonable-person standard (although it is too early to assess the outcomes of this move).

GLOSSARY

Behavioral experiences approach: Method of determining whether someone has experienced sexual harassment in which the respondent reads an example of a behavior, such as "unwanted, deliberate touching, leaning over, cornering, or pinching," and indicates how frequently (if at all) she or he experienced that behavior (cf. **direct-query approach**).

Biological model: Perspective on sexual harassment which posits that sexually harassing behavior is a function of biological sex drives. It admits that harassing behavior occurs in organizations but denies that the intent is to harass, discriminate, or dominate.

Direct-query approach: Method of determining whether someone has experienced sexual harassment in which the respondent is directly asked how frequently (if at all) she or he has been sexually harassed (cf. **behavioral experiences approach**).

Externally focused strategies: Methods of coping with or responding to sexual harassment that are problem-solving in nature. Examples include avoidance, appeasement, assertion, seeking institutional or organizational relief, and seeking social support.

Gender harassment: Category of verbal and nonverbal behaviors that convey insulting, hostile, and degrading attitudes toward women. Examples include slurs, taunts, and gestures; pornography in the workplace; and gender-based hazing or threatening behavior.

Gender saliency: Extent to which a person's gender influences how she or he is perceived and/or treated.

Gendered norms: Informal rules about the appropriateness of male and female behavior (e.g., that men should request dates from women and that women should dress provocatively to attract sexual attention).

Internally focused strategies: Methods of coping with or responding to sexual harassment characterized by attempts to manage the cognitions and emotions associated with the event. Examples include endurance, denial, detachment, reattribution, and illusory control.

Likelihood to sexually harass: Research instrument developed by John Pryor (1987) that provides several different scenarios of **quid pro quo** sexual harassment. Among other questions, respondents are asked to rate the likelihood they would act like the perpetrator in each of the scenarios (i.e., would they offer some job-related benefit in exchange for sexual favors?). Men who score high on this scale are considered to have a high likelihood of sexually harassing women.

Misogyny: Hating women, or a tendency to view women in hostile ways, especially nontraditional and feminist women.

Need for power: Strength of an individual's desire to exercise control over others.

Organizational culture: Attitudes, values, behavioral norms, and expectations shared by organization members.

Organizational model: Perspective on sexual harassment positing that sexual harassment is the result of opportunities created by organizational climate, hierarchy, and specific authority relations. For example, individuals can use their power and position in an organization to extort sexual gratification from their subordinates.

Patriarchy: Social system in which men tend to have greater economic and political dominance than women and the prevailing social beliefs tend to support and legitimize their dominance.

Quid pro quo: Latin term meaning "one thing in return for another." In sexual harassment, it is the exchange of job-related benefits or consequences for sexual favors through bribery or threat (see **sexual coercion**).

Reasonable-person standard: A standard given to judges and jurors wherein they are supposed to consider whether a reasonable person (e.g., not someone who is "hypersensitive") in the same or similar circumstances as the plaintiff (person filing the lawsuit) would consider the alleged conduct sufficiently severe or pervasive to alter the conditions of employment and create an abusive working environment (cf. **reasonable-woman standard**).

Reasonable-woman standard: An alternative to the **reasonable-person standard** in some courts (e.g., the Ninth Circuit Court of Appeals in *Ellison vs. Brady,* 1991) in which jurors are instructed to consider whether a reasonable woman in similar circumstances as the plaintiff would consider the alleged conduct sufficiently severe or pervasive to alter the conditions of employment and create an abusive working environment. By replacing the term *person* with *woman* in the standard, jurors are expected to be more sensitive to women's perceptions of social–sexual behavior at work in comparison to men's perceptions.

Sex role: A set of shared expectations about the behavior of men and women.

Sex-role spillover: Transference of gender roles to the work role. For example, when the female sex-role stereotype of being a "sexual object" is expected in the work domain, sex-role spillover occurs.

Sexual coercion: Category of behavior that includes bribes and threats, explicit or subtle, for which the perpetrator conditions some job-related benefit or consequence on sexual cooperation (see **quid pro quo**).

Sexual harassment: Unwelcome sexual advances, requests for sexual favors, and other verbal or physical conduct of a sexual nature wherein (a) submission to such conduct is made either explicitly or implicitly a term or condition of an individual's employment, (b) submission to or rejection of such conduct by an individual is used as the basis for employment decisions affecting the individual, or (c) such conduct substantially interferes with an individual's work performance or creates an intimidating, hostile, or offensive working environment.

Skewed ratios: When the proportion of one group to another (e.g., men to women) is less than or equal to roughly 5:1. For example, if a work group contains 10 men and 2 women, the ratio of women to men is skewed (see **token**).

Sociocultural model: Perspective on sexual harassment that reflects the larger society's differential distribution of power and status between the sexes. Because men tend to have more economic and political power in **patriarchal** societies, their use of aggressive and domineering sexual behaviors over women tends to be socially rewarded.

Stratified random sample: A method of sampling members of a population in which the members vary on one or more characteristics (stratifications) such that a random sample of a given proportion is drawn from each stratification. For example, if a population contains 20% managers and 80% workers and the researcher wants to draw a random sample of 10%, she or he would stratify the sample by job level (manager vs. worker) and draw a 10% random sample from each group. The resulting sample should contain 20% managers and 80% workers.

Token: In a **skewed** work group, a member of the group with numerically fewer members.

Unwanted sexual attention: Verbal and nonverbal sexual behavior such as letters, telephone calls, touching, grabbing, cornering, and sexual assault that is unwanted by the recipient but that does not imply job-related losses or benefits.

Work role: A set of shared expectations about behavior in a job.

10

Career Issues for Women and Men: Mentoring, Children, and Dual-Career Couples

Myth:	Children suffer when women try to combine both career and parenthood.
Reality:	Boys and girls of employed mothers are more likely to be independent and to hold egalitarian sex-role attitudes than children of stay-at-home mothers.
Myth:	Male and female managers are similar in terms of marital status and parenthood.
Reality:	Women managers are less likely to be married and more likely to be childless than their male counterparts.
Myth:	Careers of men and women reflect similar patterns of career development and progression.
Reality:	Traditional career development theories have been based largely on all-male samples. Women's careers are influenced to a greater degree by situational factors such as support by others, presence of children, and spousal support.

Popular myths abound regarding women and work. This is especially true for working women with children, female managers and professionals, and career-minded women. As we indicated in our introductory chapter, the workforce is increasing in diversity. Furthermore, within each group (e.g., gender, ethnicity, age), individuals differ. For example, women do not all behavior similarly at work, Hispanics do not all engage in the same activities, and older workers vary in skills significantly.

Career issues for women and men exemplify this diversity. Not only do men and women face differ career issues, but among women, there is great diversity in their career paths, obstacles, work experiences and successes. Although there are a number of text devoted to understanding careers, we believe a general discussion is essential.

In this chapter, we discuss the definitions of career and describe briefly the traditional and emerging strategies for examining careers. A brief review of the stages of one's career is followed by a discussion of issues associated with women's careers. A number of issues or factors play significant roles in both men's and women's career development that are particularly crucial for women including **mentoring,** childbearing and child care, and **dual-earner** or **dual-career** family issues.

CAREERS: TRADITIONAL DEFINITIONS AND EMERGING FORMS

What Is a Career?

Douglas T. Hall (1976), an organizational scientist and expert on careers, suggested that there are four distinct meanings of *career.* The first two definitions reflect a more traditional view of a career that emphasizes upward movement within the organization. In the first definition, a career is identified in terms of advancement, that is, in terms of movement up an organizational hierarchy or a sequence of promotions. Directionality is important in this definition; careers are assumed to move upward, not downward. This is one of the most common views of careers. Second, a career might be viewed as a profession. Although related to the view of career as advancement, this is a less common view. Certain occupations are viewed as careers when they have clear sequences for advancement. For example, lawyers proceed from law studies, then to law clerkships, and then to associate partnerships and partnerships (D.T. Hall, 1976). Other jobs do not lead to or have such clear consequences of jobs and are therefore not viewed as careers. Examples include waiters or parking lot attendants.

Although these two definitions often appear in popular writings on careers, two other definitions are common among behavioral scientists and may encompass more recent career strategies within organizations (D.T. Hall, 1976). A third definition describes careers as lifelong sequences of jobs (D.T. Hall, 1976). A career is represented by one's job history regardless of organization or level in the organizational hierarchy. According to this definition, all people who have paid work have careers. A fourth view of a career suggests that it is a lifelong sequence of role-related experiences. A career can be thought of as a way one experiences a sequence of jobs and activities involved with one's work history. It can be viewed as a lifelong process and can include careers independent of work. Therefore, the definition includes the history of a person in any role or status, not only work roles.

Emerging View of Careers

Prior to the extensive **corporate reengineering and restructuring** that were so characteristic of the 1980s and 1990s, **career management** was viewed as a lifelong process of learning about oneself, jobs, and organizations; setting personal career goals; developing strategies for achieving those goals; and revising those goals based on work and life experiences (Greenhaus, 1987). This process was viewed as a joint responsibility of the individual and the organization. The individual certainly was responsible for knowing and developing her- or himself in work-relevant ways, but the organization was also responsible in partnering with the individual, especially in helping the individual set and achieve job and organizationally relevant goals.

However, with the dramatic organizational changes in the last two decades, the balance between individual and organizational responsibility for managing careers has shifted (Nelson & Quick, 1997). The notions of career and career management are undergoing a **paradigm shift.** Lifetime employment in a single organization, which was implicit in the traditional view of careers, is becoming increasingly rare. The responsibility of managing one's career has shifted dramatically to the individual employee.

As shown in Table 10.1, the new career paradigm is characterized by **discrete exchange, occupational excellence, organizational empowerment,** and **project allegiance** (Arthur, Claman, & DeFillippi, 1995), each of which is described next.

Discrete exchange in employment refers to an exchange where the organization gains productivity while the individual gains work experience. The exchange is short-term, and periodically the relationship or **psychological contract** between the employee and the organization must be renegotiated because job skills change in value (i.e., become obsolete or replaced by technology) and organizational conditions change (i.e., **downsizing, mergers,** and so forth). Under the traditional career paradigm, the relationship between employee and employer implied an exchange in which a loyal employee would be guaranteed job security. **Occupational excellence** is achieved when the individual continually increases or acquires skills that are marketable across organizations. The focus is on achieving excellence in one's occupation and developing future job opportunities for oneself rather than specifically within one organization. Using the more traditional career paradigm, the individual would achieve excellence by enhancing organization-specific knowledge and skills, thereby benefiting one organization. **Organizational empowerment** refers to power that comes down to business units and then to employees from executive management levels. Employee creativity and innovativeness are expected to help the organization remain competitive. Employee initiative would likely be viewed positively using the new career paradigm, whereas it might be viewed by the traditional paradigm as disloyalty or disrespect (Nelson & Quick, 1997). Finally, **project allegiance** refers to commitment that the employee and the organization have to the success of a given project. Successful project completion is a win–win situation for both the organization through enhanced productivity and the individual through work experience. Project members then break up and go onto other projects. Under the traditional career paradigm, allegiance is ultimately to the corporation, and corporate policies take precedence over specific project needs.

The traditional career paradigm is far from dead, but the corporate world is in significant transition. Still, in many organizations, the norm is **vertical career progression** as depicted by Hall's first two definitions of career. However, increasingly, individuals are required to prepare and

TABLE 10.1
The New Versus Old Career Paradigms

NEW CAREER PARADIGM	OLD CAREER PARADIGM
Discrete exchange means: • explicit exchange of specified rewards in return for task performance • basing job rewards on the current market value of the work being performed • engaging in disclosure and renegotiation on both sides as the employment relationship unfolds • exercising flexibility as each party's interests and market circumstances change	*The mutual loyalty contract meant:* • implicit trading of employee compliance in return for job security • allowing job rewards to be routinely deferred into the future • leaving the mutual loyalty assumptions as a political barrier to renegotiation • assuming employment and career opportunities are standardized and prescribed by the firm
Occupational excellence means: • performance of current jobs in return for developing new occupational expertise • employees identifying with and focusing on what is happening in their adopted occupation • emphasizing occupational skill development over the local demands of any particular firm • getting training in anticipation of future job opportunities; having training lead jobs	*The one-employer focus meant:* • relying on the firm to specify jobs and their associated occupational skill base • employees identifying with and focusing on what is happening in their particular firm • forgoing technical or functional development in favor of firm-specific learning • doing the job first to be entitled to new training: making training follow jobs
Organizational empowerment means: • strategic positioning is dispersed to separate business units • everyone is responsible for adding value and improving competitiveness • business units are free to cultivate their own markets • new enterprise, spinoffs, and alliance building are broadly encouraged	*The top-down firm meant:* • strategic direction is subordinated to "corporate headquarters" • competitiveness and added value are the responsibility of corporate experts • business unit marketing depends on the corporate agenda • independent enterprise is discouraged, and likely to be viewed as disloyalty
Project allegiance means: • shared employer and employee commitment to the overarching goal of the project • a successful outcome of the project is more important than holding the project team together • financial and reputational rewards stem directly from project outcomes • upon project completion, organization and reporting arrangements are broken up	*Corporate allegiance meant:* • project goals are subordinated to corporate policy and organizational constraints • being loyal to the work group can be more important than the project itself • financial and reputational rewards stem from being a "good soldier" regardless of results • social relationships within corporate boundaries are actively encouraged

From *Organizational Behavior,* 2nd edition, by D.L. Nelson and J. Campbell Quick © 1997. Reprinted with permission of South-Western Golden Publishing, a division of International Thomson Publishing. FAX: 800-730-2215 manage their own careers with the knowledge that change is the word of the day (Buhler, 1995).

Careers as Unfolding Stages

Although career theory and research in organizations are relatively new within the social sciences (E.H. Schein, 1990), **vocational psychology** has a longer history of theory development in this area. The difference between vocational psychologists' and organizational psychologists' approaches to careers is the time span involved. Vocational psychologists and counselors focus on an individual's initial occupational choice after leaving high school or college, whereas organizational experts focus on lifelong work experiences (D.T. Hall, 1990) (For excellent reviews of vocational theories and organizational theories of career development, see Osipow (1983) and Brown (1990), respectively). However, one theme vocational psychologists and organizational experts have in common in approaching careers is a **developmental perspective.** That is, individuals pass through a series of stages in their lives that follow a specific pattern and have somewhat distinct sets of activities associated with each. Organizational career experts focus on the stages that individuals pass through during their work lives rather than prior to entering work (D.J. Levinson, 1986).

Career Stage Models. Although there are numerous career stage models, four general stages that people pass through during their careers are commonly mentioned: **establishment, advancement, maintenance,** and **withdrawal.** The first stage of an individual's career is **establishment,** where the individual begins as a newcomer to an organization. Typically, this stage begins during early adulthood between ages 18 and 25 years. Remember, however, this is using the more traditional career paradigm. Under the new or emerging career paradigm, the establishment stage could occur with some variation whenever an individual changes jobs, organizations, or careers. Usually, at this stage, the individual is highly dependent on others to learn to perform some tasks competently and to learn which tasks are essential and which require less attention (L. Baird & Kram, 1983). Often newcomers are assigned parts of larger projects that are directed by managers, and much of their work involves fairly routine tasks. During this stage, individuals develop their **psychological contract** with the organization. Specifically, individuals learn what is expected of them and what the organization will provide in return for their continued performance. As we indicated with the shift in career paradigm, the psychological contract in the workplace is evolving. What employees traditionally expected from organizations was job security, which is being replaced with individual employability. In addition, during the establishment stage, the individual must learn how to get things done using both formal and informal routes of communication. Ideally, at this stage, a newcomer will be assigned to a more senior employee who is successful, knows the organization, and is skilled with working with new employees. Mentors are valuable sources of information, advice, and support for both male and female newcomers. We discuss more about mentors and mentoring later in this chapter.

The **advancement stage** often involves new experiences including special assignments, transfers, promotions, and possibly offers from other companies. The stage is characterized by achievement, greater responsibility and authority, and upward mobility. Usually this stage occurs around age 30 to 35 (as we note later in the chapter, age ranges for all of the career stages are based on research carried out with largely all-male samples). Performance feedback becomes critical during this stage. The individual is often concerned about developing a solid work record. Tasks are performed more independently with little supervision. The focus at this stage is upward mobility, yet peer relationships are important. Finding a mentor by this stage is critical, because guidance, coaching, counseling, and friendship are keys to success. It is also during the advancement stage that childbearing and childrearing decisions, dual-career concerns, and work–home conflicts are most salient. Both child-care and dual-career concerns are discussed later in this chapter, and work–home conflicts are discussed in chapter 12.

The **maintenance** stage may be inappropriately labeled, because some individuals continue to grow in their careers although perhaps not at the same rate as in the advancement stage (Nelson & Quick, 1997). At this stage a number of personal changes occur that can either positively or negatively affect the individual and work. At this stage the individual is likely to experience a host of physical appearance changes including more wrinkles, graying and/or thinning hair, decreased stamina, and so forth. As discussed in chapter 4, perceptions of attractiveness (both perceptions by others and self-perceptions) play a significant role in our lives. Also at this stage, individuals have been in the work arena long enough to realize that their careers have or have not lived up to their dreams and expectations. During the maintenance stage, a person may take one of three career paths: star, solid citizen, or deadwood (Hellriegel, Slocum, & Woodman, 1986). Stars, of course, continue to progress upward and receive greater recognition, awards, and promotions. Solid citizens, the largest group of employees, do good work but for some reason have lower probability of moving further up the hierarchy. They have reached a

career plateau or stage where upward promotions are unlikely. Increasingly, career plateauing occurs simply because there are more qualified people for higher level positions than there are positions available. These individuals may seek employment in other organizations or may change careers altogether. Deadwood employees have little chance for promotion and often are given tasks that are not critical in developing marketable skills. The performance of these employees is likely to decline.

The **withdrawal stage** occurs around age 60. Individuals may become increasingly disengaged from work due to age discrimination or stereotyping. On the other hand, an individual may successfully bring various factions of people together for innovation or may play the role of mentor. However, this stage is usually characterized by a shift away from work and toward retirement.

WOMEN'S CAREER DEVELOPMENT

Until recently, most career research was concerned with men's careers. For a variety of reasons, women's careers often develop in different ways than men's and may pose different challenges for career researchers. Therefore, it is important to understand how current male-based career theories have developed and how women's career development departs from men's.

Critical Gaps and Issues in Women's Career Development

The developmental perspective presented earlier in this chapter is based largely on observations and research on men's careers. Although career development theories can contribute to our understanding of women's career development, these theories may not fully explain this process (Fitzgerald & Crites, 1980). For a variety of reasons, the theories previously reviewed cannot fully illuminate women's career development. One reason is that career-development models have emphasized men's aspirations and accomplishments (Gustafson & Magnusson, 1991; Roe, 1949, 1952) and are based on nearly exclusively male samples. Additionally, current theories of career development often do not include or consider variables that influence women's career decisions. For example, as a result of sex-role socialization, women are more differentially influenced by achievement motivation than men (Fitzgerald & Crites, 1980). That is, development of achievement motivation for girls depends in larger part on the experiences and support that girls receive from others. Women are likely to encounter vocational counselors who are biased and have distorted or limited views of occupations and women's "proper place" in various occupations and, therefore, implicitly (and sometimes explicitly) discourage them from entering high-pay, high-status occupations. Finally, career-stage theories that continue to be influential give little consideration to such critical issues as childbearing and childrearing (e.g., Super, 1953, 1963).

In these theories, males serve as the standard for comparison. Women are often studied in terms of how they depart from the male standard, in terms of both career choice and career development (Gutek & Larwood, 1987). Many experts (e.g., Betz & Fitzgerald, 1987; Fitzgerald & Crites, 1980) noted that women's career development is far more complexly determined and varied and less easily categorized than men's. Because, historically, women do not necessarily expect to be engaged in full-time paid work (and men do), women's careers more heavily depend on attitude, role expectations, and, generally, socialization (Gustafson & Magnusson, 1991).

Women's career development will continue to differ from men's for four reasons. First, there are different expectations for men and women regarding the appropriateness of specific jobs. These expectations affect the kinds of jobs that men and women prepare for and select. Often women are not prepared to pursue a career at all (although they often may expect to engage in paid employment during some part of their lives), whereas men are expected to participate continuously in paid work. Education is a key consideration here (Larwood & Gutek, 1987). Second, husbands and wives differ in their willingness to accommodate each other's careers. Wives are typically more willing to accommodate than husbands, so marriage has different effects on men's and women's careers. For men, marriage is career-neutral or somewhat advantageous (especially if the wife does not work outside the home). For women, however, marriage and especially having children can be among the most limiting factors for careers (Larwood & Gutek, 1987). Third, the parental role is defined differently for men and women (as we discuss in greater detail later in this chapter). Pregnancy and children are critical factors in women's career development, in large part because the mother's role typically requires more time and effort than the father's role. The stereotype is that women interrupt their careers to bear and raise children, but this is often not the case. Career theories must be flexible enough to address women who follow traditional paths as well as those who choose to have children and continue with their careers almost immediately (Larwood & Gutek, 1987). Finally, compared to men, women face more constraints in the workplace including harassment, discrimination, and stereotypes that are detrimental to career advancement (Gutek & Larwood, 1987).

Understanding how and why women's career development differs from men's becomes increasingly important as the number of women participating in the workforce increases. The proportion of women at work in the U.S. is increasing (F.D. Blau & Ferber, 1985; U.S. Department of Labor, 1983). Increased numbers of women in the labor force have been reported in other countries (Davidson & Cooper, 1983). Finally, we need to understand why 50% of the men in the workforce are distributed across 64 occupations, but only 16 occupations account for 50% of employed women (Healy, 1982; Hedges & Bemis, 1974; see chap. 7 for a discussion of occupational segregation).

Approaches to Women's Career Development

Although early work in vocational psychology and choice acknowledged differences between men and women in life patterns (Brooks, 1990), the underlying assumption of such theories (Super, 1957; Zytowski, 1969) was that homemaking and work roles were separate (Vetter, 1973), that the model life-role for women was homemaker (Betz & Fitzgerald, 1987), and that women's career commitment was naturally low (L.S. Hansen, 1978). Whereas the study of men's career development historically focused on variables describing the nature of their career choices, early research on women focused on whether women wanted to pursue a career at all. In the 1970s, the assumption that women must choose either home or career was replaced with concerns about how to combine family and career (Betz & Fitzgerald, 1987; Yogev, 1982). It was not until 1975 that women's career development began to be systematically studied (Brown et al., 1984).

Different approaches of women's career development have focused upon societal, cultural, and/or psychological factors. These approaches have identified some of the factors that create barriers for women at work or facilitate the careers of both women and men in organizations. The **sociological approach** to research on women's career development focuses on structural concerns. Specifically, this approach addresses how institutions and social practices contribute to observed differences between men and women (Berheide & Segal, 1985; Epstein, 1988; Gallos, 1989; Kanter, 1977a; Scanzoni, 1983). Observed differences between men's and women's life choices are attributed to roles, policies, and social conditions. The second approach is a **cultural approach** (Gallos, 1989) and includes both anthropological and social–psychological research. Here, the focus is on how the cultural images of men and women are shaped by social roles and life choices at home, at work, and in marriage (Yankelovich,

Sidelight 10.1 Should We Focus on Jobs or Gender When Studying Women's Careers?

Researchers studying the sociology of work (e.g., Feldberg & Glenn, 1982) have employed two very different models to explore the work behavior of men and women: the **job model** and the **gender model.** The job model treats work that people do as an **independent variable.** The emphasis here is how the actual work influences perceptions of work as well as mental and physical health. The job model is often used to explain differences among men in work perceptions and behaviors. The gender model ignores type of job and working conditions. Frequently, women's perceptions of and reactions to work are treated as a result of personal characteristics and relationships to family situations (Feldberg & Glenn, 1982). The gender model is often used to explain differences between men's and women's perceptions and behaviors.

Incorporated in both these models is the basic assumption that men are breadwinners and women are wives; in this line of research, women's employment is viewed as secondary to their primary role as wife. The models make different assumptions about the relationship between gender and work–family. According to the job model, the basic social relationships are determined by work. In the gender model, such relationships are determined by family. In the job model, the paid worker's connection to the family is as an economic provider, whereas in the gender model, the connection to the family is as wife or mother. The worker's social position in the job model is determined through work; in the gender model, it depends on the family. The individual's sociopolitical behaviors and attitudes are assumed, in the job model, to be derived from occupational socialization, class or status of the occupation, and social relationship of work. The gender model implicitly assumes that such attitudes and behaviors are derived from gender-role socialization, family roles and activities, and the relationship of household work (Feldberg & Glenn, 1982). Finally, both models make varying assumptions concerning the individual's central life interest: The job model assumes it is employment and earning money, whereas the gender model assumes it is the family.

Feldberg and Glenn (1982) suggested that when one model is used and not integrated with the other, research on men, women, and work is likely to produce biased and distorted results. First, data that do not fit the model being used are likely to be ignored. When many explanations are possible, only the ones consistent with the model in use are considered or favored. Choice of a particular model determines what variables are considered as appropriate to study and directs researchers' attention to specific issues. Thus, research that considers only one of these two perspectives is unlikely to yield a balanced picture of men's and women's experiences at work.

1981). The third is the **psychological approach,** which focuses on gender-specific ways in which men and women examine and make sense out of work (Bardwick, 1980; Belenky, Clinchy, Goldberger, & Tarule, 1986). The research on vocational and organizational career development of women often reflects a combination of these three approaches.

For example, reflecting both the sociological and cultural approaches, the classic work of Betz and Fitzgerald (1987) identifies four factors that influence women's career choices and subsequent career satisfaction and success: cultural factors, subcultural factors, immediate environment, and education. Cultural factors include societal sex-role stereotypes that convey appropriate choices and behaviors to men and women, occupational sex stereotypes that appear to be durable over time, and the lack of role models, especially for women in nontraditional jobs. Subcultural factors include socioeconomic status, race, nationality, and religion. The career experiences of women from various socioeconomic strata or women of color vary, yet we do not understand just what these experiences are. In the immediate environment, critical family-background considerations include family educational level, whether the mother works, marriage, and children. Among adults, the most consistent indicator of a woman's career development is her adult marital and family status.

Among girls, plans for marriage and children are key indicators of subsequent career progression (Betz & Fitzgerald, 1987). The influence of role models or, as we discuss later, mentors in the workplace is also an important factor in a woman's immediate environment. Finally, education has a critical influence on women's career development, especially when education is defined broadly to include the influence of counseling interventions, abilities and achievement levels, personality variables (e.g., self-concept and sex-role-related characteristics), and vocational interests, needs, and values (Betz & Fitzgerald, 1987). For example, career counselors sometimes reinforce the societal restrictions imposed on women's careers (Healy, 1982). Women who indicate a desire to enter nontraditional occupations tend to be evaluated as more deviant and in need of more counseling (A.H. Thomas & Stewart, 1971) than women entering more traditional occupations.

Hackett and Betz (1981) proposed a **self-efficacy theory** of women's career development, suggesting that gender differences in self-efficacy (i.e., the belief that you are capable of succeeding in a wide range of fields) arise from sex-role socialization and, more specifically, from differences in men's and women's opportunities. On the whole, women have fewer opportunities to engage in challenging work-relevant activities across different settings and, therefore, fewer opportunities to develop self-efficacy. Furthermore, environmental contingencies influence these beliefs.

Sex-role socialization can prevent women from developing skills and talents that would lead to self-efficacy (Hackett & Betz, 1981). For example, girls are less likely than boys to engage in mathematical or technical activities, which lowers the likelihood of strong self-efficacy for the majority of higher paying occupations (i.e., occupations that require skills in these areas).

The degrees of self-efficacy that people demonstrate interact with both their **outcome expectations** and **incentives.** Outcome expectations are beliefs about the consequences of performance. For example, a woman can believe she is very capable of being a CEO of an organization (self-efficacy). However, she may also believe that even though she can perform at an exceptional level, she will not be promoted into such a position because the organization wants a man (outcome expectations). Self-efficacy is a belief about one's ability, whereas outcome expectations reflect beliefs about what will happen if you perform well. Women who believe that good performance will not be rewarded with recognition and promotions will have less incentive to excel in the workplace than men who believe that performance will be rewarded.

Another model applicable to both men and women incorporates a variety of factors reflecting societal, cultural, and psychological involvement in career development (Gottfredson, 1981). According to the **occupational aspirations model,** people classify occupations along dimensions of sex-type, level of work, and field of work. As with other theories of women's career development (Hackett & Betz, 1981), people then assess the suitability of occupations according to **self-concept** and the amount of effort they are willing to exert to enter the occupation. Elements of self-concept that are occupationally relevant include gender, social class, IQ, interests, values, and abilities. Occupational aspirations are shaped by these elements of self-concept; certain occupations are rejected or accepted on the basis of their perceived fit with one's self-concept. Research applying this model suggests that occupations are rejected first on the basis of gender, then on the basis of social class and ability level, and finally on the basis of personal interests and values. Once a person rejects an occupation, it is unlikely that she or he will look at it again as an acceptable alternative (Brooks, 1990). The occupational aspirations model suggests that women are found in lower level jobs because these jobs are compatible with women's self-concepts and views about the accessibility of different jobs (i.e., the likelihood that they will have the opportunity to compete for jobs) (L. Brooks, 1990; Gottfredson, 1981).

Women often do not expect to work continuously throughout their lives; thus, the influence of key contextual features such as support from others, nonwork responsibilities, and spousal employment becomes critical. Therefore, in a chapter on men, women, and careers, it is essential to discuss workplace mentoring (e.g., interpersonal work support from key coworkers), the decision to marry and become a parent (e.g., nonwork responsibilities), and dual-career issues (e.g., spousal employment).

MENTORING IN THE WORKPLACE

For both men and women, mentoring is related to organizational advancement, career development, and career satisfaction (Barnier, 1982; Fagenson, 1988; Orth & Jacobs, 1971; Ragins & Cotton, 1992; Scandura, 1991). Mentoring can be beneficial at many career stages, although different kinds of mentoring may be needed at different stages (K.E. Kram, 1985; Ostroff & Kozlowski, 1993). The types of mentoring relationships available to men and women and the extent to which mentors are willing or able to help men versus women in the workplace often differ, which means that mentors may have a different influence on the careers of men and women.

What Is a Mentor?

A mentor is an experienced, productive superior who relates to a less-experienced employee and assists with his or her personal development for the benefit of the organization and the individual (K.E. Kram, 1985; Noe, 1988b). The mentoring relationship may be initiated by either party. Often **protégés** attract mentors through high performance or similarities in interest. Mentors provide both career and **psychosocial support.** Career support, which is believed to help the protégé learn the job and prepare for advancement, may include coaching, protecting, providing challenging assignments, promoting visibility, and direct sponsorship. Psychosocial support enhances the protégé's sense of competence, clarity of identity, and effectiveness in the professional role (O'Leary & Mitchell, 1990). Mentors can serve as role models, friends, and counselors and can offer protégés positive regard and acceptance (Dreher & Ash, 1990). Mentors provide protégés entry into the organization's informal social networks and help them establish alliances. Mentoring is to be distinguished from **career networks,** which involve contact with many colleagues for the purpose of mutual benefit (O'Leary & Mitchell, 1990).

For men, the early years of adult development overlap with their early career years, but these years are not so easily defined for women. Frequently, women select careers later than men, and women's early work years may be characterized by brief but repeated career interruptions. Mentoring may benefit women by increasing the likelihood that they will receive support and cooperation from peers (Ilgen & Youtz, 1986), which in turn may increase their likelihood of success. Mentoring may also reduce job stress. Women with one or more mentors report greater satisfaction and job success (Riley & Wrench, 1985). Mentors create opportunities for women to operate outside organizational norms, set high standards of performance, and publicize protégé accomplishments (Missirian, 1982). Women who are mentored report increased self-confidence and greater awareness and use of skills (Reich, 1986), which, according to previously mentioned theories, are critical to women's career development.

Barriers to Mentoring Upwardly Mobile Women

Formal and informal mentors can be instrumental in the successful career development of both men and women (for reasons previously cited, mentors can be especially useful to women). Unfortunately, as women progress to higher managerial ranks, they are more likely to be without female mentors (Warihay, 1980). Only 38% of executive managerial and administrative jobs are held by women (U.S. Bureau of Labor Statistics, 1987b), and these women are often found in such traditionally female-dominated fields as retail sales and education (U.S. Department of Labor, 1983). In addition, men hold more centralized positions that allow them to share valuable information about job openings, key assignments, and decisions within a more informal network (H.L. Smith & Grenier, 1982). Informal power through the informal sharing of information gives male mentors a wider power base than female mentors, generates a better basis to set realistic goals, provides greater visibility, and allows greater access to valuable resources (Noe, 1988b).

There is some evidence that finding a mentor is difficult for women (Noe, 1988b), as is becoming a mentor (Ragins & Cotton, 1992). Without mentors, women may find it difficult to enter an occupation, especially male-dominated occupations such as management. Most mentoring relationships are informal. However, formal mentoring programs are increasing in the public and private sectors (Roche, 1979), although the effectiveness of these programs has not been assessed. Because there are so few women in high-level organizational positions, it is very likely that when a woman does find a mentor, it will be a man.

Several barriers to establishing cross-gender mentorships have been identified (K.E. Kram, 1985; Noe, 1988a, 1980b; Ragins & Cotton, 1992). One of these is lack of access to information networks; that is, women may have limited opportunities to establish contact with potential mentors. These limited opportunities result from a lack of knowledge about how to develop informal networks, a preference for interacting with peers, or intentional exclusion of women by male managers. Although women receive equal or greater numbers of promotions than men (L.P. Stewart & Gudykunst, 1982), evidence suggests that they do not advance as far in the organizational hierarchy. Rather, women's promotions may reflect lateral movements rather than consistent upward movement. Furthermore, women are less central to men's organizational networks (especially dominant networks; Brass, 1985; Rosen et al., 1981), perhaps because they lack mentors (Noe, 1988).

A second reason why women may have difficulty finding a mentor is tokenism. Women often have high visibility due to their token status. Potential mentors may not want to enter such a relationship because of a woman's high visibility (Noe, 1988a). If the woman is unsuccessful or makes a mistake, the visibility of the mentoring relationship could damage the mentor's career. **Tokens,** especially women who obtain their positions through affirmative action, may experience resentment from men who feel that their own job security is threatened (see chap. 8 for a more detailed discussion of affirmative action). Therefore, these men do not help women succeed, thereby validating the men's perceptions that women are less competent. This is further complicated by evidence that women hired by organizations with strong affirmative action programs may develop **self-limiting attitudes** about their own competence, performance, and commitment (Chacko, 1982; Heilman et al., 1987). Therefore, a woman's success may be attributed to organizational policy (e.g., affirmative action) rather than ability. Third, negative stereotypes and attitudes toward women as managers and leaders are still common. Such stereotypes include beliefs that women are more interested in pleasant work environments than in responsibility and advancement (Rynes & Rosen, 1983). Potential mentors who accept these stereotypes are less likely to invest time and effort in advancing female protégés.

Norms regarding cross-gender mentoring relationships in organizations can be a hindrance for females seeking mentors. Men may prefer and feel more comfortable working closely with other men. Peer perceptions, too, are critical, as peers may be concerned that a cross-gender mentoring relationship will become sexual. Chapter 4 discusses a number of factors leading to interpersonal liking and attraction, and close mentoring relationships can involve a number of these factors. Perceived sexual attraction can lead to marital disruption and damaging gossip, which can undermine the effectiveness of cross-gender relationships. The conflict between wanting to develop one's protégé or subordinate and the desire to avoid awkward complications has been called the "developmental dilemma" (Burke & McKeen, 1990), and it may be a significant barrier to cross-gender mentoring relationships. Concern about perceptions of intimacy between male mentors and female protégés may lead to less frequent interactions, less one-to-one contact, and decreased effectiveness (Burke & McKeen,

1990). Finally, women themselves may inhibit mentoring by relying on ineffective power bases. Some women use indirect influence strategies such as emphasizing their own weakness or incompetence (e.g., helplessness). Others may rely more on acquiescence strategies rather than assertive strategies for interpersonal interactions.

Mentors can be valuable resources in the career development of both men and women. The consequences of women's reduced access to mentors can be substantial. Lack of a mentor may reduce the job effectiveness of women (Noe, 1988a) and may have serious consequences for the organization as well. In addition to not fully using all available human resources, organizations without mentoring programs may find themselves under legal scrutiny. The absence of cross-gender mentoring relationships can itself be a cause for litigation, on the theory that it constitutes disparate treatment of male and female employees (Noe, 1988).

CHILDBEARING, CHILD CARE, AND CAREERS

Throughout this book we discuss myths, stereotypes, and misperceptions that people hold about the roles of men and women in relation to their work. When asked to estimate the percentage of their workers who were in families where the male was the sole breadwinner to support his at-home wife and children, executives from a Harvard University seminar believed that between 40% and 70% of their workers fell into this category (D.E. Friedman, 1986). In reality, however, only approximately 10% of U.S. households fit the traditional single-earner, male head-of-household pattern. Furthermore, approximately 40% of the workforce consists of dual-earner families, and another 6% of single parents (D.E. Friedman, 1986). Approximately 80% of working women are of childbearing age, and 90% of these women will become pregnant. About 60% of men have wives who work full- or part-time (D.E. Friedman, 1986).

A substantial majority of women in the workforce will at some point have children, and a substantial majority of women with young children will continue to work. Therefore, the choice between work and family for women (as well as for men) is often illusory or is a luxury that only a small proportion of the population can afford. The question we consider here is not whether women (and men) with young children should work or should attempt to balance work and family: Most women will do both. Rather, we examine how children are likely to affect women's careers, and how women and organizations can most effectively balance the demands of work and family.

Marriage and the Decision to Bear Children

Few if any textbooks on the psychology or sociology of work discuss men's and women's decisions to marry and bear children, pregnancy discrimination, child-care options, or the effects of work on the well-being of mothers, fathers, and children. Exclusion of these topics from applied texts on work and management is not due to a lack of information. Instead, these topics have been viewed historically as "women's issues," not as mainstream employee or human resources problems (Kossck, 1990; Magid, 1983). We briefly discuss these issues as important factors in the successful career development of men and women.

Career theories, which have historically treated work and family as separate and independent domains, imply that men do not experience conflict between their careers and decisions to marry or become parents. For women, however, it is explicitly recognized that family issues, including decisions to marry and especially when or whether to have children, dramatically affect career development (Betz & Fitzgerald, 1987). For example, in a Canadian survey, 61% of women agreed that advancement in their organizations depended on putting their careers before their personal or family lives (in contrast, only 44% of male chief executives said the same thing). Over 40% of the senior female managers in this survey made the choice either to postpone having children or not to have them at all, and 19% decided either to delay marriage or not to marry. Finally, given the growing numbers of dual-earner families, decisions regarding childbearing may become more important for both partners.

Women often report conflicts between career, marriage, and family responsibilities. For example, a survey of managerial women in their 20s showed that many believed they had little time for relationships because they were concentrating on career development (Davidson & Cooper, 1992). Many women enter the workplace, begin their careers, and earn their first promotions during the same years or stages they are most able to bear children. Many of these same women postpone marriage or having children, based on the (reasonable) belief that this could substantially threaten their career progress (Davidson & Cooper, 1983; Scase & Goffee, 1989). Managerial women who attempt to juggle their careers with marriage and childbearing report high levels of stress (Davidson & Cooper, 1987, 1992; see also chap. 12). More recently, in assessments of career and family-role expectations, both parents and daughters expected the daughters to experience little frustration in balancing future career and family roles (Schroeder, Blood, & Maluso, 1992). That is, girls and young women fully expected to engage in both work and family roles, but, to date, there have been few changes in the workplace to accommodate those expectations.

Once men and women do marry and decide to have children, often the next phase of family life is pregnancy. Although there is little available empirical research on people's attitudes toward pregnant women working outside the home, there is no shortage of stereotypes about them (Davidson & Cooper, 1992).

Pregnancy and Women's Careers

Organizations historically have viewed child care as a "women's issue." However, there is little information regarding the effects of pregnancy on women's perceptions of work, nor do we know much about others' perceptions of pregnant working women. Such evidence suggests that a woman's femininity (and perhaps her sexuality, too) is rendered more salient by pregnancy (Corse, 1990). In a laboratory workplace simulation, subordinates perceived a pregnant manager more negatively, were less satisfied with their interactions, directed more social comments toward her, expected her to be passive and nurturing, and were surprised by her authoritative behavior more than with a nonpregnant female manager (Schroeder et al., 1992). Furthermore, there were no differences between male and female subordinates' reactions to the pregnant manager (Corse, 1990). These findings suggest that pregnant workers are viewed in a more stereotypically feminine manner and may be viewed more negatively as well. These findings are consistent with findings that an employed woman with an infant was evaluated less positively and received less approval than a nonemployed woman with an infant (Schroeder et al., 1992).

Our society embraces a number of social role expectations regarding pregnant women (Myers & Grasmick, 1990). Perceptions of pregnant women are sometimes described in terms of a **sick-role model** (Parsons, 1951), which emphasizes the deviancy and dependency of the sick person. Pregnant women who are viewed as "sick" are likely to be assigned fewer duties and responsibilities. However, women are less likely than men to think that pregnant women should be excused from other role responsibilities, and as socioeconomic status increases, women's adherence to the sick-role model decreases further (Myers & Grasmick, 1990). Women are more likely than men to expect pregnant women to want to return quickly to normal role responsibilities. This expectation is also positively related to socioeconomic status. Women, especially women with higher incomes and status, may feel they must balance multiple roles to protect the investments they have made, including their careers (Myers & Grasmick, 1990).

These findings have interesting implications for potential perceptions and treatment of pregnant women at work. It is evident that men subscribe

Sidelight 10.2 Children and Career Success

In this chapter, we discuss a number of studies describing men's and women's perceptions that having children limits a woman's career progress or success. Is this true?

As a society, we continue to believe that women have choices when deciding whether to work. However, only one third of working women have husbands who earn adequate incomes; the rest, at least two thirds, are either married to men whose incomes were less than $15,000 in 1984, or are single, widowed, divorced, or separated (U.S. Department of Labor, 1984). Working, therefore, is the norm for U.S. women and, increasingly, an economic necessity.

Evidence demonstrates that women are combining childbearing, family, and work (Diamond, 1987). Women do not leave their jobs after childbirth, or, if they do, they return very soon thereafter. Between 1973 and 1983, participation rates for mothers with children under 3 years of age increased from 30% to 46% (U.S. Department of Labor, 1984). However, women, especially those with children, continue to face hostility in nontraditional jobs. Working women who become pregnant face stereotypical attitudes and receive fewer promotions (J. Adams, 1984).

---

to the sick-role perception of pregnancy more strongly than do women. Men tend to believe that pregnant women should not be expected to engage in all the activities that occupied their time prior to pregnancy. There is a perception that pregnancy debilitates a woman in some way. It would be interesting to determine whether managers hesitate to assign challenging, career-enhancing tasks or projects to pregnant women. Furthermore, men are more likely than women to believe that pregnant women deserve extra protection and care (see chap. 8 for a description of legal protections regarding pregnancy). This finding may again have implications for women's career development. A pregnant woman may find it unusually difficult to locate a potential mentor if others perceive her as requiring protection from high-visibility projects. Finally, women are more likely than men to believe that a pregnant woman should look forward to getting back to her regular responsibilities and normal routine once the pregnancy is over (Myers & Grasmick, 1990).

Child Care in the United States

The influx of women into the workforce during the last two decades has altered the composition of both the workplace and family life (Silverstein,

1991). Yet, unlike 75 other countries, the United States has no comprehensive family policy to assist couples in coping with work–family conflicts (one exception is the Family and Medical Leave Act discussed in chap. 7, which provides for unpaid family leave for some workers). Work–family conflicts can contribute to stress, role conflict and overload, decreased satisfaction and commitment, absenteeism, tardiness, and turnover (Kossek & Grace, 1991), and lack of adequate child care is often a significant source of such conflicts.

A combination of factors have prompted an increase in child-care or dependent-care programs in the United States. Organizations are beginning to offer such care for several reasons: increasing competition for skilled workers due to shifts in the gender and skill mix of the workforce, changing expectations of employees, growing research evidence about negative effects of work–family conflict on productivity, and continuing shortages of quality care (Kossek & Grace, 1991). Available and affordable child care is critical to the career success and satisfaction of working women and dual-earner families. Working mothers, although they spend less time on housework, spend as much time on child care as traditional full-time mothers. Fathers in dual-career and single-earner families spend similar amounts of time on child care (Kossek, 1990; Nock & Kingston, in press). Having children can inhibit the career development of women, especially when child care is inadequate (Gwartney-Gibbs, 1988; Kossek, 1990). This is particularly true of women who work nontraditional hours (e.g., nurses) and when children become ill. Care of sick children poses a particular problem for working parents, employers, and child-care workers (Chang & Landis, 1991). There is a need to address more fully the topic of sick care for children, especially in light of evidence showing increased numbers of children attending group child care centers where the incidence of illness is greater than when child care remains with the family (Caruso, 1992; Chang & Landis, 1991).

There is evidence that quality of on-site child care can also increase women's self-efficacy by facilitating women's (and presumably men's) ability to perform both work and family roles (Kossek & Nichol, 1992). Child-care options and availability are more critical for women employed outside the home than for men for several reasons:

- Women are the primary persons responsible for housekeeping and care of children, especially when the children are ill (Bryson, Bryson, & Johnson, 1978; Nieva & Gutek, 1981b).
- Women's work and family demands are concurrent, whereas men's are sequential (D.T. Hall, 1972).

- Marriage and children interfere with women's career opportunities and progress more than work interferes with family activities (Laws, 1979.
- Children and family are often viewed by employers as burdens for women but assets for men (Bryson et al., 1978).

One explanation for this last perception is that women are more likely to interrupt their careers for marriage and childbearing than are men (Li & Currie, 1992).

More information is needed for top managerial decision makers regarding the effects of dependent-care responsibilities on job performance and the extent of the organization's responsibility to provide such care (J.J. Miller, Stead, & Pereira, 1991). Research indicates that organizations can increase productivity and reduce absenteeism when child-care programs are implemented (Chambers-Cook & Youngblood, 1984; Maume, 1991). Other findings suggest that although on-site child care is not directly related to performance, the primary performance link may be through the opportunity to perform rather than through motivation or ability (Kossek & Nichol, 1992). That is, child-care availability creates a favorable organizational climate by reducing work–family problems and allowing employees to focus on their jobs. Kossek and Nichol (1992) found that parent/employees in the organization who were on a child-care waiting list showed a frustration effect, believing that they were being denied an organizational benefit.

Employed Mothers: Effects on the Health of Women, Men, and Children

It was long assumed that women's employment was detrimental to children, particularly when child care was involved. Research has so convincingly overturned this stereotype that experts on child care have urged a **moratorium** on research searching for negative consequences of working mothers and nonfamilial child care and have asked for greater research documenting the negative consequences of not providing high-quality, affordable child care to children and their families.

Women's employment and children's experiences in nonfamiliar child-care settings can benefit both the mother's self-perceptions and well-being and the children's development (Parasuraman & Greenhaus, 1993). A *Fortune* study of employed mothers and fathers indicated that 86% of the women and 78% of the men thought children of employed parents benefited from having both as interesting role models (Chapman, 1987). Children of dual-career families hold more egalitarian sex-role attitudes

(Stephan & Corder, 1985) and are more independent (Knaub, 1986; G.L. Symons, 1984) than children in traditional families. Furthermore, the mother's work can have a positive effect on her self-esteem and emotional well-being (Barnett & Baruch, 1985; Baruch & Barnett, 1986), especially if she is employed by choice (Ross, Mirowsky, & Huber, 1983) and holds a challenging and interesting job (Valdez & Gutek, 1987). There is little evidence that involvement in multiple roles contributes to role overload and has negative consequences for a woman's health (Jacobs & Waldron, 1989). Instead, multiple roles contribute to better health for some women, through positive consequences of labor force participation and marriage.

Meneghan and Parcel's (1991) **longitudinal study** showed that the **occupational complexity** of a mother's work positively affects the home environment that the mother provides for her children. Personal resources that working mothers bring to their children including heightened self-esteem, increased locus of control, enhanced educational achievement, and increased maturity (working mothers tend to have children at a later age) all have positive effects on children's home environments (Menaghan & Parcel, 1991). Not only does a woman's employment have a positive effect on her self-esteem, but a mother's preference for a career has a positive effect on her children's self-esteem and evaluations of their own competence. We discuss the stress levels and health of working and nonworking men and women in chapter 12.

DUAL-CAREER COUPLES

Often when we discuss women's career development, we are actually describing a more complex set of work and nonwork interactions experienced by dual-earner or dual-career couples. Bruce and Reed (1991) described the **dual-career couple** as "two professional people in a marital or significant relationship in which both partners pursue a career characterized by strong commitment, personal growth and increasing levels of responsibility" (p. 1). Such couples may or may not have children. However, dual-career concerns are in no way limited to those involved in psychologically involving, upwardly mobile, or professional work (Greenhaus, 1987). Most working couples in America are better described as **dual-earners,** who are likely to need ways to balance the demands of work and home without completely segregating work responsibilities (handled by the man) and home/family responsibilities (handled by the woman).

A number of limitations within the dual-career and dual-earner research literature should be kept in mind as we review findings (A. Lewis &

Cooper, 1988). First, this research is often based exclusively on middle-class couples (Fogarty, Rapoport, & Rapoport, 1971; Pendelton, Paloma, & Garland, 1982). Second, most studies assume that both individuals are in full-time employment, but definitions of what constitutes full-time employment can vary from 20 (Pleck & Staines, 1985) to 35 (E.A. House, 1986) hours per week. Other studies include wives who are employed part-time (Pleck & Staines, 1985). Third, definitions of dual-career couples vary across studies. One of the original definitions of a two-earner couple referred to combining two jobs with childrearing (Rapoport & Rapoport, 1969). However, not all research specifies the types of jobs the two members hold, whether there are children, or the ages of the children. Fourth, research on dual-earner or dual-career couples is woman-centered; that is, there is an assumption that work is primary for men, and home and family are primary for women. Different assessment techniques are used with female and male subjects, and some questions (e.g., concerning domestic work) are asked of wives but not husbands. Finally, there is little cross-cultural research on dual-career or dual-earner couples. Much of the research has been conducted in the United States (A. Lewis & Cooper, 1988a), although the topic is receiving increasing attention in Great Britain.

In a comprehensive review of research on dual-career managers, Jeanne Brett and her colleagues (Brett, Stroh, & Reilly, 1992) discussed how dual-career managers compare with their single counterparts as well as with the traditional career model (i.e., a single breadwinner who is typically the man). The section that follows draws largely from that review.

Effects of Dual-Career Status on Comparisons Between Female and Male Managers

Comparisons of career outcomes for male and female managers are complicated by the fact that they differ substantially in a number of attributes. In particular, the majority of male managers are married and have children, whereas the majority of female managers are either single or without children. Furthermore, variables such as the spouse's status (e.g., job level, salary) may have different implications for women than for men. As a result, it is necessary to introduce many qualifiers into the following descriptions. Sometimes, male–female differences will depend on whether the managers in question are single, are in dual-career relationships, have children, and so forth.

Promotion, Mobility, and Salary.   Brett et al. (1992) found that dual-career female managers are promoted as frequently as their male peers but have less mobility. This is consistent with other research (Bielby & Bielby, 1992). Although there were no differences among the four groups compared in Brett et al.'s study (i.e., single men, single women, dual-career men, and dual-career women) in terms of the proportion who turned down job transfers during the previous 5 years, dual-career women without children were most likely to consider transfers, whereas dual-career women with children and single women were less willing to move internationally than any group of men. The decision to relocate is often a more complicated decision for women than men. Although stressful for both men and women, moving may be particularly difficult for women. Promotion and transfer occur often in the stage of a woman's career when she is also considering whether to have children. This may be a stage when women face the ambiguity or uncertainty of the effects of having children on their careers (Brett et al., 1992).

Although relative salaries of husbands and wives in dual-career relationships varied considerably in this managerial sample, 52% of dual-career females earned $5,000 more than their husbands. Only 20% of these women earned $5,000 less than their husbands. Furthermore, the jobs of dual-career females tended to be of equal or greater status than the husband's. Salary increases for female managers were smaller over a 5-year period than were salaries of single and dual-career male groups. Dual-career men's salaries increased by 63%, singles men's by 61%, and dual-career women's by only 55%. On the other hand, dual-career women received larger salaries than single women. Although more dual-career female managers occupied jobs in the better paying industries than did single men, the men's salaries were larger by 6%.

In the United States, geographic mobility and relocation are related to occupational advancement (Markham, 1987). People who move for occupational advancement are usually better off than those who do not move; this is especially true for men (Harris, 1981; Sell, 1982) and unmarried women (Mincer, 1978; Sandell, 1977; Sandell & Koenig, 1978). A married couple is more likely to move in the interest of advancing the husband's careers than the wife's. It is not surprising, then, that the husband's income is positively affected by such moves. Dual-career couples' moves also favor the husbands' careers. Although overall family income tends to increase after relocating (Mincer, 1978), wives' incomes generally decrease with moves.

Women managers may not review their career progression as advancing (like men do) because they may question whether they are getting back what they have invested. Male peers transfer more frequently and receive better salaries. Although there are apparently no differences in promotion rates, women's promotions are not always linked with relocation so their salaries do not keep up with their male peers'.

Comparisons Between Managers With or Without Children.
Brett et al. (1992) also compared dual-career women with children to
those without children. The career literature suggests that for women,
family responsibilities lead to work–family conflict. One frequent response
to this conflict is to reduce one's workload, which, in turn, often limits
women's career advancement (Parasuraman & Greenhaus, 1993). However, in the Brett sample, it appeared that dual-career women with and
without children were treated similarly. In terms of opportunities to transfer, women with children moved as frequently as those without children
and considered moves more frequently. Although one third of the dual-
career women with children withdrew their names from transfer considerations one or more times, these decisions did not significantly reduce their
rates of mobility.

The salaries of dual-career women with children were actually greater
than those of women without children; 74% of those with children earned
at least $5,000 more than their husbands, and only 11% earned $5,000 less
than their husbands. Therefore, there was little evidence that organizations
discriminated against dual-career women with children more than women
without children. However, compared to men, both these groups had fewer
opportunities for transfer and salary increases (Brett et al., 1992).

Dual-career couples without children appear similar to traditional couples (i.e., where the man is the breadwinner and the woman stays at home)
in terms of salary. In dual-career couples without children, male managers
brought more income and prestige into the family than did their wives;
at least 90% of them earned at least $5,000 more than their wives. Interest-
ingly, dual-career men with children were more reluctant to move than
either dual-career men without children or traditional men with children;
their rates of moving or promotion were lower than either comparison
group (Brett et al., 1992). Dual-career men with children moved every 5
years; dual-career men without children moved every 4 years; and traditional men with children moved every 3.5 years. Dual-career men with
children withdrew their names from move considerations more than did
traditional male earners (30% vs. 19%). On the other hand, traditional
men with children withdrew their names from transfer consideration as
frequently as did dual-career men with children. Yet the more frequent
moves of traditional male managers with children supported the notion
that they received more transfer opportunities than dual-career men with
children. The salary progression of dual-career men with children was
2% less than dual-career men without children and 7% less than traditional
men with children.

Comparing men who were married to homemakers with dual-career
men, Brett et al. (1992) found that salaries of dual-career men increased
by 63% over 5 years whereas traditional male managers' salaries increased

by 87% over the same period. This is consistent with other findings (Pfeffer & Ross, 1982). This difference may be the result of social expectations and gender stereotypes; specifically, the man is assumed to be the sole financial support of the family and the nonemployed wife provides resources and assistance (e.g., flexibility in moving, etc.) to the husband's career (Pfeffer & Ross, 1982).

Dual Careers and Work/Life Attitudes.   There were no significant differences in work attitudes among dual-career, single, or traditional family types, including attitudes toward pay, security, the work itself, and organizational commitment (Brett et al., 1992). Managers with and without children also showed similar attitudes. One exception to this pattern involves job involvement: Women were less involved than men. Also, dual-career couples were least involved, whereas single managers were the most involved. In addition, regardless of gender, managers with children were less job-involved than those without children. Dual-career women had the lowest levels of job involvement. The finding that dual-career men are as satisfied with their jobs and lives as are traditional men suggests that dual-career families may live with only modest changes in traditional family practices (Kingston, 1988). Because so many women move into and out of the workforce or hold part-time jobs, husbands and wives work full-time year-round in only one fourth of the two-job families.

Dual Careers, House Care, and Child Care

When women enter the paid workforce and work outside the home, one might expect that they would also engage in less house care and less child care. In fact, working women spend less time on housekeeping but as much time on childrearing each week as women not employed outside of the home. A related assumption suggests that with their wives working outside the home, husbands would increase their contributions to house and child care. Research data on the sharing of household and childrearing responsibilities by working husbands and wives are equivocal. There is evidence that working women continue to bear greater responsibility for home and child care than their husbands (Biernat & Wortman, 1991). For example, among dual-career couples in the United Kingdom, 79% of the women do nearly all the housework. Furthermore, men in dual-career families average 6 more hours of free time per week than their wives (Henwood, Rimmons, & Wicks, 1987). Husbands are most likely to participate in home and child care more when their wives are psychologically involved with their own work (Yogev & Brett, 1985) and when the men are engaged in fewer hours of paid work (Biernat & Wortman, 1991;

Pleck, 1983). Cross-cultural research also shows that female managers spend more time with their children than do male managers (Larwood & Wood, 1977, 1979; A. Lewis & Cooper, 1988).

Couples share more of the housework if the wives earn a larger share of the family income (Ishii-Kuntz & Coltrane, 1992). The degree to which husbands restructure their work for family activities depends on a number of work and home-care variables. Men will restructure or make changes to accommodate work–family demands depending upon their occupation and their career stage (Brett & Yogev, 1989). Male managers do the least restructuring, whereas male professionals (e.g., doctors, psychotherapists) do the most. Men in an established career stage also do more restructuring. The more paid help that the family receives with child care or housework, the more restructuring men are likely to do. On the other hand, men's restructuring is not related to number of hours worked per day, number of extra work activities, frequency of travel, or psychological involvement in work (Brett & Yogev, 1989). One explanation that Brett and Yogev provide is that men who see more need for restructuring may also see the need for more outside help. Furthermore, there is a negative relationship between men's self-efficacy and amount of restructuring. Those men who restructure may feel that they are not handling things well (Brett & Yogev, 1989).

Wives' attempts to restructure their work are also related to a range of work and nonwork variables (Brett & Yogev, 1989). Women doing extra work activities and who are highly involved in their work do significantly less restructuring. Like men, women's restructuring is not related to number of hours worked per day, travel, or career stage. Nonwork variables that predict women's restructuring include family stage and number of family–work activities. Women with young children do more restructuring than women with older children. Furthermore, women who spend more time on housework and child care do more restructuring. A woman's restructuring is not related to number of children, family involvement, paid help with housework and child care, or her self-efficacy (Brett & Yogev, 1989). Finally, a woman's level of restructuring does not predict her husband's level or vice versa. Therefore, different factors are associated with restructuring for men and women.

SUMMARY

Women are not new to the workforce, and current expectations are that 95 of 100 women will work outside the home sometime in their lives

(Betz & Fitzgerald, 1987). Most married women work outside the home, including more than 61% of mothers with children under 18 years of age and 52% of mothers with preschoolers. However, much of what we know about careers can be labeled "the vocational development of middle-class males" (Tyler, 1977, p. 40). During the last several decades, interest in women's work lives and careers has increased. Yet few theories exclusively address women's career development and even fewer theories attempt to understand minority male and female career development without using White men as the referent or comparison group (Betz & Fitzgerald, 1987; Osipow, 1983).

Experts on career development state repeatedly that, although women's career development is similar to men's, there are enough differences to warrant different theories (Larwood & Gattiker, 1987; Osipow, 1983). Women encounter experiences in society, in their education, and at work (e.g., discrimination) that men do not. Researchers need to consider how the family and competing external work environments affect both men and women and to identify other factors that distinguish men's and women's career-related experiences.

Because women often are socialized to expect some work interruptions, continuous employment throughout a woman's life (compared to a man's) may be more heavily influenced by support from and expectations of others, decisions to marry or have children, and the spouse's career. Mentoring relationships are important to the success of both men and women in the workplace. Mentoring provides valuable informal support, including coaching, as well as psychosocial support. Yet, there are numerous barriers to mentoring for women, including few female mentors as one moves up the organizational hierarchy. In male-dominated occupations, women will likely have male mentors and may have limited opportunities to establish contact with potential mentors due to unfavorable features associated with the status of token. Lack of a mentor, however, may reduce job effectiveness for women.

One myth or misperception about young, married, working women is that they will interrupt their work lives for extended periods of time to bear and care for children. Although women do stop work briefly to have children, the majority return to work after a very brief interruption. The duration of the "interruption" may be more driven by harsh economic realities (i.e., unpaid maternity leaves under the Family Leave Act) than by consideration of the welfare of the mother, child, and family.

There is also evidence that prior to her departure from the workplace, a pregnant woman is often viewed as a sick person or, at best, as temporarily disabled. Men tend to more strongly hold this view than do other women. It is not surprising, then, that pregnant women find it difficult to establish and maintain mentoring relationships.

Although lack of adequate child care often may be a source of work–family stress, quality child care and dependent-care programs have positive effects on working mothers. On-site care can enhance women's self-efficacy in handling work–family conflicts. However, more research is needed on the specific links between child-care features and child development. Also, accommodation and care for sick children have received little attention, in terms of both research and practical opportunities for working mothers. There is evidence that children of employed mothers and fathers benefit from having both as strong, interesting role models.

Finally, with increasing numbers of women of childbearing age participating in the workforce, the work and family experiences of dual-career couples have become more important. Occupational advancement is associated with mobility, and dual-career women tend to have less mobility yet similar rates of promotion to men. Dual-career women with children receive larger salaries than women without children yet, compared to men, both these groups have few salary increases. Men and women also hold similar work attitudes except in terms of job involvement, where dual career females show the lowest levels of job involvement.

GLOSSARY

Advancement stage: Second stage of career progression, which involves new experiences including transfers and promotions and is characterized by achievement, greater responsibility, and upward mobility.

Career management: Lifelong process of learning about oneself, jobs, and organizations; setting personal career goals; developing strategies for achieving those goals; and revising those goals based on work and life experiences.

Career network: Contact with many colleagues for mutual benefit.

Career plateau: A point in an employee's career where he or she might be doing good work but for some reason has a lower probability of moving up the organizational hierarchy.

Career salience: When one's career plays a very important and vital role in one's life and decisions.

Corporate reengineering and restructuring: Process of changing how different parts of an organization are separated from and interconnected to each other. The structure creates and reinforces relationships within and among groups in the organization. Furthermore, the structure of an organization shapes various interpersonal and group processes within the workplace.

Cultural approach: An approach to studying women's careers focusing on how the cultural images of men and women are shaped by social roles and life choices at home, at work, and in marriage.

Developmental perspective: Perspective whereby individuals are studied as they pass through a series of stages in their lives. The stages follow a specific pattern and involve distinct sets of activities.

Discrete exchange: An exchange where the organization gains productivity and the individual gains work experience.

Downsizing: Reduction in labor force within an organization.

Dual-career couple: Two professional people in a significant relationship (e.g., marriage) where both partners pursue careers that are characterized by strong commitment, personal growth, and high levels of responsibility.

Dual-earner: A person in a significant relationship (e.g., marriage) where both partners have jobs that may or may not be professional, upwardly mobile, or involving.

Establishment stage: Stage when individual begins as a newcomer to an organization.

Gender model: Model to explore the work behavior of men and women where perceptions of and reactions to work are treated as a result of personal characteristics and relationships to family situations.

Independent variable: In experimental research, a variable that is manipulated while its effect on another variable is observed.

Job accessibility: Availability of jobs in a geographical area.

Job model: Model that has been used to explore the work behavior of men and women. It emphasizes how actual work influences perceptions of work as well as mental and physical health and is often used to explain differences among men and women in work perceptions and behaviors.

Longitudinal study: Type of research in which the investigator observes the same people over and over again; there are several measurements over an extended period of time.

Maintenance stage: The third stage in career development where a number of personal changes occur and a person takes one of three career paths: star, solid citizen, or deadwood.

Mentoring: Relationship where an experienced, productive manager or employee relates to a less-experienced employee and assists with his or her personal development for the benefit of the individual and the organization.

Merger: When two organizations join together under one structure.

Occupational aspirations model: Model which posits that people classify occupations along dimensions of sex-type, level of work, and field of work and then assess the suitability of occupations consistent with their self-concept and amount of effort they are willing to exert.

Occupational complexity: Degree to which an occupation requires the incumbent to possess intelligence and skill in order to perform complex tasks that require decision-making and responsibility.

Occupational excellence: Quality whereby an individual continually increases or acquires skills that are marketable across organizations.

Organizational empowerment: Power that comes down to business units and then to employees from executive levels.

Outcome expectations and incentives: Beliefs about the consequences of performance.

Paradigm shift: Movement from one model or pattern to another.

Project allegiance: Commitment that the employee and the organization have to the success of a given project.

Protégé: Less experienced participant in a mentoring relationship who receives assistance with personal development from a more senior and experienced employee.

Psychological Approach: Approach to studying women's careers that focuses on gender-specific ways in which men and women examine and make sense of work.

Psychological contract: Implicit or unspoken understanding between the employee and the organization usually involving what they expect from each other.

Psychosocial Support: A type of support a mentor often provides; includes enhancing the protégé's sense of competence, providing friendship, and offering positive regard and acceptance.

Sociological approach: Study of women's careers focusing on how social institutions and practices contribute to observed differences between men and women.

Self-efficacy: A component of self-concept that deals with one's perceived abilities and competencies to deal with a given task.

Self-concept: A complex collection of information that somehow is held together as oneself.

Self-limiting attitudes: Attitudes that result from negative self-evaluations and cause people to limit their range of career options and have limited confidence, assertiveness, and presentation of competence.

Sick role model: Model used to examine perceptions of pregnant women. Using this model, pregnancy is viewed as a deviant role, implying dependency of a sick person.

Tokens: The underrepresented members in a group where, for example, there is a 85:15 ratio of men to women or vice versa; they are people who differ from the majority on a readily observable demographic characteristic like gender, age, or race.

Vertical career progression: Progression up the organizational hierarchy, often through promotions.

Vocational psychology: The study of individual factors such as interests and situational factors that lead to occupational choice and satisfaction.

Withdrawal stage: Stage that occurs later in life (around age 60) when employees may become increasingly disengaged from work due to stereotyping, health factors, skill deterioration, or discrimination.

11

Gender and Leadership

Profiles of Women Leaders

Carol Stephenson, president and CEO of Stentor Resources Centre, Inc., an alliance of nine major Canadian telephone companies. Stephenson began her career as a telephone operator at Bell Canada while finishing her undergraduate education at the University of Toronto. After graduation she entered Bell's management trainee program, where she progressed to plant manager of a switching center. There, she supervised 60 men, mostly engineers and technical specialists who were tired of being "overmanaged." She responded to their heed by becoming a resource person, allowing the employees to self-manage as long as performance levels remained high. Her success led to more promotions, and she eventually became vice-president of operator services. Here, her span of control included over 3,000 operators, mostly women, who, she discovered, were bright, articulate, and well educated. Again, using her penchant for empowerment, she altered these operators' jobs from providing routine information to promoting products and services that generated millions of dollars in new revenues. Following her success in line-level positions, she became vice-president of regulatory affairs, a policy position. Subsequently, she was promoted to group vice-president at Stentor and then appointed as president and CEO. She credits her success to powerful female role models in her family (her grandmother owned and operated a business school and her mother was a nurse), a critical yet supportive husband, supportive and influential mentors throughout her career, and her own willingness to accept risky positions and challenging assignments. Furthermore, she values her "female" style of management, which includes an ability to listen and speak clearly and honestly, to mediate between conflicting parties and views, and to brighten the workplace with a new sense of style.

—Source: Stephenson (1997)

Rebecca Mark, executive, Enron Corp., an international energy business. Mark doesn't shy away from using her feminine charms to secure multimillion-dollar contracts in developing nations such as Brazil and India. Eschewing "dress for success" formulas of dark-colored, below-the-knee masculine suits, Mark chooses between tight pants and a red and white jacket for a lunch with the major clients, and a fluorescent red–orange miniskirted suit for a speech before a crowd dressed in dull gray and navy. And with any outfit are the 3-inch stiletto heels. Mark admits that although her fashion flare provides a bit of theater, helping her to make important deals with influential political and business leaders, her business and interpersonal savvy have helped her rise to the level of imminent CEO. Having impressed a colleague in a previous job in Houston, Mark was handpicked as the finance chief of a new, risky upstart business, Enron, which developed out of energy deregulation. Soon, Mark's job was to open new markets for private energy plants that could sell power to utilities. Mark capitalized on a chance meeting with a Brazilian energy consultant to develop a market for Enron in Brazil. After many meetings and negotiations with heads of state in Brazil and Bolivia, Mark captured the Brazilian energy market for Enron. She met with similar success in India. Mark grew up on a farm east of Kansas City, Missouri, where she learned the value of hard work.

She moved to Texas, earning her BA in psychology and an MA in international business at Baylor University. Once her career began to develop, she completed a Harvard MBA. In addition to having a flare for style and theatrics, Mark is a consummate negotiator and compromiser. She is willing to take short-term losses to gain a long-term win–win solution netting a far more profitable arrangement for Enron. Analysts predict that if she isn't picked off by another company, Mark, 44, may be the first female CEO in the highly male-oriented energy business.

—Source: Mack (1998)

Leadership is a concept that pervades all ages, generations, cultures, and domains of life. Whether one discusses mythological heroes who overcame tremendous obstacles to obtain divine leadership powers (Campbell 1949) or the challenges of U.S. businesses to remain competitive in a global economy, leadership remains an essential qualification for progress. As the two very different profiles of successful female leaders depicted at the beginning of this chapter demonstrate, there is no one best way to lead and be effective. This chapter summarizes the major theories of leadership in organizations and examines the implications for female and male leaders. Next, research examining comparisons of male and female leaders is reviewed. Finally, additional challenges facing female leaders and organizations that strive to fully utilize their leadership resources are discussed.

DEFINITIONS AND THEORIES
OF LEADERSHIP

Scholars in a number of disciplines, ranging from psychology to military science, have written extensively on leadership, and a number of theories, perspectives, and definitions of leadership exist.

What Is Leadership?

Although definitions and perspectives on leadership vary widely, most experts on the topic agree that leadership implies influence that goes beyond normal role requirements (Yukl & Van Fleet, 1992). A supervisor, for example, who orders workers to complete tasks within a certain period of time is influencing these workers but not leading them. The workers are simply responding to the role demands of the supervisor. On the other hand, a supervisor who inspires workers to achieve difficult goals amid mounting obstacles is exhibiting leadership. In the latter case, the supervisor's influence is greater than the rewards and punishments legitimately accorded to him or her due to organizational position. To this end, it is important to distinguish between leadership and management, keeping in mind that most of the research on leaders looks at managers. Nonetheless, Robinson (1989) summarized the difference between managing and leading. Whereas managing others involves directing others, competing, using hierarchy, emphasizing consistency and sameness, using slow decision-making, seeking permission, being averse to risks, making individual contributions, and seeing people as an expense, leading others involves guiding and developing others, collaborating, using networks, emphasizing diversity and flexibility, making fast decisions and judgments, taking risks, being a team player, and seeing people as an asset.

One implication of the distinction between management and leadership is that the people who are nominally in charge of a work group (e.g., the lines of authority depicted on an organizational chart) are not necessarily its leaders. In chapter 6, we distinguish between structural power (i.e., formal authority) and personal power (i.e., influence over others). This distinction is maintained here. In this chapter, leadership refers to extra-role influence, not necessarily to the formal position one holds in an organization.

Traditional Theories of Leadership

Theories of leadership can be characterized broadly as being concerned with who leads (i.e., characteristics of leaders), how they lead (i.e., leader behaviors), under what circumstances the lead (i.e., situational theories), or who follows the leader (i.e., relational theories). Examples of all four approaches are presented next.

Trait Approaches.   Over the millennia, great leaders were believed to possess special traits or attributes that distinguished them from other people. According to this "great-man" or "great-person" theory, leaders seemed to have extraordinary ambition, clear and articulate vision, and a winning personality that drew people to them. Sir Francis Galton, a member of an eminent European family which included Charles Darwin, argued that the traits which distinguished great leaders from others were inherited. Early systematic research in which the traits of a broad variety of leaders were compared with a broad variety of people who were not described as leaders found very few consistent differences (Mann, 1959; Stogdill, 1948). Recently, however, there has been a renewed interest in learning whether leaders possess certain traits or characteristics to a greater extent than do nonleaders. We return to this in our discussion of charismatic and transformational leadership later in the chapter.

Behavioral Approaches.   The behavioral approach focuses on what leaders do as opposed to what traits they possess. Researchers at the Ohio State University asked employees (and others) what types of behaviors or acts they observed in their leaders. A long list of behaviors were collected, which the researchers determined fell into two categories: consideration (C) and initiating structure (IS) (see Fleishman, 1973 for a summary of this research). Consideration encompasses behaviors that demonstrate a concern for people, their needs, and their relationships with others; initiating structure encompasses concern for organizing and accomplishing tasks. Because these factors are uncorrelated, a particular leader can demonstrate both C and IS behaviors, one or the other, or neither (although, by definition, a person who does not engage in either C or IS behaviors is not a leader). The elegance and simplicity of this model led to a proliferation of programs to teach leadership skills. Most notably, Blake and Mouton's (1964) managerial grid emphasized the importance of utilizing a high degree of both C and IS behaviors.

This simple two-factor taxonomy dominated the research on leadership in the 1950s and 60s; however, it did not appear to capture the richness and complexity of what leaders did. In this era of high technology, rapid communication and transportation, globalization, and increasing diversity of human resources, leaders must draw on a broad range of behaviors and skills to navigate their businesses through tumultuous waters. Leaders are constantly communicating (both speaking and listening), making decisions, strategizing, deciphering information, building relationships, expanding networks, and solving problems (Lipman-Bluman, 1996; Yukl & Van Fleet, 1992). Leadership researcher Gary Yukl and his colleagues developed a more specific list of behaviors that most managers engage in from time to time depending on the situation. These including planning and organizing, problem solving, clarifying, informing, monitoring, motivating, consulting, recognizing, supporting, managing conflict and team building, networking, delegating, developing and mentoring, and rewarding (see Yukl & Van Fleet, 1992; Yukl, Wall, & Lepsinger, 1990).

In general, the two-factor approach to leadership has not revealed a great deal about what makes an effective leader (Yukl & Van Fleet, 1992). Although subordinates seem to be more satisfied with their jobs if their leaders use a lot of C behaviors (see Yukl & Van Fleet, 1992), both domains of behaviors (i.e., C and IS) as well as the more specific sets of behaviors identified by Yukl et al. (1990) are needed for effective leadership. The behavioral theories tend to overlook the importance of the situation and the interaction between the situation and the leader's traits and styles in determining how effective a particular leader will be.

Situational Theories. Would Adolf Hitler have become such a powerful figure in the mid-1920s and 1930s if Germany hadn't suffered devastating economic losses from World War I? Would Martin Luther King, Jr., been an influential leader if he had lived a century earlier—or later? Of course, we can't answer these questions empirically, but asking them points out the importance of considering the situation when we study leadership style, behavior, and effectiveness.

Looking more closely at leadership in organizations, Stewart (1976) noted that when deciding how to interact with subordinates, peers, or the public, leaders consider the extent to which the work environment they manage is predictable versus certain and unhurried versus rushed, and whether work tasks are sustained for a long period of time or are broken up by other distractions or requirements. Other researchers have focused on the interpretations or **attributions** leaders make about why subordinates act the way they do (especially for poor performance) in deciding how to handle subordinates (Green & Mitchell, 1979). For example, if the leader believes that the subordinate did not have the proper tools or equipment, then she or he is likely to try to change the situation (e.g., provide the tools). However, if the leader believes the subordinate was lazy or lacked the required abilities, then she or he is more likely to punish the employee or provide remedial training.

Situational theories of leadership try to explain leader style, behavior, or effectiveness by understanding how aspects of the situation shape leaders' behavior. Although situational approaches remind us of the importance of external conditions, most people, including scholars, believe that leaders not only are products of their environments but also shape their situations.

Contingency theories of leadership take the view that the personal characteristics of leaders, such as their traits, behaviors, and preferred leadership styles, interact with characteristics of the situations in which they lead, such as the degree to which group members get along, subordinates' skills and professionalism, or the degree to which work tasks are routine and predictable, in determining how successful leaders will be. There are several different contingency theories. Some focus on overall leadership effectiveness (e.g., Fiedler's contingency theory, R.E. Fiedler, 1978; and path-goal theory, House & Mitchell, 1974), whereas others focus on the acceptance and effectiveness of leaders' decisions (e.g., normative decision model, Vroom & Jago, 1974; Vroom & Yetton, 1973) and even the need for leadership (Kerr & Jermier's substitutes for leadership theory, 1978). Table 11.1 summarizes the major contingency theories. Regardless of their focus, these theories share the assumption that certain types of leader skills, styles, or approaches are more or less effective

TABLE 11.1
Summary of Leadership Contingencies Theories and Models

Theory or model	Important personal leadership characteristics	Important situational characteristics	Expected outcomes
Fiedler's Contingency Theory	Leader style, measured by the LPC (Least Preferred Coworker) scale • High LPC scorers prefer "person-oriented" leadership • Low LPC scorers prefer "task-oriented" leadership	Group atmosphere—degree to which group members get along Task structure—extent to which the task is clearly understood vs. ambiguous Leader power—amount of authority the leader has in the group	If situation characteristics are all favorable (good leader–member relations, high task structure, and high authority), or if they are all poor, the low-LPC leader should be more effective than the high-LPC leader. The latter is expected to do well when the situation is moderately favorable (some aspects are good, others are not).
Path-Goal Theory	Leader behaviors/styles • Directive leadership • Supportive leadership • Participative leadership • Achievement-oriented leadership	Subordinate characteristics (locus of control and/or ability) Environmental forces (task characteristics, formal authority systems, primary work group)	Depending on the situational characteristics, leaders use one of the four styles of leadership to influence subordinates' perceptions and to motive them. This leads to role clarity, expectations of meeting goals, job satisfaction, and improved performance.
Substitutes for Leadership[a]	Leader behaviors • Reward and punishment behaviors • Instrumental and supportive behavior	Subordinate characteristics (ability experience, training, need for independence, professional orientation, or indifference toward organizational rewards Task characteristics (unambiguous and routine, self-providing feedback, or intrinsically satisfying) Organizational characteristics (formal, inflexible, highly specified and active advisory and staff functions, closely knit, cohesive groups, rewards not in leader's control, or spatial distance between superior and subordinates)	When neutralizers (subordinate, task, or organizational characteristics) are present, leaders do not need to exhibit reward/punishment or instrumental/supportive behaviors (depending on the nature of the neutralizer) to achieve group effectiveness. The neutralizer substitutes for the need for leadership. When the neutralizer is not present (e.g., tasks are ambiguous and novel instead of unambiguous and routine), leadership is needed (e.g., the leader needs to be instrumental and supportive) to achieve group effectiveness.

Continues

TABLE 11.1
Continued

Theory or model	Important personal leadership characteristics	Important situational characteristics	Expected outcomes
Vroom–Yetton Decision Tree Model	Leader decision styles • Authoritarian • Consultative • Delegation • Group based	Questions the leader asks about the subordinates and about the situation in which the decision needs to be made: • Quality solution needed? • Leader has sufficient information? • Problem structured? • Subordinate acceptance needed? • If solved alone, subordinates would accept? • Subordinates share goals? • Conflict likely?	Leader follows a decision tree containing these seven questions. Depending on the pattern of answers, a feasible set consisting of one or more of seven decision styles (based on the four described to the left) can be used to make the decision. If the leader chooses a style in the feasible set, the decision is more likely to be successful than if a style not in the feasible set is chosen.

Note: From Fiedler (1967), House & Mitchell (1974), Kerr & Jermier (1978), Podsakoff et al., (1966),Vroom & Yetton (1973).
[a]In this theory, important situational characteristics are called "neutralizers."

under different conditions. In more technical terms, characteristics of the situation moderate (make more or less important) the degree to which a personal characteristic of the leader will be associated with good outcomes for the group or organization.

Scientific investigations into the accuracy or validity of contingency theories have yielded mixed results. For example, critics have argued that although several studies support Fiedler's predictions, many other studies contradict the theory's predictions (Korman, 1974). The substitutes for leadership theory (Kerr & Jermier, 1978) was rigorously tested by Podsakoff, MacKenzie, and Bommer (1996), who noted that past research on the substitutes theory did not support the theory's predictions. Instead, Podsakoff et al. (1996) found that characteristics of subordinates (e.g., being intolerant of organizational rewards), of the task (e.g., the extent to which the task directly provided performance feedback to the worker), and of the organization (e.g., the extent to which the organization followed formal rules and guidelines) had strong and direct effects on many outcomes believed to be influenced by good leadership, such as worker satisfaction, commitment to the organization, and the extent to which subordinates experience **role ambiguity,** regardless of what leaders did or what style they used. Similarly, critics of path-goal theory found that the model was unable to support many of its predictions (Schriesheim & DeNisi, 1981). Thus, although contingency theories of leadership entice us to view leadership in a more comprehensive and integrated manner than other leadership theories, it appears that more refinement or different conceptualizations of leadership are needed.

Relational-Based Theories. A more recent development in our understanding of leadership has been to move away from traits, behaviors, styles, or situational characteristics that determine leadership. Instead, leadership is viewed in terms of relationships between leaders and followers. The quality of these relationships determines how the leader and the follower respond to each other and how effective a team, group, or organization will be. Relationship-based leadership theories are based on social-exchange theory, which states that people will remain committed to a relationship to the extent that the benefits they receive from the relationship outweigh the costs of being in the relationship (Luthans, 1998). In leadership terms, both the leader and the followers commit to working together (i.e., the followers are willing to be led and the leader is willing to provide direction and support) as long as members find the relationship mutually satisfying.

An influential relationship-based leadership theory is the *leader–member exchange* (LMX) model by Dansereau, Graen, and Haga (1975).

Also called the vertical dyad linkage model, LMX theory claims that leaders change their style of leadership depending on the quality of the relationship they have with a particular subordinate or follower. The leader provides more decision latitude, authority, and consideration for subordinates who are able to take on more responsibility. These followers become part of the leader's "in group" and the level of exchange between these followers and the leader is relatively high. The leader spends considerable time developing and mentoring ingroup followers, and in return, they become loyal, dependable, and hardworking. Subordinates who merely comply with the formal requirements of the job description become part of the leader's "out group." The level of exchange between these followers and the leader is much lower and more formal than between ingroup members. The leader provides less consideration and communicates with them less often and, in return, the followers merely fulfill their formal job or role obligations. By dividing subordinates into in groups and out groups, the leader is able to more effectively channel energy toward relationships that promise a high yield of rewards.

Leadership in the New Era

Pick up any business magazine or newspaper, or any of dozens of new books on leadership, management, and organizational change, or, better yet, talk to people who are working in almost any industry, and you'll quickly learn that organizations are changing rapidly. The rapid pace of technological developments affects not only the speed and the way in which products are designed and manufactured but also the types of services that are offered. A large Midwestern bank, for example, gives customers at remote branches, real estate offices, and even supermarkets an opportunity to interact directly with corporate experts via videoconferencing in order to apply for mortgages, make investments, or complete other complex services. Technology is changing the way people communicate: Cell phones, faxes, videoconferencing, and e-mail are breaking down the formality of interpersonal communication, increasing the speed with which information is exchanged and acted upon, and closing geographical and psychological gaps. Organizational structures are also shifting from rigid, hierarchically structured bureaucracies to lean, **decentralized,** employee-managed organizations, or a host of temporary structures, including **boundaryless organizations** and **virtual organizations,** in which organizations offering complementary services or specialized skills join together for a limited business venture. Amid all of the technological and organizational advances is a burgeoning multiethnic, multiracial labor force not only demanding full and equal access to employment opportunities but expressing the need to have their ethnic, racial, or gender-related talents and virtues valued and fully utilized instead of homogenized into preexisting White-male frameworks. According to a report prepared in the late 1980s, women and people of color including African-Americans, Hispanics, and Asians will make up the majority of new growth in the labor market over the next 2 decades (Johnston & Packer, 1987). With unemployment in the late 1990s at the lowest level in almost 3 decades, drawing upon the full multiracial, multiethnic labor force is not only a moral obligation but a business necessity.

The demands on and opportunities for leaders during these turbulent times, therefore, are immense. A simple, single-faceted approach (such as just traits, just behaviors, or just interaction skills) is insufficient for understanding all of the attributes leaders must possess and all the strategies they must enact in order to thrive. In this section, we address some of the more relevant and influential modern approaches to understanding leadership—transformational leadership and connective leadership—and also report advice from U.S. business leaders and management consultants and scholars about leadership in this turbulent era.

Transformational Leadership

Transformational leadership is "the process of influencing major changes in the attitudes and assumptions of organizational members . . . and building commitment for major changes in the organization's objectives and strategies" (Yukl & Van Fleet, 1992, p. 174). Transformational leadership goes beyond the day-to-day, reward/punishment-based styles described in "transactional" theories of leadership (e.g., leader–member exchange, Ohio State leadership studies). Transactional leadership produces incremental changes in the way followers behave, whereas transformational leadership produces fundamental changes in followers' beliefs and attitudes about the organization. Many scholars have argued that transformational leadership is critical for organizational effectiveness in an age of increasing turbulence and uncertainty.

Although many theories of transformational leadership exist (e.g., Burns, 1978; Conger & Kanungo, 1987; R.J. House, 1977), Bass' theory (1985) is more fully developed and has received more attention than most. Bass (1985) argued that leaders need to use both transactional and transformational leadership styles, albeit with a higher concentration of the latter. The transformation styles are labeled "the four I's":

1. Idealized influence: moral, outwardly focused behavior that inspires admiration, trust, and identification among followers.

2. Inspirational motivation: possessing charisma and vision.
3. Intellectual stimulation: inspiring creativity, innovation, and risk taking among followers.
4. Individualized consideration: attention to followers' growth needs by acting as a coach and mentor (Avolio, Waldman, & Yammarino, 1991).

There are three salient transactional leadership styles: contingent reward, management by exception, and laissez-faire. Contingent reward involves the exchange of rewards for desired results. Management by exception takes two forms: active (monitoring deviations from expectations and taking corrective action) or passive (waiting for mistakes to occur and then taking corrective action). Laissez-faire is characterized as the absence or avoidance of leadership and is neither transactional nor transformational (Bass & Avolio, 1994). Bass and Avolio argued that the most effective leaders engage primarily in transformational behaviors (the four I's), somewhat fewer contingent reward behaviors, and proportionately fewer management-by-exception and laissez-faire leadership behaviors.

A recent review (Lowe, Kroeck, & Sivasubramaniam, 1995) supported Bass and Avolio's (1994) claim. Across 39 published and unpublished studies that measured Bass' transformational and transactional leadership dimensions with real leaders in real organizations (as opposed to hypothetical leaders or contrived laboratory studies), individuals who used transformational skills were rated by their subordinates as more effective than those who led primarily with transactional styles. Furthermore, transformational leadership was associated with objective organizational measures of success (e.g., profit, percentage of goals met, or supervisory performance appraisals) more than was transactional leadership.

Connective Leadership

Organizational sociologist and management consultant Jean Lipman-Blumen (1996) described the new era that organizational, political, and social leaders face as the "connective era." This era replaces the physical era in which territorial boundaries defined a leader's domain and the geopolitical era in which political and ideological differences defined the boundaries of leader's influence. Although single-faceted leadership styles such as competitiveness and authoritarianism may have sufficed in previous eras, they are not sufficient (yet not completely obsolete) in the connective era. Two forces, interdependence and diversity, provide significant new challenges for leaders in the connective era. These forces summarize the conditions of change and turbulence described previously. First, with the rapid growth in technology and the breakdown of geopolitical boundaries, everything is connected to everything else. Second, as the world becomes smaller, due to these influences, recognition of diversity in cultures, values, preferences, styles, skin color, abilities, gender, and so forth is essential. Leaders in the connective era must draw upon a wealth of styles and abilities, especially those that emphasize mutuality and inclusiveness, to harness the forces of interdependence and diversity.

Lipman-Blumen (1996) is specifically concerned about the multitude of ways that leaders can achieve success for their organizations. She has done considerable research in developing a model of achievement styles for connective leaders (summarized in Table 11.2). Many of these styles are not new. The revelation is that connective leaders must draw on all or a substantial mix of many of these styles to achieve success, and that leaders must use their styles in accordance with the following principles:

- *Denatured Machiavellianism:* Unlike the self-interested "ends-justify the means" leader of Machiavelli's *The Prince,* the connective leader follows principled instrumentality in which the self and others are used ethically to achieve group goals or solve important organizational problems.
- *Authenticity and accountability:* If the leader always places organizational and societal goals above personal glory, then others will accept seemingly contradictory behavior, such as eliminating a satisfactorily performing subsidiary. Furthermore, when leaders communicate regularly and honestly with a wide range of stakeholders, accountability and trust increase.
- *The politics of commonalities:* Connective leaders take the widest view of problems, strategies, and solutions to foster a view of all the interconnected parts of systems and humanity.
- *Adopting a long-term perspective:* Although leaders exploit rapid change and temporariness, they must always consider the long-term impact of their decisions, making sure they can remain flexible in their efforts to achieve ultimate organizational and societal goals.
- *Leadership through expectation:* By empowering others to handle significant responsibilities, the connective leader is able to accomplish more tasks while also building a web of trusting relationships.
- *Personal odyssey for life's mission:* Connective leaders actively seek to better understand themselves, the organization, and the societies in which they live and interact.

Leaders in the connective era draw on many talents, skills, and styles in a principled, ethical manner to build effective, enduring relationships

TABLE 11.2

Achievement Styles for Connective Leadership

Category	Style	Focus	Example/description
Direct	Intrinsic	Focus on personal mastery or execution of a task. Derive pleasure from the work itself. Enjoy creativity, individual innovation, self-reliance, and autonomy.	People for whom doing their best is more important than beating the competition.
	Competitive	Focus on measuring themselves against an external standard, typically their competitors' accomplishments. Treat most situations as contests.	People for whom winning is the most important goal.
	Power	Focus on controlling, influencing, and coordinating people, tasks, resources, and situations. Enjoy taking charge and dominating.	People for whom coordinating and controlling and seeing results are not always just for personal glory but also for achieving important organizational or societal goals.
Relational	Collaborative	Focus on working with others to achieve mutual goals. Enjoy smooth-working, long-term relationships with others and short-term, energized, high-intensity collaborations.	People who realize that long-term success is often more feasible when working together rather than working competitively.
	Contributory	Focus on providing support to help significant others achieve mutual goals.	Stereotypically, women have capitalized on contributory styles to support spouses or children's goals, but these styles are also used effectively by leaders who find that helping others achieve goals forwards a mutual agenda.
	Vicarious	Focus on encouraging and guiding others to their goals. Identify with the dreams and goals of other leaders. Do not participate directly in the tasks of the other achiever.	People for whom personal happiness comes from watching the success of others, such as mentors or sports fans.
Instrumental	Personal	Focus on using all their personal resources, including intellect, humor, charm, physical attractiveness, persuasive skills, and social status, to achieve success.	Charismatic leaders like J.F. Kennedy, M.L. King, Jr., and Steve Jobs (see also the highlight on Rebecca Marks, beginning of chapter) who possess special characteristics that draw others into their goals and aspirations.
	Social	Focus on using relationships with others to achieve desired goals. Tend to build elaborate networks with people who have specific strengths, skills, or connections that will be useful to the achiever at some point.	Not just social climbers, but people who recognize the importance of building relationships with others.
	Entrusting	Assume that others share their goals and trust that others will use their talents and rise to the occasion when needed. Rely on trust and positive expectations.	People who arouse intrinsic desires in others to meet challenging goals for the good of the group, organization, or society.

Note: Data from Lipman-Blumen (1996).

with followers, constituents, and even business competitors in order to successfully harness the forces of interdependence and diversity that shape the modern landscape.

Advice for Leaders in the Modern Era

The changes to the world business community described previously are well understood among progressive business leaders, management consultants, and scholars. Francis Hesselbein and her associates at the Peter Drucker Foundation for Nonprofit Management compiled a collection of essays and advice on leadership challenges and opportunities from these leaders and scholars (Hesselbein, Goldsmith, & Beckhard, 1996). Although this information does not compare with scientific theory and empirical research, it does provide insights into the future direction of leadership. Follow-up scientific investigations will lend credence or doubt to the truthfulness of their insights. The following themes have been gleaned from these essays (see also exemplars of these themes in Table 11.3).

Vision.   By definition, leaders in this turbulent era face complex issues and forces that must be carefully evaluated, balanced, and integrated to develop a successful strategy. Many stakeholder groups, including organizational members at all levels, customers, shareholders, and community members, are demanding to have a voice and an important role in shaping and guiding the organization's agenda. Leaders need to develop and articulate their vision for achieving success for the organization (Kanter, 1996). Furthermore, this vision must resonate with the goals and aspirations of the constituents (Kouzes & Posner, 1996), must create a sense of community among stakeholders so that everyone is guided by a common purpose (Pinchot, 1996), and must serve as a "glue" that keeps autonomous and even competing entities within organizations united for a common purpose (Handy, 1996; Pinchot, 1996).

Sharing Leadership.   The concept of empowering employees to make decisions and take responsibility has been an incipient value of the **Human Relations Movement,** and it has not lost its value in over 50 years. In fact, it has broadened from the concept of simple delegation to fully charging leadership responsibilities among all members of the organization (W. Bridges, 1996; Handy, 1996) to the concept of "servant leadership," where the organizational hierarchy is turned upside down and "top" managers consider themselves servants to a fully empowered workforce (Greenleaf, 1977). Pinchot (1996) offered a unique leadership-sharing model in which empowered subunits of organizations compete

TABLE 11.3

Exemplars of Leadership Themes

Theme	Exemplar
Theme 1: Vision	**Frances Hesselbein,** currently president of the Peter F. Drucker Foundation for Nonprofit Management and chairman of the Board of Governors of the Josephson Institute for the Advancement of Ethics. Hesselbein is credited as the outstanding leader of the voluntary sector. From 1976 to 1990, Hesselbein was CEO of Girl Scouts of America. In 1976, Girl Scouts had over 3 million members and was run by over 650,000 volunteers. Cookie sales grossed a third of a billion dollars annually, but the Girl Scouts had not kept up with the increasing social changes of the previous decades. The Girl Scouts remained a White, middle-class club. Hesselbein worked with her board and management team to debate the purpose and mission of the scouts. From this emerged a new mission: "To help each girl reach her own potential." To pursue this mission, Hesselbein wanted to triple minority membership. She and her colleagues succeeded by creating a community in which local leaders felt inspired and empowered to achieve this goal. Through participatory leadership and respect for all opinions, Hesselbein was able to unite people with different and sometimes opposing goals. Her willingness to listen and respect all points of view helped build cohesion within the organization instead of divisiveness.
Theme 2: Sharing	**Max De Pree,** CEO of Herman Miller, one of the largest producers of office furniture. De Pree has build his company's reputation as one of the most creative innovators of the industry because he trusts the strengths of all Hermann Miller employees. For motivation, Herman Miller has long utilized the Scanlon plan, which rewards employees with financial gains from their suggestions for improving productivity. De Pree is also unafraid to surround himself with advisors and managers who have better skills and abilities than he, being unafraid to "abandon himself to the strength of others."
Theme 3: Credibility	**Anita Roddick,** founder of The Body Shop. Roddick has built a successful international business by emphasizing such business goals as a concern for the environment, trade with developing nations instead of aid, education instead of advertising pressure for customers, and promotion of social causes and volunteerism among employees and customers. When Roddick travels to Body Shop locations she stays in the homes of employees and talks to them about their hopes for themselves and their ideas for the company. Roddick is the daughter of Italian immigrants to Great Britain. She started her small company in 1976 as a way to support her family and soon realized that her organization would be guided by holistic principles. She didn't shy away from making profit but quickly turned those profits into ways of helping achieve the company's social goals. For example, she invested 8 million pounds to build a soap factory in one of the worst slum areas in Glasgow, believing that the people of Glasgow could be employed consumers instead of disaffected social burdens. Recently, Roddick stepped down as CEO of The Body Shop, believing it was time for new leadership in the company.

Continues

TABLE 11.3
Continued

Theme	Exemplar
Theme 4: Communication	**Robert Galvin,** CEO of Motorola. Galvin envisioned the power of self-managing teams in the early 1970s and was one of the first leaders of a large U.S. company to enable leadership capacities among all workers. This was accomplished through communication and feedback so that employees understood how their own piece of the business contributed to the grand corporate scheme. Galvin also encourages healthy debate and challenges to top executive initiatives. Employees who successfully challenge inappropriate premises of top executives are amply rewarded.
Theme 5: Integration and Strategy	**Mitch Snyder,** homeless advocate. Snyder is known for unrelenting devotion to achieve adequate housing for the homeless of Washington, D.C. Although his vision is singular, his strategies are not. Harnessing a coalition of volunteers, community groups, and religious leaders, Snyder first attempted to use a power strategy to commandeer a building to shelter the homeless. When this strategy failed, he initiated a Ghandi-like fast to bring attention to his coalition's cause. As his strength slowly ebbed and he slipped from consciousness, the federal government finally agreed to fund a 6 million dollar shelter near the White House.

Note: From Lipman-Bluman (1996), O'Toole (1995), Pinchot (1996).

with other service units for internal or external customers. Leadership at the subunit level is needed to mobilize the unit to meet and exceed customer expectations, and executive leadership is needed not only to build healthy competition among subunits but also to keep subgroups united toward common purposes. Regardless of the model or style of employee empowerment that is achieved in an organization, sharing leadership requires mutual trust, respect for differences and diversity, acceptance of feedback and criticism, skills in collaboration, and an ability to align with agreed-upon goals (Kouzes & Posner, 1996; Pinchot, 1996; Work, 1996).

Credibility.   Respect and authority are earned, not granted. Typically, leaders gain credibility when they work their way through many areas of the business and are constantly willing to do the work and make the sacrifices they ask others to do (Handy, 1996; Kouzes & Posner, 1996). Kouzes and Posner also suggested that leaders gain credibility by achieving small, early successes toward a larger goal. When stakeholders experience small wins, their vision of, confidence in, and commitment to the overall strategy solidity. Another critical feature of credibility is character. Leaders who act with honesty, are forward-looking, and behave in accordance with their values and goals inspire trust and devotion.

Communication.   Integral to all the attributes of successful leadership is communication. Articulating a vision, empowering and enabling subordinate leaders, building trust, and establishing credibility all require leaders to open free-flowing channels of communication. Leaders need to share information honestly and openly, although Bardwick (1996) suggested that leaders reduce information overload by simplifying and amplifying key messages. Concomitantly, leaders need to be effective listeners and to gather information, opinions, advice, and feedback from all important constituents including employees, customers, stockholders, and community members (Bardwick, 1996; Pinchot, 1996).

Integration and Strategy.   The forces of a complex, global, interdependent, and diversified business environment require top-level integration and task-oriented strategic planning. Employee empowerment, reliance on temporary labor forces, and organizational structures run the risk of disintegration without specific guidance on how disparate units will work toward the common goals envisioned by the corporate leadership. Vision and persuasion communication skills alone are not sufficient to bring success. Specific action plans, objective goals, and mechanisms for pulling together loosely connected organizational units are essential ingredients for realizing the organization's vision for success (Bardwick, 1996; W. Bridges, 1996).

GENDER AND LEADERSHIP

When researchers or the general public evaluate the effectiveness of male and female leaders, or the potential for women or men to lead, it is important to determine whether comparisons are based on stereotypical conceptions of male and female leaders or whether such comparisons are based on observed behaviors, traits, or styles of male and female leaders. Even when comparisons are based on "unbiased" observations, situational cues and role demands can influence the leadership-related behaviors we observe. In other words, women and men may lead differently because they occupy situations that call for different styles of leadership. The following sections review the research literature on both people's perceptions and judgments of male and female leaders and observed differences and similarities in the way some men and women lead. We also discuss the implications of stereotypes of male and female leaders and provide theoretical explanations for these findings.

Stereotypes of Male and Female Leaders: Implications for How They Are Judged

Since the early 1970s, researchers have repeatedly shown that many traits associated with management and leadership (e.g., competitiveness, leadership ability, self-confidence, and desire for responsibility) are seen as "male" traits (Brenner et al., 1989; Heilman et al., 1989; Powell & Butterfield, 1979, 1989; V.E. Schein, 1973, 1975). Our stereotypes of "leader" seem to overlap substantially with the male stereotype. Female managers (especially successful ones) appear to be viewed as a "different type" of woman (see chap. 3 on stereotypes).

The implications of these stereotypes for evaluations of male and female leaders and managers have been well documented in the research literature. Even when resumes, work products, or work records are identical, women are typically perceived as less competent, as less effective, and as having less management/leadership potential than men (e.g., Goldberg, 1968; Paludi & Strayer, 1985). The tendency to evaluate male leaders more favorably than female leaders is consistently found across numerous studies where the work product or performance is the same (Swim, Borgida,

Maruyama, & Myers, 1989). Although the pro-male bias is somewhat small, it is particularly prominent when male and female leaders in a stereotypically masculine context such as management are evaluated.

Other, more subtle forms of bias have been documented. For example, it is more likely that women's success on a masculine task will be attributed to luck or effort than to ability, compared to men (e.g., Deaux & Emswiller, 1974; Deaux & Farris, 1977), whereas women's failure is more likely to be attributed to lack of ability than to bad luck (Deaux & Taynor, 1973). Women managers may be more likely to be assigned dull, unchallenging tasks compared to men (Mai-Dalton & Sullivan, 1981; M.S. Taylor & Ilgen, 1981), which may have serious implications for promotion opportunities.

With the increasing awareness of the illegality of gender discrimination in performance evaluations, gender bias is less likely to be observed in overt performance judgments. Yet stereotypes continue to influence reactions to male and female leaders in subtle ways. For example, Butler and Geis (1990) found that women and men were rated as equally competent by their group members in a controlled laboratory experiment. Trained observers, however, found consistent differences in group members' nonverbal, affective responses to male and female leaders. That is, female leaders received fewer positive nonverbal responses from their group members (e.g., head nodding, eye contact displaying approval) and more negative responses than male leaders. These findings were more negative when female leaders took a more active (vs. passive) leadership role. One explanation for these findings is that when a woman assumes an active leadership role, it is contrary to traditional sex-role expectations and evokes negative emotions among followers. Thus, although group members claimed that male and female leaders were equally effective, they tended to have more negative nonverbal reactions to female leaders.

In a number of other areas of leadership, researchers have studied observers' judgments of male and female leaders, leaders' judgments of their own styles, or more objective behavioral differences in the way women and men lead. However, before we review this research it is important to summarize the conditions that influence whether stereotypes guide our judgments of women and men (see also chapter 3). Generally, female managers and leaders, compared to males, are viewed more stereotypically (and thus less competently) when the salience of their gender is heightened. Such conditions prevail in three situations:

1. When raters must make judgments without job-relevant information (e.g., when raters are reviewing brief resumes or short vignettes of performance; Heilman, Martell, & Simon, 1988).

2. When candidates are judged on tasks that are stereotypically cross-gender specific (e.g., when women are rated in "masculine" jobs such as management, or when men are rated in "feminine" jobs such as nursing; Heilman, 1983; Nieva & Gutek, 1981).
3. When women are substantially outnumbered in a group, such that they appear to be tokens (Kanter, 1977a).

Bearing in mind these conditions under which stereotypes guide judgments, we examine the research on gender differences in perceptions of leadership and in actual leadership behaviors.

Emergent Leadership

An important aspect of leadership is being perceived as a leader by others. A natural way to study these perceptions is to form groups without an assigned leader and observe who emerges in that role. Measures of emergent leaders are based on group participants' or independent observers' perceptions of who leads the group. Distinctions between who leads in task-oriented and social-oriented domains are often examined as well. Because masculinity is associated with **agentic/instrumental** characteristics such as competitiveness, task-structuring, and assertiveness, whereas femininity is associated with **communal/expressive** characteristics such as helpfulness, expressiveness, and consideration, it is important to distinguish among the types of situations where men and women may differentially emerge as leaders.

A classic study of emergent leadership conducted by Megargee (1969) was described in chapter 4 on language and power. However, it is valuable to discuss the findings in terms of leadership implications. Megargee measured the research participants' personality trait of "dominance" and paired male and female subjects who were high and low on this trait on a task demanding leadership. In this task one person instructed the other on what color bolts to install into a specially designed panel. The "follower" could not see the leader's side of the panel and thus was dependent on the leader's instructions. In same-sex pairs, the high-dominance person emerged as leader more often than the other. Similarly, high-dominance men emerged more often as leaders when paired with low-dominance females. The interesting finding was that low-dominance men were significantly more likely to emerge as leaders when paired with high-dominance women. Although these women did not emerge as leaders in these pairings, they were more likely than other women to choose that their male partner be the leader. In other words, these high-dominance women displayed their dominance by choosing who was the leader. Actually

phenomenon (her case is described at the beginning of chap. 7). Her style was described as tough, masculine, and unfriendly. Among recommendations given to improve her style, she was told she needed to act more femininely and wear more makeup. American Psychological Association members argued to the U.S. Supreme Court that judgments of her fitness for partnership were based on stereotyping, not on her actual performance (Fiske, Bersoff, Borgida, Deaux, & Heilman, 1991). She was devalued because she was a woman who used a masculine style.

Because modern theories of management exalt the glories of participative, democratic leadership (e.g., Likert, 1967; Peters & Waterman, 1982), one might infer that women are better leaders than men, because their upbringing and gender-role socialization supply them with more talent to lead participatively (e.g., Loden, 1985). As encouraging as this sounds, restricting women's leadership styles to one acceptable type (participative) ultimately may be destructive. The very notion of participative versus autocratic decision-making grew out of contingency theories that prescribe the effective use of both forms of decision-making under different circumstances (Jago & Vroom, 1982; Vroom & Yetton, 1973). To use leadership talent fully, women need to be free to use the same spectrum of leadership styles that we afford men.

Consideration, initiating structure, and participative–autocratic decision-making styles describe broad dimensions of leadership behavior. Because of the wide variation in leadership styles within groups (e.g., among men and among women), it is understandable why there are not big differences between groups (e.g., between women and men) on these global leadership dimensions. Closer inspection of more specific styles of leadership may reveal interesting gender associations. In the next section, we look at dimensions of transformational and connective leadership styles.

Gender Comparisons of Transformational and Connective Leadership

As mentioned in the discussion on transformational leadership, the crux of transformational leadership is building trust, respect, and admiration in followers so that effective changes for the organization can be realized (Bass, 1985). Transformational leaders empower their followers to think creatively and act responsibly in both autonomous and cooperative settings. There is some evidence that women are more skilled in several aspects of transformational leadership than men (Denmark, 1993), but research examining gender differences in transformational styles of leadership is scarce, and gender is rarely mentioned in the transformational leadership literature. A handful of studies that have compared male and female leaders on transactional and transformational leadership find that female leaders, compared to male leaders, are more likely to be perceived by their followers as transformational leaders (Bass, Avolio, & Atwater, 1996; Bycio, Hackett, & Allen, 1995; Druskat, 1994). In a study involving student resident hall leaders, both men and women reported using individual consideration more than any other transformational or transactional leadership style (Komives, 1991). The only gender difference in leadership styles was found with intellectual stimulation, on which men rated themselves higher than women. Further research is needed to determine whether transformational leadership in fact is the province of women leaders.

The connective leader achievement styles outlined by Lipman-Blumen (1996) have also been examined in research on transformational leadership. Leaders who achieve their goals by building effective relationships with followers are more likely to be perceived as transformational than leaders who achieve through competition and using power over people (Lipman-Blumen, Handley-Isaksen, & Leavitt, 1983).

Lipman-Blumen's leader achieving styles (discussed earlier in this chapter) were examined among a national group of elite female college leaders as well as among a group of men and women who were not leaders (i.e., **controls,** Offerman & Beil, 1992). Although the male nonleaders compared to female nonleaders used competition, power, and social instrumental achieving styles, the elite female leaders compared to both male and female nonleaders used more intrinsic, reliant, and collaborative achieving styles. Female leaders, therefore, appear to use styles of achieving consistent with transformational leadership, that is, achieving success by working well with others. Because the study did not contain a sample of elite male college leaders, gender differences in leadership styles or achieving patterns cannot be assumed.

In another study, male and female leaders (resident hall directors) were compared on transformational and transactional leadership styles and on leadership achieving styles (Komives, 1991). Leaders rated their own achieving, transformational, and transactional leadership styles. Furthermore, their followers (resident hall assistants) rated their leaders' styles on these same dimensions. Men tended to associate their direct achieving styles (styles that focus on the use of the self as the sole source of leadership) with both transformational and transactional leadership, whereas both female leaders and followers of either gender associated relational achieving styles (i.e., cooperating with and using others) with transformational leadership only. The author concluded that followers perceive relational achieving styles to contribute to transformational leadership, which is consistent with female leaders' views of themselves but not with male leaders' views. The results of Komives' research supports Leavitt and Lipman-Blumen's (1980) assertion that today's leaders need to move from the "competitive edge" to the "connective edge."

The Bottom Line: Are Men More Effective Leaders Than Women?

In the preceding sections, we examined differences and similarities in the stereotypes we have about male and female leaders, the tendency for men or women to emerge as leaders, and the ways and styles in which women and men lead. We have said fairly little, however, about whether there are gender differences in the effectiveness of leaders. There is some debate about whether men are better leaders, whether women are better leaders, or whether men and women are equally effective as leaders. Alice Eagly and her associates (Eagly, Karau, & Makhijani, 1992) provided the most compelling evidence of gender differences and similarities in overall leadership effectiveness. They collected all of the published research articles, unpublished papers, book chapters, and dissertations that compared the effectiveness of male and female leaders. Effectiveness in these studies could be assessed by objective performance measures, such as the speed of solving puzzles, tests of business knowledge, and worker productivity measures. However, effectiveness was more likely to be assessed by subjective measures such as subordinates', peers' , or supervisors' ratings of leaders' overall effectiveness as leaders, their ability to lead, their effort or motivation to perform well, or their followers' ratings of satisfaction with their leader. Averaging over all of these studies, Eagly et al. (1995) found that men and women were equally effective. Furthermore, men and women tended to be rated as equally effective on both objective and subjective measures. However, men tended to be rated as slightly more effective than women on measures of their ability to lead. Female leaders tended to obtain higher satisfaction ratings compared to male leaders. In studies conducted in organizational settings (about 75% of the studies), interesting differences were observed across type of organization. There was a fairly strong bias in favor of male leaders in military settings and slightly less so in first-line management positions. Female leaders, however, were favored in education, government, and social service settings and, to some extent, in business settings. Women were also rated as more effective in second-line or middle-level management positions. Eagly et al. (1995) concluded that, on balance, women and men lead equally well. Men are rated as more effective leaders in situations that are highly masculine and highly male dominated, such as the military. Although women tend to be rated as more effective in female-dominated settings such as social services and education, they are making gains over their male counterparts in some traditionally masculine domains such as business and middle management.

Sidelight 11.1   Debate: Do Women and Men Differ in Their Leadership Styles?

Yes

Judy Rosener, a professor in the Graduate School of Management at the University of California, Irvine, argues that women have an advantage over men in being able to use an interactive leadership style. This style emphasizes collaborative versus top-down decision-making, valuing group as well as individual contributions and interpersonal as well as technical skills, empowering workers at all levels, and providing multidimensional feedback and performance evaluations. According to Rosener, women are comfortable with ambiguity because they are used to juggling many tasks and roles. Furthermore, women can easily change plans and roles because they are used to handling unpredictable family responsibilities. Finally, because they have learned to simultaneously satisfy different and conflicting needs of spouses, family members, and coworkers, women have developed a crucial leadership skill: negotiation (Rosener, 1990, 1997). Other writers also argue that women have a greater capacity than men to employ leadership styles requiring interpersonal sensitivity and empowerment (e.g., Loden, 1985).

No

Gary Powell, a professor of management at the University of Connecticut, concludes that when you weigh the differences in the styles, preferences, and traits of male and female leaders, not only do you find only a few differences, which are of little magnitude, the differences tend to balance each other out so that, overall, there are no practical differences in the ways women and men lead. Powell summarized the major studies that have investigated differences in male and female leadership styles and ability and found that although men tend to have greater company loyalty, motivation to advance within the company, and attentiveness to power structures compared to women, women tend to have greater administrative ability, interpersonal skills and sensitivity, written skills, energy, and work standards compared to men. There are practically no gender differences in task versus interpersonal styles of leadership, although women tend to use participative leadership more than do men. Powell argues that any gender differences in leadership style can be explained by situational factors. When women are in situations requiring autocratic leadership (e.g., the military), they are more likely to be autocratic than democratic. Similarly, men tend to use participative leadership styles in situations that require it (Powell, 1993, 1997).

(From Walsh, 1997)

THE GLASS CEILING: A SPECIAL CHALLENGE FOR WOMEN

Many authors agree that in addition to the stressors of management and leadership faced by men and women alike, female managers' stress is compounded by gender-specific conditions such as work–family conflict, sexual harassment, and wage discrimination, which are reviewed in other chapters of this book. The odds of reaching top leadership positions in organizations are extremely low, even for White males. Consider the additional hurdles faced by women and especially women of color, and one quickly gains respect for female leaders.

Despite the tremendous increase of women in the workforce generally, and in management and entrepreneurial endeavors specifically (Davidson & Cooper, 1992; Morrison, White, & Van Velsor, 1992), women remain conspicuously absent among the highest ranking, top paying, and most powerful corporate positions (Morrison & Von Glinow, 1990). Motivated by the women's movement of the 1960s, many women aspire to and are achieving status in traditionally male work domains. Contemporary labor statistics indicate that women occupy approximately 30 to 40% of lower and midlevel management positions in organizations, compared to less than 20% in the early 1970s (cited in Powell, 1993). However, only 2 to 5% of top executive positions (e.g., corporate officers) are held by women. This finding has been termed the *glass ceiling*.

This glass ceiling has been described as "a barrier so subtle that it is transparent, yet so strong that it prevents women and minorities from moving up the management hierarchy" (Morrison & Von Glinow, 1990, p. 200). It appears to exist at the general management level in many businesses. Morrison et al. (1992) indicated that only 2.6% of Fortune 500 corporate officers were women, and that this percentage decreases as company size increases. The number of female CEOs in the Fortune 500 can be counted on one hand (Morrison et al. 1992; Powell, 1993). The U.S. Department of Labor's survey of Fortune 500 organizations found that the glass ceiling exists at lower levels than addressed by previous definitions (U.S. Department of Labor, 1991).

Explanations for the Glass Ceiling Effect: Fewer Skills or Unfair Barriers?

Human capital theory, one explanation for the glass ceiling, posits that women have not advanced to top-level positions because they have not attained the same levels of education and experience or developed the same leadership skills and abilities as men (as described by Terborg, 1977). This theory suggests that as women gain these necessary experiences and characteristics, they will be represented equally at top management levels. However, the Feminist Majority Foundation reported that at the present rate of advancement, it will take until about the year 2465 for women's presence in executive suites to be equal men's (1991; cited in Morrison et al., 1992). Moreover, all evidence indicates that there are few, if any, real differences in women's and men's qualifications to lead (see preceding review, as well as Dobbins & Platz, 1986 ; Morrison & Von Glinow, 1990; Powell, 1993; Stroh et al., 1992).

It is more plausible that women face many more barriers than men in their quest to reach top leadership positions in organizations. Morrison and Von Glinow (1990) discussed sex (and race) stereotyping and systemic barriers. Stereotyping theory suggests that women are discriminated against by power holders because of a perceived lack of fit with top leadership positions (discussed in detail in chap. 7). We documented earlier how stereotypical perceptions lead to devalued opinions of women managers (discussed in chap. 3). Decision makers who hold these views are likely to place women in positions consistent with their assumed value to the organization. Thus, women may be denied opportunities to advance at the same rate as men because systematic biases in review processes may lead to unfair promotion decisions. Recent research using computer simulation provides compelling evidence that stereotypes and biases against women as leaders explain the extreme paucity of women in top levels of management (Martell, 1998; Martell, Lane, & Emrich, 1996).

Systemic barriers that nurture the glass ceiling involve organizational conditions that mirror the prejudices of broader society. In other words, these barriers can't be attributed directly to people's stereotypes and prejudices but are attributed to the "system" more broadly. Discrimination occurs because the organization is structured such that women are systematically disadvantaged in comparison to men in their efforts to navigate their careers to top executive levels. Structural discrimination is typified by gender-concentrated occupations that pay less and involve little power. Women are unlikely to advance to top organizational levels because they are not adequately represented in career paths that lead to those positions (Morrison, 1996). Despite the idealistic scenario portrayed in the movie *Working Girl,* people are not often promoted to important managerial jobs from clerical positions.

Women in managerial career paths still may have difficulty attaining top executive positions, in part because they are often not given the same developmental opportunities as their male peers. It is important not only to be employed in a career path leading to the executive suite but also to be given challenging job assignments that increase one's visibility to organizational decision makers (McCall, Lombardo, & Morrison, 1988; McCauley, Ruderman, Ohlott, & Morrow, 1994; Morrison, 1996). Three categories of developmental opportunities that are important for proving oneself suitable for top management were described by Ohlott, Ruderman, and Morrow (1994). *Job transition* involves changes in a job's content, status, or location and challenges the manager to effectively structure a new and unfamilar situation. *Task-related characteristics* involve risks and challenges in the existing job that give managers opportunities to test and learn from new courses of action, such as turning around a troubled operation. *Obstacles* are difficulties faced in the job such as a difficult boss or lack of personal support.

Male and female managers attending management development seminars were surveyed to assess gender differences in these key developmental experiences (Ohlott, Ruderman, & Morrow, 1994). Men reported significantly more task-related developmental components in their jobs compared to women. These differences remained after age, tenure, education, and job type were taken into account. Women reported significantly less personal support in their jobs than men. In another sample of managers, Stroh et al. (1992) found that women and men had the same level of education, worked in the same industries, indicated the same willingness to relocate, and took very few, if any, career breaks (i.e., to raise a family). However, even in this sample of very similar male and female managers, women received significantly less pay than men. If women are not equitably rewarded for their efforts to be good leaders, this must affect their motivation to aspire to top executive levels of management.

Other systemic barriers include **tokenism** and **bicultural stressors** (discussed in chap. 7 and 12). The heightened visibility and unrealistic expectations characteristic of tokenism create conditions for failure (Kanter, 1977b), affecting not only the person in the token position but also other women in the pipeline. When the token woman fails, decision makers are less likely to risk placing other women in that position. Finally, women in management face the dual stressors of being a female (which is associated with discrimination, greater work–family stress, and greater likelihood of being sexually harassed) and being a manager. Women may deliberately choose not to pursue top positions because of the compounded stressors from both these demanding domains of life. Whether women are directly discriminated against in their attempts to advance to top organizational levels, or whether the "system" makes women's advancement more difficult than men's (i.e., woman have to put up with being tokens as well as managing stressors from multiple roles more so than do men), the glass ceiling remains a formidable barrier for women leaders.

Breaking the Glass Ceiling

Some women have made it to the top in organizational management (or very close to it). Through interviews and surveys, researchers have examined the characteristics of these women that helped them break the glass ceiling (Morrison et al., 1992; Scandura, 1991). Scandura (1991) surveyed 176 female executives (80 of whom identified a male peer, who also completed the survey) in order to obtain a profile of women who had surpassed glass-ceiling boundaries. Participants in the study came from service industries, manufacturing, government, retail industries, and small businesses. Over 80% of the sample were within three decision levels to the top of their organizations and, on average, they controlled budgets of over $2.5 million. Thus, women in this sample truly held top-level positions in their companies and had themselves broken the glass ceiling. Interestingly, 80% of the women in the sample came from relatively small companies, and most women were in service and retail industries. Thus, the glass-ceiling breakers were unlikely to come from the largest, most powerful organizations.

Scandura (1991) found that these exceptional women were more similar to their male peers in the study than they were different. Although comparisons between men and women in this study are potentially biased, due to the way men were selected for the study (they were nominated by the female participants), it is worth noting that these women, like their male peers, possessed college degrees, averaged 13 years of experience in their current type of work, had at least one mentor during their career, and worked in "line" as opposed to "staff" positions. On the other hand, women held more egalitarian sex-role socialization attitudes than did the men and were less optimistic about their future upward mobility than men. Within the female sample, having had a mentor was positively related to salary and perceptions of being promoted in the future. Also, female executives who had children under 18 reported lower career expectations, higher levels of stress, and more thoughts of quitting, even though many of their companies made accommodations for family concerns.

In summary, female executives succeeded with many of the same characteristics as did male executives (Scandura, 1991). Good education, hard work, line responsibilities, and mentors were keys to their success. Additionally, women's positive attitudes about egalitarian sex roles facilitated their upward mobility. Although the presence of children tended to be negatively associated with career aspirations, almost half of these executive women did have children under 18, suggesting that it is not impossible to have a family and be a successful executive.

These findings were mirrored in the Center for Creative Leadership's (CCL) study of female executives (Morrison et al., 1992). These researchers conducted in-depth interviews with 76 women in or near to general management positions across the United States. The researchers also found that, contrary to previous assumptions, these women tended to be in their early 40s (not older), to be married, and to have children. Furthermore, they tended to be in or to have had line positions where they were responsible for profit and loss. They faced pressures not only from the job itself (e.g., difficult decisions, angry customers, disgruntled employees, endless phone calls) but also from their pioneer role as a woman in the position and from the strain of family obligations and work–family conflict.

Morrison et al. (1992) reported that these women succeeded by taking risks, pursuing line responsibility, managing people effectively, and having mentors—much like male executives who had been studied in an earlier CCL project. Unlike the men, however, these women had to manage within a "narrow band of acceptable behavior" (p. 47). Although accumulated evidence indicates that managerial women are more like men than unlike them (i.e., Eagly et al., 1992), these women had to deal with perceptions by bosses, subordinates, peers, and customers that only certain forms of leadership are acceptable for women (e.g., Jago & Vroom, 1982). Thus, they had to be more concerned about their image than men, walking a fine line between behaving too masculinely (lest they be pegged as too aggressive) or too femininely (lest they be pegged as too soft).

The glass ceiling has been documented in non-U.S. organizations as well. Davidson and Cooper (1992) reviewed European and Australian literature and surveys and found that, like their U.S. peers, top female managers in these countries are woefully underrepresented. Women managers are more heavily represented in service organizations (e.g., government, education and training, and professional services) than in manufacturing and in staff and specialist positions than in general management. Davidson and Cooper (1992) also described the barriers and stressors facing female leaders. In addition to handling the stress of management jobs themselves, European and Australian female managers deal with societal prejudices about women in management, tokenism, dual-career stress (or the stigma of being a "single career woman"), and work–family conflict, a list quite similar to that for U.S. female managers. At least in Western societies, the glass ceiling and the factors supporting it are ubiquitous, and the current methods of surpassing it are similar. Perhaps the greatest obstacle facing leadership in organizations concerns equal access to leadership positions for those with talent, whether female or male, Euro-American or not.

Leadership and the Glass Ceiling for Non-White Women

The leadership research reviewed to this point has focused primarily if not exclusively on White women. Women of color may have been included in studies examining gender differences and similarities in leadership perceptions, styles, and behaviors, but since their numbers were low, analysis by race was seldom conducted. Since women of color are marginalized in our society because of their gender and their race, they merit special attention (Morrison, 1996; Y.S. White, 1990).

Women of color are very scarce in executive-level management positions. Morrison and Von Glinow (1990) reported that in the early 1980s, the number of minorities (including men) holding top executive positions in U.S. corporations could be counted on one's fingers. Non-White women face the same barriers impeding White women's access to top leadership positions. Additional burdens due to ethnic and racial prejudices and stereotypes make their journey to the top especially difficult. For example, to the extent that White men are the influential leaders who are likely to be mentors for young managers, they are likely to choose "like" protégés: White men. White women may offer some discomfort, but not to the same extent as would African-American, Hispanic, or Asian women (Nkomo & Cox, 1989).

Research examining the barriers faced by non-White women in achieving leadership success has yielded mixed results. Y.S. White (1990) interviewed several female African-American business leaders, most of whom were vice presidents in their organizations. They stated that although their companies publicly supported affirmative action/equal opportunity initiatives, they saw very little change happening on the inside. Very few African-American women were promoted to line positions, the pipeline to upper management. African-American men and White women were more likely to benefit from affirmative action policies than were African-American women. Yet these women also noted that the factors accounting for their own success were much the same as those mentioned by White women for breaking the glass ceiling: taking risky, highly visible job assignments, networking and mentoring, and having strong technical, managerial, and social skills.

A few field studies and experiments have examined the extent to which stereotypes associated with being both non-White (e.g., Black) and female bias raters' judgments of African-American women's managerial competence. McRae (1994) examined the extent to which sex stereotypes influence judgments of Black male and female managerial candidates in a sample of Black male and female managers. The researchers created resumes of equally qualified Black women and Black men and sent these to a sample of managers who were asked to judge their potential for success in either a financial management position (a stereotypically male-job) or a benefits manager position (a stereotypically female job). The managers rated the Black women as more suitable (i.e., had greater potential to work effectively, complete tasks, and do technical work) for the benefits manager position than for the financial manager position. Black men were rated as equally suitable for either type of position. This study suggests that sex stereotypes affect Black women but not Black men.

Nkomo and Cox (1989) investigated the "double whammy versus double advantage hypothesis" for the upward mobility of Black managers. "Double whammy" implies that the stereotypes of being both African-American and female are addictive. "Double advantage" implies that Black women are advantaged in comparison to Black men for two reasons: Black culture is matriarchal, so Black women have higher status than Black men, and hiring or promoting a Black woman is perceived as counting as two affirmative action points (but, in fact, does not). A survey of a large number of male and female Black managers in the United States that examined their upward mobility patterns (e.g., number of promotions, promotion rates, organizational size, and other control factors) found few gender differences. Black men were older, had more seniority, and had higher salaries than Black women; however, Black women had higher self-rated job performance and were more satisfied with their advancement rate. Black women's and men's upward mobility rates were equal, and they reported equal levels of satisfaction with their careers. When differences in education and prior experience were accounted for, there were no gender differences in promotion rates and managerial level. Thus, it appears that Black women are neither advantaged nor disadvantaged in comparison to Black men.

It is hard to draw conclusions about the processes affecting non-White women's advancement to top executive positions. First, the research is too sparse to make firm conclusions. Second, full experimental designs that vary race and sex of both targets and raters need to be incorporated into future research. Third, factors affecting women from cultures and ethnic backgrounds other than African American need to be studied. However, the data regarding non-White women in top executive positions are clear: There are extremely few non-White women in top leadership positions in U.S. organizations.

SUMMARY

Leadership is typically viewed as the ability to influence and motivate people beyond what is required of them by their jobs or situations. To this end, leaders help groups achieve goals by guiding, developing, and challenging group members as well as by making important decisions, taking risks, being a team player, and valuing others. Leadership scholars have attempted for decades to understand the qualities of good leaders. In behavioral terms, leaders initiate structure, direction, and organization of group tasks as well as provide support and concern for group members. However, leadership in today's complex environment requires a great range of behaviors. In fact, some scholars have suggested that the environment in which leaders operate is very significant in determining what leadership styles or behaviors will be effective. Characteristics of situations that influence the effectiveness of various leadership styles include the skills and professionalism of the subordinates, the types of decisions that need to be made, and the predictability or ambiguity of the tasks that need to be accomplished, among other factors. Research on situational and contingency theories of leadership has provided mixed support.

Recent advances in leadership theory have focused on the relational qualities of good leaders. Transactional theories, such as leader–member exchange theory, suggest that leaders can maximize their outcomes by developing high-quality relationships with select followers while providing more routine guidance to other members. Transformational leaders go beyond day-to-day exchanges with group members to promote fundamental changes in people and organizations by enacting idealized influence, inspirational motivation, intellectual stimulation, and individualized consideration for others. Finally, connective leaders rely on a wide variety of achievement styles including principled instrumentality, authenticity, interdependence, long-range vision, positive expectations, and personal growth to help guide people and organizations through a highly interconnected yet diverse social, political, and business universe.

Because there appears to be no one best way to lead, leaders must rely on a great wealth of resources, both within themselves and within the people they lead. Good leadership, therefore, must be fostered among a wide variety of people. Particularly, good leadership must be fostered in both men and women. Women, however, have to face many hurdles and obstacles in being perceived and treated as effective leaders. Especially in the male-dominated profession of management, women are perceived as not as competent as men. Women's successes tend to be attributed to luck or hard work as opposed to natural ability, and their failures tend to be attributed to poor abilities. Furthermore, women tend to be perceived as leaders when the situation highlights traditional sex-role stereotypes of women, such as when groups are working on typically masculine tasks or when women are token members of their groups. Furthermore, women tend to not emerge as leaders in contrived, short-lived laboratory studies of leadership. In the real world, however, there are very few gender differences in who emerges as a leader and in the types of behaviors and styles that are used to lead. The exception is that female leaders tend to lead more democratically than do male leaders. This may be due, in part, to social penalties that women face if they use typically masculine forms of leadership such as autocratic decision styles. Most importantly, regardless of how women are perceived as leaders, the cumulative evidence strongly suggests that women and men are equally effective as leaders across many different types of situations.

Despite the apparent similarity in the way men and women lead and the fact that women tend to be equally effective as men as leaders, women still face significant barriers in rising to top levels of management in business organizations. Explanations for the glass-ceiling effect include both systemic barriers and bicultural stressors. For example, women more often than men are placed in occupations that do not have clear paths to top management, or they are not given developmental opportunities to prove their leadership capabilities. Women also not only have to perform exceptionally well in their paid work roles but also have to deal with tokenism, discrimination, sexual harassment, and work–family conflict. These stressors are compounded for non-White women, who must also combat racism in order to convince a White majority of their leadership potential.

To break the glass ceiling, efforts are needed at both the personal level and the organizational level to dispel stereotypes about women's leadership abilities and to eliminate the structural barriers that keep women from advancing to top levels of management.

GLOSSARY

Agentic/instrumental: Concern for one's own self-interests. Includes traits such as forceful, aggressive, independent, and ambitious.

Attributions: Process through which individuals attempt to determine the causes of others' behavior.

Boundaryless organization: Organization in which chains of command are eliminated, spans of control are unlimited, and rigid departments give way to empowered teams.

Communal/expressive: Concern for one's relationship with other people. Includes traits such as affectionate, gentle, appreciative, and sensitive.

Controls (control group): Research participants who do not receive the experimental manipulation of interest in the study. Useful for comparing the difference in outcomes for those who do not receive the experimental manipulation.

Decentralization: Extent to which authority and decision-making are spread throughout all levels of an organization rather than being reserved for top management.

Field study: Research conducted in naturalistic settings such as a real organization.

Human relations movement: Perspective on organizational behavior that recognizes the importance of social processes in work settings.

Laboratory study: Research conducted in artificial settings in which the researcher can carefully control all conditions of the study.

Role ambiguity: Uncertainty about the requirements of a job.

Sex-role stereotypes: A structured set of inferential relations that link personal attributes to the social categories of female and male.

Systemic barriers: Obstacles that are explicitly caused by systems and/or policies in organizations (as opposed to personal biases) which unfairly disadvantage certain groups. For example, a policy in a commercial airline that pilots must have 5 years of flying experience in the military represents a systemic barrier for women being selected for commercial pilot positions, because until recently women were not allowed to fly in the military.

Bicultural stressors: Stressors that arise from possessing two or more cultural identities that can involve discrimination or negative stereotyping. Bicultural stressors can compound these stressors or they can pose conflicting stressors. For example, an African-American woman may experience the stress of being African-American and female, both of which are stressful in U.S. society. Furthermore, under some circumstances these stressors can conflict with one another. For example, the African-American value of protecting and standing up for others of their own race (including African-American men) can conflict with the stress of being a woman being abused by a man.

Tokenism: Status of being perceived as a token (i.e., member of small, visible minority). Typically tokens are perceived stereotypically, are

expected to perform better than anyone else, and are expected to fulfill
stereotypical roles for their token status.

Virtual organization: Highly flexible, temporary organization formed
by a group of companies that join forces to exploit a specific opportunity.

12

Stress, Health, and Gender

Stress Hitting More Workers

Susan Burns works with babies who often are sick or injured. Some babies die, making her job particularly stressful. The neonatal nurse practitioner at St. Joseph's Hospital in Tucson, Ariz., works in what most people would consider a high-stress job. Yet 90 percent of American workers say they experience high levels of stress in the workplace at least once or twice a week.

And while some stress is not necessarily bad, the number of workers adversely affected by stress is rapidly growing and may be costing employers more than $100 billion a year, according to the National Institutes for Occupational Safety and Health. A Lou Harris and Associates poll indicates U.S. industry loses about 286 million workdays per year in stress-related absenteeism.

—(From Madrid, 1994)

The individual costs associated with stress are staggering in terms of personal health costs, lost health, lost income, damaged interpersonal relations both at home and at work, and loss of interest in life. Furthermore, worker stress is extremely costly to organizations. Accidents cost U.S. companies over $32 billion each year, and approximately 75 to 85% of these are due to stress at work (J. W. Jones, 1984; Matteson & Ivancevich, 1987). Heart disease (which we discuss later in the chapter) is associated with work/family stress and is responsible for approximately 135 million workdays lost annually. Sixty percent of long-term employee disability cases result from psychological or psychosomatic problems, and $26 billion is spent annually on disability payments and medical bills. Both organizations and individuals lose opportunities due to stress (Matteson & Ivancevich, 1987).

We begin this chapter by defining stress and describing two general models of work stress: the job characteristics model and the organizational model. Each model has identified and emphasized different sources of stress at work; these sources of work stress are described. Next, we discuss approaches for linking gender with stress and health outcomes. Some explanations of the effects of stress on health may differ depending on whether we are referring to men or women. In the next section, physical and mental/emotional consequences of workplace stress are presented. Stress reduction strategies are described, including both individual and organizational-level interventions. Stressors that are particularly relevant for women, as well as their health consequences, are described. The chapter concludes with a brief discussion of how workplace stress affects members of minority groups.

STRESS AND WORK

Although it is widely acknowledged that work is a significant source of stress for individuals, it is sometimes difficult to say exactly why work might be stressful or what might be done to reduce work stress. There are many different definitions of stress and many different models or theories of how and why work might be stressful.

What Is Stress?

"**Stress**" is a Latin term and was used in the 17th century to convey hardship, adversity, or affliction (Davidson & Cooper, 1992). In the 18th century, the term was used to denote force, pressure, strain, or strong effort and referred to people's organs or mental powers (Hinkle, 1973). Today stress is an ambiguous term and experts do not always agree on its definition. **Stress** is a complex set of emotional, physiological, and mental states in response to demands from an action or situation (Greenberg & Baron, 1997; Hellriegel et al., 1986). It involves interplay between a person and that person's environment. **Stressors,** various factors in an environment that promote stress among individuals, can include demands from a job, family, friends, or coworkers or internal personal demands. Often stress and stressors are distinguished from **strain** or **distress,** which refer to the effects of stress. These include adverse or negative psychological, physical, behavioral, and organizational consequences that may result from stressful circumstances (Nelson & Quick, 1997).

Conceptualizations of stress vary depending on your perspectives on work. In particular, labor and managerial groups in organizations define stress differently (L. Murphy, 1988). Literature examining stress from the perspective of labor tends to discuss stress in terms of objective physical and environmental stressors. Stressors identified in this literature include lack of control over work content and process, unrealistic task demands, lack of supervisory and management understanding, and lack of predictability and security about job future. The managerial literature tends to emphasize personality traits (e.g., Type A behavior pattern), lifestyle behaviors, interpersonal relations, and family problems as key stressors. These different conceptualizations of stress are associated with different research approaches and often result in different resolutions or interventions for stress reduction. Labor groups tend to advocate health and safety committees and increased worker participation as stress-reduction strategies. Managerial groups tend to advocate individual stress management programs and training (L. Murphy, 1988). Later in this chapter, we discuss methods of reducing work stress.

Models of Work Stress

There are numerous models of work stress, which can be categorized into one of two general groups: job characteristics models and organizational models. The first group evolved from the labor tradition of investigating the "objective" characteristics of the work environment and their relationship to psychological and especially to physical health. Much of the research in this tradition has been conducted in Sweden and England and is described in some detail in the next section of this chapter. This research reflects an interdisciplinary approach involving psychologists, sociologists, and medical health professionals.

Job Characteristics Model of Stress. Karasek (1979) and colleagues developed a framework that describes characteristics of jobs associated with stress. As Figure 12.1 indicates, stress is associated with two work variables: **psychological demands** and **decision latitude or control** (R. Karasek & Theorell, 1990; Theorell, 1991). Psychological job demands most often refer to time pressures but can also involve fear of losing one's job or skill obsolescence. Job demands also include the physical demands of work. Decision latitude is a combination of **task authority** and **skill discretion.** *Task authority* is the autonomy one has to make decisions, whereas *skill discretion* refers to the breadth or variety of skills usable on the job. Occupations can be categorized along stress or strain levels. For example, active jobs are those with high psychological demands and high degrees of control or decision latitude, such as surgeons or rock climbers. These jobs are generally characterized by learning and growth and generally high productivity. High energy, which is often converted into action, is associated with these jobs. However, there is only average psychological strain in these jobs.

Low-strain jobs (e.g., natural scientists, architects, or repair personnel) are characterized by low psychological demands and high decision latitude. There is lower than average strain or risk of illness in these jobs. In **passive jobs,** both decision latitude and psychological demands are low (R. A. Karasek, 1979; Theorell, 1991). Although these jobs are associated with nonenergetic responses, they have none of the relaxation features of low-strain jobs. There is a gradual decline of skills and abilities from lack of use. Incumbents are not asked to meet significant job challenges, nor are they allowed to initiate projects or activities on the job. In passive jobs, there are average levels of psychological strain and illness risk. Because there is low job demand, incumbents encounter few stressors. When a stressor occurs, however, it tends to result in individual strain. Finally, high-strain jobs are associated with the greatest psychological strain for the individual including fatigue, anxiety, depression, and physical

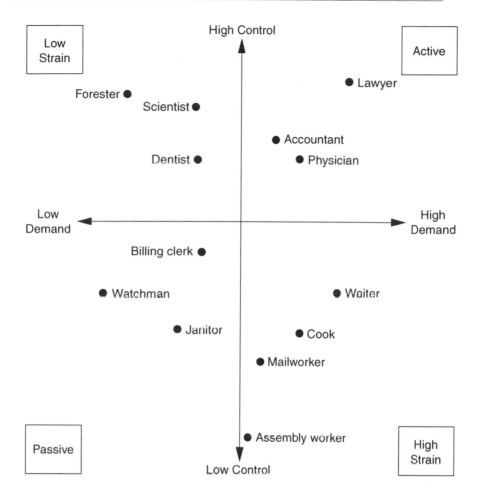

FIG. 12.1. Karasek model of occupational stress, with average scores for various occupations. High and low levels of two components, demand and control, determine its four quadrants. Figure reprinted from T. Theorell (1991). On cardiovascular health in women: Results from epidemiological and psychological studies in Sweden. (pp 187–206). In M. Frankenhaeuser, U. Lundberg, & M. Chesney. *Women, work, and health*. Plenum Press: New York. Reprinted with permission from Plenum Publishing. Copyright 2000.

illness. High-strain jobs (e.g., assembly line workers, waitresses, or garment workers) are characterized by high job demands and low control or decisional latitude. Relief from stress responses to such work can be accomplished by allowing freedom of action in performing the formal job tasks, as well as freedom to engage in informal rituals or activities at work such as coffee breaks, smoking breaks, or even fidgeting (R. Karasek & Thorell, 1990).

Organizational Stress Model.   The second approach to studying stress can be found in the management research literature. There are several theories of management stress, coping, and well-being (Edwards, 1992; see Eulberg, Weekley, & Bhagat, 1988, for a review of managerial stress theories). The organizational stress approach focuses more on the characteristics of the individual or the individual's perceptions of the work environment than on documenting the presence of objective environmental stressors. This approach suggests that stress is an interactive process between characteristics of the individuals (Nelson & Quick, 1997) and characteristics of the environment (Lazarus, 1966; Lazarus & Folkman, 1984). Although some environmental stressors might be present in a given situation, their actual effects on a person may depend upon a variety of individual characteristics (e.g., fit with the environment, cognitive appraisal, discrepancy between ego-deal and self-image).

Sources of Stress

The job characteristics and organizational stress models previously described refer to broad orientations toward research on work and stress. One concentrates on the characteristics of the work itself and the other on characteristics of the individuals. Within these broad research orientations, a number of specific models have been proposed to identify sources of work-related stress (Cooper, 1986; Matteson & Ivancevich, 1987; Offermann & Armitage, 1993). All of these models identify task, social or societal, organizational, and individual or personal characteristics that are sources or antecedents of stress (R. L. Kahn & Byosiere, 1992). Many models also discuss properties or characteristics of the individual that influence the degree to which a stressor has an impact (positive or negative) on the individual. A generic diagram of the major factors that appear to play significant roles in work-related stress is presented in Fig. 12.2. The models discussed subsequently focus on five general sources of stress: characteristics of the job (task demands), the individual's role in the organization (role demands), relationships at work, organizational structure/climate, and nonwork factors (Cooper, 1986; Matteson & Ivancevich, 1987; Nelson & Quick, 1997).

Task Demands.   Two of the most stressful conditions at work are change and lack of control. Change is a pervasive and ever-present characteristic of today's workplace. With change comes uncertainty and a lack of predictability in job tasks and responsibilities. U.S. organizations in the 1980s were constantly undergoing mergers, acquisitions, and downsizing, which certainly created uncertainty for employees (Nelson & Quick, 1997). Definitions of jobs and job duties have also been changing rapidly

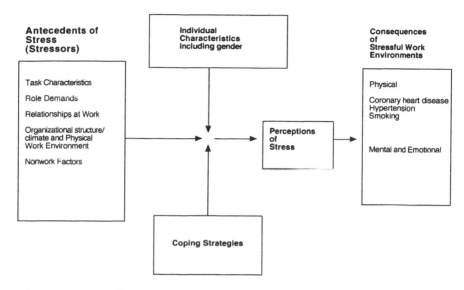

FIG. 12.3. General Model of Stress: Antecedents, Intervening Variables, and Consequences.

in many organizations. Uncertainty about one's future, one's duties, and relationships within organizations is a significant source of stress.

Lack of control is also a significant source of workplace stress. Lack of control may be caused by a number of task factors including the inability to predict the timing of tasks, to make decisions that influence important work outcomes, or to select the methods or tools needed to successfully complete a task (Nelson & Quick, 1997). Combined with lack of control, **work overload** or **work underload** in a job can create stress. As discussed later in the chapter, individuals in jobs with low control and high work loads have greater incidence of heart attacks. Other task demands contributing to stressful work environments include new technologies, which workers may perceive as a threat to their job security.

Role Demands.   Work roles are by definition demanding but can be made much more demanding (and therefore stressful) as the result of role conflict and role ambiguity. Role conflict is an incompatibility between the expectations of parties or between aspects of a single role (Greenberg & Baron, 1997). There are three general types of role conflict: interrole, intrarole, and person-role conflict. **Interrole conflict** is perhaps the most familiar and is caused by conflicting expectations from two separate roles, such as employee and parent. An example of this is the employee who has a deadline to meet but also has a child who is the starting pitcher in her Little League baseball game. **Intrarole conflict** refers to conflicting expectations related to a single role, such as employee. For example, a physician might be expected to provide quality time with patients but also may have a daily quota of patients to see. Finally, **person-role conflicts** exist when employees are expected to behave in ways that violate personal values or beliefs (Nelson & Quick, 1997). For example, employees in organizations that are involved in unethical activities (e.g., price-rigging) may experience stress because their work roles require them to engage in activities that they believe to be wrong. Similarly, individuals working for organizations whose products or services are fraudulent (e.g., employees of a "psychic hotline") or inherently dangerous (e.g., employees of cigarette manufacturers) may experience conflicts between their beliefs and the behaviors they are required to carry out at work.

   Role ambiguity, another cause of stress, refers to an individual's uncertainty about what actions to take to fulfill a job. Interestingly, levels of role ambiguity differ from country to country (M. F. Peterson, Smith, et al., 1995). For example, in countries where people prefer to act as members of groups rather than as individuals, there is relatively low role ambiguity.

   Interpersonal Demands.   Relationships with other people at work are a major source of stress. Examples of interpersonal demands include abrasive personalities, sexual harassment, responsibility for others, or leadership style, and lack of social support. For example, a coworker who is talented but who is also blunt or aggressive can be a significant source of day-to-day stress. Some roles expose individuals to high levels of interpersonal demands. For example, supervisors must listen to complaints, mediate disputes, promote cooperation, and motivate, reward, and punish employees. Individuals working in service occupations must deal with irate customers or with multiple demands on their time and attention. Individuals working in emergency services (e.g., police, firefighters, emergency room staff) must deal with people in pain and distress. These tasks are all likely to be stressful. Finally, relationships between supervisors and subordinates can be a source of interpersonal stress. For example, various leadership styles, task-oriented and directive versus participative, may create stress for employees with particular personalities (Nelson & Quick, 1997).

   Physical Work Environment.   Although there is legislation designed to protect the health and well-being of employees, the physical conditions under which work is carried out continue to be a significant source of stress and concern. Some jobs take place in extreme environments (e.g., working outdoors in very hot or cold temperatures), require strenuous activities such as lifting heavy objects, or involve contact with hazardous substances. Many individuals work in jobs where dangerous physical conditions cause them considerable stress. These include construction workers, road maintenance workers, and auto mechanics. However, they may also include lab technicians, medical researchers, chemists, and biologists who work with toxic substances or life-threatening viruses. In addition to the interpersonal demands faced by police officers, firefighters, and other public safety personnel, the threat of violence, accidents, and bodily harm can be a significant source of stress.

Organizational Structure/Climate. Organizations may be structured such that individuals are concerned about opportunities for career growth or progression. There may not be clear paths for employees who want to plan their careers. Organizational structures may also lead to role conflicts, role ambiguity, or other role difficulties that cause stress. For example, an organization might be structured such that responsibility for a large project is diffused over several organizational units, with little incentive or few mechanisms for these units to cooperate. This is likely to be a source of stress for everyone working on this project.

Furthermore, work may be structured so that stress is promoted. For example, shiftwork is common in organizations that require continuous operations. **Shiftwork** requires that the work period extend beyond the normal workday, increasing the likelihood of conflicts with other demands upon the employee. In addition to heightening work–nonwork conflicts, shiftwork can be a significant source of stress if it disrupts sleep or rest patterns. Finally, organizational climate can enhance or inhibit stress. Some organizations have a ruthlessly aggressive or competitive climate, whereas others nurture employees and their families.

Nonwork Demands. Not all work stress is caused by factors in the immediate work environment. Events that occur outside of work can generate stress that may be carried back to work (L. T. Thomas & Ganster, 1995). Nonwork stressors include stressful life events and hassles of daily life (Nelson & Sutton, 1990). For example, there are life events that in many cases are inevitable yet remain highly stressful: death of a spouse, divorce, injury or death to one's child, unwanted pregnancy, and so forth. Individuals who experience these events are more likely to become ill than individuals who do not, and the more stressful events one experiences, the larger the risk to one's health (Holmes & Masuda, 1974). Daily hassles are those countless minor irritations that seem to make up for their low intensity by their high frequency of occurrence. These hassles include household hassles (e.g., preparing meals), time pressure hassles (e.g., sitting in traffic yet running late), and financial hassles. Work and nonwork stressors combine with individual characteristics (e.g., Type A behavior, level of anxiety, tolerance for ambiguity, neuroticism) to lead to individual and organizational symptoms of strain, most notably poor health and disease (such as coronary heart disease, poor mental health, chronically poor performance, and frequent and severe accidents).

In a multifactor model of stress and female managers, similar factors were identified that contribute to women's stress and negative health (Offermann & Armitage, 1993). However, a number of factors unique to women contribute to stress. Examples have been discussed throughout this text and include negative societal attitudes toward women in particular occupations (e.g., male-dominated fields), male–female power differences at work, and differential access to organizational networks as a function of gender, sexual harassment, tokenism, and sexual discrimination.

Work–Family Conflict.   Both early research on work and family and the popular press have perpetuated the myths that work and family are separate domains, that each has its own rules or laws of behavior, and that each can be studied independently of each other (Kanter, 1977c). The perception that work and family are separate domains appears to be linked closely to traditional sex-role stereotypes and beliefs that portray men as breadwinners and women as wives and mothers who nurture (Voydanoff, 1987). However, there is clear evidence that work and family domains affect one another.

Greenhaus and Beutell (1985) defined work–family conflict as "a form of interrole conflict in which the role pressures from the work and family domain are mutually incompatible in some respect. That is, participation in the work (family) role is made more difficult by participation in the family (work) role" (p. 77). Although individuals in multiple roles may not experience continual work–family conflict, even intermittent conflict can be quite stressful.

The literature is not clear on the precise nature of the relationship between work, family, and stress. Some researchers believe that work and nonwork are positively related (spillover effect); that is, the quality of work might affect the quality of nonwork. If, for example, one's work life is busy and active, one's nonwork life may also be characterized by high activity (Elizur, 1992). A second suggested relationship between work and nonwork is compensatory in nature. Here work and nonwork are negatively related. For example, if work is dull, then the individual will compensate by engaging in exciting or satisfying nonwork activities. The scarcity hypothesis has also been used to examine work–family interrelationships. According to this perspective, people have limited time and energy to invest in work and family, and investment in one area (e.g., work) will generally lead to a scarcity of resources (e.g., time and attention) in another.

Work–family conflict has been examined by assessing the interference of work with the family and vice versa (Gutek, Searle, & Klepa, 1991). Although individual research findings are not always consistent, it is clear that work and family life affect each other. R. W. Burke (1989) reported that when these domains conflict, such conflict appears to have equally serious effects on both work and individual well-being. Frone, Russell, and Cooper (1992), studying the relative permeability of work and family boundaries, found that work interfered with family life more often than family life interfered with work. In a Canadian sample of private-sector employees, Higgins, Duxbury, and Lee (1992) reported similar findings. Burden and Googins (1987; Ferber, O'Farrell, & Allen, 1991) found that 86% of employees rated their job performance as good or unusually good and only 59% rated their family performance that way.

The research literature suggests that work obligations take priority over family obligations, particularly for men. Employment is a critical part of men's personal identity (Vodaynoff, 1987), and it is socially acceptable for men to give higher priority to work than to family. There appears to be greater interdependence between work and family among women, and women are more likely than men to experience stress as the result work–family conflict. For example, women with high role conflict experience greater job dissatisfaction and absenteeism than men with high conflict. Job stress is also more directly related to women's experience of role conflict than men's (Greenglass, Pantony, & Burke, 1989).

The preceding paragraphs might lead you to conclude that work is a source of unnecessary stress for women. In fact, work may have a number of beneficial effects on women, including increased decision-making within the marriage, increased sense of competence, increased family living standards, and enhanced social class (Blood, 1965; Nieva, 1985; Safilios-Rothschild & Dijkens, 1978). Furthermore, there is little evidence that women's employment harms their children or marriage. On the other hand, men's work status significantly effects the family and men themselves. Unemployment has devastating effects on men, including loss of power and respect within the family (Braginsky & Braginsky, 1975; Nieva, 1985). The man's power over his wife and children seems to be derived from his job (Aldous, 1969), and loss of a job can mean considerably more for a man than the simple loss of income.

Although women tend to encounter more stressors at work than do men, women also appear to have better coping strategies (Korabik & McDonald, 1991), which may help them handle that stress. For example, women experience greater role overload and conflict than men. Yet Rosenfield (1980) found that when both partners work, men showed more psychosomatic symptoms and greater sadness than their wives. R. Burke and Weir (1976) found that husbands of working wives performed less well and were less satisfied with their jobs and marriages. On the other hand, Karasek, Lindell, and Gardell (1981) found that the presence of a working spouse increased strain on the working woman but not on the working man. T. D. Jick and Mitz (1985) suggested that these conflicting findings may be the result of numerous factors, including whether subjects had children, ages of children, types of job held by men and women, and amounts of control or decision latitude.

GENDER, STRESS, AND
HEALTH OUTCOMES

In 1900, life expectancies for women and men were 48 years and 46 years, respectively. In 1990, these numbers were 79 years and 72 years, respectively. Males die at higher rates than females in all age groups from 4 to 85 years (Powell, 1993; U.S. Dept. of Commerce, 1991). Male mortality in the United States is twice as high as female mortality for suicide, homicide, motor vehicular and other accidents, lung cancer and related cancers, emphysema and other chronic pulmonary diseases, heart disease, and chronic liver diseases. Higher rates of death for men are due largely to sex differences in risky behaviors, specifically cigarette smoking and alcohol consumption (Waldron, 1991, 1986). Although women report more acute and nonfatal chronic illnesses, such as depression, headaches, dizziness, and stomach upsets (Verbrugge, 1985), men suffer more major ailments like heart disease and cancer. Yet women must cope with a unique set of stressors that men do not encounter (or at least encounter less frequently) at work, such as sex discrimination, gender stereotyping, social isolation, and conflicting work–family demands (Powell, 1993). Although women's life expectancies still exceed men's, their advantage has decreased in recent years, especially for persons over 45 years (Rodin & Ickovics, 1990). This shift may be attributable to lifestyle changes, including shifts in women's work roles (Frankenhaeuser, Lundberg, & Chesney, 1991). We discuss three of the explanations provided for observed differences in stress-related outcomes among women and men and explore how experts view the role of work in women's lives.

Explaining Female–Male Differences
in Stress Outcomes

Work-stress experts have identified three general sources of sex or gender differences in stress: genetic, structuralist, and social/psychological (Jick

& Mitz, 1985; Payne, 1988). **Genetic sources** are inborn tendencies to experience stress and strain that are not substantially affected by situation or psychological factors. There are genetic factors related to male–female differences in stress, but on the whole, research support for this explanation of why men and women differ so much in terms of work stress is somewhat limited. For example, it is generally agreed that male hormones contribute to men's greater readiness for aggression and competitiveness, which may in turn expose them to more stressors. However, behavior of this sort is strongly shaped by social experiences and learning, and it is difficult to sort out the roles of biology versus society in determining male aggressiveness or combativeness.

Second, differences between men's and women's experiences of and reactions to work-related stress might be attributable to their different **roles** within the organization (Kanter, 1977a). The **structuralist position** suggests that different work stressors are associated with different work situations. Women experience greater work distress because they occupy jobs that have fewer opportunities for mobility and influence, are the subject of strong and largely negative stereotypes, are involved with less powerful work, have fewer mentors and female support groups, earn lower salaries, and encounter greater career blocks (Jick & Mitz, 1985). Women's jobs tend to have high demands and low control, which researchers have associated with high strain (Karasek, 1979; Piechowski, 1992).

Evidence supports a structuralist explanation for sex differences in stress and health (LaCroix & Haynes, 1987). Although there has been a great influx of women into the labor force, women continue to be segregated into relatively small numbers of lower level occupations (see chap. 8). The jobs held by men and women often differ in terms of physical and psychosocial work environments, and these different work environments may be associated with different perceptions of stress and different stress-related health consequences. For example, women make up a greater proportion of the "working class" than men (LaCroix & Haynes; E. O. Wright, Costello, Hachen, & Sprague, 1982). Jobs held by women are often characterized by tedious and repetitive tasks, low authority and autonomy, limited upward mobility, and underutilization of skills; there are infrequent opportunities for decision-making and usually no supervisory responsibilities in these jobs. Even within the same occupations, power is allocated unequally among men and women (Wolf & Fligstein, 1979; E. O. Wright et al., 1982). Women have less control over the work of other people than do men, even men in similar jobs. Tasks assigned to men and women in the same jobs differ systematically (Kraft, 1984), with women performing more supportive activities (consistent with gender stereotypes) and fewer delegating and decision-making tasks.

Male managers describe the demands of leadership/authority roles (e.g., disciplining subordinates, being the boss, managing/supervising people, etc.) as their most significant source of stress, but for female managers the most significant source of stress is the organization. Female managers report that the most important causes of stress include a lack of support or encouragement from supervisors, lack of consultation and communication, lack of power and influence, lack of clarity of job roles/job duties, inadequate promotion, and inadequate feedback about one's work (Davidson & Cooper, 1983). It appears that men experience stress from engaging in various job-related requirements, whereas women experience stress from what they perceive is not available to them—organizational power and support to perform job requirements.

The third explanation for sex differences in stress involves **social/ psychological factors** and focuses on women's and men's different internal responses to stressful situations. Cognitive appraisal of stress and strategies for coping with stress are mechanisms for explaining differences in stress symptoms between men and women. For example, men and women sometimes experience similar symptoms in response to stress, but men are less likely to interpret such symptoms as strain. Similarly, men and women sometimes cope with stressors in different ways. For example, in dealing with a difficult colleague, men may be more likely to actively resolve their differences (through either negotiation or confrontation), whereas women may be more likely to take the colleague's point of view or to build cooperation.

Models for Linking Work With Health

How does working outside the home relate to one's physical and mental health? This question was posed and pursued following women's entrance into the workforce in significant numbers. Because the vast majority of White males have been employed historically, the implicit assumption was that work was the norm for men. With greater numbers of women (especially White females) entering employment, society, the scientific community, and the popular press debated whether such employment was beneficial or harmful to women. Three models have emerged linking paid work with health, specifically women's health (Sorensen & Verbrugge, 1987). In the **health-benefits model,** work is believed to have direct beneficial effects on health, including opportunities to build self-esteem and confidence in one's decision-making, social support, financial reward, greater feelings of control, and experiences that enhance one's life satisfaction. All of these factors are believed to contribute to the health of paid workers, especially women. Employed women appear healthier than nonemployed women in terms of risk factors for chronic diseases (LaCroix & Haynes, 1987). Waldron and Lye (1989) found that employment tends to increase a person's social support, and this may have a positive effect on women's health.

The **job-stress model** stipulates that stress and strain of employment can harm women's mental and physical well-being. It suggests that women are particularly vulnerable to increased health risks especially given their dual responsibilities of work and family (Sorensen & Verbrugge, 1987). This model focuses on objective features of work that lead to distress or strain, including time pressures, workload, pacing, job ambiguity, low decision latitude, close supervision, and highly routinized work. The relationship between objective job stressors and health depends on two factors: the individual's perceptions and psychological resources, and the demands of other stressors and obligations outside of work. The focus in this approach has largely been on cardiovascular disease as a health outcome. Although there is a widespread belief that work is a source of significant stress for women and is harmful to their health, there is little evidence to support this view (Wegman & Fine, 1990).

The **role-expansion model** suggests that paid work offers indirect advantages to the worker. One's work role contributes to positive health through increased opportunities for rewards and satisfaction. Furthermore, different roles (worker, spouse, parent) can compensate for each other (Frankenhaeuser et al., 1991). That is, satisfaction in one role can compensate for strain in another. Multiple role involvement can be positive because it expands one's resources and rewards including self-esteem, control, and social support (Sorensen & Verbrugge, 1987).

Numerous studies have found that involvement in multiple roles (including worker, spouse, and parent) contributes to better health (Jacobs & Waldron, 1989). For example, single women have significantly higher levels of stress symptoms than married parents (Fong & Amatea, 1992). Although work can be a significant source of stress for both men and women, it is possible that the health benefits of working outweigh the health risks that result from stress on the job.

These three models focus on different variables and suggest different patterns of relationships among work and health. There is evidence to support two of the three models (i.e., data support important predictions of the health-benefits and role-expansion models), but it is likely that none of these models provides a complete picture. On the whole, there is evidence that work may have both health-promoting and health-damaging effects (Frankenhaeuser et al., 1991).

Sidelight 12.1   Methodological Challenges
in Research on Gender
and Stress

Let's examine two methodological considerations in evaluating the results of stress research on men and women. First, a comparison group of adults who are not in the labor force is required to adequately assess the effects of labor force participation. For employed women, a readily available comparison group is full-time homemakers (Waldron, 1991). However, it is difficult to find an adequate comparison group for working-age men. Men who are not working either are or are perceived to be deviant in many characteristics, including their health. Much of the research on effects of work on health outcomes has focused on women in their prime working ages and then shifted to men and women at retirement ages. The latter comparisons may yield different results because work effects at older ages may differ from those at prime ages due to physiological differences and social norms concerning the acceptability of being out of work (especially for men). The three models used here to investigate the effects of work on health (i.e., health-benefits, job-stress, and role-expansion models) suggest that the question of how work affects health did not become interesting or viable until women entered the workforce. Men have little flexibility in choosing whether they should work because there is such a strong sex-role norm that they ought to work.

A second methodological problem in studying the effects of work on health is that it is difficult to distinguish cause from effect or to separate the effects of labor-force participation on health from the effects of health on the labor force. Although women who work outside the home generally enjoy better health than women who do not, this finding does not necessarily mean that work has beneficial effects on women's health (Repetti, Matthews, & Waldron, 1989). Women in good health, for example, may seek employment more readily than women who are less well. Furthermore, women who are in good health tend to retire later in life. Older workers generally tend to be in better health than retirees (Minkler, 1981; Palmore, Burchett, Fillenbaum, George, & Wallman, 1985). Cause–effect interpretations are particularly ill-advised with correlational data, but longitudinal data can present similar challenges (Waldron & Jacobs, 1989). Results from longitudinal research (Haynes, Eaker, & Feinleib, 1984; Kotler & Wingard, 1989; Waldron & Jacobs, 1988, 1989) indicate that, on average, work has no significant effects on risk of coronary heart disease or mortality among women. For example, among middle-aged or older women who are White and married, work has no effect on general health, but for married Black women and unmarried White women, work has a positive effect on health. This may be due to social support received from coworkers. In addition to depending on race and marital status, the effects of work may also depend on type of occupation and whether the woman has children (Haynes et al., 1984). Also, women who work appear not to adversely affect their husbands' health, especially with respect to coronary heart disease (Haynes et al., 1984).

CONSEQUENCES OF STRESS

There are numerous documented consequences of stressful work environments. Physical outcomes include coronary heart disease (CHD), hypertension, and smoking, and stress can also affect the mental well-being of workers. Each of these is discussed in this section.

Physical Outcomes

There are a number of physical outcomes of stress at work. As Figure 12.1 indicates, a stressful work environment will not necessarily lead to these negative outcomes. Rather, the strength of the links between stress and negative health outcomes depends on a number of individual factors including personality variables. However, there is evidence of some consistent links among characteristics of the work environment, gender, and physical outcomes.

Work Environment and Coronary Heart Disease.   Several studies (e.g., J. V. Johnson, 1986; J. V. Johnson, Hall, & Theorell, 1989; Theorell, 1991) have shown that three environmental factors interact to increase one's risk of stress-related illness: job demands, decision latitude, and social support. Although researchers expected that the incidence of CHD would increase among women when they entered the workforce, there is no such evidence to date (Theorell, 1991). However, the risk of myocardial infarction (a heart disorder) is higher for both men and women when they hold hectic or monotonous jobs (Alfredson, Spetz, & Theorell, 1985). This might imply higher risks for women, because many "women's" jobs have these characteristics. Women with jobs where high percentages of employees report subjective symptoms such as fatigue and headaches also experience increased risks of CHD. This is not so for men, although men may be less inclined to report such symptoms.

Women in jobs that involve overtime (at least 10 hours per week) are at greater risk of hospitalization due to myocardial infarction (Alfredson et al., 1985). The opposite is found for men: Moderate amounts of overtime are associated with lower risk. Overtime at work may be more harmful to women than to men because it increases work–family conflicts (Theorell, 1991). Men in jobs described as both hectic and low in learning components have higher incidence of hospitalization. Although such jobs are the most significant predictor of men's risk, they do not predict hospitalization rates for women.

Jobs that are characterized by high demands and low control, such as air traffic control, are viewed as more stressful. Furthermore, these positions tend to be associated with increased risk of CHD. Among women, risk of CHD is higher for clerical workers, for the self-employed, and for employees in private institutions. Workload is associated with both CHD and hypertension (i.e., high blood pressure; Ironson, 1992). However, the precise contributions of workload to particular health outcomes are not clear (Ironson, 1992; Magnus, Matroos, & Strackee, 1983; Maschewsky, 1982; Orth-Gomer, 1979). Problems with social relations at work can also increase CHD risk for both men and women. However, a man's risks can be buffered by a supportive wife. Support from coworkers can also buffer stress for both men and women (Ironson, 1992).

In one study, men and women in the United States who were initially free of CHD were followed for 9 years. In this large-scale research, work, even in low-prestige jobs, was not an additional risk factor for CHD (Haynes & Feinlieb, 1980). However, the risk of CHD was two to three times higher among female clerical workers with two to three children or who were married to blue-collar workers. Also, clerical workers with nonsupportive bosses and who suppressed anger were at higher risk. Furthermore, high Type A women were twice as likely to develop heart disease as Type A males (Baruch, Biener, & Barnett, 1987).

Gender and Hypertension.   In general, women are at lower risk of developing high blood pressure and heart disease than men. It is not clear whether this difference is hereditary, hormonal, or due to environmental factors (Pickering et al. 1991). Hypertension was found to be more prevalent among men (16%) than women (5%) and more common among older and more overweight individuals in seven worksites (i.e., a daily newspaper, a federal health agency, a brokerage firm, a beverage company, a hospital, a sanitation department, an auto repair center, and a retail warehouse; Schlussel, Schnall, Zimbler, Warren, & Pickering, 1990). Also, married individuals have less hypertension than single people (Miall, 1987), and hypertension is more common among less well-educated people (Hypertension Detection and Follow-up Program Cooperative Group, 1987). The only group of women who experience disease rates equal to those of men are mothers working in clerical jobs (Haynes & Feinlieb, 1980).

Emotions such as anger, anxiety, and happiness all tend to increase blood pressure among women. For both men and women, a consistent determinant of blood pressure is the perception that one's job is stressful. Potential sources of domestic stress are also related to blood pressure. Pickering et al. (1991) found that marriage was associated with higher blood pressure as measured in the workplace. If an individual also had children, this was associated with higher blood pressure at home.

Women actually respond to stressors as if they have two full-time jobs (i.e., paid work and home work), and these findings are consistent with the Framingham Heart Study (Pickering et al., 1991). For example, arousal levels for women physicians are not much different between work and leisure hours (Theorell, 1991). This is consistent with the possibility that it is difficult for these women to combine household and paid work responsibilities. Further evidence of sex differences in stress patterns in the evening after work suggests that male managers' norepinephrine (a factor associated with stress) decreases during the evening hours whereas female managers' increases. Women managers tend to "wind up" at night, whereas male managers "wind down" (Frankenhaeuser, 1991a). In addition to physiological differences, women report greater feelings of tiredness and time pressure.

Smoking, Gender, and Health.

Smoking is related to coronary heart disease for both women and men (Barboriak, Anderson, & Hoffman, 1984) and is more strongly associated with coronary occlusion or blockage among women. Women are somewhat protected from heart disease prior to menopause, but menopause tends to occur 1 to 2 years earlier among women who smoke (Jick, Porter, & Morrison, 1977). Smoking is associated with increased risk for lung cancer and lung disease for both men and women (Harris, 1983; U.S. Department of Health and Human Services, 1983, 1984). Women who smoke also increase health risks for infants and are more likely to experience preterm births (U.S. Department of Health and Human Services, 1980).

In 1955 and 1977, women who worked were more likely to smoke than full-time homemakers (Haenszel, Shimkin, & Miller, 1956; Waldron, 1980). More recent surveys reveal little or no relationship between smoking and work status. However, there may be an indirect relationship between working and smoking. Work may increase stress, and stress is related to smoking (Biener, 1988; Chesney, 1991). Hourly and salaried workers experience similar time pressures (66 vs 67%) but differ on the ability to unwind after work (35 vs 51%) and job strain (31 vs. 45%), with salaried employees reporting more stress. One explanation linking stress to smoking suggests that stress leads to negative affect such as depression, tension, and anger directed toward oneself. Negative affect, in turn, leads to coping response, one of which involves smoking. Both salaried workers and homemakers who reported time pressures or difficulty unwinding (stress) scored higher on negative mood states. Cigarette smoking is used by women to cope with stress and negative mood (Chesney, 1991).

Jobs, Gender, and Stress. Karasek's (1979) demand–control model suggests that having a significant psychological workload interacts with having few adequate resources or little control to result in "high-strain" job situations. Workers in such high-strain jobs include most clerical workers, computer operators, saleswomen, telephone operators, waitresses, assemblers, and nursing aides (Cranor, Karasek, & Carlin, 1981). Stress and associated health outcomes in these jobs are of particular concern given the increasing numbers of women entering these positions. Great increases were expected between 1982 and 1995 among clerical workers, computer operators (46.1% increase), switchboard operators (28.7% increase), and order clerks (19.2% increase) (Hartmann, Kraut, & Tilly, 1986; Haynes, 1991), all of whom use computers extensively. Computerization appears to have increased rather than decreased problems for women, including increased sex segregation of jobs, which relegates women to lower status, lower pay, and higher stress jobs and occupations (Haynes, 1991). Clerical work is often characterized by underutilization of skills, lack of autonomy, low levels of responsibility, sustained attentional demand, and social isolation (Mackay & Cox, 1984). Such lack of control and high job demands are related to increases in systolic and diastolic blood pressure, excretion of catecholamines, hypertension, cardiovascular disease, and mortality (Haynes, LaCroix, & Lupine, 1987.

Mental and Emotional Health Consequences

Karoshi is a Japanese word meaning "death by overwork." This is certainly an extreme result of stress. The most common types of psychological distress are depression, burnout, and psychogenic disorders (Nelson & Quick, 1997). Depression and burnout at a minimum contribute to lower employee performance, lower interest in work, and fatigue. Psychogenic disorders are physical ailments that begin as psychological problems.

In much of the literature on stress and mental or emotional health, women tend to report more symptoms than men. However, these differences in reporting may reflect a response bias rather than true differences in symptoms. Men, in general, talk less about their health than women. Women who work outside the home show less depression (Schwartzberg & Dytell, 1989; Thoits, 1983, 1986) and greater psychological health and

---

Sidelight 12.2   A Biopsychosocial Model of Gender and Stress

Marianne Frankenhaeuser's (1991a, 1991b) biopsychosocial model of sex differences in occupational stress incorporates several features of the epidemiological, cognitive appraisal, and demand–control models. Her simple model indicates that health and well-being result from both one's cognitive assessment and one's bodily reactions to more objective environmental demands. Her model draws from multidisciplinary research in medicine, psychology, and sociology. The model emphasizes the influence of a person's attitudes and values on bodily stress responses. Thus, sex differences in values are reflected in physiological indicators of stress, and changes in values should be associated with changes in physiological indicators of stress (Frankenhaeuser, 1991a). During many decades of careful, systematic research, Frankenhaeuser (1991a) accumulated evidence to support her model. For example, laboratory research during the 1970s consistently found sex differences between men's and women's responses to achievement situations. Women were less prone to respond to such situations with increased epinephrine secretion. At rest, men and women were similar, but in challenging situations, men consistently secreted more epinephrine (Frankenhaeuser, 1988, 1983). More intense and frequent neuroendocrine stress responses in men may be associated with greater vulnerability to coronary heart disease. Frankenhaeuser also found that differences in reactivity (response) patterns in men and women may be influenced by social factors. She hypothesized that women in traditionally male occupations would respond the same as men in terms of psychoendocrine stress indicators. She found that such women tended to respond to achievement demands with increases in epinephrine secretion similar to men's (1991a). She also proposed that women were more vulnerable than men when faced with situations in which, by tradition or stereotype, they were expected to show competence (e.g., emphasis on social skills such as maintaining good group relationships; Lundberg, de Chateau, Wenberg, & Frankenhaeuser, 1981). Frankenhaeuser found that women secreted as much epinephrine, nonepinephrine, and cortisol as men in these situations.

---

self-esteem (Barúch & Barnett, 1986) than women who do not. Although some argue that combining work and family leads to role overload (Barúch & Barnett, 1986; Pleck, 1985), others report that women's perceptions of role overload come from the mother role, not the worker role (Barúch & Barnett, 1986). This may be due to the nature of the mother role; mothers are responsible for the well-being and satisfaction of others although they may in fact have little control over these outcomes. There are few differences between employed and nonemployed mothers with respect to total amount of family stress on specific components of family stress, including overload (Schwartzberg & Dytell, 1989). However, employed women report less support from their spouses (i.e., they expect more support) and nonemployed women report less support from their children than do employed women. Although work can have beneficial effects on women's mental health, balancing work, marriage, and parenting can create psychological distress (Crosby, 1984). Women tend to experience role overload associated with the motherhood role, which is a source of psychological distress (Barnett & Barúch, 1986). Having preschool children is associated with poorer mental health among employed women (McLanahan & Adams, 1987; Wortman, Biernat & Lang (1991). In general, however, women's work roles appear to have positive effects on women's psychological and physical well-being. Nonemployed wives and mothers may experience more anxiety when they feel stress in family roles than do wives and mothers who are employed (Barnett & Barúch, 1985). Family stress is related to negative mental health, especially depression (Barúch et al., 1987).

Chronic role strains (which occur over an extended period of time) or daily hassles may have more detrimental effects on workers' mental and physical health than acute life events (Kesler, Price, & Wortman, 1985). Such stressors are more common (e.g., job pressures, work–family conflicts, etc.), yet less research has been devoted to them than to other stressors (for an exception, see Pearlin, Lieberman, Meneghan, & Mullen, 1981). Although women report greater daily work–family conflicts than men (Wortman, Biernat, & Lang, 1991), women tend to be more critical of themselves as spouses and parents than are men. Chronic role strain for women includes annoyance at not being able to complete home projects (e.g., cleaning, child-care responsibilities). All of these stressors can decrease mental health.

STRESS REDUCTION: COPING STRATEGIES AND INTERVENTIONS

Numerous strategies have been designed to reduce stress. These strategies can be categorized into two general groups: individual and organizational-level strategies. Although a few individual strategies are discussed here, we focus more on organizational approaches to addressing work–family conflict, stress, and health issues.

Individual Strategies for Reducing Stress

The research literature suggests a number of methods for reducing stress and dealing with conflict. Some effective individual strategies include managing a positive lifestyle, physiological techniques (e.g., relaxation, exercise, and meditation), and cognitive techniques.

Exercise and individual biofeedback have been shown to decrease stress (Matteson & Ivancevich, 1988). Enhancing one's physical fitness is one of the best things a person can do to reduce stress and its harmful effects. Exercise has been associated with less heart disease and lower cholesterol (J. D. Brown, 1991). Another individual technique for coping with stress is meditation where the individual sits quietly, with eyes closed, relaxed and breathing slowly. During meditation (preferably once or twice a day for 10–20 minutes), individuals clear their minds of unsettling thoughts. Related to meditation is relaxation training, where people learn how to first tense and then relax their muscles (Benson, 1975). Such relaxation techniques can be used to prevent tension. The presence of pets decreases a person's physiological reactions during stressful tasks, more so than even the presence of a friend (Allen, Blascovich, Tamaka, & Kelsey, 1991). Finally, cognitive techniques can be used to avoid excessive worrying or thoughts in which we magnify the effects of a negative situation (Greenberg & Baron, 1997). For example, humor can be used to address negative marital (Krokoff, 1991) and work stressors.

Coping responses to stress have been classified in various ways. In general, however, these responses can be grouped into three categories (Ashford, 1988; Lazarus & Launier, 1978; Moos, 1976): **appraisal-focused coping,** where the individual attempts to redefine the meaning of the situation; **problem-focused coping,** where the individual attempts to deal with the problem directly; and **emotion-focused coping,** where the individual attempts to change the emotions aroused by the stressors (Ashford, 1988; Moos & Billings, 1982). In appraisal-focused coping, both cognitive redefinition and cognitive avoidance are involved (Moos & Billings, 1982). To some degree, these coping strategies are similar to the cognitive techniques described previously. Through **cognitive redefinition** a person can redefine stressors in positive terms (e.g., challenge) rather than in negative terms (e.g., threat). On the other hand, **cognitive avoidance** may enable the individual to reduce stress by not dwelling on a current problem and focusing his or her energies elsewhere.

A major element of problem-focused coping is information seeking (Ashford, 1988). By obtaining more information, the individual increases the predictability of a situation and thus enhances her or his sense of control when dealing with problems (Ashford, 1988; S. E. Taylor, 1983). A particularly useful type of information is feedback, specifically feedback regarding the antecedents and consequences (rewards or negative outcomes) of various stressors.

Regulation, resigned acceptance, and emotional discharge are strategies used during emotion-focused coping (Moos & Billings, 1982). Both regulation and resigned acceptance are strategies that contain emotions, whereas discharge reflects active expression of emotion. Although emotional discharge is dissimilar to the other coping strategies, it is still considered a coping strategy (Moos & Billings, 1982).

Organizational Interventions and Policies

I/O psychology has a long history of investigating and developing activities that can be used to address health issues at work, especially health-protection strategies. During recruitment, realistic job previews can narrow the gap between the individual's expectations and the requirements of the job (Lambert, 1992). Further prevention can occur at the selection stage. Through careful and valid testing procedures, individuals who possess specific requisite skills can be matched appropriately to jobs or situations with particular skill demands. For example, an organization might match a Type A individual with a less stressful organizational unit (Matteson & Ivancevich, 1987). Socialization of individuals, especially at the preentry stage, regarding the norms and practices of the organization may also be an effective stress-reduction intervention (Matteson & Ivancevich, 1987).

One of the primary areas where I/O psychologists can help organizations decrease the stress of work environments is **job design.** Job-design research typically addresses the match between the task demands of the job and individual's capabilities. Concern for employee health would expand the role of job design in two ways (Ilgen, 1990). First, organizations would design healthier jobs. As we have pointed out, control over the activities in one's life not only is a critical element in psychological well-being (Karasek, 1979; Murphy, 1988), but it also has a positive effect on the immune system as reflected in better physical health (Ilgen, 1990). Jobs can be redesigned to increase workers' participation in decision-making concerning tasks that affect them and to increase job autonomy, especially work-schedule autonomy (Murphy, 1988). Jobs can be also designed to reduce excessively high demands, which have been found repeatedly, in conjunction with low control (Karasek, 1979), to significantly predict high-stress jobs (Westman & Eden, 1992). Through job redesign, specific forms of conflict between work and family can be accommodated without perpetuating sex segregation of occupations (Glass & Camarigg, 1992; Hughes, Galinsky, & Morris, 1992). I/O psychologists know a great deal about motivational issues related to job performance and learning in training programs. Motivational issues are a key concern in health-promotion activities (Ilgen, 1990), especially in encouraging employees to choose behaviors that promote sound mental and physical health.

HEALTH ISSUES UNIQUE TO WOMEN

Our discussion of the relationship between stress and health outcomes for men and women would not be complete without addressing health concerns and issues specific to women's reproductive cycle and capacity. In the following sections, we briefly examine relationships between work stress and women's reproductive phase, menopause, and premenstrual syndrome.

Reproduction, Women's Health, and Work

Fertility has decreased over the last century in both Europe and North America (Hagenfeldt, 1991). One explanation for the fertility decline in the United States is referred to as the "European pattern"—later marriages and high celibacy rates. Contributing to this pattern are women's higher status and extended education and employment (because childbearing and childcaring can impede women's work outside the home, they reduce the family size; Hagenfeldt, 1991; Van de Walle & Kuodel, 1980).

Fertility is related to women's educational status. In the United States, 80 to 87% of the women born between 1940 and 1944 who did not complete high school were mothers by age 25, compared with 52 to 60% of those born at the same time who completed college. In 1973, the average number of children born to women with 0 to 11 years of education was 3.0, whereas the average for women with more than 13 years of education was 1.7 (Pratt, Mosher, Bachrach, & Horn, 1984). Early pregnancy, especially during the teens, inhibits girls' educational and future economic possibilities in all cultures (Hagenfeldt, 1991). As discussed in chapter 10, the decision to have children and the timing of childbearing and childrearing can significantly impact women's career choices and career advancement.

Women, Work, and Menopause

In the United States, **menopause** occurs on average at approximately age 51. This is a time when most women are working outside the home either part time or full time (McKinlay, 1988). Working women experience fewer menopause symptoms and are better able to cope with family and relationship stresses than women who are not employed outside the home (Sarrel, 1991). However, there has been little research on the effects of menopause on work performance.

With the onset of menopause, the production of certain hormones decreases. With decreases in these hormones, women can experience a number of physical and emotional symptoms. One physiological symptom is known as hot flashes or warm flushes. At least 80% of women develop these before and after menopause, often along with some sleep disturbance (Sarrel, 1991). Long-term hormonal changes can be associated with **osteoporosis.** Therefore, menopausal women may be at greater risk for wrist, vertebral, or hip fractures. However, these fractures often do not occur until after women have left the workforce (after age 65 years). Hormonal changes can affect other organs as well and result in numbness, small-joint pain, urinary urgency and incontinence, vaginal dryness, and dyspareunia, palpitations, headaches, anxiety attacks, depression, and altered memory functions (Sarrel, 1991). These symptoms are not specific to menopausal women; they occur in response to hormonal deficiencies regardless of the cause. In one study, hot flashes, depression, and sexual dysfunction occurred in more than 30% of postmenopausal women for 5 years and in over 25% of the women for more than 10 years (Bengtsson, 1973). Sleep disturbances, hot flashes, anxiety attacks, and depression, all symptoms that negatively affect work and sexual relationships, may also be considered stressors (Sarrel, 1991).

For postmenopausal women, cardiovascular disease is the leading cause of mortality in the United States and results in three to four times the annual number of deaths as lung, breast, endometrial, and ovarian cancers combined (National Center for Health Statistics, 1988). Although estrogen replacement therapy (ERT) reduces the risk of heart attacks and strokes (Bush, Barrett-Connor, & Cowan, 1987), after menopause, the incidence of cardiovascular disease among women is similar to men's (Colditz, Willett, & Stampfer, 1987). In the United States, numerous studies indicate that employed women show less psychological anxiety and depression and better health than homemakers. Yet, self-report data suggest that women are moderately affected at work by such menopausal symptoms as sleep disturbances, hot flashes, and, to a lesser degree, anxiety attacks (Sarrel, 1991).

Premenstrual Syndrome, Work, and Health

There continues to be some controversy among clinical and counseling psychologists regarding premenstrual syndrome (PMS). PMS is characterized by numerous somatic, affective, cognitive, and behavioral symptoms or disturbances. In fact, one of the points of controversy is the large list of symptoms associated with PMS (symptoms that either men or women could have). However, diagnosis of the syndrome depends on the timing of the symptoms: a sudden onset in the second half of the menstrual cycle, and a disappearance of symptoms with the appearance of full menstrual flow. A subset of symptoms includes irritability, depression, loss of energy, food cravings, loss of sexual interest, bloatedness, and breast tenderness.

Emotional PMS symptoms are reported to be more distressing for women than physical symptoms (A. Collins, 1991). There is a feeling of loss of control. Women describe themselves as impatient, intolerant, spiteful, vindictive, faultfinding, quarrelsome, and quick-tempered (Dalton, 1984). PMS sleep disturbances can leave women feeling tired or exhausted at work. Yet, there is little evidence of lowered intellectual performance among employees with PMS (Clare, 1985; Sommer, 1982). Long-term consequences of PMS may lead to deterioration of interpersonal relationships, perceived inefficiency at work, and feelings of inadequacy, hopelessness, and guilt. At work, approximately 10% of women with PMS are estimated to need some kind of medical treatment for PMS-related conditions (Andersch, 1980).

PMS sufferers score higher on somatic anxiety, muscular tension, and indirect aggression and lower on socialization (A. Collins et al., 1986; Hallman, 1987). PMS may be more common among women who have difficulty dealing with life's stressful events and are dissatisfied with their work (Clare, 1983; Siegal, Johnson, & Sarason, 1979; Wood, Larsen, & Williams, 1979). However, the effects of work on PMS are not known. Women at work tend to hide the fact that they suffer from PMS because they are afraid it may affect promotion opportunities.

Concentrating and interacting with other people are the aspects of work performance most affected by PMS (A. Collins, 1991). Women in management receive less social support for their symptoms than do women in service jobs. Women with PMS tend to experience more role conflict and also report less satisfaction with themselves as parents and wives, as well as with their professional role, during the PMS phase. They engage in more self-blame and feelings of inadequacy (A. Collins, 1991).

STRESS, WORK, AND ETHNIC MINORITIES

Although workers' health problems are receiving increased attention (K. James, 1994; Kizer, 1987; Matteson & Ivancevich, 1988), less research has addressed the nature and effects of stress on minority employees

(Ford, 1985). Because the proportion of minority group members in the workforce is increasing (Johnson & C. Packer, 1987), it seems more important than ever to determine whether individual and organizational antecedents of stress vary for minority and nonminority employees.

There is empirical evidence that perceived discrimination and prejudice at work contribute to minority group members' stress. For example, among African-American workers, perceived discrimination at work is associated with increased blood pressure (S. A. James, LaCroix, Kleinbaum, & Strogatz, 1984). Perceptions of discrimination also contribute to work distress, depression, and several physiological symptoms among African-American workers (Erlich & Larcom, 1992; Frone, Russell, & Cooper, 1990). Both minority and nonminority workers who perceive discrimination against minorities in their work group show higher levels of stress than those who do not (Gutierres, Saenz, & Green, 1992). This suggests that perceptions of unfair discrimination may have pervasive negative impacts on employees.

Although minority children are more likely to respond to school requirements and to study more when their mother's work is demanding and regulated (Piotrokowski & Katz, 1982), in general, minority employees' work status has less positive effects on their families. Minority workers have worse jobs and lower incomes than White workers, which negatively affects their families (Ferber et al., 1991; Harrison, 1989). When employed, especially at higher levels in an organization, African-Americans may experience heightened career stress resulting from attempts to demonstrate their competence by excessively working. Mutual feelings of distrust between Black managers, peers, and superiors, and participation in organizational policies that are not in the best interests of Blacks, also contribute to stress (Latack, 1989). Although, in one study most employees report being satisfied with their work, African-Americans, compared to Whites and Mexican-Americans, experienced the highest levels of stress, both work- and non-work-related, and had the most chronic health problems (J. Jackson & Antonuicci, 1989). Other researchers have found few differences in stress levels among men from various racial and ethic groups, although African-American women experienced less work–family stress than White women or other women of color (Fernandez, 1981).

Career experiences of minorities in predominantly White organizations have been studied extensively (D. A. Thomas & Alderfer, 1989). The literature on African-Americans suggests that minority experiences at work may be largely bicultural, in the sense that the dominant culture in the workplace is likely to reflect the experiences, preferences, and biases of White employees. Stress is experienced when one moves back and forth between one's own culture and the dominant culture (E. T. Bell, 1986).

Research on minority women may provide a framework for understanding how minorities choose the level and degree to which they will move between the two cultures and the tensions associated with those shifts. Three patterns of bicultural life structures have been found among women (E. T. Bell, 1986). The first is *career-oriented* women. Black women have social networks in both the Black and White communities, and stress results from attempts to balance the two cultures. Black *community-oriented* women are deeply involved in the Black community and experience social and emotional distance from the dominant culture. Stress results from inadequate resources in their own culture and insufficient social support (D. A. Thomas & Alderfer, 1989). *Family-oriented* women are centered on family; work is secondary. Stress here is experienced as unfulfilled career aspirations.

Given the increasing proportion of ethnic minorities entering the workforce, it becomes critical for organizations to understand whether factors that contribute to stress among majority group members have similar negative effects for minority group members, and to identify and understand the unique factors that contribute to stress among minority members. With such information, organizations can design intervention programs or individuals can learn methods to cope with such stress (K. James, 1994).

SUMMARY

Stress is a complex set of reactions to demands from an action or situation, often involving an interaction between a person and that person's environment. Although there are numerous ways of thinking about work stress, two general models of work stress, the job characteristics model and the organizational model, have dominated the work literature. Historically each model has focused on different occupations and emphasizes different sources of stress at work. The job characteristics model evolved from the labor tradition (e.g., factory occupations) and emphasizes the objective characteristics of jobs that contribute to stress. These include jobs that have high or low psychological demands and low decision latitude or control. The organizational stress model focuses more on the individual's characteristics and perceptions of the work environment as important in understanding workplace stress. Sources of work stress that have been identified using these models include task demands of the job, the individual's role in the organization or role demands, relationships at work, organizational structure/climate, and nonwork factors including work–family conflicts. One important factor that may influence the effects of these sources of stress on a person's perceptions of stress and subsequent health is a person's gender. Approaches for linking gender with stress and health outcomes include genetic, structuralist, and social/psychological. These approaches suggest that men and women may differ in their reactions to stress and provide a number of reasons for such differences. Furthermore, the effects of a stressor on health may differ depending on whether we are referring to men or women.

Stress can adversely affect an individual's health and is linked to coronary heart disease, hypertension, and smoking. The effects of workplace stressors may place women at greater health risk than men, in part due to the types of jobs women are likely to occupy. Women typically occupy and continue to enter occupations that are considered "high strain" jobs. These jobs involve significant psychological workloads yet have little decision latitude; they include clerical work, sales, and food services jobs.

Strategies to reduce workplace stressors include individual and organizational strategies. Individual strategies include exercise, individual biofeedback, and a number of cognitive techniques designed to help individuals either avoid dwelling on stressful events or redefine those events. One theme that has emerged throughout this text is that for each content area of work described (e.g., leadership, careers, etc.), there are unique issues that women either face in or bring to the workplace. Regarding stress and health, women face additional potential stressors and health concerns including fertility issues, menopause, osteoporosis, and premenstrual syndrome. These issues may influence how women react to workplace stressors or may interact with workplace stressors to influence work satisfaction and performance. Increasingly, stress researchers are investigating not only how workplace stressors influence the majority of male workers but also how ethnic minorities are affected by such stressors and what additional stressors may affect minority members' health.

GLOSSARY

Appraisal-focused coping: Method of coping where the individual attempts to redefine the meaning of the situation.

Cognitive avoidance: Psychological mechanism where an individual reduces stress by not dwelling on a problem and by focusing his or her energies elsewhere.

Cognitive redefinition: Psychological process whereby a person can redefine stressors in more positive terms.

Decision latitude/control: A combination of task authority and skill discretion one possesses in a given job.

Emotion-focused coping: Method of coping where the individual attempts to change the emotions aroused by the stressor.

Genetic sources: Source of stress involving inborn tendencies with little or no variation due to situational or psychological factors.

Health-benefits model: Model wherein work is assumed to have direct and beneficial effects on one's health.

Interrole conflict: Conflict expectations from two separate roles, such as employee and parent.

Intrarole conflict: Conflicting expectations related to a single role, such as employee.

Job design: Grouping certain tasks into a particular job.

Job stress model: Model which indicates that stress and strain of employment can harm women's (not necessarily men's) mental and physical well-being, especially because of dual responsibilities of work and family.

Menopause: When a woman has had no menstrual periods for 1 year.

Osteoporosis: Bone thinning from loss of calcium, which makes bones susceptible to breaking.

Passive jobs: Jobs characterized by low decision latitude and low psychological demands (e.g., a somewhat boring job).

Person-role conflict: Conflict arising when employees are expected to behave in ways that violate personal values or beliefs.

Problem-focused coping: Method of coping where the individual attempts to deal with the problem directly.

Psychological demands: Time pressures on the job; also fear of losing one's job or skills becoming out of date (obsolete).

Role ambiguity: An individual's uncertainty about what actions to take to fulfill a job.

Role-expansion model: Model which suggests that paid work offers advantages to workers indirectly through increased opportunity for rewards and satisfaction.

Roles: A recurring set of actions of an individual that are appropriately interrelated with the repetitive activities of another self, so as to yield a predictable outcome.

Shiftwork: Work period that extends beyond the normal workday.

Skill discretion: Breadth or variety of skills usable on the job.

Social/psychological factors: Sources of stress that focus on women's and men's differential internal responses to stressful situations.

Strain (distress): Effects of stress on an individual.

Stress: A complex set of emotional, physiological, and mental states in response to demands from an action or situation.

Stressors: Factors in an environment that promote stress among individuals.

Structuralist position: A major source of stress; suggests that different work stressors are associated with different work situations.

Task authority: The autonomy or independence one has to make decisions about pertinent matters.

Work overload: Situation where demands and stimulation of a job reach beyond a worker's capabilities.

Work underload: Situation where demands and stimulation of a job are so low that the job is boring.

IV

WHAT DO WE DO WITH
WHAT WE KNOW AND
DO NOT KNOW?

13

Managing Diversity: Research and Interventions

- The managers and executives of an organization have, in the past, always been male. Fearing a lawsuit, the organization aggressively recruits female MBAs.
- Roberto is hired as a sales manager to help increase marketing in local and regional Hispanic communities.
- An organization that has lost top job applicants because of limited dual-career opportunities creates a program to identify opportunities for spouses (primarily female) early in the recruitment process.
- Concerned about the relatively small numbers of girls pursuing advanced science and math courses, the principal of a high school creates a mentoring program to help girls identify and link up with successful women in science, math, medicine, and other similar fields.

All of these examples represent efforts of organizations or schools to increase opportunities for women or members of minority groups. They are driven by a number of motives (e.g., desire to increase market share or to avoid lawsuit, or concern over limited opportunities available to or taken by members of some groups), and they take a number of forms. All can be thought of as specific facets of a more general strategy of "managing diversity."

The term *managing diversity* is in some ways unfortunate, because it suggests that the increasing diversity of the workforce is a problem to be managed. As shown in this chapter, this is to some extent true. Diversity can bring problems, but it can also bring unique opportunities. Managing diversity focuses on minimizing the challenges and maximizing the opportunities presented by workforce diversity.

The purpose of this chapter is to integrate a number of the issues, perspectives, and findings discussed in chapters 1 through 12 under the general heading of "managing diversity." That is, we will use organizations' efforts to deal with the increasing diversity of the U.S. workforce as a springboard for discussing interventions and strategies for dealing with many of the issues and problems described in the preceding chapters.

We begin with a brief discussion of what managing diversity might mean and the various reasons organizations might have for dealing with diversity-related questions. We then discuss some specific processes that interfere with organizational and societal efforts to open opportunities to a more diverse population. We follow this with a discussion of some of the steps that might be taken to build gender-inclusive organizations. Finally, we discuss specific interventions designed to deal with several of the issues raised in chapters 1 through 12.

WHAT DOES IT MEAN
TO MANAGE DIVERSITY?

The demographic makeup of the U.S. workplace is changing rapidly. For most of our history, the substantial majority of the paid workforce (particularly in full-time, semiskilled, skilled, managerial, and professional jobs) has been drawn from a relatively narrow slice of society—White males. This is no longer the case. The large majority of new entrants into the workforce are now females and/or members of minority groups and immigrants. Population changes (e.g., Baby Bust), increased globalization of the marketplace, increased accessibility of the workplace for disabled people and others traditionally denied equal employment opportunities, and other factors noted previously have led to projections that the U.S. workplace will be more demographically diverse in the year 2000 than ever before (Johnston & Packer, 1987; Offermann & Gowing, 1990). As a result, organizations must develop methods of dealing with both the problems and the opportunities posed by a diverse workforce. Organizations that take planned, proactive steps to ease the transition from a relatively homogeneous workforce to an increasingly diverse one are said to be managing diversity.

Two basic approaches might be taken in dealing with diversity. The first is to change people to fit the organization. That is, you can keep everything in the organization exactly as it has been in the past (when the workforce was more homogeneous) and use selection, training, socialization, and rewards to make new workers more similar to the workforce you are accustomed to dealing with. The second strategy is to change the organization to fit the people. That is, if new workers have different interests, values, and norms, it might be necessary to change the way the organization works to accommodate these differences. Most interventions designed to manage diversity seem to do a little of both (i.e., change the people and change the organization), but in many cases, the strategy of choice will be to change the organization to fit the workforce. The main reason for choosing this approach is that it is very difficult to change people, whereas organizations and the systems used to operate organizations are more amenable to change.

One way of thinking about what managing diversity means is to think of the problems organizations might face if they do nothing in response to the changing demographic makeup of the U.S. workforce. Organizations that ignore the increasing diversity of the workforce, essentially maintaining their current cultures, personnel policies, and values, may experience difficulties in staffing and may experience increasing levels of intergroup conflict. For example, organizations that have traditionally relied on high levels of time commitment from their employees (e.g., requiring them to work substantial amounts of overtime, to report to work with minimal notice, to work evenings and weekends) may be less attractive to people who are unable or unwilling to make these commitments (e.g., mothers and fathers with young children). Organizational cultures that are "macho" may be less attractive to women or members of different ethnic groups.

Organizations are under no legal obligation to change in response to changes in the workforce, but many organizations will find that they have no choice. The supply of workers who "fit" the existing policies and culture simply may not be sufficient to meet the demand.

A second reason for attempting to manage diversity is that it may be more profitable to change the organization to fit the current workforce than to ignore or resist changes in the workforce. Researchers suggest that companies can create or maintain a competitive advantage by attracting and harnessing a multicultural workforce. Such companies will certainly face a number of challenges (e.g., increased intergroup conflict; Cox & Blake, 1991), but the advantages of overcoming these challenges are often seen as outweighing the costs. Thus, a wide range of ideas and programs for managing diversity have been offered by practitioners and theorists (see S.E. Jackson, 1992, for a summary).

Some researchers define managing diversity as "a variety of management issues and activities related to hiring and effective utilization of personnel from different cultural backgrounds" (Cox & Blake, 1991, p. 45). The philosophy underlying most diversity initiatives is that going beyond simple compliance with equal employment opportunity and affirmative action legislation and court orders is a sound business strategy. Organizations in which all individuals enjoy full and equal opportunities for employment are thought to be more competitive than those in which a narrowly drawn group dominates. The assumption behind many interventions designed to help organizations manage diversity is that workers from a wide range of backgrounds and groups have much to offer and that organizations are more likely to maximize the benefits of such a workforce if they adjust to the changing realities of the labor market.

Managing Diversity: Theory and Philosophy

On the whole, the literature on managing/valuing diversity is more anecdotal than theoretically or empirically driven. Nonetheless, there have been some attempts to structure and guide these efforts. Drawing on models of societal acculturation processes, Cox (1991) developed a model that categorizes organizations on the extent to which they exhibit gender, racial, and ethnic integration. These criteria illustrate the range of issues involved in managing diversity and provide benchmarks for evaluating organizational responses to the increasing diversity of the workforce. Cox (1994) proposed six criteria for evaluating the extent to which organizations value and accommodate diversity:

1. Structural integration—representation of minorities (White women and racially and ethnically diverse women and men) at all levels of the organization.
2. Informal integration—inclusion in social networks in the organization.
3. Removal of cultural bias—lack of prejudice and discrimination.
4. Organizational identification—extent to which there are gender and racial and ethnic differences in commitment and attachment to the organization.
5. Reduction of interpersonal conflict—lack of group-based tension and interpersonal friction.
6. Degree of acculturation—extent to which cultural differences are resolved and dealt with.

Given these six criteria, there are many different ways you might characterize organizational responses to workforce diversity (e.g., an organization might provide high levels of structural and informal integration but still have lingering cultural bias, high levels of conflict, or low levels of identification with the organization among several demographic groups). However, Cox suggested that a few specific models for acculturation can be defined and that these describe many organizations.

In assimilated organizations, minorities are expected to adopt the norms and values of the dominant group, that is, they are expected to lose their distinct cultural identity (these organizations follow the "change the people" strategy). Assimilated organizations are frequently characterized by low structural and informal integration, high levels of discrimination and prejudice, and large intergroup differences in organizational attachment favoring the dominant group. Because the perceived odds of surviving overt conflict are low for minority groups, intergroup conflict is likely to be low.

Plural organizations are characterized by diversity in numbers but not always in spirit. Steps may taken to include various groups by adherence to equal opportunity and affirmative action policies, but these may lead to backlash (i.e., dominant group members' feelings of reverse discrimination) and higher levels of intergroup conflict, which in turn can strengthen the barriers between groups. In plural but culturally separated organizations, neither the dominant nor the minority groups do much to adapt to one another. In these organizations, people may work side by side, but for all intents and purposes, they are members of different organizations.

Truly multicultural organizations are characterized by full structural and informal integration, minimal prejudice or discrimination, minimal subgroup differences in organizational attachment, and low levels of conflict. Cox admitted that very few organizations are truly multicultrual but provided suggestions for achieving this status. We use his suggestions as a framework for describing various components of change efforts designed to enhance gender equity in the workplace and for evaluating the merit of these programs.

The studies reviewed in chapters 1 through 12 suggest that few women work in truly multicultural organizations. For example, we noted in several chapters that despite progress in recent years, barriers still exist to women's full structural integration in the workplace. Women are more likely to be judged by their appearance than men, are more likely to make career sacrifices during their childbearing years than men, and are more likely to be the targets of sexual harassment. Although explicit and intentional discrimination against women may be declining, there are numerous subtle forms of discrimination against women, such as the tendency of men to exclude women from influential social networks, that substantially hamper women's chances of success in the workplace. Prejudice and discrimination against women are probably not as widespread as 30 years ago, but they are still important facts of life, particularly in nontraditional fields (e.g., science, management, top leadership positions). All of these factors suggest that the workplace is still, on the whole, less favorably inclined toward women than toward men (although there are certainly jobs, occupations, and organizations where the reverse might be true). It appears, then, that a great deal of work remains to be done in managing the gender diversity of the workforce. However, before we describe efforts to increase women's opportunities to participate fully in the workplace, it is useful to ask whether efforts to manage diversity actually work. That is, it is useful to assess the impact of some of the interventions designed to foster true multiculturalism on the workers whom these programs are designed to help and on the organizations that implement these programs.

Does Managing Diversity Work?

A growing body of both anecdotal (case study) and empirical research supports the idea that initiatives designed to help manage diversity (or other similarly labeled initiatives, such as workplace flexibility (Hall & Parker, 1993) can substantially benefit both workers and organizations (S.E. Jackson, 1992). Internal evaluations of these programs demonstrate that carefully constructed, integrated, comprehensive efforts to manage and value diversity that are supported by top management reap dividends to these organizations in the form of greater attraction and retention of White women and racially and ethnically diverse workers, greater representation of diverse groups of people in all levels and sectors of the organization, more positive public image, and increased capability of achieving strategic company objectives (see S.E. Jackson, 1992, for a review; see also Hall & Parker, 1993). Cox and Blake (1991), reviewing a wide body of corporate-specific evaluations of managing diversity initiatives, suggested that such efforts have the potential to help organizations attract and retain the most talented workforce, reduce turnover/withdrawal costs (e.g., women and members of minority groups who feel their skills are being used effectively may be less than likely to leave and more likely to be productive), improve marketing success (e.g., a diverse workforce may be more likely to understand product and service needs of diverse consumers), and inspire greater creativity and improved problem solving (e.g., heterogeneous groups can be more successful in generating more and better potential solutions to problems than homogeneous groups).

Several recent studies have examined the effects of diversity initiatives across organizations on a number of key criteria; we will cite two examples from a large and complex literature. Wright, Ferris, Hiller, and Kroll (1995) reviewed stock valuation data on firms that either had won the U.S. Department of Labor's Exemplary Voluntary Efforts Award (which is given for high-quality affirmative action programs) or had announced major settlements in discrimination suits. Analyses of data collected over several years suggest that firms with proactive strategies for managing diversity performed better than firms that experienced major problems with discrimination.[1] The *Affirmative Action Review: A report to the President* (1995) identified substantial gains in employment opportunities for women and members of racial and ethnic minority groups and suggested that organizational policies to increase multiculturalism are likely to be responsible for at least some of this gain. Despite the rhetoric from both opponents and proponents of efforts to increase diversity, it is very difficult to determine precisely the impact of these programs, because they have been implemented at the same time as numerous other societal changes have occurred (e.g., better educational opportunities for women and members of minority groups). Nevertheless, the authors of the White House review suggested that organizational efforts to provide greater access and a more hospitable climate for a diverse workforce have substantially increased employment opportunities.

The literature on initiatives aimed at managing diversity suggests that they can succeed but that the criteria for evaluating their success are not always obvious. For example, organizations might concentrate on "getting their numbers right" by hiring more women and minority group members. These efforts can solve a short-term problem but are unlikely to bring

---

[1]It is important to note, however, that the Department of Labor award or the discrimination settlement itself could be responsible for changes in stock prices.

Sidelight 13.1   Diversity Without Discrimination?

Does valuing diversity imply that you will discriminate on the basis of race and gender to redress imbalances in the workforce? This is the assumption usually made in discussions of programs to increase diversity in organizations. Consider, for example, California's Proposition 209 (see chap. 7); this proposition

1. Prohibits the state, local governments, districts, public universities, colleges, and schools, and other government instrumentalities from discriminating against or giving preferential treatment to any individual or group in public employment, public education, or public contracting on the basis of race, sex, color, ethnicity, or national origin.
2. Does not prohibit reasonably necessary, bona fide qualifications based on sex and actions necessary for receipt of federal funds.
3. Mandates enforcement to extent permitted by federal law.
4. Requires uniform remedies for violations. Provides for severability of provisions if invalid.

Many of the opponents of this proposition have attacked it on the assumption that this law will make it difficult to increase or even maintain the diversity of private- and public-sector organizations in California. Proponents of Proposition 209 sometimes share this assumption and argue that any attempt to broaden opportunities for women or minority group members must involve reverse discrimination. The implicit notion in this debate is that "preferential treatment" is necessary if we wish to see any changes in employment opportunities for members of protected groups.

In one sense, both the opponents and proponents of Proposition 209 are right. If nothing else changes in society and organizations, it is probably unrealistic to assume that substantial changes will occur without some sort of race- or gender-conscious personnel policies. However, as we stress throughout this chapter, the assumption that nothing else will or should change in organizations as the workforce changes is fundamentally wrong. There is, for example, clear evidence of changes in the way that children are socialized into sex roles (e.g., "Bring Your Daughter to Work Day"), and it is reasonable to believe that these changes will have a major impact on male–female interactions in the workplace. The assumption that reverse discrimination is a necessary component of increasing diversity is part of a larger assumption that nothing else is happening, or likely to happen, to break down the barriers to full participation in the workplace that currently exist. We are not as pessimistic about the prospects for broad (albeit slow) societal changes as some of the opponents or proponents of Proposition 209 seem to be.

the organization long-term success and may in fact plant the seeds for long-term disaster unless they are accompanied by systematic efforts to adapt to the changing workforce. For example, an organization with a traditional "macho" culture may provide an uneasy working environment for women. Even though they are hired into this organization, it is unlikely that women will thrive, and the organization may encounter more problems with sex discrimination in promotion and rewards as a result of its efforts to obtain more favorable employment statistics.

Two things are necessary for a successful diversity initiative. First, in designing a diversity initiative, it pays to critically examine the criteria used to define success, particularly if those criteria focus narrowly on short-term results. For example, there is little to be gained by hiring or promoting women into environments that virtually guarantee their failure. A diversity initiative that aims to bring women into an organization, without providing the support or climate necessary for them to perform effectively and compete fairly with their male colleagues, makes the mistake of focusing on proximal success criteria (i.e., number of women hired) while ignoring long-term prospects for success. Second, it is important to realize that diversity is a complex construct and that the most obvious aspects of diversity (e.g., gender, skin color) can be the least important ones. Demographic diversity often implies diversity in experiences, values, interests, patterns of interaction, and methods of communication, and all of these aspects of workforce diversity can create both opportunities and problems for organizations. We have already noted potential opportunities and contributions that arise as a result of increasing diversity; it is also useful to understand some of the problems organizations are likely to encounter as their workforce becomes increasingly diverse.

Intergroup Conflict: Diversity's Downside

Although the literature in this area argues forcefully for the advantages of multiculturalism, there are identifiable downsides to diversity. In particular, diverse groups are more prone to conflict, stereotyping, and bias than homogeneous groups. Thus, one critical component of managing diversity is understanding how and why diversity may lead to conflict and taking concrete steps to head off such conflict.

Psychologists have studied relationships and conflicts among groups for more than a century, and a number of models and theories can used to understand how diversity might contribute to conflict. We review two major theoretical foundations of intergroup relations—realistic conflict theory and social identity theory—and discuss their relevance for efforts to manage diversity.

Realistic Conflict Theory.   Realistic conflict theory (RCT) suggests that when there are multiple, distinct groups in an organization, conflict is likely to occur. This conclusion is based on the assumptions that people will try to maximize their own outcomes and the outcomes of people similar to them, and that the interests of different groups are not always compatible (D.M. Taylor & Moghaddam, 1994). If groups within an organization have or are seen to have different interests, RCT suggests that conflict, prejudice and stereotyping are completely normal and predictable.

RCT has a number of implications for managing diversity programs and has been applied in a number of different ways. One application is in the creation and management of teams of organizations. This theory suggests that conflict can be reduced if members of a diverse group see themselves as a unified team rather than a collection of different interest groups. One strategy for developing this unified approach is to develop and define goals that are widely accepted by team members. Consistent with predictions of RCT theory, members of diverse demographic groups working toward a common goal are more likely to discard their background differences in favor of solving a problem. A second application of RCT to managing diversity is the management of intergroup confrontations in organizations. This might occur when, for example, a coalition composed of a members of a particular demographic group, such as a women's group or an African-American group, challenges the existing power holders, such as Euro-American men. Blake and Mouton (1986) summarized their program of research and consultation in organizations dealing with many different kinds of intergroup conflict, which has demonstrated that diverse groups working together on superordinate goals can resolve conflict and achieve solutions that are more creative and effective than would be expected from more homogeneous groups.

Social Identity Theory.   Social identity theory asserts that individuals seek to belong to groups that develop or enhance a positive self-identity and that self-identity is naturally enhanced when one's ingroup is positively distinguished from the outgroup. Tajfel and his colleagues (as described by D.M. Taylor & Moghaddam, 1994) have demonstrated through decades of research that groups formed on the basis of even the most trivial of circumstances (e.g., tendencies to underestimate or overestimate the number of dots in a grouping) develop cognitively distorted perceptions of ingroup and outgroup members that result in biased evaluations (i.e., negative outgroup attitudes) and discriminatory treatment (e.g., inequitable reward distribution). Furthermore, these processes are just as powerful in groups created by arbitrary, trivial criteria as groups created by meaningful, value-laden criteria (Moghaddam & Stringer, 1986).

Social identity theory makes the important point that ingroup/outgroup processes are natural, perhaps inevitable social realities. People exist as members of social groups, and they strive for positive self-evaluation by maintaining or creating positive ingroup evaluations. Unfortunately, people also tend to evaluate groups other than their own more negatively. Several diversity intervention strategies have attempted to reduce negative biases in perceptions of outgroup members. In chapters 3, 4, and 7, we noted that stereotyped impressions of women and men occur in a variety of circumstances, especially those in which the gender of the job type does not match the gender of the target, we lack job-relevant information about targets of evaluation and know little more than their gender (Heilman, 1983), targets are in token positions in groups, or attractive women are placed in male-typed jobs (Heilman & Stopeck, 1985). In all of these situations, gender is made more salient than other information about the target, leading people to use "male" versus "female" to define social groups. This suggests one strategy for developing interventions: redefining group identity around job-relevant criteria (e.g., developing strong identities with work teams) rather than around gender.

A Common Theme for Developing Interventions. Both realistic conflict theory and social identity theory suggest that identification with (and positive biases toward) your own group, combined with relatively negative perceptions of other groups, are important sources of intergroup conflict. Realistic conflict theory assumes that different groups often have different interests, and thus there is often a realistic basis for disagreements. Social identity theory suggests that even where there are no meaningful differences to argue about, our tendency to view people like ourselves positively and people unlike ourselves negatively will lead to conflicts between groups. Both theories suggest that conflict can be reduced by shifting its focus. That is, if groups can be defined in terms of their functions rather than their demographic characteristics, it may be possible to head off the conflicts that naturally emerge when a diverse population shares the same space (or organization).

Conflict is less likely if workers think of themselves as members of a team, department, or organization first, and members of groups defined in terms of gender, race, or ethnicity second. Although programs designed to develop highly cohesive teams in organizations are not often thought of as diversity programs, they may be central to reducing the potential downside of diversity. Two approaches seem especially promising. First, consistent with realistic conflict theory, it is possible to build cohesive teams by either identifying or stimulating interest in a goal that transcends differences among team members. For example, Sherif's "robbers cave" studies demonstrated that conflict within diverse groups could be reduced by engaging the group in valued activities that could not be accomplished by members working alone, or by creating competition between groups (Sherif, Harvey, White, Hood, & Sherif, 1961). Similar experiments in the contexts of labor-management conflict (Blake, Shepard, & Mouton, 1964) and school desegregation (Aronson, Stephan, Sikes, Blaney, & Snapp, 1978) have shown that team-building interventions of this sort can reduce conflict within teams.

A second approach involves reducing the salience of gender, race, or other demographic characteristics (thus reducing the likelihood that groups will be formed around these characteristics). As we noted in several earlier chapters, gender is most salient when men or women are in a substantial minority in a particular job or organization or when the stereotypes of the job do not fit the stereotypes of men and women. To a large extent, this problem may be self-correcting (albeit slowly). As more women enter jobs that have traditionally been dominated by men, the stereotypes of jobs are likely to change and the statistical rarity of women must, by definition, change. Bringing more women into particular jobs or occupations is not the only way to reduce the salience of gender in defining social groups, but it is likely that at least some of the conflicts that emerge as workforces begin to diversify will be less intense as diversity becomes the norm.

APPROACHES TO DEVELOPING GENDER-INCLUSIVE ORGANIZATIONS

Our focus in this book is examining the role of gender in understanding behavior and experiences in organizations. As we noted in several of the preceding chapters, work and work organizations are often seen as the male domain, and women are often rejected in this realm or at least less welcome than men. Suppose you wanted to develop an organization in which gender was not especially relevant to decisions such as who is hired, fired, or promoted, and in which both men and women were welcomed equally as participants in the workforce. There are several things you might do to create a pluralistic climate and culture, to train employees and managers, to orient new members, and to increase the involvement of women in decision making. A few examples are discussed next.

First, you could increase the structural integration of women, that is, increase their chances to compete for jobs. Second, you might ease their entry into and movement within an organization. Third, it would be important to change the climate, culture, and procedures of the organization itself. A point we have already made several times bears repeating: Simply hiring or promoting members of protected groups in an organization that has traditionally excluded them, without making any other changes in the organization, is self-defeating. Thus, a number of steps beyond structural integration are necessary and useful for building a gender-inclusive workplace.

Structural Integration

Structural integration implies that there is no correlation between demographic group membership and job status (Cox, 1994). The focus of this book is on gender in organizations, and for our purposes, assessments of structural integration involve assessments of how well women are represented in different areas and levels of an organization. Interventions designed to increase structural integration are likely to involve removing barriers to hiring and retaining women and creating incentives to increase their structural representation. It is important to emphasize that a gender-inclusive organization is not defined solely in terms of its head count. Much of the debate over diversity has been obscured by an undue focus (on the parts of components and proponents of diversity programs) on numerical representation. Numerical equality in all job categories is not the goal of most diversity programs, nor is it the ultimate criterion for evaluating these programs. Rather, an assumption of most diversity programs is that changes in organizations and in society in general will, in the long run, substantially reduce the numerical imbalance currently seen in many occupations and organizations. In this sense, numerical equality is not so much a goal as a by-product of organizational inclusiveness. Nevertheless, it makes sense to argue that a gender-inclusive organization will probably have women and men represented throughout the organization, and that an organization that has few women in jobs outside of the "pink-collar ghetto" is unlikely to be thought of as gender inclusive. Rather, it seems reasonable to assume that an organization that cannot or does not attract and retain women probably presents structural barriers (which may or may not be intentional) to women's entry into and success in the organization. Some tools and approaches for increasing structural integration are discussed next.

Affirmative Action.   In chapter 8, we noted that affirmative action requirements are poorly understood by the public, and that much of the controversy over affirmative action may involve activities that are not required and sometimes not even permitted by law (e.g., setting firm quotas). There are, however, several steps under the heading of affirmative action that an organization can take to integrate women into the organization. The first step in an affirmative actin program is usually to develop

vigilant and consistent enforcement of equal opportunity laws and requirements. Many organizations employ human resource specialists whose
main responsibility is to see that hiring, firing, promotion, and transfer
decisions conform to the requirements of state and federal equal employment opportunity laws and policies. This strict scrutiny has probably made
personnel decisions slower and more costly, but by monitoring personnel
decisions carefully, organizations probably reduce both the likelihood of
discrimination on the basis of sex, race, or religion and their vulnerability
to EEO litigation.

Affirmative action starts with careful enforcement of antidiscrimination
laws, but it usually goes further, incorporating active efforts to attract,
hire, train, and develop members of underrepresented groups. Next we
discuss three activities that might be considered part of an overall affirmative action strategy. None of these involve setting quotas or preferential
hiring; rather they involve making resources available and making changes
in organizational policies to increase the likelihood that women will join
and progress through an organization.

Incentives for Managers. Most of the time, if a goal is truly
important to an organization, the organization will monitor progress toward
achieving that goal and provide incentives and rewards for accomplishing
it. Thus, one way to determine whether an organization is truly interested
in the structural integration of women into the workforce is to examine
the incentives available to managers and executives to move this process
along. As K. Murphy and Cleveland (1995) noted, organizations often
give lip service to human resource activities (e.g., performance appraisals)
but provide no meaningful rewards for doing them well and no meaningful
sanctions for doing them poorly. Organizations can show their commitment to structural integration by providing and advertising meaningful
incentives to managers for identifying and developing successful female
employees and for increasing the skills held by and the opportunities open
to women in the organization.

For example, organizations often provide awards for success in increasing diversity. More importantly, many organizations are beginning to include diversity-related activities as part of the performance appraisal of
managers and executives. We see this strategy as particularly useful because
it helps move the organization away from an emphasis on the short-term
"numbers game" (e.g., diversity awards are sometimes given to organizations that hire many women or members of minority groups, even though
these organizations have done little to create conditions for success for these
new hires) toward an emphasis on developing a diverse workforce.

In evaluating an incentive program, it is useful to ask both what behaviors are rewarded and how substantial the rewards really are. Diversity

programs are most likely to succeed if the rewards and incentives are large enough to be meaningful (and if the sanctions for failing to take steps to increase diversity are also meaningful) and the emphasis is on developing long-term success stories rather than providing positive numbers in the short term.

HRM Policy and Benefit Changes. Organizations that want to attract and retain a high-quality workforce need to develop human resource policies that satisfy diverse needs. For example, with more mothers of young children in the workforce, family-friendly benefits arc likely to become increasingly important in attracting and retaining women. Friedman and Galinsky (1992) noted that a number of forces are pushing the idea of family-friendly benefits. Businesses may feel the need to adopt family-friendly policies and benefits because of union pressure (whose memberships are also changing to reflect the diversity of the workforce), increased media attention on work and family issues, government mandates, or expectations on the part of employees (both male and female). There arc also financial incentives to developing family-friendly policies; surveys of representative samples of workers are showing that family care distractions result in significant productivity loss for men and women (Galinsky & Hughes, 1987). For example, parents of children who are not in supervised care (e.g., latchkey kids) are absent an average of 13 days a year compared to an average of 7 to 9 days (Friedman & Galinsky, 1992). Parents of preschoolers reported having a difficult to a very difficult time finding adequate, let alone high-quality, child care. Finally, as the population ages, baby boomers in the prime of their careers are likely to find themselves side-tracked by elder-care problems.

The needs of a diverse workforce go beyond making adequate child- and elder-care arrangements. Employees are demanding more flexibility in their jobs to manage both work and nonwork domains. Flexible working hours, flexible benefits, and alternative work arrangements, such as telecommuting, job sharing, and part-time employment, are among the options believed to increase workers' control and balance of their work and nonwork demands (C.S. Rogers, 1992). Also, needs of dual-career couples (regardless of the presence of children) can be addressed with spouse job-referral networks.

Friedman and Galinsky (1992) noted that organizational perspectives toward work–family issues often evolve through a series of discrete stages. At Stage 1, organizations do not view work–family issues as business issues and are concerned that adoption of such policies will jeopardize perceptions of equity (i.e., they would be used only by women). Only a few isolated, not well-coordinated solutions to work–family problems arc implemented, and most consider only child-care arrangements. During

Stage 2, the focus on child care is expanded to include other issues such as elder care and relocation. More coordinated effort in managing companies' work–family initiatives becomes evident as full-time or part-time responsibility for these matters is allocated to an individual or group, and top-management commitment begins to emerge. At Stage 3, work–family issues are integrated into organization-wide diversity and gender equity management. There is a movement toward a life-cycle approach that broadens the concept of work–family to work–life needs. The organization's culture reflects the value of the "whole" individual, and standards for promotion and career development are concordant with work–life issues.

There is no clear explanation for how organizations progress through these stages or become halted at suboptimal stages. Meyer and Berry (1995), reporting on the development of a measure of workplace flexibility, showed that workplace flexibility was strongly related to the number of family-friendly policies provided by respondents' organizations and to supervisory support for respondents' child-care needs.

Diversity at the Top.   Cox (1994) suggested that structural integration at all levels of the organization is important in developing inclusive organizations. One specific step he suggested is to increase women's or minority group members' representation on key decision-making bodies. Special advisory committees are widely used by organizations, both to educate organization members about diverse perspectives or issues faced by the organization and to provide visible evidence of the organization's willingness to incorporate these diverse perspectives.

There are several examples in organizations where decision-making teams have been deliberately composed to reflect multiple dimensions of diversity. Aldefer (1992), for example, described a special task force set up in XYZ Corporation (a pseudonym) to evaluate candidates for managerial advancement. The task force was racially and gender balanced. Furthermore, half of the task force members were closely aligned with the company's race relations improvement process and half were not. Analysis of data comparing the task force's evaluations of managerial candidates versus recommendations of the candidates' departments revealed not only that the task force recommended more women and minorities for advancement than did the departments but also that the task force's recommended candidates were better qualified than the departments' preferred candidates (Alderfer, 1992). These data challenge the notion that groups concerned with diversity are less interested in merit than are other groups.

As part of their overall diversity management programs, several organizations have instituted special advisory groups to inform top management of key concerns of the constituencies they represent. For example, Xerox

Corporation has supported Black caucus groups, Hispanic caucus groups, and women's caucus groups for over 2 decades (Sessa, 1992). Coopers & Lybrand, a professional services organization, has built its diversity initiatives on the concept of a strategic grass roots approach, in which groups concerned with diversity vis-à-vis organizational effectiveness can, with organizational support, experiment with trial programs and initiatives. Evaluations of their projects are reviewed by top management, who decide whether the programs/initiatives will be institutionalized more broadly in the organization (DeLuca & McDowell, 1992).

Constructing advisory committees that represent diverse groups can become a double-edged sword, however. One particularly difficult issue is burnout. It is not unusual to find that those few women or members of minority groups who have risen to critical managerial levels of the organization are overburdened with committee assignments. Their presence on such committees will be desired and deemed important by the organization, but the extra service load these workers often experience can interfere with their primary job responsibilities. Organizations that routinely assign a few women and minority group members to task forces, committees, and diversity projects, may create conditions guaranteeing that these same individuals will fail. Nevertheless, if carefully managed, task forces and advisory committees can promote inclusiveness, both through the substantive suggestions developed by these committees and through the message sent to organization members about the organization's commitment to increasing diversity.

Informal Integration

Structural integration efforts help to attract, hire, and promote women, but they do not necessarily establish the support systems that most successful employees rely on to get their work done and to advance their careers. In particular, establishing strong and helpful social networks is often a critical part of success in modern organizations, and if women or members of minority groups are excluded from these informal social networks, they will find it much harder to perform or progress in the organization. Thus, one important goal of a diversity effort should be to reduce barriers to joining and accessing influential social networks in organizations (Cox, 1994).

There is evidence that individuals who are well connected to the social networks of organizations have greater political awareness, are more likely to be considered ingroup members, are more likely to be friends with influential people in the organization, are more cognizant and aligned with the organization's history, goals, and values, and are likely to achieve performance proficiency more quickly than those less well socialized

(Chao, O'Leary-Kelly, Wolf, Klein, & Gardner, 1994). Among the options for enhancing informal integration identified by Cox (1991), the creation and support of mentoring programs have received the most attention (Ostroff & Kozlowski, 1993).

Mentoring programs. Higher level organizational members who are committed to assisting the career development of lower level protégés are often referred to as mentors. As discussed in chapter 10, mentors provide both psychosocial benefits (e.g., friendship, support, counseling, and role modeling) and career-related benefits (e.g., coaching, increased visibility, sponsoring, and protection; K.E. Kram, 1985). A number of field studies have shown that people who have mentors experience greater job satisfaction, greater career mobility, faster promotion rates, and higher salaries than those without mentors (Chao, Walz, & Gardner, 1992; Cotton, 1995; Fagenson, 1989; Whitely, Dougherty, & Dreher 1991).

Recognizing the importance of mentoring relationships, many organizations have instituted formal mentoring programs. The distinction between formal and informal mentoring programs is that a senior organizational member is assigned to a new member in the former case, whereas such relationships develop naturally in the latter case. Formal mentoring programs may also train mentors on how to provide mentoring functions, might monitor the quality and quantity of interactions between mentors and protégés, and might use special events to build and highlight mentoring relationships (Henry, Stockdale, Hall, & Deniston, 1994; Newby & Heide, 1992). However, some concern has been raised about whether formal mentoring programs can be as effective as informal mentoring relationships (e.g., because informal relationships arise as the result of friendship or interest on the part of the mentor, whereas formal relationships represent additional job duties; see Chao et al., 1992; Keele, Buckner, & Bushnell, 1987; Noe, 1988b). Chao et al. (1992) examined the success of mentoring among alumni at a Midwestern university who were employed in a variety of occupations and organizations. The sample included individuals who were informally mentored, were formally mentored (i.e., participated in a formal mentoring program), or were not mentored. Both formally and informally mentored respondents reported greater socialization and job satisfaction than nonmentored respondents, but informally mentored respondents had significantly higher (i.e., more positive) responses on these items than did formally mentored respondents. Furthermore, informally mentored respondents received higher salaries than did formally mentored or nonmentored respondents. Cotton (1995), replicating Chao et al.'s study on a national sample of social workers, engineers, and journalists, found that both formally and informally mentored respondents were more satisfied with their jobs, were more organizationally committed, had higher organizational self-esteem, were more satisfied with opportunities for promotion, and were more committed to their careers than were nonmentored respondents. Moreover, there was no significant difference between formally and informally mentored protégés on these outcomes. There were also no gender differences on reports of being either formally or informally mentored or on the outcomes measured.

Although Chao et al. (1992) and Cotton (1995) reached different conclusions about the relative effectiveness of formal and informal mentoring, their results taken together are encouraging to organizations endeavoring to promote mentoring relationships. First, both studies found that mentoring, whether formal or informal, is related to positive career outcomes for both the individual and the organization (i.e., greater job satisfaction, promotion rates, salaries, etc.). Second, it is possible that in cases where formal mentoring was less effective than informal mentoring, the formal mentoring programs may not have been well constructed or managed (Cotton, 1995). The findings also suggests that high-quality mentoring programs can be constructed. Research is needed to determine how formal mentoring programs can be constructed and managed to maximize effectiveness.

Creating Pluralism. Mentoring programs help to break barriers to integrating a diverse workforce into the social networks of the organization by enlisting the aid and sponsorship of powerful members of those networks. A second strategy for increasing informal integration is to change the climate and culture of the organization to make inclusiveness a norm rather than an exception. Efforts in this direction are sometimes labeled "creating pluralism."

Cox (1994) and others contrast monolithic organizations, in which the values and norms of the dominant group are viewed as superior to those of other groups, and in which all members of the organization are expected to conform to and identify with those values and norms, to pluralistic organizations. A pluralistic organization is one in which differences between individuals and groups are acknowledged and accepted and there is no assumption that there is one best way for all. For example, many organizations have the policy of publicly acknowledging individual achievements, which strikes most Americans as a good idea. However, this sort of policy may cause anxiety and discomfort to members of cultures who believe individuals should remain modest about their accomplishments. Although the policy may be well intentioned and may seem completely acceptable (and even laudable) to most members of the organization, its adoption could be a real barrier to success for some employees.

In monolithic organizations, the assumption is that people will change to fit the place (i.e., people are expected to adapt to the culture of the organization). In pluralistic organizations, the assumption is that as the workforce changes, organizations should also change. Furthermore, it is assumed that increasing contact between members of different cultures will change everyone and will decrease artificial barriers to the integration of a diverse workforce into the social networks of an organization. It is well established in social psychology that simple contact between groups can reduce antagonism and misunderstanding (Baron & Byrne, 1994), but it is also well known that changes in relationships between culturally distinct groups can occur very slowly. Many organizations have implemented structured programs to accelerate the pace of developing pluralistic cultures.

Programs and policies aimed at creating or increasing a sense of pluralism are designed first and foremost to increase the awareness of diversity and sensitivity to cultural differences (Cox, 1994). At least some of the resistance to promoting diversity is attributable to a simple lack of understanding of the different perspectives members of various groups sometimes take when interpreting events in the organization. Critics of diversity programs sometimes complain that an undue emphasis on differences can increase hostility and misunderstanding among groups, and they have a point. Diversity training programs may meet with less resistance and may have a better chance of success if they recognize both commonalities and differences among groups in an organization. For example, we have noted several examples of male–female differences in use of language, leadership style, and ways of handling work–family conflicts. These differences are real and important, but the idea that men and women come from completely different cultures is an oversimplification and potentially a barrier to their effective cooperation.

Once people become aware of similarities and differences among groups in the organization, the second goal of diversity training programs is often to influence their interpretation of diversity (Conference Board, 1994). Diversity can be seen as a problem (e.g., a source of conflict, reverse discrimination) or as an opportunity (e.g., diversity may help you reach a broader range of markets); an important goal of many diversity training programs is to encourage people to accept and value diversity. Finally, diversity training programs are used to develop skills in dealing with people who have different values, norms, and experiences.

One of the advantages of a homogeneous, monolithic organization is that employees do not have to learn how to deal with differences. For members of the dominant culture, a monolithic organization is likely to be more comfortable and easier to work with, and if everyone else simply adapted to that culture, life would be easier (at least for members of the dominant group). As the workforce becomes more diverse, members of the dominant culture will need to develop skills in recognizing areas of

Table 13.1
Stages in Diversity Training

Stage	Knowledge	Skill	Application of skill
Unconsciously incompetent	Low	Low	Low
Consciously incompetent	High	Low	Low
Consciously competent	High	High	Low
Unconsciously competent	High	High	High

communality and difference, working with diverse teams and organizations, and handling conflicts that arise as a result of differences in values, perceptions, and experiences.

Table 13.1 illustrates a four-stage model that is often used to describe the goals and outcomes of diversity training (Conference Board, 1994). Before receiving training, many workers lack knowledge of or skills in dealing with diversity ("unconsciously incompetent").

Training can increase knowledge about diversity, but unless it also helps individuals develop skills in dealing with people from different backgrounds or cultures, training may not help move toward a pluralistic organization (workers who know about diversity issues but lack skills for dealing with these issues are described as "consciously incompetent"). As skills in dealing with a diverse workforce are developed, workers develop competence but must work to apply these skills ("consciously competent"). Finally, with practice, workers no longer have to think about diversity issues but rather can apply these skills without a great deal of effort ("unconsciously competent").

Like training programs, orientation programs provide a formal mechanism to convey the organization's commitment to diversity and gender equity. Rather than specifically targeting attitudes, however, orientation programs can outline the organization's overall diversity strategy and philosophy and introduce new employees to various benefit options such as flexible work schedules, corporate-sponsored day care, flexible career tracks, and so forth. Most importantly, orientation programs provide one of the first organizational socialization activities, which can have a powerful effect on communicating the company's norms, values, and expectations toward diversity (see, e.g., VanMaanen & Schein, 1979). In addition to training and orientation activities, a number of steps might be taken to make both the formal and the informal organization more gender inclusive. Several of these are outlined next.

Additional Steps Toward Inclusiveness

Chapters 1 through 12 outlined a number of similarities and differences in men's and women's experiences in organizations. One theme in many of these chapters is that differences in the way men and women are treated by society, organizations, superiors, peers, and subordinates can create barriers to women's full participation in the workplace. Creating a truly gender-inclusive organization might involve interventions targeted at many of these issues. Two areas for intervention involve changing attitudes and beliefs about women and men in organizations and changing organizational structures and practices to reflect the needs and preferences of a gender-diverse workforce.

Changing Stereotypes.   The stereotypes we hold about men and women in the workplace are central to many of the issues we have discussed in this book, and an obvious area for intervention in developing gender-inclusive organizations is in changing stereotypes. Stereotypes are learned early and are deeply ingrained in our culture, but there are reasons to be optimistic about reducing stereotyping in the workplace. In particular, there is evidence that prejudice, stereotyping, and discrimination can be reduced by something as simple as open discussion and debate (Baron & Byrne, 1994; Elliot, 1986; Gaertner & Dovido, 1986).

The rationale for this approach (i.e., reducing reliance on stereotypes by discussing them) is that stereotypes are unconscious structures that we use to classify and simplify our perceptions of others. As people become aware of their reliance on stereotypes and of the content of those stereotypes, they will become less likely to fall back on this unconscious categorization strategy and more likely to play attention to other aspects of men and women when interacting with them in work settings.

Interventions should focus not only on reducing reliance on stereotypes but also on changing the content of those stereotypes. One illustration of this approach is in women's athletics, where terms like "girl power" are used to turn around the stereotype that girls and women are not interested or talented in athletics and to highlight their prowess in a number of fields. In women's volleyball, the phrase "serves like a girl" has been transformed into phrases like "serves like a girl—right in your face." In the workplace, stereotypical beliefs about women's lack of interest in or talent for particular occupations or tasks (e.g., math and science-related activities) can be changed by showing examples of exemplary women and, more important, examples of male–female similarity in settings in which artificial barriers to women's success have been removed (e.g., noncombat military specialties).

Sexuality and Productivity.   Many discussions of workplace attraction and romance begin with the assumption that sexuality in the workplace is a problem. Sometimes it is a problem; however, the assumption that normal interpersonal relationships (which are likely to include attraction and romance) are necessarily or even often a problem in the workplace should not go unchallenged. One reason for challenging this assumption that action taken on the basis of this assumption seems to fall more heavily on women than on men. That is, when a workplace romance is seen as a problem, one response is often to remove the woman. For example, the armed services are currently discussing resegregation of military training after reports of sexual harassment of female trainees.

Empirical research on the influence of sexuality in organizations is growing rapidly, and we may soon have data to address whether (and under what conditions) sexuality is a problem in the workplace. It is also important to examine whether (and under what conditions) suppression of sexuality in the workplace is a problem. One obvious area for intervention is to develop and advertise clear guidelines regarding romantic and sexual interactions in the workplace and to closely examine the rationale (or lack thereof) for such guidelines. Recent Supreme Court cases (e.g., *Burlington Industries, Inc. v. Ellereth*) suggest the need for such guidelines in the area of sexual harassment, but a good case can be made for clarifying norms regarding sexuality in the workplace. By spelling out what is or is not permissible and why, organizations can resolve many murky areas for both management and employees. For example, dating among coworkers is usually allowed (organizations usually have no good basis for a blanket refusal), but dating between supervisors and subordinates sometimes is not or may require special accommodations (e.g., it is usually not good policy for a supervisor to evaluate the performance of a subordinate if a romantic relationship exists).

The process of developing guidelines for workplace sexuality may be more important than the guidelines themselves. You can think of the process of developing these guidelines as a sort of organizational development activity, in which you are forced to examine assumptions (e.g., what sorts of relationships should be regulated and why) and to consider the outcomes that are most likely to result from different policies (e.g., will a policy that forces transfers when supervisors and subordinates become involved fall more heavily on men or on women?). We noted earlier that organizations often use task forces to obtain input from multiple constituencies; this is an area where such task forces might be especially useful. By encouraging input from men and women, an organization is less likely to develop a one-sided policy for dealing with attraction and romance in the workplace.

Changing Discourse. The way we talk about men, women, and work influences the way we think about these topics, and one of the most important interventions in developing gender-inclusive organizations may be to change the way we talk. Feminist scholars have long noted that terms we use to designate leaders often imply a male model (e.g., *chairman* and terms used to refer specifically to women (e.g., titles ending in *ess* or *ette*) often imply a junior or second-class status. *He* is often used as a generic term for workers, especially supervisors, managers, and executives (e.g., "when a supervisor provides feedback, he helps subordinates identify developmental needs"). Critics of diversity programs sometimes ridicule attempts to monitor and change the way we describe men's and women's experiences at work, but the issue is far from trivial. The first step in changing the way people think about men and women at work is probably to change the way they talk about this issue, and efforts to reduce the use of sexist language (e.g., publication manuals for journals and book publishers now routinely include sections describing ways to replace sexist terms) are likely to have a substantial payoff.

In addition to changing what people say, there is some benefit to educating workers about differences in the ways men and women use language. Both the popular and scientific literatures describe male–female differences in language use, and some of these are particularly relevant to the workplace. First, there is considerable evidence that men and women use different language styles in mixed-gender groups. There are a number of specific differences, but in general, males tend to be more dominant and aggressive in mixed-gender groups (e.g., they interrupt more and make more suggestions and demands). These differences can be interpreted as differences in ability to lead or interest in leading others, even when there are no true differences on these dimensions. Second, men in work settings tend (contrary to the popular stereotype) to talk more than women. This can be mistaken for male–female differences in verbal fluency or (as previously noted) in leadership.

Language differences are an important topic in gender-oriented diversity training. There is evidence that both men and women misinterpret communication that does not conform to their preferred style of language. As Table 13.1 suggests, training is most likely to succeed if it both alerts men and women to differences in language use and provides them with exposure to and practice in using specific communication skills (e.g., listening skills, or skills in interpreting others' communication styles).

Stress Reduction. One of the most significant sources of stress for working women is the conflict between their work and family roles. This conflict is significantly more severe if organizational policies and practices interfere with nonwork roles. For example, Cox (1994) noted that in some organizations, long hours are the norm, extensive travel is expected, and meetings or critical activities are often scheduled at the very beginning or the very end of the day. All of these features can exaggerate existing work–family conflicts. Because home and family roles are still predominantly the responsibility of women, the stress of working in such an organization can be especially severe for female employees.

One key to building a gender-inclusive organization is to recognize and remove unnecessary stressors, particularly those that differentially affect men and women. Some of these changes are relatively easy to implement (e.g., don't schedule meetings at times when working mothers are likely to have peak child-care needs; reduce travel requirements and replace travel with telecommuting or video conferencing). Others (e.g., on-site child care) might be costly, but the benefits of reducing work–family conflicts, stress, and time lost and increasing productivity can far exceed the costs. The most difficult stress-reduction interventions, however, involve substantial changes to the climate and culture of work organizations. As we note subsequently, work-related stress is often the result of difficulties in establishing and maintaining priorities among the various roles we carry out. Some of the most successful stress-reduction interventions may be those that encourage workers to take a more balanced approach to integrating their work and nonwork roles.

Changing the Climate and Culture of Organizations. American organizations tend to expect and reward high levels of dedication and commitment, long hours, and placing the demands of work ahead of the demands of nonwork responsibilities. This is sometimes referred to as a "high-work, low-family" orientation, the notion being that work should be a top priority in employees' lives, which in turn is based on the assumption that someone other than the employee (for all intents and purposes, his wife) will take care of responsibilities outside of the world of paid work. To a large extent, the climate and culture of many American organizations (particularly in the managerial and professional ranks) reflect a set of beliefs about the importance of work versus nonwork roles that is both outdated and exclusionary. The changing demographics of the workforce, (e.g., single-income families with one spouse providing full-time home and child care are now a rarity) make it increasingly unlikely that all workers can or should fit the profile that many organizations still demand. More important, changing societal values make this sort of organization increasingly unattractive to both men and women.

The assumption that work is a top priority is one example of a broader issue. Work organizations have been built largely on a male model. That is, the attributes that are valued, the priorities that are established, the structures that are put in place, and the climate, culture, and dominant language, all reflect the ideas, assumptions, and biases of the men who built these organizations. Most U.S. organizations were built by and for men (usually White men), and it should come as no surprise that men fit better than women in many instances. Perhaps the biggest challenge in building organizations that fit women as well as men is to examine critically the values and assumptions that define work and work organizations. In the monolithic organizations that typified the post–World War II boom, women were expected to adapt to the organization (if they sought employment at all), and the chances of success were typically small unless individual women changed to fit the values, biases, and assumptions of their male coworkers. In building pluralistic organizations, men, women, and the organization will have to adapt, and the values that defined yesterday's organization may not be the same as those that define tomorrow's.

SUMMARY

Diversity in the workforce brings both opportunities and challenges; *managing diversity* is a term used to describe policies and actions designed to maximize the benefits and minimize the costs of workforce diversification. Programs to manage diversity often combine efforts to increase the representation of women and members of minority groups at all levels in the organization with efforts to change the policies, structure, climate, and culture of organizations to better fit the current workforce. Much of the public debate regarding diversity has focused on head counts, but the most critical issues in managing diversity are not merely hiring and promoting members of underrepresented groups but rather changing organizations to give every individual a fair chance to compete and succeed. One of many diversity programs is to move toward pluralistic organizations, in which diversity is both recognized and valued. In the context of gender diversity, pluralism implies that organizations will to some extent change to adapt to the changing gender composition of the workforce. Rather than forcing women to adopt male values, attitudes, norms, and behaviors, pluralistic organizations adapt to changing workforce demographics.

There is evidence that programs to increase acceptance of diversity can also contribute to the bottom line, by enhancing an organization's ability both to attract and retain a diverse workforce and to relate to a diverse clientele. However, diversity can be a source of conflict, and a key goal of programs designed to enhance diversity should be to reduce and resolve these conflicts.

The starting point for developing gender-inclusive organizations is to increase women's representation at all levels and in all sectors of the organization. However, integration into the informal social networks of the organization might be just as important as numerical equality. Training, mentoring, and organizational change efforts might all be used to advance this goal. Additional ways to enhance gender inclusiveness include programs to reduce stereotypes, a careful examination of policies and practices that seem to have different effects for men and women (e.g., policies regarding workplace romance), changes in the way we refer to men and women in the workplace, and programs to reduce the extra sources of stress encountered by women in many work settings. The most important changes might be to the climate and cultures of organizations. As noted in several of the earlier chapters, work organizations are for the most part built by and for men, and they generally reflect male assumptions, values, norms and biases. The biggest challenge will be to reconstruct organizations to reflect a more balanced set of views.

GLOSSARY

Acculturation: Extent to which cultural differences are resolved and dealt with in an organization.

Informal integration: Inclusion of women and members of minority groups in social networks in the organization.

Managing diversity: Taking planned, proactive steps to ease the transition from a relatively homogeneous workforce to an increasingly diverse one.

Mentors: Higher level organizational member who assists the career development of a lower level protégé.

Monolithic Organization: Organization in which the values and norms of the dominant group are viewed as superior to those of other groups, and in which members are expected to conform to and identify with those values and norms.

Pluralistic organization: Organization in which differences between individuals and groups are acknowledged and accepted, and in which there is no assumption that there is one best way for all.

Realistic conflict theory: Theory suggesting that conflict occurs because people try to maximize their own outcomes and the outcomes of people similar to them under conditions where the interests of different groups are not compatible.

Social identity theory: Theory that individuals seek to belong to groups that develop or enhance a positive self-identity.

Structural integration: Representation of women and members of minority groups at all levels of an organization.

References

Abbey, N. (1982). Sex differences in attributions for friendly behavior: Do males misperceive females friendliness? *Journal of Psychology, 42,* 830–838.

Abbey, A., & Melby, C. (1986). The effects of nonverbal cues on gender differences in perceptions of sexual intent. *Sex roles, 15,* 283–298.

Abu-Laban, S. M. (1981). Women and aging: A futuristic perspective. *Psychology of Women Quarterly, 6*(1), 85–98.

Adams, J. (1984). Women at West Point: A three-year perspective. *Sex Roles, 11,* 525–542.

Adams, G. R., & Huston, T. L. (1975). Social perceptions of the middle-aged varying in physical attractiveness. *Developmental Psychology, 95,* 76–83.

Adams, G. R., & LaVoie, J. C. (1974). The effect of student's sex, conduct, and facial attractiveness on teacher expectancy. *Education, 95,* 76–83.

Adarand Constructors, Inc. v. Peña, 63 U.S.L.W. 4523, (1995).

Affirmative action review: A report to the President. (1995). Washington, DC: Office of the President, White House.

Alberts, J. K. (1992). Teasing and sexual harassment: Double-bind communication in the workplace. In L. A. M. Perry, L. H. Turner, & H. M. Sterk (Eds.), *Constructing and reconstructing gender: The links among communication, language and gender* (pp. 185–196). Albany, NY: SUNY Press.

Aldefer, C. P. (1992). Changing race relations embedded in organizations: Report on a long-term project with the XYZ corporation. In S. E. Jackson (Ed.), *Diversity in the workplace: Human resource initiatives* (pp. 138–166). New York: Guilford Press.

384

Alderman L. (1995, February 1). Your work life: Surviving an office romance without jeopardizing your job. *Money, 24.*

Aldous, S. (1969). Occupational characteristics and male role performance in the family. *Journal of Marriage and the Family, 31,* 707–712.

Alfredson, L., Spetz, C. L., & Theorell, T. (1985). Type of occupation and near-future hospitalization for myocardial infarction and some other diagnoses. *International Journal of Epidemiology, 14,* 378–388.

Allen, K. M., Blascovich, J., Tomaka, J., & Kelsey, R. M. (1991). Presence of human friends, and pet dogs as moderators of autonomic responses to stress in women. *Journal of Personality and Social Psychology, 61,* 582–589.

Alliger, G. M., & Williams, K. J. (1993). Using signal-contingent experience sampling methodology to study work in the field: A discussion and illustration examining task perceptions and mood, *Personnel Psychology, 46,* 525–549.

Allport, G. W. (1954). *The nature of prejudice.* Reading, MA: Addison-Wesley.

Altemeyer, R. A., & Jones K. (1974). Sexual identity, physical attractiveness and seating position as determinants of influences in discussion groups. *Canadian Journal of Behavioral Science, 6,* 357–375.

American Heart Association. (1984a). *Exercise and your heart.* Dallas, TX: author.

American Heart Association. (1984b). *Nutritional counseling for cardiovascular health.* Dallas, TX: Author.

Anatomy of a debacle: A behind-the-scenes look at how Thomas's nomination blew apart—and led to the hearings that stunned the nation. (1991). *Newsweek, 118*(17), 26–32.

Ancker-Johnson, B. (1975). Physicist. *Educational Horizons, 53,* 116–121.

Andersch, B. (1980). *Epidemiological, hormonal, and water balance studies in pre-menstrual tension.* Unpublished doctoral dissertation, University of Gothenburg: Sweden.

Anderson, C. J., & Fisher, C. (1991). Male–female relationships in the workplace: Perceived motivations in office romance. *Sex Roles, 25,* 163–180.

Anderson, R., & Nida, S. A. (1978). Effect of physical attractiveness on opposite- and same-sex evaluations. *Journal of Personality, 46,* 401–413.

Ansari, M. A. (1989). Effects of leader sex, subordinate sex, and subordinate performance on the use of influence strategies. *Sex Roles, 20,* 283–193.

Apostal, R. A., & Helland, C. (1993). Commitment to and role changes in dual career families. *Journal of Career Development, 20,* 121–129.

Argyle, M., Alkema, F., & Gilmour, K. (1971). The communication of friendly and hostile attitudes by verbal and nonverbal signals. *European Journal of Social Psychology, 2,* 385–402.

Argyle, M., Lalljee, M., & Cook, M. (1968). The effects of responsibility on interaction in a dyad. *Human Relations, 21,* 3–17.

Argyle, M., Salter, V., Nicholson, H., Williams, M., & Burgess, P. (1970). The communication of inferior and superior attitudes by verbal and nonverbal signals. *British Journal of Social and Clinical Psychology, 9,* 222–231.

Aries, E. (1977). Male–female interpersonal styles in all male, all female, and mixed groups. In A. G. Sargent (Ed.), *Beyond sex roles* (pp. 292–299). New York: West.

Arthur, M. B., Claman, P. H., & DeFillippi, R. J. (1995, November). Intelligent enterprise, intelligent careers. *Academy of Management Executive,* pp. 7–22.

Arvey, R. (1979). Unfair discrimination in the employment interview: Legal and psychological aspects. *Psychological Bulletin, 86,* 736–765.

Arvey, R. D., & Cavanaugh, M. A. (1995). Using surveys to assess the prevalence of sexual harassment: Some methodological problems. *Journal of Social Issues, 51,* 39–52.

Ashford, S. J. (1988). Individual strategies for coping with stress during organizational transitions. *Journal of Applied Behavior Science, 24,* 19–36.

Ashmore, R. D., & Del Boca, F. K. (1986) (Eds.). *The social psychology of female–male relations: A critical analysis of central concepts.* Orlando, FL: Academic Press.

Averill, J. R. (1982). *Anger and aggression: An essay on emotion.* New York: Springer-Verlag.

Avolio, B. J., Waldman, D. A., & Yammarino, F. J. (1991). Leading in the 1990s: The four I's of transformational leadership. *Journal of European Industrial Training, 15,* 9–16.

Baird, J. E., Jr., & Bradley, P. H. (1979). Styles of management and communication: A comparative study of men and women. *Communication Monographs, 46,* 101–111.

Baird, L., & Kram, K. (1983, Spring). Career dynamics: Matching the superior/subordinate relationship. *Organizational Dynamics,* Spring, *13,* 46–64.

Bales, R. F., & Slater, P. E. (1955). Role differentiation in small decision-making groups. In T. Parsons, R. T. Bales, & J. Olds (Eds.), *Family, socialization and interaction process* (pp. 5–128), Glencoe, IL: Free Press.

Balswick, J. O., & Peek, C. W. (1971). The inexpensive male: A tragedy of American society. In A. Skolnick & J. H. Skolnick (Eds.), *Intimacy, family and society* (pp. 237–244). Boston: Little, Brown.

Bandy, N. (1989). *Relationships between male and female employees at Southern Illinois University.* Unpublished doctoral dissertation, College of Education, Southern Illinois University, Carbondale.

Barak, A., Pitterman, Y., & Yitzhaki, R. (1995). An empirical test of the role of power differential in originating sexual harassment. *Basic and Applied Social Psychology, 17,* 497–518.

Barboriak, J. J., Anderson, A. J., & Hoffmann, R. G. (1984, March). *Smoking and coronary artery occlusion in female heart patients.* Paper presented at the American Heart Association Conference on Cardiovascular Disease Epidemiology, Tampa, FL.

Bardwick, J. (1980). The season's of a woman's life. In D. McGuigan (Ed.), *Women's lives: New theory, research, and policy.* Ann Arbor: University of Michigan Center for Continuing Education for Women.

Bargh, J. A., & Raymond, P. (1995). The naive misuse of power: Nonconscious sources of sexual harassment. *Journal of Social Issues, 51,* 85–96.

Bargh, J. A., Raymond, P., Pryor, J., & Strack, F. (1995). The attractiveness of the underling: An automatic power sex association and its consequence for sexual harassment and aggression. *Journal of Personality and Social Psychology, 64,* 123–152.

Barker, M. A. (1997). Remedying gender-based wage discrimination: The comparable worth approach. In P. Dubeck & K. Borman (Eds.), *Women and work: A reader* (pp. 375–381). New Brunswick, NJ: Rutgers University Press.

Barnett, R. C. (1975). Sex differences and age trends in occupational preference and occupational prestige. *Journal of Counseling Psychology, 22,* 35–38.

Barnett, R. C., & Baruch, G. K. (1985). Women's involvement in multiple roles and psychological distress. *Journal of Personality and Social Psychology, 49,* 135–145.

Barnett, R. C., & Baruch, G. K. (1987). Social roles, gender, and psychological distress. In R. C. Barnett, L. Biener, & G. K. Baruch (Eds.), *Gender and stress* (pp. 122–143). New York: Free Press.

Barnett, R. C., & Marshall, N. L. (1991). The relationship between women's work and family roles and their subjective well-being and psychological distress. In M. Frankenhaeuser, V. Lundberg, & M. Chesney (Eds.), *Women, work & health: Stress and opportunities* (pp. 111–136). London: Plenum Press.

Barnier, L. A. (1982). A study of the mentoring relationship: An analysis of its relation to career and adult development in higher education and business. *Dissertation Abstracts International, 42* (7-A), 3012–3013.

Baron, R. A., & Bryne, D. (1994). *Social psychology.* Boston: Allyn & Bacon.

Barreca, R. (1991). *They used to call me Snow White . . . But I drifted: Women's strategic use of humor.* New York: Viking Penguin.

Bar-Tal, D., & Saxe, L. (1976). The effects of physical attractiveness and its relationship to sex-role stereotyping. *Sex Roles, 2,* 123–133.

Bartol, K. M., & Martin, D. C. (1986). Women and men in task groups. In R. D. Ashmore & F. K. Del Boca (Eds.), *The social psychology of female–male relations: A critical analysis of central concepts* (pp. 259–310). Orlando, FL: Academic Press.

Bartol, K. M., & Butterfield, D. A. (1976). Sex effects in evaluating leaders. *Journal of Applied Psychology, 61,* 446–454.

Baruch, G. K., & Barnett, R. C. (1986). Role quality, multiple role involvement and psychological well-being in midlife women. *Journal of Personality and Social Psychology, 51,* 578–585.

Baruch, G. K., Biener, L., & Barnett, R. C. (1987). Women and gender in research on work and family strerss. *American Psychologist, 42,* 130–136.

Basow, S. (1986). *Gender stereotypes: Traditions and alternatives.* Monterey, CA: Brooks/Cole.

Bass, B. M. (1981). Individual capability, team response, and productivity. In E. A. Fleishman & M. D. Dunnette (Eds.), *Human performance and productivity.* Hillsdale, NJ: Lawrence Erlbaum Associates.

Bass, B. M. (1985). *Leadership and performance beyond expectations.* New York: The Free Press.

Bass, B. M., & Avolio, B. J. (1994). Introduction. In B. M. Bass & B. J. Avolio (Eds.), *Improving organizational effectiveness through transformational leadership.* Newbury Park, CA: Sage.

Bass, B. M., Avolio, B. J., & Atwater, L. E. (1996). The transformational and transactional leadership of men and women. *Applied Psychology: An International Review, 45,* 5–34.

Bassili, J. N. (1981). The attractiveness stereotype: Goodness or glamor? *Basic and Applied Social Psychology, 2,* 235–252.

Baumann, M. (1976). Two features of "women's speech." In B. L. DuBois & I. Crouch (Eds.), *The sociology of the languages of American women* (pp. 33–40). San Antonio, TX: Trinity University.

Beck, J. B., Ward-Hull, C. J., & McLear, P. M. (1976). Variables related to women's somatic preferences of the male and female body. *Journal of Personality and Social Psychology, 34,* 1200–1210.

Beehr, T. A., & Gilmore, D. C. (1982). Applicant attractiveness as a perceived job-relevant variable in selection of management trainees. *Academy of Management Journal, 25,* 607–617.

Belenky, M., Clinchy, B., Goldberger, N., & Tarule, J. (1986). *Women's ways of knowing.* New York: Basic Books.

Bell, E. T. (1986). *The power within: Bicultural life structures and stress among black women.* Unpublished doctoral dissertation, Case Western Reserve University, Cleveland, OH.

Bell, M. (1984). Teaching of the heart. *Journal of the American Medical Association, 252,* 2684.

Bem, S. L. (1974). The measurement of psychological androgyny. *Journal of Consulting and Clinical Psychology, 42,* 155–162.

Bem, S. L. (1975). Keep sex role adaptability: One consequence of gender identity psychological androgyny. *Journal of Personality and Social Psychology, 31,* 634–643.

Bem, S. L. (1979). Theory and measurement of androgyny: A reply to the Pechazler–Tetenbaum and Locksley–Colter critiques. *Journal of Personality and Social Psychology, 37*(6), 1047–1054.

Bengtsson, C. (1973). Ischaemic heart disease in women. A study based on a randomized population sample of women and women with myocardial infarction in Goteborg, Sweden. *Acta Medica Scandinavica, 5,* 1–128.

Bennett-Alexander, D. D., & Pincus, L. B. (1998). *Employment law for business* (2nd ed.). Boston: Irwin McGraw-Hill.

Benson, H. (1975). *The relaxation response.* New York: William Morrow.

Berger, J., Fisek, H., Norman, R. Z., & Zelditch, M., Jr. (1977). *Status characteristics in social interaction: An expectation states approach.* New York: Elsevier.

Berger, J., & Zelditch, M. (1985). *States, rewards, and influence. How expectations organize behavior.* San Francisco: Jossey-Bass.

Bernard, J. (1972). *The sex games.* New York: Atheneum.

Berryman, C. L. (1980). Attitudes toward male and female sex-appropriate and sex-inappropriate language. In C. L. Berryman & V. A. Eman (Eds.), *Communication, language, and sex* (pp. 195–216). Rowley, MA: Weinberg House.

Berryman-Fink, C., & Wheeless, V. E. (1987). Male and female perceptions of women as managers. In L. P. Stewart & S. Ting-Toomey (Eds.), *Communication, gender, and sex roles in diverse interaction contexts* (pp. 85–95). Norwood, NJ: Ablex.

Berscheid, E., Dion, K. K., Walster, E., & Walster, G. W. (1971). Physical attractiveness and dating choice: A test of the matching hypothesis. *Journal of Experimental Social Psychology, 7,* 173–189.

Berscheid, E., & Walster, E. (1969). *Interpersonal attraction.* Reading, MA: Addison-Wesley.

Berscheid, E., & Walster, E. (1972). Beauty and the beast. *Psychology Today, 5,* 42–46.

Best, D. L., Williams, J. E., & Briggs, S. R. (1980). A further analysis of the affective meanings associated with male and female sex-type stereotypes. *Sex Roles, 6,* 735–746.

Betz, M., & O'Connell, L. (1989). Work orientations of males and females: Exploring the gender socialization approach. *Sociological Inquiry, 59,* 318–330.

Betz, N., & Fitzgerald, L. (1987). *The career psychology of women.* New York: Academic Press.

Beutell, N. J., & Greenhaus, J. H. (1982). Interrole conflict among married women: The influence of husband and wife characteristics on conflict and coping behavior. *Journal of Vocational Behavior, 21,* 99–110.

Biaggio, M., Watts, D., & Brownell, A. (1990). Addressing sexual harassment: Strategies for prevention and change. In M. Paludi (Ed.), *Ivory power: Sexual harassment on campus* (pp. 213–230). Albany, NY: SUNY Press.

Bielby, D. D., & Bielby, W. T. (1988). Women's and men's commitment to paid work and family: Theories, models and hypothesis. In B. A. Gutek, A. H. Stromberg, & L. Larwood (Eds.), *Women and work: An annual review* (Vol. 3, pp. 249–264). Thousand Oaks, CA: Sage.

Bielby, W. T., & Bielby, D. D. (1992). I will follow him: Family ties, gender-role beliefs, and reluctance to relocate for a better job. *Journal of Sociology, 97,* 1241–1267.

Bielby, W. T., & Baron, J. N. (1984). A woman's place is with other women: Sex segregation within organizations. In B. F. Riskin (Ed.), *Sex segregation in the workplace* (pp. 27–55). Washington, DC: Academy Press.

Bielby, W. T., & Baron, J. N. (1986). Men and women at work: Sex segregation and statistical discrimination. *American Journal of Sociology, 91,* 759–799.

Biener, L. (1988). Coping and adaptation. In R. C. Barnett, L. Biener, & G. K. Baruch (Eds.), *Gender and stress* (pp. 332–349). New York: Free Press.

Biernat, M., & Wortman, C. B. (1991). Sharing of home responsibilities between professionally employed women and their husbands. *Journal of Personality and Social Psychology, 61,* 844–861.

Black, H. K. (1974). Physical attractiveness and similarity of attitude in interpersonal attraction. *Psychological Reports, 35,* 403–406.

Blake v. City of Los Angeles, 15 FEP 77 (1977).

Blake, R. R., & Mouton, J. S. (1964). *Managing intergroup conflict in industry.* Houston, TX: Gulf.

Blake, R. R., & Mouton, J. S. (1986). From theory to practice in interface problem solving. In S. Worchel & W. G. Austin (Eds.), *Psychology of intergroup relations* (2nd ed., pp. 67–82). Chicago: Nelson-Hall.

Blake, R. R., Shepard, H. A., & Mouton, J. S. (1964). *Managing intergroup conflict in industry.* Houston, Tex., Gulf Pub. Co.

Blau, F. D. (1978). The data on women workers, past, present and future. In A. H. Stromberg & S. Harkness (Eds.), *Women working: Theories and facts in perspective* (pp. 29–62). Palo Alto, CA: Mayfield.

Blau, F. D., & Ferber, M. A. (1985). Women in the labor market: The last 20 years. In L. Larwood, A. H. Stromberg, & B. A. Gutek (Eds.), *Women and work: An annual review* (vol. 1, pp. 19–49). Thousand Oaks, CA: Sage Publishing.

Blau, F. D., & Ferber, M. A. (1987). Occupations and earnings of women workers. In K. S. Koziara, M. H. Moskow, & L. D. Tanner (Eds.), *Working women: Past, present, future*. Washington, DC: Bureau of National Affairs.

Blau, P. (1956). Social mobility and interpersonal relations. *American Sociological Review, 21,* 290–295.

Blood, R. O. (1956). Uniformities and diversities in campus dating preference. *Journal of Marriage and Family Living, 18,* 37–45.

Blood, R. O., Jr. (1965). Long range causes and consequences of the employment of married women. *Journal of Marriage and the Family, 27,* 43–47.

Bodine, A. (1975). Sex differentiation in language. In B. Thorne & N. Henley (Eds.), *Language and sex difference and dominance* (pp. 130–151). Rowley, MA: Newbury House.

Bolick, C., & Nestleroth, S. (1988). *Opportunity 2000: Creative affirmative action strategies for a changing work force.* Washington, DC: U.S. Government Printing Office.

Boor, M., Wartman, S., & Reuben, D. (1983). Relationship of physical appearance and professional demeanor to interview evaluations and rankings of medical residency applicants. *Journal of Psychology, 113,* 61–65.

Bornstein, R. F. (1989). Exposure and affect: Overview and meta-analysis of research, 1968–1987. *Psychological Bulletin, 106,* 265–289.

Bradac, J. J., Hemphill, M. R., & Tardy, C. H. (1981). Language style on trial: Effects of "powerful" and "powerless" speech upon judgements of victims and villains. *Western Journal of Speech Communication, 45,* 327–341.

Bradford, D. L., Sargent, A. G., & Sprague, M. S. (1980). The executive man and woman: The issue of sexuality. In D. A. Neugarten & J. M. Shafritz (Eds.), *Sexuality in organizations* (pp. 17–28). Oak Park, IL: Moore.

Bradley, P. H. (1981). The folk-linguistics of women's speech. An empirical examination. *Communication Monographs, 48,* 73–90.

Braginsky, D. D. & Braginsky, B. M. (1975). Surplus people: Their lost faith and self. *Psychology Today, 9,* 69–72.

Brass, D. J. (1985). Men's and women's networks. A study of interaction patterns and influence in an organization. *Academy of Management Journal, 28,* 327–343.

Brenner, O. C., Tomkiewicz, J., & Schein, V. E. (1989). The relationship between sex role stereotypes and requisite management characteristics revisited. *Academy of Management Journal, 32,* 662–669.

Brett, J. B., & Stroh, L. K. (1997). Jumping ship: Who benefits from an external labor market strategy? *Journal of Applied Psychology, 82,* 331–341.

Brett, J. M., Stroh, L. K., & Reilly, H. H. (1992). What's it like being a dual-career manager in the 1990s. (p. 138–167) In S. Zedeck (Ed). *Work, family and organizations*. Frontiers in Industrial and Organizational Psychology. *v. 5*. Jossey-Bass: San Francisco.

Brett, J. B., & Yogev, S. (1989). Restructuring work for family. How dual-earner couples with children manage. In E. B. Goldsmith (Ed.), *Work and family: Theory, research and applications* (pp. 159–174). Newbury Park, CA: Sage.

Bridges, J. S. (1981). Sex-typed may be beautiful but androgynous is good. *Psychological Reports, 48,* 267–272.

Bridges, J. S. (1988). Sex differences in occupational performance expectations. *Psychology of Women Quarterly, 12,* 75–90.

Bridges, W. (1996). Leading the de-jobbed organization. In F. Hesselbein, M. Goldsmith, & R. Beckhard (Eds.), *The leader of the future: New visions, strategies, and practices for the next era* (pp. 11–18). San Francisco: Jossey-Bass.

Brief, A. P., & Nord, W. R. (1990). *Meaning of occupational work: A collection of essays*. Lexington, MA: Lexington.

Brislin, R. W., & Lewis, S. A. (1968). Dating and physical attractiveness: Replication. *Psychological Reports, 22,* 976.

Brooks, L. (1990). Recent developments in theory building. In D. Brown, & L. Brooks (Eds.), *Career choice and development: Applying contemporary theories to practice* (pp. 364–294). San Francisco: Jossey-Bass.

Broverman, L. L., Vogel, S. R., Broverman, D. M., Clarkson, F. E., & Rosenkrantz, P. S. (1972). Sex-role stereotypes: A current appraisal. *Journal of Social Issues, 28,* 59–78.

Brown, J. D. (1991). Staying fit and staying well: Physical fitness as a moderator of life stress. *Journal of Personality and Social Psychology, 60,* 555–561.

Brown, V., & Geis, F. L. (1984). Turning lead into gold: Leadership by men and women and the alchemy of social consensus. *Journal of Psychology, 46,* 811–824.

Brownmiller, S. (1984). *Femininity*. New York: Fawcett Books.

Bruce, W. M., & Reed, C. M. (1991). *Dual-career couples in the public sector*. Westport, CT: Quorum.

Bryne, D., & Clore, G. L. (1970). A reinforcement model of evaluative responses. *Personality: An International Journal, 1,* 103–128.

Bryson, R., Bryson, J. B., & Johnson, M. F. (1978). Family size, satisfaction & productivity in dual-career couples. *Psychology of Women Quarterly, 3,* 67–77.

Bucholz, B. B. (1966, June 23). Slow gains for women who would be partners. *New York Times,* p. 10.

Buhler, P. (1995, July). Managing in the '90's. *Supervision,* 24–26.

Bulzarik, M. (1978). Sexual harassment at the workplace: Historical notes. *Radical America, 12,* 25–43.

Burden, D. S., & Googins, B. (1987). *Balancing job and homelife study: Managing work and family stress in corporations*. Boston: Boston University School of Social Work.

Bureau of National Affairs (1988). *Corporate Affairs: Nepotism, office romance and sexual harassment*. Washington, DC: Bureau of National Affairs.

Burke, R. J. (1989). Some antecedents and consequences of work, family conflicts. In E. B. Goldsmith (Ed.), *Work and family: Theory, research, and applications* (pp. 287–302). Newbury Park, CA: Sage.

Burke, R. J., & Weir, T. (1976). Relationship of wives' employment status to husband, wife, pair satisfaction, and performances. *Journal of Marriage and the Family, 38,* 279–287.

Burke, R. V., & McKeen, C. T. (1990). *Mentor relationships in organizations. Issues, strategies and prospects for women.* Unpublished manuscript, York University: Toronto, Canada.

Burley, D. P. (1990). Corporate secrets: What so often gets dismissed as teasing can be torture—with long-term effects. *Executive Female, 13,* 23.

Burlington Industries, Inc. v. Ellerth S. Ct. 97-569, Lexiss 4217 (1998).

Burns, J. M. (1978). *Leadership.* New York: Harper & Row.

Burrell, G. (1984). Sex and organization analysis. *Organization Studies, 5,* 97–118.

Bush, T. L., Barrett-Conner, E., Cowan, L. D., Rosner, B., Speizer, F. E., & Hennekeos, C. H. (1987). Cardiovascular mortality and non-contraceptive use of estrogen in women. *Circulation, 75,* 1102–1109.

Bussey, K., & Bandura, A. (1984). Influence of gender constancy and social power on sex-linked modeling. *Journal of Personality and Social Psychology, 47,* 1292–1302.

Bussey, K., & Perry, D. G. (1982). Same sex imitation: The avoidance of cross-sex models or the acceptance of same-sex models? *Sex Roles, 8,* 773–784.

Butler, D., & Geis, F. L. (1990). Nonverbal affect responses to male and female leaders. Implication for leadership evaluation. *Journal of Psychology, 58,* 48–59.

Bycio, P., Hackett, R. D., & Allen, J. S. (1995). Further assessments of Bass's (1985) conceptualization of transactional and transformational leadership. *Journal of Applied Psychology, 80,* 468–478.

Byrne, D. (1971). *The attraction paradigm.* New York: Academic Press.

Byrne, D., Clore, G. L., & Smeaton, G. (1986). The attraction hypothesis: Do similar attitudes affect anything? *Journal of Personality and Social Psychology, 51,* 1167–1170.

Byrne, D., & Neuman, J. H. (1992). The implications of attraction research for organizational issues. In K. Kelley (Ed.), *Issues, theory, and research in industrial/organizational psychology* (pp. 29–70). Amsterdam: North Holland.

Caballero, M., & Pride, W. (1984). Selected effects of salesperson sex and attractiveness in direct mail advertisements. *Journal of Marketing, 48,* 94–100.

Campbell, J. (1949). *The hero with a thousand faces.* New York: Pantheon.

Cantor, J. R. (1976). What is funny to whom? The role of gender. *Journal of Communication, 26,* 164–172.

Caplan, N., & Nelson, S. D. (1973). On being useful: The nature and consequences of psychological research on social problems. *American Psychologist, 28,* 199–211.

Carbonell, J. L. (1984). Sex roles and leadership revisited. *Journal of Applied Psychology, 69*(1), 44–49.

Carli, L. (1982). *Are women more social and men more task-oriented? A meta-analytic review of sex differences in group interaction, reward allocation, coalition formation and cooperation in the prisoner's dilemma game.* Unpublished manuscript, University of Massachusetts, Amherst.

Caruso, G. L. (1992). Patterns of maternal employment and child care for a sample of two-year olds. *Journal of Family Issues, 13,* 297–311.

Case, S. S. (1988). Cultural differences not deficiencies: An analysis of managerial women's language. In S. Rose & L. Larwood (Eds.), *Women's careers: Pathways and pitfalls* (pp. 41–63). Praeger: New York.

Cash, T. F., Gillen, P., & Burns, S. D. (1977). Sexism and "beautism" in personnel consultant decision-making. *Journal of Applied Psychology, 62,* 301–310.

Cashin, J., Stockdale, M. S., & Shearer, V. (1993). *The 1993 Survey of Sexual Harassment at SIUC.* Department of Psychology, Southern Illinois University at Carbondale.

Chacko, T. I. (1982). Women and equal employment opportunity: Some unintended effects. *Journal of Applied Psychology, 617,* 119–123.

Chambers-Cook, K., & Youngblood, S. A. (1984). Child care assistance can improve employee attitudes and behavior. *Personnel Administrator, 29,* 45–52.

Chao, G. T., Walz, P. M., & Gardner, P. H. (1992). Formal and informal mentorships: A comparison on mentoring functions and contrast with nonmentored counterparts. *Personnel Psychology, 45,* 619–636.

Chao, G. T., O'Leary-Kelly, A. M., Wolf, S., Klein, H. J., & Gardner, P. D. (1994). Organizational socialization: Its content and consequences. *Journal of Applied Psychology, 79,* 730–743.

Chapman, F. S. (1987, February 16). Executive guilt: Who's taking care of the children? *Fortune,* pp. 30–37.

Chase, I. D. (1975). A comparison of men's and women's intergenerational mobility in the United States. *American Sociological Review, 40,* 483–509.

Chassin, L., Zeiss, A., Cooper, K., & Reaven, J. (1985). Role perceptions, self-role congruence and marital satisfaction in dual worker couples with pre-school children. *Social Psychology Quarterly, 48,* 301–311.

Chesanow, N. (1992, July). Do office affairs ruin careers? *New Woman, 22,* pp. 84–87.

Chesney, M. A. (1991). Women, work-related stress, and smoking. In M. Frankenhaeuser, V. Lundberg, & M. Chesney (Eds.), *Women, work and health: Stress and opportunities* (pp. 139–156). London: Plenum.

Christensen, D., & Rosenthal, R. (1982). Gender and nonverbal decoding skills as determinants of interpersonal expectancy effects. *Journal of Psychology, 42,* 75–87.

Clare, A. W. (1983). Psychiatric and social aspects of premenstrual complaint. In. *Psychological Medicine Monograph (Suppl. 4).* Cambridge, UK: Cambridge University Press.

Clare, A. W. (1985). Hormones, behaviour and the menstrual cycle. *Journal of Psychosomatic Research, 29,* 225–233.

Clawson, J.G., & Kram, K. E. (1984, May–June). Managing cross gender mentoring. *Business Horizons, 27,* 22–32.

Cleveland, J. N., & Kerst, M. E. (1993). Sexual harassment and perceptions of power: An under-articulated relationship. *Journal of Vocational Behavior, 42*, 49–67.

Cleveland, J. N., & McNamara, K. (1996). Understanding sexual harassment: Contributions from research on domestic violence and organizational change. In M. S. Stockdale (Ed.), *Women and work: Vol. 6. Sexual harassment* (pp. 217–240). Thousand Oaks, CA: Sage.

Clifford, M. M. (1975). Physical attractiveness and academic performance. *Child Study Journal, 5*, 201–209.

Clifford, M. M., & Walster, E. (1973). The effect of physical attractiveness on teacher expectations. *Sociology of Education, 46*, 248–258.

Cohn S. (1996). Human capital theory. In P. Dubeck & K. Borman (Eds.), *Women and work: A reader* (pp. 107–110). New Brunswick, NJ: Rutgers University Press.

Cohen, S. I., & Bunker, K. A. (1975). Subtle effects of sex role stereotypes on recruiter hiring decisions. *Journal of Applied Psychology, 60*, 566–572.

Coker, D. R. (1984). The relationship among concepts and cognitive maturity in preschool children. *Sex Roles, 10*, 19–31.

Colby, L. (1991, June). Regulating love. *Personnel*, p. 23.

Colditz, G. A., Willett, W. C., & Stampfer, M. J. (1987). Menopause and the risk of coronary heart disease in women. *New England Journal of Medicine, 316*, 1105–1110.

Collins, A. (1991). Premenstrual distress: Implications for women's working capacity and quality of life. In M. Frankenhaeuser, U. Lyndberg, & M. Chesney (Eds.), *Women, work and health: Stress and opportunities* (pp. 239–254). New York: Plenum.

Collins, A., Lundstrom, W., Nordstrom, L., Nilsson, C. G., Hamfelt, A., & Eneroth, P. (1986). Psychoneuroendocrinological characteristics of premenstrual tension: Effects of treatment with vitamin B. In L. Dennerstein & I. Frazer (Eds.), *Hormones and behavior* (pp. 183–196). Amsterdam: Elsevier.

Collins, E. G. C., & Blogett, T. B. (1981). Sexual harassment: Some see it some won't. *Harvard Business Review, 59*, 77–94.

Collins, E. G. C. (1983). Managers and lovers. *Harvard Business Review, 61*(5), 142–153.

Colwill, N. (1982). *The new partnership*. Palo Alto, CA: Mayfield.

Colwill, N. L., & Lips, H. M. (1988). Corporate love: The pitfalls of workplace romance. *Business Quarterly, 53*(1), 89–91.

Condon, J. W., & Crano, W. D. (1988). Inferred evaluation and the relation between attitude similarity and interpersonal attraction. *Journal of Personality and Social Psychology, 54*, 789–797.

Conference Board. (1994). *Diversity training: A research report* (Report No. 1083-94-RR). New York: The Conference Board.

Conger, J. A., & Kanungo, R. N. (1987). Toward a behavioral theory of charismatic leadership in organizational settings. *Academy of Management Review, 12*, 637–647.

Conklin, N. F. (1974). Toward a feminist analysis of linguistic behavior. *The University of Michigan Papers in Women's Studies, 1*(1), 51–73.

Conte, A. (1997). Legal theories of sexual harassment (pp. 50–83). In W. O'Donohue (Ed.). *Sexual harassment: Theory, research, and treatment.* Needham Heights, MA: Allyn and Bacon.

Coombs, R. H., & Kenkel, W. F. (1966). Sex differences in dating aspirations and satisfaction with computer-selected partners. *Journal of Marriage and the Family, 28,* 62–66.

Cooper, C. L. (1986). Job distress: Recent research and the emerging role of the clinical occupational psychologist. *Bulletin of the British Psychological Society, 39,* 325–331.

Cooper, C. L., & Payne, R. (1988). *Causes, coping and consequences of stress at work.* Chichester, England: Wiley.

Corse, S. J. (1990). Pregnant managers and their subordinates: The effects of gender expectations on hierarchical relationships. *The Journal of Applied Behavioral Sciences, 26,* 25–47.

Coser, R. L. (1960). Laughter among colleagues. *Psychiatry, 23,* 81–95.

Cottle, M. (1998, May). Turning boys into girls. *Washington Monthly, 30*(5), 32(5).

Cotton, J. L. (1995, May). *Protege outcomes from formal and informal mentoring.* Paper presented at the Society for Industrial and Organizational Psychology meeting, Orlando, FL.

County of Washington v. Gunther, 25 FEP 1521 (1981).

Cox, T., Jr. (1994). *Cultural diversity in organizations: Theory, research, and practice.* San Francisco: Berrett-Koehler.

Cox, T. H., & Blake, S. (1991). Managing cultural diversity: Implications for organizational competitiveness. *The Executive, 5*(3), 45–56.

Crandall, R. (1972). Field extension of the frequency-affect findings. *Psychological Reports, 31,* 371–374.

Crandall, V. C. (1963). Achievement. In H. W. Stevenson (Ed.), *Child psychology: 62nd yearbook of the National Society for the Study of Education.* Chicago: University of Chicago Press.

Cranny, C. J., Smith, P. C., & Stone, E. F. (Eds.) (1992). *Job satisfaction: How people feel about their jobs and how it affects performance.* New York: Lexington.

Cranor, L. A., Karasek, R. A., & Carlin, C. J. (1981). *Job characteristics and office work: Findings and health implications.* Paper presented at the National Institute for Occupational Safety and Health Conference on Occupational Health Issues Affecting Clerical/Secretarial Personnel, Cincinnati, OH.

Crawford, M., & Marecek, J. (1989). Psychology reconstructs the female: 1968–1988. *Psychology of Women Quarterly, 13,* 147–165.

Crosby, F. (1982). *Relative deprivation and the working woman.* New York: Oxford University Press.

Crosby, F. (1984). Job satisfaction and domestic life. In M. D. Lee & R. N. Kanungo (Eds.), *Management of work and personal life.* New York: Praeger.

Crosby, F., & Nyquist, L. (1977). The female register. An empirical study of Lakoff's hypotheses. *Language in Society, 6,* 313–322.

Crull, P. (1982). Stress effects of sexual harassment on the job: Implications for counseling. *American Journal of Orthopsychiatry, 52*, 539–544.

Culbertson, A. L., Rosenfeld, P., Booth-Kewley, S., & Magnusson, P. (1992). *Assessment of sexual harassment in the Navy: Results of the 1989 Navy-wide survey* (NPRDC TR-92-11). San Diego, CA: Navy Personnel Research and Development Center.

Dalton, K. (1984). *The premenstrual syndrome and progesterone therapy.* London: Heineman.

Dansereau, F., Graen, G., & Haga, W. J. (1975). A vertical dyad linkage approach to leadership in formal organizations. *Organizational Behavior and Human Performance, 13*, 46–78.

Darley, J. M., & Fazio, R. H. (1980). Expectancy confirmation processes arising in the social interaction sequence. *American Psychologist, 35*, 867–881.

Davidson, M. J., & Cooper, C. L. (1984). Occupational stress in female managers: A comparative study. *Journal of Management Studies, 21*, 185–205.

Davidson, M. J., & Cooper, C. L. (1987). Female managers in Britain—A comparative review. *Human Resource Management, 26*, 217–242.

Davidson, M. J., & Cooper, C. L. (1992). *Shattering the glass ceiling: The woman manager.* London: Chapman.

Deaux, K. (1976). *The behavior of women and men.* Monterey, CA: Brooks/Cole.

Deaux, K. (1979). Self-evaluations of male and female managers. *Sex Roles, 5*, 571–580.

Deaux, K., & Emswiller, T. (1974). Explanations of successful performance on sex-linked tasks: What is skill for the male is luck for the female. *Journal of Personality and Social Psychology, 29*(1), 80–85.

Deaux, K., & Farris, E. (1977). Attributing causes for one's own performance: The effects of sex norms, and outcomes. *Journal of Research in Personality, 11*(1), 59–72.

Deaux, K., & Lewis, L. L. (1984). Structure of gender stereotypes. Interrelationships among components of gender label. *Journal of Personality and Social Psychology, 46*, 991–1004.

Deaux, K., & Major, B. (1987). Putting gender into context: An interactive model of gender related behavior. *Psychological Review, 94*, 369–389.

Deaux, K., & Taynor, J. (1973). Evaluation of male and female ability: Bias works two ways. *Psychological Reports, 32*(1), 261–262.

Del Boca, F. K., & Ashmore, R. D. (1980). Sex stereotypes through the life cycle. In L. Wheeler (Ed.), *Review of personality and social psychology* (Vol. 1, pp. 163–192). Beverly Hills, CA: Sage.

DeLuca, J. M., & McDowell, R. N. (1992). Managing diversity: A strategic "grass-roots" approach. In Jackson, S. E. et al. (Eds.), *Diversity in the workplace: Human resources initiatives* (pp. 227–247). New York: Guilford Press.

Denmark, F. L. (1993). Women, leadership and empowerment. *Psychology of Women Quarterly, 17*, 343–356.

Denmark, F. L., Ruzzo, N. F., Frieze, I. H., & Sechzei, J. A. (1988). Guidelines for avoiding sexism in psychological research: A report of the ad hoc committee on nonsexist research. *American Psychologist, 43*, 582–585.

Diamond, E. (1987). Theories of career development and the reality of women at work. In B. A. Gutek & L. Larwood (Eds.), *Women's career development* (pp. 15–27). Newbury Park, CA: Sage.

Dierks-Stewart, K. (1980). Sex differences in nonverbal communication: An alternative perspective. In C. L. Berryman & V. A. Eman (Eds.), *Communication, language, and sex* (pp. 112–121). Rowley, MA: Newbury House.

Dillard, J. P. (1987). Close relationships at work: Perceptions of the motives and performance of relational participants. *Journal of Social and Personal Relationships, 4,* 179–193.

Dillard, J. P., & Broetzmann, S. M. (1989). Romantic relationships at work: Perceived changes in job-related behaviors as a function of participant's motive, partner's motive, and gender. *Journal of Applied Social Psychology, 19,* 93–110.

Dillard, J. P., & Witteman, H. (1985). Romantic relationships at work: Organizational and personal influences, *Human Communication Research, 12,* 99–116.

Dion, K. K. (1972). Physical attractiveness and evaluations of children's transgressions. *Journal of Personality and Social Psychology, 24,* 207–213.

Dion, K. K. (1974). Children's physical attractiveness and sex as determinants of adult punitiveness. *Development Psychology, 10,* 772–778.

Dion, K. K. (1977). The incentive value of physical attractiveness for young children. *Personality and Social Psychology Bulletin, 3,* 67–70.

Dion, K. K., & Berscheid, E. (1974). Physical attractiveness and peer perception among children. *Sociometry, 37,* 1–12.

Dion, K. K., Berscheid, E., & Walster, E. (1972). What is beautiful is good. *Journal of Personality and Social Psychology, 24,* 285–290.

Dipboye, R. L. (1987). Problems and progress of women in management. In K. S. Koziara, M. S. Moskow, & L. D. Tanner (Eds.), *Working women: Past, present, and future* (pp. 118–153). Washington, DC: BNA Books.

Dipboye, R. L., Arvey, R. D., & Terpstra, D. E. (1977). Sex and physical attractiveness of raters and applicants as determinants of resume evaluations. *Journal of Applied Psychology, 62,* 288–294.

Dipboye, R. L., Fromkin, H. L., & Wiback, K. (1975). Relative importance of applicant sex, attractiveness, and scholastic standing in evaluation of job applicant resumes. *Journal of Applied Psychology, 60,* 39–43.

Dobbins, G. H., & Platz, S. J. (1986). Sex differences in leadership: How real are they? *Academy of Management Review, 11*(1), 118–127.

Dobrzynski, J. H. (1996, February 28). Viewing barriers to women's careers. *Wall Street Journal,* p. d2.

Dothard v. Rawlinson, 15 FEP 11 (1977).

Dovidio, J. F., & Ellyson, S. L. (1982). Decoding visual dominance: Attributions of power based on the relative percentages of looking while speaking and looking while listening. *Social Psychology Quarterly, 45,* 106–113.

Dovidio, J. F., Ellyson, S. L., Keating, C. F., Heltman, K., & Brown, C. E. (1988). The relationship of social power to visual displays of dominance between men and women. *Journal of Personality and Social Psychology, 54,* 233–242.

Dreher, G. F., & Ash, R. A. (1990). A comparative study of mentoring among men and women in managerial, professional and technological positions. *Journal of Applied Psychology, 75,* 539–546.

Dreher, G. F., Dougherty, T. W., & Whitely, W. (1989). Influence tactics and salary attainment. A gender-specific analysis. *Sex Roles, 20,* 535–550.

Druskat, V. U. (1994). Gender and leadership style: Transformational and transactional leadership in the Roman Catholic Church. *Leadership Quarterly, 5,* 99–119.

Dunn, D. (1997a). Gender and earnings. In P. Dubeck & K. Borman (Eds.), *Women and work: A handbook* (pp. 61–64). New York: Garland.

Dunn, D. (1997b). Sex-segregated occupations. In P. Dubeck & K. Borman (Eds.), *Women and work: A handbook* (pp. 91–93). New York: Garland.

Eagly, A. H. (1983). Gender and social influence: A social psychological analysis. *American Psychologist, 38,* 971–981.

Eagly, A. H. (1987). *Sex differences in social behavior: A social-role interpretation.* Hillsdale, NJ: Lawrence Erlbaum Associates.

Eagly, A. H., Ashmore, R. D., Makhijani, M. G., Long, L. C. (1991). What is beautiful is good, but . . . A meta-analytic review of research in the physical attractiveness stereotype. *Psychological Bulletin, 110,* 109–128.

Eagly, A. H., & Johnson, B. T. (1990). Gender and leadership style: A meta-analysis. *Psychological Bulletin, 108,* 233–256.

Eagly, A. H., & Karau, S. J. (1991). Gender and the emergence of leaders: A meta-analysis. *Journal of Personality and Social Psychology, 60*(5), 685–710.

Eagly, A. H., Makhijani, M. G., & Klonsky, B. G. (1992). Gender and the evaluation of leaders: A meta-analysis. *Psychological Bulletin, 111*(1), 3–22.

Eakins, B. W., & Eakins, R. G. (1978). *Sex differences in human communication.* Boston: Houghton Mifflin.

Edelsky, C. (1981). Who got the floor? *Language in Society, 10,* 383–421.

Eder, D., & Hallinan, M. T. (1978). Sex differences in children's friendships. *American Sociological Review, 43,* 237–250.

Edwards, J. R. (1992). A cybernetic theory of stress coping and well-being in organizations. *Academy of Management Review, 17,* 238–274.

Efran, M. G. (1974). The effect of physical appearance on the judgment of guilt, interpersonal attraction, and severity of recommended punishment in a simulated jury task. *Journal of Research in Personality, 8,* 45–54.

Eisenbert, P., & Lazarsfield, P. F. (1938). The psychological effects of unemployment. *Psychological Bulletin, 35,* 358–391.

Elias, M. (1995). *Touting oneself can work against women.* USA Today, Thursday, June 29, p. 01D.

Ellsworth, P. C., Carlsmith, J. M., & Hensen, A. (1972). The stare as a stimulus to flight in human subjects: A series of field experiments. *Journal of Applied Psychology, 21,* 302–311.

Ellyson, S. L., & Dovidio, J. F. (Eds.) (1985). *Power, dominance, and nonverbal behavior.* New York: Springer-Verlag.

Elizur, D. (1992). Work and nonwork relations: The corical structure of work and home life relationship. *Journal of Organizational Behavior, 12,* 313–322.

Ellison v. Brady, 924 F.2d 872, 9th Cir. (1991).

Ely, R. J. (1994). The effects of organizational demographics and social identity on relationships among professional women. *Administrative Science Quarterly, 39,* 89–117.

Emerson, R. M. (1962). Power-dependence relations. *American Sociological Review, 27,* 31–40.

The Employment Situation. (1998, July 2). USDA-98-271 [on-line]. Available: stats.bls.gov.newrel.htms.

Epstein, C. F. (1987). Multiple demands and multiple roles: The conditions of successful management. In F. J. Crosby (Ed.), *Spouse, parent, worker. On gender and multiple roles* (pp. 23–35). New Haven, CT: Yale University Press.

Epstein, C. F. (1988). *Sex, gender, and social order.* New Haven, CT: Yale University Press.

Equal Employment Opportunity Commission. (1980). Guidelines on discrimination because of sex (Sect. 1604.11). *Federal Register, 45,* 74676–74677.

Equal Employment Opportunity Commission (1995). *2nd quarter report to the chairman.* Washington, DC: Office of Program Operations.

Erez, M., Borochov, O., & Mannheim,-B. (1989). Work values of youth: Effects of sex or sex role typing? *Journal of Vocational Behavior, 34,* 350–366.

Erkert, S. (1983). Exploring sex differences in expectancy, attribution, and academic achievement. *Sex Roles, 9,* 217–231.

Erlich, H. J., & Larcon, B. E. K. (1992). *The effects of prejudice and ethnoviolence on workers' health.* Paper presented at the 2nd American Psychological Association/National Institute of Occupational Safety and Health Conference on Work Stress and Health, November, Washington, DC.

Etzioni, A. (1975). *A comparative analysis of complex organizations* (rev. ed.). New York: Free Press.

Eulberg, J. R., Weekley, J. A., & Bhagat, R. S. (1988). Models of stress in organizational research: A metatheoretical perspective. *Human Relations, 41,* 331–350.

Evans, G. W., & Howard, R. B. (1973). Personal space. *Psychological Bulletin, 80,* 334–344.

Exline, R. V. (1963). Explorations in the process of person perception: Visual interaction in relation to competition, sex, and need for affiliation. *Journal of Personality, 31,* 1–20.

Exline, R. V., Ellyson, S. L., & Long, B. (1975). Visual behavior as an aspect of power role relationships. In P. Pliner, L. Krames, & T. Alloway (Eds.), Nonverbal communication of aggression. Proceedings of the 4th annual Symposium on Communication and Affect held at Erindale College, University of Toronto, March 28–30, 1974.

Eyler, D. R., & Baridon, A. P. (1992a, May–June). Far more than friendship. *Psychology Today, 25,* 59–67.

Eyler, D. R., & Baridon, A. P. (1992b). Managing sexual attraction in the workplace. *Business Quarterly, 56*(3), 19–26.

Fagenson, E. A. (1988). The power of a mentor: Protégés' and nonprotégés' perceptions of their own power in organizations. *Group and Organization Studies, 13,* 182–192.

Fagenson, E. A. (1989). The mentor advantage: Perceived career/job experiences of protégés versus nonprotégés. *Journal of Organizational Behavior, 10,* 309–320.

Fagenson, E. A. (1992). Mentoring—Who needs it? A comparison of protégés' and non-protégés' needs for power achievement, affiliation and autonomy. *Journal of Vocational Behavior, 41,* 48–60.

Fain, T. C., & Anderson, D. L. (1987). Sexual harassment: Organizational context and diffuse status. *Sex Roles, 5/6,* 291–311.

Falbo, T., Hazen, M. D., & Linimon, D. (1982). The costs of selecting power bases or messages associated with the opposite sex. *Sex Roles, 8,* 147–157.

Falbo, T., & Peplau, L. A. (1980). Power strategies in intimate relations. *Journal of Personality and Social Psychology, 35,* 537–547.

Fallon, A. E., & Rozin, P. (1985). Sex differences in perceptions of desirable body shape. *Journal of Abnormal Psychology, 94*(1), 102–105.

Faragher v. Boca Raton, S. Ct. 97-282, Lexis, 4216 (1998).

Farley, L. (1978). *Sexual shakedown: The sexual harassment of women on the job.* New York: McGraw-Hill.

Feingold, A. (1990). Gender differences in effects of physical attractiveness on romantic attraction: A comparison across five research paradigms. *Journal of Personality and Social Psychology, 59,* 981–993.

Feldberg, R. L., & Glenn, E. N. (1979). Male and female: Job vs. gender models in the sociology of work. *Social Problems, 26,* 525–535.

Feldberg, R. L., & Glenn, E. N. (1982). Male and female: Job vs. gender models in the sociology of work. In R. Kahn-Hut, A. K. Daniels, & R. Colvard (Eds.), *Women and work: Problems and perspectives* (pp. 65–80). New York: Oxford University Press.

Feldman, R. S. (1998). *Social psychology.* Englewood Cliffs, NJ: Prentice-Hall.

Ferber, M. A., O'Farrell, B., & Allen L. (1991). *Work and family: Policies for a changing workforce.* Washington, DC: National Academy Press.

Fernandez, J. P. (1981). *Racism and sexism in corporate life: Changing values in American business.* Lexington, MA: Lexington.

Fidell, L. S. (1975). Empirical verification of sex discrimination in hiring practices in psychology. In R. K. Unger & F. L. Denmark (Eds.), *Women: Dependent or independent variable?* New York: Psychological Dimensions.

Fiedler, F. E. (1967). *A theory of leadership effectiveness.* New York: McGraw-Hill.

Fiedler, F. E. (1978). Contingency model and the leadership process. In L. Berkowitz (Ed.), *Advances in experimental social psychology* (Vol. 11, pp. 60–112). New York: Academic Press.

Fine, G. A. (1986). Friendships in the workplace. In V. J. Derlega, & C. B. A. Winstead (Eds.), *Friendship and social interaction* (pp. 188–206). New York: Springer-Verlag.

Fine, M. G., Johnson, F. L., Ryan, M. S., & Lutfiyya, M. N. (1987). Ethical issues in defining and evaluating women's communication in the workplace. In L. P. Stewart & S. Ting-Toomey (Eds.), *Communication, gender, and sex role in diverse interaction contents* (pp. 105–118). Norwood, NJ: Albex.

Fisher, A. B. (1996). What's so funny, jokeboy? *Fortune,* December 9, 1996, v. 134 n.11, p. 220(1).

Fisher, A. B. (1994, October 3). Getting comfortable with couples in the workplace. *Fortune, 130,* 138–144.

Fishman, P. M. (1983). Interaction: The work women do. In B. Thorne, C. Kramarae, & C. N. Henley (Eds.), *Language, gender, and society* (pp. 89–101). Rowley, MT: Newbury House.

Fiske, S. T. (1993). Controlling other people: The impact of power on stereotyping. *American Psychologist, 48,* 621–628.

Fiske, S. T., Bersoff, D. N., Borgida, E., Deaux, K., & Heilman, M. E. (1991). Social science research on trial: Use of sex sterotyping research. *American Psychologist, 46,* 1049–1060.

Fiske, S. T., & Taylor, S. E. (1991). *Social cognition* (2nd ed.). McGraw-Hill: New York.

Fitzgerald, L. F. (1993). Sexual harassment: Violence against women in the workplace. *American Psychologist, 48,* 1070–1076.

Fitzgerald, L. F., & Crites, J. O. (1980). Toward a career psychology of woman. What do we know? What do we need to know? *Journal of Counseling Psychology, 27,* 44–62.

Fitzgerald, L. F., Gelfand, M. J., & Drasgow, F. (1995). Measuring sexual harassment: Theoretical and psychometric advances. *Basic and Applied Social Psychology, 17,* 425–445.

Fitzgerald, L. F., & Shullman, S. L. (1993). Sexual harassment: A research analysis and agenda for the 1990s. *Journal of Vocational Behavior, 42,* 5–27.

Fitzgerald, L. F., Shullman, S. L., Bailey, N., Richards, M., Swecker, J., Gold, Y., Ormerod, A. J., & Weitzman, L. (1988). The dimensions and extent of sexual harassment in higher education and the workplace. *Journal of Vocational Behavior, 32,* 152–175.

Fitzgerald, L. F., Swan, S., & Fischer, K. (1995). Why didn't she just report him? The psychological and legal implications of women's responses to sexual harassment. *Journal of Social Issues, 51,* 117–138.

Fleishman, E. A. (1973). Twenty years of consideration and structure. In E. A. Fleishman & J. G. Hunt (Eds.), *Current developments in the study of leadership* (pp. 1–40). Carbondale: Southern Illinois University Press.

Fleming, J. (1983a). Black women in black and white college environment: The making of a matriarch. *Journal of Social Issues, 39*(3), 41–54.

Fleming, J. (1983b). Sex differences in the educational and occupational goals of Black college students: Continued inquiry into the Black matriarchy theory. In M. S. Horner & C. Nadelson (Eds.), *The challenge of change.* New York: Plenum.

Folkman, S., & Lazarus, R. S. (1980). An analysis of coping in a middle-aged community sample. *Journal of Health and Social Behavior, 21,* 219–239.

Folkman, S., & Lazarus, R. S. (1985). If it changes it must be progress: Study of emotion and coping during three stages of a college examination. *Journal of Personality and Social Psychology, 48,* 150–171.

Forman, A. K., & Pressley, G. (1987). Ethnic culture and corporate culture: Using Black styles in organization. *Communication Quarterly, 35,* 293–307.

Fogarty, M. P., Rapoport, R., & Rapoport, R. N. (1971). *Sex, career and family: Including an international review of women's roles.* London: George Allen & Unwin.

Fong, M. L., & Amatea, E. S. (1992). Stress and single professional women: An exploration of causal factors (Special Issue: Women and health). *Journal of Mental Health Counseling, 14,* 20–29.

Ford, D. L. (1985). Job-related stress of the minority professional. In T. A. Beehr & R. S. Bhagat (Eds.), *Human stress and cognition in organizations* (pp. 287–323). New York: Wiley.

Frankenhaeuser, M. (1983). The sympathetic–adrenal and pituitary–adrenal response to challenge: Comparison between the sexes. In T. M. Dembroski, T. H. Schmidt, & G. Blumchen (Eds.), *Biobehavioral bases of coronary heart disease* (pp. 91–105). Basel, Switzerland: Karger.

Frankenhaeuser, M. (1988). Stress and reactivity patterns at different stages of the life cycle. In P. Pancheri & L. Zichella (Eds.), *Biorhythms and stress in the phipco-pathology of reproduction* (pp. 31–40). New York: Hemisphere.

Frankenhaeuser, M. (1989). A biopsychosocial approach to work life issues. *International Journal of Health Services, 19,* 748–758.

Frankenhaeuser, M. (1991a). The psychophysiology of sex differences as related to occupational status. In M. Frankenhaeuser, W. Lundberg, & M. Chesney (Eds.), *Women, work and health: Stress and opportunities* (pp. 39–61). New York: Plenum.

Frankenhaeuser, M. (1991b). The psychophysiology of workload, stress, and health: Comparison between the sexes. *Annals of Behavioral Medicine, 13,* 197–204.

Frankenhaeuser, M., Lundberg, V., & Chesney, M. (1991). *Women, work and health: Stress and opportunities.* New York: Plenum.

Franklin, C. W. (1984). *The changing definition of masculinity.* New York: Plenum.

Frazier, P. A., Cochran, C. C., & Olson, A. M. (1995). Social science research on lay definitions of sexual harassment. *Journal of Social Issues, 51,* 21–37.

French, J., Jr., & Raven, B. (1959). The bases of social power. In C. Cartwright (Ed.), *Studies in social power.* Ann Arbor: University of Michigan Press.

Friedman, A. (1987). Getting powerful with age: Changes in women over the life cycle. *Israel Social Science Research, 5,* 76–86.

Friedman, A., Tzukerman, Y., Wienberg, H., & Todd, J. (1992). The shift in power with age: Changes in perceptions of the power of women and men over the life cycle. *Psychology of Women Quarterly, 16,* 513–525.

Friedman, D. E. (1986). Child care for employees' kids. *Harvard Business Review,* pp. 28–32.

Friedman, D. E., & Galinsky, E. (1992). Work and family issues: A legitimate business concern. In S. Zedeck (Ed.), *Work, families, and organizations* (pp. 168–207). San Francisco: Jossey-Bass.

Friedman, H., & Zebrowitz, L. A. (1992). The contribution of typical sex differences in facial maturity to sex role stereotypes. *Personality and Social Psychology Bulletin, 18,* 430–438.

Friend, R. M., & Vinson, M. (1974). Leaning over backwards: Jurors' responses to defendants' attractiveness. *Journal of Communication, 24,* 1124–1129.

Frieze, I., & Ramsey, S. (1976). Nonverbal maintenance of traditional sex roles. *Journal of Social Issues, 32,* 133–141.

Fritz, J. H. (1997). Men's and women's organizational peer relationships: A comparison. *Journal of Business Communication, 34,* 27–46.

Frone, M. R., Russell, M., & Cooper, M. L. (1990). *Occupational stressors, psychosocial resources, and psychological distress: A comparison of Black and White workers.* Paper presented at the annual meeting of the Academy of Management, August.

Frone, M. R., Russell, M., & Cooper, M. L. (1992). Prevalence of work–family conflict. Are work and family boundaries asymmetrically permeable? *Journal of Organizational Behavior, 13,* 723–729.

Fulmer, R. M. (1977). *Practical human relations.* Homewood, IL: Irwin.

Gabarro, J. J. (1986). The development of working relationships. In J. Lorsch (Ed.), *The handbook of organizational behavior* (pp. 172–189). Englewood Cliffs, NJ: Prentice-Hall.

Gaertner, S., & Dovido, J. (1986). *Prejudice, discrimination and racism.* New York: Academic Press.

Galensky, E., & Hughes, D. (1987). *The Fortune magazine study.* New York: Families and Work Institute.

Gallos, J. V. (1989). Exploring women's development: Implications for career theory, practice and research. In M. B. Arthur, D. T. Hall, & B. S. Lawrence (Eds.), *Handbook of career theory* (pp. 110–132). Cambridge, UK: Cambridge University Press.

Galtung, J. (1974). *A structural theory of revolutions.* Rotterdam University Press: Rotterdam.

Gannon, L., Luchetta, T., Rhodes, K., Pardee, L., & Segrist, D. (1992). Sex bias in psychological research. *American Psychologist, 47,* 389–396.

Gardenswartz, L., & Rowe, A. (1994). *Diverse teams at work: Capitalizing on the power of diversity.* Homewood, IL: Irwin.

Garlick, B., Dixon, S., & Allen, P. (Eds.) (1992). *Stereotypes of women in power.* Westport, CT: Greenwood Press.

Geddes, D. (1992). Sex roles in management: The impact of varying power of speech style on union members' perception of satisfaction and effectiveness. *The Journal of Psychology, 126,* 589–607.

Gelfand, M. J., Fitzgerald, L. F., & Drasgow, F. (1995). The structure of sexual harassment: A confirmatory analysis across cultures and settings. *Journal of Vocational Behavior, 47,* 164–177.

General Electric Co. v. Gilbert, 429 U.S. 125 (1976).

Giles, H. (1977). *Language, ethnicity, and intergroup relations.* NY: Academic Press.

Giles, H., Bourhis, R. Y., & Taylor, D. M. (1977). Towards a theory of language in ethnic group relations. In H. Giles (Ed.), *Language, ethnicity, and intergroup relations* (pp. 307–348). New York; Academic Press.

Giles, H., & Powesland, P. F. (1975). *Speech style and social evaluation.* Academic Press: London.

Giles, H., Robinson, W. P., & Smith, P. M. (Eds.) (1980). *Language: Social psychological perspectives.* Oxford: Pergamon.

Giles, H., Taylor, P. M., & Bourhis, R. Y. (1973). Towards a theory of interpersonal accommodation through speech: Some Canadian data. *Language in Society, 2,* 177–192.

Gillen, B. (1981). Physical attractiveness: A determinant of two types of goodness. *Personality and Social Psychology Bulletin, 7,* 277–281.

Gillen, B., & Sherman, R. C. (1980). Physical attractiveness and sex as determinants of trait attributions. *Multivariate Behavioral Research, 15,* 423–437.

Gillespie, D. L., & Leffler, A. (1987). The politics of research methodology in claims-making activities: Social science and sexual harassment. *Sexual Problems, 34,* 490–501.

Gilley, H. M., & Summers, C. S. (1970). Sex differences in the use of hostile verbs. *Journal of Psychology, 76,* 33–37.

Gitter, A. G., Black, H., & Mostofsky, D. I. (1972). Race and sex in the communication of emotion. *Journal of Social Psychology, 88,* 273–276.

Glass, J., & Camarigg, V. (1992). Gender, parenthood, and job family compatibility. *American Journal of Sociology, 98,* 131–151.

Glick, P., Zion, C., & Nelson, C. (1988). What mediates sex discrimination in hiring decisions? *Journal of Personality and Social Psychology, 55,* 178–186.

Goffman, E. (1959). *Presentation of self in everyday life.* New York: Anchor.

Goldberg, P. (1968, April 5). Are women prejudiced against women? *Transaction, 5,* 28–30.

Goodman, E. (1979). It's not a question of style. *Spokeswomen, 9,* 16.

Gottfredson, L. S. (1981). Circumscription and compromise. A developmental theory of occupational aspirations. *Journal of Counseling Psychology Monograph, 28,* 545–579.

Gough, H. G., & Heilbron, A. B. (1980). *Adjective check list manual.* Palo Alto, CA: Consulting Psychologists Press.

Gould, S. J. (1981). *The mismeasure of man.* New York: Norton.

Graham, A. (1973, December). The making of a nonsexist dictionary. *Ms., 2,* 12–16.

Gray, J. (1992). *Men are from Mars, women are from Venus.* New York: HarperCollins.

Green, M. (1982). A Washington perspective on women and networking: The power and pitfalls. *Journal of NAWDAC, 46,* 7–21.

Green, S. G., & Mitchell, T. R. (1979). Attributional processes of leaders in leader–member exchanges. *Organizational Behavior and Human Performance, 23,* 429–458.

Greenberg, J., & Baron, R. A. (1997). *Behavior in organizations: Understanding and managing the human side of work.* Englewood Cliffs, NJ: Prentice-Hall.

Greenglass, E. R., Pantony, K., & Burke, R. J. (1989). A gender-role perspective on role conflict, work stress, and social support. In E. B. Goldsmith (Ed.), *Work and family: Theory, research and application* (pp. 317–328). Newbury Park, CA: Sage.

Greenhaus, J. H. (1987). *Career management.* Chicago: Dryden Press.

Greenhaus, J. H., & Beutell, N. J. (1985). Sources of conflict between work and family roles. *Academy of Management Review, 10,* 76–88.

Greenhaus, J. H., & Parasuraman, S. (1986). Vocational and organizational behavior, 1985: A review. *Journal of Vocational Behavior, 29,* 115–176.

Greenhaus, J. H., Parasuraman, S., & Wormley, W. M. (1990). Effects of race on organizational experiences, job performance evaluations, and career outcomes. *Academy of Management Journal, 33,* 64–86.

Greenleaf, R. K. (1977). *Servant leadership: A journey into the nature of legitimate power and greatness.* New York: Paulist Press.

Griscom, J. I., (1992) Women and power: Definition, dualism, and difference. *Psychology of Women Quarterly, 16,* 389–414.

Gruber, J. E. (1989). How women handle sexual harassment: A literature review. *Sociology and Social Research, 74,* 3–9.

Gruber, J. E. (1992). A typology of personal and environmental sexual harassment: Research and policy implications for the 1992. *Sex Roles, 26,* 447–464.

Gruber, J. E., & Bjorn, L. (1982). Blue collar blues: The sexual harassment of women autoworkers. *Work and Occupations, 9,* 271–298.

Gruber, J. E., & Bjorn, L. (1986). Women's responses to sexual harassment: An analysis of sociocultural, organizational and personal resource models. *Social Science Quarterly, 67,* 814–826.

Gruber, J. E., Smith, M., & Kauppinen-Toropainen, K. (1996). Sexual harassment types and severity: Linking research and policy. In M. S. Stockdale (Ed.), *Sexual harassment in the workplace: Perspectives, frontiers, and response strategies* (pp. 151–173). Thousand Oaks, CA: Sage.

Gruber, K. J., & White, J. W. (1986). Gender differences in the perceptions of self's and others' use of power strategies. *Sex Roles, 15,* 109–118.

Guelzow, M. S., Bird, G. W., & Koball, E. H. (1991). An exploratory path analysis of the stress process for dual-career men and women. *Journal of Marriage and the Family, 53,* 151–164.

Guitierres, S. E., Saenz, D., & Green B. (1992). *Occupational stress and health among Anglo and ethnic minority university employees.* Paper presented at the Second American Psychological Association, National Institute of Occupational Safety and Health Conference on Work Stress and Health, November, Washington, DC.

Gupta, N., Jenkins, Jr., G. D., & Beehr, T. A. (1983). Employee gender, gender similarity, and supervisor–subordinate cross-evaluations. *Sex Roles, 8,* 174–184.

Gutek, B. A. (1985). *Sex in the workplace: Impact of sexual behavior and harassment on women, men and organizations.* San Francisco: Josey-Bass.

Gutek, B. A. (1992). Understanding sexual harassment at work. *Notre Dame Journal of Law, Ethics and Public Policy, 6,* 335–358.

Gutek, B. A. (1993). Responses to sexual harassment. In S. Oskamp & M. Costanzo (Eds.), *Gender issues in contemporary society* (pp. 197–216). Newbury Park, CA: Sage.

Gutek, B. A. (1997). Sexual harassment policy initiatives. In W. O'Donohue (Ed.), *Sexual harassment: Theory, research, and treatment* (pp. 185–198). Boston: Allyn & Bacon.

Gutek, B. A., Cohen, A. G., & Konrad, A. M. (1990). Predicting social–sexual behavior at work: A contact hypothesis. *Academy of Management Journal, 33,* 560–577.

Gutek, B. A., & Koss, M. P. (1993). Changed women and changed organizations:

Consequences of and coping with sexual harassment. *Journal of Vocational Behavior, 42,* 28–48.

Gutek, B. A., & Larwood, L. (1987). Introduction: Women's careers are important and different. In B. A. Gutek & L. Larwood (Eds.), *Women's career development* (pp. 7–14). Newbury Park, CA: Sage.

Gutek, B. A., Larwood, L., & Stromberg, A. (1985). Women at work. In C. Cooper & I. Robertson (Eds.), *Review of industrial/organizational psychology* (Vol. 1). Chichester, UK: Wiley.

Gutek, B. A., & Morasch, B. (1982). Sex ratios, sex-role spillover and sexual harassment of women at work. *Journal of Social Issues, 38,* 55–74.

Gutek, B. A., Morasch, B., & Cohen, A. (1983). Interpreting social–sexual behavior in a work setting. *Journal of Vocational Behavior, 22,* 30–48.

Gutek, B. A., & O'Connor, M. (1995). The empirical basis for the reasonable woman standard. *Journal of Social Issues, 51,* 151–166.

Gutek, B. A., O'Connor, M., Melancon, R., & Greer, T. (1998, June). *Using realistic stimulus materials to study gender effects and the reasonable woman standard in hostile environment cases of harassment.* Paper presented at the 1998 meeting of the Society for the Psychological Study of Social Issues, Ann Arbor, MI.

Gutek, B. A., Repetti, R. L., & Silver, D. L. (1988). Nonwork roles and series at work. In C. L. Cooper & R. Payne (Eds.), *Causes, coping and consequences of stress at work* (pp. 141–174). Chichester, UK: Wiley.

Gutek, B. A., Searle, S., & Klepa, L. (1991). Rational versus gender role explanation for work–family conflict. *Journal of Applied Psychology, 76*(4), 560–572.

Gutmann, D. (1987). *Reclaimed powers: Towards a new psychology of men and women in later life.* New York: Basic Books.

Gwartney-Gibbs, P. (1988). Women's work experience and the rusty skills hypothesis. A reconceptualization and re-evaluation of evidence. In B. A. Gutek, A. H. Stromberg, & L. Larwood (Eds.), *Women and work: An annual review* (Vol. 3, pp. 169–188). Newbury Park, CA: Sage.

Haas, A. (1979). Male and female spoken language differences: Stereotypes and evidence. *Psychological Bulletin, 86,* 616–626.

Haas, L. (1990, December). Gender equality–social policy. *Journal of Family Issues, 11,* 401–423.

Haavio-Mannila, E., Kauppinen-Toropainen, K., & Kandolin, I. (1988). The effect of sex composition of the workplace on friendship, romance, and sex at work. In B. A. Gutek, A. H. Stromberg, & L. Larwood (Eds.), *Women and work: An annual review* (Vol. 3, pp. 123–137). Thousand Oaks, CA: Sage.

Hacker, B. C., & Hacker, S. (1987). Military institutions and the labor process: Noneconomic sources of technological change, women's subordination, and the organization of work. *Technology and Culture, 28,* 743–775.

Hackett, G., & Betz, N. E. (1981). A self-efficacy approach to the career development of women. *Journal of Vocational Behavior, 18,* 326–339.

Haenszel, W., Shimkin, M. B., & Miller, H. P. (1956). Tobacco smoking patterns in the United States. *Public Health Monograph, 45,* 1–105.

Hagenfeldt, K. (1991). Reproductive technologies, women's health, and career choices. In M. Frankenhaeuser, U. Lundberg, & M. Chesney (Eds.), *Women, work and health: Stress and opportunities* (pp. 207–223). New York: Plenum.

Hall, D. T. (1972). A model of coping with role conflict: The role behavior of college educated women. *Administrative Science Quarterly, 17,* 471–489.

Hall, D. T. (1976). *Careers in organizations.* Glenview, IL: Scott, Foresman.

Hall, D. T. (1990). Career development theory in organizations. In D. Brown, & L. Brooks (Eds.), *Career choice and development: Applying contemporary theories to practice* (pp. 422–454). San Francisco: Jossey-Bass.

Hall, D. T., & Parker, V. A. (1993, Summer). The role of workplace flexibility in managing diversity. *Organizational Dynamics, 22,* 5–18.

Hall, D. T., & Richter, J. (1988). Balancing work life and home life: What can organizations do to help? *Academy of Management Executives, 2,* 213–223.

Hall, R., & Sandler, B. (1982). *The classroom climate: A chilly one for women?* Washington, DC: Association of American Colleges, Project on the Status and Education of Women.

Hamilton, D. L. (1979). A cognitive–attributional analysis of stereotyping. *Advances in Experimental Psychology, 12,* 53–81.

Hamilton, M. C. (1991). Masculine bias in the attribution of personhood. *Psychology of Women Quarterly, 15,* 393–402.

Handy, C. (1996). The new language of organization and its implications for leaders. In F. Hesselbein, M. Goldsmith, & R. Beckhard (Eds.), *The leader of the future: New visions, strategies, and practices for the next era* (pp. 3–10). San Francisco: Jossey-Bass.

Hanisch, K. A. (1996). An integrated framework for studying the outcomes of sexual harassment: Consequences for individuals and organizations. In M. S. Stockdale (Ed.), *Sexual harassment: Perspectives, frontiers, and response strategies* (pp. 174–198). Thousand Oaks, CA: Sage.

Hansen, L. S. (1978). Promoting female growth through a career development curriculum. In L. S. Hansen & R. S. Rapoza (Eds.), *Career development and Counseling of women.* Springfield, IL: Thomas.

Hansen, R. D., & O'Leary, V. E. (1985). Sex-determined attributions. In V. E. O'Leary, R. K. Unger, & B. S. Wallston (Eds.), *Women, gender and social psychology* (pp. 67–100). Hillsdale, NJ: Lawrence Erlbaum Associates.

Hare-Mustin, R. T., & Maracek, J. (1988). The meaning of difference: Gender theory, post-modernism and psychology. *American Psychologist, 43,* 455–464.

Harless v. Duck, 14 FEP 1616 (1977).

Harris v. Forklift Systems, Inc., U.S. U10433, 1993.

Harris, R. J. (1981). Rewards of migration for income attainment, 1968–1973. *Social Science Quarterly, 62,* 275–293.

Harris, V. E. (1983). Cigarette smoking among successive birth cohorts of men and women in the United States during 1900–1980. *Journal of the National Cancer Institute, 71,* 473–479.

Harris-Kessler, A. (1985). The debate over equality for women in the work place: Recognizing differences. In L. Larwood, A. H. Stromberg, & B. A. Gutek (Eds.), *Women and work: An annual review* (Vol. 1, pp. 141–161). Beverly Hills, CA: Sage.

Harrison, A. D. (1989). Black working women. In R. L. Jones (Ed.), *Black adult development and aging*. Berkeley, CA: Cobb & Henry.

Hartmann, H. (1979). Capitalism, patriarchy and job segregation by sex. In Z. R. Eisenstein (Ed.), *Capitalist patriarchy and the case for socialist feminism*. New York: Monthly Review Press.

Hartmann, H. I., Kraut, R. E., & Tilly, L. A. (Eds.) (1986). Effects of technological change: Employment levels and occupational shifts. *Computer chips and paper clips: Technology and women's employment* (Vol. 1, pp. 62–126). Washington, DC: National Academy Press.

Haslett, B. J., Geis, F. L., & Carter, M. R. (1992). *The organizational woman: Power and paradox*. Norwood, NJ: Ablex.

Hatch, M. J. (1993). The dynamics of organizational culture. *Academy of Management Review, 18,* 657–693.

Haynes, S. G. (1991). Effect of job demands, job control, and new technologies in the health of employed women: A review. In M. Frankenhaeuser, V. Lundberg, & M. Chesney (Eds.), *Work, work and health: Stress and opportunities* (pp. 157–169). New York: Plenum.

Haynes, S. G., Eaker, E. D., & Feinleib, M. (1984). The effect of employment, family, and job stress on coronary heart disease patterns in women. In E. B. Gold (Ed.), *The changing risk of disease in women: An epidemiological approach* (pp. 37–48). Lexington, MA: Health.

Haynes, S. G., & Feinlieb, M. (1980). Women, work, and coronary heart disease: Prospective findings from the Framingham heart study. *American Journal of Public Health, 70,* 133–141.

Haynes, S. G., LaCroix, A. Z., & Lippin, T. (1987). The effect of high job demands and low control on the health of employed women. In J. C. Quick, R. Rasbhagat, J. Dalton & J. D. Quick (Eds.), *Work stress and health care* (pp. 93–110). New York: Praeger.

Healy, C. C. (1982). *Career development: Counseling definitions, through the life stages*. Boston: Allyn & Bacon.

Hearn, J., & Parkin, W. (1987). *Sex at work: The power and paradox of organization sexuality*. New York: St. Martin's Press.

Hearn, J., Sheppard, D. L., Tancred-Sheriff, P., & Burrell, G. (1989). *The sexuality of organization*. Newbury Park, CA: Sage.

Hedges, J. N., & Bemis, S. E. (1974). Sex stereotyping: Its decline in skilled trades. *Monthly Labor Review, 97,* 4–22.

Heilman, M. E. (1983). Sex bias in work settings: The lack of fit model. In B. M. Staw & L. L. Cummings (Eds.), *Research in organizational behavior* (Vol. 5, pp. 269–298). Greenwich, CT: JAI.

Heilman, M. E. (1984). Information as a deterrent against sex discrimination: The effects of applicant sex and information type on preliminary employment decisions. *Organizational Behavior and Human Performance, 33,* 174–186.

Heilman, M. E. (1994). Affirmative action: Some unintended consequences for working women. *Research in Organizational Behavior, 16,* 125–169.

Heilman, M. E., Block, C. J., Martell, R. F., & Simon, M. C. (1989). Has anything changed? Current characterizations of men, women, and managers. *Journal of Applied Psychology, 74*(6), 935–942.

Heilman, M. E., Block, C. J., & Stathatos, P. (1997). The affirmative action stigma of incompetence. *Academy of Management Journal, 40,* 603–625.

Heilman, M. E., Lucas, J. A., & Kaplow, S. R. (1990). Self-derogating consequences of sex-based preferential selection. The moderating role of initial self-confidence. *Organizational Behavior and Human Decision Processes, 46,* 202–216.

Heilman, M. E., Martell, R. F., & Simon, M. C. (1988). The vagaries of sex bias: Conditions regulating the undervaluation, equivaluation, and overvaluation of female job applicants. *Organizational Behavior and Human Decision Processes, 41,* 98–110.

Heilman, M. E., McCullough, W. F., & Gilbert, D. (1996). The other side of affirmative action: Reactions of nonbeneficiaries to sex-based preferential selection. *Journal of Applied Psychology, 81,* 346–357.

Heilman, M. E., Rivero, J. C., & Brett, J. F. (1991). Skirting the competence issue: Effects of sex-based preferential selection on task choices of women and men. *Journal of Applied Psychology, 76,* 99–105.

Heilman, M. E., & Saruwatari, L. R. (1979). When beauty is beastly: The effects of appearance and sex on evaluations of job applicants for managerial and nonmanagerial jobs. *Organizational Behavior and Human Performance, 23,* 360–372.

Heilman, M. E., Simon, M. C., & Repper, D. P. (1987). Intentionally favored, unintentionally harmed? The impact of gender-based preferential selection on self-perceptions and self-evaluations. *Journal of Applied Psychology, 72,* 62–68.

Heilman, M. E., & Stopeck, M. H. (1985). Being attractive, advantage or disadvantage? Performance-based evaluations and recommended personnel actions as a function of appearance, sex, and job type. *Organizational Behavior and Human Decision Processes, 35,* 202–215.

Hellriegel, D., Slocum, J. W., & Woodman, R. W. (1986). *Organizational behavior.* St. Paul, MN: West.

Hendrick, C., & Hendrick, S. (1983). *Liking, loving, and relating.* Monterey, CA: Brooks/Cole.

Henley, N. M. (1972). *Body politics: Power, sex, and nonverbal communication.* Englewood Cliffs, NJ: Prentice-Hall.

Henley, N. M. (1973–1974). Power, sex, and nonverbal communication. *Berkeley Journal of Sociology, 18,* 1–26.

Henley, N. M. (1989). Molehill or mountain: What we know and don't know about the masculine as generic English. In M. Crawford & M. Gentry (Eds.), *Gender and thought: Psychological perspectives* (pp. 59–78). New York: Springer-Verlag.

Henley, N. M., & Karamarae, C. (1991). Gender, power and noncommunication. In N. Coupland, H. Giles, & J. M. Wiemann (Eds.), *"Miscommunication" and problematic talk* (pp. 18–43). Newbury Park, CA: Sage.

Henley, N., & Thorne, B. (1977). Womanspeak and manspeak. Sex differences and sexism in communication, verbal and nonverbal. In A. G. Sargent (Ed.), *Beyond sex roles* (pp. 201–218). St. Paul, MN: West.

Henry, J. S., Stockdale, M. S., Hall, M., & Deniston, W. (1994). A formal mentoring program for junior female faculty: Description and evaluation. *Initiatives, 56*(2), 37–46.

Henwood, M., Rimmer, L., & Wicks, M. (1987). *Inside the family: Changing roles of men and women.* London: Family Policies Study Centre.

Hess, B. B., & Ferree, M. M. (1987). *Analyzing gender: A handbook of social science research.* Newbury Park, CA: Sage.

Hesselbein, F., Goldsmith, M., & Beckhard, R. (Eds.) (1996). *The leader of the future: New visions, strategies, and practices for the next era.* San Francisco: Jossey-Bass.

Higgins, C. A., & Duxbury, L. E. (1992). Work–family conflict: A comparison of dual-career and traditional-career men. *Journal of Organizational Behavior, 13,* 389–411.

Higgins, C. A., Duxbury, L. E., & Irving, R. H. (1992, February). Work–family conflict in the dual-career family. *Organizational Behavior and Human Decision Processes,* pp. 51–75.

Hiley, D. R. (1987). Power and values in corporate life. *Journal of Business Ethics, 6,* 343–353.

Hill, C. T., & Stull, D. E. (1981). Sex differences in effects of social and value similarity in same-sex friendship. *Journal of Personality and Social Psychology, 41,* 488–502.

Hilpert, F., Kramer, C., & Clark, R. A. (1975). Participants' perceptions of self and partner in mixed-sex dyads. *Central Status Speech Journal, 26,* 52–56.

Hinkin, T. R., & Schriesheim, C. A. (1990). Relationships between subordinate perceptions of supervisor influence tactics and attributed bases of supervisory power. *Human Relations, 43,* 221–237.

Hinkle, L. E. (1973). The concept of stress in the biological and social sciences. *Science, Medicine, and Man, 1,* 31–48.

Hoffman, L. W. (1986). Work, family and the child. In M. S. Pallak & R. O. Perloff (Eds.), *Psychology and work: Productivity, change, and employment* (pp. 173–220). Washington, DC: American Psychological Association.

Hoffman, L. W. (1989). Effects of maternal employment in the two parent family. *American Psychologist, 44,* 283–292.

Hofstede, G. (1984). Motivation, leadership, and organization: Do American theories apply abroad? In D. Kolb, I. Rubin, & J. McIntyre (Eds.), *Organizational psychology: Readings on human behavior in organizations* (pp. 309–330). Englewood Cliffs, NJ: Prentice-Hall.

Hole, J., & Levine, E. (1971). *Rebirth of feminism.* New York: Quadrangle.

Holmes, T. H., & Masuda, M. (1974). Life change and illness susceptibility. In B. S. Dohrenwend & B. P. Dohrenwend (Eds.), *Stressful life events: Their nature and effects* (pp. 45–72). New York: Wiley.

Hooks, J. M. (1947). *Women's occupations through seven decades* (U.S. Department of Labor Women's Bureau, Bull. 218). Washington, DC: U.S. Government Printing Office.

Horai, J. (1976). The effects of sensation seeking, physical attractiveness of stimuli, and exposure frequency on liking. *Social Behavior and Personality, 4,* 241–246.

Horn, P., & Horn, J. (1982). *Sex in the office: Power and passion in the workplace.* Reading, MA: Addison-Wesley.

House, E. A. (1986). Sex role orientation and mental satisfaction in dual and one provider couples. *Sex Roles, 14,* 245–259.

House, R. J. (1977). A 1976 theory of charismatic leadership. In J. G. Hunt & L. L. Larson (Eds.), *Leadership: The cutting edge.* Carbondale: Southern Illinois University Press.

House, R. J., & Mitchell, T. R. (1974, Fall). Path-goal theory of leadership. *Contemporary Business, 3,* 81–98.

Hudson, J. W., & Henze, L. S. (1969). Campus values in male selection: A replication. *Journal of Marriage and the Family, 31,* 772–775.

Hughes, D., Galinsky, E., & Morris, A. (1992). The effects of job characteristics or marital quality: Specifying linking mechanism. *Journal of Marriage and the Family, 54,* 31–42.

Hulin, C. L., Fitzgerald, L. F., & Drasgow, F. (1996). Organizational influences on sexual harassment. In M. S. Stockdale (Ed.), *Sexual harassment in the workplace: Perspectives, frontiers, and response strategies* (pp. 127–150). Thousand Oaks, CA: Sage.

Huston, T. L. (1973). Ambiguity of acceptance, social desirability, and dating choice. *Journal of Experimental Social Psychology, 9,* 32–42.

Huston, T. L. (Ed.) (1974). *Foundations of interpersonal attraction.* New York: Academic Press.

Hutt, C., & Ounsted, C. (1966). The biological significance of gaze aversion with particular inference to the syndrome of infantile autism. *Behavioral Science, 11,* 346–356.

Hyde, J. S. (1990). Meta-analysis and the psychology of gender differences. *Signs: Journal of Women in Culture and Society, 16,* 55–73.

Hyde, J. S. (1985). *Half the human experience: The psychology of women.* Lexington, MA: Health.

Hymes, D. (1972). Models of the interaction of language and social setting. In J. J. Gumpebz & D. Hymes (Eds.), *Directions in socio-linguistics: The ethnopathy of communication* (pp. 35–71). New York: Holt, Rinehart & Winston.

Ibarra, H. (1992). Homophily and differential returns: Sex differences in network structure and access in an advertising firm. *Administrative Science Quarterly, 37,* 422–447.

Iglehart, A. P. (1979). *Married women and work: 1957 and 1976.* Lexington, MA: Lexington, Heath.

Ilgen, D. R. (1990). Health issues at work: Industrial–organizational psychology opportunities. *American Psychologist, 45,* 273–283.

Ilgen, D. R., & Youtz, M. A. (1986). Factors affecting the evaluation and development of minorities in organizations. In K. M. Rowland & G. R. Ferris (Eds.), *Research in personnel and human resource management* (Vol. 4, pp. 307–337). Greenwich, CT: JAI.

Ironson, G. (1992). Work, job stress and health. In S. Zedeck (Eds.), *Work, families and organizations* (pp. 33–69). San Francisco: Jossey-Bass.

Ishii-Kuntz, M., & Coltrane, S. (1992). Predicting the sharing of household labor:

Are parenting and housework distinct? *Sociological Perspectives, 35,* 629–647.

Izraeli, D. N., & Izraeli, D. (1985). Sex effects in evaluating leaders: A replication study. *Journal of Applied Psychology, 70,* 540–546.

Jackson, B. (1978). *Stages of Black identity development.* Unpublished manuscript, University of Massachusetts at Amherst, School of Education.

Jackson, L. A. (1983a). The influence of sex, physical attractiveness, sex role, and occupational sex-linkage on perceptions of occupational suitability. *Journal of Applied Social Psychology, 13,* 31–44.

Jackson, L. A. (1983b). Gender, physical attractiveness and sex role in occupational treatment discrimination: The influence of trait and role assumptions. *Journal of Applied Social Psychology, 13,* 443–458.

Jackson, L. A., Gardner, P. D., & Sullivan, L. A. (1992). Explaining gender differences in self-pay expectations: Social comparison standards and perceptions of fair pay. *Journal of Applied Psychology, 77,* 651–663.

Jackson, S. E. (1992). *Diversity in the workplace: Human resource initiatives.* New York: Guilford.

Jacobson, S. K., & Berger, C. R. (1974). Communication and justice: Defendant attributes and their effect on the severity of his sentence. *Speech Monographs, 41,* 282–286.

Jago, A. G., & Vroom, V. H. (1982). Sex differences in the incidence and evaluation of participative leader behavior. *Journal of Applied Psychology, 67,* 776–783.

James, K. (1994). Social identity, work stress, and minority workers health. In G. Puryear Keita & S. L. Sauter (Eds.), *Stress in the 90's: A changing workforce in a changing workplace* (pp. 127–146). Washington, DC: American Psychological Association.

James, S. A., La Croix, A. Z., Kleinbaum, D. G., & Strogatz, D. S. (1984). John Henryism and blood pressure differences among Black men: II. The role of occupational stressors. *Journal of Behavioral Medicine, 7,* 259–275.

Jamison, K. (1983). Managing sexual attraction in the workplace. *Personnel Administrator, 28*(8), 45–51.

Jaroff, L. (1996). Assembly-line sexism? Charges of abusing women—and angry denials—rock a Midwestern Mitsubishi auto plant. *Time, 147*(19), 56–60.

Jensen, A. (1980). *Bias in mental testing.* New York: The Free Press.

Jenson v. Eveleth Taconite Co., 824 F. Supp. 847, D. Minn. (1993).

Jick, H., Porter, J. & Morrison, A. A. (1977). Relation between smoking and age of natural menopause. *Lancet, 325 i,* 1354.

Jick, T. D., & Mitz, L. F. (1985). Sex differences in work stress. *Academy of Management Review, 10,* 408–420.

Johnson, B. J., & Waldman, E. (1983). Most who maintain families receive poor labor market returns. *Monthly Labor Review, 106,* 30–34.

Johnson, C. B., Stockdale, M. S., & Saal, F. E. (1991). Persistence of men's misperceptions of friendly cues across a variety of interpersonal encounters. *Psychology of Women Quarterly, 15,* 463–475.

Johnson, F. L. (1983). Political and pedagogical implications of attitudes towards women's language. *Communication Quarterly, 31,* 133–138.

Johnson, J. V. (1986). *The impact of workplace social support, job demands and work control upon cardiovascular disease in Sweden* (Report No. 1). Stockholm: Division of the Social Psychology of Work, Department of Psychology, University of Stockholm.

Johnson, P. (1976). Women and power: Toward a theory of effectiveness. *Journal of Social Issues, 32,* 99–110.

Johnson, P. B., & Goodchild, J. D. (1976). How women get their way. *Psychology Today, 10,* 69–70.

Johnson, W. B., & Packer, A. H. (1987). *Workforce 2000: Work and workers for the twenty-first century.* Indianapolis, IN: Hudson Institute.

Jones, E. E. & Pittman, T. S. (1982). Toward a general theory of strategic self-presentation. In J. Suls (Ed.). *Psychological perspectives on the self.* Hillsdale, NJ: Erlbaum.

Jones, J. W. (1984). A cost evaluation for stress management. *EAP Digest, 1,* 34–39.

Josefowitz, N. (1982). Sexual relationships at work: Attraction, tranference, coercion or strategy. *Personnel Administrator, 27*(3), 91–96.

Kacmar, K. M., & Hochwarter, W. A. (1992, August). *Rationalizing inconsistent findings: A field investigation of demographic effects on interview outcomes.* Paper presented at the National Academy of Management Meetings, August.

Kahn, A. (1984). The power war: Male response to power loss under equality. *Psychology of Women Quarterly, 8,* 234–247.

Kahn, R. L. (1972). The justification of violence: Social problems and social resolutions. *Journal of Social Issues, 28,* 155–175.

Kahn, R. L., & Byosiere, P. (1992). Stress in organizations (pp. 571–650). In M. D. Dunnette & L. M. Hough (Eds.). *Handbook of Industrial and Organizational Psychology.* Palo Alto, CA: Consulting Psychologist Press, Inc.

Kane, T. R., Suls, J., & Tedeschi, J. T. (1977). Humour as a tool of social interaction. In A. J. Chapman, & H. C. Foot (Eds.), *It's a funny thing, humor* (pp. 13–16). Oxford, UK: Pergamon.

Kanter, R. M. (1996). World-class leaders: The power of partnering. In F. Hesselbein, M. Goldsmith, & R. Beckhard (Eds.), *The leader of the future: New visions, strategies, and practices for the next era* (pp. 89–98). San Francisco, Jossey-Bass.

Kanter, R. M. (1975). Women and the structure of organizations: Explorations in theory and behavior. In M. Millman & R. M. Kanter (Eds.), *Another voice: Feminist perspectives in social life and social sciences.* Garden City, NY: Anchor/Doubleday.

Kanter, R. M. (1977a). *Men and women of the corporation.* New York: Basic Books.

Kanter, R. M. (1977b). Some effects of proportions on group life: Skewed sex ratios and responses to token women. *American Journal of Sociology, 82,* 965–990.

Kanter, R. M. (1977c). *Work and family in the United States: A critical review and agenda for research and policy:* New York: Russell Sage Foundation.

Kaplan, R. M. (1978). Is beauty talent? Sex interaction in the attractiveness halo effect. *Sex Roles, 4,* 195–204.

Kaplan, R. (1991). *Beyond ambition.* San Francisco: Jossey-Bass.

Karasek, R. A. (1979). Job demands, job decision latitude and mental strain. *Administrative Science Quarterly, 24,* 285–308.

Karasek, R., & Theorell, T. (1990). *Healthy work: Stress, productivity, and the reconstruction of working life.* New York: Basic Books.

Karasek, R., Lindell, J., & Gardell, B. (1981). *Patterns of health in association with job and non-job stressors for Swedish white collar workers.* Working paper, Columbia University, New York.

Kaslow, F. W., & Schwartz, L. L. (1978). Self-perceptions of the attractive, successful female professional. *Intellect, 106,* 313–315.

Kay, B., & Neeley, J. N. (1982). Sexuality and aging: A review of current literature. *Sexuality and Disability, 5*(1), 38–46.

Keele, R. L., Buckner, K., & Bushnell, S. J. (1987). Formal mentoring programs are no panacea. *Management Review, 76,* 67–68.

Kelman, H. C. (1961). Processes of opinion change. *Public Opinion Quarterly, 25,* 57–78.

Kenkel, W. T. (1963). Observational studies of husband–wife interaction in family decision-making. In M. Sussman (Ed.), *Sourcebook in marriage and the family* (pp. 144–156). Boston: Houghton Mifflin.

Kerr, S., & Jermier, J. M. (1978). Substitutes for leadership. Their meaning and measurement. *Organizational Behavior and Human Performance, 22,* 375–403.

Kessler, R. C., & McRae, J. A. (1982). The effects of wives' employment on the mental health of married men and women. *American Sociological Review, 47,* 216–227.

Kessler, R. C., Price, R. H., & Wortman, C. B. (1985). Social factors in psychopathology. Stress, social support, and coping processes. *Annual Review of Psychology, 36,* 531–572.

Keyes, R. (1980). *The height of your life.* Boston: Little, Brown.

Kilbourne, B. S., & England, P. (1997). Occupational skill, gender and earnings. In P. Dubeck & K. Borman (Eds.), *Woman and work: A handbook* (pp. 68–70). Garland: New York.

Kimble, C. E., Yoshikawa, J. C., & Zehr, H. S. (1981). Vocal and verbal assertiveness in same-sex and mixed-sex groups. *Journal of Psychology, 40,* 1047–1054.

King, M. C. (1975, June). Oppression and power: Unique status of the Black woman in the American political system. *Social Science Quarterly, 56,* 116–128.

Kingston, P. W. (1988). The work and family connection. *Journal of Social Behavior and Personality, 3,* 55–60.

Kipnis, D. (1974). Inner direction, other direction, and achievement motivations. *Human Development, 17,* 321–343.

Kipnis, D. (1984). The use of power in organizations and in interpersonal settings. In S. Oskamp (Ed.), *Applied Social Psychology Annual, 5,* 179–210. Beverly Hills, CA: Sage.

Kipnis, D. (1990). *Technology and power.* New York: Springer-Verlag.

Kipnis, D., & Consentino, J. (1969). Use of leadership powers in industry. *Journal of Applied Psychology, 53,* 460–466.

Kipnis, D., & Schmidt, S. M. (1982). *Profile of organizational influence strategies.* San Diego, CA: University Associates.

Kipnis, D., & Schmidt, S. M. (1983). An influence perspective on bargaining within organizations. In M. H. Bazerman & R. J. Lewicki (Eds.), *Negotiating in organizations.* Beverly Hills, CA: Sage.

Kipnis, D., & Schmidt, S. M. (1988). Upward-influence styles: Relationship with performance evaluations, salary, and stress. *Administrative Science Quarterly, 33,* 528–542.

Kipnis, D., Schmidt, S. M., & Wilkinson, I. (1980). Interorganizational influence tactics: Explorations in getting one's own way. *Journal of Applied Psychology, 65,* 440–452.

Kizer, W. M. (1987). *The healthy workplace: A blueprint for corporate action.* New York: Wiley.

Kleck, R. E., & Rubenstein, C. (1975). Physical attractiveness, perceived attitude similarity, and interpersonal attraction in an opposite-sex encounter. *Journal of Personality and Social Psychology, 31,* 107–114.

Kleck, R. E., Richardson, S. A., & Ronald, L. (1974). Physical appearance cues and interpersonal attraction in children. *Child Development, 43,* 305–310.

Knaub, P. K. (1986). Growing up in a dual career family! The children's perceptions. *Human Relations, 35,* 431–437.

Komarovsky, M. (1962). *Blue collar marriage.* New York: Vintage.

Komives, S. R. (1991). Gender differences in the relationship of hall directors' transformational and transactional leadership and achieving styles. *Journal of College Student Development, 32,* 155–165.

Korabik, K. (1981). Changes in physical attractiveness and interpersonal attraction. *Basic and Applied Social Psychology, 2,* 59–65.

Korabik, K. (1990). Androgyny and leadership style. *Journal of Business Ethics, 9,* 9–18.

Korabik, K., & McDonald, L. M. (1991). Sources of stress and ways of coping among male and female managers. *Journal of Social Behavior and Personality, 6,* 1–14.

Korman, A. K. (1974). Contingency approaches to leadership: An overview. In J. G. Hunt & L. L. Larson (Eds.), *Contingency approaches to leadership.* Carbondale: Southern Illinois University Press.

Korsmeyer, C. (1981). The hidden joke: Generic uses of masculine terminology. In M. Vetterling-Braggin (Ed.), *Sexist language: A modern philosophical analysis* (pp. 116–131). Totawa, NJ: Littlefield, Adams.

Koslowsky, M., & Schwarzwald, J. (1993). The use of power tactics to gain compliance: Testing aspects of Raven's (1988) theory of conflictual situations. *Social Behavior and Personality, 21,* 135–144.

Koss, M. P. (1990). Changed lives: The psychological impact of sexual harassment. In M. Paludi (Ed.), *Ivory power: Sexual harassment on campus.* Albany, NY: SUNY Press.

Kossek, E. E. (1990). Diversity in child care assistance needs: Employee problems, preferences, and work related outcomes. *Personnel Psychology, 43,* 769–791.

Kossek, E. E., & Grace, P. (1991). Taking a strategic view of employee child care assistance: A cost–benefit model. *Human Resource Planning, 13,* 189–202.

Kossek, E. E., & Nichol, V. (1992). Effects of on-site child care on employee attitudes and performance. *Personnel Psychology, 45,* 485–509.

Kotler, P., & Wingard, D. L. (1989). The effect of occupational, marital, and parental roles on morality: The Alameda County Study. *American Journal of Public Health, 79,* 607–612.

Kouzes, J. M., & Posner, B. Z. (1996). Seven lessons for leading the voyage to the future. In F. Hesselbein, M. Goldsmith, & R. Beckhard (Eds.), *The leader of the future: New visions, strategies, and practices for the next era* (pp. 99–110). San Francisco: Jossey-Bass.

Kraft, P. (1984). *Computer programming. Do males and females do the same work?* Paper presented at the Office of Technology Assessment Symposium on the Impacts of Office Automation and Computer Mediated Work on the Quality of Worklife, Washington, DC.

Kram, K. E. (1983). Phases of the mentor relationship. *Academy of Management Journal, 26,* 608–625.

Kram, K. E. (1985). *Mentoring at work.* Glenview, IL: Scott, Foresman.

Kram, K., & Isabella, L. (1985). Mentoring alternatives: The role of peer relationships in career development. *Academy of Management Journal, 28,* 110–132.

Kramer, C. (1974a). Folklinguistics. *Psychology Today, 8,* 82–85.

Kramer, C. (1974b). Stereotypes of woman's speech: The word from cartoons. *Journal of Popular Culture, 8,* 624–630.

Kramer, C. (1974c). Women's speech: Separate but unequal? *Quarterly Journal of Speech, 60,* 14–24.

Kramer, C. (1977). Perceptions of female and male speech. *Language and Speech, 20,* 151–161.

Kramer, R. M. (1978, April 5–8). *Some determinants of commitment levels in premarital relationship.* Paper presented at the Annual Conference of the Rocky Mountain Psychological Association, Denver, CO.

Kramarae, C. (1974, February). Women's speech: Separate but unequal? *Quarterly Journal of Speech, 60,* 14–24.

Kramerae, C. (1978). Women's and men's ratings of their own and ideal speech. *Communication Quarterly, 26*(2), 271.

Kramarae, C. (1980). Introduction. In C. L. Berryman & V. A. Eman (Eds.), *Communication, language, and sex* (pp. 1–7). Rowley, MA: Newbury House.

Kramarae, C. (1981). *Women and men speaking: Frameworks for analysis.* Rowley, MA: Newbury House.

Kramarae, C. (1982). Gender: How she speaks. In E. B. Ryan & H. Giles (Eds.), *Attitudes towards language variation: Social and applied contexts* (pp. 84–98). London: Edward Arnold.

Kramerae, C., Thorne, B., & Henley, N. (1978). Review essay: Perspectives on language and communication. *Signs, 3,* 638–651.

Kravitz, D. A., Harrison, D. A., Turner, M. E., Levine, E. L., Chaves, W., Brannick, M. T., Denning, D. L., Russell, C. J., & Conrad, M. A. (1997). *Affirmative action: A review of psychological and behavioral research.* Bowling Green, OH: Society for Industrial and Organizational Psychology.

Kravitz, D. A., & Platania, J. (1993). Attitudes and beliefs about affirmative action: Effects of target and/or respondent sex and ethnicity. *Journal of Applied Psychology, 78,* 928–938.

Krokoff, L. J. (1991). Job distress is no laughing matter in marriage, or is it? *Journal of Social and Personal Relationships, 8,* 5–25.

Kurth, S. B. (1970). Friendships and friendly relations. In G. J. McCall, M. M. McCall, N. K. Denzin, G. D. Suttles, & S. B. Kurth (Eds.), *Social relationships* (pp. 136–170). Chicago: Aldine.

Labov, W. (1972). *Sociolingusitic patterns.* Philadelphia: University of Pennsylvania Press.

Lach, D. H., & Gwartney-Gibbs, P. A. (1993). Sociological perspectives on sexual harassment and workplace dispute resolution. *Journal of Vocational Behavior, 42,* 102–115.

Lakoff, R. (1973). Language and woman's place. *Language in Society, 2,* 45–79.

Lakoff, R. (1975). *Language and woman's place.* New York: HarperCollins.

LaCroix, A. Z., & Haynes, S. G. (1987). Gender differences in the health effects of workplace roles. In R. C. Barnett, L. Brener, & G. K. Baruch (Eds.), *Gender and stress* (pp. 96–121). New York: Free Press.

LaFrance, M. (1992). Gender and interruptions: Individual infraction or violation of the social order? *Psychology of Women Quarterly, 16,* 497–512.

Lambert, S. J. (1992). The combined effects of job and family characteristics or the job satisfaction, job involvement, and intrinsic motivation of men and women workers. *Journal of Organizational Behavior, 12,* 341–363.

Landrine, H. (1985). Race × Class stereotypes of women. *Sex Roles, 13*(1/2), 65–75.

Landy, D., & Sigall, H. (1974). Beauty is talent: Task evaluation as a function of the performer's physical attractiveness. *Journal of Personality and Social Psychology, 29,* 299–304.

Larwood, L., & Gattiker, V. E. (1987). A comparison of the career paths used by successful women and men. In B. A. Gutek & L. Larwood (Eds.), *Women's career development* (pp. 129–156). Newbury Park, CA: Sage.

Larwood, L., & Gutek, B. A. (1987). Working toward a theory of women's career development. In B. A. Gutek & L. Larwood (Eds.), *Women's career development* (pp. 170–183). Newbury Park, CA: Sage.

Larwood, L, & Wood, M. M. (1977). *Women in management.* Lexington, MA: D.C. Heath.

Latack, J. C. (1989). Work, stress and careers: A preventative approach to maintaining organizational health. In M. B. Arthur, D. T. Hall, & B. S. Lawrence (Eds.), *Handbook of career theory* (pp. 252–274). Cambridge, UK: Cambridge University Press.

Laws, J. L. (1979). *The second X: Sex role and social role.* New York: Elsevier.

Lazarus, R. S. (1966). *Psychological stress and the coping stress.* New York: McGraw-Hill.

Lazarus, R. S., & Folkman, S. (1984). *Stress, coping, and adaptation.* New York: Springer-Verlag.

Lazarus, R. S., & Launier, R. (1978). Stress related transactions between person and environment. In L. A. Pervin & M. Lewis (Eds.), *Perspectives in international psychology* (pp. 189–217). New York: Plenum.

Leahy, R. L., & Shirk, S. R. (1984). The development of classificatory skills and sex-trait stereotypes in children. *Sex Roles, 10,* 281–292.

Leavitt, H. J., & Lipman-Blumen, J. (1980, Summer). A case for the relational manager. *Organizational Dynamics, 20,* 27–41.

Lengnick-Hall, M. L. (1995). Sexual harassment research: A methodological critique. *Personnel Psychology, 48,* 841–864.

Lerner, M. J., & Karabenick, S. A. (1974). Physical attractiveness, body attitudes and self-concept in late adolescents. *Journal of Youth and Adolescence, 3,* 307–316.

Lerner, R. M., Orlos, J. B., & Knapp, J. R. (1976). Physical attractiveness, physical effectiveness and self-concept in late adolescence. *Adolescence, 11,* 313–326.

Lever, J. (1978). Sex differences in the complexity of children's play and games. *American Sociological Review, 43,* 471–483.

Levinson, D. J. (1986). A conception of adult development. *American Psychologist, 41,* 3–13.

Levitin, T., Quinn, R. R., & Staines, G. L. (1971). Sex discrimination against the American working woman. *American Behavioral Scientist, 15,* 237–254.

Levy, P. E., & Baumgardner, A. H. (1991). Effects of self esteem and gender on goal choice. *Journal of Organizational Behavior, 12,* 529–541.

Lewis, A., & Cooper, C. L. (1988). The transition to parenthood in dual earner couples. *Psychological Medicine, 18,* 477–486.

Lewis, K. E., & Bierly, M. (1990). Toward a profile of the female voter: Sex differences in perceived physical attractiveness and competence of political candidates. *Sex Roles, 22,* 1–12.

Lewis, S. N. C., & Cooper, C. L. (1988). Stress in dual earners families. In B. A. Gutek, A. H. Stromberg, & L. Larwood (Eds.), *Women and work: An annual review* (Vol. 3, pp. 139–168). Newbury Park, CA: Sage.

Li, P. S., & Currie, D. (1992). Gender differences in work interruptions as unequal effects of marriage and childrearing: Findings from a Canadian national survey. *Journal of Comparative Family Studies, XXIII,* 217–229.

Likert, R. (1967). *The human organization: Its management and value.* New York: McGraw-Hill.

Littlepage, G. E., Nixon, C. T., & Gibson, C. R. (1992). Influence strategies used in meetings. *Journal of Social Behavior and Personality, 7,* 529–538.

Lindesmith, A., Strauss, A. L., & Denzin, N. K. (1977). *Social psychology.* New York: Holt, Rinehart & Winston.

Lipmen-Blumen, J. (1984). *Gender roles and power.* Englewood Cliffs, NJ: Prentice-Hall.

Lipman-Blumen, J. (1996). *The connective edge: Leading in an interdependent world.* San Francisco: Jossey-Bass.

Lipman-Blumen, J., Handley-Isaksen, A., & Leavitt, H. J. (1983). Achieving styles in men and women: A model, an instrument, and some findings. In J. T. Spence (Ed.), *Achievement and achievement motives: Psychological and sociological approaches* (pp. 147–204). San Francisco: Freeman.

Lips, H. M. (1986). *Self-schema theory and gender-related behaviors: Research on some correlates of university women's participation in mathematics science and athletic activities.* (ERIC Document Reproduction Service No.

ED 263517 ERIC Clearinghouse on Counseling and Personnel Services: Washington, DC.

Lips, H. M. (1988). *Sex and gender: An introduction.* Mountain View, CA: Mayfield.

Lips, H. M. (1991). *Women, men, and power.* Mountain View, CA: Mayfield.

Lobel, S. A. (1993). Sexuality at work: Where do we go from here? *Journal of Vocational Behavior, 42,* 136–152.

Lobel, S. A., Quinn, R. E., St. Clair, L., & Warfield, A. (1994). Love without sex: The impact of organizational intimacy between men and women at work. *Organizational Dynamics, 23*(1), 5–16.

Lockheed, M. E., & Hall, K. P. (1976). Conceptualizing sex as a status characteristic: Applications to leadership training strategies. *Journal of Social Issues, 32*(3), 111–123.

Locksley, A., Borgida, E., Brekke, N., & Hepburn, C. (1980). Sex stereotypes and social judgement. *Journal of Applied Psychology, 39,* 821–831.

Lodahl, T. M., & Kejner, M. (1965). The definition and measurement of job involvement. *Journal of Applied Psychology, 49,* 24–33.

Loden, M. (1985). *Feminine leadership or how to succeed in business without being one of the boys.* Toronto, ON: Ca. Time Books.

Loden, M., & Rosener, J. B. (1991). *Workplace America! Managing employee diversity as a vital resource* Homewood, IL: Irwin.

Lord, R. G., & Maher, K. J. (1991). *Leadership and information processing linking perceptions and performance.* London: Unwin Hyman.

Lorence, J. (1987). A test of "gender" and "job" models of sex differences in job involvement. *Social Forces, 66,* 121–143.

Lott, B. (1981). A feminist critique of androgyny: Toward elimination of gender attributions for learned behavior. In C. Mayo & N. Henley (Eds.), *Gender and nonverbal behavior* (pp. 171–180). New York: Springer Verlag.

Lott, B. (1987). Sexist discrimination as distancing behavior: I. A laboratory demonstration. *Psychology of Women Quarterly, 11,* 47–58.

Lowe, K. B., Kroeck, K. G., & Sivasubramaniam, N. (1995, April). *Effectiveness correlates of transformational and transactional leadership: A meta-analytic review.* Paper presented at the 10th Annual Meeting of the Society for Industrial and Organizational Psychology, Orlando, FL.

Lowenthal, M. F., Thurnber, M., & Chiriboga, D. (1975). *Four stages of life: Comparative study of women and men facing transitions.* San Francisco: Jossey-Bass.

Loy, P. H., & Stewart, L. P. (1984). The extent and effects of the sexual harassment of working women. *Sociological Focus, 17,* 31–43.

Lubman, S. (1996). 'Ebonics' has roots in black pride movement. *Knight-Ridder/ Tribune News Service,* Dec. 22, 1996, p1222K5680.

Lundberg, V., deChateau, P., Winberg, J., & Frankenhaeuser, M. (1981). Catecholamide and cortisol excretion patterns in three-year-old children and their patients. *Journal of Human Stress, 7,* 3–11.

Luthans, F. (1998). *Organizational behavior* (8th ed.). Boston: Irwin-McGraw Hill.

Maas, H. S., & Kuypers, G. N. (1974). *From thirty to seventy: A forty-year longitudinal study of changing life styles and personal development.* San Francisco: Jossey-Bass.

Maccoby, E. E., & Jacklin, C. N. (1974). *The psychology of sex differences.* Stanford, CA: Stanford University Press.

Mack, T. (1998, May 18). High finance with a touch of theater. *Forbes,* pp. 140.

Mackay, C., & Cox, T. (1984). Occupational stress associated with visual display unit operation. In B. Pierce (Ed.), *Health hazards of UDTs* (pp. 137–144). New York: Wiley.

Mackie, M. (1987). *Constructing women and men: Gender socialization.* Toronto, ON: Holt, Rinehart & Winston of Canada.

MacKinnon, C. A. (1979). *Sexual harassment of working women.* New Haven, CT: Yale University Press.

Madden, H. F. (1985). The persistence of pay differentials: The economics of sex discrimination. In L. Larwood, A. Stromberg, & B. Gutek (Eds.), *Women and work: An annual review* (Vol. 1, pp. 76–114). Greenwich, CT: JAI.

Madrid, D. (1994). Stress Hitting More Workers, Gannett News Service, 12-29-94. [www.elibrary.com/s/eduma . . . 9624@library_gedtype=OnO&dinst=].

Magid, R. Y. (1983). *Childcare initiatives for working parents: Why employers get involved.* New York: American Management Association.

Magnus, K., Matroos, A. W., & Strackee, J. (1983). The self-employed and the self-driven: Two coronary prone sub-populations from the Zeist study. *American Journal of Epidemiology, 118,* 799–805.

Mai-Dalton, R. R., & Sullivan, J. J. (1981). The effects of manager's sex on the assignment to a challenging or dull task and reasons for the choice. *Academy of Management Journal, 24,* 603–618.

Mainiero, L. A. (1986). A review and analysis of power dynamics in organizational romance. *Academy of Management Review, 11,* 750–762.

Mainiero, L. A. (1989). *Office romance: Love power, and sex in the workplace.* New York: Rawson.

Mandler, G. (1984). *Mind and body.* New York: Norton.

Mann, R. D. (1959). A review of the relationship between personality and performance in small groups. *Psychological Bulletin, 56,* 241–270.

Markham, W. T. (1987). Sex, relocation and occupational advancement: The "real cruncher" for women. In A. H. Stromberg, L. Larwood, & B. A. Gutek (Eds.), *Women and work: An annual review* (Vol. 2, pp. 207–231). Newbury Park, CA: Sage.

Maroldo, G. K. (1982). Shyness and love on a college campus. *Perceptual and Motor Skills, 55,* 819–824.

Marshall, J. (1984). *Women managers: Travellers in a male world.* Chichester, UK: Wiley.

Marshall, R., & Paulin, B. (1987). Employment and earnings of women: Historical perceptive. In K. S. Koziara, M. H. Moskow, & L. D. Tanner (Eds.), *Working women: Past, present and future* (pp. 1–36). Washington, DC: Bureau of National Affairs, Industrial Relations Research Association.

Martell, R. F. (1996). Sex discrimination at work. In P. Dubeck & K. Borman (Eds.), *Women and work: A handbook* (pp. 329–331). New York: Garland.

Martell, R. F. (1998, June). *When just a little gender bias hurts women a lot: A computer simulation.* Paper presented at the Society for the Psychological Study of Social Issues Annual Convention, Ann Arbor, MI.

Martell, R. F., Lane, D. M., & Emrich, C. G. (1996). Male–female differences: A computer simulation. *American Psychologist, 51,* 157–158.

Martin, C. L., & Halverson, C. F. (1983). Gender constancy: A methodological and theoretical analysis. *Sex Roles, 1,* 775–790.

Martin, J., Price, R. L., Bies, R. J., & Powers, M. E. (1987). Now that I can have it, I'm not sure I want it. In B. A. Gutek & L. Larwood (Eds.), *Women's career development* (pp. 42–65). Newbury Park, CA: Sage.

Martindale, M. (1991). *Sexual harassment in the military: 1988* (Report). Arlington, VA: Defense Manpower Data Center.

Martinko, M. J., & Gardner, W. L. (1987). The leader/member attribution process. *Academy of Management Review, 12,* 235–249.

Marvelle, K., & Green, S. K. (1980). Physical attractiveness and sex bias in hiring decisions for two types of jobs. *Journal of the National Association for Deans, Administrators, and Counselors, 44,* 3–6.

Maschewsky, W. (1982). The relation between stress and myocardial infarction. *Social Science and Medicine, 16,* 455–462.

Mathes, E. W. (1975). The effects of physical attractiveness and anxiety on heterosexual attraction over a series of five encounters. *Journal of Marriage and the Family, 37,* 769–773.

Matteson, M. T., & Ivancevich, J. M. (1987). *Controlling work stress: Effective human resource and management strategies.* San Francisco: Jossey-Bass.

Matteson, M. T., & Ivancevich, J. M. (1988). Health promotion at work. In C. L. Cooper & I. Robertson (Eds.), *International review of industrial and organizational psychology* (pp. 279–306). New York: Wiley.

Maume, D. J., Jr. (1991). Child-care expenditures and women's employment turnover. *Social Forces, 70,* 495–508.

Maupin, R. J. (1993). How can women's lack of upward mobility in accounting organizations be explained? *Group and Organization Management, 18,* 132–152.

Maurer, T. J., & Taylor, M. A. (1991, April). *How important is rater sex in sex bias in evaluation?* Paper presented at the annual meeting of the Society of Industrial and Organizational Psychology, St. Louis, MO.

Mayer, J. (1983, May 25). TV anchor women never die, they get replaced by the young. *Wall Street Journal,* pp. 1, 21.

McAdams, D. P. (1982). Experiences in intimacy and power: Relationships between social motives and autobiographical memory. *Journal of Personality and Social Psychology, 42,* 292–302.

McAdams, D. P., & Losoff, M. (1984). Friendship motivation in fourth and sixth graders: A thematic analysis. *Journal of Social and Personal Relationships, 1,* 11–27.

McArthur, L. Z. (1982). Judging a book by its cover: A cognitive analysis of the relationship between physical appearance and stereotyping. In A. Hastorf & A. M. Isen (Eds.), *Cognitive social psychology.* New York: Elsevier.

McBroom, W. H. (1987). Changes in sex-role expectations: A five year longitudinal comparison. *Sex Roles, 11,* 583–592.

McCall, W. W., Jr., Lombardo, M. M., & Morrison, A. M. (1988). *The lessons of experience: How successful executives develop on the job.* Lexington, MA: Lexington.

McCleland, D. C., Atkinson, G. W., Clark, R. A., & Lowell, E. L. (1953). *The achievement motive.* New York: Appleton-Century-Crofts.

McClelland, D. C. (1975). *Power: The inner experience.* New York: Irvington.

McDonnell Douglas Corp. v. Green, 411 U.S. (1973).

McGhee, P. E. (1979). The role of laughter and humor in growing up female. In C. B. Kopp (Ed.), *Becoming female: Perspectives on development* (pp. 183–206). New York: Plenum.

McGrath, J. E. (1976). Stress and behavior in organizations. In M. D. Dunnette (Ed.), *Handbook of industrial and organizational psychology* (pp. 1351–1395). Chicago: Rand McNally.

McHugh, M. C., Koeske, R. D., & Frieze, I. H. (1986). Issues to consider in conducting nonsexist psychological research: A guide for researchers. *American Psychologist, 41,* 879–890.

McKee, J. P., & Sherriffs, A. C. (1957). The differential evaluation of males and females. *Journal of Personality, 25,* 356–371.

McKelvie, S. J., & Matthews, S. J. (1976). Effects of physical attractiveness and favourableness of character of liking. *Psychological Reports, 35,* 1223–1230.

McKinlay, S. (1988). *Social factor and responses to menopause* (Conference on Menopause). Bethesda, MD: National Institutes of Health.

McLanahan, S. C., & Adams, J. (1987). Parenthood and psychological well being. *Annual Review of Sociology, 13,* 237–257.

McRae, M. B. (1994). Influence of sex role stereotypes on personnel decisions of Black managers. *Journal of Applied Psychology, 79,* 306–309.

Mead, M. (1980). A proposal: We need taboos on sex at work. In D. A. Neugarten & J. M. Shafritz (Eds.), *Sexuality in organizations* (3rd ed., pp. 53–56). Oak Park, IL: Moore.

Megargee, E. I. (1969). Influence of sex roles on the manifestation of leadership. *Journal of Applied Psychology, 53,* 377–382.

Menaghan, E. G., & Parcel, T. L. (1991). Determining children's home environments: The impact of maternal characteristics and current occupational and family conditions. *Journal of Marriage and the Family, 53,* 417–431.

Meritor Savings Bank, FSB v. Vinson, 477 U.S. 57 (1986).

Meyer, J., & Berry J. O. (1995, May). *Development and validation of a measure of workplace flexibility.* Paper presented at the Society for Industrial and Organizational Psychology Conference, Orlando, FL.

Miall, N. E. (1987). Some personal factors influencing arterial blood pressure. In J. Stamler, R. Stamler, & T. N. Pullman (Eds.), *The epidemiology of hypertension* (pp. 69–80). New York: Grune & Stratton.

Miller, A. G. (1970). Role of physical attractiveness in impression formation. *Psychonomic Science, 19,* 241–243.

Miller, G. (1980). The interpretation of nonoccupational work in modern society: A preliminary discussion and typology. *Social Problems, 27,* 381–390.

Miller, J. J., Stead, B. A., & Pereira, A. (1991). Dependant care and the workplace: An analysis of management and employee perceptions. *Journal of Business Ethics, 10,* 863–869.

Mincer, J. (1978). Family migration decisions. *Journal of Political Economy, 86,* 749–773.

Minkler, M. (1981). Research on the health effects of retirement: An uncertain legacy. *Journal of Health and Social Behavior, 22,* 117–130.

Mishra, J. M., & Harell, R. (1989, May–June). Managing today's hot workplace issues, *Management World, 18,* 26–29.

Missirian, A. K. (1982). *The corporate connection: Why women need mentors to reach the top.* Englewood Cliffs, NJ: Prentice-Hall.

Mitchell, K. R., & Orr, F. E. (1976). Heterosexual social competence, anxiety, and self-judged physical attractiveness. *Perceptual and Motor Skills, 43,* 553–554.

Moghaddam, F. M., & Stringer, P. (1986). "Trivial" and "important" criteria for social categorization in the minimal group paradigm. *Journal of Social Psychology, 126,* 345–354.

Molm, L. D. (1985). Gender and power use: An experimental analysis of behavior and perceptions. *Social Psychology Quarterly, 48,* 285–300.

Molm, L. D. (1986). Gender, power, and legitimation: A test of three theories. *American Journal of Sociology, 91,* 1356–1386.

Moos, R. H. (Ed.) (1976). *Human adaptation. Coping with life crisis.* Lexington, MA: Heath.

Moos, R. H., & Billings, A. G. (1982). Conceptualizing and measuring coping resources and processes. In L. Goldberger & S. Breznitz (Eds.), *Handbook of stress* (pp. 212–230). New York: The Free Press.

Morris, D. (1971). *Intimate Behavior.* New York: Random House.

Morrison, A. M. (1996). *The new leaders: Leadership diversity in America.* San Francisco: Jossey-Bass.

Morrison, A. M., & Von Glinow, M. A. (1990). Women and minorities in management. *American Psychologist 45*(2), 200–208.

Morrison, A. M., White, R. P., Van Velsor, E., & The Center for Creative Leadership. (1987). *Breaking the Glass Ceiling: Can women reach the top of America's largest corporations?* Reading, MA: Addison-Wesley.

Mumby, D. K., & Putnam, L. L. (1992). The politics of emotion: A feminist reading of wounded rationality. *Academy of Management Review, 17,* 465–487.

Murphy, K., & Cleveland, J. (1995). *Understanding performance appraisal: Social, organizational and goal-oriented perspectives.* Newbury Park, CA: Sage.

Murphy, K., & Davidshofer, C. (1998). *Psychological testing: Principles and applications* (4th ed.). Englewood Cliffs, NJ: Prentice-Hall.

Murphy, L. (1988). Workplace interventions for stress reduction and prevention. In C. L. Cooper & R. Payne (Eds.), *Causes, coping & consequences of stress at work* (pp. 301–339). Chichester, UK; London: Wiley.

Murphy, S. K. (1989). Influences of sex composition and topic management in initial interactions. In C. M. Lont & S. A. Friedley (Eds.), *Beyond boundaries: Sex and gender diversity in communication* (pp. 75–94). Fairfax, VA: George Mason University Press.

Myers, S. T., & Grasmick, H. G. (1990). The social rights and responsibilities of pregnant women: An application of the Parsons's sick role model. *Journal of Applied Behavioral Sciences, 26,* 157–172.

National Center for Health Statistics. (1988). *Vital statistics of the United States, 1986: Vol. II. Mortality Parts A and B* (DHHS Publication Nos. 88-1122 and 88-1114). Washington, DC: Public Health Service, U.S. Government Printing Office.

National Committee on Pay Equity. (1986, April). *Newsletter.* Washington, DC: Author.

Neff, W. S. (1985). *Work and human behavior.* New York: Aldine.

Nelson, D. L., & Quick, J. C. (1997). *Organizational behavior: Foundations, realities, and challenges.* St. Paul, MN: West.

Nelson, D. L., & Sutton, C. (1990). Chronic work stress and coping: A longitudinal study and suggested new directions. *Academy of Management Journal, 33,* 659–689.

Newby, T. J., & Heide, A. (1992). The value of mentoring. *Performance Improvement Quarterly, 5,* 2–15.

Newcombe, N., & Arnkoff, D. (1979). Effects of speech style and sex of speaker on person perception. *Journal of Personality and Social Psychology, 37,* 1293–1303.

Newell, C. E., Rosenfeld, P., & Culbertson, A. L. (1995). Sexual harassment experiences and equal opportunity perceptions of Navy women. *Sex Roles, 32,* 159–168.

Nieva, V. F. (1985). *Work and family linkages.* In L. Larwood, A. H. Stromberg, & B. A. Gutek (Eds.), *Women and work: An annual review* (Vol. 1, pp. 162–190). Newbury Park, CA: Sage.

Nieva, V. F., & Gutek, B. A. (1981a). *Sex segregation, women and work: A psychological perspective.* New York: Praeger.

Nieva, V. F., & Gutek, B. A. (1981b). *Women and work: A psychological perspective.* New York: Praeger.

Nieva, V. F., & Gutek, B. A. (1980). Sex effects on evaluation. *Academy of Management Review, 5,* 267–276.

Nkomo, S. M., & Cox, T. L., Jr. (1989). Gender differences in the upward mobility of black managers: Double whammy or double advantage. *Sex Roles, 21,* 825–839.

Noe, R. A. (1988a). An investigation of the determinants of successful assigned mentoring relationships. *Personnel Psychology, 41,* 457–479.

Noe, R. A. (1988b). Women and mentoring: A review and research agenda. *Academy of Management Review, 13,* 65–78.

Nowak, C. A. (1976). *Youthfulness, attractiveness, and the midlife woman: An analysis of the appearance signal in adult development.* Paper presented at the Annual Meeting of the Midwestern Psychological Association, Chicago, March.

Nowak, C. A., Karuza, J., & Namikas, J. (1976). *Youth, beauty, and the midlife woman: The double whammy strikes again.* Paper presented at the Conference on Women in Midlife Crisis, Cornell University, Ithaca, NY.

Nyquist, L. V., & Spence, J. T. (1986). Effects of dispositional dominance and sex role expectations on leadership behaviors. *Journal of Personality and Social Psychology, 50,* 87–93.

Oakland school board amends Ebonics policy. (1997, January 16). CNN Interactive. US News Interactive. (CNN. com)

O'Connor, J. M. (1997, October). Statistics in corporate downsizing cases: Unfulfilled promise for plaintiffs. *Labor Law Review,* 627–638.

Offermann, L. R., & Armitage, M. A. (1993). Stress and the woman manager: Sources, health outcomes, and interventions. In E. A. Fagenson (Ed.), *Women in management: Trends, issues, and challenges in managerial diversity* (pp. 131–161). Newbury Park, CA: Sage.

Offermann, L. R., & Beil, C. (1992). Achievement styles of women leaders and their peers: Toward an understanding of women and leadership. *Psychology of Women Quarterly, 16,* 37–56.

Offermann, L. R., & Gowing, M. K. (1990). Organizations of the future. *American Psychologist, 45,* 95–108.

Offermann, L. R., & Schrier, P. E. (1985). Social influence strategies: The impact of sex, role, and attitudes toward power. *Personality and Social Psychology Bulletin, 11,* 286–300.

Officers for Justice v. Civil Service Commission, 11 FEP 815 (1975).

Ohlott, P. J., Ruderman, M. N., & McCauley, C. D. (1994). Gender differences in managers' developmental job experiences, *Academy of Management Journal, 37,* 46–67.

O'Keefe, E. S. C., & Hyde, J. S. (1983). The development of occupational sex-role stereotypes: The effects of gender stability and age. *Sex Roles, 39,* 481–492.

O'Leary, V. E., & Harrison, A. O. (1975, September). *Sex role stereotypes as a function of race and sex.* Paper presented at the annual convention of the American Psychological association, Chicago.

O'Leary, V. E. (1977). *Toward understanding women.* Monterey, CA: Brooks/ Cole.

O'Leary, V. E., & Mitchell, J. M. (1990). Women connecting with women: Networks and mentors. In S. S. Lie & V. E. O'Leary (Eds.), *Storming the tower* (pp. 58–73). New York: Nichols/G P Publishing.

Olson, J. E., & Frieze, I. H. (1987). Income determinants for women in business. In A. H. Stromberg, L. Larwood, & B. A. Gutek (Eds.), *Women and work: An annual review* (Vol. 2, pp. 173–206). Newbury Park, CA: Sage.

Orth-Gomer, K. (1979). Ischemic heart disease and psychological stress in Stockholm and New York. *Journal of Psychosomatic Research, 23,* 165–173.

Osipow, S. H. (1983). *Theories of career development.* Englewood Cliffs, NJ: Prentice-Hall.

Ostroff, C., & Kozlowski, S. W. J. (1993). The role of mentoring in the information gathering processes of newcomers during early organizational socialization. *Journal of Vocational Behavior, 42,* 170–183.

O'Sullivan, C. S., Cole, C. A., & Moseley, S. (1982, April). *Content and structure of gender stereotypes.* Paper presented at the meeting of the Southwestern Psychological Association, Dallas, TX.

O'Toole, J. (1995). *Leading change: Overcoming the ideology of comfort and the tyranny of custom.* San Francisco: Jossey-Bass.

Oyster, C. K. (1992). Perceptions of power: Female executives' descriptions of power usage by "best" and "worst" bosses. *Psychology of Women Quarterly, 16,* 527–533.

Paetzold, R. L., & O'Leary-Kelly, A. M. (1996). The implications of U.S. Supreme Court and Circuit Court decisions for hostile environment sexual harassment cases. In M. S. Stockdale (Ed.), *Sexual harassment in the workplace: Perspectives, frontiers, and response strategies* (pp. 85–104). Thousand Oaks, CA: Sage.

Paetzold, R. L., & Shaw B. (1994). A postmodern feminist view of "reasonableness" in hostile environment sexual harassment. *Journal of Business Ethics, 13,* 681–691.

Paludi, M. A., & Strayer, L. A. (1985). What's in an author's name? Differential evaluations of performance as a function of author's name. *Sex Roles, 12,* 353–361.

Parasuraman, S., & Greenhaus, J. H. (1993). Personal portrait: The life style of the woman manager. In E. A. Fagenson (Ed.), *Women in management: Trends, issues and challenges in managerial diversity* (pp. 186–211). Newbury Park, CA: Sage.

Parsons, T. (1951). *The social system.* New York: The Free Press.

Parsons, T., & Bales, R. F. (1955). *Family socialization and interaction process.* New York: The Free Press.

Patzer, G. L. (1985). *The physical attractiveness-phenomenon.* New York: Plenum.

Payne, R. (1988). Individual difference in the study of occupational stress. In C. H. Cooper & R. Payne (Eds.), *Causes, coping & consequences of stress at work* (pp. 209–232). Chichester, UK: Wiley.

Pazy, A. (1986). The persistence of pro-male bias despite identical information regarding causes of success. *Organizational Behavior and Human Decision Processes, 38,* 366–377.

Pearlin, L. I., Lieberman, M. A., Meneghan, E. G., & Mullen, J. T. (1981). The stress process. *Journal of Health and Social Behavior, 22,* 337–356.

Pellegrini, R. J., Hicks, R. A., & Meyers-Winton, S. (1979). Situational affective arousal and heterosexual attraction: Some effects of success, failure, and physical attractiveness. *Psychological Record, 29,* 453–462.

Pendleton, B. F., Paloma, M. M., & Garland, T. N. (1982). An approach to quantifying the needs of dual career families. *Human Relations, 35,* 69–82.

Peters, T. J., & Waterman, R. H., Jr. (1982). *In search of excellence: Lessons from America's best-run companies.* New York: Harper & Row.

Peterson, J. L., & Miller, C. (1980). Physical attractiveness and marriage adjustment in older American couples. *Journal of Psychology, 105,* 247–252.

Peterson, M. F., Smith, P. B, Akande, A., Ayestaran, S., Bochner, S., Callan, V., Guk Cho, N., Correia Jesvino, J., D'Amorim, M., Francois, P., Hofmann, K., Koopman, P., Leung, K., Keng Lim, T., Mortazavi, S., Munene, J., Radford, M., Ropo, A., Savage, G., Setiadi, B., Sinha, T. N., Sorenson, R., & Viedge, C. (1995). Role conflict, ambiguity & overload: A 21-Nation Study. *Academy of Management Journal, 38,* 429–452.

Pettigrew, T. (1964). *A profile of the Negro American.* Princeton, NJ: Van Nostrand.

Pfeffer, J. (1981). *Power in organizations.* Boston: Pitman.

Pfeffer, J., & Ross, J. (1982). The effects of marriage and a working wife on occupational and wage attainment. *Administrative Science Quarterly, 27,* 66–80.

Pheterson, G. I., Kiesler, S. B., & Goldberg, P. A. (1971). Evaluation of the performance of women as a function of their sex achievement and personal history. *Journal of Applied Psychology, 19,* 114–118.

Philips, S. V. (1980). Sex differences and language. *Annual Review of Anthropology, 9,* 523–544.

Phillips, v. Martin Marietta Corp., 400 U.S. 542 (1971).

Pickering, T. G., James, G. D., Schnall, P. L., Schlussel, L. R., Pieper, C. F., Gerin, W., & Karasek, R. A. (1991). Occupational stress and blood pressure: Studies in working men and women. In M. Frankenhaeuser, V. Lundberg, & M. Chesney (Eds.), *Women, work & stress: Stress and opportunities* (pp. 171–186). London: Plenum.

Piechowski, L. D. (1992). Mental health and women's multiple roles. *Families in Society, 73,* 131–139.

Pierce, C. A. (1994, April). *A meta-analytic test of the male taller social norm in mate selection.* Paper presented at the meeting of the Eastern Psychological Association, Providence, RI

Pierce, C. A., Byrne, D., & Aguinis, H. (1996). Attraction in organizations: A model of workplace romance. *Journal of Organizational Behavior, 17,* 5–32.

Pietropinto, A. (1986, July). Sex in the workplace. *Medical Aspects of Human Sexuality, 20,* 17–22.

Piliavin, J. A., & Martin, R. (1978). The effects of sex composition on style of social interaction. *Sex Roles, 4,* 281–296.

Pinchot, G. (1996). Creating organizations with many leaders. In F. Hesselbein, M. Goldsmith, R. Beckhard (Eds.), *The leader of the future: New visions, strategies, and practices for the next era* (pp. 25–39. San Francisco: Jossey-Bass.

Player, M. A. (1988). *Employment discrimination law.* St. Paul, MN: West.

Pleck, J. H. (1976). The male sex role: Definitions, problems, and sources of change. *Journal of Social Issues, 32,* 155–164.

Pleck, J. H. (1981). *The myth of masculinity.* Cambridge, MA: MIT Press.

Pleck, J. H. (1983). Husbands' paid work and family roles: Current research issues. In I. H. Lopata & J. Pleck (Eds.), *Research in the interweave of social roles: Women and men.* Greenwich, CT: JAI.

Pleck, J. H. (1985). *Working wives/working husbands.* Beverly Hills, CA: Sage.

Pleck, J. H., & Staines, G. L. (1985). Work schedules and family life in two-earner couples. *Journal of Family Issues, 6,* 68–82.

Pliner, P., Chaiken, S., & Flett, G. L. (1990). Gender differences in concern with body weight and physical appearance over the life span. *Personality and Social Psychology Bulletin, 16,* 263–273.

Podsakoff, P. M., MacKenzie, S. B., & Bommer, W. H. (1996). Meta-analysis of the relationships between Kerr and Jermier's substitutes for leadership and employee job attitudes, role perceptions, and performance. *Journal of Applied Psychology, 81,* 380–399.

Polacheck, S. (1981). Occupational self-selection: A human capital approach to sex differences in occupational structure. *Review of Economics and Statistics, 58,* 60–69.

Powell, G. N. (1993). *Women and men in management.* Newbury Park, CA: Sage.

Powell, G. N. (1997). Gender and leadership: Vive la difference? In M. Walsh (Ed.), *Women, men, and gender: Current debates* (pp. 298–305). New Haven, CT: Yale University Press.

Powell, G. N. (1986, July–August). What do tomorrow's managers think about sexual intimacy in the workplace? *Business Horizons, 29*(4), 30–35.

Powell, G. N., & Butterfield, D. A. (1994). Investigating the "glass ceiling" phenomenon: An empirical study of actual promotions to top management. *Academy of Management Journal, 37,* 68–86.

Powell, G. N., & Butterfield, D. A. (1989). The "good manager": Did androgyny fare better in the 1980s? *Group and Organization Studies, 14*(2), 216–233.

Powell, G. N., & Butterfield, D. A. (1979). The "good manager": Masculine or androgynous? *Academy of Management Journal, 22,* 395–403.

Powell, G. N., & Mainiero, L. A. (1990). What managers need to know about office romances. *Leadership and Organization Development Journal, 11,* i–iii.

Powell, G. N., & Posner, B. Z. (1983). Stereotyping by college recruiters. *Journal of College Placement, 64,* 63–65.

Prather, J. (1971). Why can't women be more like men? A summary of the sociopsychological factors hindering women's advancement in the profession. *American Behavioral Scientist, 15*(2), 172–182.

Pratt, W. F., Mosher, W., Bachrach, C., & Horn, M. (1984). Understanding U.S. fertility. *Population Bulletin, 39,* 1–42.

Price-Waterhouse v. Hopkins, 109 5. Ct. 1775 (1989).

Pruett, B. M. (1989). Male and female communicator style differences: A meta-analysis. In C. M. Lont & S. A. Friedley (Eds.), *Beyond boundaries: Sex and gender diversity in communication* (pp. 107–120). Fairfax, VA: George Mason University Press.

Pryor, J. B. (1987). Sexual harassment proclivities in men. *Sex Roles, 17,* 269–290.

Pryor, J. B. (1995). The psychosocial impact of sexual harassment on women in the U.S. military. *Journal of Social Issues, 17,* 581–604.

Pryor, J. B., LaVite, C. M., & Stoller, L. M. (1993). A social psychological analysis of sexual harassment: The person/situation interaction. *Journal of Vocational Behavior, 42,* 68–83.

Quinn, R. E., & Judge, N. A. (1978, July). The office romance: No bliss for the boss. *Management Review, 67,* 43–49.

Quinn, R. E., & Lees, P. L. (1984). Attraction and harassment: Dynamics of sexual politics in the workplace. *Organizational Dynamics, 13*(2), 35–46.

Rabidue v. Osceola Refining Company, 805 F.2d 611 (6th Cir. 1986), cert. denied, 481 U.S. 1041 (1987).

Raciot, B. M., Day, D. V., & Lard, R. G. (1991). Type A behavior pattern and goal setting under different conditions of choice. *Motivation and Emotions, 4,* 67–79.

Radtke v. Everett, 61 FEP Cases 1644, Mich. (1993).

Ragins, B. R., & Cotton, J. L. (1992). Gender and willingness to mentor in organizations. *Journal of Management, 19,* 97–111.

Ragins, B. R., & Scandura, T. A. (1992, April/May). *Antecedents and consequences of sexual harassment.* Paper presented at the 1992 Society for Industrial/Organizational Psychology Conference, Montreal, PQ.

Ragins, B. R., & Sundstrom, E. (1989). Gender and power in organizations: A longitudinal perspective. *Psychological Bulletin, 105,* 51–88.

Ragins, B. R., & Sundstrom, E. (1990). Gender and perceived power in manager–subordinate relations. *Journal of Occupational Psychology, 63,* 273–287.

Rahim, M. A., & Afza, M. (1993). Leader power, commitment, satisfaction, compliance, and propensity to leave a job among U.S. accountants. *Journal of Social Psychology, 133,* 611–625.

Rankin, R. A., & Cannon, A. (1998, April 2). Judge: At worse, Clinton was 'offensive.' *The Denver Post,* p. 1A+.

Ralph, J. B., Goldberg, M. L., & Passow, A. H. (1966). *Bright underachievers.* New York: Teacher's College Press.

Rapoport, R., & Rapoport, R. N. (1969). The dual-earner family: A variant pattern and social change: *Human Relations, 22,* 3–30.

Rapp, E. (1992, February). Dangerous liaisons. *Working Woman, 17,* 56–61.

Reich, M. H. (1986). The mentor connection. *Personnel, 63,* 50 56.

Reis, H. T., & Wright, S. (1982). Knowledge of sex-role stereotypes in children aged 3 to 5. *Sex Roles, 8,* 1049–1056.

Repetti, R. L., Matthews, K. A., & Waldron, I. (1989). Effects of paid employment on women's mental and physical health. *American Psychologist, 44,* 1394–1401.

Reskin, B. F. (1984). *Sex segregation in the workplace: Trends, explanations, and remedies.* Washington, DC: National Academy Press.

Reskin, B. F., & Padavic, I. (1994). *Women and men at work.* Thousand Oaks, CA: Pine Forge, Press.

Rice, R. W., Bender, L. R., & Vitters, A. G. (1980). Leader, sex, follower attitudes toward women and leadership effectiveness: A laboratory experiment. *Organizational Behavior and Human Performance, 25,* 46–78.

Rice, R. W., Instone, D., & Adams, J. (1984). Leader, sex, leader success, and leadership process: Two field studies. *Journal of Applied Psychology, 69,* 12–32.

Riger, S. (1991). Gender dilemmas in sexual harassment policies and procedures. *American Psychologist, 46,* 497–505.

Riger, S. (1992). Epistemological debates, feminist voices: Science, social values, and the study of women. *American Psychologist, 47,* 730–740.

Riggio, R. E., & Throckmorton, B. (1988). The relative effects of verbal and nonverbal behavior, appearance, and social skills on evaluations made in hiring interviews. *Journal of Applied Social Psychology, 18,* 331–348.

Riley, S., & Wrench, D. (1985). Mentoring among women lawyers. *Journal of Applied Social Psychology, 15,* 374–386.

Roberts, T. (1991). Gender and the influence of evaluations on self-assessments in achievement settings. *Psychological Bulletin, 109,* 297–308.

Robinson v. Jacksonville Shipyards, Inc., 760 F Supp 1486, M.D. Fla. (1991).

Robinson, D. G. (1989, June). The 1990's: From managing to leading. *Supervisory Management, 7.*

Roche, G. R. (1979). Much ado about mentors. *Harvard Business Review, 57,* 14–31.

Rodin, J., & Ickovics, J. R. (1990). Women's health: Review and research agenda as we approach the 21st century. *American Psychologist, 45,* 1018–1034.

Rodin, J., Silberstein, L., & Striegel-Moore, R. (1984). Women and weight: A normative discontent. *Nebraska Symposium on Motivation.* v. 32, 267–307.

Roe, A. (1949). Psychological examinations of eminent biologists. *Journal of Consulting Psychology, 13,* 225–246.

Roe, A. (1952). Early determinants of vocational choice. *Journal of Counseling Psychology, 4,* 212–217.

Rogers, C. R. (1951). *Client-centered therapy.* Boston: Houghton Mifflin.

Rogers, C. S. (1992). The flexible workplace: What have we learned? *Human Resource Management, 31,* 182–199.

Roman, M. (1990, October 29). Women, beware: An MBA doesn't mean equal pay. *Business Week, 61,* 57.

Rosen, B., & Jerdee, T. H. (1974). Influence of sex-role stereotypes on personnel decisions. *Journal of Applied Psychology, 59,* 9–14.

Rosen, B., Templeton, M. E., & Kirchline, K. (1981). First few years on the job: Women in management. *Business Horizons, 24*(12), 26–29.

Rosenbaum, M. E. (1986a). Comment on a proposed two-stage theory of relationship formation: First, repulsion: Then, attraction. *Journal of Personality and Social Psychology, 51,* 1171–1172.

Rosenbaum, M. E. (1986b). The repulsion hypothesis: On the nondevelopment of relationships. *Journal of Personality and Social Psychology, 51,* 1156–1166.

Rosener, J. B. (1990, November–December). Ways women lead. *Harvard Business Review, 68,* 119–125.

Rosener, J. B. (1997). Leadership and the paradox of gender. In M. Walsh (Ed.), *Women, men, and gender: Current debates* (pp. 294–297). New Haven, CT: Yale University Press.

Rosenfield, S. (1980). Sex differences in depression: Do women always have higher rates? *Journal of Health and Social Behavior, 21,* 33–42.

Rosenkrantz, P., Vogel, S. R., Bee, H., Broverman, I. K., & Broverman, D. M. (1968). Sex-role stereotypes and self-concepts in college students. *Journal of Consulting and Clinical Psychology, 32,* 287–295.

Rosenthal, D. B., & Hautaluoma, J. (1988). Effects of importance of issues, gender, and power of contenders on conflict management style. *Journal of Social Psychology, 128,* 699–701.

Ross, C. E., Mirowsky, J., & Huber, J. (1983). Dividing work, sharing work and in-between. Marriage patterns and depression. *American Sociological Review, 48,* 809–823.

Ross, J., & Ferris, K. R. (1981). Interpersonal attraction and organizational outcome: A field experiment. *Administrative Science Quarterly, 26,* 617–632.

Rowe v. General Motors, 4 FEP 445 (1972).

Rowe, M. P. (1996). Dealing with harassment: A systems approach. In M. S. Stockdale (Ed.), *Sexual harassment in the workplace: Perspectives, frontiers, and response strategies* (pp. 241–270). Thousand Oaks, CA: Sage.

Rubin, Z. (1970). Measurement of romantic love. *Journal of Psychology, 16,* 265–273.

Rubin, Z. (1973). *Liking and loving: An invitation to social psychology.* New York: Holt, Rinehart & Winston.

Rubin, Z. (1980). *Children's friendships.* Cambridge, MA: Harvard University Press.

Rush, M. C., Phillips, J. S., & Lord, R. G. (1981). Effects of a temporal delay in ratings on leader behavior descriptions: A laboratory investigation. *Journal of Applied Psychology, 66*(4), 442–450.

Rynes, S., & Rosen, B. (1983). A comparison of male and female reactions to career advancement opportunities. *Journal of Vocational Behavior, 22,* 105–116.

Saal, F. E. (1996). Men's misperceptions of women's interpersonal behaviors and sexual harassment. In M. S. Stockdale (Ed.), *Sexual Harassment in the Workplace: Perspectives, frontiers, and response strategies* (pp. 67–84). Thousand Oaks, CT: Sage.

Saal, F. E., Johnson, C. B., & Weber, N. (1989). Friendly or sexy? It may depend on whom you ask. *Psychology of Women Quarterly, 13,* 263–276.

Sachdev, I., & Bourhis, R. Y. (1984). Minimal majorities and minorities. *European Journal of Social Psychology, 14,* 35–52.

Sachdev, I., & Bourhis, R. Y. (1985). Social categorization and power differentials in group relations. *European Journal of Social Psychology, 15,* 415–434.

Sachs, J., Lieberman, P., & Erickson, D. (1973). Anatomical and cultural determinants of male and female speech. In R. W. Shuy & R. W. Fasold (Eds.), *Language attitudes.* Washington, DC: Georgetown University Press

Sackett, P. R., DuBois, C. L., & Noe, R. (1991). Tokenism in performance evaluation: The effects of work group representation on male–female and White–Black differences in performance ratings. *Journal of Applied Psychology, 76,* 263–267.

Sacks, H., Schegloff, E. A., & Jefferson, G. (1974). A simplist systematics for the organization of turn-taking for conversation. *Language, 50,* 696–735.

Safilios-Rothschild, C., & Dijkens, M. (1978). Handling unconventional asymmetries. In R. Rapaport & R. Rapoport (Eds.), *Working couples.* New York: Harper & Row.

Sagrestano, L. M. (1991). *Gender issues in social influence: A review of empirical research.* Unpublished manuscript.

Sagrestano, L. M. (1992). Power strategies in interpersonal relationships. *Psychology of Women Quarterly, 16,* 481–495.

Salancik, G. R., & Pfeffer, J. (1977, Winter). Who gets power—and how they hold on to it: A strategic-contingency model of power. *Organizational Dynamics, 5,* 3–35.

Sandell, S. H. (1977). Women and the economics of migration. *Review of Economics and Statistics, 59,* 406–414.

Sandell, S. H., & Koenig, P. J. (1978). The migration of young families: An economic perspective. In F. L. Mott. (Ed.), *Women, work, and the family* (pp. 95–111). Lexington, MA: D.C. Heath.

Sanford, S., & Eder, D. (1984). Adolescent humor during peer interaction. *Social Psychology Quarterly, 47,* 235–243.

Sarason, S. B. (1973). Jewishness, Blackness, and the nature–nurture controversy. *American Psychologist, 28,* 960–971.

Sargent, A. G. (1977). *Beyond sex roles.* St. Paul, MN: West.

Sarrel, P. M. (1991). Women, work, and menopause. In M. Frankenhaeuser, U. Lundberg, & M. Chesney (Eds.), *Women, work and health, stress and opportunities* (pp. 225–237). New York: Plenum.

Sattell, J. W. (1983). Men, inexpressiveness and power. In B. Thorne, C. Kamarae, & N. Healey (Eds.), *Language, gender and society* (pp. 119–124). Rowley, MA: Newburg House.

Scandura, T. A. (1991). *Breaking the glass ceiling in the 1990s* (Technical Report). Washington, DC: U. S. Department of Labor, Women's Bureau.

Scandal and the second term: Monkey business. (1997). *The Economist, 342,* 21–23.

Scanzoni, J. (1983). *Shaping tomorrow's family: Theory and policy for the 21st century.* Beverly Hills, CA: Sage.

Scase, R., & Goffee, R. (1989, September). *Women in management—Towards a research agenda.* Paper presented at British Academy of Management Conference.

Scheflen, A. E. (1972). *Body language and social order.* Englewood Cliffs, NJ: Prentice-Hall.

Schein, E. H. (1973). Personal change through interpersonal relationships. In W. G. Bennis, D. E. Berlew, E. H. Schein, & F. I. Steele (Eds.), *Interpersonal dynamics* (3rd ed.). Homewood, IL: Dorsey.

Schein, E. H. (1990). Organizational culture. *American Psychologist, 45,* 109–119.

Schein, E. H. (1991). What is culture? In P. Frost, L. Moore, M. Louis, C. Lundberg, & J. Martin (Eds.), *Reframing organizational culture* (pp. 243–253). Newbury Park, CA: Sage.

Schein, V. E. (1973). Relationship between sex role stereotypes and requisite management characteristics. *Journal of Applied Psychology, 57,* 95–100.

Schein, V. E. (1975). Relationships between sex role stereotypes and requisite management characteristics among female managers. *Journal of Applied Psychology, 60*(3), 340–344.

Schein, V. E. (1977). Individual power and political behavior in organizations: An inadequately explored reality. *Academy of Management Review, 2,* 64–72.

Schein, V. E., & Mueller, R. (1992). Sex role stereotyping and requisite management characteristics: A cross cultural look. *Journal of Organizational Behavior, 13,* 439–447.

Schneider, B. (1987). The people make the place. *Personnel Psychology, 40,* 437–453.

Schneider, B. E. (1982). Consciousness about sexual harassment among heterosexual and lesbian women workers. *Journal of Social Issues, 38,* 75–98.

Schneider, J. W., & Hacker, S. L. (1973). Sex role imagery and the rise of the generic "man" in introductory texts. *American Sociologist, 8,* 12–18.

Schneider, K. T., Swan, S., & Fitzgerald, L. F. (1997). Job-related and psychological effects of sexual harassment in the workplace: Empirical evidence from two organizations. *Journal of Applied Psychology, 82,* 401–415.

Schriesheim, C. A., & DeNisi, A. (1981). Task dimensions as moderators of the effects of instrumental leadership: A two sample applicated test of path–goal leadership theory. *Journal of Applied Psychology, 66,* 589–597.

Schroeder, K. A., Blood, L. L., & Maluso, D. (1992). An intergenerational analysis of expectations for women's career and family roles. *Sex Roles, 26,* 273–291.

Schultz, T. (1982, May). In defense of the office romance. *Savvy, 3,* 54–64.

Schlussel, Y. R., Schnall, P. L., Zimbler, M., Warren, K., & Pickering, T. G. (1990). The effect of work environments in blood pressure: Evidence from seven New York organizations. *Journal of Hypertension, 8,* 679–685.

Schuman, H., Steeh, C., & Bobo, L. (1985). *Racial attitudes in America: Friends and interpretations.* Cambridge, MA: Harvard University Press.

Schutte, J. G., & Light, J. M. (1978). The relative importance of proximity and status for friendship choices in social hierarchies. *Social Psychology, 41,* 26–264.

Schwartz, F. (1970). *Sex roles and leadership dynamics: A study of attitude toward the female sex role.* Senior honor's thesis, University of Pennsylvania, Philadelphia.

Schwartz, F. N. (1989). Management women and the facts of life. *Harvard Business Review, 11,* 65–76.

Scott, K. P. (1980). Perceptions of communication competence: What's good for the goose is not good for the gander. In C. Kramarae (Ed.), *The voices and words of women and men* (pp. 199–208). Oxford, UK: Pergamon.

Schwartzberg, N. S., & Dytell, R. S. (1989). Family, stress and psychological well-being among employed and nonemployed mothers. In E. B. Goldsmith (Ed.), *Work and family theory research and applications* (pp. 175–190). Newbury Park, CA: Sage.

Schwimmer, E. (1980). The limits of economic ideology: A comparative anthropological study of work concept. *International Social Science Journal, 32,* 517–531.

Sedmak, N. J., & Vidas, C. (1994). *Primer of equal employment opportunity* (6th ed.). Washington, DC: BNA Books.

Seligman, C. R., Tucker, G. R., & Lambert, W. E. (1972). The effects of speech style and other attributes on teacher's attitudes toward pupils. *Language in Society, 1,* 131–142.

Sell, R. R. (1982). A research note on the demography and occupational relocation. *Social Forces, 60,* 859–865.

Sessa, V. I. (1992). Managing diversity at the Xerox Corporation: Balanced workforce goals and caucus groups. In S. E. Jackson (Ed.), *Diversity in the workplace: Human resource initiatives* (pp. 37–64). New York: Guilford.

Sexual harassment: Naval operations. (1992). *The Economist, 324,* 29.

Sharabany, R., Gershoni, R., & Hoffman, J. E. (1981). Girlfriend, boyfriend:

Age and sex differences in intimate friendship. *Developmental Psychology, 17,* 800–808.

Shae, E. A. (1972). Differential impact of negative stereotypes in employee selection. *Personnel Psychology, 25,* 333–338.

Sheidlower, J. (1997, January). Sex talk. *Esquire, 127*(1), 29.

Sherriffs, A. C., & McKee, J. P. (1957). Qualitative aspects of beliefs about men and women. *Journal of Personality, 25,* 451–464.

Shields, S. A. (1975). Functionalism, Darwinism, and the psychology of women: A study in social myth. *American Psychologist, 30,* 739–754.

Shockey, M. L. (1997). Women and part-time work. In P. Dubeck & K. Borman (Eds.), *Women and work: A handbook* (pp. 7–9). New York: Garland.

Siegal, J., Johnson, J., & Sarason, I. (1979). Life changes and menstrual discomfort. *Journal of Human Stress, 5,* 41–46.

Silveira, J. (1972). Thoughts on the politics of touch. *Women's Press* (Eugene, OR), *1,* 13.

Silveira, J. (1980). Generic masculine words and thinking. In C. Kramarae (Ed.), *The voices and words of women and men* (pp. 165–178). Oxford, UK: Pergamon.

Silverstein, L. B. (1991). Transforming the debate about child care and maternal employment. *American Psychologist, 46,* 1025–1032.

Smelser, N. J. (1980). Vicissitudes of work and love in Anglo American society. In N. J. Smelser & E. H. Erikson (Eds.), *Themes of work and love in adulthood* (pp. 105–119). Cambridge, MA: Harvard University Piers.

Smith, H. L., & Grenier, M. (1982). Sources of organizational power for women: Overcoming structural obstacles. *Sex Roles, 8,* 733–746.

Smith, A., & Stewart, A. J. (1983). Approaches to studying racism and sexism in Black women's lives. *Journal of Social Issues, 39*(3), 1–15.

Smits, G. J., & Cherhoniak, I. M. (1976). Physical attractiveness and friendliness in interpersonal attraction. *Psychological Reports, 39,* 171–174.

Snyder, M. E., Berseheid, E., & Matwychuk, A. (1988). Orientations toward Personal Selection: Differential reliance on appearance and personality. *Journal of Personality and Social Psychology, 54,* 972–979.

Sommer, B. (1982). Cognitive behavior and the menstrual cycle. In R. C. Friedman (Ed.), Behavior and the menstrual cycle (pp. 101–128). Basel, Switzerland: Marcel Dekker.

Sorell, G. T., & Nowak, C. A. (1981). The role of physical attractiveness as a contributor to individual development. In R. M. Lerner & N. S. Busch-Rossnagel (Eds.), *Individuals as producers of their development: A life-span perspective* (pp. 389–446). Orlando, FL: Academic Press.

Sorensen, G., & Verbrugge, L. M. (1987). Women, work and health. *Annual Review of Public Health, 8,* 235–251.

Sowell, T. (1990). *Preferential politics: An international perspective.* New York: William Morrow.

Spaeth, J. L. (1985). Job power and earnings. *American Sociological Review, 50,* 603–617.

Spangler, E., Gordon, M. A., & Pipkin, R. M. (1978). Token women: An empirical test of Kanter's hypothesis. *American Journal of Sociology, 84,* 160–170.

Spelman, D., Crary, M., Kram, K. E., & Clawson, J. G. (1986). Sexual attraction at work: Managing the heart. In L. L. Moore (Ed.), *Not as far as you think* (pp. 69–91), Lexington, MA: Lexington.

Spence, J. T., Helmreich, R., & Stapp, J. (1974). The Personal Attributes Questionnaire: A measure of sex-role stereotypes and masculinity–femininity. *Journal of Applied Psychology Catalog of Selected Documents in Psychology, 4*, 127.

Spence, J. T., & Sawin, L. L. (1985). Images of masculinity and femininity: A reconceptualization. In V. E. O'Leary, R. K. Unger, & B. S. Wallston (Eds.), *Women, gender and social psychology* (pp. 35–66). Hillsdale, NJ: Lawrence Erlbaum Associates.

Spencer, B. A., & Taylor, G. S. (1988). Effects of facial attractiveness and gender on causal attributions of managerial performance. *Sex Roles, 19*, 272–285.

Spigelman, M., & Schultz, K. (1981, June). *Attitudes towards obesity.* Paper presented at the annual convention of the Canadian Psychological Association, Toronto, ON.

Spruell, G. R. (1985). Daytime drama: Love in the office. *Training and Development Journal, 39*(2), 20–23.

Staff, (1988, February 15). Love in the office. *Newsweek, 111*, 48–52.

Staines, G., Tavris, C., & Epstein Jayarantne, T. (1974) The queen-bee syndrome. *Psychology Today, 7*, 55–60.

State, County, and Municipal Employees v. Washington, 38 FEP 1353 (1985).

Stein, A. H. (1971). The effects of sex-role standards for achievement and sex-role preference in three determinants of achievement motivation. *Developmental Psychology, 4*, 219–231.

Stein, A. H., & Bailey, M. M. (1973). The socialization of achievement orientation in females. *Psychological Bulletin, 80*, 345–366.

Stephan, C. W., & Corder, J. (1985). The effects of dual-career families on adolescents' sex-role attitudes,work and family plans, and choices of important others. *Journal of Marriage and the Family, 47*, 921–929.

Stephensons, C. (1997, January 15). Toward a female model of leadership. *Vital Speeches, 63*(7), 202+.

Sternberg, R. J. (1988). Triangulating love. In R. J. Sternberg & M. L. Barnes (Eds.), *The psychology of love* (pp. 119–138). New Haven, CT: Yale University Press.

Stewart, R. (1976). *Contrasts in management.* Maidenhead, Berkshire, UK: Mc-Graw-Hill.

Stewart, L. P., & Gudykunst, W. B. (1982). Differential factors influencing the hierarchical level and member of promotions of males and females within an organization. *Academy of Management Journal, 25*, 586–597.

Stockdale, M. S. (1997). *The direct and moderating influences of sexual harassment pervasiveness, coping strategies, and gender on work-related outcomes.* Unpublished manuscript, Department of Psychology, Southern Illinois University, Carbondale.

Stockdale, M. S. (1996). What we know and what we need to learn about sexual harassment. In M. S. Stockdale (Ed.), *Sexual harassment in the workplace: Perspectives, frontiers, and response strategies* (pp. 3–25). Thousand Oaks, CA: Sage.

Stockdale, M. S., Vaux, A., & Cashin, J. (1995). Acknowledging sexual harassment: A test of alternative models. *Basic and Applied Social Psychology, 17,* 469–496.

Stockdale, M. S., & Vaux, A. (1993). What sexual harassment experiences lead respondents to acknowledge being sexually harassed? A secondary analysis of a university survey. *Journal of Vocational Behavior, 43,* 221–234.

Stogdill, R. M. (1948). Personal factors associated with leadership: A survey of the literature. *Journal of Psychology, 25,* 35–71.

Stokes, S. J., & Bickman, L. (1974). The effect of the physical attractiveness and role of the helper on help seeking. *Journal of Applied Social Psychology, 4,* 286–294.

Stover, D. L. (1997). The stratification of women within organizations. In P. Dubeck & K. Borman (Eds.), *Women and work: A reader* (pp. 317–320). New Brunswick, NJ: Rutgers University Press.

Stordtbeck, F. L., & Mann, R. D. (1956). Sex role differentiation in jury deliberations. *Sociometry, 19,* 3–11.

Stroebe, W., Insko, C. A., Thompson, V. D., & Layton, B. D. (1971). Effects of physical attractiveness, attitude similarity, and sex on various aspects of interpersonal attraction. *Journal of Personality and Social Psychology, 18,* 79–91.

Stroh, L. K., Brett, J. M., & Reilly, A. H. (1992). All the right stuff: A comparison of female and male managers' career progression. *Journal of Applied Psychology, 77,* 251–260.

Studd, M. V., & Gattiker, U. E. (1991). The evolutionary psychology of sexual harassment in organizations. *Ethology and Social Biology, 12,* 249–290.

Summerhayes, D. L., & Suchner, R. W. (1978). Power implications of touch in male–female relationships. *Sex Roles, 4,* 103–110.

Sunnafrank, M. (1992). On debunking the attitude similarity myth. *Communication Monographs, 59,* 164–179.

Super, D. E. (1957). *The psychology of careers.* New York: Harper & Row.

Super, D. E. (1963). The definition and measurement of early career behavior: A first formulation. *Personnel and Guidance Journal, 41,* 775–780.

Super, D. E. (1953). A theory of vocational development. *American Psychologist, 8,* 185–190.

Sutherland, E., & Veroff, J. (1985). Achievement, motivation and sex-roles. In V. E. O'Leary, R. K. Unger, & B. S. Wallston (Eds.), *Women, gender, and social psychology* (pp. 101–128). Hillsdale, NJ: Lawrence Erlbaum Associates.

Swacker, M. (1975). The sex of the speaker as a sociolinguistic variable. In B. Thorne & N. Henley (Eds.), *Language and sex difference and dominance.* Rowley, MA: Newbury House.

Swim, J., Borgida, E., Maruyama, G., & Myers, D. G. (1989). Joan McKay versus John McKay: Do gender stereotypes bias evaluations? *Psychological Bulletin, 105*(3), 409–429.

Symons, J. L. (1993). A champion disqualified. *Executive Female, 16,* 56.

Symons, G. L. (1984). Career lives of women in France and Canada: The case of managerial women. *Work and Occupations, 11,* 331–352.

Szwajkowski, E., & Larwood, L. (1991). Rational decision processes and sex discrimination: Testing "rational" bias theory. *Journal of Organizational Behavior, 12,* 507–527.

Tajfel, H. (1974). Social identity and intergroup behavior. *Social Science Information, 13,* 65–93.

Tajfel, H. (1978). *Differentiation between social groups: Studies in the social psychology of intergroup relations.* New York: Academic Press.

Tangri, S., Burt, M. R., & Johnson, L. B. (1982). Sexual harassment at work: Three explanatory models. *Journal of Social Issues, 38,* 33–54.

Tavris, C. (1991). The mismeasure of woman: Paradoxes and perspectives in the study of gender. In J. D. Goodchilds (Eds.), *Psychological perspectives on human diversity in America* (pp. 87–136). Washington, DC: American Psychological Association.

Tavris, C. (1992). *The mismeasure of woman.* New York: Simon & Schuster.

Tavris, C., & Wade, C. (1984). *The longest war: Sex differences in perspective.* New York: Harcourt Brace Jovanovich.

Taylor, D. M., & Moghaddam, F. M. (1994). *Theories of intergroup relations: International social psychological perspectives.* Westport, CT: Praeger.

Taylor, M. S., & Ilgen, D. R. (1981). Sex discrimination against women in initial placement decisions: A laboratory investigation. *Academy of Management Journal, 24*(4), 859–865.

Taylor, S. E. (1983). Adjustments to threatening events. *American Psychologist, 39,* 1161–1173.

Taynor, J., & Deaux, K. (1975). Equity and perceived sex differences: Role behavior as defined by the task, the mode, and the actor. *Journal of Personality and Social Psychology, 32,* 381–390.

Terborg, J. R. (1977). Women in management: A research review. *Journal of Applied Psychology, 62,* 647–664.

Terpstra, D. E., & Baker D. D. (1992). Outcomes of federal court decisions on sexual harassment. *Academy of Management Journal, 35,* 181–190.

Theorell, T. (1991). On cardiovascular health in women: Results of epidemiological and psychosocial studies in Sweden (pp. 187–204). In M. Frankenhaeuser, V. Lundberg, & M. Chesney (Eds.), *Women, work and health: Stress and opportunities.* London: Plenum.

Thomas, A. H., & Stewart, N. R. (1971). Counselor response to female clients with deviate and conforming career goals. *Journal of Counseling Psychology, 18,* 352–357.

Thomas, D. A., & Alderfer, C. P. (1989). The influence of race on career dynamics: Theory and research on minority career experiences. In M. B. Arthur, D. T. Hall, & B. S. Laurence (Eds.), *Handbook of career theory* (pp. 133–158). Cambridge, UK: Cambridge University Press.

Thomas, L. T., & Ganster, D. C. (1995). Impact of family-supportive work variables on work–family conflict and strain: A control perspective. *Journal of Applied Psychology, 80,* 6–15.

Thorne, B., & Henley, N. (1975). *Language and sex differences and dominance.* Rowley, MA: Newbury House.

Thorne, B., Kramarae, C., & Henley, N. (1983). Language, gender and society: Opening a second decade of research. In B. Thorne, C. Kramarae, & C. N.

Henley (Eds.), *Language, gender and society* (pp. 7–24). Rowley, MA: Newbury House.

Thornton, B., & Linnstaedter, L. (1975). *Effects of perceived attractiveness and sex-role interests on interpersonal attraction.* Unpublished manuscript (ERIC Document Reproduction Service No. ED 134 896).

Thornton, B., & Linnstaedter, L. (1980). The influence of physical attractiveness and sex-role congruence on interpersonal attraction. *Representative Research in Social Psychology, 11,* 55–63.

Thoits, P. (1983). Multiple identities and psychological well-being. *American Sociological Review, 48,* 174–187.

Thoits, P. A. (1986). Multiple identities: Explaining gender and marital status differences in distress. *American Sociological Review, 51,* 259–272.

Tiefer, L. (1987). Social constructionism and the study of human sexuality. In P. Shaver & C. Hendrick (Eds.), *Sexual gender* (Vol. 7, p. 70–94). Newbury Park, CA: Sage.

Till, F. (1980). *Sexual harassment: A report on the sexual harassment of students.* Washington, DC: National Advisory Council on Women's Educational Programs.

Toner, M. (1998). White-black vernacular gap widening: Linguists warn of 'bad omen' for American society. *The Atlanta Journal and Constitution,* February 15, 1998, p. A06.

Touhey, J. C. (1979). Sex-role stereotyping and individual differences in liking for the physically attractive. *Social Psychology Quarterly, 42,* 285–289.

Triandis, H. C., Loh, W. D., & Levin, L. A. (1966). Race, status, quality of spoken English and opinions about civil rights as determinants of interpersonal attitudes. *Journal of Applied Psychology, 3,* 468–472.

Truax, K., Cordova, D. I., Wood, A., Wright, E., & Crosby, F. (1998). Undermined? Affirmative action from the target's point of view. In Swim, J., Stangor, C. et al. *Prejudice: The target's perspective.* (pp. 171–188). San Diego: Academic Press, Inc.

Tuddenham, R. D., McBride, P., & Zahn, V. (1958). The influence of the sex composition of the group upon yielding to a distorted norm. *Journal of Psychology, 46,* 243–251.

Turner, M. E., & Pratkanis, A. R. (1994). Affirmative action as help: A review of recipient reactions to preferential selection and affirmative action. *Basic and Applied Social Psychology, 15,* 43–69.

Tyler, C. (1977). The encounter with poverty—Its effect on vocational psychology. In H. J. Peters & J. C. Hanson (Eds.), *Vocational guidance and career level.* New York: Macmillan.

Unger, R. K. (1983). Through the looking glass; No wonderful yet! (The reciprocal relationship between methodology and models of reality). *Psychology of Women Quarterly, 8,* 9–32.

Unger, R. K. (1979). Toward a redefinition of sex and gender. *American Psychologist, 34,* 1085–1094.

Unger, R., & Crawford, M. (1992). *Women and gender: A feminist psychology.* New York: McGraw-Hill.

UAW v. Johnson Controls, Inc., 499 U.S. 187 (1991).

United Nations. (1991). *The world's women: Trends and Statistics, 1970–1990.* New York: United Nations Publications.

U.S. Bureau of the Census. (1975). *Historical Statistics of the United States: Colonial Times to 1970.* Part I. Washington, DC: U.S. Government Printing Office.

U.S. Bureau of the Census. (1984). Male–female differences in work experiences, occupation and earnings: 1984. In *Current population reports* (Household Economic Studies, Series P. 70, No. 10). Washington, DC: Government Printing Office.

U.S. Bureau of the Census. (1992). *Statistical Abstracts of the United States: 1992.* Washington, DC: U.S. Government Printing Office.

U.S. Bureau of Labor Statistics. (1987a). *Employment and earnings* (Vol. 34, No. 4, p. 29). Washington, DC: U.S. Government Printing Office.

U.S. Bureau of Labor Statistics. (1987b). *Statistical abstract of the United States* (107th ed.). Washington, DC: U.S. Department of Commerce.

U.S. Department of Commerce. (1991). *Statistical abstract* (111th ed.). Washington, DC: Government Printing Office.

U.S. Department of Commerce. (1997). *Statistical abstract of the United States.* (117th ed., pp. 398–399). Washington, DC: Author.

U.S. Department of Health and Human Services. (1984). *The health consequences of smoking—Chronic obstruction lung disease: A report of the surgeon general* (DHHS Publication No. PHS 84-50205). Washington, DC: U.S. Government Printing Office.

U.S. Department of Labor. (1983). Women's employment in occupations and industries. In *Time of Change: 1983 Handbook on Women Workers* (Bulletin 298). Washington, DC: U.S. Government Printing Office.

U.S. Department of Labor. (1984). *Facts on women workers.* Washington, DC: Author.

U.S. Department of Labor. (1991). *A report on the glass ceiling initiative.* Washington, DC: Secretary's Office, U.S. Department of Labor.

U.S. Department of Health and Human Services. (1980). *The health consequences of smoking for women: A report of the surgeon general* (DHHS Publication No. 5396). Washington, DC: U.S. Government Printing Office.

U.S. Department of Health and Human Services. (1983). *The health consequences of smoking—Cardiovascular disease: A report of the surgeon general* (USDHHS Publication No. 84-50204). Washington, DC: U.S. Government Printing Office.

U.S. Department of Labor. (1995). *The glass ceiling fact-finding report: Good for business—Making full use of the nation's human capital.* Washington, DC: Author.

U.S. Department of Labor, Bureau of Labor Statistics. (1977). *U.S. Working women: A databook.* Washington, DC: U.S. Government Printing Office.

U.S. Department of Labor, Bureau of Labor Statistics, Women's Bureau. (1984). *Facts on women workers* (909–710). Washington, DC: U.S. Government Printing Office.

U.S. Department of Labor, Bureau of Labor Statistics, Women's Bureau. (1993). *Facts on Working Women.* Report No. 93-2 Washington, DC: U.S. Government Printing Office.

United States Merit Systems Protection Board. (1981). *Sexual harassment in the federal workplace.* Washington, DC: U.S. Government Printing Office.

United States Merit Systems Protection Board. (1988). *Sexual harassment in the federal government: An update.* Washington, DC: U.S. Government Printing Office.

United States Merit Systems Protection Board. (1995). *Sexual harassment in the Federal workplace: Trends, progress, and continuing challenges.* Washington, DC: U.S. Government Printing Office.

Valdez, R. L., & Gutek, B. A. (1987). Family roles: A help or a hindrance for working women. In B. A. Gutek & L. Larwood (Eds.), *Women's career development* (pp. 157–169). Newbury Park, CA: Sage.

Van de Walle, E., & Kuodel, J. (1980). Europe's fertility transition: New evidence and lessons for today's developing world. *Population Bulletin, 34,* 1–42.

VanMaanen, J., & Schein, E. (1979). Toward a theory of organizational socialization. In B. M. Staw (Ed.), *Research in organizational behavior* (Vol. 1, pp. 209–264). Grenewich, CT: JAI.

Vaughn, L. S., & Wittig, M. A. (1981). Women's occupations, competence, and role over-load as determinants of evaluation of others. *Journal of Applied Social Psychology, 10,* 398–415.

Vaux, A. (1993). Paradigmatic assumptions in sexual harassment research: Being guided without being misled. *Journal of Vocational Behavior, 42,* 116–135.

Verbrugge, L. M. (1985). Gender and health: An update on hypotheses and evidence. *Journal of Health and Social Behavior, 26,* 156–182.

Veroff, J. (1969). Social comparison and the development of achievement motivation. In C. P. Smith (Ed.), *Achievement-related motives in children.* New York: Russell Sage Foundation.

Vetter, L. (1973). Career counseling for women. *Counseling Psychologist, 4,* 54–67.

Vollmer, F. (1976). Why do men have higher expectancy than women? *Sex Roles, 14,* 351–362.

Voydanoff, P. (1987). *Women's work, family and health.* In K. S. Koziara, M. H. Moskow, & L. D. Tanner (Eds.), *Working women: Past, present and future* (pp. 69–96). Washington, DC: Bureau of National Affairs.

Vroom, V. H., & Yetton, P. W. (1973). *Leadership and decision-making.* Pittsburgh, PA: University of Pittsburgh Press.

Vroom, V. H., & Jago, A. G. (1974). Decision making as a social process: Normative and descriptive models of leader behavior. *Decision Sciences, 5,* 743–769.

Wagman, M. (1967). Sex differences in types of daydreams. *Journal of Personality and Social Psychology, 7,* 329–332.

Walby, S. (1986). *Patriarchy at work: Patriarchal and capitalist relations in employment.* Minneapolis: University of Minnesota Press.

Waldron, I. (1980). Employment and women's health. *International Journal of Health Services, 10,* 435–454.

Waldron, I. (1986). What do we know about causes of sex differences in mortality? A review of the literature. *Population Bulletin of the United Nations,* No. 18-1985, 59–76.

Waldron, I. (1991). Effects of labor force participation on sex differences in mortality & morbidity. In M. Frankenhaeuser, V. Lundberg, & M. Chesney (Eds.), *Women, work and health: Stress and opportunities* (pp. 17–38). New York: Plenum.

Waldron, I., & Jacobs, J. (1988). Effects of labor force participation on women's health: New evidence from a longitudinal study. *Journal of Occupational Medicines, 30,* 977–983.

Waldron, I., & Jacobs, J. (1989). Effects of multiple roles on women's health: Evidence from a national longitudinal study. *Women and Health, 15,* 3–19.

Waldron, I., & Lye, D. (1989). Employment, unemployment, occupation and smoking. *American Journal of Preventive Medicine, 5,* 142–149.

Walker, N. (1981). Do feminists ever laugh? Women's humor and women's right. *International Journal of Women's Studies, 4,* 1–9.

Walsh, M. R. (Ed.) (1997). *Women, men and gender: Ongoing debates.* New Haven, CT: Yale University Press.

Walster, E., Aronson, V., Abrahams, D., & Rottman, L. (1966). Importance of physical attractiveness in dating behavior. *Journal of Personality and Social Psychology, 4,* 508–516.

Warihay, P. D. (1980). The climb to the top: Is the network the route for women? *Personnel Administrator, 25*(4), 55–60.

Wegman, D. H., & Fine, L. J. (1990). Occupational health in the 1990s. *Annual Review of Public Health, 11,* 89–103.

Weiss, L., & Lowenthal, M. F. (1975). Life-course perspectives on friendship. In M. F. Lowenthal, M. Thurnher, & D. Chiriboga (Eds.), *Four stages of life.* San Francisco: Jossey-Bass.

Weitz, S. (1976). Sex differences in nonverbal communication. *Sex Roles, 2,* 175–184.

Wentworth, D. K., & Anderson, L. R. (1984). Emergent leadership as a function of sex and task type. *Sex Roles, 11*(5b), 513–524.

Westhoff, L. A. (1985). *Corporate romance.* New York: Times Books.

Westman, M., & Eden, D. (1992). Excessive role demand and subsequent performance. *Journal of Organizational Behavior, 13,* 519–529.

White, L. K., Booth, A., & Edwards, J. N. (1986). Children and marital happiness—Why the negative correlation. *Journal of Family Issues, 7,* 131–147.

White, J. W. (1988). Influence tactics as a function of gender, insult, and goal. *Sex Roles, 18,* 433–448.

White, Y. S. (1990). Understanding the Black woman manager's interaction with the corporate culture. *The Western Journal of Black Studies, 14,* 182–186.

Whitely, W., Dougherty, T. W., & Dreher, G. F. (1991). Relationship of career mentoring and socioeconomic origin to managers' and professionals' early career progress. *Academy of Management Journal, 34,* 331–351.

Wiener, R. L. (1995). Social analytic jurisprudence in sexual harassment litigation: The role of social framework and social fact. *Journal of Social Issues, 51,* 167–180.

William, S. D., & Best, D. L. (1990). *Measuring sex stereotypes: A multination study.* Newbury Park, CA: Sage.

Williams, J. E., & Bennett, S. M. (1975). The definition of sex stereotypes via the adjective check list. *Sex Roles, 1,* 327–337.

Williams, J. E., & Best, D. L. (1982). *Measuring sex stereotypes: A thirty-nation study.* Beverly Hills, CA: Sage.

Williams, J. E., & Giles, H. (1978). The changing status of women in society: An intergroup perspective. In H. Tajfel (Ed.), *Differentiation between social groups* (pp. 431–446). Academic Press: London.

Williams, K. B., & Cyr, R. R. (1992). Escalating commitment to a relationship: The sexual harassment trap. *Sex Roles, 27,* 47–71.

Willis, F. N., Jr. (1966). Initial speaking distance as a function of the speakers' relationship. *Psychonomic Society, 5,* 221–222.

Wilson, E. O. (1975). *Sociobiology: The new synthesis.* Cambridge, MA: Harvard University Press.

Winstead, B. A. (1986). Sex differences in same-sex friendships. In V. J. Derlega & B. A. Winstead (Eds.), *Friendship and social interaction* (pp. 81–99). New York: Springer-Verlag.

Winther, D. A., & Green, S. B. (1987). Another look at gender-related differences in leadership behavior. *Sex Roles, 16,* 41–56.

Wittig, M. A. (1985). Metatheoretical dilemmas in the psychology of gender. *American Psychologist, 40,* 800–810.

Wolf, W. C., & Fligstein, N. D. (1979). Sexual stratification: Differences in power in the work setting. *Social Forces, 58,* 94–107.

Women as bosses: The problems they face. (1983, July 11). *U.S. News and World Report,* pp. 56–57.

Women's wit and wisdom. (1991). Hong Kong: Running Press.

Wood, C., Larsen, L., & Williams, R. (1979). Social and psychological factors in relation to premenstrual tension and menstrual pain. *Australian and New Zealand Journal of Obstetrics and Gynaecology, 19,* 111–115.

Wood, W. (1987). Meta-analytic review of sex differences in group performance. *Psychological Bulletin, 102,* 53–71.

Wood, W., Polek, D., & Aiken, C. (1985). Sex differences in group task performance. *Journal of Psychology, 48,* 63–71.

Wooley, H. T. (1910). Psychological literature: A review of the recent literature on the psychology of sex. *Psychological Bulletin, 7,* 335–342.

Work, J. W. (1996). Leading a diverse workforce. In F. Hesselbein, M. Goldsmith, & R. Beckhard (Eds.), *The leader of the future: New visions, strategies, and practices for the next era* (pp. 71–80). San Francisco: Jossey-Bass.

Working Women's Institute. (1975). *Sexual harassment on the job: Results of a preliminary survey* (Research Series, Report No. 1). New York: Author.

Wortman, C., Biernat, M., & Lang, E. (1991). *Coping with role overload.* In M. Frankenhaeuser, V. Lundberg, & M. Chesney (Eds.), *Women, work, and health: Stress and opportunities* (pp. 85–110). New York: Plenum.

Wright, E. O., Costello, C., Hachen, D., & Sprague, J. (1982). The American class structure. *American Sociological Review, 47,* 709–726.

Wright, P., Ferris, S. P., Hiller, J. S., & Keroll, M. (1995). Competitiveness through management of diversity: Effects on stock price valuation. *Academy of Management Journal, 38,* 272–287.

Wright, P. H. (1982). Men's friendships, women's friendship and the alleged inferiority of the latter. *Sex Roles, 8,* 1–20.

Yankelovich, D. (1981). *New rules: Searching for self and fulfillment in a world turned upside down.* New York: Random House.

Yoder, J. D. (1991). Rethinking tokenism: Looking beyond numbers. *Gender and Society, 5,* 178–192.

Yogev, S. (1982). Happiness in dual career couples: Changing research, changing values. *Sex Roles, 8,* 593–605.

Yogev, S., & Brett, J. M. (1985). Patterns of work and family involvement among single and dual-career couples. *Journal of Applied Psychology, 70,* 754–768.

Yukl, G., & Falbe, C. M. (1990). Influence tactics and objectives in upward, downward, and lateral influence attempts. *Journal of Applied Psychology, 75,* 132–140.

Yukl, G., & Van Fleet, D. D. (1992). Theory and research on leadership in organizations. In M. D. Dunnette & L. M. Hough (Eds.), *Handbook of industrial and organizational psychology* (2nd ed., vol. 3) (pp. 147–198). Palo Alto, CA: Consulting Psychologists Press.

Yukl, G., Wall, S., & Lepsinger, R. (1990). Preliminary report on validation of the management practices survey. In K. E. Clark & M. B. Clark (Eds.), *Measures of leadership.* West Orange, NJ: Leadership Library of America.

Yukl, G. A. (1981). *Leadership in organizations.* Englewood Cliffs, NJ: Prentice-Hall.

Zajonc, R. B. (1968). Attitudinal effects of mere exposure. *Journal of Personality and Social Psychology Monograph Supplement, 9*(2, Pt. 2), 1–27.

Zimbardo, P. G. (1972). The pathology of imprisonment. *Society, 9*(6).

Zimbardo, P. G., & Meadow, W. (1974). *Becoming sexist in one easy laugh: Sexism in Reader's Digest.* Paper presented at the Annual Meeting of the Western Psychological Association, San Francisco.

Zimmerman, D. H., & West, C. (1975). Sex roles interruptions and silences in conversations. In B. Thorne & N. Henley (Eds.), *Language and sex: Difference and dominance* (pp. 105–129). Rowley, MA: Newbury House.

Zytowski, D. G. (1969). Toward a theory of career development for women. *Personnel and Guidance Journal, 47,* 660–664.

Author Index

Subject Index